Sandip Sinharay

Springer
Tokyo
Berlin
Heidelberg
New York
Hong Kong
London
Milan
Paris

H. Yanai, A. Okada, K. Shigemasu,
Y. Kano, J.J. Meulman (Eds.)

New Developments in Psychometrics

Proceedings of the International Meeting of the
Psychometric Society IMPS2001

Osaka, Japan, July 15-19, 2001

With 128 Figures

 Springer

Haruo Yanai
Professor, Research Division
National Center for University Entrance Examinations
2-19-23 Komaba, Meguro-ku,
Tokyo 153-8501, Japan

Akinori Okada
Professor, Department of Industrial Relations
School of Social Relations
Rikkyo (St. Paul's) University
3-34-1 Nishi Ikebukuro, Toshima-ku,
Tokyo 171-8501, Japan

Kazuo Shigemasu
Professor, Department of Multi-Disciplinary Sciences - Life Sciences
Graduate School of Arts and Sciences
University of Tokyo
3-8-1 Komaba, Meguro-ku,
Tokyo 153-8902, Japan

Yutaka Kano
Associate Professor
Graduate School of Human Sciences
Osaka University
Suita, Osaka 565-0871, Japan

Jacqueline J. Meulman
Professor, Data Theory Group
Faculty of Social and Behavioral Sciences
Linden University
P.O. Box 9555, 2300 RB Leiden, The Netherlands

Library of Congress Cataloging-in-Publication Data applied for.

ISBN 4-431-70343-8 Springer-Verlag Tokyo Berlin Heidelberg New York

Printed on acid-free paper

Typesetting: Editors
Printing and binding: Hicom, Japan
SPIN: 10888997

Preface

The International Meeting of the Psychometric Society (IMPS2001) was held July 15–19, 2001, at the Osaka University Convention Center, Osaka, Japan. The meeting was the successor to the 11th European Meeting of the Psychometric Society held at Lueneburg, Germany, in 1999, and is a part of the long history of the Psychometric Society, which was established in 1936. It is significant that the IMPS2001 was the first meeting of the Psychometric Society held outside North America or Europe, and it was also the first meeting of the Psychometric Society designated as *international*. Our expectations were modest, but we were very happy to host 313 participants from 19 countries around the world although the meeting was held in Japan, far from most of those countries.

The IMPS2001 was organized under the auspices of the Psychometric Society and the Organizing Committee of the IMPS2001. It was co-sponsored by the Behaviormetric Society of Japan, the Japan Statistical Society, the Japanese Psychological Association, and the faculty of Human Sciences of Osaka University, with the support of 28 cooperative societies in Japan. Further, we would like to acknowledge the Commemorative Association for the Japan World Exposition (1970), and the 26 other organizations whose financial assistance enabled us to publish this volume of conference proceedings.

The science program comprised 2 keynote lectures, 10 invited lectures, 5 symposia, 20 invited sessions, 13 contributed sessions, and 6 poster sessions. The details of the program can be found in the December issue of *Psychometrika*, 2001, pp. 599–608. In all, nearly 250 presentations were delivered. We estimate that both the number of presentations and the number of participants were the largest among the meetings of the Psychometric Society so far. We are grateful to a number of the past presidents of the society for the success of this meeting. Of those, we express our thanks first Dr. Ivo Molenaar, who encouraged us to organize the meeting in Japan, and also to Dr. Susan Embretson, who, as the president of the Psychometric Society, permitted us to join the trustees' meeting in June 1999 at the University of Kansas, and who was instrumental in the decision to organize the IMPS2001 in Japan. We also thank Dr. Yoshio Takane, one of the presidents of the Psychometric Society, for giving us useful suggestions for editing the conference volume. In addition, we thank Drs. Shizuhiko Nishisato, Fumiko Samejima, Lawrence Hubert, Michael W. Browne, David Thisssen, and William Stout for their agreement at the trustees' meeting to have the first meeting of the Psychometric Society in Japan.

We would like mention that we were deeply grateful for the efforts shown by all those concerned with the preparations for the IMPS2001. As noted earlier, many participants traveled a long distance to Japan and presented informative talks at a number of different sessions. In order to thank all who were involved with the IMPS2001, we feel a responsibility to publish this volume of conference proceedings (IMPS2001). It took some time to find an appropriate publisher. In December 2001, however, we announced to all participants who attended the meeting and gave their presentations that we would publish the proceedings of the IMPS2001 as scheduled, and that if they were willing to present their papers, we would welcome submissions until April 20, 2002.

All submitted papers were sent to two reviewers to evaluate whether they were worthy of publication. From their recommendations, we made a final selection of 80 papers. We believe that readers of this volume will agree that the selected papers cover a wide range of topics and perspectives related to recent developments in psychometrics both in theory and in application. We would like to thank all the reviewers who read the papers and made helpful comments for revision. The names of the reviewers are listed on page viii. Without their efforts, this conference volume could not have succeeded.

We regret to report that during the preparation of this volume for publication, Dr. Chikio Hayashi passed away suddenly. Dr. Hayashi was the honorary adviser of the meeting, and he also was one of the invited lecturers. Before the meeting, he gave generously of his advice, drawing on his experience in organizing many international meetings. We the editors greatly appreciate Dr. Hayashi's contributions and express our sincere sympathy to his family.

Finally, the editors thank the staff of Springer-Verlag Tokyo for their support and dedication and for providing us the opportunity to publish this volume of proceedings, which we earnestly hope will contribute to new developments in psychometrics in the twenty-first century.

Editorial Committee
Haruo Yanai, Chief, National Center for University Entrance Examinations, Tokyo
Akinori Okada, Rikkyo (St. Paul's) University, Tokyo
Kazuo Shigemasu, University of Tokyo, Tokyo
Yutaka Kano, Osaka University, Osaka
Jacqueline J. Meulman, Leiden University, Leiden

November 10, 2002

Greetings

Writing as the 2001-2002 President, on behalf of the Psychometric Society I wish to commend the Organizing and Program Committees of the Osaka 2001 International Meeting of the Psychometric Society (IMPS2001) on an historic and dramatically successful conference. This first "international" meeting of the Society (all previous meetings being North American or European meetings) was an exhilarating intellectual experience. In addition to the two keynote lectures, there was an impressive array of hour-long invited lectures, invited symposiums, invited sessions, contributed sessions, and poster sessions. Indeed, with over 250 papers read and over 300 participants, it must have been the largest meeting ever of the Society. Of course, meeting size alone does not guarantee success. However, having attended many North American and European Society meetings, I can personally testify that IMPS2001 was one of the Society's most successful meetings.

The meeting was not only an intellectual success, but was also a great social success. The informal American phrase, "A good time was had by all!" sums it up nicely. A social high point was the Kyoto banquet, a joyous and sumptuous affair held in a beautiful setting with traditional Japanese cultural touches. The organizational aspects of the meeting were superb. The organizers boldly conceived of the idea of a Japanese meeting, started very early in approaching the Society Board of Trustees, laid careful and meticulously thorough plans, involved a large number of people from all over the world (37 people from 9 countries serving on the International Program Committee), and then raised the money and spent the enormous amount of time an undertaking of this scope and complexity requires.

Now, we are fortunate that this historic event will be intellectually preserved and widely communicated by this IMPS2001 Conference Volume. I am personally honored to be an author of one of the 80 papers selected for the volume. The Editorial Committee of the Conference Volume is to be commended for carrying out this challenging and important task. The diversity and the large number of articles reflect the diversity and health of the Society. Indeed, the IMPS meeting and Conference Volume are excellent examples of the Society's current emphasis on diversifying intellectually and geographically.

Special thanks go to Professor Haruo Yanai for his tireless efforts as Chair of the IMPS2001 Conference Committee and as Editor-in-Chief of the Editorial Committee of the IMPS2001 Conference Volume. Thanks go to the other members of the Conference and Editorial Committees: Professors Akinori Okada, Kazuo Shigemasu, Yutaka Kano and Jacqueline Meulman serving on both committees. Thanks go to Osaka University for providing a superb site for the meeting. Thanks go to the many organizations who provided generous financial assistance for this undertaking. Finally, thanks go to the many participants of IMPS2001, with special thanks to those contributing to this Conference Volume.

William Stout

Professor Emeritus William Stout
Department of Statistics, University of Illinois, and
Consultant, Educational Consulting Service

Reviewers

A
Kohei Adachi
Shotaro Akaho
Hideki Asoh
B
Peter M. Bentler
Ulf Böckenholt
Kenneth A. Bollen
Giuseppe Bove
C
Naohito Chino
D
Mark de Rooij
F
Yasunori Fujikoshi
Wing K. Fung
G
John G. Gower
Patrick J.F. Groenen
H
Tomokazu Haebara
Tamaki Hattori
Andy Heath
Willem Heiser
Takahiro Hoshino
Aapo Hyvärinen
I
Masanori Ichikawa
Hiroshi Ikeda
Tarow Indow
Hidetoki Ishii
Manabu Iwasaki
K
Allan Karde
Henk Kiers
Sadanori Konishi
Pieter M. Kroonenberg
Naoki Kuramoto
Manabu Kuroki
L
Carlo Lauro
Sik-Yum Lee
Jiajuan Liang
M
Tadahiko Maeda
Shin-ichi Mayekawa

Gideon J. Mellenbergh
Hisao Miyano
Masahiro Mizuta
Robert Mokken
Ivo W. Molenaar
Ab Mooijaart
Yoshiya Moritani
Takashi Murakami
Eiji Muraki
Noboru Murata
In Jae Myung
N
Masanori Nakagawa
Shizuhiko Nishisato
Hiroyuki Noguchi
O
Haruhiko Ogasawara
Tatsuo Otsu
Tadasu Oyama
S
Albert Satorra
Kenpei Shiina
Kojiro Shojima
Klaas Sijtsma
Xin-Yuan Song
Maarten Speekenbrink
Nariaki Sugiura
Takakazu Sugiyama
T
Masaaki Taguri
Yoshio Takane
Kazuhisa Takemura
Yutaka Tanaka
Jos M.F. ten Berge
David Thissen
U
Maomi Ueno
V
Wim J. van der Linden
Rossana Verde
W
Hiroshi Watanabe
Y
Kazunori Yamaguchi
Yoshiro Yamamoto
Ryozo Yoshino

Conference Committee

Haruo Yanai (Chair of Organizing Committee)
National Center for University Entrance Examinations

Akinori Okada (Vice Chair of Organizing Committee)
Rikkyo (St. Paul's) University

Kazuo Shigemasu (Chair of International Program Committee)
University of Tokyo

Yutaka Kano (Chair of Local Organizing Committee)
Osaka University

International Program Committee

Phipps Arabie	U.S.A.	Peter M. Bentler	U.S.A.
Jos ten Berge	Neth.	Ulf Bockenholt	U.S.A.
Hamparsum Bozdogan	U.S.A.	Michael W. Browne	U.S.A.
J. Douglas Carroll	U.S.A.	Susan Embretson	U.S.A.
Constantino Arce Fernandez	Spain	Yasunori Fujikoshi	Japan
John C. Gower	U.K.	Willem J. Heiser	Neth.
Lawrence Hubert	U.S.A.	Masanori Ichikawa	Japan
Hiroshi Ikeda	Japan	Tarow Indow	U.S.A.
Yutaka Kano	Japan	Henk A. L. Kiers	Neth.
Rolf Langeheine	Germany	Carlo Lauro	Italy
Wim J. van der Linden	Neth.	Jacqueline J. Meulman	Neth.
Robert J. Mislevy	U.S.A.	Ivo W. Molenaar	Neth.
Takashi Murakami	Japan	Eiji Muraki	U.S.A.
Shizuhiko Nishisato	Canada	Akinori Okada	Japan
James O. Ramsay	Canada	Juergen Rost	Germany
Fumiko Samejima	U.S.A.	Albert Satorra	Spain
William Stout	U.S.A.	Yoshio Takane	Canada
David Thissen	U.S.A.	Haruo Yanai	Japan

Honorary Adviser

Chikio Hayashi (The Institute of Statistical Mathematics, Professor Emeritus)

Contents

Part 1 Key Note Speeches and Invited Lectures

Part 2 Structural Equation Modeling and Factor Analysis

Part 3 Item Response Theory (IRT) and Adaptive Testing

Part 4 Testing in General

Part 5 Multivariate Statistical Methods

Part 6 Scaling

Part 7 Classification Method

Part 8 Independent Component Analysis and Principal Component Analysis

Part 1

Key Note Speeches and Invited Lectures

Psychometric Engineering as Art: Variations on a Theme

David Thissen[1]

[1]L.L. Thurstone Psychometric Laboratory, University of North Carolina at Chapel Hill, Davie Hall, CB#3270, Chapel Hill, NC, 27599, USA

Summary. The Psychometric Society is "devoted to the development of Psychology as a quantitative rational science." Engineering is often set in contradistinction with science; art is sometimes considered different from science. Why, then, juxtapose the words in the title: *psychometric*, *engineering*, and *art*? Because an important aspect of quantitative psychology is problem-solving, and engineering solves problems. And an essential aspect of a good solution is beauty—hence, art. In overview and with examples, this presentation describes activities that are quantitative psychology as engineering and art—that is, as design. Extended illustrations involve systems for scoring tests in realistic contexts. Allusions are made to other examples that extend the conception of quantitative psychology as engineering and art across a wider range of psychometric activities.

Key words. Psychometrics, quantitative psychology, design

1 Introduction[2]

The purpose of the Psychometric Society is "to encourage the development of Psychology as a quantitative rational science" (Thurstone 1937 p 227). To empha-

---

[2] This chapter is based on the Presidential Address presented at the 66th Annual Meeting of the Psychometric Society held in King of Prussia, Pennsylvania, USA, on June 24, 2001. The address was also presented on July 16 at the 2001 International Meeting of the Psychometric Society held in Osaka, Japan. Portions were published in *Psychometrika*, as "Psychometric Engineering as Art" (December, 2001; *66*, pp. 473-486, © The Psychometric Society), and are reprinted with permission.

Thanks to R. Darrell Bock, Paul De Boeck, Lyle V. Jones, Cynthia Null, Lynne Steinberg, and Howard Wainer for constructive comments on early drafts of this ms. And thanks to Val Williams, Mary Pommerich, Lee Chen, Kathleen Rosa, Lauren Nelson, Maria Orlando, Kimberly Swygert, Lori McLeod, Bryce Reeve, Fabian Camacho, David Flora, Viji Sathy, Michael Edwards, and Jack Vevea for their many contributions to some of the research that illustrates this commentary. Of course, any flaws in the argument or its presentation remain the author's.

size that, *Psychometrika* carried the subtitle "devoted to the development of psychology as a quantitative rational science" from the first volume in 1936 until the 1984 cover redesign. It is clear, both from the historical record and from observation of the current activities of the Society's members, that psychometrics is about science.

Engineering is often set in contradistinction with science; art is sometimes considered to be very different from science. Why, then, juxtapose the words in the title: psychometric, engineering, and art?

1.1 Engineering

An important aspect of quantitative psychology is problem-solving, and engineers solve problems. Indeed, one of the origins of psychometric thought was engineering, in that L.L. Thurstone was originally trained as an engineer, and was employed as an instructor at the Engineering College of the University of Minnesota before he began graduate study in Education, and then Psychology, at the University of Chicago (Jones 1998). Ledyard Tucker made a transition from a career as an engineer to become Thurstone's student. Many other quantitative psychologists have also come from engineering backgrounds. Nevertheless, quantitative psychology is devoted to the advancement of science; what might it mean to speak of *psychometric engineering*?

A description by Lewis (1996 p 92) of the distinction between engineers and all others is cogent:

> There are two kinds of people in the world, according to a tired joke: those who divide the world into two kinds of people and those who don't. I'm one of the ones who do. I divide the world into engineers and everyone else. Being an engineer isn't a matter of training or expertise, or at least not the way I use the term. Engineers look at every problem as a puzzle they can solve, as long as they're smart, systematic, and ingenious enough and look at it from the right angle. The rest of the world looks at problems as, well, problems. Things that make their lives worse. Obstacles. Barriers. Something you call an engineer to take care of for you.

If engineering solves problems, how then does engineering differ from science? In his acceptance lecture of the Allen Newell Award of the Association for Computing Machinery, Frederick Brooks (1996 p 62) put it succinctly: "The scientist *builds in order to study*; the engineer *studies in order to build*" (emphasis in the original). The title of Brooks' lecture was "The computer scientist as toolsmith II," and he argued that computer science is misnamed—that its problems of design are properly engineering.

I would extend Brooks' distinction between scientists and engineers to create a special category for psychometricians: We study in order to build tools (largely) in order (for others) to study. Those in the psychometric tradition very occasionally do science. An example is, of course, Thurstone's (1927) *law of comparative judgment,* which is both a minimal sort of psychological process theory and the basis for many statistical procedures for data analysis (including much of item response theory). But most often we build tools for others to use to understand their data, or to test their theories. We should understand that is our goal, and reward its accomplishment. Brooks (1996 p. 62) suggests that

> Sciences legitimately take the discovery of facts and laws as a proper end in itself ... But in design, in contrast with science, novelty in itself has no merit. If we recognize our artifacts as tools, we test them by their usefulness and their costs, not their novelty.

Further, Brooks (1996 p 62) suggests that unhappy trends arise in a confusion of science and engineering; as his final specific point, we writes:

> As we honor the more mathematical, abstract, and "scientific" parts of our subject more, and the practical parts less, we misdirect young and brilliant minds away from a body of challenging and important problems that are our peculiar domain, depriving these problems of the powerful attacks they deserve.

What have been some of the most prominent contributions of the psychometric community? Factor analysis, and its offspring, structural equation modeling. Psychological scaling models and procedures, and more recently multidimensional scaling. Statistical theories about data arising from psychological tests. A large number of techniques in multivariate statistics, including technology for research synthesis (meta-analysis). There are others as well; but they have in common that they are tools.

I suggest we think of ourselves as a tool-making discipline, because it is our tool-making that is our greatest contribution to psychological science. If we think that way in what we choose to do, in what we choose to publish (both as authors and as editors and reviewers), and in our evaluations of our colleagues, we advance the psychometric tradition.

1.2 Art

If psychometrics is engineering, what is its relation with art? Engineering is (primarily) design, and many qualities of good design are esthetic. Design is art.

What do psychometricians design? Models. Algorithms. Statistical procedures. If we look at those as art, as well as engineering, we can learn a good deal from an artist's reflections. Here are two of those attributed to Pablo Picasso:

"Art is a lie that enables us to realize the truth."[3] Juxtapose that comment with George Box's (1979 p 2) oft-quoted remark that "models, or course, are never

---

[3] Quotations attributed to P. Picasso, as used in the text, are from the website http://painting.about.com/hobbies/painting/library/blpicassoquotes.htm, which does not provide sources. Paul De Boeck has kindly provided the likely original source for the first of the two quotes, "Art is a lie that makes us realize truth" (Picasso, 1923, p. 315). Barr (1946, pp. 270-271) reprinted the text of that statement by Picasso, attributing the interview to Marius de Zayas; the fact that the original conversation was conducted in Spanish likely accounts for slightly differing English translations.

true, but fortunately it is only necessary that they be useful." Our models are lies, but they may be evaluated by the standards of engineering (Is the model useful?) and art (Or is this science?: Does the model enable us to realize the truth?). Good models, although they may be lies, fall on the positive side of J.W. Tukey's (1962 pp 13-14) dictum: "Far better an approximate answer to the *right* question, which is often vague, than an *exact* answer to the wrong question, which can always be made precise" (emphasis in the original).[4]

"Bad artists copy. Good artists steal."[5] A similar idea is often expressed in a remark suggesting that we "stand on the shoulders of giants," but the idea is the same: Some of the most original (and useful) work steals (or, to be more polite, "borrows") from that which has gone before. Recall the list of some of the most important contributions of quantitative psychology, and consider the many incremental contributions that have made those approaches to data analysis so useful?

Models are art. The methods required to properly associate models and data involve engineering. And the beauty of the enterprise appears when psychometric engineering solves real-world problems.

1.3 Design

Design is the integration of art and engineering. Psychometrics uses design to solve problems that arise in modeling and data analysis in the behavioral sciences. Practicing psychometricians design models, and algorithms to perform statistical computations. Of course, the first goal of design should be to solve the problem; thus, design is engineering. Many would like our designs to be intellectually and esthetically pleasing; so design should be artistic. Artists steal, so design should borrow from what has gone before.

Practitioners of psychometrics can learn a good deal from those, perhaps in other disciplines, who study design for its own sake. An important aspect of good design is to know when to use what has gone before, and when to take an entirely different approach to the problem. In his acceptance lecture of the Turing Award

---

[4] Howard Wainer has informed me that John Tukey kept a file labeled "juicy quotes," that included the following line from Herbert Robbins (1952, p. 529): "It is often better to have reasonably good solutions of the proper problems than optimum solutions of the wrong problems." Tukey's version is more-often quoted, probably because it exhibits a superior turn of phrasing; but it makes an interesting transition to the next idea to note that Tukey borrowed the line.

[5] Picasso's line has gained prominence after being (mis-)quoted by Steve Jobs as "Good artists copy; great artists steal," in the PBS documentary *Triumph of the Nerds* written by Bob Cringely. As an illustration of the concept (theft), the actor Noah Wylie, playing Steve Jobs in the TNT movie *Pirates of Silicon Valley*, delivers Jobs' line. Another illustration of theft in art arises from the fact that the pseudonym "Robert X. Cringely" (Bob Cringely on the byline of *Triumph of the Nerds*) was alleged in a lawsuit to be stolen from the publication *Infoworld*. The name had been created as a *nom de plume* for a collection of columnists, including Mark Stevens, the writer of *Triumph of the Nerds*.

of the Association for Computing Machinery, Frederick Brooks (in press) told the following story:[6]

> Here's an example: In designing a wing for our house, I had to do a professional music studio... This thing had to be this size and shape to accommodate two grand pianos, a string octet, and a one foot teaching margin around the octet for the teacher to go around and look over people's shoulders, and various other constraints. Now the difficulty is that, given all the other constraints as to where this could be attached to the existing house...

> Ah, there's a covenant in the deed that says there's a setback line of fifteen feet from the property line. Oops. And, the town law says you can't cast a shadow on the winter solstice on your neighbor's property, and that gives a seventeen-foot setback line.

The studio would not fit between the exiting house and the setback lines. Brooks continued:

> Well, I wrestled for two weeks with this problem at the architectural design level; I pushed, I pulled, I massaged, I turned this way and that, and no good solution could readily be found. And finally it occurred to me that I was working in the wrong frame of reference and I said "Why not hire a lawyer and go to the city council and try to get a variance?" Well, that's a pretty expensive and lengthy process too.

> And then the right answer occurred to me, and I went to the neighbor and said, "Would you sell me a five-foot strip of land?" And he said, "I'll be glad to."... Now we have a new property line, ... and we're free and clear. Thinking in a different frame made all the difference in the architectural design.

Approaching the problem ingeniously, "breaking set," or thinking in the right "frame of reference," are aspects of good design.

2 Illustrations

The idea is that psychometric activity involves a sequence of three conceptual stages: 1) engineering (defining a problem to be solved), 2) art (that involves lies and stealing), and 3) design of a solution.

The illustrations that follow are drawn largely from our recent work on the subject of *Test Scoring* (Thissen and Wainer 2001); they include examples of quantitative psychology as engineering, using models (are they lies if they are not entirely true?) and theft (is it stealing if the sources are properly cited?). These illustrations fall most readily to hand, because they reflect some of our work of the past decade. However, a property of these particular illustrations is that they solve

---

[6] The published version of Brooks' address, *The design of design*, has not appeared at the time of this writing; this version of the story is derived from a transcription of the original address.

relatively narrowly-defined problems in test theory; that should not be taken to indicate that this is a paean to applied research; it is not. These illustrations describe basic research that solves fairly narrowly defined problems. Additional examples, some of which exhibit more data-analytic generality, can easily be found in other areas of quantitative psychology. All such examples illustrate the basic research that is quantitative psychology.

2.1 The North Carolina End-of-Grade Tests

The engineering problem to be solved

The context for the development of the North Carolina End-of-Grade (NC EOG) tests in 1992 was the desire for a set of "end of grade" tests in Reading and Mathematics for grades three through eight. The goal of these tests was to measure the correspondence between student progress and state-specified curricular objectives. While the test was designed to report individual student-level scores, the primary objective involved aggregate reporting at school district and state levels, to demonstrate annual progress toward greater educational accomplishment. A desire to represent the curriculum extensively created a demand for multiple forms of each test at each grade level, to provide sufficient items to measure large numbers of curricular objectives without making the tests inordinately long for individual students.

A plan for timely reporting of results required that the tests be locally scored, quickly (in a matter of days)—that specification precluded the common practice in large-scale testing of centralized automated scoring and post-operational equating of the multiple forms. (It also meant that the test would include only machine-scored multiple-choice items.) For a number of reasons it appeared desirable to use item response theory (IRT) to provide the scale for the test scores. However, to provide comparable scores on each form, the plan required tables translating each summed score into a corresponding estimate of proficiency (linearly transformed onto the integer reporting scale). While tradition in IRT might have made use of response-pattern scores, the use of response-pattern scores was judged unacceptable for some of the consumers of the test results. Many teachers, students, and parents (not to mention newspaper reporters) expect students who answer the same number of questions correctly to receive the same scale score on a test. Because response-pattern scores do not have that property, and because a purpose of the scores on this test was that they be highly visible, we eschewed response-pattern scoring.

In planning the testing program, we added a plan to place the scores on a so-called "developmental" or "vertically equated" scale, to enhance the interpretability of the scores. Such scales permit an evaluation of year to year growth, a feature that is absent from tests scored entirely normatively within grade level.

The art of theft

We used the three-parameter logistic (3PL) model (Birnbaum 1968) for the multiple-choice item responses. [Of course, Birnbaum's 3PL model was based on extensive borrowing, most notably from Lord (1953), Finney (1952), and Berkson (1944, 1953).] Data on the same item tryout forms collected in adjacent grades (3 and 4, 4 and 5, 5 and 6, and so on) were used to estimate the difference between the distributions of proficiency for those grades (Williams et al. 1998), using Bock and Aitkin's (1981) improvement of Bock and Lieberman's (1970) estimation procedures. (Because we were using ideas IRT has borrowed from Thurstone (1925, 1938), we also created the developmental scale using Thurstone's (1938) procedure and compared the results [Williams et al. 1998].)

For use as pieces of the solution to the requirement for IRT-based tables translating summed scores into scale scores, we were able to collect the following contributions: Yen (1984) had observed that IRT provides the basis for likelihood-based scale scores for summed scores, even for models like the 3PL for which the summed score is not a sufficient statistic, and response-pattern scoring is optimal. Yen also proposed an approximate computational procedure for maximum likelihood estimates of proficiency for summed scores, making use of an approximation offered by Lord and Novick (1968 pp 524-526). However, essentially simultaneously with the publication of Yen's (1984) paper, Lord and Wingersky (1984), showed how to eliminate the approximation in the computation of the summed-score likelihood through the use of a recursive algorithm. The Lord and Wingersky (1984) paper was on the subject of equating, and its terse presentation of the recursive algorithm provided no direct clue that it might also be useful for test scoring.

Bock and Mislevy (1982) had re-introduced to IRT the idea of expected *a posteriori* (EAP) scoring for response patterns (that idea had originally been suggested by Lazarsfeld, 1950). Assembling all of those ideas produced a quick computational procedure for tables translating summed scores into the corresponding expected values of proficiency (Thissen et al. 1995; Thissen and Orlando, 2001).

The design

We used IRT to link the scales for proficiency for all grades; a linear transformation of that scale to have an average of 150 and a standard deviation of 10 in grade 5 became the reporting scale for the scores. Because all items in the original large-scale item tryout were calibrated on the same scale, alternate forms could be constructed within grades and linked to that common scale implicitly using IRT, removing the need for post-operational equating of the forms.

Tables translating summed scores into the corresponding expected values of proficiency, computed using the algorithm described by Thissen et al. (1995) and Thissen and Orlando (2001), are used to provide scores on the alternate forms. While the computations involved in creating these score-translation tables are sufficiently tedious that they require modern computational machinery, both the theory underlying the scores and the presentation of the score-translation tables themselves are very simple—much more simple than the response-pattern scoring that has been traditional in IRT. The procedure has been used in each of the past nine years to create scoring tables for each form. Decentralized scanning and score-translation using these tables means that each of the (approximately) half million Reading and Mathematics tests are scored within days after administration at the end of each school year.

With respect to broader design issues in quantitative psychology, our work with the posterior distributions for summed scores provided initial bases for a new item calibration system based on score-group frequencies rather than response patterns (Chen 1995; Chen and Thissen 1999), and a useful approach to the goodness-of-fit problem for IRT models (Orlando 1997; Orlando and Thissen 2000).

2.2 Score Combination

The engineering problem to be solved

It is becoming increasingly common practice in educational measurement in the U.S. to design assessments that include both multiple-choice items and con-structed-response items. There are usually large numbers of multiple-choice items, to provide breadth of content coverage and consequent reliability and validity; the constructed-response items are usually "larger" and more time-consuming, and are administered largely for their putative positive effects on instruction. The North Carolina Tests of Computer Skills is an example. It includes both a multiple-choice test measuring knowledge of topics relevant to personal-computer usage and a performance test in which the examinee is scored on the accomplishment of pre-specified word-processing tasks and responses to open-ended questions using a database and a spreadsheet. A smaller example, described more extensively in several chapters of Thissen and Wainer (2001), is a Reading test from Wisconsin that included sixteen multiple-choice items and four open-ended (constructed-response) items; the latter were rated by judges on a four-point (0-3) scale.

The problem to be solved is to provide a single score (if that is appropri-ate—that is, if all of the items are indicators of a common construct) combining the responses to the multiple-choice and open-ended items.

The art of theft

A traditional solution using IRT to score combinations of multiple-choice item re-sponses and ratings of constructed responses involves the use of item response-pattern scoring. Such a solution is used, for example, for the National Assessment of Educational Progress (NAEP), which uses the three-parameter logistic model for multiple-choice items and the generalized partial credit model (Muraki 1992, 1997) for constructed response items (Mislevy et al. 1992). However, in many cases, as was the case with the NC EOG tests, item response-pattern scoring has unattractive features for a large-scale test subject to intense public scrutiny, so another plan was required. Solutions from the traditional test theory, involving scoring weights assigned arbitrarily to each section, seemed unattractive.

Looking at the problem from a different perspective, the mechanics of IRT provide a solution, based on our work on IRT for summed scores (Thissen and Orlando 2001; Thissen et al. 2001).

The design

Our proposed solution to the problem of combining responses to items of different kinds (like multiple-choice items and rated constructed-response items) has been to use the mechanics of IRT to assign scores (EAPs) to response patterns of summed scores on the separate sections (Rosa et al. 2001). This procedure uses IRT for summed scores to compute the likelihood for the multiple-choice items using Birnbaum's (1968) model, and then separately for the constructed-response items using Samejima's (1969, 1997) model. Then the two likelihoods are combined, as though they represented very large "items"; including the population distribution yields the joint likelihood for the "pattern" of responses comprising the multiple-choice and constructed-response summed scores. EAPs computed from those joint likelihoods may be linearly transformed to become reported scores that are comparable across the many alternate forms of the tests that are required each year for administration at various times, re-tests, and so on.

While the mechanics of IRT are used behind the scenes to produce the scoring system, the consequent scoring procedure is nearly as simple as that involved in the summed-score translation tables for the NC EOG tests described in the previous section. Here, the score-translation tables are two-way arrays, indexed by the summed scores on the two sections, with entries corresponding to scale scores.

Sequelae

We have subsequently developed a straightforward system based on linear combinations of scores derived from the parts of tests to approximate IRT combined scores (Thissen et al. 2001). That system may also be used as the basis for a scoring system for computerized adaptive tests (CATs) that are assembled using multi-item units, or testlets. If a CAT adaptively administers blocks of items (instead of using an item-by-item selection algorithm), then each of those blocks may be analogous to a section of a paper-and-pencil test. For a two-stage CAT, there are two sections; one way to score the combination is to compute the expected value of proficiency for the pattern of summed scores—that is, the summed score on the first block and the summed score on the second block. If the CAT has three or more stages, the scoring algorithm generalizes straightforwardly.

Such a scoring system is not as efficient as item-by-item response-pattern scoring, if the IRT model is correct. On the other hand, it is not as difficult to explain to non-psychometric audiences as response-pattern scoring, because in many cases the scoring system can be exhaustively tabulated as summed-score to scale-score translation tables. The approximation to this system can use weighted sums of (transformed) block scores (Thissen et al. 2001); a scoring system based on linear combinations may be even more widely acceptable.

It is important in solving engineering problems that the design solves all aspects of the problem. If one considers only statistical optimality, then IRT response-pattern scores may be demonstrably "best" in many situations. However, in the real-world use of tests, the engineering problem may also include other requirements, such as a need to explain the scoring algorithm to a variety of audiences. It may be necessary to think differently, and to yield some degree of statistical optimality, to arrive at a satisfactory solution for the overall problem.

2.3 Approximate IRT Pattern Scoring

The solution to one apparently narrowly-defined problem can often plant seeds that grow into many other solutions. That was the case with our early work on summed scores as they relate to IRT, which prompted the conception of a new item calibration system and a new scheme for evaluating goodness of fit of the models. Again in this illustration, what began as a solution to the problem of combining scores on multiple-choice and open-ended sections of a test grew into a scoring system for more complicated computerized adaptive tests with two or more parts. Ultimately, in an arc that has become a complete circle, we have taken the idea of a linear approximation for IRT scale scores back to simplify response-pattern scoring under some circumstances.

Conventional IRT response-pattern scoring involves elaborate computations for each response pattern. For example, the expected a posteriori (EAP) estimate of the underlying latent variable θ is

$$\text{EAP}(\theta \mid \mathbf{x}) = \int \left[\prod_i T(x_i) \right] \phi(\theta) d\theta, \tag{1}$$

in which $T(x_i)$ is the trace line, derived from the item response model, for the response x to the ith item in the response pattern $\mathbf{x}$, and $\phi(\theta)$ is the population distribution. In practice, the integration is carried out numerically; see Thissen and Orlando (2001 pp 103-114).

Such scale scores are valuable for many reasons: They can be computed in the presence of randomly missing data, whereas that presents a problem for summed scores. They can be comparable for alternate forms of the test or questionnaire (because that is simply a particular kind of missing data). They are on a scale that is likely to have nicely linear relations with other variables. They are well-suited to the analysis of growth or change, or for use in procedures that, for example, decompose scores or growth trajectories into clusters, because their scaling and distributional properties are well-behaved.

But such scale scores are also little used in research in psychology, because they are difficult to compute. Special IRT software is required to perform the necessary operations using the trace lines, as shown on the screen; it is not something one "does in SAS."

During the past year, we have specialized our testlet-scoring scheme (developed for computerized adaptive tests with groups of items) to create a linear scoring system for responses to individual items. For each response pattern, there is a weighted sum of item values, a sum of the weights, and then computation of a weighted average that gives essentially the same answer as the traditional IRT computation described in Eq. 1. Specifically,

$$EAP*(\theta \mid x) = \frac{\sum_i w_x^i EAP_x^i}{\sum_i w_x^i - (I-1)};$$

(2)

this computation involves only a set of values for each item response, EAPs indexed by the item i (for $i = 1, 2, \ldots I$) and the response x, and a set of similarly-indexed weights w. The values and weights can be tabulated; then the approximate EAP*s *can* be computed using standard statistical software such as SAS or SPSS.

While we have shown that this approximation works poorly when the 3PL model is used for the trace lines (Thissen et al. 2000), subsequent study has shown that it appears to work very well for Samejima's (1969, 1997) graded model (which includes the 2PL model as a special case). That the approximation "works very well" means that the approximate scores are usually within a few hundredths of a z-score unit of the exact value, and the loss of reliability entailed in the approximation appears to be most often in the third decimal place (Steinberg and Thissen, unpublished ms, 2001). This approximation merits further study, which it is receiving at this time. However, with it we hope to make IRT much more practicable for relatively small-scale measurement in psychological research.

2.4 Augmented Subscores

The engineering problem to be solved

A request for "diagnostic information" is a challenge often encountered in the construction of large-scale tests of educational achievement, such as the NC EOG Mathematics Test or the NC Tests of Computer Skills. While such tests usually include groups of items that cover distinguishable subject matter, those groups of items are usually too small in number to yield reliable "subscores." To a point, psychometricians can solve the problem by avoiding it, by saying that there are too few items to produce reliable scores on diagnostic portions of the tests. However, when state legislators threaten to pass laws requiring that the test provide diagnostic information, a solution that provides defensible results may be better than refusal.

The art of theft

In work at the Educational Testing Service in the U.S., Howard Wainer proposed the multivariate generalization of Kelley's (1927, 1947) "regressed true score estimate" as a potential solution to this problem. Kelley's regressed true score estimates have been largely a subject of academic curiosity for much of the past century: They are discussed in many textbooks on test theory, because the elegance of the derivation is unquestioned, producing as it does, the regression of an unknowable variable on an observed variable. But they are almost never used in practice, because they do nothing; Kelley's regression reduces the variance of the estimates, but does not change their order, so on a norm-referenced test there is no difference whatever between using the usual summed score or the regressed estimates.

Wainer observed that the multivariate generalization of Kelley's regressed estimates of true scores differs in important ways from the univariate procedure: The multivariate regressed estimates may be very different from the raw scores from which they are computed. Further, the regressed estimates may be much more reliable than the simple summed scores of small subsets of items on a test. "Wainer subscores" (as we have called them at times) are based on "borrowing strength" (Tukey 1961; p 277 in the Jones 1986 reprint) from all of the items on the test in scoring each of several parts, by computing an estimate of the score for each part that is regressed on all of the part-scores. [Of course, as is often the case with developments such as this, the same results have been obtained more than once. Cronbach et al. (1972 pp 309*ff*) described "multivariate estimation of universe scores" in their classic text on generalizability theory.]

The complete version of augmentation works like this: If a test has three parts (for example, a mathematics test with sections about algebra, geometry, and probability and statistics), then one could compute three raw subscores, one for each of the three parts. Because each of those three subscores is based on only one-third as many items as the entire test, each subscore is likely to be relatively unreliable. However, estimates of the correlation of each of those subscores with the corresponding true score can be computed (by estimating reliability), and estimates of the correlations among the three true scores can be computed by correlating the summed scores. Those estimates can be assembled into the algebra of regression to yield multiple regression equations that predict each true score as a linear combination of all three simple summed subscores. Those predictions of the true subscores may be much more accurate (reliable) than the individual subscores. Unlike univariate Kelley regressed estimates, the multivariate procedure changes the order of the scores: A high score on the algebra section for a person who also obtains high scores on geometry and probability/statistics is predicted to be higher, while the same high algebra score for a person who scores lower on the other two sections is predicted to be lower.

Motivated by a desire for subscores on the NC EOG Mathematics Test and the NC Tests of Computer Skills, we have extended Wainer's proposal to work entirely within the context of IRT (Wainer et al. 2001). The integration of IRT with the multivariate Kelley regression system permits the IRT to carry the burden of between-form linking, so comparable subscores can be computed from multiple forms without *post hoc* equating.

The design

Several steps are involved in the computation of augmented subscores for a large-scale test, especially if IRT is used for multiple forms. Wainer et al. (2001) provide several examples; the steps are simply listed here:

1. Calibrate the items, using an IRT model, within each part of the test for which a subscore is to be computed.
2. Compute the correlations among the IRT estimates of proficiency for each sub-part of the test. Then combine those correlations with the reliability estimates obtained in step (1) to obtain the regression coefficients for each "true" subscore.
3. Regressed subscores are computed as a set of linear combinations of the conventional (IRT) estimates of proficiency for each part of the test.

These developments permit reliable subscores to be computed for each of many alternate forms that use IRT to ensure between-form comparability of scores. The system is completely general and may find many applications in large-scale testing; setting aside the tedious nature of some of the computations, its concepts are straightforward and the presentation of the results is remarkably simple.

3 Expanding Horizons

The illustrations presented here have been test theory, because that has been our area of research for some time. It is also currently the area of research for many active members of the Psychometric Society. I won't say "too many" because according to either *Time* magazine (Goldstein 2001) or *The New York Times* (Henriques and Steinberg 2001) there is a shortage of psychometricians in the U.S.—meaning persons who work in test theory.

However, it appears from recent programs of the annual meeting of the Psychometric Society that there are proportionally too many of us. There are problems in psychological research that test theorists are ill-equipped to solve. For example, recordings of single-channel event-related potentials are a commonly-used source of data in biological psychology and neuroscience; the statistical problems associated with the analysis of such data are fascinating (see, for example, Raz et al. 2001). However, traditionally-oriented groups of quantitative psychologists have been slow to turn attention to this and other new problems in data analysis in the behavioral sciences, such as the analysis of the essentially spatial data that arise from functional magnetic resonance imaging (fMRI) recordings (see, e.g., Laidlaw et al. 1995).

How can we re-invigorate our problem-solving discipline of design, within the context of institutions that may not see psychology as a design-oriented discipline? How can we maintain the continuity of our intellectual history while renewing ourselves with the need to design solutions for new problems? Those question are the challenge for the future of quantitative psychology, and the Psychometric Society.

4 Concluding Remarks

L.L. Thurstone's (1937) presidential address to the Psychometric Society concluded (p. 232):

> Let us remember that a psychological theory is not good simply because it
> is cleverly mathematical, that an experiment is not good just because it
> involves ingenious apparatus and that statistics are merely the means for
> checking theory with experiment. In the long run we shall be judged in
> terms of the significance, the fruitfulness and the self-consistency of the
> psychological principles that we discover.

I would modify the last line, in this age of collaboration, to read "that we help
discover." As science has grown in the sixty-five years since the founding of the
Psychometric Society, we have become part—the tool-making part—of a very
large community of specialized individuals engaged in psychological science. Let
us do our part well, by recognizing the needs of the larger community and providing artistic engineering: good design.

References

Barr AH (1946) Picasso: Fifty years of his art. The Museum of Modern Art, New York

Berkson J (1944) Application of the logistic function to bio-assay. Journal of the American
Statistical Association 39:357-375.

Berkson J (1953) A statistically precise and relatively simple method of estimating the bio-
assay with quantal response, based on the logistic function. Journal of the American
Statistical Association 48:565-599.

Birnbaum A (1968) Some latent trait models and their use in inferring an examinee's ability. In: Lord FM, Novick MR, Statistical theories of mental test scores. Addison-
Wesley, Reading, MA, pp 395-479

Bock RD, Aitkin M (1981) Marginal maximum likelihood estimation of item parameters:
an application of the EM algorithm. Psychometrika 46:443-459

Bock RD, Lieberman M (1970) Fitting a response model for n dichotomously scored items.
Psychometrika 35:179-197

Bock RD, Mislevy RJ (1982) Adaptive EAP estimation of ability in a microcomputer environment. Applied Psychological Measurement 6:431-444

Box GEP (1979) Some problems of statistics and everyday life. Journal of the American
Statistical Association 74:1-4

Brooks FP (1996) The computer scientist as toolsmith II. Communications of the ACM
39:61-68

Brooks FP (in press) The design of design. Communications of the ACM

Chen WH (1995) Estimation of item parameters for the three-parameter logistic model using the marginal likelihood of summed scores. Unpublished doctoral dissertation, The
University of North Carolina at Chapel Hill

Chen WH, Thissen D (1999) Estimation of item parameters for the three-parameter logistic model using the marginal likelihood of summed scores. British Journal of Mathematical and Statistical Psychology 52:19-37

Cronbach LJ, Gleser GC, Nanda H, Rajaratnam N (1972) The dependability of behavioral measurements: Theory of generalizability for scores and profiles. John Wiley & Sons, New York

Finney DJ (1952) Probit analysis: A statistical treatment of the sigmoid response curve. Cambridge University Press, London

Goldstein A (2001, March 12) Making another big score. Time 157:66-67

Henriques DB, Steinberg J (2001, May 20) Errors plague testing industry. The New York Times, pp A1, A22-23

Jones LV (1998) LL Thurstone's vision of psychology as a quantitative rational science. In: Kimble GA, Wertheimer M (eds) Portraits of pioneers in psychology, vol III. Lawrence Erlbaum Associates, Mahwah, NJ, pp 84-102

Kelley TL (1927) The interpretation of educational measurements. World Book, New York

Kelley TL (1947) Fundamentals of statistics. Harvard University Press, Cambridge, MA

Lazarsfeld PF (1950) The logical and mathematical foundation of latent structure analysis. In: Stouffer SA, Guttman L, Suchman EA, Lazarsfeld PF, Star, SA, Clausen JA, Measurement and Prediction. Wiley, New York, pp 362-412

Laidlaw DH, Fleischer KW, Barr AH (1995, September) Bayesian Mixture Classification of MRI Data for Geometric Modeling and Visualization. Poster presented at the First International Workshop on Statistical Mixture Modeling, Aussois, France. (Retrieved from the Worldwide Web: http://www.gg.caltech.edu/~dhl/aussois/paper.html)

Lewis B (1996, March 15) IS survival guide. Infoworld 21:96

Lord FM (1953) The relation of test score to the trait underlying the test. Educational and Psychological Measurement 13:517-548

Lord FM, Novick M (1968) Statistical theories of mental test scores. Addison Wesley, Reading, MA

Lord FM, Wingersky MS (1984) Comparison of IRT true-score and equipercentile observed-score "equatings." Applied Psychological Measurement 8:453-461

Mislevy RM, Johnson EG, Muraki E (1992) Scaling procedures in NAEP. Journal of Educational Statistics 17:131-154

Muraki E (1992) A generalized partial credit model: Application of an EM algorithm. Applied Psychological Measurement 16:159-176

Muraki E (1997) A generalized partial credit model. In: van der Linden W, Hambleton RK (eds) Handbook of modern item response theory. Springer, New York, pp 153-164

Orlando M (1997) Item fit in the context of item response theory. Unpublished doctoral dissertation, The University of North Carolina at Chapel Hill

Orlando M, Thissen D (2000) New item fit indices for dichotomous item response theory models. Applied Psychological Measurement 24:50-64

Picasso P (1923) Picasso speaks—A statement by the artist. The Arts 3:315-326

Raz J, Turetsky BI, Dickerson LW (2001) Inference for a random wavelet packet model of single-channel event-related potentials. Journal of the American Statistical Association 96:409-420

Robbins H (1952) Some aspects of the sequential design of experiments. Bulletin of the American Mathematical Society 58:527-535

Rosa K, Swygert K, Nelson L, Thissen D (2001) Item response theory applied to combinations of multiple-choice and constructed-response items—scale scores for patterns of summed scores. In: Thissen D, Wainer H (eds) Test Scoring. Lawrence Erlbaum Associates, Mahwah, NJ, pp 253-292

Samejima F (1969) Estimation of latent ability using a response pattern of graded scores. Psychometric Monograph No 17

Samejima F (1997) Graded response model. In: van der Linden W, Hambleton RK (eds) Handbook of modern item response theory. Springer, New York, pp 85-100

Thissen D, Flora D, Reeve B, & Vevea J L (2000, July) Linear Approximations for Item Response Theory Response Pattern Scores. Paper presented at the annual meeting of the Psychometric Society, Vancouver, BC, Canada

Thissen D, Nelson L, Rosa K, McLeod LD (2001) Item response theory for items scored in more than two categories. In: Thissen D, Wainer H (eds) Test Scoring. Lawrence Erlbaum Associates, Mahwah, NJ, pp 141-186

Thissen D, Nelson L, Swygert K (2001) Item response theory applied to combinations of multiple-choice and constructed-response items—approximation methods for scale scores. In: Thissen D, Wainer H (eds) Test Scoring. Lawrence Erlbaum Associates, Mahwah, NJ, pp 293-341

Thissen D, Orlando M (2001) Item response theory for items scored in two categories. In: Thissen D, Wainer H (eds) Test Scoring. Lawrence Erlbaum Associates, Mahwah, NJ, pp 73-140

Thissen D, Pommerich M, Billeaud K, Williams VSL (1995) Item response theory for scores on tests including polytomous items with ordered responses. Applied Psychological Measurement 19:39-49

Thissen D & Wainer H (eds) (2001) Test Scoring. Lawrence Erlbaum Associates, Mahwah, NJ

Thurstone LL (1925) A method of scaling psychological and educational tests. Journal of Educational Psychology 16:433-449

Thurstone LL (1927) The law of comparative judgment. Psychological Review 34:278-286

Thurstone LL (1937) Psychology as a quantitative rational science. Science 85:227-232

Thurstone LL (1938) Primary mental abilities. University of Chicago Press, Chicago, IL

Tukey JW (1961) Data analysis and behavioral science or learning to bear the quantitative man's burden by shunning badmandments. Unpublished ms reprinted in LV Jones (ed) (1986), The collected works of John W Tukey, Vol III, Philosophy and principles of data analysis: 1949-1964. Wadsworth & Brooks-Cole, Monterey, CA, pp 187-389

Tukey JW (1962) The future of data analysis. Annals of Mathematical Statistics 33:1-67. (Reprinted in LV Jones (ed) (1986), The collected works of John W Tukey, Vol III, Philosophy and principles of data analysis: 1949-1964. Wadsworth & Brooks-Cole, Monterey, CA, pp 391-484)

Wainer H, Vevea JL, Camacho F, Reeve B, Rosa K, Nelson L, Swygert K, Thissen D (2001) Augmented scores—"borrowing strength" to compute scores based on small numbers of items. In: Thissen D, Wainer H (eds) Test Scoring. Lawrence Erlbaum Associates, Mahwah, NJ, pp 343-387

Williams VSL, Pommerich M, Thissen D (1998) A comparison of developmental scales based on Thurstone methods and item response theory. Journal of Educational Measurement 35:93-107

Yen WM (1984) Obtaining maximum likelihood trait estimates from number-correct scores for the three-parameter logistic model. Journal of Educational Measurement 21:93-111

Vectors and Matrices in Psychometrics with Special Emphasis on Generalized Inverse and Projection Matrices

Haruo Yanai[1]

1) Research Division, National Center for University Entrance Examinations,
2-19-23, Komaba, Meguro, Tokyo, 153-8501, Japan   *yanai@rd.dnc.ac.jp*

Summary. This paper illustrates uses of vectors and matrices in psychometric problems with special emphasis on generalized inverse and projection matrices. As examples of recommended uses of vectors, the idea of covariance ratio is first introduced, which is useful in determining the weights for high school subjects taken at the university entrance examinations. Secondly, results on the range of a correlation coefficient are summarized and generalized by extensive uses of generalized inverse and projection matrices. Thirdly, previous results showing that multiple correlation and canonical correlations can be computed from a singular correlation matrix, are explained and by extending these results, some new results are introduced, and the relationships on multiple, canonical and partial canonical correlations among some sets of residual variables are discussed. Our emphasis given in this paper is that uses of vectors and matrices allow one to understand the complex problems in psychometrics quite easily without making use of complicated algebra.

Key words. projection matrix (projector), generalized inverse matrix, multiple correlation, canonical correlation, range of correlation, correlation between residual variables

1 Introduction

Thurstone (1935) published his book entitled "Vector of Mind", in which he tried to represent scores of intelligent tests in terms of vectors, and proposed the idea that the number of fundamental abilities required to solve items in intelligent tests coincides with the number of dimensions of the space these vectors span. The emphasis in this book is that the correlation coefficient between two variables can be represented by the cosine of the angle between the corresponding two vectors. Gulliksen (1950) developed classical test theory by extensive uses of vectors and showed that vectors of raw scores are decomposed into the sum of two orthogonal vectors, one corresponding to the vector of true scores, and the other to that of error scores.

1.1 Simple examples of vector notation

First, we give three simple examples to show how uses of vectors help us solve some problems in psychometrics. We first consider the case where two variables $\mathbf{x}$ and $\mathbf{y}$ with the same variance are given. Throughout the paper variables are represented as n dimensional vectors, and the inner product between $\mathbf{x}$ and $\mathbf{y}$ is written as $(\mathbf{x}, \mathbf{y})$. The norms of these vectors are written as $\|\mathbf{x}\|$ and $\|\mathbf{y}\|$. The correlation coefficient between $\mathbf{x}$ and $\mathbf{y}$ can be defined as $r(\mathbf{x}, \mathbf{y}) = (\mathbf{x}, \mathbf{y})/(\|\mathbf{x}\| \|\mathbf{y}\|)$. Since two variables $\mathbf{x}$ and $\mathbf{y}$ have a same variance, we have $\|\mathbf{x}\| = \|\mathbf{y}\|$, thus establishing that the covariance between the sum of the two variables and the difference score between them vanishes since $(\mathbf{x} + \mathbf{y}, \mathbf{x} - \mathbf{y}) = \|\mathbf{x}\|^2 - \|\mathbf{y}\|^2 = 0$ (See, Fig. 1.). If both $\|\mathbf{x}\| = \|\mathbf{y}\|$ and $(\mathbf{x}, \mathbf{y}) = 0$ hold simultaneously, then $r(\mathbf{x} + \mathbf{y}, \mathbf{x}) = 1/\sqrt{2} = 0.707$, which is surprisingly high contrary to our intuition, since the two variables have the zero correlation (See, Fig. 2.). If $\|\mathbf{x}\| = \|\mathbf{y}\|$, then $\|\mathbf{x} + \mathbf{y}\|^2 \le \|\mathbf{x}\|^2$ implies $r(\mathbf{x}, \mathbf{y}) \le -0.5$, which implies that the variance of the total score of the two variables x and y becomes smaller than the variance of a variable. This implies that one must take a note of the magnitude of correlations among variables, if one tries to make a composite score by summing scores across variables (See, Fig. 3.).

1.2 The covariance ratio

The idea of covariance ratio was first introduced by Stanley and Wang (1970) and it was named as the covariance ratio by a Japanese Statistician (Takeuchi, 1986), and has been used as a method of analysis of university entrance examination data in Japan. We give a brief sketch of the theory of covariance ratio. Given p variables $x_1, x_2, \cdots, x_p$, we minimize $\left\| x_j - b_j \sum_{k=1}^{p} x_k \right\|^2$ over b_j. Then, $b_j = (\mathbf{x}_j, \mathbf{t})/(\mathbf{t}, \mathbf{t}) = r(\mathbf{x}_j, \mathbf{t}) \dfrac{\|\mathbf{x}_j\|}{\|\mathbf{t}\|} = \dfrac{\|P(\mathbf{t})\mathbf{x}_j\|}{\|\mathbf{t}\|}$ where $\mathbf{t} = \sum_{k}^{p} x_k$ and $P(\mathbf{t}) = t(t't)^{-1}t'$ is the orthogonal projector onto $S(\mathbf{t})$, the space spanned by t. Observe that $\sum_{j=1}^{p} b_j = 1$. The b_j is called the covariance ratio reflecting the magnitude of the relationship of variable x_j to the total score t. When $p = 2$ and two variables x_1 and x_2 have the same variance, $b_1 = b_2 = 1/2$. We give a numerical example of covariance ratios. In Japan, the joint first

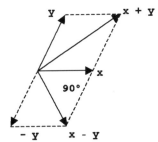

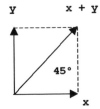

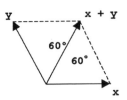

Fig. 1. Correlation between the sum of two variables and the difference of those

Fig. 2. Correlation between the sum of two uncorrelated variables and each variable

Fig. 3. When the variance of the sum of two variables is smaller than the variance of each variable

(Throughout Figs 1, 2 and 3, the variances of
all the variables are assumed to be equal)

stage achievement (JFSA) test was introduced in 1979 for applicants to the national and public universities. The JFSA test covers Japanese languages, social studies, mathematics, science and foreign languages. Scores of each sub-test ranged from 0 to 200. Covariance ratios of these five subjects computed from the JFSA test data obtained in 1979 were 12.50, 16.14, 27.13, 25.27 and 18.96, respectively. Covariance ratios of mathematics and science were relatively high compared to those of the other subjects, almost twice those of other subjects. This can be shown immediately by drawing parallelogram.

2 Restriction on the range of a correlation coefficient

If $r(\mathbf{x}, \mathbf{y}) = 0.5$ and $r(\mathbf{y}, \mathbf{z}) = 0.5$, the minimum value that $r(\mathbf{x}, \mathbf{z})$ can attain is -0.5 and the maximum is 1. More generally, Glass and Collins (1970) and Hubert (1972) discussed the restriction on the range of the correlation coefficient. Earlier results of these authors and some new results can be summarized in the following property.

Property 1: Given three variables $\mathbf{x}$, $\mathbf{y}$ and $\mathbf{z}$, let $r(\mathbf{x}, \mathbf{y}) = a$, $r(\mathbf{y}, \mathbf{z}) = b$ and $r(\mathbf{x}, \mathbf{z}) = c$ where both a^2 and b^2 are strictly less than 1. Then, the following eight statements are equivalent.

(ia) $\qquad ab - \sqrt{(1 - a^2)(1 - b^2)} \le c \le ab + \sqrt{(1 - a^2)(1 - b^2)}$

(ib) $\qquad bc - \sqrt{(1 - b^2)(1 - c^2)} \le a \le bc + \sqrt{(1 - b^2)(1 - c^2)}$

(ic) $$ac - \sqrt{(1-a^2)(1-c^2)} \le b \le ac + \sqrt{(1-a^2)(1-c^2)}$$

(ii) $$-1 \le \frac{(c-ab)}{\sqrt{(1-a^2)}\sqrt{(1-b^2)}} \le 1, \text{ where}$$

$$r(\mathbf{x}, \mathbf{z}/\mathbf{y}) = \frac{(r(\mathbf{x},\mathbf{z}) - r(\mathbf{x},\mathbf{y})r(\mathbf{y},\mathbf{z}))}{\sqrt{1-r(\mathbf{x},\mathbf{y})^2}\sqrt{1-r(\mathbf{y},\mathbf{z})^2}} \text{ is the partial}$$

correlation coefficient between $\mathbf{x}$ and $\mathbf{z}$ eliminating $\mathbf{y}$.

(iii) $R^2(\mathbf{x}, \mathbf{y}/\mathbf{z}) = (b^2 + c^2 - 2abc)/(1-a^2) \le 1$, where $R^2(\mathbf{x}, \mathbf{y}/\mathbf{z})$ is the squared multiple correlation coefficient predicting $\mathbf{z}$ from $\mathbf{x}$ and $\mathbf{y}$.

(iv) $$R^2(\mathbf{y}, \mathbf{z}/\mathbf{x}) = (a^2 + c^2 - 2abc)/(1-b^2) \le 1$$

(v) $$(1 + 2abc - a^2 - b^2 - c^2) \ge 0$$

(vi) $\begin{pmatrix} 1 & c \\ c & 1 \end{pmatrix} - \begin{pmatrix} a \\ b \end{pmatrix} \begin{pmatrix} a & b \end{pmatrix} = \begin{pmatrix} 1-a^2 & c-ab \\ c-ab & 1-b^2 \end{pmatrix}$ is positive semi-definite.

Proofs are easy, and we do not elaborate the proofs here. Instead, we consider the special case in which $c^2 = 1$. From (1b), it follows that if $c = 1$, then $a = b$, and thus $r(\mathbf{x}, \mathbf{z}/\mathbf{y}) = 1$ follows from (ii), and $R(\mathbf{x}, \mathbf{y}/\mathbf{z}) = R(\mathbf{y}, \mathbf{z}/\mathbf{x}) = 1$ follows from (iii) and (iv). Similarly, if $c = -1$, then $a = -b$, thus $r(\mathbf{x}, \mathbf{z}/\mathbf{y}) = -1$ and $R(\mathbf{x}, \mathbf{y}/\mathbf{z}) = R(\mathbf{y}, \mathbf{z}/\mathbf{x}) = 1$ follow immediately. If $a = b = c$, then from (v), we have $a \ge -0.5$.

Olkin (1981) extended this result to the case where three sets of variables are available. We will give some extensions of Olkin's result in the final section of this paper.

3 Uses of generalized inverse and projection matrices in multivariate analysis

In this section, we will review some essential properties of generalized inverse and projection matrices, and how these properties have been used in earlier published Psychometrikas, and some statistical books and journals.

The concept of projection matrices plays an important role in psychometrics and statistics. Rao and Mitra (1971) demonstrated various uses of generalized inverse and projection matrices in statistics. It is well known that a square matrix P is said to be an orthogonal projector if and only if P satisfies both

(a) $P^2 = P$ and   (b) $P' = P$.   (1)

The generalized inverse matrix of A was first introduced as the matrix A^+ satisfying the following four conditions, i.e.,

(c) $AA^+A = A$ (d) $A^+AA^+ = A^+$

(e) $(AA^+)' = AA^+$ and (f) $(A^+A)' = A^+A$,   (2)

where A^+ is called the Moore-Penrose inverse matrix (the MP inverse) of A. Rao (1962) introduced a weaker g-inverse A^- which satisfies only

$$\text{(g)} \quad AA^-A = A .$$

Note that the MP inverse is uniquely determined while a weaker g-inverse is not. We give a numerical example. Let $A = \begin{pmatrix} 1 & 1 \\ 1 & 1 \end{pmatrix}$. Then $A^- = \begin{pmatrix} a & b \\ c & d \end{pmatrix}$

where $a + b + c + d = 1$ is not unique, while $A^+ = (\frac{1}{4}) \begin{pmatrix} 1 & 1 \\ 1 & 1 \end{pmatrix}$ is unique. In

psychometrics, Tucker et al. (1971) was the first to define multiple correlation coefficients using the MP-inverse of a singular correlation matrix A. Kaiser (1976) defined the image and anti-image correlation matrices in terms of the MP inverse of A. Khatri (1976) extended Tucker's result by replacing the MP inverse by a weaker inverse A^-. Motivated by these results, Takeuchi, Yanai and Mukherjee(1982) tried to represent various methods of multivariate statistical methods in terms of orthogonal projection matrices and generalized inverses. Given a set of vectors X spanning the subspace $S(X)$, the orthogonal projectors defined onto $S(X)$ and its ortho-complement subspace $S(X)^\perp$ can be defined as

$$P(X) = X(X'X)^-X' \quad \text{and} \quad Q(X) = I_n - P(X) , \qquad (3)$$

respectively. Note that $P(X)$ is not only invariant for any choice of g-inverses of $X'X$ 'but also invariant for any choice of a matrix X spanning $S(X)$. This invariance property helped identify mutual relationships among various methods of multivariate analysis. Let $P(Y) = Y(Y'Y)^-Y'$ be the orthogonal projector onto $S(Y)$. Further, let $R_{XX} = X'X$, $R_{YY} = Y'Y$ and $R_{XY} = X'Y$ be covariance matrices among variables in X, those in Y and between those in X and Y, respectively. Then the squared canonical correlation between X and Y, which we denote by $cc_j^2(X,Y)$, is equal to

$$\lambda_j(P(X)P(Y)) = \lambda_j((X'X)^-X'Y(Y'Y)^-Y'X) = \lambda_j(R_{XX}^-R_{XY}R_{YY}^-R_{YX})$$
$$(4)$$

which is invariant for any choice of g-inverses of R_{XX} and R_{YY} (Rao, 1981). To illustrate, let

$$R_{XX} = R_{YY} = R_{XY} = R_{YX} = \begin{pmatrix} 1 & 1 \\ 1 & 1 \end{pmatrix} , \quad \text{and}$$

$$H = R_{XX}^- R_{XY} R_{YY}^- R_{YX} = \begin{pmatrix} a & a \\ 1-a & 1-a \end{pmatrix}.$$

Then irrespective of any choice of a in H, we have $\lambda_1(H) = 1$ and $\lambda_2(H) = 0$. If Y has a single variable y, then

$$\lambda_1(P(X)P(\mathbf{y})) = \mathbf{y}'P(X)\mathbf{y}/\mathbf{y}'\mathbf{y} = (\mathbf{r}_{X\mathbf{y}})'R_{XX}^- \mathbf{r}_{X\mathbf{y}} = R^2(X/\mathbf{y}), \quad (5)$$

which is the squared multiple correlation coefficient (SMC). If $R_{XX} = \begin{pmatrix} 1 & 1 \\ 1 & 1 \end{pmatrix}$

and $(\mathbf{r}_{X\mathbf{y}})' = (a, a)$, then we have $R^2(X/\mathbf{y}) = \begin{pmatrix} a & a \end{pmatrix} \begin{pmatrix} 1 & 1 \\ 1 & 1 \end{pmatrix}^- \begin{pmatrix} a \\ a \end{pmatrix} = a^2$,

which is exactly the SMC($\mathbf{y}$) based on $X = (\mathbf{x}_1, \mathbf{x}_2)$. Under the condition that $a^2 \neq 1$, the correlation matrix R between $\mathbf{y}$ and $X = (\mathbf{x}_1, \mathbf{x}_2)$, and its Moore-Penrose inverse R^+ can be written as

$$R = \begin{pmatrix} 1 & a & a \\ a & 1 & 1 \\ a & 1 & 1 \end{pmatrix} \text{ and } R^+ = \begin{pmatrix} 1 & -a/2 & -a/2 \\ -a/2 & 1/4 & 1/4 \\ -a/2 & 1/4 & 1/4 \end{pmatrix} /(1-a^2),$$

thus

$$Q = (\mathbf{q}_1, \mathbf{q}_2, \mathbf{q}_3) = I_3 - RR^+ = \begin{pmatrix} 0 & 0 & 0 \\ 0 & 1/2 & -1/2 \\ 0 & -1/2 & 1/2 \end{pmatrix}.$$

$\mathbf{q}_1$ is a null vector, while both $\mathbf{q}_2$ and $\mathbf{q}_3$ are non-null. It follows that SMC($\mathbf{y}$) based on X is a^2, while both SMC($\mathbf{x}_1$) based on $\mathbf{x}_2$ and $\mathbf{y}$, and SMC($\mathbf{x}_2$) based on $\mathbf{x}_1$ and $\mathbf{y}$ are 1. The results given here illustrate an example of Theorem 1 by Khatri (1976). It is important to realize that the SMC can be computed even from a singular correlation matrix, using generalized inverse matrices.

If either X or Y is a null matrix, or both are null matrices, then $\lambda_j(P(X)P(Y)) = 0$, thus all the canonical correlation coefficients are null. In this connection, if either $\mathbf{x} = 0$ or $\mathbf{y} = 0$, then $cc_1^2(\mathbf{x}, \mathbf{y}) = \lambda_1(P(\mathbf{x})P(\mathbf{y})) = 0 = r(\mathbf{x}, \mathbf{y})^2$, which implies that the correlation coefficient $r(\mathbf{x}, \mathbf{y})$ is 0 if either the values of $\mathbf{x}$ and/or those of $\mathbf{y}$ are constant. In addition, Yanai and Mukherjee (1987) extended Tucker's result by replacing the MP inverse by a weaker g-inverse in constructing image and anti-image correlation matrices. We give some extensions of Yanai and Mukherjee (1987) by introducing the matrix of the form $X = (X_1, X_2, \cdots, X_p)$ where X_j is the matrix of the standardized observations of p_j variables. Excluding X_j from X, we construct the matrix of the form $X_{(i)} = (X_1, \cdots, X_{j-1}, X_{j+1}, \cdots, X_p)$. Then the anti-image matrix can be defined by $X_A = (X_{A1}, \cdots, X_{Ap})$, where $X_{Aj} = Q(X_{(j)})X_j$, $j = 1, \cdots, p$. Noting that $S(X_A)$ is a subspace of $S(X)$, the anti-image matrix can be expressed as

$$X_A = P(X)X_A = XR^- D \tag{6}$$

where $D = \begin{pmatrix} D_1 & O & \cdots & O \\ O & D_2 & \cdots & O \\ \cdots & \cdots & \cdots & \cdots \\ O & O & \cdots & D_p \end{pmatrix}$ and $I - D_j = (X'_j P(X_{(j)})X_j)$, since $X'X_A =$

D. Further, the covariance matrix of X_A can be expressed as $(X_A)'X_A = DR^- D$. Note that diagonal elements of $I - D_j$ are $1 - \text{SMC}(\mathbf{x}_{jk})$ $(k = 1, ..., p_j)$ based on $X_{(j)}$. If all matrices X_j include a single variable x_j, then D_j is equal to $1 - \text{SMC}(\mathbf{x}_j)$ based on $X_{(j)}$, which was exactly the same as that given by Yanai and Mukherjee (1987). As far as the theory of projection matrices is concerned, orthogonal projection matrices are special cases of oblique projection matrices. For interesting properties of oblique projectors, see Rao and Yanai (1979), and Takane and Yanai (1999).

4 Correlation, multiple correlation, and canonical correlation between two sets of residual variables

Jewell and Bloomfield (1983) first showed that canonical correlation coefficients between two sets of vectors X and Y, whose joint dispersion matrix is

$$R_{22} = \begin{pmatrix} R_{XX} & R_{XY} \\ R_{YX} & R_{YY} \end{pmatrix} = \begin{pmatrix} X'X & X'Y \\ Y'X & Y'Y \end{pmatrix}, \tag{7}$$

are precisely the same as the canonical correlations associated with the dispersion matrix; i.e.,

$$R_{22}^{-1} = \begin{pmatrix} R^{XX} & R^{XY} \\ R^{YX} & R^{YY} \end{pmatrix} \tag{8}$$

where it is partitioned in accordance with the partition of R. This result was interpreted in terms of projection matrices and was further extended by Baksalary, Puntanen, and Yanai (1992) and Yanai and Puntanen (1993). We will give a series of results obtained by these authors and extend them later.

Property 2: (Baksalary, Puntanen, and Yanai,1992) Let X and Y be $n \times q$ and $n \times q$ matrices. Consider the residual matrix predicting Y from X and that of X from Y, that is, $Q(X)Y$ and $Q(Y)X$. Then, the following four quantities are identical if $cc_j(X, Y) < 1$.

(i) $cc_j^2(X, Y)$

(ii) $cc_j^2(Q(Y)X, Q(X)Y)$

(iii) $\lambda_j(R_{XX}^{-1}R_{XY}R_{YY}^{-1}R_{YX})$

(iv) $\lambda_j(R^{XY}(R^{YY})^{-1}R^{YX}(R^{XX})^{-1})$.

We omit the proofs of the property 2. If $X = (\mathbf{x})$ and $Y = (\mathbf{y})$, the equivalence between (i) and (ii) of Property 2 implies $r(Q(\mathbf{y})\mathbf{x}, Q(\mathbf{x})\mathbf{y})^2 = r(\mathbf{x}, \mathbf{y})^2$. However, we can prove a stronger result.

Property 3: $r(Q(\mathbf{y})\mathbf{x}, Q(\mathbf{x})\mathbf{y}) = -r(\mathbf{x}, \mathbf{y})$ if $r(\mathbf{x}, \mathbf{y}) \neq \pm 1$.

Proof : For a proof of Property 3, first observe that

Lemma 1: $X'Q(Y)Q(X)Y = -X'P(Y)Q(X)Y = -X'Q(Y)P(X)Y$

which leads to

$$\mathbf{x}'Q(\mathbf{y})Q(\mathbf{x})\mathbf{y} = -\mathbf{x}'P(\mathbf{y})Q(\mathbf{x})\mathbf{y} = -\mathbf{x}'Q(\mathbf{y})P(\mathbf{x})\mathbf{y}.$$

Thus, if $(\mathbf{x}, \mathbf{y}) \neq 0$, then $\mathbf{x}'Q(\mathbf{y})\mathbf{x}/\mathbf{y}'Q(\mathbf{x})\mathbf{y} = \mathbf{x}'\mathbf{x}/\mathbf{y}'\mathbf{y}$, establishing

$$r(Q(\mathbf{y})\mathbf{x}, Q(\mathbf{x})\mathbf{y}) = \frac{\mathbf{x}'Q(\mathbf{y})Q(\mathbf{x})\mathbf{y}}{\sqrt{\mathbf{x}'Q(\mathbf{y})\mathbf{x}}\sqrt{\mathbf{y}'Q(\mathbf{x})\mathbf{y}}} = \frac{-\mathbf{x}'P(\mathbf{y})Q(\mathbf{x})\mathbf{y}}{\sqrt{\mathbf{x}'Q(\mathbf{y})\mathbf{x}}\sqrt{\mathbf{y}'Q(\mathbf{x})\mathbf{y}}}$$

$$= \frac{-\mathbf{x}'\mathbf{y}(\mathbf{y}'\mathbf{y})^{-1}\sqrt{\mathbf{y}'Q(\mathbf{x})\mathbf{y}}}{\sqrt{\mathbf{x}'Q(\mathbf{y})\mathbf{x}}} = \frac{-\mathbf{x}'\mathbf{y}(\mathbf{y}'\mathbf{y})^{-1}\sqrt{\mathbf{y}'\mathbf{y}}}{\sqrt{\mathbf{x}'\mathbf{x}}} = \frac{-\mathbf{x}'\mathbf{y}}{\|\mathbf{x}\| \|\mathbf{y}\|} = -r(\mathbf{x}, \mathbf{y}).$$

If $(\mathbf{x}, \mathbf{y}) = 0$, then $r(Q(\mathbf{y})\mathbf{x}, Q(\mathbf{x})\mathbf{y}) = -r(\mathbf{x}, \mathbf{y})$ obviously holds. This result follows immediately from the following geometrical consideration. Let the angle between two vectors $\mathbf{x}$ and $\mathbf{y}$ be $\theta(\mathbf{x}, \mathbf{y})$ and let the angle between two residual vectors $Q(\mathbf{x})\mathbf{y}$ predicting $\mathbf{y}$ from $\mathbf{x}$ and $Q(\mathbf{y})\mathbf{x}$ predicting $\mathbf{y}$ from $\mathbf{x}$ be $\theta(Q(\mathbf{x})\mathbf{y}, Q(\mathbf{y})\mathbf{x})$. Then it follows that

$$r(Q(\mathbf{x})\mathbf{y}, Q(\mathbf{y})\mathbf{x}) = \cos(\theta(Q(\mathbf{x})\mathbf{y}, Q(\mathbf{y})\mathbf{x})) = \cos(180^0 - \theta(\mathbf{x}, \mathbf{y}))$$

$$= -\cos(\theta(\mathbf{x}, \mathbf{y})) = -r(\mathbf{x}, \mathbf{y}),$$

thus establishing the desired result (See, Fig. 4.) (Q.E.D.)

It is interesting to note that the proof of (i) $\Leftrightarrow$ (ii) of the property 2 can be done similarly in terms of geometrical notation, since the maximum canonical correlation can be defined as the cosine of the minimum angle, which we denote as $\theta(S(X), S(Y))$ between the two vectors spanning $S(X)$ and $S(Y)$, respectively (See, Fig. 5.).

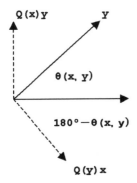

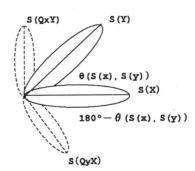

Fig. 4. Vector representaion of correlation between the residual vector of **y** on **x** and that of **x** on **y**

Fig. 5. Matrix representaion of canonical correlation between the residual matrix of Y on X and that of X on Y

If $Y = (\mathbf{y})$, then the equivalence (i) and (ii) of Property 2 implies

Property 4: $R(Q(\mathbf{y})X/Q(X)\mathbf{y}) = R(X/\mathbf{y})$

where $R(Q(\mathbf{y})X/Q(X)\mathbf{y})$ is the multiple correlation coefficient predicting $Q(X)\mathbf{y}$ from $Q(\mathbf{y})X$, while $R(X/\mathbf{y})$ is the multiple correlation coefficient predicting **y** from X.

Property 5: Consider the orthogonal projection matrices $P(X,Y)$ and $Q(X,Y)$, onto the subspaces $S(X,Y)$ and $S(X,Y)^{\perp}$, respectively. They are decomposed into

$$P(X,Y) = P(X) + P(Q(X)Y) = P(Y) + P(Q(Y)X) \tag{9}$$

and

$$Q(X,Y) = Q(Q(X)Y)Q(X) = Q(Q(Y)X)Q(Y). \tag{10}$$

The proof of (9) was first given by Theorem 5 of Rao & Yanai (1979), but we give here a geometrical proof , using the decomposition of $S(X,Y)$ as the direct sum of two orthogonal subspaces, that is, $S(X,Y) = S(X) \oplus S(Q(X)Y) = S(Y) \oplus S(Q(Y)X)$.

The above decomposition leads to the following decompositions of the squared multiple correlation of **y** on $X = (X_1, X_2)$, $i.e.$,

$$R(X/\mathbf{y})^2 = R(X_1/\mathbf{y})^2 + R(Q(X_1)X_2/\mathbf{y})^2 = R(X_2/\mathbf{y})^2 + R(Q(X_2)X_1/\mathbf{y})^2.$$

The proof of (10) follows immediately from (9), since $Q(X,Y) = I - P(X,Y)$.

Property 6: Let $B(X/Y)$ and $B(Y/X)$ be matrices of regression coefficients predicting Y from X, and predicting X from Y, respectively. Further, let $B(Q(Y)X/Q(X)Y)$ and $B(Q(X)Y/Q(Y)X)$ be matrices of regression coefficients predicting $Q(X)Y$ from $Q(Y)X$ and those predicting $Q(Y)X$ from $Q(X)Y$, respectively. Then

(i) $B(Q(Y)X/Q(X)Y) = -B(X/Y)$,　(ii) $B(Q(X)Y/Q(Y)X) = -B(Y/X)$,

(iii) $B(Q(Y)X/Q(X)Y)B(Q(X)Y/Q(Y)X) = B(X/Y)B(Y/X)$,

(iv) $cc_j^2(X,Y) = \lambda_j(B(X/Y)B(Y/X))$
$$= \lambda_j(B(Q(Y)X/Q(X)Y)B(Q(X)Y/Q(Y)X)).$$

Proof : First, we prove (i). Using Lemma 1, we can prove

$$\begin{aligned}
B(Q(Y)X/Q(X)Y) &= (X'Q(Y)X)^{-1}X'Q(Y)Q(X)Y \\
&= -(X'Q(Y)X)^{-1}X'Q(Y)P(X)Y \\
&= -(X'Q(Y)X)^{-1}X'Q(Y)X(X'X)^{-1}X'_iY \\
&= -(X'X)^{-1}X'Y = -B(X/Y).
\end{aligned}$$

The statement (ii) can be proved similarly. (iii) follows from (i) and (ii). (iv) follows, since

$$\lambda_j(B(X/Y)B(Y/X)) = \lambda_j((X'X)^{-1}X'Y(Y'Y)^{-1}Y'X) = cc_j^2(X,Y).$$

Corollary to Property 6:

If $X = (\mathbf{x})$ and $Y = (\mathbf{y})$, we have

(i) $b(Q(\mathbf{y})\mathbf{x}/Q(\mathbf{x})\mathbf{y}) = -b(\mathbf{x}/\mathbf{y})$　(ii) $b(Q(\mathbf{x})\mathbf{y}/Q(\mathbf{y})\mathbf{x}) = -b(\mathbf{y}/\mathbf{x})$

(iii) $b(Q(\mathbf{y})\mathbf{x}/Q(\mathbf{x})\mathbf{y})b(Q(\mathbf{x})\mathbf{y}/Q(\mathbf{y})\mathbf{x}) = b(\mathbf{x}/\mathbf{y})b(\mathbf{y}/\mathbf{x}) = r(\mathbf{x},\mathbf{y})^2$,

where $b(\mathbf{x}/\mathbf{y})$ and $b(\mathbf{y}/\mathbf{x})$ are the regression coefficients of $\mathbf{x}$ predicting $\mathbf{y}$, and that of $\mathbf{y}$ predicting $\mathbf{x}$, and $b(Q(\mathbf{y})\mathbf{x}/Q(\mathbf{x})\mathbf{y})$ and $b(Q(\mathbf{x})\mathbf{y}/Q(\mathbf{y})\mathbf{x})$ are that of $Q(\mathbf{y})\mathbf{x}$ predicting $Q(\mathbf{x})\mathbf{y}$, and that of $Q(\mathbf{x})\mathbf{y}$ predicting $Q(\mathbf{y})\mathbf{x}$.

Note that (iv) of Property 6 is a natural extension of the known result given by (iii) of the above Corollary.

Suppose that the correlation matrix R_{33} for three sets of variables X, Y and Z is given in the partitioned form by

$$R_{33} = \begin{pmatrix} R_{XX} & R_{XY} & R_{XZ} \\ R_{YX} & R_{YY} & R_{YZ} \\ R_{ZX} & R_{ZY} & R_{ZZ} \end{pmatrix} = \begin{pmatrix} X'X & X'Y & X'Z \\ Y'X & Y'Y & Y'Z \\ Z'X & Z'Y & Z'Z \end{pmatrix} \quad . \qquad (11)$$

Let the generalized inverse matrix of R be

$$R_{33}^{-1} = \begin{pmatrix} R^{XX} & R^{XY} & R^{XZ} \\ R^{YX} & R^{YY} & R^{YZ} \\ R^{ZX} & R^{ZY} & R^{ZZ} \end{pmatrix} \qquad (12)$$

given in accordance with the partition of R_{33}. Let $cc_j(Q(Z)X, Q(Z)Y)$ be the jth partial canonical correlation coefficient between X and Y eliminating Z.

Further, let $R_{XX/Z} = R_{XX} - R_{XZ}R_{ZZ}^- R_{ZX}, R_{YY/Z} = R_{YY} - R_{YZ}R_{ZZ}^- R_{ZY}$

and $R_{XY/Z} = R_{XY} - R_{XZ}R_{ZZ}^- R_{ZY}$. Then we have

Property 7: (Yanai and Puntanen, 1993) The following four quantities are mutually identical:

(i) $cc_j^2(Q(Z)X, Q(Z)Y)$ (ii) $cc_j^2(Q(Y, Z)X, Q(X, Z)Y)$
(iii) $\lambda_j(R_{XY/Z}R_{YY/Z}^{-1}R_{YX/Z}R_{XX/Z}^{-1})$ (iv) $\lambda_j(R^{XY}(R^{YY})^{-1}R^{YX}(R^{XX})^{-1})$

Proofs are omitted. In view of the equivalence between (i) and (ii), we have $r^2(Q(\mathbf{x}, Z), Q(\mathbf{y}, Z) = r^2(Q(\mathbf{y}, Z)\mathbf{x}, Q(\mathbf{x}, Z)\mathbf{y})$. However, we can prove a stronger result, using Property 3 and (10).

Property 8: $r(Q(\mathbf{x}, Z)\mathbf{y}, Q(\mathbf{y}, Z)\mathbf{x}) = -r(Q(Z)\mathbf{x}, Q(Z)\mathbf{y})$ if $R(Z/\mathbf{x}) \neq 1$ and $R(Z/\mathbf{y}) \neq 1$ where $r(Q(Z)\mathbf{x}, Q(Z)\mathbf{y})$ is the partial correlation between $\mathbf{x}$ and $\mathbf{y}$ eliminating Z.

Property 9: Let $B(Q(Y, Z)X/Q(X, Z)Y)$ and $B(Q(X, Z)Y/Q(Y, Z)X)$ be matrices of regression coefficients predicting $Q(X, Z)Y$ from $Q(Y, Z)X$ and those predicting $Q(Y, Z)X$ from $Q(X, Z)Y(Y, Z)$, respectively. Then,

(i) $B(Q(Y, Z)X/Q(X, Z)Y) = -B(Q(Z)X/Q(Z)Y)$
(ii) $B(Q(X, Z)Y/Q(Y, Z)X) = -B(Q(Z)Y/Q(Z)X)$
(iii) $\lambda_j(B(Q(Y, Z)X/Q(X, Z)Y)B(Q(X, Z)Y) = cc_j^2(Q(Z)X, Q(Z)Y)$.

Proof : Using (10) and property 6, it follows that

$$B(Q(Y, Z)X/Q(X, Z)Y) = B(Q(Q(Z)Y)(Q(Z)X)/Q(Q(Z)X)(Q(Z)Y))$$
$$= -B(Q(Z)X/Q(Z)Y),$$

thus establishing (i). (ii) can be proved similarly. (iii) follows immediately from (i) and (ii).

5 Extension of Olkin's result

In order to extend Property 2, Olkin (1981) considered range restrictions for the matrix of product moment correlations R_{33} given by (11). He considered the following two cases: (i) the case when all submatrices but R_{XX} are fixed. (ii) the case when all sub-matrices but R_{XY} are fixed. For the first case, Olkin showed that positive-definiteness of R_{22} is equivalent to positive-definiteness of R_{YY} and the condition

$$R_{XX} > R_{XY} R_{YY}^{-1} R_{YX} \ . \tag{13}$$

By uses of generalized inverse and projection matrices, Olkin's result can be extended in such a way that positive semi-definiteness of (11) is equivalent to either both positive semi-definiteness of R_{YY} and the condition

$$R_{XX} > R_{XY} R_{YY}^- R_{YX} \tag{14}$$

or both positive definiteness of R_{YY} and

$$R_{XX} \geq R_{XY} R_{YY}^- R_{YX} \tag{15}$$

Thus, if $R_{XX} = \begin{pmatrix} 1 & r_{x1x2} \\ & 1 \end{pmatrix}$, then $-1 \leq r(x_1, x_2/Y) \leq 1$, where

$$r(x_1, x_2/Y) = \frac{r(x_1, x_2) - q(x_1, x_2/Y)}{\sqrt{(1 - q(x_1, x_1/Y))}\sqrt{(1 - q(x_2, x_2/Y))}} \ , \quad \text{and}$$

$$\begin{pmatrix} q(x_1, x_1/Y) & q(x_1, x_2/Y) \\ q(x_2, x_1/Y) & q(x_2, x_2/Y) \end{pmatrix} = \begin{pmatrix} r_{x1y1} & r_{x1y2} & \cdots\cdots & r_{x1yq} \\ r_{x2y1} & r_{x2y2} & \cdots\cdots & r_{x2yq} \end{pmatrix} R_{YY}^- \begin{pmatrix} r_{x1y1} & r_{x2y1} \\ r_{x1y2} & r_{x2y2} \\ r_{x1y3} & r_{x2y3} \\ \cdots & \cdots \\ r_{x1yq} & r_{x2yq} \end{pmatrix} \ .$$

Observe that (13) and (14) imply $cc_j^2(X, Y) < 1$. Olkin's result in (ii) can be extended in such a way that positive definiteness of (11) and positive semi-definiteness of R_{zz} implies positive semi-definiteness of

$$\begin{pmatrix} R_{XX} & R_{XY} \\ R_{YX} & R_{YY} \end{pmatrix} - \begin{pmatrix} R_{XZ} \\ R_{YZ} \end{pmatrix} R_{ZZ}^- \begin{pmatrix} R_{ZX} & R_{ZY} \end{pmatrix}$$

$$= \begin{pmatrix} R_{XX} - R_{XZ} R_{ZZ}^- R_{ZX} & R_{XY} - R_{XZ} R_{ZZ}^- R_{ZY} \\ R_{YX} - R_{YZ} R_{ZZ}^- R_{ZX} & R_{YY} - R_{YZ} R_{ZZ}^- R_{ZY} \end{pmatrix}$$

$$= \begin{pmatrix} X' \\ Y' \end{pmatrix} Q(Z) \begin{pmatrix} X & Y \end{pmatrix} = \begin{pmatrix} X'Q(Z)X & X'Q(Z)Y \\ Y'Q(Z)X & Y'Q(Z)Y \end{pmatrix} \geq O. \tag{16}$$

Observe that (16) implies either

$$X'Q(Z)X - (X'Q(Z)Y)(Y'Q(Z)Y)^- Y'Q(Z)X$$
$$= X'Q(Y,Z)X = X'X - X'P(Y,Z)X \geq O, \tag{17}$$

or

$$Y'Q(Z)Y - (Y'Q(Z)\dot{X})(X'Q(Z)X)^-(X'Q(Z)Y) = Y'Q(X,Z)Y$$
$$= Y'Y - Y'P(X,Z)Y \geq O. \tag{18}$$

Observe that (17) implies $cc_j(X,(Y,Z)) \leq 1$ for any j and (18) implies $cc_j(Y,(X,Z)) \leq 1$ for any j. Furthermore, it can be said that both (17) and (18) implies $cc_j(Q(Z)X, Q(Z)Y) \leq 1$. It is obvious that obtained results are natural extensions of equivalences among (ii), (iii), (iv) and (vi) in Property 1. The above results can be summarized in the following Property.

Property 10: The following five statements are mutually equivalent.

(1) $cc_j(X,(Y,Z)) \leq 1$, (2) $cc_j(Y,(X,Z)) \leq 1$, (3) $cc_j(Q(Z)X, Q(Z)Y) \leq 1$
(4) The matrix given by (17) is positive semi-definite.
(5) Both the matrix given by (16) and the matrix R_{ZZ} are' positive semi-definite.

Takane and Shibayama (1991) and Yanai and Takane (1992) proposed constrained principal component analysis and constrained canonical correlation analysis by means of projectors. Recently, Nishisato and Baba (1999) studied the conditional forced classification method of the dual scaling (Nishisato,1980) in terms of the orthogonal projector.

Acknowledgement: The author wishes to acknowledge Professor Yoshio Takane (Mcgill University, Canada) and two anonymous reviewers for their helpful comments on earlier drafts of this paper.

References

Baksalary,J.K., Puntanen,S., and Yanai,H.(1992) Canonical correlation associated with symmetric reflexive g-inverse of the dispersion matrix. Linear Algebra and its Applications 176:61-74.

Glass,G.V., and Collins,J.R.(1970) Geometric proof of the restrictions of possible value of r(x,y) when r(x,z) and r(y,z) are fixed. Educational and Psychological Measurement 30: 37-39.

Gulliksen,H. (1950) Theory of Test Scores, John Wiley & Sons, New York

Hubert,L.J.(1972) A note on the restriction of ranges for Pearson product moment correlation. Educational and Psychological Measurement 32:767-770.

Jewell,N.P. and Bloomfield,P.(1983) Canonical correlations of past and future for time series: definition and theory.Annals of Statistics 11:837-847

Kaiser,H.(1976). Image and anti-image covariance matrix from a correlation matrix that may be singular. Psychometrika 41:295-300.

Khatri,C.G.(1976) A note on multiple and canonical correlations for a singular covariance matrix. Psychometrika, 41:465-470.

Nishisato,S.(1980) Analysis of Categorical Data: Dual Scaling and its Applications, University of Tronto Press

Nishisato,S. and Baba,Y.(1999) On contingency, projection and forced classification. Behaviormetrika 26:207-219

Olkin,I.(1981) Range restrictions for product moment correlation matrices. Psychometrika 46:469-472

Rao,C.R.(1962) A note on a generalized inverse of a matrix with applications to problems in mathematical satatistics. J. Royal Statistical Society B,24:152-158

Rao,C.R. and Mitra, S.K.(1971) Generalized inverse of matrices and its applications . Wiley.

Rao,C.R. and Yanai,H.(1979) General definition of a projector, Its decomposition and applications to statistical problems. J. of Statistical Planning and Inference 3:1-17

Stanley,J.C. and Wang,M.D.(1970) Weighting test items and test-item options. An overview of the analytical and empirical literature. Educational and Psychological Measurement 30:21-35

Takane,Y. and Shibayama,T.(1991) Principal component analysis with external information on both subjects and variables. Psychometrika 56:97-120

Takane,Y.and Yanai,H.(1999) On oblique projectors. Linear Algebra and its Applications 289:297-310

Takeuchi,K.(1986) How to evaluate posterior weights of subjects in the entrance examination, Report on the meeting in charge of university entrance examination. 7:500-501

Takeuchi,K., Yanai,H., and Mukherjee,B.N.(1982) The foundation of multivariate Analysis. Wiley Eastern

Tucker,L.R.,Cooper,L.G. and Meredith,W.M.(1972) Obtaining squared multiple correlation from a correlation matrix which may be singular. Psychometrika, 37:143-148.

Thurstone,L.L.(1935) Vectors of Minds. Univ. of Chicago Press

Yanai,H. and Mukherjee,B.N.(1987) A generalized method of image analysis from an inter correlation matrix which may be singular. Psychometrika, 52:555-564.

Yanai,H., and Puntanen,S.(1993) Partial canonical correlation associated with g-inverses of the dispersion matrix, In K.Matsushita (Ed.) Statistical sciences and data analysis, pp253-264, Statistical Science and Data Analysis..

Yanai,H., and Takane,Y.(1992) Canonical correlation analysis with linear constraints. Linear Algebra and its Applications, 176:75-89.

Early Statistical Modelling of Latent Quantities: The History of Distance Measurement by Triangulation

Willem J. Heiser

Psychometrics and Research Methodology, Department of Psychology, Leiden University, PO Box 9555, 2300 RB Leiden, The Netherlands

Summary. Measurement of long distances in astronomy and geodesy has an interesting history involving the inception of several statistical concepts, such as least absolute deviations, least squares, maximum likelihood, and robustness.

Geographical maps are models of locations on Earth. Maps at a small scale rely on some map projection method and knowledge of latitude and longitude. Maps at a larger scale became to be be based on angle measurement in triangulation networks, without information on latitude or longitude. Absolute size of the Earth was estimated by measuring amplitude and length of a meridian arc. Map making projects of Mercator, the Blaeu family, the Cassini family, and Ino are discussed, as well as theoretical contributions of Frisius, Snellius, Galilei, and Gauss.

Key words. Geodesy, map projection, intersection, resection, least squares

1 History of Statistics Starts With History of Measurement

Measurement in the social and behavioral sciences is predominantly concerned with the determination of latent quantities. Latent scores arise in classical test theory, item response theory, various forms of scaling, and factor analysis alike. Psychometricians often assume rather too lightly that the older sciences have the privilege of being able to directly measure manifest quantities, because variables like length and mass would generally be determined by use of measuring rods and pairs of scales. However, many – if not most – interesting achievements in physical and astronomical measurement did not at all involve direct determination of the quantities involved.

In the third century B.C., the great scholar Eratosthenes of Cyrene (276 – 195 B.C.), chief librarian of the Museum in Alexandria, determined the circumference of the Earth without leaving the library. He had heard stories about a well in Syene (now Aswan), approximately 50 days of travel southeast of Alexandria by camel caravan, where the Sun's rays fall straight down into its deep waters at high noon on the longest day of the year. Erastosthenes noted that at Alexandria, at the same date and time, the Sun has an altitude of about 83 degrees. The zenith distance is the angle from the zenith to the Sun's position at noon, and equals 90 degrees minus the altitude. Eratosthenes knew from geometry that the ratio of the distance between Alexandria and Syene to the circumference of the Earth must be equal to the ratio of an arc distance to a full circle of 360 degrees, and that the arc distance is equal to the zenith distance. He could now calculate the circumference of the Earth from his measurement of the zenith distance at Alexandria (7.2°, or about 1/50 of a full circle) and the estimated travel distance to Syene (5000 stadia), as 50 x 5000 = 250,000 stadia (or 39,375 km, if one takes one stadium as 157.5 meters). Although the exactness of this estimate is still not settled (Rawlins, 1982), Eratosthenes' method provided a remarkable and sound approach to measuring a quantity that cannot be directly observed.

In the first published multidimensional scaling analysis in *Psychometrika*, Klingberg (1941) analyzed the psychological distances between the seven Great Powers at the verge of World War II. When I first saw this example it hit me right between the eyes, as it showed so very clearly, in a photograph of a physical model with seven spheres held together with bamboo sticks, the major opposition between Italy and Germany vis-à-vis USA, France and Britain, the eccentric position of Russia, and the ambivalence towards Japan. Since Klingberg measured the same distances at several points in time, he could also monitor the changing relations between the Nations as the World War set in. What we have here is again a method that allows us to identify quantities that cannot be directly observed.

What multidimensional scaling achieves seemed so fundamental to me that I couldn't believe that no one else had tried earlier to convert distance information into spatial relations. Thus it became an urgent question for me to find out what kind of distance measurement had been developed in the classical sciences.

In the course of following the path back to the roots, it became also evident to me that we have to change the way in which we look at the history of statistics. Traditional history of statistics usually starts from probability theory, especially combinatorial chance (David, 1962). Recent writers are increasingly aware of statistics as a separate field, with a history of its own (Porter, 1986; Daston, 1988; Gigerenzer et al., 1989; Hacking, 1990). Also, Stigler (1986) has done much to show that the integration of probability theory and statistics only started taking place in the 19th century. Yet what these authors appear to have in common is the tenet that statistics is about uncertainty and chance. An exception is the admirable book by Hald (1990), who gives a balanced account of the contemporaneous development and mutual interaction of probability theory, statistics in astronomy and demography, and life insurance mathematics.

My own conviction is that statistics originates from measurement, including counting, and including the measurement of uncertainty. Measurement is a fundamental scientific activity that aims at quantification (for a fascinating perspective, see Porter, 1995). We may either want to measure one parameter, such as the circumference of the Earth, or a whole set of parameters, such as the positions of the seven Great Powers in psychological space. Sometimes, but not always, we may also want to measure the standard error of some measurement procedure under replication, or the tail probability of some test statistic. When we measure or count too much, we need statistical modelling, and when we measure or count too little, we need statistical inference. As I hope to show in this paper, quite a number of statistical ideas originated in the context of the measurement of distance.

2 Instrument Makers in the Low Countries

We start our history at the time of the Scientific Revolution. Around 1600 the instrument maker was central to the new science that was moving away from Aristotelian verbal-logical methodology and started embracing the experimental (i.e., observational) method. The Low Countries were in their commercial heydays and stood at the forefront of this revolution, producing theoretical underpinnings as well as practical tools for measurement.

For measuring weight and force, Simon Stevin (1548-1620, Brugge) continued work on statics where Archimedes had left it, and developed the concept of center of gravity, useful for determination of weight of all kinds of bodies (Dijksterhuis, 1943). For measuring time, Christiaan Huygens (1629-1695, The Hague) developed the first high-precision pendulum clock (Yoder, 1988). For measuring the world and the universe, refined angle-measuring instruments were developed, and applied in new ways. Especially these last developments are relevant for the history of distance measurement. We will first discuss the contributions of Gemma Frisius (1508-1555), Gerard Mercator (1512-1594) and Willem Blaeu (1571-1638). Then we treat the work of Willebrordus Snellius (1580-1626) separately.

2.1 Gemma Frisius

Gemma (Jemme Reinerszoon) Frisius was born in 1508 in Dokkum (Friesland), educated in Groningen after the early death of his parents, and then sent to the university of Leuven (Louvain, Belgium), where he became professor of mathematics and medicine somewhere between 1537 and 1539, teaching and writing until his death in 1555.

In his early work *De Principiis Astronomiae et Cosmographicae* (1530), he was the first to describe how longitude may be determined by using a clock. Estimates of longitude were usually based on travelers' accounts, which could rarely be trusted. Travelers either kept no records or, as Ptolemy warned, through "their love of boasting they magnify distances" (Wilford, 2000, p. 35). He also developed several new astronomical instruments, such as the *Flemish Astrolabe*, the back of which bears his universal stereographic celestial projection. In *De Astrolabe Catholico* (1556) he introduced this projection theoretically, and explained the use of the shadow square or geometrical quadrant on an astrolabe (simple theodolite, or Holland circle), in taking geographical measurements without reference to latitude and longitude.

This remarkable coordinate-free approach had already been described in an Appendix to a new edition of *Cosmographicus Liber Petri Apiani* (1533), called *Li-*

bellus de locorum describendorum ratione[1]. In 16 pages Gemma Frisius gave the foundation of position measurement by triangulation (Haasbroek, 1968). According to De Vocht (1961, cited in Haasbroek, 1968, p. 11), "its importance can hardly be gauged: for it revealed the final definite way of representing any country with its towns ... by means of a series of triangles with one common basis which could be measured with preciseness so that it led to accurate distances and became the beginning of actual geography; subsequent times have only been able to add to it more facilities in the checking and the registering of the various elements".

Frisius' method was based on angle measurements made with an astrolabe consisting of a circle divided into four quadrants, each in turn divided into 90 degrees, with a sight rule fastened at the center. The circle was to be positioned horizontally, with the origin of the circular scale oriented towards the magnetic North with a compass. By measuring the angle of some tower or any other landmark with respect to the North, East, South, or the West, he could determine all angles between any three landmarks by calculation. For instance, in the triangle Brussels–Antwerp–Leuven, the angle between the South and Brussels is 25° towards the west, looking from Antwerp; from the same position, the angle between the South and Leuven is 4° eastwards; and finally, looking from Brussels the angle between the East and Leuven is 14° towards the South. Translating the origin to Leuven, it follows that the angle between Brussels and Antwerp as seen from Leuven must be 90° – 4° – 14° = 72°. As psychometricians, we cannot fail to notice the striking analogy of this procedure with being able to reconstruct the correlation between two manifest variables from their factor loadings!

Angles are sufficient to produce a map up to a scale factor. To determine a definite scale and thus the actual distances, some common baseline should be measured as accurately as possible. Since Hellenistic times, surveyors had used counting the revolutions of a wheel to measure long distances. However, these perambulators (or odometers) were hard to use when there were obstacles in the terrain, like buildings or rivers. Two more accurate methods based on right-angled triangles are described in *Libellus*. One method uses the *scala geometrica* to measure the angle toward the distant object at the corner opposite to the right angle, on the baseline of known length. The required distance then is the cotangent of the measured angle times the baseline distance. The second method does not require angle measurement, only straight-line- and right-angle adjustment. Suppose a baseline of 30 feet extends from A to B, with a right angle at A towards distant object T (a tower, for example). Then, starting at A, walk 40 feet back (away from T) and position a stick C so that TAC forms a straight line. Next, walk parallel with AB (at a right angle with TAC), and position a new stick D so that TBD forms a straight line. Once the distance CD is measured, the distance TC follows from the proportionality $(CD - AB) : CD = AC : TC$. In Frisius' example, $CD = 36$, so that $TC = 240$ and the required distance $TA = 240 - 40 = 200$.

---

[1] In 1537, a Dutch edition was published, called *Een boecxken seer nut ende Profitelijc allen Geographiens leerende hoemen eenighe plaetsen beschrijven ende het verschil oft distantie derselver meten sal welck tevoren noyt ghesien en is gheweest* [A booklet very useful and profitable for all geographers, teaching how to describe several places and to measure their difference or distance, which was never seen before].

Perhaps Frisius' most fundamental contribution, described in Chapter V (Pouls, 1999), was the *method of intersection*, still one of the basic measurement methods used by surveyors today. From some baseline of known length, one measures the two angles of the endpoints with respect to the distant object. Once we know two angles and one distance in any triangle, the remaining angle and the remaining distances can be determined by the Law of Sines. As the method of intersection does not require angle measurement with respect to a meridian, it does not need the use of a compass, thus eliminating an important source of error.

Gemma Frisius did not actually produce a map of Flanders by his own methods. The triangulation shown in his famous booklet was just an example: some of the adjacent towns in the network were so far apart that the curvature of the earth would prevent their towers to be spotted by the naked eye. First to be surveyed by triangulation was probably the Duchy of Brabant; Jacob van Deventer, a fellow student of Frisius, published a map based on that survey in 1536.

2.2 Gerardus Mercator

Gerardus Mercator[2] (Gerard de Cremer, 1512-1594) was born in Rupelmonde (Flanders), went to the Latin school at 's Hertogenbosch in the Netherlands, and then studied humanities and philosophy at the University of Leuven. After a personal crisis induced by religious worries he settled in metropolitan Antwerp and travelled around, after which period he returned to Leuven–determined to become a builder of navigation instruments, in order to contribute to the great adventure of his time: the exploration of the world. This quest brought him to Gemma Frisius, under whom he studied geodesy, astronomy and geometry. He learnt to be an engraver and instrument maker from the goldsmith Gaspar à Myrica. Working together, they constructed a state-of-the-art terrestrial globe in 1535-1536 and an equally excellent celestial globe in 1537. Mercator started engraving maps: one of Palestine in 1537, a small map of the world in 1538, and a map of Flanders in 1540. The world map was largely copied from the Frisius globe, but was the first to name North America and used a new projection of the French cartographer Orontius Finaeus (*cf.* Blondeau, 1993, p. 48), in which the two hemispheres were drawn in a double cordiform shape.

In 1552 Mercator moved to Duisburg (Germany), where he opened a cartographic workshop and continued to work on his famous big map of the world, finished in 1569. This map gave improved coastlines of South America and more accurate contours of Asia, including South-east Asia, but persisted in the Greek myth of a large continent around the southern pole, *Terra Australis*. However, its most important innovation was the cylindrical projection that bears Mercator's name.

---

[2] Mercator's portrait copied from the Web: http://www.math.utwente.nl/~jagers/Book/

The *Mercator projection* has equidistant, straight meridians, and parallels of latitude that are straight, parallel, and perpendicular to the meridians. The parallels are spaced more widely as one moves away from the equator. The effect of these features is that all lines of constant bearing are shown straight. Thus a sailor could follow a single compass setting based on the bearing of the straight line connecting the point of departure and the point of destination on the map (*cf.* Snyder, 1993, p. 45). Not only gives the Mercator projection correct directions, its simple rectangular coordinate system also allows one to interpolate longitude and latitude easily.

2.3 Willem and Joan Blaeu

Joan Blaeu was born in 1596 in Alkmaar. He was the son of Willem Janszoon Blaeu (1571-1638), an instrument maker who also produced globes and maps and who travelled, in 1594, to Denmark to study under the great astonomer Tycho Brahe, becoming his assistant at the atronomical observatory Uraniborg on the island of Hven. Then the Blaeu family moved to Amsterdam, where father set up a shop and a printing press, to print and sell works on navigation, astronomy, literature and theology. The son started to study Law at Leiden University, gaining his doctorate in 1620, and learned the mapmaking trade from his father, succeeding him in 1638 as the official mapmaker of the VOC (United East-India Company).

Goss (1997) gives the following description of the beginning of what was to be a very succesful enterprise: "The business partnership of father and son began in 1630 with the publication of an atlas called *Atlantis Appendix, sive pars altera ... nunc primum editas*, which contained sixty maps. The title is an allusion to an earlier atlas, published by the Amsterdam mapmaker Jodocus Hondius the younger, who published the later editions of the Atlas of Gerard Mercator until 1629. At the death of Hondius in that year, Willem Janszoon Blaeu bought several of his copper plates to add to his own then small plate stock with the intention of compiling and publishing an atlas of his own. In the preface to an early edition of his Appendix in 1631, Blaeu wrote: 'Abraham Ortelius, the celebrated geographer of Philip II, king of Spain, made a *Theatrum Orbis Terrarum*, in which are maps of different parts of the world, some representing the ancient state of things, and others the modern. Whatever praise and thanks that incomparable man may have merited by his work, and with whatever appreciation the educated public may have received it, nevertheless this *Theatrum* has its defects. Later the great mathematician Gerard Mercator began to prepare, with tremendous labour and at tremendous expense, the publication of his *Atlas*, but death overtook him [in 1595], so that he left his work incompleted. By that its value is very considerably decreased, because he was able to complete Europe only (with the exception of Spain).' (...) Blaeu's use of the title *Appendix* or later on, *Atlantis Appendix*, was an astute commercial decision designed to link his new work with a well-established and well-respected work which was by then nearing the end of its effective commercial life (...)." (Goss, 1997, pp. 10-11).

The expanded 1631 edition, containing ninety-eight maps, was called *Appendix Theatri A. Orteli et Atlantis G. Mercatoris*, and a long series of ever growing atlases followed, requiring three volumes in 1640, four in 1645, five in 1654, six in 1655. Finally, the *Atlas Major* published in 1662 contained six hundred maps.

What made these maps so impressive was their richness in detail and elegant artwork. Although often they were also remarkably accurate, even the maps at a larger scale were not yet based upon anything like triangulation. Apart from the magnificent World map in Mercator projection, most of them were done with classical equirectangular, conic and stereographic projections[3]. The Blaeu family could draw upon an extensive informer network and the rich archives of the VOC. Strong points of their maps were the accurate outlines of Indonesia and the western portion of Australia (called *Hollandia Nova*), the intentional omission of unobserved lands like *Terra Australis*, and the excellent map of Japan provided by the Italian Jesuit Martino Martini, who travelled throughout China and the Far East. Martini determined for the first time with any degree of accuracy the astronomical position of many towns, and had first-hand knowledge of previously unknown geographical features, such as the fact that Korea is a peninsula (Goss, 1997, p. 222).

3 Snellius' Contributions to Modern Geodesy

Willebrordus Snellius (Willebrord van Roijen Snell, 1580-1626) succeeded his father Rudolph as professor of Physics and Mathematics at Leiden University in 1613. He found a new approximation of π by polygons, reaching 34 decimals with only a 2^{30}-sided polygon thanks to an acceleration of Archimedes' method (courteously staying behind his teacher Ludolphus van Ceulen, who calculated 35 decimals right). Snell wrote his name in the Book of Science by the discovery of the Law of refraction of light in different media (Snell's Law).

What did Snellius do for geodesy? He invented the *method of resection*, applying it from the roof of his house to determine the distance towards the spire of the Townhall of Leiden (Haasbroek, 1968). In the method of resection, one determines the location of some point O by measuring the directions from O towards (at least) three points (A, B, C) of which the location is known. The location of O can then be calculated by using trigonometric relations in the circumscribed circles of the triangles AOB and BOC.

Snell's resection method was described in his book *Eratosthenes Batavus: De Terrae Ambitus Vera Quantitate* (1617) [The Dutch Eratosthenes: About the Real Size of the Circumference of the Earth]. He needed the distance from the roof of his house to the Townhall to set up a small triangulation network for finding the distance from Leiden to the nearby town of Zoeterwoude, which in turn served as a baseline for finding the distance from Leiden to The Hague by intersection, which in turn served as a baseline for a triangulation of Holland. The most northern town in this triangulation network was Alkmaar, the most southern one Bergen op

---

[3] It should be noted, however, that Willem Blaeu also published *The Light of Navigation* in 1612, which contained new and corrected astronomical and nautical tables and a new set of see charts, all drawn on Mercator's projection (Hall, 1994)

Zoom. From astronomical measurements in these towns, he estimated the amplitude of the arc of the meridian of Alkmaar up to its intersection point with the parallel circle of Bergen op Zoom. From the triangulation network he computed the length of that arc. Amplitude and length of an arc suffice for finding the circumference of the earth (for a very thorough treatment, see Haasbroek, 1968).

It turned out that Snellius' estimate of the size of the earth was 38,639.160 km, which is 3.65% too small (the correct size is 40,103.381 km). Considering Eratosthenes' original estimate of 39,375 km (under the previous assumption of the length of one stadium), which is 1.82% too small, we see in hindsight that the Dutch Eratosthenes failed in his major goal, despite all efforts to boost precision!

Eratosthenes Batavus is nevertheless considered a classic in the geodetic literature because it presented the first serious detailed triangulation and introduced several technical innovations. Using a linked sequence of baselines was new. As his unit of length, Snellius used the Rijnlandse roede (Rhineland rood). Although the rood was divided into 12 feet and a foot into 12 inches, Snellius worked with 10th and 100th parts of roods, following a decimal system in the footsteps of Simon Stevin. Some of the base distances were measured by the newly invented surveyor's chain (Rathborne, 1616), angle measurements by instruments of first quality, made by Willem Blaeu. Finally, it is interesting to note that Snellius sometimes used the average when he had two estimates of the same quantity.

4 Galilei's Statistical Analysis of Astronomical Data

The reflecting telescope with which Galileo Galilei[4] (1564-1642) studied the skies had been manufactured by himself, from first principles, after he had heard of its invention by Sacharias Janssen, spectacle maker of Middelburg, Zeeland, in 1608. [According to some, the telescope was invented by Hans Lippershey, also from Middelburg, around the same time.] In 1628, Galilei was challenged by Chiaramonti to prove that Tycho Brahe's *Stella Nova* (new star) that shocked the world in 1572 was <u>not</u> *sublunar*, that is, not closer to Earth than the Moon. In his *Dialogo* (1632), Galilei gives a detailed statistical analysis of several estimates of this distance made by others, like Brahe, Camerarius, Reinhold, Frisius and Ursinus. According to Hald (1990, p. 149-150), "His discussion may be summarized as follows:

1. There is only one number which gives the distance of the star from the center of the earth, the true distance.
2. All observations are encumbered with errors, due to the observer, the instruments, and the other observational conditions.

---

[4] Galilei's portrait copied from the Web: http://www.th.physik.uni-frankfurt.de/~jr/gif/phys/s_galileo1.jpg

3. The observations are distributed symmetrically about the true value; that is, the errors are distributed symmetrically about zero.
4. Small errors occur more frequently than large errors.
5. The calculated distance is a function of the direct angular observations such that small adjustments of the observations may result in a large adjustment of the distance."

This set of assumptions has a distinctively modern flavor, and if one replaces 'distance of the star' with 'score of the subject' and 'center of the earth' with 'origin of the scale', assumptions 1–4 come close to describing classical test theory[5]. In order to decide between the two hypotheses about the distance from the Earth to Stella Nova and to the Moon, Galilei writes: "Those observations must be called the more exact, or the less in error, which by the addition of substraction of the fewest minutes restore the star to a possible position. And among the possible places, the actual place must be believed to be that in which there concur the greatest number of distances, calculated on the most exact observations" (Galilei, as quoted in Hold, 1990, p. 150). As Hold demonstrates, the badness-of-fit function used by Galilei was the sum of the absolute deviations from the fitted value.

It appears that what is being done here not only anticipates the least absolute value principle and maximum likelihood estimation, but also presents the first meta analysis to resolve a delicate issue by pooling the scant evidence.

5 Triangulating the World

The first country to be triangulated after Holland was France. Louis XIV's influential minister of finance, Jean Baptiste Colbert, believed that he needed reliable topographical maps for his great ambitions in building roads and canals to boost economic progress, but to his utter dismay nobody could tell him where they were or how to make them. Hence he had to resort to asking an Italian, Giovanni Domenico Cassini, professor at Bologna, astronomer to the Pope, and surveyor of waterworks and fortifications, to help with surveys by which such maps could be constructed. In 1673, Cassini became French citizen, changing his name into Jean Dominique, and for the next hundred years the Cassinis–father, son, grandson, and greatgrandson–surveyed and mapped the whole of France (Wilford, 2000, ch. 8).

The English started a national survey as a military project, setting up a government's agency for topographic mapping, the Ordnance Survey, only in 1791. The survey of India was founded by James Rennel in 1765, Captain Cook used triangulation to map the coast of Newfoundland between 1763 and 1767, while mapping New Zealand between 1768 and 1771, and surveying much of the Pacific during his last voyage between 1776 and 1779. In the United States, triangulation was not yet an issue, because precision was not a first priority in a land with great wilderness and moving frontiers.

---

[5] Note that assumption 5 is much less common in the behavioral sciences

The first modern maps of Japan were produced by Tadataka Ino[6] (1745-1818) in the period 1800-1816. This great geographer and mathematician, who still is admired by many as one of the symbols of the modernization of Japan, with his spirit of hard work and belief in scientific knowledge, was born in a village near the Pacific Ocean in the Prefecture of Chiba. Before his scientific career, he was engaged in family business of brewing and dealings with rice, as well as being actively involved in helping the poor.

After retiring at the age of 50, Ino moved to Tokyo, then known as Edo, to study astronomy under Yoshitoki Takahashi. As for others before him, estimating the size of the Earth provided the challenge that motivated his plan to make a geographical survey of Japan along its full length, from North to South. To make a start, Ino asked the local government for permission to survey the Southeastern coast of Hokkaido. The shogunate granted this permission, reasoning that this detailed geographic information would be useful in defending Japan's nothern parts. After this initial success, it took him 16 years to survey the rest of the country. He spent 3,736 days on the road, logged a total of 43,708 km on foot, and made 150,000 directional measurements (Source: *Encyclopedia Nipponica* 2001). The "Ino Maps" were published by his students three years after his death, and became famous for their great accuracy. From the data he collected, Ino estimated the length of one degree of latitude as 110.75 kilometers. This figure implies a perimeter of 39,870 km, which is only 0.58% off the correct value.

6 Gauss' First Example of Least Squares

At the age of 14, Carl Friedrich Gauss[7] (1777-1855) received a stipend from the duke of Brunswick which allowed him to study and publish without restraint. He quickly became a very productive and famous mathematician and astronomer. After his benefactor was killed while fighting for the Prussian army, Gauss had to find a job, and at age 30, he went to Göttingen to become director of the Observatory. In *Theoria Motus Corporum Coelestium in Sectionibus Conicis Solem Ambientium* (1809) [Theory of the Motion of Heavenly Bodies Moving About the Sun in Conic Sections], Gauss gave a probabilistic justification of Legendre's Least Squares criterion published in 1805, showing that is a maximum likelihood method when

---

[6] Ino's portrait copied from: http://www.iptp.go.jp/museum_e/stamp/h7/sstamp-006.html

[7] Gauss' portrait copied from: http://www-history.mcs.st-andrews.ac.uk/history/PictDisplay/Gauss.html

the errors are normal. Then he got into a priority dispute, not only with Legendre, but also with Laplace, who published his central limit theorem in 1809, and applied it to justify Least Squares in a memoir of the French Académie (1810), and again in his major work *Théorie Analytique des Probabilités* (1812).

Then Gauss thought of something better. In *Theoria Combinationis Observationem Erroribus Minimis Obnoxiae: Pars Prior* (1823), *Pars Posterior* (1923), and *Supplementum*(1828) [Theory of the Combination of Observations Least Subject to Errors: Part One, Part Two, Supplement], he proved his *minimum variance* (or Gauss-Markov) theorem: of all linear combinations of measurements estimating an unknown, the least squares estimate has the greatest precision in terms of the root mean squared error (Stewart, 1995, p. 220-226). Note that this result does not depend on the distribution of errors, and that it is not asymptotic!

In discussing his first example of least squares in the *Supplementum*, Gauss writes (Stewart, 1995, p. 147): "Since the method described in this memoir finds its most frequent and natural application in calculations arising from the higher geodesy, I hope my readers will be grateful if I illustrate the principles with some examples drawn from this subject". He then gives a detailed analysis of a triangulation of Friesland and Groningen, based on nine triangles among nine towns, among which Dokkum, the birthplace of Gemma Frisius. Gauss notes that a previous analysis by De Krayenhof had a root mean squared error of 5.1247 degrees, while he himself obtained 2.7440 degrees. Although the error is almost halved, the previous method (by Snellius) was not terribly far off.

That Gauss invented least squares triangulation was no coincidence. During the years 1817-1825, geodesy was his main preoccupation, because he took up a project that involved the triangulation of Hannover, for which he did most of the fieldwork himself (Cung, 2001). Because of the survey, he invented the *heliotrope*, which is an instrument that reflects the Sun's rays in a controllable horizontal direction. He also started teaching regular courses in "Higher Geodesy", and wrote the two-volume book *Untersuchungen Über Gegenstände der Höheren Geodäsie* (1843 and 1846), after having invented in 1822 several new map projections of the transverse Mercator type. These methods are especially suited for mapping regions that mostly extend North-South, and are still among the most used today (Snyder, 1993, p. 159-161). Geodesy also started him off in differential geometry.

7 Conclusion

It can be no accident that accurate long distance measurement was developed in the Low Countries, where distant churches are abundant and easily spotted, in a period that the circumstances were favorable for science to flourish. From the history of triangulation it becomes clear that measurement naturally leads to a variety of statistical considerations, and that statistical models were fitted long before the word statistics was ever used. Measurement problems of geodesy and astronomy have some ground in common with psychometrics. The fact that different methods are used, depending on scale, reminds us of the different worlds of item response theory and factor analysis, which operate at different aggregation levels. However, it appears that psychometrics is not much bothered by the Galilean observation that small changes in data values may lead to large changes in estimates, especially when the distances are very long.

References

Blondeau RA (1993) Mercator van Rupelmonde. Lannoo, Tielt (Belgium)

Cung, N (2001) "Carl Friedrich Gauss." (3 October 2001); 8 pars. Online: Internet. 29 July 2002 (http://www.geocities.com/RainForest/Vines/2977/gauss/g_bio.html)

Daston L. (1988) Classical Probability in the Enlightenment. Princeton University Press, Princeton, NJ

David FN. (1962) Games, Gods and Gambling. Charles Griffin, London

Dijksterhuis EJ (1943) Simon Stevin. Martinus Nijhof, 's-Gravenhage (The Netherlands)

Gigerenzer G, Swijtink Z, Porter T, Daston L, Beatty J, Krüger L (1989) The Empire of Chance: How Probability Changed Science and Everyday Life. Cambridge University Press, Cambridge

Goss J (Ed., 1997) Blaeu's The Grand Atlas of the 17th Century World. Publ. In cooperation with Royal Geographical Society London by Barnes & Noble Books, New York

Haasbroek ND (1968) Gemma Frisius, Tycho Brahe and Snellius and Their Triangulations. Rijkscommissie voor Geodesie, Delft (The Netherlands)

Hacking I (1990) The Taming of Chance. Cambridge University Press, Cambridge

Hald A (1990) A History of Probability and Statistics and Their Applications Before 1750. John Wiley, New York

Hall MB (1994) The Scientific Renaissance 1450-1630. Dover Publications, New York

Klingberg FL (1941) Studies in measurement of the relations among sovereign states. Psychometrika 6: 335-352.

Porter TM (1986) The Rise of Statistical Thinking 1820-1900. Princeton University Press, Princeton, NJ

Porter TM (1995) Trust in Numbers: The Pursuit of Objectivity in Science and Public Life. Princeton University Press, Princeton, NJ

Pouls HC (1999) Een nuttig en profijtelijk boekje voor alle geografen, Gemma Frisius. Nederlandse Commissie voor Geodesie, Delft (The Netherlands)

Rathborne A (1616) The Surveyor in Foure Bookes. W. Burre, London

Rawlins D (1982) Eratosthenes' geodest unraveled: was there a high-accuracy Hellinistic astronomy. Isis 73: 259-265

Snyder JP (1993) Flattening the Earth: Two Thousand Years of Map Projections. University of Chicago Press, Chicago IL

Stewart GW (1995) [Translation and commentary] Theoria Combinationis Observationem Erroribus Minimis Obnoxia by Carl Friedrich Gauss. SIAM, Philadelphia, PA.

Stigler SM (1986) The History of Statistics: The Measurement of Uncertainty before 1900. Harvard University Press, Cambridge, MA

Wilford JN (2000) The Mapmakers, 2nd rev. edn. Vintage Books, New York

Yoder JG (1988) Unrolling Time: Christiaan Huygens and the Mathematization of Nature. Cambridge University Press, Cambridge

Relationships among Various Kinds of Eigenvalue and Singular Value Decompositions

Yoshio Takane

McGill University, 1205 Dr. Penfield Avenue Montreal QC H3A 1B1
takane@takane2.psych.mcgill.ca

Summary. Eigenvalue decomposition (EVD) and/or singular value decomposition (SVD) play important roles in many multivariate data analysis techniques as computational tools for dimension reduction. A variety of EVD and SVD have been developed to deal with specific kinds of dimension reduction problems. This paper explicates various relationships among those decompositions with the prospect of exploiting them in practical applications of multivariate analysis.

Key words: Ordinary and Generalized Eigenvalue Decompositions (EVD and GEVD), Ordinary, Product, Quotient, Restricted, and Generalized Singular Value Decompositions (SVD, PSVD, QSVD, RSVD, and GSVD), Canonical Correlation Analysis (CANO), Constrained Principal Component Analysis (CPCA).

1 Introduction

In many multivariate data analysis (MVA) techniques, we look for best reduced-rank approximations of (some functions of) data matrices. In principal component analysis (PCA), for example, we obtain a reduced-rank approximation of a (standardized) data matrix or that of a covariance (or correlation) matrix. In canonical correlation analysis (CANO), we obtain a reduced-rank approximation of $P_G P_H$, where $P_G = G(G'G)^- G'$ and $P_H = H(H'H)^- H'$ (with $^-$ indicating a generalized inverse (g-inverse) of a matrix) are orthogonal projectors formed from the two sets of data matrices, G and H. Eigenvalue (or spectral) decomposition (EVD) and/or singular value decomposition (SVD) play important roles in this rank-reduction process.

Standard PCA has recently been extended to accommodate external information on both rows and columns of data matrices (CPCA; Takane and Shibayama 1991, Takane and Hunter 2001). Similar extensions have also been made to CANO (GCCANO; Takane and Hwang 2002, Takane et al. 2002, Yanai and Takane 1992). These techniques first decompose data matrices or projectors formed from the data matrices according to the external information. Decomposed matrices are then subjected to a rank-reduction process. Again, EVD or SVD plays important roles in the rank-reduction process.

Ordinary EVD and SVD have been extended in various ways: Generalized EVD (GEVD), Product SVD (PSVD), Quotient SVD (QSVD), Restricted SVD (RSVD), Generalized SVD (GSVD), etc. GEVD obtains EVD of a square (often symmetric and/or nonnegative definite (nnd)) matrix with respect to another nnd matrix. PSVD obtains SVD of a product of matrices without explicitly forming the product. QSVD obtains SVD of a rectangular matrix with respect to another rectangular matrix. RSVD extends QSVD to a triplet of matrices. GSVD obtains SVD of a matrix under non-identity nnd metric matrices. There are interesting relationships among these decompositions. For example, it is well known that SVD($P_G P_H$) mentioned above is simply related to GSVD($(G'G)^- G'H(H'H)^-, G'G, H'H$) (i.e., GSVD of $(G'G)^- G'H(H'H)^-$ with row metric $G'G$ and column metric $H'H$) (Takane and Shibayama 1991, Takane and Hunter 2001; see also the application section below). In this paper we systematically investigate these relationships and suggest ways to exploit them in practical applications of multivariate analysis.

In what follows, U and V denote (full) orthogonal matrices of order m and n, respectively, and X, X_1, and X_2 denote square nonsingular matrices of appropriate orders. Diag($\cdots$) indicates a block diagonal matrix with matrices in parentheses constituting its diagonal blocks. Sp(A) and Ker(A) indicate, respectively, the range and the null spaces of A. Let C^- denote a g-inverse of C. The following conditions called Moore-Penrose Conditions characterize various kinds of g-inverse matrices.

$$CC^-C = C, \tag{1}$$

$$C^-CC^- = C^- \quad \text{(reflexivity)}, \tag{2}$$

$$(CC^-)' = CC^- \quad \text{(least squares)}, \tag{3}$$

and

$$(C^-C)' = C^-C \quad \text{(minimum norm)}. \tag{4}$$

Conditions (3) and (4) may, respectively, be generalized into:

$$(SCC^-)' = SCC^- \quad \text{(S-least squares)}, \tag{5}$$

and

$$(TC^-C)' = TC^-C, \quad \text{(T-minimum norm)}, \tag{6}$$

where S and T are nnd matrices (called metric matrices). Matrices C_l^- and C_m^- denote a least squares and a minimum norm g-inverse of C, respectively, satisfying (1) and (3), and (1) and (4), respectively.

2 Various Decompositions

2.1 SVD

Let A be an m by n matrix of rank a, and let D be an m by n semi-diagonal matrix of the form $D = \begin{bmatrix} {}_a\Delta_a & {}_a0 \\ 0_a & 0 \end{bmatrix}$, where ${}_a\Delta_a$ is a positive definite (pd) diagonal matrix of order a. (We sometimes write ${}_a\Delta_a$ as Δ.) Then, matrix decomposition

$$A = UDV' \tag{7}$$

is called (complete) SVD of A and is denoted by SVD(A). Let U and V be partitioned according to the partition of D above. That is, $U = [U_1, U_2]$, and $V = [V_1, V_2]$, where U_1 is m by a, and V_1 is n by a. Then,

$$A = U_1 \Delta V_1'. \tag{8}$$

This is called incomplete SVD of A. In most data analysis applications only the incomplete version of SVD is of direct interest. In this paper, however, the word SVD refers to the complete SVD unless otherwise specified. Note that $\text{Sp}(A) = \text{Sp}(U_1)$, $\text{Ker}(A') = \text{Sp}(U_2)$, $\text{Sp}(A') = \text{Sp}(V_1)$, and $\text{Ker}(A) = \text{Sp}(V_2)$. (It should be understood that some blocks in partitioned matrices may be null. For example, in the above $D = [\Delta, 0]$ and $U = U_1$ if $m = a$, and $D' = [\Delta, 0]$ and $V = V_1$, if $n = a$.)

The diagonal elements in Δ are assumed to be all distinct and in decreasing order of magnitude, and columns of U and V are arranged accordingly. Let $U_{(r)}$ and $V_{(r)}$ denote the matrices with the first $r(\leq a)$ columns of U_1 and V_1, and let $\Delta_{(r)}$ denote the matrix with the leading diagonal block of order r in Δ. Then, $A_{(r)} = U_{(r)} \Delta_{(r)} V_{(r)}'$ gives the best rank r approximation to A in the least squares sense. That is, the above $A_{(r)}$ gives the minimum of $\text{SS}(A - A_{(r)}) = \text{tr}(A - A_{(r)})'(A - A_{(r)})$ over all matrices of rank r (Eckart and Young 1936; see ten Berge (1993) for an elegant proof of this property). It is this best reduced-rank approximation property that makes SVD extremely useful in multivariate analysis. Mirsky (1960) later showed that this optimality was not restricted to the SS norm. It holds generally for all unitarily (orthogonally) invariant norms.

The following property of SVD is important from a computational point of view (Takane and Hunter 2001, Theorem 1):

Property 1. Let B and C be columnwise orthogonal matrices, i.e., $B'B = I$ and $C'C = I$. Let $A = UDV'$ denote SVD(A), and let $BAC' = U^*D^*V^{*\prime}$ denote SVD(BAC'). Then, $U^* = BU$ (or $U = B'U^*$), $V^* = CV$ (or $V = C'V^*$), and $D^* = D$.

2.2 EVD

Let S be an *nnd* matrix of order n and of rank a. Let $\tilde{D}^2$ denote an *nnd* diagonal matrix of order n with Δ^2 as the leading diagonal block. Then,

$$S = V\tilde{D}^2 V' \qquad (9)$$

is called (complete) EVD of S and is denoted as EVD(S). Matrix S can also be expressed as

$$S = V_1 \Delta^2 V_1', \qquad (10)$$

which is called incomplete EVD of S. When S is obtained by $A'A$, EVD(S) can be derived from SVD(A) by $S = A'A = V\tilde{D}^2 V' = V_1 \Delta^2 V_1'$, where $\tilde{D}^2 = D'D$. Alternatively, if S is obtained by AA', then $S = AA' = UDD'U' = U_1\Delta^2 U_1'$. As in the SVD of A, $S_{(r)} = V_{(r)}\tilde{\Delta}^2_{(r)} V'_{(r)}$ gives the best rank r approximation of S in the least squares sense.

2.3 PSVD

Let A be as defined earlier, and let C be a p by n matrix. The pair of decompositions,

$$A = UDX' \quad \text{and} \quad C' = (X')^{-1} JV', \qquad (11)$$

is called PSVD of the matrix pair, A and C, and is denoted by PSVD(A, C) (Fernando and Hammarling 1988). Here,

$$D = \begin{bmatrix} {}_h\Delta_h & {}_h0_s & {}_h0_t & {}_h0 \\ {}_t0_h & {}_t0_s & {}_tI_t & {}_t0 \\ 0_h & 0_s & 0_t & 0 \end{bmatrix}, \quad \text{and} \quad J = \begin{bmatrix} {}_hI_h & {}_h0_s & {}_h0 \\ {}_s0_h & {}_sI_s & {}_s0 \\ {}_t0_h & {}_t0_s & {}_t0 \\ 0_h & 0_s & 0 \end{bmatrix},$$

where, $h = \text{rank}(AC')$, $s = \text{rank}(C) - h$, $t = \text{rank}(A) - h$, and ${}_h\Delta_h$ is diagonal and *pd*. It follows that

$$AC' = U(DJ)V' \qquad (12)$$

gives SVD of AC'. Note that portions of X corresponding to the last column block of D (and the last row block of J) are not unique (although this usually does not cause much difficulties).

PSVD of two matrices can be easily extended to the product of three matrices, A, $B(q \times m)$, and C. Let $A = X_1 D X_2'$, $B = U E X_1^{-1}$, and $C' = (X_2')^{-1} JV'$. Then, $BAC' = U(EDJ)V'$ gives the SVD of BAC'. PSVD of the matrix triplet, A, B and C, is denoted by PSVD(A, B, C). Here, D, E, and J are of the following form

$$E = \begin{bmatrix} {}_hI_h & {}_h0_s & {}_h0_k & {}_h0_j & {}_h0_i & {}_h0 \\ {}_j0_h & {}_j0_s & {}_j0_k & {}_jI_j & {}_j0_i & {}_j0 \\ {}_i0_h & {}_i0_s & {}_i0_k & {}_i0_j & {}_iI_i & {}_i0 \\ 0_h & 0_s & 0_k & 0_j & 0_i & 0 \end{bmatrix},$$

$$D = \begin{bmatrix} {}_h\Delta_h & {}_h0_s & {}_h0_t & {}_h0_k & {}_h0_j & {}_h0 \\ {}_s0_h & {}_sI_s & {}_s0_t & {}_s0_k & {}_s0_j & {}_s0 \\ {}_k0_h & {}_k0_s & {}_k0_t & {}_kI_k & {}_k0_j & {}_k0 \\ {}_j0_h & {}_j0_s & {}_j0_t & {}_j0_k & {}_jI_j & {}_j0 \\ {}_i0_h & {}_i0_s & {}_i0_t & {}_i0_k & {}_i0_j & {}_i0 \\ 0_h & 0_s & 0_t & 0_k & 0_j & 0 \end{bmatrix}, \quad \text{and} \quad J = \begin{bmatrix} {}_hI_h & {}_h0_s & {}_h0_t & {}_h0 \\ {}_s0_h & {}_sI_s & {}_h0_t & {}_s0 \\ {}_t0_h & {}_t0_s & {}_tI_t & {}_t0 \\ {}_k0_h & {}_k0_s & {}_k0_t & {}_k0 \\ {}_j0_h & {}_j0_s & {}_j0_t & {}_j0 \\ 0_h & 0_s & 0_t & 0 \end{bmatrix},$$

where $h = \text{rank}(BAC')$, $s = \text{rank}(AC') - h$, $t = \text{rank}(C) - \text{rank}(AC')$, $k = \text{rank}(A) - \text{rank}(BA) - \text{rank}(AC') + h$, $j = \text{rank}(BA) - h$, and $i = \text{rank}(B) - \text{rank}(BA)$.

In multivariate analysis, there are many situations in which SVD of a product of two or more matrices is obtained. One classical example is inter-battery factor analysis, where a best reduced-rank approximation of the product of two sets of variables, G and H, is obtained. As another example, Koene and Takane (1999) recently proposed a regularization technique for multi-layered feed-forward neural networks. This method obtains a best reduced-rank approximation of YW, where Y is the matrix of input variables, and W is the matrix of estimated weights associated with the connections from input variables to hidden units. Takane and Yanai (2002) used PSVD of a matrix triplet (Zha 1991b) to show what kind of g-inverse of BAC' is necessary for $\text{rank}(A - AC'(BAC')^- BA) = \text{rank}(A) - \text{rank}(BAC')$, to hold. The result generalizes the Wedderburn-Guttman theorem (Guttman 1944, 1957; Wedderburn 1934).

2.4 QSVD

Let A and C be as defined in PSVD. The pair of decompositions,

$$A = UDX' \quad \text{and} \quad C = VJX', \tag{13}$$

is called QSVD of A with respect to C and is denoted by QSVD(A, C) (Van Loan, 1976). Matrices D and J are of the form

$$D = \begin{bmatrix} {}_h\Delta_h & {}_h0_s & {}_h0_t & {}_h0 \\ {}_t0_h & {}_t0_s & {}_tI_t & {}_s0 \\ 0_h & 0_s & 0_t & 0 \end{bmatrix}, \quad \text{and} \quad J = \begin{bmatrix} {}_hI_h & {}_h0_s & {}_h0_t & {}_h0 \\ {}_s0_h & {}_sI_s & {}_s0_t & {}_s0 \\ 0_h & 0_s & 0_t & 0 \end{bmatrix},$$

where Δ is pd and diagonal, and $h = \dim(\text{Sp}(A') \cap \text{Sp}(C'))$, $s = \dim(\text{Ker}(A) \cap \text{Sp}(C'))$, and $t = \dim(\text{Sp}(A') \cap \text{Ker}(C))$. As in PSVD, the portions of X pertaining to the last block are not unique.

Let N be such that $\text{Sp}(N) = \text{Ker}(C)$. (This matrix N could be V_2 if $C'C = V\tilde{D}^2V' = V_1D_1^2V_1'$ represents the EVD of $C'C$.) Define further $C_{N/A'A}^- = Q_{N/A'A}C_l^-$, where $Q_{N/A'A} = I - N(N'A'AN)^-N'A'A$ (and C_l^- is a least squares g-inverse of C). Then, $\text{PSVD}(A, C_{N/A'A}^-) = \text{SVD}(AC_{N/A'A}^-)$ is obtained from $\text{QSVD}(A, C)$ by

$$
\begin{aligned}
AC_{N/A'A}^- &= AQ_{N/A'A}^- C_l^- \\
&= UDX'Q_{N/A'A}(X')^{-1}J_l^- V' \\
&= UDQ_{N^*/D'D}J_l^- V' \\
&= U(DJ_{N^*/D'D}^-)V',
\end{aligned} \tag{14}
$$

where $N^* = X'N$, and $J_{N^*/D'D}^- = Q_{N^*/D'D}J_l^-$. Note that in going from the first equation to the second we used $(X')^{-1}J_l^- V' \in \{C_l^-\}$ if $C = VDX'$ (Rao and Mitra 1971, Complement 3.2 (iv)). Leading diagonals in $DJ_{N^*/D'D}^- = \text{diag}(\Delta, 0, 0, 0)$ have nonzero and finite singular values of A with respect to C. (All improper (infinite and indeterminate) singular values become zero in $\text{SVD}(AC_{N/A'A}^-)$.) Note that $A'A = XD'DX'$, and that $X'Q_{N/A'A}(X')^{-1} = I - N^*(N^{*'}D'DN^*)^- N^{*'}D'D = Q_{N^*/D'D}$. Note also that

$$
J_l^- = \begin{bmatrix} I & 0 & 0 \\ 0 & I & 0 \\ Z_1 & Z_2 & Z_3 \\ E_1 & W_2 & E_3 \end{bmatrix}, \quad \text{but} \quad J_{N^*/D'D}^- = \begin{bmatrix} I & 0 & 0 \\ 0 & I & 0 \\ 0 & 0 & 0 \\ E_1^* & E_2^* & E_3^* \end{bmatrix},
$$

where Z_i's and E_i's, and E_i^*'s $(i = 1, \cdots, 3)$ are arbitrary.

G-inverse, $C_{N/A'A}^- = Q_{N/A'A}C_l^-$, satisfies (1), (3), and (6) of the extended Moore-Penrose Conditions, namely

$$
CC_{N/A'A}^- C = C, \tag{15}
$$

$$
(CC_{N/A'A}^-)' = CC_{N/A'A}^- \qquad \text{(least squares)}, \tag{16}
$$

and

$$
(A'AC_{N/A'A}^- C)' = A'AC_{N/A'A}^- C \qquad (A'A\text{-minimum norm}). \tag{17}
$$

The first two of these conditions follow immediately from $CQ_{N/A'A} = C$. The last condition follows from $A'AC_{N/A'A}^- C = A'AQ_{N/A'A}$, (the latter is clearly symmetric), and from

$$
A'AQ_{N/A'A} = C'AC \tag{18}
$$

for some Λ. That is, $A'AC_{N/A'A}^- C = A'AQ_{N/A'A} = A'AQ_{N/A'A}C_l^- C = C'ACC_l^- C = C'AC = A'AQ_{N/A'A}$. G-inverse, $J_{N^*/D'D}^- = Q_{N^*/D'D}J_l^-$, has a similar property. The fact that $C_{N/A'A}^-$ can be expressed as $Q_{N/A'A}C_l^-$ (and that $J_{N^*/D'D}^-$ can be expressed as $Q_{N^*/D'D}J_l^-$) is sufficient, but not necessary, for the above three conditions ((1), (3), and (6)) to hold. In terms of the expression of $J^-_{N*/D'D}$ given above, the zero matrix in the third row and the third column block could be arbitrary in order to satisfy the three conditions.

The name "Quotient" SVD derives from the fact that it obtains SVD of $AC^-_{N/A'A}$, which is analogous to taking the quotient (a/c) of two numbers (De Moor 1991, De Moor and Golub 1991). QSVD used to be called GSVD by computational matrix algebraists (Golub and Van Loan 1989, Paige 1986, Paige and Saunders 1981, Van Loan 1976). This was quite confusing because the same terminology has been used by French data analysts for a different decomposition. See below. GSVD in the sense of computational matric algebraists has recently been renamed into QSVD (De Moor and Golub 1991).

2.5 RSVD

Let A, B, and C be as introduced earlier. The triplet of decompositions,

$$A = X_1 D X'_2, \quad B = U E X'_1, \quad \text{and} \quad C = V J X'_2, \tag{19}$$

is called RSVD of A with respect to B and C and is denoted by RSVD(A, B, C) (De Moor and Golub 1991, Zha 1991a). Here,

$$D = \begin{bmatrix} {}_h\Delta_h & {}_h0_s & {}_h0_t & {}_h0_k & {}_h0_j & {}_h0 \\ {}_s0_h & {}_sI_s & {}_h0_t & {}_s0_k & {}_s0_j & {}_s0 \\ {}_k0_h & {}_k0_s & {}_k0_t & {}_kI_k & {}_k0_j & {}_k0 \\ {}_j0_h & {}_j0_s & {}_j0_t & {}_j0_k & {}_jI_j & {}_j0 \\ {}_i0_h & {}_i0_s & {}_i0_t & {}_i0_k & {}_i0_j & {}_i0 \\ 0_h & 0_s & 0_t & 0_k & 0_j & 0 \end{bmatrix}, \quad E = \begin{bmatrix} {}_hI_h & {}_h0_j & {}_h0_i & {}_h0 \\ {}_s0_h & {}_s0_j & {}_s0_i & {}_s0 \\ {}_k0_h & {}_k0_j & {}_k0_i & {}_k0 \\ {}_j0_h & {}_jI_j & {}_j0_i & {}_j0 \\ {}_i0_h & {}_i0_j & {}_iI_i & {}_i0 \\ 0_h & 0_j & 0_i & 0 \end{bmatrix},$$

and

$$J = \begin{bmatrix} {}_hI_h & {}_h0_s & {}_h0_t & {}_h0_k & {}_h0_j & {}_h0 \\ {}_s0_h & {}_sI_s & {}_h0_t & {}_s0_k & {}_s0_j & {}_s0 \\ {}_t0_h & {}_t0_s & {}_tI_t & {}_t0_k & {}_t0_j & {}_t0 \\ 0_h & 0_s & 0_t & 0_k & 0_j & 0 \end{bmatrix},$$

where $h = \rho_{abc} - \rho_{ab} - \rho_{ac} + \text{rank}(A)$, $s = \rho_{ab} - \rho_{abc} + \text{rank}(C)$, $t = \rho_{ac} - \text{rank}(A)$, $k = \rho_{abc} - \text{rank}(A) - \text{rank}(B)$, $j = \rho_{ab} - \rho_{abc} + \text{rank}(B)$, and $i = \rho_{ab} - \text{rank}(A)$ with $\rho_{abc} = \text{rank}\begin{bmatrix} A & B' \\ C & 0 \end{bmatrix}$, $\rho_{ab} = \text{rank}[A, B']$, $\rho_{ac} = \text{rank}\begin{bmatrix} A \\ C \end{bmatrix}$.

SVD$((B^-_{M/AA})'AC^-_{N/A'A})$ follows from RSVD(A, B, C), where M is such that Sp$(M) = $ Ker(B) (which is analogous to N for C). Note that $(B^-_{M/AA'})'A$ $C^-_{N/A'A} = U(K^-_{M*/DD'})'DJ^-_{N*/D'D}V'$, where U and V are, respectively, matrices of left and right singular vectors, and $(K^-_{M*/DD'})'DJ^-_{N*/D'D}$ a diagonal matrix of nonzero finite singular values of $(B^-_{M/AA'})'AC^-_{N/A'A}$. (All other singular values of A with respect to B and C become zero.) Matrix $B^-_{M/AA}$ has similar properties to those possessed by $C^-_{N/A'A}$.

2.6 GEVD (QEVD)

Let T be an nnd matrix of the same order as S. The pair of decompositions,

$$S = X \tilde{D}^2 X' \quad \text{and} \quad T = X \tilde{J}^2 X', \tag{20}$$

is called GEVD of S with respect to T and is denoted by GEVD(S,T). Here, $\tilde{D}^2 = \text{diag}(\Delta^2, 0, I, 0)$ (where Δ^2 is diagonal and pd), and $\tilde{J}^2 = \text{diag}(I, I, 0, 0)$. The four diagonal blocks in these matrices pertain to $\text{Sp}(S) \cap \text{Sp}(T)$, $\text{Ker}(S) \cap \text{Sp}(T)$, $\text{Sp}(S) \cap \text{Ker}(T)$, and $\text{Ker}(S) \cap \text{Sp}(T)$, and their sizes reflect the dimensionality of these subspaces. As in QSVD (and PSVD), portions of X pertaining to the last block are usually non-unique.

Let $W = (X')^{-1}$. In the more traditional approach to GSVD, this W may be of more direct interest. This W has the property of simultaneously diagonalizing both S and T. That is, $W'SW = \tilde{D}^2$, and $W'TW = \tilde{J}^2$. De Leeuw (1982) has given a complete solution to this problem. Let $T = FF'$ be a full rank square root decomposition of T, and let N be a columnwise orthogonal matrix such that $\text{Ker}(T) = \text{Sp}(N)$. Let $W = [W_1, W_2]$, where W_1 and W_2 correspond with $\text{Sp}(T) = \text{Sp}(F)$ and $\text{Ker}(T) = \text{Sp}(N)$, respectively. Define $Q_{N/S} = (I - N(N'SN)^- N'S)$. (This is analogous to $Q_{N/A'A}$ in QSVD.) Then, W can be obtained by

$$W_1 = Q_{N/S}(F')^+ + Q_{N/S} N Z_1, \tag{21}$$

and

$$W_2 = N W_2^* D^*, \tag{22}$$

where W_1^* and W_2^* are complete sets of eigenvectors of $F^+ Q'_{N/S} S Q_{N/S} (F')^+$ and $N'SN$, respectively, $^+$ indicates the Moore-Penrose inverse ($F^+ = (F'F)^{-1}F'$ and $(F')^+$ is its transpose), and Z_1 is arbitrary. D^* is such that $D^* = \begin{bmatrix} \Delta_2^{-1} & 0 \\ 0 & Z_2 \end{bmatrix}$, where Δ_2^2 is the diagonal matrix of nonzero eigenvalues of $N'SN$, and Z_2 is a nonnull (but otherwise arbitrary) square matrix. Note that $\text{Sp}(Q_{N/S}N)$ pertains to the joint null space of S and T, that is, $\text{Ker}(S) \cap \text{Ker}(T)$. The fact that W is usually non-unique corresponds with the fact that X is usually non-unique.

If $S = A'A$ and $T = C'C$, where A and C are those used in QSVD, GEVD(S,T) is obtained from QSVD(A,C) by setting $S = X\tilde{D}^2 X'$ and $T = X'\tilde{J}^2 X$, where $\tilde{D}^2 = D'D$, and $\tilde{J}^2 = J'J$. In fact, QSVD was invented initially (Van Loan, 1976) to obtain GEVD$(A'A, C'C)$ without explicitly calculating $A'A$ and $C'C$.

2.7 GSVD

Let A be as defined earlier, and let K and L be nnd matrices of order m and n, respectively. Then, the triplet of matrix decompositions

$$A = X_1 D X_2', \quad K = (X_1')^{-1} \tilde{E}^2 X_1^{-1}, \text{ and } L = (X_2')^{-1} \tilde{J}^2 X_2^{-1}, \qquad (23)$$

is called GSVD of A with metric matrices K and L. Matrix D is similar to that in PSVD, and $\tilde{E}^2 = \text{diag}(I, 0, 0, I, I, 0)$ and $\tilde{J}^2 = \text{diag}(I, I, I, 0, 0, 0)$ are themselves *nnd*, and are obtained by $\tilde{E}^2 = E'E$ and $\tilde{J}^2 = J'J$. Let $R_K' = \tilde{E} X_1^{-1}$, and $R_L = (X_2')^{-1} \tilde{J}$, and define $(R_K')_*^- = X_1 \tilde{E}^+$, and $(R_L)_*^- = \tilde{J}^+ X_2'$ (where $^+$ indicates the Moore-Penrose inverse). Then, $(R_K')_*^- R_K' A R_L (R_L)_*^- = X_1 (\tilde{E}^+ \tilde{E} D \tilde{J} \tilde{J}^+ X_2' = X_1 D^* X_2'$. (Matrix $(R_K')_*^-$ satisfies (1), (2), (3), and (6) of the extended Moore-Penrose Conditions with $T = (X_1 X_1')^{-1}$, while $(R_L)_*^-$ satisfies (1), (2), (3), and (5) with $S = X_2 X_2'$. Leading diagonals of D^* have nonzero generalized singular values of A under metric matrices K and L. GSVD of A under metric matrices K and L is denoted by $\text{GSVD}(A, K, L)$.

$\text{GSVD}(A, K, L)$ is typically calculated as follows: Let $K = F_K F_K'$ and $L = F_L F_L'$ denote full rank square root decompositions of K and L. Let $F_K' A F_L = U * D * V^{*'}$ be $\text{SVD}(F_K' A F_L)$. Then, $P_{F_K} A P_{F_L} = X_1 \tilde{D} X_2'$, where P_{F_K} and P_{F_L} are orthogonal projectors defined by F_K and F_L, $U = F_K (F_K' F_K)^{-1} U^*$, $\tilde{D} = D^*$, and $V = F_L (F_L' F_L)^{-1} V^*$. Note that $X_1' K X_1 = \tilde{E}^2$, and $X_2' L X_2 = \tilde{J}^2$.

There is an important property associated with GSVD of a matrix, which is analogous to Property 1 mentioned in the section entitled SVD (Takane and Hunter 2001, Theorem 2).

Property 2. Let B and C be such that BAC' can be formed. Let $BAC' = UDV'$ denote $\text{GSVD}(BAC', K, L)$, and let $A = U^* D^* V^{*'}$ denote $\text{GSVD}(A, B'KB, C'LC)$. Then, $U = K^- KBU^*$, $V = L^- LCV^*$ and $D = D^*$, or $U^* = (B'KB)^- B'KU$, $V^* = (C'LC)^- C'LV$ and $D^* = D$.

3 Applications

How can we effectively use these decompositions in representative methods of multivariate analysis? Let us take canonical correlation analysis (CANO) and constrained principal component analysis (CPCA; Takane and Shibayama 1991, Takane and Hunter 2001) as examples.

As is well known, CANO between G and H amounts to $\text{SVD}(P_G P_H)$ or equivalently to $\text{GSVD}((G'G)^- G'H(H'H)^-, G'G, H'H)$. The former obtains canonical scores directly, while the latter obtains weights applied to G and H to obtain the canonical scores. Property 2 mentioned above indicates there is a simple relationship between the two decompositions. Let $P_G P_H = UDV'$ represent $\text{SVD}(P_G P_H)$, and let $(G'G)^- G'H(H'H)^- = X_1 D^* X_2'$ represent $\text{GSVD}((G'G)^- G'H(H'H)^-, G'G, H'H)$. Then, $U = GX_1$ (or $X_1 = (G'G)^- G'U$), $V = HX_2$ (or $X_2 = (H'H)^- H'V$), and $D = D^*$. It may look as if the dimensionality of the former problem is usually much larger than the latter. Thus, it is wise to obtain the latter first and then derive the former from it. However, the dimensionality of the former can also be directly reduced using Property 1 in SVD. Let Y_G and Y_H denote orthonormal bases for $\mathrm{Sp}(G)$ and $\mathrm{Sp}(H)$, respectively. Then, P_G and P_H can be written as $P_G = Y_G Y_G'$ and $P_H = Y_H Y_H'$, respectively. Let $Y_G' Y_H = UDV'$ denote $\mathrm{SVD}(Y_G' Y_H)$. Then, $\mathrm{SVD}(P_G P_H) = \mathrm{SVD}(Y_G(Y_G' Y_H)Y_H')$ is obtained by $Y_G UDV' Y_H'$.

In GCCANO (Takane and Hwang 2002, Takane et al. 2002), the situation is only slightly more complicated. In GCCANO, matrices from which projectors are formed (that is, matrices analogous to G and H in standard CANO) are obtained by products of two or more matrices. However, the structure of the computational problem remains essentially the same.

CPCA, on the other hand, involves five matrices. CPCA of a data matrix Z with two external information matrices, G and H, and two metric matrices, K and L, is denoted by $\mathrm{CPCA}(Z, G, H, K, L)$, and it subsumes a number of existing MVA techniques as special cases. For example, CANO between G and H follows when $Z = I$, $K = I$ and $L = I$. CPCA amounts to $\mathrm{GSVD}(P_{G/K} Z P_{H/L}', K, L)$ or equivalently to $\mathrm{GSVD}((G'KG)^- G'KZLH(H'LH)^-, G'KG, H'LH)$. Again by Property 2, there is a simple relationship between the two decompositions. Let $G^* = R_K' G$, $H^* = R_L' H$, and $A^* = R_K' A R_L$. Then, $R_K' P_{G/K} Z P_{H/L}' R_L = P_{G^*} A^* P_{H^*}$, where P_{G^*} and P_{H^*} are orthogonal projectors defined by G^* and H^*, respectively. Let Y_{G^*} and Y_{H^*} be matrices of orthonormal bases spanning $\mathrm{Sp}(G^*)$ and $\mathrm{Sp}(H^*)$, respectively. Then, $P_{G^*} A^* P_{H^*} = Y_{G^*} Y_{G^*}' A^* Y_{H^*} Y_{H^*}'$. Let $Y_{G^*}' A^* Y_{H^*} = UDV'$ be $\mathrm{SVD}(Y_{G^*}' A^* Y_{H^*})$. Then, $\mathrm{SVD}(Y_{G^*}(Y_{G^*}' A^* Y_{H^*})Y_{H^*}')$ is obtained by $Y_{G^*} UDV' Y_{H^*}'$. From this, $\mathrm{GSVD}(P_{G/K} Z P_{H/L}', K, L)$ is obtained by $(R_K')^- Y_{G^*} UDV' Y_{H^*}' R_L^-$ and $\mathrm{GSVD}((G'KG)^- G'KZLH(H'LH)^-, G'KG, H'LH)$ is obtained by $(G^{*'} G^*)^- G^{*'} UDV' H^* (H^{*'} H^*)^-$.

The above procedures represent more conventional procedures for computing CANO (and GCCANO), and CPCA. In the light of the new breed of SVD's discussed in this paper, we have other options, which may yield numerically more stable solutions. Virtually any one of the EVD's and SVD's discussed in this paper can be used to obtain solutions for CANO and CPCA by preprocessing matrices appropriately. This is summarized in the following table. Which one to use in which situation depends on the size of matrices involved (e.g., EVD of $A'A$ is much faster than SVD of A when A is very tall), how crucial the numerical accuracy is, etc. In both CANO and CPCA, $Q_{N/S} = I$ (i.e., $\mathrm{Sp}(S) \cap \mathrm{Ker}(T) = \{0\}$) which simplifies the formula considerably.

A little more elegant way of computing $\mathrm{CANO}(G, H)$ is to combine more than one kind of decomposition. $\mathrm{CANO}(G, H)$ may be solved by obtaining $\mathrm{QSVD}(\mathrm{PSVD}(I, G', H'), G', H')$, which De Moor (1991) calls QPPQ-SVD, or by $\mathrm{PSVD}(\mathrm{QSVD}(I, G, H), G, H)$, which De Moor calls PQQP-SVD. Similarly, $\mathrm{CPCA}(A, G, H, K, L)$ may be solved by $\mathrm{QSVD}(\mathrm{PSVD}(A^*, G^{*'}, H^{*'}), G^{*'},$

Table 1. CANO and CPCA Solutions by Various EVD's and SVD's.

	CANO(G, H)	CPCA(Z, G, H, K, L)
SVD	$A = P_G P_H$	$A = R'_K P_{G/K} Z P'_{H/L} R_L$
EVD	$S = P_H P_G P_H$	$S = R'_L P_{H/L} Z' K P'_{H/L} R_L$
PSVD	$A = G'H,\ B = G(G'G)^-,$ $C = H(H'H)^-$	$A = G'ZH,\ B = G(G'G)^-,$ $C = H(H'H)^-$
QSVD	$A = P_G H,\ C = H$	$A = R'_K P_{G/K} ZLH,\ C = R'_L H$
RSVD	$A = G'H,\ B = G,\ C = H$	$A = G'KZLH,\ B = R'_K G,\ C = R'_L H$
GEVD	$S = H'P_G H,\ T = H'H$	$S = H'LZ'KP_{G/K} ZLH,\ T = H'LH$
GSVD	$A = (G'G)^- G'H(H'H)^-,$ $K = G'G,\ L = H'H$	$A = (G'KG)^- G'KZLH(H'LH)^-,$ $K = GKG,\ L = H'LH$

$H^{*\prime}$) or PSVD(QSVD(A^*, G^*, H^*), G^*, H^*). Since A^*, G^*, and H^* are themselves products of two matrices, an even more sophisticated approach is to eliminate the multiplications to form these products altogether.

References

de Leeuw J (1982) Generalized eigenvalue problems with positive semi-definite matrices. Psyhometrika 47: 87–93

De Moor B (1991) Generalizations of the OSVD: Structure, properties and applications. In: Vaccaro RJ (ed) SVD and signal processing, II: Algorithms, analysis and applications. Elsevier, Amsterdam, pp 83–98

De Moor BLR, Golub GH (1991) The restricted singular value decomposition: Properties and applications. SIAM Journal: Matrix Analysis and Applications 12: 401–425

Eckart C, Young G (1936) The approximation of one matrix by another of lower rank. Psychometrika 1: 211–218

Fernando KV, Hammarling SJ (1988) A product induced singular value decomposition for two matrices and balanced realization. In: Datta BN, Johnson CR, Kaashoek MA, Plemmons R, Sontag E (eds) Linear algebra in signal systems and control. SIAM, Philadelphia, pp 128–140

Golub GH, Van Loan CF (1989) Matrix computations (2nd Ed). Johns Hopkins University Press, Baltimore

Guttman L (1944) General theory and methods of matric factoring. Psychometrika 9: 1–16

Guttman L (1957) A necessary and sufficient formula for matric factoring. Psychometrika 22: 79–81

Koene R, Takane Y (1999) Discriminant component pruning: Regularization and interpretation of multi-layered back-propagation networks. Neural Computation 11: 783–802

Mirsky L (1960) Symmetric gage functions and unitarily invariant norms. Quarterly Journal of Mathematics 11: 50–59

Paige CC (1986) Computing the generalized singular value decomposition. SIAM Journal: Scientific Computing 7: 1126–1146

Paige CC, Saunders MA (1981) Towards a generalized singular value decomposition. SIAM Journal: Numerical Analysis 18: 398–405

Rao CR, Mitra SK (1971) Generalized inverse of matrices and its applications. Wiley, New York

Takane Y, Shibayama T (1991) Principal component analysis with external information on both subjects and variables. Psychometrika 56: 97–120

Takane Y, Hunter MA (2001) Constrained principal component analysis: A comprehensive theory. Applicable Algebra in Engineering, Communication and Computing 12: 391–419

Takane Y, Hwang, H (2002) Generalized constrained canonical correlation analysis. Multivariate Behavioral Research 37: 163–195

Takane Y, Yanai H, Hwang H (2002) An improved method for generalized constrained canonical correlation analysis. Submitted to Computational Statistics and Data Analysis.

ten Berge JMF (1993) Least squares optimization in multivariate analysis. DSWO Press, Leiden

Van Loan CF (1976) Generalizing the singular value decomposition. SIAM Journal: Numerical Analysis 13: 76–83

Wedderburn JHM (1934) Lectures on matrices. Colloquium Publications 17, Providence, American Mathematical Society

Yanai H, Takane Y (1992) Canonical correlation analysis with linear constraints. Linear Algebra and Its Applications 176: 75–89

Zha H (1991a) The restricted singular value decomposition of matrix triplets. SIAM Journal: Matrix Analysis and Applications 12: 172–194

Zha H (1991b) The product singular value decomposition of matrix trplets. BIT 31: 711–726

Power of χ^2 Goodness-of-fit Tests in Structural Equation Models: the Case of Non-Normal Data

Albert Satorra

Universitat Pompeu Fabra. Barcelona, Ramon Trias Fargas 25-27, 08005-Barcelona, Spain.

Summary. In the context of structural equation models, we investigate the asymptotic and finite sample size distribution of competing χ^2 goodness-of-fit test statistics. We allow for a) the data to be non-normal, b) the estimation method to be non-optimal, and c) the model to be misspecified. Power of the test is computed distinguishing whether asymptotic robustness (AR) holds or not. The power of the various test statistics is compared, asymptotically and using Monte Carlo simulation. A scaled version of a normal-theory (NT) goodness-of-fit test statistic for ULS analysis is included among the test statistics investigated.

Keywords. minimum-distance, non-normality, misspecification, asymptotic χ^2 statistic, non-centrality parameter, power of the test.

1 Introduction

In the analysis of structural equation models (SEM) we often need to assess the power of a χ^2 goodness-of-fit test (see Satorra and Saris, 1985 and, more recently, MacCallum, Browne and Sugawara, 1996). In SEM, typically a vector σ, say, of population first- and second-order moments of manifest variables, is expressed as a vector-valued function $\sigma = \sigma(\vartheta)$ of unknown model parameters ϑ, of a parameter space $\mathcal{F}$. The vector ϑ is estimated by fitting $\sigma = \sigma(\vartheta)$ to the corresponding vector of sample moments s, where $\text{plim}_{n \to \infty} s \to \sigma$, and n is sample size. In this set-up, of special relevance is the goodness-of-fit test of the null hypothesis $H_0 : \sigma = \sigma(\vartheta)$, $\vartheta \in \mathcal{F}$. Alternative χ^2 goodness-of-fit tests are nowadays available in the standard software for SEM analysis. Typically, $n-1$ times the minimum of the fitting function is asymptotically χ^2 distributed when the model and specific distribution conditions, usually restrictive, do hold. In an asymptotically distribution-free (ADF) setting, Browne (1984) proposes a residual-based χ^2 goodness-of-fit test that is asymptotically χ^2 distributed under general conditions. As an alternative, Satorra and Bentler (1994) propose a family of corrections for normal-theory (NT) based χ^2 goodness-of-fit tests that for small and medium size samples outperform ADF methods (see, e.g., Hu, Bentler and

Kano, 1992; Curran, West and Finch, 1996). Parallel to these developments, the so-called work on asymptotic robustness (AR) (see, e.g., Satorra, 2002, and references therein) has shown the validity of NT statistics far beyond the assumption of normality of manifest variables; in particular, standard NT-based χ^2 goodness-of-fit test statistics can be asymptotically χ^2 distributed despite severe non-normality of the data.

Thus, when dealing with non-normal data, researchers are confronted with the choice of competing χ^2 goodness-of-fit test statistics. The present paper investigates the performance of various of these test statistics in a general setting that allows for non-normal data and misspecification of the models. The present paper pursues the work of Satorra (2001), by expanding the class of statistics considered and the Monte Carlo illustration.

The following notation will be used. For a symmetric matrix A, v (A) is the vector obtained from vec(A) by eliminating the duplicated elements associated with the symmetry of A; D and D^+ are matrices defined by the identities vec$A = D$v (A) and v $(A) = D^+$vec(A), for a symmetric matrix A, with "+" denoting Moore-Penrose inverse. We use the standard notation $\oplus_{i=1}^m A_i$ for the direct sum of matrices. By $\chi^2(r, \lambda)$ we denote the non-central χ^2 distribution of r degrees of freedom (df) and non-centrality parameter (ncp) λ. The central χ^2 distribution of r df is denoted simply by χ_r^2. By $O_p(1)$ we indicate that a stochastic quantity (scalar or vector) is bounded in probability (as sample size $n \to \infty$).

2 Data and Model Set-up

Consider independent samples $\{z_{gi}\}_{i=1}^{n_g}$, $g = 1, \ldots, G$, from G populations or groups, where z_{gi} is a $p_g \times 1$ vector of observable variables associated with the ith individual of group gth. Let $S_g = \frac{1}{n_g} \sum_{i=1}^{n_g} z_{gi} z_{gi}'$ be the $p_g \times p_g$ matrix of sample cross-product moments and $s = (s_1', \ldots, s_G')'$ be the $p^* \times 1$ vector of sample moments, where $s_g = $ v (S_g), $p^* = \sum_{g=1}^G p_g^*$ and $p_g^* = p_g(p_g + 1)/2$. Let Σ_g be the probability limit of S_g (as $n_g \to \infty$) and $\sigma = (\sigma_1', \ldots, \sigma_G')'$ the vector of population moments, where $\sigma_g = $ v (Σ_g). The matrices S_g and Σ_g are assumed to be non-singular.

As in Satorra (2001), in the case of no model misspecification, we assume

$$z_{gi} = \Lambda_g \xi_{gi} \quad g = 1, \ldots, G, \tag{1}$$

where

$$\Lambda_g = (\Lambda_g^{(0)}, \Lambda_g^{(1)}, \ldots, \Lambda_g^{(L_g)})$$

and

$$\xi_{gi} = (\xi_{g0i}', \xi_{g1i}', \ldots, \xi_{gL_gi}')'$$

are conformable partitions of Λ_g ($p_g \times m_g$) and ξ_{gi} ($m_g \times 1$), with $m_g = \sum_{\ell=0}^{L_g} m_{g\ell}$. Here $\Lambda_g^{(\ell)}$ is a $p_g \times m_{g\ell}$ matrix of coefficients, and $\xi_{g\ell i}$ is a random

$m_{g\ell} \times 1$ vector. Three types of vector-variables $\xi_{g\ell i}$ are distinguished according to the value of the sub-index ℓ: the ξ_{g0i}, that are assumed fixed across sample replications; the $\xi_{g\ell i}$, $\ell = 1, \ldots, L_g - 1$, that are assumed distribution-free with finite second-order moments; and the $\xi_{gL_g i}$, that are assumed to be normally distributed. When the fixed or normal components are absent from (1), $E(z_{gi}) = 0$.

For each g here, assume that

a)

$$\lim_{n_g \to +\infty} \frac{1}{n_g} \sum_{i=1}^{n_g} \xi_{g0i} = \mu_{0g} \quad \text{and} \quad \lim_{n_g \to +\infty} \frac{1}{n_g} \sum_{i=1}^{n_g} \xi_{g0i}\xi_{g0i}' = \Phi_g^{(0)},$$

for suitable $m_{g0} \times 1$ vector μ_{0g} and $m_{g0} \times m_{g0}$ matrix $\Phi_g^{(0)}$.

b) $\{\xi_{g\ell i}\}_i$ is an iid sequence, $\ell = 1, \ldots, L_g$.

c) $\xi_{g1i}, \ldots, \xi_{gL_g i}$ are uncorrelated with zero mean and respective variance matrices $\Phi_g^{(1)}, \ldots, \Phi_g^{(L_g)}$.

Owing to a) and b), $Q_g = \frac{1}{n_g} \sum_{i=1}^{n_g} \xi_{gi}\xi_{gi}' \to \Phi_g = \oplus_{\ell=0}^{L_g} \Phi_{g\ell}$, in probability. Consider now a model with $\Phi_g = \Phi_g(\vartheta)$, $\Lambda_g = \Lambda_g(\tau)$ and $\Phi_g^{(L_g)} = \Phi_g^{(L_g)}(\tau)$, where ϑ is in the interior of a t-dimensional space $\mathcal{F}$ and τ (t^*-dimensional, $t^* < t$) is a sub-vector of ϑ. This implies a moment structure $\sigma = \sigma(\vartheta)$, $\vartheta \in \mathcal{F}$. To allow for model misspecificaton, we just assume that $\sigma = \sigma(\vartheta) + \frac{1}{\sqrt{n}}\delta$, where δ is a finite $p^* \times 1$ vector induced by the misspecification of the model (this implies a sequence of local alternatives; see Stroud (1972)). When $\delta = 0$, we say the model holds *exactly* (see Satorra, 2001, for an specific model form of this misspecification). For further use, we define the Jacobian $p^* \times q$ matrix $\Delta = \partial\sigma(\vartheta)/\partial\vartheta'$ and we let $\Delta_\perp$ be an orthogonal complement of Δ, i.e., $\Delta_\perp$ is a $p^* \times (p^* - q)$ matrix of full-column rank such that $\Delta_\perp' \Delta = 0$.

3 MD Estimation and Testing

3.1 General Formulation

Consider the minimum distance (MD) estimator

$$\hat{\vartheta} = \operatorname{argmin}_{\vartheta \in \mathcal{F}} \{s - \sigma(\vartheta)\}' \hat{V} \{s - \sigma(\vartheta)\}, \tag{2}$$

where $\hat{V}$ ($p^* \times p^*$) converges in probability to V, a positive definite matrix, and $\mathcal{F}$ is a q–dimensional compact subset of $\mathcal{R}^q$. Assume that $\hat{\vartheta}$ in (2) is unique for all s, $\Delta'V\Delta$ ($q \times q$) is non-singular, and the true value of ϑ is in the interior of $\mathcal{F}$. In particular, consider the NT-MD method discussed in Section 3.2 below, and the equally weighted MD (EW-MD) (also known as ULS) where $\tilde{V} = \oplus_{g=1}^{G} \frac{n_g}{n} \tilde{V}_g$, with $\tilde{V}_g = \frac{1}{2}D'D$ and $n = n_1 + \ldots + n_G$

(this is the same as minimizing $\sum_g \frac{n_g}{2n} \text{tr} (S_g - \Sigma_g(\vartheta))^2$). Crucial to this set-up is the asymptotic variance matrix Γ_s of s. Under standard conditions, a consistent estimator of Γ_s is just given by $\hat{\Gamma}_s = \oplus_{g=1}^{G} \frac{n}{n_g} \hat{\Gamma}_{s_g}$, where $\hat{\Gamma}_{s_g} = \frac{1}{n_g-1} \sum_{i=1}^{n_g} (d_{gi} - s_g)(d_{gi} - s_g)'$ and $d_{gi} = v(z_{gi} z_{gi}')$.

A Wald-type test statistic for testing the goodness-of-fit of the model $H_0 : \sigma = \sigma(\vartheta), \vartheta \in \mathcal{F}$, is

$$T_V = n(s - \hat{\sigma})' \hat{\Delta}_\perp \left(\hat{\Delta}'_\perp \hat{\Gamma}_s \hat{\Delta}_\perp \right)^+ \hat{\Delta}'_\perp (s - \hat{\sigma}), \tag{3}$$

where $\hat{\Delta}_\perp$ and $\hat{\Gamma}_s$ are consistent estimators of $\Delta_\perp$ and Γ_s, respectively. According to the standard theory of Wald-test statistics, T_V is asymptotically χ^2 distributed with df equal to $r = \text{rank} (\Delta'_\perp \Gamma_s \Delta_\perp)$, and ncp

$$\lambda = \delta' \Delta_\perp (\Delta'_\perp \Gamma_s \Delta_\perp)^+ \Delta'_\perp \delta \quad (= \lambda(T_V)). \tag{4}$$

Here $\delta = \sqrt{n}(\sigma^0 - \sigma_0)$, where $\sigma^0 (= \sigma_n^0)$ and σ_0 are the respective population counterparts of s and $\hat{\sigma}$. When $\hat{\Gamma}_s$ is non-singular, then

$$T_V = n(s - \hat{\sigma})' \left\{ \hat{\Gamma}_s^{-1} - \hat{\Gamma}_s^{-1} \hat{\Delta} \left(\hat{\Delta}' \hat{\Gamma}_s^{-1} \hat{\Delta} \right)^{-1} \hat{\Delta}' \hat{\Gamma}_s^{-1} \right\} (s - \hat{\sigma}).$$

In the case of one-sample covariance structure analysis, this is the residual-based χ^2 goodness-of-fit introduced by Browne (1984). Clearly, the asymptotic α-level test of H_0 *rejects* when $T_V > c_\alpha$, where c_α is the critical value of the test, i.e. $Pr\{\chi_r^2 > c_\alpha\} = \alpha$. Associated to a specific vector $\delta \neq 0$, the (asymptotic) power of the test is given by

$$\text{power} = Pr\{\chi^2(r, \lambda) > c_\alpha\}, \tag{5}$$

with r and λ as defined above.

From equation (4) we see that the ncp λ associated with T_V, $\lambda(T_V)$, may change with Γ_s, i.e., with the specific distribution of the data. That is, for the same misspecification parameter δ, the power of the test may change with different departures from non-normality.

3.2 The NT-MD Approach

When $\{z_{gi}\}_i$ is iid normal (normal theory, NT), Γ_s takes the form

$$\Gamma_s^* = \oplus_{g=1}^{G} \pi_g^{-1} 2D^+ (\Sigma_g \otimes \Sigma_g - \mu_g \mu_g' \otimes \mu_g \mu_g') D^{+'}, \tag{6}$$

with $\mu_g = E(z_{gi})$. Define $\Omega = 2 \oplus_{g=1}^{G} \pi_g^{-1} D^+ (\Sigma_g \otimes \Sigma_g) D^{+'}$. $V^* = \oplus_{g=1}^{G} \pi_g V_g^*$, with $V_g^* = \frac{1}{2} D'(\Sigma_g^{-1} \otimes \Sigma_g^{-1})D$, and let $\hat{\Omega}$ and $\hat{V}^*$ be the respective matrices Ω and V^* with π_g and Σ_g substituted by $\frac{n_g}{n}$ and S_g, respectively. MD estimation with $V = V^*$ will be called NT-MD, an estimation method that is known to be asymptotically equivalent to maximum likelihood (ML) estimation.

A χ^2 goodness-of-fit test statistics associated with NT-MD estimation is $T_{NT-MD} = n(s - \hat{\sigma})'\hat{V}(s - \hat{\sigma})$. Consider now the NT-version of the residual-based goodness-of-fit χ^2 test statistic,

$$T_V^* = n(s - \hat{\sigma})'\hat{\Delta}_\perp \left(\hat{\Delta}'_\perp \hat{\Omega}_s \hat{\Delta}_\perp \right)^+ \hat{\Delta}'_\perp (s - \hat{\sigma}), \qquad (7)$$

where "hat" indicates substitution of population values for the specific MD estimates. In particular, we consider $T_{V^*}^*$ (NT-MD) and $T_{\tilde{V}}^*$ (EW-MD). Note that $T_{V^*}^*$ and $T_{\tilde{V}}^*$ involve only first- and second-order sample moments, since $\hat{\Omega}$ is used instead of $\hat{\Gamma}_s$. Satorra and Bentler (1991) study the asymptotic robustness of this statistic for instrumental variable (IV) estimation.

Under the setting of the present paper, it can be shown that $T_{V^*}^*$, $T_{\tilde{V}}^*$ and T_{NT-MD} (and the T_{ML} associated to ML estimation) are all asymptotically equal, so we denote as T^* any of these statistics. For general distribution of the data, T^* will not be asymptotically χ^2 distributed, while T_V is asymptotically χ^2 distributed under general conditions. The theory of AR for T_V^*, for a general weight matrix V, can be found in Satorra (2002).

Under normality, with possible misspecification of the model, the T^* are asymptotically equivalent to T_V and (asymptotically) distributed as $\chi^2(r, \lambda)$ with $r = \text{rank} (\Delta'_\perp \Gamma_s^* \Delta_\perp)$ and

$$\lambda = \delta'\Delta_\perp (\Delta'_\perp \Omega \Delta_\perp)^{-1} \Delta'_\perp \delta \quad (= \lambda(T^*)). \qquad (8)$$

In the general case of non-normality, however, the asymptotic distributions of T^* and T_V do not necessarily coincide, with T^* deviating possibly from an asymptotic χ^2 distribution.

3.3 The Scaled Test Statistics

To improve the χ^2 approximation, Satorra and Bentler (1994) suggest an scaling correction to T^*. Let $U = V^* - V^* \Delta J^{-1} \Delta' V^*$, with $J = \Delta' V^* \Delta$, and

$$c = \frac{1}{r}\text{tr} \{U\Gamma_s\} = \frac{1}{r}\text{tr} \{V^*\Gamma_s - J^{-1}\Delta'V^*\Gamma_s V^*\Delta\}. \qquad (9)$$

The scaled (adjusted for mean) chi-square goodness-of-fit test statistic is

$$\bar{T} = T^*/\hat{c}, \qquad (10)$$

where $T^* = T_{V^*}$ and $\hat{c}$ is a consistent estimator of c. Since, as argued above, $T_{V^*}^*$ and $T_{\tilde{V}}^*$ are asymptotically equivalent to T_{V^*}, such scaling correction applies, with no modification, to $T_{\tilde{V}}^*$, leading to the scaled statistic $\bar{T}_{\tilde{V}}^* = T_{\tilde{V}}^*/\hat{c}$. Since the scaled versions of T_{V^*} and $T_{\tilde{V}}^*$ (and of T_{ML}) are all asymptotically equivalent, $\bar{T}$ is used to denote any of these scaled statistics. Under NT, $c = 1$ and then T_V, T^* and $\bar{T}$ are (asymptotically) equivalent and distributed as $\chi^2(r, \lambda)$, with $\lambda = \lambda(T^*)$ as in (8).

Under general conditions, T^* is distributed asymptotically as a mixture of independent non-central χ^2 distributions of 1 df. Thus, it follows from Satorra and Neudecker (1997) that the asymptotic mean of T^* is tr $\{U\Gamma_s\} + \lambda$, with $\lambda = \lambda(T^*)$ as in (8); that is, in a general setting of non-normality, the asymptotic mean of $\bar{T}$ is

$$m_{\bar{T}} = (\text{tr}\,\{U\Gamma_s\} + \lambda(T^*))\,/c = r + \lambda(T^*)/c, \qquad (11)$$

with $\lambda(T^*)$ and c given respectively in (8) and (9). Consequently, the ncp $\lambda(\bar{T})$ associated with $\bar{T}$ equals $\lambda(T^*)/c$, not necessarily equal to $\lambda(T_V)$ of (4) with $V = V^*$. This has practical implications, as it implies that when $c \neq 1$, $\bar{T}$ and T_{V^*} may differ in asymptotic power. Thus, comparison of the performance of $\bar{T}$ and T_V with respect to power is worth pursuing. We now investigate this issue, both for NT-MD and EW-MD analyses.

3.4 Power of the Test and AR

The asymptotic power of the test of $H_0 : \sigma = \sigma(\vartheta)$, $\vartheta \in \mathcal{F}$, based on T_V is given by (5). The ncp is given by (4) in the general setting, and by (8) when the manifest variables are normally distributed.

For normal data, the power of the goodness-of-fit test based on T_{ML} or T_{NT-MD} can be evaluated using the procedure proposed in Satorra and Saris (1985). The procedure uses (5) with λ replaced by the value of the test statistic obtained when the (null) model H_0 is analyzed with σ^0 replacing s.

The same procedure can be used for computing the ncp associated to T_V and $\bar{T}$. Indeed, from (11), when $\bar{T}$ is referred to a $\chi^2(r, \lambda)$ distribution with $\lambda = \lambda(T^s)/c$, i.e. the value of the test statistic $\bar{T}$ when the null model H_0 is fitted with σ^0 and c replacing s and $\hat{c}$ respectively. For non-normal data, however, to apply this procedure we require the fourth-order moment matrix Γ_s, in the case of T_V, or c, in the case of $\bar{T}$. We will see that when AR holds, Γ_s or c are not needed to compute power.

We now summarize AR results of relevance for computing the power of the χ^2 tests (see Satorra (2002) for more details of AR theory in the present model context). Related to model (1), consider the following conditions for asymptotic robustness (model and distribution conditions, MC and DC):

MC: *The distinct elements of the matrices $\Phi_g^{(\ell)}$, $g = 1, \dots, G$, $\ell \leq L_g - 1$, [1] are free parameters of the model.*

DC: *The random sequences $\{\xi_{g1i}\}_i, \{\xi_{g2i}\}_i, \dots, \{\xi_{gL_gi}\}_i$ are iid and mutually independent (not only uncorrelated).*

---

[1] *The structural 1 in $\Phi_g^{(0)}$ (induced by the 1 in ξ_{g0i}) is not regarded as a parameter of the model $(g = 1, \dots, G)$.*

In practice, MC implies that the variances and covariances of possibly non-normal constituents of the model are not restricted by the model, not even across groups (restrictions, however, are allowed on the variances and covariances of normally distributed constituents of the model). Condition DC imposes that random constituents of the model, usually stated as being mean-independent (e.g., factors and errors) now are required to be mutually independent. For example, DC does not permit heteroscedasticity (e.g., variance of the error that changes with the value of the regressor).

The theory of AR states that under MC and DC some of the asymptotic distributions obtained under the assumption of normality of manifest variables (NT assumption) carry over to non-normal data. In particular, the NT-based χ^2 goodness-of-fit test is asymptotically distributed as χ^2 despite severe non-normality of manifest variables. That is, when MC and DC hold, T^* and T_V are asymptotically equivalent and (asymptotically) distributed as $\chi^2(r, \lambda)$, with λ as in (8); i.e., $\lambda(T_{V*}) = \lambda(T^*)$. Its practical implication is that under AR the ncp associated to T_V, T^* and $\bar{T}$ can be obtained using Satorra and Saris (1985) procedure applied to, for example, T_{V*} (information on the fourth-order moment matrix Γ_s is not needed in this case).

4 Monte Carlo Illustration

Monte Carlo simulation will now be used to illustrate the theory of Section 3 and to assess the finite sample performance of the various χ^2 goodness-of-fit tests discussed. We consider a simple model setting of one-factor model with six manifest variables

$$z_j = \lambda_j F + \varepsilon_j, \quad j = 1, .., 6, \tag{12}$$

where F is the common factor, $\varepsilon_1, \ldots, \varepsilon_6$ are the errors (unique factors), λ_j and $\psi_j = \text{var}(\varepsilon_j)$ $(j = 1, \ldots, 6,)$ are loading and variance parameters respectively. Two alternative model specifications are introduced: the unrestricted model (UM), in which the λ_j 's and ψ_j 's are unrestricted parameters, and the restricted model (RM) in which $\psi_j = \psi$. In both specifications, $\text{var}(F) = 1$. The df of models UM and RM are 9 (21 moments minus 12 free parameters) and 14 (21 moments minus 7 parameters), respectively.

Non-normality in manifest variables and misspecification of the model is introduced by the following data generating process (DGP) of the simulated data:

$$z_j = \lambda_{j1} F_1 + \lambda_{j2} F_2 + \varepsilon_j, \quad j = 1, \ldots, 6, \tag{13}$$

where F_1 and F_2, and $\varepsilon_1, \ldots, \varepsilon_6$, are χ_1^2 distributed conveniently scaled and such that 1) $\{\varepsilon_j\}_j$ are mutually independent and independent also of F_1 and F_2; 2) $\text{var}(F_1) = \text{var}(F_2) = 1$, $\text{cov}(F_1, F_2) = \phi$ (varying in the study); 3) $\text{var}(\varepsilon_j) = 0.3$, $j = 1, \ldots, 6$; and 4) $\lambda_{11} = \lambda_{42} = 1$, $\lambda_{21} = \lambda_{31} = \lambda_{52} = \lambda_{62} = 0.8$, and 0 otherwise. When $\phi = 1$, equation (12) holds exactly for both UM and RM; when $\phi < 1$, equation (12) is misspecified. The presence (or not) of model misspecification is indicated by $MISS = 1$ (or $= 0$).

Note that MC and DC are satisfied under UM (since the parameterisation of UM is equivalent to the one that sets unconstrained the variances of all the non-normal random constituents of the model, while restricts one loading to a non-zero value), and DGP ensures independence among the random constituents of the model.

Under RM, however, AR does not hold (since RM restricts by equality the variances of the ϵ_j, non-normally distributed constituents of the model). Whether AR holds or not is indicated by $AR = 1$ or $= 0$.

A basic sample size of the study is $n = 150$. This "moderate" sample size is then increased till the empirical (Monte Carlo) and theoretical (asymptotic) distributions reach an accurate fit for all test statistics. This leads us to increase sample size till $n = 8000$. Accuracy of the fit between empirical and asymptotic distribution is visualized by the cumulative distribution function (CDF) plots, and indicated by the Kolmorogov-Smirnov statistics. The assumption of a sequence of local alternatives is introduced by setting $\phi = 1 - 0.1\sqrt{120/n}$.

Our Monte Carlo study considers 5000 replications for each cell design. The three test statistics considered are: T_V, i.e., Browne's (1984) residual-based χ^2 goodness-of-fit test statistic; $\bar{T}$, Satorra-Bentler's (1994) scaled NT χ^2; and T_{NT-MD}, the un-scaled NT χ^2 test statistic. In the tables and graphs, these statistics are denoted respectively as rchi2, sbchi2 and chi2. Independent replications apply for NT-MD and EW-MD analyses. Note that for EW-MD, the statistics rchi2, sbchi2 and chi2 are, respectively, $T_{\tilde{V}}$, $\bar{T}_{\tilde{V}}{}^*$ and $T_{\tilde{V}}{}^*$.

CDF plots are obtained for each set of 5000 replications. Here, however, we report only the most representative ones. These are plots showing the empirical (Monte Carlo) and asymptotic CDF functions for the three test statistics, rchi2, sbchi2 and chi2.

The theoretical (asymptotic) CDF have been obtained as follows. When $AR = 1$, the ncp is the population value of T_{NT-MD} for NT-MD ($T_{\tilde{V}}^*$ for EW-MD). When AR $= 0$, we first obtain an approximation of Γ_s averaging over 2000 replications (with independence of the 5000 replications of the Monte Carlo study) the sample fourth-order moment matrix $\hat{\Gamma}_s$ of a sample of size n of the specified DGP. This average is used as the true Γ_s to compute the ncp.[2]

Figure 1 shows the CDF for $MISS = 0$, $AR = 1$, and $n = 150$. This is a case of AR where all the three χ^2 statistics have the same asymptotic distribution, shown in the graph by a continuous line. Here chi2 and sbchi2 adhere closely to the asymptotic distribution. The empirical rejection rates for both statistics are close to the nominal 5% level. As expected from the

---

[2] With empirical data, we would use as population value the estimate $\hat{\Gamma}_s$ based on the sample data.

theory of AR, here the empirical distribution of chi2 is very close to its asymptotic χ^2 distribution (despite the severe non-normality of the data). In contrast, rchi2 differs markedly from the χ^2 distribution, despite the fact that rchi2 is an statistic robust to non-normality (and asymptotically equal to the chi2 and sbchi2, in the present case). Note that the empirical rejection rate of rchi2 is markedly higher than the desired nominal 5% level.

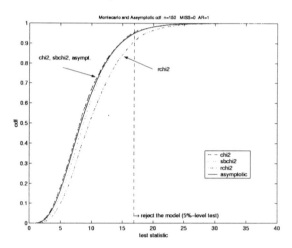

Fig. 1. Cumulative distribution functions for MISS=0, AR=1 and $n = 150$.

Figure 2 shows the results for $AR = 1$ and $MISS = 1$, sample size $n = 150$. This is a case of AR, thus we have a common asymptotic non-central χ^2 distribution for all the three test statistics (the solid line of the graph). The various test statistics adhere reasonable well to the common asymptotic distribution. The three test statistics attain similar power at the nominal 5% level.

Figure 3 corresponds to $MISS = 1$ and $AR = 0$, with $n = 150$. Here the asymptotic χ^2 distributions differ among statistics. For sbchi2, the empirical and asymptotic distribution are very close to each other, while for rchi2 the empirical distribution deviates markedly from its asymptotic (theoretical) distribution. Since this is a case where AR does not hold, the chi2 is expected to deviates from a χ^2 distribution (hence the graph does not show the asymptotic distribution of this statistic).

We now increase sample size till achieving an accurate fit between the simulated and asymptotic CDFs for rchi2. The Monte Carlo results for varying sample size are summarized in Table 1, a table that shows the Kolmogorov-Smirnov (K-S) deviations between empirical and asymptotic distributions and the ncp used to compute the asymptotic distributions. Figure 4 shows the CDF graphs in this case of a very large sample size, $n = 8000$.

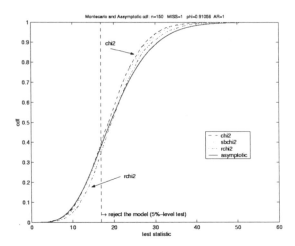

Fig. 2. Cumulative distribution functions for MISS=1, AR=1 and $n = 150$.

Figure 4 illustrates the empirical and asymptotic performance of the three test statistics in the case of a very large sample size. We see a reasonable accurate fit between the empirical to asymptotic distributions, with substantial power difference among the two competing statistics, sbchi2 and rchi2, with rchi2 achieving more power than sbchi2.

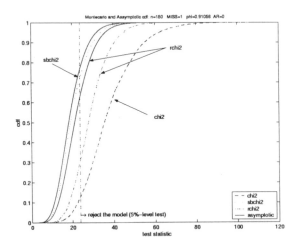

Fig. 3. Cumulative distribution functions for MISS=1, AR=0 and $n = 150$

As seen in Table 1, the K-S values (maximum absolute difference among the simulated and asymptotic CDF) for sbchi2 are below .07 for a variety of conditions. This is not the case of rchi2, which requires a very large sample

Table 1. K-S discrepancies between simulated and asymptotic distributions and ncp. Estimation methods NT-MD.

n	AR	MISS	chi2	sbchi2	rchi2	λ_{sb}	λ_r
150	1	0	0.026	0.050	0.125	0.000	0.000
150	0	0	0.617	0.068	0.244	0.000	0.000
150	1	1	0.066	0.050	0.050	11.135	11.135
150	0	1	0.427	0.056	0.320	5.123	8.028
1000	0	1	0.476	0.027	0.131	8.049	16.641
2000	0	1	0.478	0.023	0.090	8.898	19.404
4000	0	1	0.481	0.025	0.052	9.567	21.539
8000	0	1	0.483	0.026	0.037	10.055	23.183

size (in fact $n = 8000$!) to achieve an accurate fit between the empirical and asymptotic distribution. K-S values are omitted for chi2 when $AR = 0$, since this statistic is not expected to be χ^2 distributed in this case. The last two columns of the table show the ncp of the asymptotic distributions, for sbchi2 and rchi2 statistics. From inspection of these two columns, we see that when $AR = 0$ the (asymptotic) power of the rchi2 outperforms sbchi2 (the ncp for rchi2 is larger than for sbchi2).

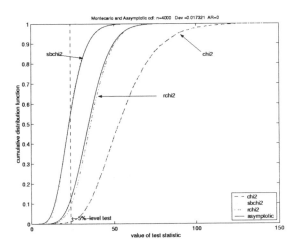

Fig. 4. Cumulative distribution functions for MISS=1, AR=0 and $n = 8000$.

The same pattern of results as described for NT-MD are for EW-MD, with no appreciable changes on power values when comparing NT-MD with EW-MD. It is remarkable that the performance of $T^*_{V^*}$ is the same as $T^*_{\tilde{V}}$, both in terms of power and small sample behaviour, the same being true for the scaled version of both statistics.

5 Acknowledgement

Comments by Nicholas T. Longford on a previous version of this paper are very much appreciated. This research was supported by grant BEC2000-0983 of the Spanish Ministry of Science and Technology.

References

1. Browne, M.W. (1984): Asymptotically distribution-free methods for the analysis of covariance structures. British Journal of Mathematical and Statistical Psychology, **37**, 62–83
2. Curran, P. J., West, S. G., and Finch, J. F. Curran, P. J., West, S. G., and Finch, J. F. (1996): The robustness of test statistics to nonnormality and specification error in confirmatory factor analysis, Psychological Methods, **1**, 16–29.
3. Hu, L., Bentler, P. M., and Kano, Y. (1992): Can test statistics in covariance structure analysis be trusted?, Psychological Bulletin, **112**, 351–362.
4. MacCallum, R., Browne, M.W. and Sugawara, H.M. (1996). Power analysis and determination of sample size for covariance structure modeling, Psychological Methods, **1**, 130-149.
5. Satorra, A. (2001): Goodness-of-fittesting of structural equation models with multiple-group data and nonnormality. In: Cudeck, R., du Toit, S. and Sörbom D. (eds) Structural Equation Modeling: Present and Future, A Festschrift in honor of Karl G. Jöreskog, SSI Scientific Software: Lincolnwood, IL.
6. Satorra, A. (2002): Asymptotic robustness in multiple-group linear-latent variable models, Econometric Theory **18**, 297-232.
7. Satorra, A. & P.M. Bentler (1991): Goodness-of-fit test under IV estimation: asymptotic robustness of a NT test statistic. In Proceedings of the Fifth International Symposium on Applied Stochastic Models and Data Analysis. R. Gutierrez y M.J. Valderrama (Edts.) (pp. 555-567). World Scientific: London.
8. Satorra, A. & Bentler, P.M. (1994): Corrections to test statistics and standard errors in covariance structure analysis, In: Latent variable analysis in developmental research, A. van Eye and C.C. Clogg, (edts), pp. 285-305, SAGE Publications: Thousand Oaks, CA
9. Satorra, A. & Neudecker, H. (1997): On the asymptotic distribution of χ^2 based test statistics in the analysis of moment structural models, Bulletin of the International Statistical Institute (Proceedings, Actes, Book 2), pp. 251-254.
10. Satorra, A. & W.E. Saris (1985): Power of the likelihood ratio test in covariance structure analysis, Psychometrika **50**, 83-89.
11. Stroud, T.W.F. (1972): Fixed alternatives and Wald's formulation of the noncentral asymptotic behavior of the likelihood ratio statistic, The Annals of Statistics, **43**, 447-454.

The Respondent-Generated Intervals Approach to Sample Surveys: From Theory to Experiment

S. James Press[1] and Judith M. Tanur[2]

[1]University of California, Riverside
[2]State University of New York, Stony Brook

SUMMARY. We describe a new method for asking questions involving recall in surveys, called Respondent-Generated Intervals (RGI). We ask respondents for lower and upper bounds for the true answer to a factual question, as well as their best guess. For example, "How many times did you visit your doctor last year?" Also, "What is the largest value the true value is likely to be, and what is the smallest value the true value is likely to be?" Bayesian and other estimators are proposed. We describe several empirical studies that have used, and are using the RGI protocol.

Key Words: Bayes Estimation, Brackets, Cognitive Science, Hierarchical Model, Range Information, Recall, Response Bias.

1 Introduction

1.1 Definition of RGI

Consider a factual question that requires a respondent (R) to recall a numerical amount, perhaps the amount or frequency of a behavior. Assume that R is sincerely trying to recall the quantity accurately, not attempting to deceive, and actually has information about the answer. We refer to the quantitative item being requested as *usage*. R must render a subjective assessment of his/her usage. It is common in surveys to have Rs answer within a preset (set by the analyst) interval rather than specifically, especially for sensitive questions. The current procedure is different, however, in that the interval is not preset, but it is generated by R (Respondent Generated Interval, RGI); see Press, 1999, and 2002. The bounds also provide more information that can be used for estimating population parameters.

The RGI protocol for questionnaire design has its origins in Bayesian assessment procedures wherein an entire prior distribution for an individual is assessed by connecting a collection of points on the individual's subjective probability distribution via a sequence of elicitation questions (see, e.g., Schlaifer, 1959, Ch. 6; Hogarth, 1980, App. B and C, and Press, 1989, Ch.4).

R's degree of belief (subjective probability) about the correctness of a factual recalled quantity is characterized by an entire probability distribution for R, not just a single point. For example, R may have a normal subjective probability distribution for the number of doctor visits in the last year, say $N(4,1)$, so that s/he believes that it is most likely that he/she visited 4 times last year (modal value), with a standard deviation of 1. But usually we ask for just one point on this distribution. Perhaps we can improve the accuracy of R's recall by measuring several points on his/her recall distribution. It would be ideal to ask R many additional questions about his/her recall of the usage quantity to assess many points on his/her recall distribution. But respondent burden, the cost of added interviewer time, etc., argue against many additional questions. We therefore describe a procedure that involves adding just two bounds-questions, and we examine the possible benefits accruing from such an addition.

1.2 **Related Research**

There are other survey procedures that also request that respondents provide bounds type information under certain circumstances. Usually, these other procedures ask respondents to select their response from among several (analyst-generated) pre-assigned intervals (sometimes called "brackets"). According to Kennickel, 1997, the use of "bounds", or "range" information to collect partial information in a sample survey may date back to the 1967 Survey of Consumer Finances conducted by the Survey Research Center at the University of Michigan. In that survey respondents who did not want to, or were unable to, give dollar values for their asset values were given the opportunity to respond anyway by selecting a particular range from several that were supplied with the questionnaire. The 1977 Survey of Consumer Credit, also conducted by the Survey Research Center at the University of Michigan collected all dollar responses by providing respondents with pre-assigned ranges, and asking them to select one that is appropriate, reasoning that because asking only for ranges would be less revealing, and therefore less threatening, response rates would be increased.

Kennickell, 1997 described the 1995 Survey of Consumer Finances (SCF), carried out by the National Opinion Research Center in Chicago, as including opportunities for the respondents who answered either "don't know", or "refuse", to select from eight pre-assigned ranges, or to provide their own upper and lower bounds ("volunteered ranges"). These respondents were addressing what are traditionally recognized as *sensitive* questions about their assets. By contrast with the survey approach taken in the current work, where the respondent is asked for both a basic response and upper and lower bounds, in the SCF, the respondent is given a choice to either give a basic response, or to select from one of several pre-assigned ranges, or to provide volunteered bounds. The pre-assigned intervals are supplied on "range cards" designed for situations in which the respondent has indicated that he/she does not desire to provide the specific usage quantity requested.

Another related technique that has been proposed is called "unfolding brackets" (see Heeringa, Hill and Howard, 1995). In this approach, respondents are asked a sequence of binary ("yes/no") types of "bracketing questions" which successively narrow the range in which the respondent's true value might lie. For example, the respondent might be asked whether the amount sought, such as the amount of household financial assets of a given type, in a given year, say stocks and bonds, is greater than $10,000. If the response is "yes", the respondent might then be asked whether the amount is greater than $20,000. Questions of this type can continue, or they can be stopped at any time. The questioning can continue until a desired pre-assigned bracketing range is obtained. Finding optimal bracketing breakpoints can be a complex problem.

Several issues about these bounds-related techniques are not yet resolved: whether any of these approaches (RGI, Range Techniques, or Unfolding Brackets, or other such techniques) yields more accurate answers than the traditional approach; how these methods compare to one another under various circumstances; or how these different options affect response rate. It may also be that merely asking respondents for their bounds information (RGI), but not also asking for their "basic usage responses", will be sufficient to improve accuracy and response rate, and might be even better than asking for both bounds information and basic usage.

2 Estimation of the Population Mean

2.1 Bayesian Point Estimation

A Bayesian hierarchical model that involved Markov Chain Monte Carlo estimation of the population mean was developed in Press, 1999. That model was used in the various empirical tests of the RGI procedure described in Section 3. More recently (see Press, 2002), an alternative modeling and estimation procedure was found to be much simpler and more intuitively appealing. Because it is newer, we next describe the more recent estimation procedure.

Let y_i, a_i, b_i denote the basic usage quantity response, the lower bound response, and the upper bound response, respectively, of respondent i, i = 1,...,n. Suppose that the y_i's are all normally distributed. It is shown in Press, 2002 that in such a situation, the posterior distribution of the population mean, say θ_0, is given by:

$$\theta_0 | data \sim N(\bar{\theta}, \omega^2), \tag{1}$$

where the posterior mean, $\tilde{\theta}$, is expressible as a weighted average of the usage quantities, the y_i's, and the weights are expressible approximately as simple algebraic functions of the bounds. ω^2 denotes the posterior variance; it is discussed in below.

The posterior mean is given by:

$$\tilde{\theta} = \sum_1^n \lambda_i y_i \tag{2}$$

where the λ_i's are weights that are given approximately by:

$$\lambda_i = \frac{\left(\dfrac{1}{\dfrac{(b_i - a_i)^2}{k_1^2} + \dfrac{(b_0 - a_0)^2}{k_2^2}} \right)}{\sum_1^n \left(\dfrac{1}{\dfrac{(b_i - a_i)^2}{k_1^2} + \dfrac{(b_0 - a_0)^2}{k_2^2}} \right)}, \quad \sum_1^n \lambda_i = 1. \tag{3}$$

Here, a_0 denotes the smallest of all of the a_i's and b_0 denotes the largest of all of the b_i's. k_1 and k_2 denote pre-assigned multiples of standard deviations that correspond to how the bounds should be interpreted in terms of standard deviations from the mean. For example, for normally distributed data it is sometimes assumed that such lower and upper bounds can be associated with 3 standard deviations below, and above, the mean, respectively. With this interpretation, we would take $k_1 = k_2 = 6$, to represent the length of the interval between the largest and smallest values that the true value of the answer to the recall question might be for respondent i. If desired, we might take $k_1 = k_2 = k = 4, 5, 6, 7, 8$, and study how the estimate of the population mean varies with k.

We note the following characteristics of this estimator:

1) The weighted average is simple and quick to calculate, without requiring any computer-intensive sampling techniques.

2) In the special case in which the interval lengths in Eqs. (3) are all the same, the weighted average reduces to the sample mean, $\bar{y}$, where the weights all equal (1/n).

This result suggests that the weighted average estimator and the sample mean estimates of the population mean will differ most when the respondents provide the most disparate interval lengths from one another.

3) The longer the interval a respondent gives, the less weight is applied to that respondent's usage quantity in the weighted average. The length of respondent i's interval seems intuitively to be a measure of his/her degree of confidence in the usage quantity he/she gives, so that the shorter the interval, the greater degree of confidence that respondent seems to have in the usage quantity he/she reports. (Of course a high degree of confidence does not necessarily imply an answer close to the true value.)

4) Since the weights sum to one, and must all be non-negative, they can be thought of as a probability distribution over the values of the usage quantities in the sample. So λ_i represents the probability that $y = y_i$ in the posterior mean.

5) From Eqs. (3) we see that if we take $k_1 = k_2$, the k's cancel out and the λ_i weights no longer depend upon the k's.

6) If we define the precision of a distribution as its reciprocal variance, the quantity $\left\{ \dfrac{(b_i - a_i)^2}{k_1^2} + \dfrac{(b_0 - a_0)^2}{k_2^2} \right\}$ was found to be the variance in the posterior

distribution corresponding to respondent i (see Press 2002), and therefore, its reciprocal represents the precision corresponding to respondent i. Summing over all respondents precisions gives:

$$\text{total precision} = \sum_{1}^{n} \left(\frac{1}{\dfrac{(b_i - a_i)^2}{k_1^2} + \dfrac{(b_0 - a_0)^2}{k_2^2}} \right) \qquad (4)$$

So another interpretation of λ_i is that it is the proportion of the total precision in the data attributable to respondent i.

2.2 Bayesian Interval Estimation

It was shown in Press, 2002 that the variance of the posterior distribution is given approximately by:

$$\omega^2 = \cfrac{1}{\sum_{1}^{n}\left(\cfrac{1}{\cfrac{(b_i - a_i)^2}{k_1^2} + \cfrac{(b_0 - a_0)^2}{k_2^2}}\right)} \tag{5}$$

Comparison with Eqs. (4) shows that the posterior variance is exactly the reciprocal of the total precision. Moreover, the posterior variance depends upon the k's even if we take $k_1 = k_2$. In that case, the posterior variance is given by:

$$\omega^2 = \cfrac{1}{\sum_{1}^{n}\left(\cfrac{k^2}{(b_i - a_i)^2 + (b_0 - a_0)^2}\right)} \tag{6}$$

Because the posterior distribution of the population mean, θ_0, is normal, it is straightforward to find credibility intervals for θ_0. For example, a 95% credibility interval for θ_0 is given by:

$$(\tilde{\theta} - 1.96\omega, \tilde{\theta} + 1.96\omega). \tag{7}$$

That is,

$$P\{(\tilde{\theta} - 1.96\omega \le \theta_0 \le \tilde{\theta} + 1.96\omega) | data\} = 95\%. \tag{8}$$

2.3 Weighted Average Bounds Estimation

We can generate a family of alternative point estimates of the population mean by using a weighted average of the assessed average bounding endpoints, $\bar{a}$ and $\bar{b}$, where

$$\bar{a} \equiv \frac{1}{n}\sum_i a_i, \quad \bar{b} \equiv \frac{1}{n}\sum_i b_i .$$

Such a weighted average point estimator of the population mean is given by:

$$\bar{m} = \delta\bar{a} + (1 - \delta)\bar{b}, \qquad 0 \le \delta \le 1.$$

But how should we select δ ? If δ and $(1-\delta)$ are each taken to be ½, we have an equal weighting, and $\overline{m}$ becomes a *midpoint estimator* $\overline{m} = (\overline{a}+\overline{b})/2$.

To account for respondent error in assessing the bounds, calculate the standard deviations of the bounds and use weights that are proportions of total variances, a common practice (see, Sect. 2.1 and, e.g., Kish, 1965, p. 432). We could also express the weights in terms of the *precisions* of the average bounds, that is, the reciprocals of the variances of the average bounds. An unequally weighted estimator would be sensible in situations in which we expect there might be substantial discrepancies between the uncertainties in assessing a_i versus those in assessing b_i.

2.4 Multiple Imputation

It might be of interest to impute missing usage information from respondents who do not provide usage information, but provide bounds information. In such cases, we could impute the missing usage data and use the bounds information to constrain the multiple imputation (Kennickell, personal communication). We have used the midpoint estimator to impute values for item nonresponse (without use of multiple imputation). The results, discussed below, seem very promising.

2.5 Comparing Interval Estimators

We evaluate several competing interval estimators in the RGI context: traditional confidence intervals, Bayesian credibility intervals as described above, and the ARGI, or Average Respondent-Generated Intervals ($\overline{a},\overline{b}$). Because the extremes of respondent belief are reflected in the intervals provided by RGI respondents, the ARGI will typically cover the true population values (minimizing response bias), while the other two interval estimators are less likely to cover the true population values. We have found these expectations to hold in the experimental studies described below.

3.   The Experiments

Several empirical studies were designed to examine the functioning of RGI under a broad range of conditions. Questions that we have attempted to address in our experiments are:

a) How would RGI work with sensitive questions, such as "income"?
b) Does the ordering of the basic usage and bounds questions matter?
c) Does an option to choose between usage and bounds questions affect response rate?

d) Can wording of the bounds questions be improved to aid respondents' understanding?

e) Can we ask only for bounds information (RGI) without asking for basic usage and still improve accuracy and response rate?

3.1 Campus Surveys

At each of our campuses we carried out a paper-and-pencil survey, asking students about quantitative aspects of their campus life that could be verified by appropriate campus offices.

The usage question was always asked before the bounds question. The form of the bounds question was "Please fill in the blanks – There is almost no chance that the number of credits I earned by the beginning of this quarter was less than _____, and almost no chance that it was more than _____." Sample sizes for many questions were reduced because (1) we used half the sample to test another form of the bounds question, since discarded and (2) not all students gave permission to access their records for verification purposes. For four questions about fees, however, all respondents were asked the RGI format and no individual verification was needed as these fees are uniform across full-time students. Thus we have much bigger sample sizes for these questions.

3.2 The Census Experiment

This experiment was designed to vary the order of asking the bounds and usage questions, test if the RGI procedure can be used in a telephone interview, test its usefulness for sensitive questions, and broaden our universe of Rs past college students.

This experiment used extensive cognitive pretesting for the form of the interval question. In a split-panel experiment 75 percent of the Rs were asked the two bounds questions first, followed by the usage question and 25% received the reverse ordering.

From a frame of households that filed joint tax returns having wage and salary income for the previous five consecutive years, a sample of about 2000 households was drawn. From this sample the Census Bureau obtained a quota of 500 CATI interviews. Rs answered questions about their income from salary/wages and from interest/dividends for the past two years, and for the change in both types of income over the previous five years. Since the frame information also included data from administrative records about household income, we could verify the responses.

3.3 The HMO experiment

A new experiment was fielded in order to test if *R*s are willing to answer the bounds question without being offered the usage question, and to explore which option they choose if permitted a choice between the bounds and usage questions.

Mail questionnaires went out in Oct., 2001, to 3000 female members of a Health Maintenance Organization (HMO) asking questions for which the answers can be verified from the HMO files. There are five groups of *R*s: a control group asked the usage quantity only, another control group asked the questions in the form currently used by the HMO (respondents classify themselves into one of several predetermined interval options), a group that received only the bounds questions, and two groups that were offered a choice of answering the bounds or the interval question (bounds offered first to one group, second to the other).   Results have not yet been analyzed.

4. Results

The accuracy and nonresponse results described in this section were obtained using the modeling and estimation procedure developed in Press, 1999. There hasn't yet been time to see how these results would compare to what might be obtained using the newly developed model (see the discussion at the beginning of Section 2, and Press, 2002).

4.1 Accuracy of Point Estimates

We calculated the signed percentage of the true values that the errors (deviations from truth) constitute. These percents vary widely, from less than 1 percent to close to 500 percent. We also see that several quantities seem to be estimated very badly regardless of estimation method used, notably both the change variables in the Census experiment, especially when the usage question is asked before the bounds question. We speculate that respondents find it difficult to report these changes, as they must not only recall two quantities but also carry out a calculation, a process fraught with opportunities for error. Also estimated particularly badly are the number of traffic tickets on both campuses and the number of library fines at SUSB. These are the most sensitive questions on the questionnaires for the campus experiments, both asking for reports of negative behaviors.

In 19 of the 30 questions tabulated (18 in the campus experiments and 12 in the Census experiment), one of the estimators arising from the RGI procedure had the smallest absolute percentage error. There was also a remarkable similarity of performance of the estimators (with the possible exception of the Bayesian estimator that uses the sample median for the prior mean). In 22 out of 30 cases the estimators are unanimous in either under-estimating or over-estimating truth.

4.2 Accuracy of Interval Estimates

Because our experiments were all designed to offer verification data for the group being studied, we can see whether the intervals being calculated cover the true values. Note that for this argument we are making a rather unusual use of intervals. Rather than asking whether an interval calculated for a sample covers the true population value, in this case we are thinking about our samples rather as if they were populations and asking whether the calculated intervals cover the average true values for the group of people questioned.

For the interval estimates, we found that the ARGI covered the average true value in 23 of the 30 questions, while the traditional 95% confidence interval covered the average true value for only 17 of the 30 questions.

Next we consider the order variation in the Census Experiment, asking if the length of the ARGI is different if the usage question is asked before or after the bounds questions. We found that for the questions on salary and wages (and their five-year change) the ARGI is always smaller when the questions are ordered with the basic usage question first. These questions are ones for which the information is probably best known to the respondents. The trend is exactly reversed, however, for the questions about interest and dividends (and their five-year change) where the information is probably not as well known to respondents. (Interest and dividends do not appear on regular paychecks, and often a respondent's only information about them may come from a year-end summary used to prepare income taxes.) For these questions, the shorter ARGI is found when respondents are asked the bounds questions first. We must refine our hypothesis and speculate that respondents give shorter intervals in the usage quantity first condition when they can utilize their usage response as an anchor, if they are confident of their usage response. When respondents are not sure about their recall of the usage quantity, however, that anchoring effect is either not available or not useful.

4.3 Reduction of Item Nonresponse

To investigate whether the RGI procedure reduces item nonresponse we use data from the paper-and-pencil campus experiments. Those Rs who gave an interval but did not give a usage quantity constitute an appreciable percentage of those who did not give a usage quantity and thus were potential nonresponders to each item. Indeed, those percentages are never less than 4% and twice are over 40%. We can interpret these results as estimated conditional probabilities of giving an interval among those who did not give a usage quantity. We can use the midpoint of the RGI as a point estimator and the ARGI as an interval estimator, for those respondents who offered interval but no usage quantity responses, and inquire into the accuracy of these estimates for the fee data (where sample sizes are large and verification data unnecessary because of the uniformity of the fees across respondents). We find that the average midpoints overestimate usage for 3 or the 4 cases, but the ARGI cover the true value in all cases.

Thus in the Campus Experiments in a substantial proportion of cases, Rs who do not supply an estimate of usage quantities do supply intervals which are reasonably accurate, thus reducing the amount of item non-response appreciably. In the Census Experiment, although many Rs did not supply usage quantities, in only a few such cases did they supply bounds information. Why these differences? There may be an effect of the sensitivity of the questions, sensitive questions about income in the Census Experiment, less sensitive questions in the Campus Experiments. There may also be a mode effect. In the paper-and-pencil Campus Experiments it was easy to fill in part of a question; it is less easy to answer part of a question posed by an interviewer over the telephone. The type of respondent, type of interviewer, and survey sponsor may matter. The Campus Experiments involved undergraduate student Rs, students distributing questionnaires, and an "academic" survey. The Census Experiment interviewed Rs from established households, who were presented with questions from professional interviewers representing the US Census Bureau. Overall, there was greater respondent cooperation in this government survey by telephone than we found in our earlier campus-based experiments.

5. Conclusions

We have found that the RGI technique yielded promising results in improving the accuracy of point and interval estimation and in reducing item non-response in cases of low cooperation.

References

Evans M, Swartz T (1995). Methods for Approximating Integrals in Statistics With Special Emphasis on Bayesian Integration Problems, *Statistical Science*, Vol. 10, No.3, pp.254-272.

Heeringa SG, Hill, DH, Howell, DA (1995). Unfolding Brackets for Reducing Item Non-Response in Economic Surveys, *Health and Retirement Study Working Paper Series*, Paper No. 94-029, Institute for Social Research, University of Michigan, June, 1995.

Hogarth R (1980). *Judgment and Choice: The Psychology of Decision,* New York: John Wiley and Sons, Inc.

Kennickell AB (1997). Using Range Techniques with CAPI in the 1995 Survey of

Consumer Finances, Jan., 1997, Board of Governors of the Federal Reserve System, Washington, D.C. 20551.

Kish L (1965) *Survey Sampling*. New York: John Wiley and Sons.

Marquis KH, Press SJ (1999). Cognitive Design and Bayesian Modeling of a Census Survey of Income Recall, *Proceedings of the Federal Committee on Statistical Methodology Conference*, Washington, DC, Nov. 16, 1999, pp.51-64 (see http://bts.gov/fcsm).

Press SJ (1989). *Bayesian Statistics: Principles, Models and Applications*, New York: John Wiley and Sons, Inc.

Press SJ (1999). Respondent-Generated Intervals for Recall in Sample Surveys, manuscript, Department of Statistics, University of California, Riverside, CA 92521-0138 , Jan., 1999. http://cnas.ucr.edu/~stat/press.htm.

Press SJ (2002). "Respondent-Generated Intervals For Recall in Sample Surveys", Technical Report No. 272, July, 2002, Department of Statistics, University of California, Riverside.

Press SJ, Marquis KH (2001) Bayesian Estimation in a U. S. Census Bureau Survey of Income Recall Using Respondent-Generated Intervals. *Journal of Research in Official Statistics*, Amsterdam: Eurostat.

Press SJ, Marquis KH (2002) Bayesian Estimation in a U.S. Government Survey of Income Using Respondent-Generated Intervals. *Proceedings of the Sixth World Meeting of the International Society for Bayesian Analysis*, May, 2000, Crete, Greece; Amsterdam: Eurostat.

Press SJ, Tanur JM (2000) Experimenting with Respondent-Generated Intervals in Sample Surveys, with discussion. Pages 1-18 in Monroe G. Sirken (ed.) *Survey Research at the Intersection of Statistics and Cognitive Psychology*, Working Paper Series #28, National Center for Health Statistics, U.S. Department of Health and Human Services, Center for Disease Control and Prevention.

Press SJ, Tanur JM (2001). Respondent-Generated Interval Estimation to Reduce Item Nonresponse, in *Applied Statistical Science V*, Nova Science Publishers, pp. 39-49, M. Ahsanullah, J. Kennyon, S.K. Sarkar (Eds.). See also, http://cnas.ucr.edu/~stat/press.htm

Press SJ, Tanur JM (2002).   "Cognitive and Econometric Aspects of Responses to Surveys as Decision-Making", Technical Report No. 271, June, 2002, Department of Statistics, University of California, Riverside.

Schlaifer H (1959). *Probability and Statistics for Business Decisions*, New York: McGraw-Hill Book Co., Inc.

Student Profile Scoring for Formative Assessment

Louis V. DiBello[1], William Stout[2]

[1]Director K-12 Assessment Research and Development, Educational Testing Service, Rosedale Road, Princeton, NJ, USA
[2]Professor Emeritus, Department of Statistics, University of Illinois, Urbana, IL 61801, USA; Past President Psychometric Society; Private Consultant: Director ETS External Diagnostic Research Team;

Summary. This paper is adapted from an invited address delivered by Professor Stout and a symposium presentation delivered by Dr. DiBello at the 2001 International Meeting of the Psychometric Society, Osaka, Japan. This first IMPS meeting to be held in Japan was an auspicious occasion for bringing together statisticians and psychometricians from Japan with their North American and European colleagues. It provided an important forum for discussing new opportunities for assessment in the twenty-first century that result from a fortuitous conjunction of heightened public attention to school effectiveness and new psychometric methods that allow the practical operationalization of more complex cognitive models. In this paper we recall the term formative assessment as it is used in education, and define a class of scoring procedures called student profile scoring. We describe the formative aspects of the mostly summative US No Child Left Behind legislation. We outline the simple cognitive modeling that is reflected in the reparameterized unified model. We close with a call to psychometricians for a paradigm shift that moves the testing industry beyond an almost exclusive focus on low dimensional, data reductionist methods to include student profile scoring based on richer, substantively-grounded models.

Key words. Unified model, Diagnostic testing, Formative assessment, Student profile scoring, Item response modeling

1 Opportunities for Assessment

This paper is especially directed to psychometricians and offers some reflections on recent work in which we focus on assessment that promotes teaching and learning. The discussion centers on the context in which psychometrics is applied rather than

The views expressed in this paper are entirely those of the authors and do not reflect the views of Educational Testing Service, the University of Illinois, or the Psychometric Society. We thank Michal Beller, Henry Braun, Carolyn Crone, Dan Eignor, Tom VanEssen, Wendy Yen, an anonymous referee and an Editor for comments that improved the text. The paper's warp and woof and final manifestation remains the sole responsibility of the authors.

the psychometrics per se. For we psychometricians to help solve real problems in education it will be necessary for us to appreciate and address contextual issues, outside the test, as part of our work in designing assessments.

The U.S. No Child Left Behind (NCLB) legislation establishes standards-based testing as an engine for nation-wide school improvement and has resulted in a heightened need for useful assessment within the American K-12 setting. We use the requirements of this legislation as a framework for our discussion.

We view formative assessment in its natural manifestation as an aspect of effective teaching and also as a characteristic of more formal assessments. A general category of scoring methods called student profile scoring is outlined as a tool for furthering the aims of formative assessment.

As an example of a student profile scoring method that can meet the needs of formative assessment we highlight one particularly effective and practical method that is based on a reparameterization of the unified model.

We conclude with a call to psychometricians to heed the demands of our clients for new assessments that are designed to provide richer, more pertinent, more useful, and usable information.   Unless psychometricians comprehend the special significance of current client needs coupled with practical student profile scoring methods and seize the occasion, the momentum will pass to other groups who will act without the benefit of psychometric science. Psychometrics as a profession will have evaded its responsibility and schooling will be the worse for it.

1.1   Age of Assessment

The NCLB Act of 2001 is shaping the early years of the 21st century in American education into an age of standardized testing (US Federal Government 2001). This legislation seeks to improve schooling across America by establishing rigorous student performance standards within each state, means for school-level accountability, and sanctions for not reaching targets. The goals of the legislation are to raise the performance of all students to clearly specified expectations, and, in particular, to close performance gaps between subpopulations. Spurred originally by the standards movement, and further stimulated by the No Child Left Behind legislation, states are now squarely in the business of producing and administering high stakes, end-of-year, standards-based accountability tests.

The NCLB legislation adds enormous pressure to quickly expand standards-based accountability testing. Whether these state tests will succeed in their school reform purpose is not yet established. We argue that there is a good chance, with courageous leadership from psychometrics, that the accountability tests can be well conceived, and designed in such a way that they measure what is relevant to schooling and report information that is useful for instructional decision making. To exercise this leadership, psychometrics must make a quantum leap to another level that adds to our tool kit, alongside of our highly tuned unidimensional methods, new student profile scoring methods that can be based on richer substantively-grounded models, and that can recover ample formative value from existing assessments and direct the effective design of new formative assessments.

1.2 Formative Assessment

The term *formative assessment* is adapted from the program evaluation literature, and refers to assessment whose purpose is to provide information that can be used to improve the student or program that is being assessed. Educational assessment is formative if it promotes and facilitates better teaching and learning. Formative assessment typically considers process as well as outcome. Formative assessment activities often are designed to have instructional value in themselves.

Formative assessment most often refers to K-12 classroom assessment but can be applied more broadly. As developed by Black and Wiliam (Black and Wiliam 1998, Black et al. 2002, Wiliam and Black 1996, Wiliam 2000), formative assessment is a matter of teacher behavior. Teachers are good formative assessors when they engage in activities that allow them to know what their students understand, and then use that knowledge to plan and deliver instruction.

An assessment is called formative only if the assessment results are used and actually do improve teaching and learning (Black et al. 2000). Intent to provide useful information is not enough. The intent must be consummated in order for an assessment to be formative. Therefore the assertion that an assessment is formative is a validity claim.

The term *diagnostic test* refers to a test that identifies deficiencies but may or may not indicate what to do about them (Black et al. 2000). A formative assessment often includes a diagnostic component, but a diagnostic test might not be formative.

1.3 Student Profile Scoring

We use the term *student profile scoring* to refer to any assessment design and scoring method that provides more than a single score. We purposely use a broad definition that includes sub-scoring methods as well as a host of other methods that are well known within psychometrics. They include the reparameterized unified model with MCMC estimation software as noted above (Hartz 2002), the rule space approach (Tatsuoka 1985, 1990, 1995), multidimensional item response theory (Reckase 1997), latent class analysis (von Davier and Yamamoto unpublished), Bayes nets (Mislevy 1997, Mislevy et al. 1999), hybrid approaches such as Yamamoto's HYBRID model (Yamamoto 1989, 1991), and others.

These approaches differ in a number of ways, including suitability and effectiveness for specific purposes; cost to set up, manage and run; and computing efficiency. Some of these methods are new and they vary in the extent to which they have been applied to real data and real testing settings.

One important example of student profile scoring accompanies the College Board PSAT/NMSQT™. A descriptive score report called the Score Report *Plus*™ has been provided operationally since October 2001 for the PSAT/NMSQT. For each student the report suggests up to three skills to improve in each of the three areas of verbal, mathematics, and writing. An adaptation of the rule space approach is used (Tatsuoka 1995, DiBello, Crone and Narcowich 2001).

The descriptive score information reported in the PSAT/NMSQT Score Report *Plus* is intended for low stakes uses.   Consequently, moderate reliability of mastery/nonmastery skill classifications is acceptable (of course scale score reliability is required to be high to maintain SAT™ score predictability).

Early experience with the PSAT/NMSQT indicates that the skill information extracted from the test is useful and is valued.   Field data is anecdotal and validity studies of the use of the skill information are planned, but we believe that these positive initial reactions result from the validity and usefulness of the information. The extracted skills information represents, however imperfectly, an underlying reality of skill levels that is important and useful to report to students, parents and teachers.   Based on this experience we strongly suggest that many tests not designed for cognitive diagnosis should be able to support useful student profile scoring.

Furthermore, experience with retrofit cases is valuable for learning more about student profile scoring and comparing various methods.   More such experimental attempts are warranted and necessary in order to better understand the dimensions of the problem, best methods and likely benefits.

Ideally a formative assessment is designed from the beginning for the purpose of high quality skills diagnosis of students, with an expectation of high classification reliability and validity.   Such assessment design work is occurring now at Educational Testing Service in several groups including the K-12 research and development group, as well as outside of ETS.   This work is laying the groundwork for the next generation of assessment that truly supports teaching and learning –formative assessment.

1.4   Call for Large Scale Formative Tests

The NCLB tests are designated for accountability purposes.   Starting in the 2002-2003 school year, states are required to test annually once in each of three grade spans (grades three through five, six through nine, and ten through twelve), to test all children, and to test mathematics and reading.   Testing at more grades and an additional content area, science, is to be added in the 2005-2006 and 2007-2008 school years, respectively.   The tests must be aligned with state academic standards. Adequate yearly progress (AYP) targets are set for each year, hence the accountability focus.   Consistent failure to meet the AYP targets triggers real sanctions for a school.   These aspects of the law make the NCLB tests summative, high stakes tests.   But these labels tell only half the story.   The other half has to do with formative uses of test results that also are mandated by the law.

A provision of the No Child Left Behind legislation that is particularly relevant to the central issue of this paper is the following: "A State's academic assessment system must produce individual student interpretive, descriptive, and diagnostic reports that ... help parents, teachers, and principals to understand and address the specific academic needs of students ..." (Title I of US NCLB 2001).

The U.S. Department of Education has announced its intention to interpret this requirement broadly, providing as much latitude and flexibility as possible within the provisions of the law. As of the time of this writing, specific interpretive regulations have not been developed, criteria for compliance have not been established, and federal technical assistance has not been made available to help states comply with the provision. Psychometrics and the testing industry have a wide-open opportunity to lead in defining and serving these testing purposes.

Note that this provision uses the term diagnostic. And the requirement that the reports will help parents and teachers address specific learning needs of students is a formative requirement. The provision thereby adds a formative purpose to the overall summative purpose, making the NCLB tests both summative and formative.

This true formative specification should be distinguished from a false formative function. Any recurring summative test could *seem* to serve an effective formative purpose as follows. If the summative results are not "good," then the "formative" advice would be to improve the program. But, without more detail about what kinds of improvement, this feedback would be useless for school improvement.

Imagine a favorite American football team in which the coaches are never allowed to watch the game or see tapes of the game. The coaches call in plays from a closed locker room for the players to carry out. The only information the coaches are given each week is the final score after the game is over. If they lost, then they are expected to do better next week. This is a tough way to build a winning season. The summative information – final score – serves little useful formative function. Not so different is the teacher who is given in mid-summer last year's summative scores and expected to "do better" next year.

But the NCLB provision quoted above, even given the timing of the tests at the end of the school year, does make the NCLB tests formative, at least potentially. The joint purposes of the NCLB tests represent a summative and formative duality.

Psychometrics has an opportunity and a professional responsibility to develop testing methods and approaches that provide the kind of information that can have a significant impact on the improvement of schooling. We believe that formative assessment as envisioned by the legislative provision quoted above is reasonable, sensible, and possible using new psychometric methods. Practical methods such as the reparameterized unified model provide a capability for accomplishing much of what was envisioned in the NCLB legislation and the standards-based educational reform efforts that preceded it. This model exists now, is based upon sound science, is ready for practical applications, is straightforward to apply to various testing analysis and design situations, and provides a large measure of what this legislation envisions and other testing situations demand.

2 Modeling for Formative Assessment

2.1 Brief Retrospective of Assessment for Learning

The goal of cognitive diagnosis and the use of assessment to promote learning is not new. Robert Glaser (1963) called for testing to be used to promote individualized adaptive instruction. The linear logistic trait model (Fischer 1973) is perhaps the first approach for connecting cognition to a psychometric model, but was designed not for producing student profiles, but for decomposing item difficulties into difficulty factors. As noted earlier, Black and Wiliam play a large role in defining the area of assessment for learning and formative assessment (op. cit.).

The Office of Naval Research funded a major line of research in the late 1980's and early 1990's. An ONR/ACT conference on Cognitive Diagnostic Assessment in 1993 reports four currently important approaches: the unified model, Bayes nets, rule space, Martin and Van Lehn's connectionist approach (Nichols et al. 1995).

A recent National Research Council Report on cognitive assessment is a call for assessments for learning. (Pellegrino, Chudowski and Glaser 2001).

An incomplete list of other important contributors that are not mentioned in this paper include: Wiley and Haertel (1996), Embretson (1998), Doignon and Falmagne (1985), Wilson and Draney (1997), Junker and Sijtsma (2001).

2.2 Strategies for Formative Assessment

Test clients and consumers are now demanding richer information from tests. The NCLB tests, for example, must be based on state performance standards. States, school systems and individual schools are asking for, in addition to scale scores, student profile scores that reflect performance on those underlying standards.

The temptation is great to retreat to what has worked in the past, unidimensional scoring, and to claim that richer information demands are untenable, based perhaps upon reliability arguments. Concerns about reliability are legitimate and pertinent to valid test use, but an enlightened notion of reliability must be applied that takes into account the use of the profile information, as well as the differences between scale score reliability and classification reliability for student profiles. Traditional methods for estimating reliability as well as standards for adequate or required levels of reliability are not particularly apposite to the formative purposes required by NCLB legislation.

Setting about to improve traditional unidimensional score methods is unlikely to achieve much. Existing unidimensionally scored tests are highly engineered to be best possible, under existing political, social and economic constraints. A better strategy is to introduce entirely new ideas, methods and approaches for achieving the goals of formative assessments. We have now an opportunity to apply the fruits of research in learning, cognition and instruction and to exploit student profile scoring methods in order to extract useful information from existing or newly designed assessments that improves teaching and learning and prepares students for high stakes summative assessments and more generally for success in school and beyond.

2.3 Probabilistic Unified Model

The unified model was developed as an IRT-like model that would express the stochastic relationship between item response and status of underlying skills (DiBello Stout and Roussos 1995). Although a thorough discussion of the model is beyond the scope of this paper, we present here just enough to demonstrate the simplicity and richness of the modeling.

As a starting point, we assume an underlying conjunctive latent response model as employed within the rule space (Tatsuoka 1985, 1995) and later within the latent response models of Maris (1999). In this simple conception, a fixed test is considered, with say I items. A moderately sized set of skills is selected that are important to the client and believed to be well measured by the test. Either the test exists or is to be built with the goal of effective skill classification of students. Each item is coded for the skills it requires. Settling on an appropriate list of skills at the right level of granularity is an important step (VanEssen 2001).

A student is modeled as having an unobservable profile of skill proficiencies $\underline{\alpha} = (\alpha_1,...,\alpha_K)$, where $\alpha_k = 1$ means that skill k is mastered and $\alpha_k = 0$ means that skill k is not mastered. The relationship between item response and skills is modeled as conjunctive in the following sense. An item is considered to involve a certain subset of the K skills. The latent response to that item for that student is correct if and only if the student has mastered *all* the skills required by that item. If one or more of those required skills is not mastered, the latent response is incorrect.

This latent response model provides an idealized response pattern for a given knowledge state. It is not claimed that students behave in this deterministic fashion.

The relationship between items and required skills can be expressed through an item-skill incidence matrix called the Q matrix.

$$Q = (q_{i,k})$$

where

$$q_{i,k} = \begin{cases} 1 & \text{means that item i requires skill k} \\ 0 & \text{means that item i does not require skill k} \end{cases}$$

A student's observed response is considered to be a "noisy" version of the latent response. The unified model starts by identifying a number of specific factors that explain the divergence of observed from latent response on an item.

Strategy: The Q matrix presumes a predominant solution strategy for each item, and specifies for each item a particular set of skills that are required by that strategy for successfully answering that item. In general other strategies may be available to solve this problem that require different mixes of skills. If the student chooses to employ a strategy different from that embodied in the Q matrix, his or her observed response to this item may not be the same as the latent response. Parameter $d_i =$ probability across the population that the Q strategy is selected for item i.

Completeness: The Q matrix offers a manageable set of skills that are available to be coded as required for individual items. For various reasons, we may decide to leave out of the Q matrix some skills that are important for a particular item. For example, Samejima (1995) would leave out higher order thinking skills from the Q matrix, as inherently not discretizable. We would leave out skills of much finer granularity than the others, in order to keep the total number of skills in bounds. We would leave out a skill that occurs in only one item. For a given item i, a parameter c_i is used as an index of the extent to which the Q matrix is complete for that item.

We introduce a continuous student ability parameter η to represent overall ability outside of the skills of the Q matrix. In contrast to the specified detail of the skills listed in the Q matrix, abilities outside the Q matrix are modeled as simply as possible. By this we do not intend to imply that the non-Q abilities are less important, but we do make a conscious focus on the cognitive aspects that are modeled more explicitly in the Q matrix. Although the non-Q abilities are crudely modeled by η, the η functions as a variable that is able to soak up variation, and appears to considerably enhance classification performance.

Positivity: A person may be a master of a skill k and yet apply it incorrectly to an item i. That may be because the particular instance of that skill within that item is particularly challenging, so that even masters of that skill can misapply it in that item. Conversely a non-master of skill k may correctly apply it to a particular item because the instance of it is easy. Note that neither of these cases need result from "slips" or "guesses." We introduce two parameters for each item-skill pair.

$\pi_{i,k}$ = P(apply skill k correctly in item i|skill k is mastered)

$r_{i,k}$ = P(apply skill k correctly in item i|skill k is not mastered)

Slips: Given that everything else has been done correctly, a response that should have been correct may be recorded incorrectly. We call this a slip and introduce the slip parameter p = probability of committing a slip.

Thus the unified model assigns parameters for each of these factors, and provides a parametric expression for the probability of a correct response to an item, given the student's mastery/non-mastery skill pattern.

$$P(X_i = 1|\underline{\alpha} = (\alpha_1,...,\alpha_K),\eta) =$$

$$(1-p)\left\{d_i\left[\prod_{k=1}^{K}(\pi_{i,k})^{q_{i,k}\alpha_k}(r_{i,k})^{q_{i,k}(1-\alpha_k)}\right]P_0(\eta+c_i)+(1-d_i)P_0(\eta-b_i)\right\}$$

Here η = continuous ability outside of the Q skills.

P_0 = one parameter logistic with $a=1$ and 1.7 present.

b_i = difficulty parameter for non-Q strategy.

$0 \le c_i \le 3$ is the item completeness index.

$c_i \approx 0$ implies other (unspecified) skills important for answering item i correctly.

$c_i \approx 3$ implies specified attributes in Q suffice to control examinee response to i.

Several different assumptions of conditional independence are made. For further details see DiBello, Stout and Roussos (1995) and Hartz (2002).

2.4   Advantages and Features of the Unified Model

The unified model demonstrates several important characteristics. Rather than IRT θ, the latent space now is $(\underline{\alpha},\eta)$, where a skill profile vector $\underline{\alpha} = (\alpha_1,...,\alpha_K)$ tells mastery or nonmastery for each of the list of important skills being diagnosed by the test, and a continuous parameter η indicates ability outside the cognitive Q matrix. The aspects of the model that result from the four sources above – strategy, completeness, positivity and slips – capture more of the reality of the process of responding. In that sense the model is more true to reality and should lead to more accurate and valid diagnosis.

One may object that the model is still far too simple, that it is not consistent with known dynamic aspects of cognition, and that it does not express the rich complexity of interactions between item characteristics and cognitive function. All of these arguments are true, but the unified model is now well within the bounds of the feasible. Statistical approaches inherently cannot deal with the full complexities of cognitive processing in responding to assessment tasks. Nonetheless, the unified model appears to be able to provide exactly the kind of profile scoring that is called for by the cited NCLB provision and by other demands for formative assessments.

The original unified model lacked a practical calibration method and the $\pi_{i,k}$'s and $r_{i,k}$'s were non-identifiable. Hartz (2002) in her PhD thesis reparameterized the model, cast it into a hierarchical Bayesian framework and programmed a Markov Chain Monte Carlo (MCMC) parameter estimation procedure called ARPEGGIO[1]. Hartz chose a particularly intuitive and useful reparameterization:

$$\pi^*_i = \prod_{k=1}^{K} \pi_{i,k} \text{ and } r^*_{i,k} = \frac{r_{i,k}}{\pi_{i,k}}.$$

These $K+1$ *-parameters are identifiable. Further, of much greater importance, the *-parameters are interpretable by non-technical test clients or test developers.

π^*_i is a conditional difficulty, and

$r^*_{i,k} = \dfrac{r_{i,k}}{\pi_{i,k}}$ measures the inverse information strength of skill k within item i.

In particular, the quantity $(1 - r^*_{i,k})$ is a penalty factor for skill k in item i. If $r^*_{i,k}$ is low, then the penalty in item i for non-mastery of skill k is high. If $r^*_{i,k}$ is high, then the penalty is low. Once a test is calibrated that is well fit by the unified model, the values of the $r^*_{i,k}$ tell how well skill k is tapped by each item, and ultimately by the test. This provides a psychometrically sound method to empirically support expert judgment-based standards or skills alignments to items.

Classification reliability has been investigated in analyses of PSAT/NMSQT test-retest data, ACT math test data, and simulation studies. The results are quite good and can be found in Hartz (2002) and Hartz, Roussos and Stout (unpublished).

The unified model also provides a data-driven model revision procedure that makes the model robust to model misspecification. Deciding which skills to include or omit in the Q matrix allows for some control over the number of parameters. This control is critical to be able to achieve tractability (Hartz 2002).

---

[1] The software named ARPEGGIO provides a hierarchical Bayes MCMC parameter estimation procedure for the reparameterized unified model (Hartz 2002). A patent has been applied for. The patent application and software are wholly owned by Educational Testing Service. It is anticipated that the software will be renamed.

3 Vision for the Present

3.1 Complex Models

Models are tools for understanding and prediction, with no necessary claims to verisimilitude. Particular models attain standing within a field if they are tractable, provide a framework for substantive theories, and demonstrate good empirical prediction. Demands for substantive plausibility are often muted.

The dominance within modern testing practice of unidimensional IRT models is not correlative to some conveniently simple substantive reality. Its success results from the conceptually important modeling of ability as independent of individual tests or populations and, as a result, its great utility in developing ability estimates, estimates of meaningful item parameters, estimates of reliability, and its support of theoretical and practical equating and scaling methods. Suitability of a unidimensional model generally would not be argued on psychological or cognitive grounds, but on grounds of "fit," the extent to which data and model-based parameter estimates are internally consistent.

So as not to put too fine a point on this argument, the success of unidimensional methods suggests that low dimensional logistical or normal ogive models *can* for some purposes adequately summarize an underlying psychological reality. In fact this is just the crux of our argument. On one hand, the practical adequacy of a model representation is never solely the result of data reduction based on parsimony. It must always be based upon suitability to the purpose. On the other hand, desires for finer grained match to reality must balance against costs and consequences – technical and human. Model suitability is not an issue of logic or degree of match to reality. Is the model useful? Does its use move us forward?

Note that complexity in itself is not the goal. We seek the simplest models that reflect enough of a rich substantive reality that we can accomplish our formative goals. Simplicity and parsimony are still paramount values in our view. The difference between what we argue here and much of current psychometric practice is that in our view parsimony does not trump substantive adequacy.

The reparameterized unified model is an example of a model that is useful, even when much more parsimonious models may fit well. It is best envisioned in circumstances in which substantive experts say that a particular Q matrix must hold, at least approximately. That is the situation with the NCLB tests. By building the skills foundation for the NCLB tests on state standards, as is legally required, these tests represent a ripe setting for application of the unified model.

3.2 Conclusion

Psychometricians now must rise to the challenge to build a conceptual and methodological infrastructure for supporting improved testing that helps to increase the utility of testing in general, and that promotes K-12 teaching and learning.

The purposes of assessment today that touch the interactions between learning, teaching and assessment demand effective student profile scoring. An approach like the unified model and ARPEGGIO offers an underlying psychometric method that is rich enough to support greater information demands, and simple enough to apply now in a straightforward manner, for research and operational purposes.

A paradigm shift in testing is called for and in fact is occurring. The shift is characterized by the use of complex models, provision of student profile scores, and assessment design in context. It will have the effect of moving the testing industry beyond the unidimensional methods that have served, and continue to serve, so well into a new realm of assessment that promotes teaching and learning.

References

Black PJ, Wiliam D (1998) Inside the black box: raising standards through classroom assessment. Phi Delta Kappan, 80 (2), 139-148

Black PJ, Harrison C, Lee C, Marshall B, Dylan W (2002) Working inside the black box: assessment for learning in the classroom. London, UK: King's College London Department of Education and Professional Studies

DiBello L, Stout W, Roussos L (1995) Unified cognitive/psychometric diagnostic assessment likelihood-based classification techniques. In: Nichols P, Chipman S, Brennen R (eds) Cognitively diagnostic assessment. Hillsdale , NJ: Earlbaum. 361-389

DiBello L, Crone C, Narcowich M (2001) Descriptive score reporting on a national standardized test. NCME presentation, Seattle, WA

Doignon JP, Falmagne JC (1985) Spaces for the assessment of knowledge. International Journal of Man-Machine Studies 23: 175-196

Embretson SE (1998) A cognitive design system approach to generating valid tests: Application to abstract reasoning. Psychological Methods 3: 380-396

Fischer GH (1973) The linear logistic test model as an instrument in educational research. Acta Psychologica 37: 359-374

Glaser, R. (1963). Instructional technology and the measurement of learning outcomes: Some questions. American Psychologist 18: 519-521

Hartz, SM (2002) A bayesian framework for the Unified Model for assessing cognitive abilities: Blending theory with practicality. PhD Thesis: U Illinois, Urbana-Champaign

Junker BW, Sijtsma K (2001) Cognitive assessment models with few assumptions, and connections with nonparametric item response theory. Applied Psychological Measurement 25(3): 258-272

Maris E (1999) Estimating multiple classification latent class models. Psychometrika, 64 (2): 187-212

Martin J, Van Lehn K (1995) A Bayesian approach to cognitive assessment. In: Nichols P, Chipman S, Brennen R (eds) Cognitively diagnostic assessment. Hillsdale , NJ: Earlbaum. pp 141-166

Mislevy RJ (1997) Probability-based inference in cognitive diagnosis. In Nichols P, Chipman S, Brennan R (eds) Cognitively diagnostic assessment. Hillsdale NJ: Erlbaum, pp 43-71

Mislevy RJ, Almond RG, Yan D, Steinberg LS (1999). Bayes nets in educational assessment: Where do the numbers come from? In: Laskey KB, Prade H (eds) Proc 15th conference on uncertainty in artificial intelligence. San Francisco: Morgan Kaufmann, pp 437-446

Nichols P, Chipman S, Brennen R (1995) Cognitively diagnostic assessment. Hillsdale , NJ: Earlbaum

Pellegrino JW, Chudowski N, Glaser R (2001) Knowing what students know: The science and design of educational assessment. Washington, DC: National Academy Press

Reckase MD (1997) The past and future of multidimensional item response theory. Applied Psychological Measurement 21(1): 25-36

Samejima F (1995) A cognitive diagnosis method using latent trait models: Competency space approach and its relationship with DiBello and Stout's unified cognitive-psychometric diagnosis model. In: Nichols P, Chipman S, Brennen R (eds) Cognitively diagnostic assessment. Hillsdale , NJ: Earlbaum, pp 391-410

Tatsuoka KK (1985) A probabilistic model for diagnosing misconceptions by the pattern classification approach. J Educational Statistics 10:55-73

Tatsuoka KK (1990) Toward an integration of item-response theory and cognitive error diagnosis. In Frederiksen N, Glaser R, Lesgold A, Shafto MG (eds) Diagnostic monitoring of skill and knowledge acquisition. Hillsdale, NJ: Erlbaum, pp 453-488

Tatsuoka KK (1995) Architecture of knowledge structures and cognitive diagnosis: statistical pattern recognition and classification approach. In: Nichols P, Chipman S, Brennen R (eds) Cognitively diagnostic assessment. Hillsdale , NJ: Earlbaum. pp 327-359

US Government (2001) No Child Left Behind Act of 2001. Federal legislation

VanEssen T (2001) Developing skills, descriptions and steps for improvement on a national standardized test. NCME presentation. Seattle, WA

Wiley DE, Haertel EH (1996). Extended assessment tasks: Purposes, definitions, scoring, and accuracy. In Kane MB, Mitchell R (eds), Implementing performance assessments: Promises, problems, and challenges. Mahwah, NJ: Erlbaum

Wiliam D, Black PJ (1996) Meanings and consequences: a basis for distinguishing formative and summative functions of assessment? British Educational Research Journal, 22(5), 537-548

Wiliam D (2000, November) Integrating summative and formative functions of assessment. Paper presented at First annual conference of the Association for Educational Assessment-Europe held at Prague, Czech Republic

Wilson M, Draney K (1997) Developing maps for student progress in the SEPUP Assessment System. U California, Berkeley: BEAR Report Series, SA-97-2

Yamamoto K (1989) HYBRID model of IRT and latent class models. Research Report. RR-89-41. Princeton, NJ: Educational Testing Service

Yamamoto K (1991) Performance modeling that integrates latent trait and class theory. Research Report. RR-91-01. Princeton, NJ: Educational Testing Service

Part 2
Structural Equation Modeling and Factor Analysis

The Determinants of the Bias in Minimum Rank Factor Analysis (MRFA)

Gregor Sočan and Jos M.F. ten Berge

Heijmans Institute, University of Groningen, Grote Kruisstraat 2/1, 9712 TS Groningen, The Netherlands

Summary. Minimum Rank Factor Analysis (MRFA), see Ten Berge (1998), and Ten Berge and Kiers (1991), is a method of common factor analysis which yields, for any given covariance matrix Σ, a diagonal matrix Ψ of unique variances which are nonnegative and which entail a reduced covariance matrix $\Sigma-\Psi$ which is positive semidefinite. Subject to the above constraints, MRFA minimizes the amount of common variance left unexplained when we take any fixed small number of common factors. Shapiro and Ten Berge (2002) have derived the asymptotic bias of the unexplained common variance, its variance, and also the asymptotic covariance matrix of the unique variances. The present research deals with the impact of sample size, population minimum rank, number of extracted factors and standardization of the sample covariance matrix on the bias of unexplained common variance and total common variance. Special attention was paid to situations where the asymptotic theory does not apply. The results indicate that the bias could present a practical problem only if the population minimum rank was unnaturally low or if the sample size was small.

Key words: proper communality estimates, unexplained common variance, asymptotic bias, simulations

1 Introduction

Factor analysis aims to decompose the covariance matrix Σ of p observed variables into a covariance matrix Σ_c of common parts of the variables and a diagonal matrix Ψ of uniquenesses. In the ideal case, Σ_c would be factored as $\mathbf{FF}'$, where $\mathbf{F}$ is a $p \times r$ matrix of factor loadings. In that case, the decomposition would be

$$\Sigma = (\Sigma - \Psi) + \Psi = \mathbf{FF}' + \Psi \tag{1}$$

In practice, a solution with a small number of factors is sought, thus we are typically willing to trade the exact reproduction of Σ_c for the parsimony of a low-dimensional solution. The factor analysis decomposition can now be written as

$$\Sigma = \mathbf{FF'} + (\Sigma_c - \mathbf{FF'}) + \Psi \tag{2}$$

where the first part on the right-hand side corresponds to the variance, explained by the r extracted common factors (explained common variance or ECV), and the second term corresponds to the variance due to the $p-r$ ignored common factors (unexplained common variance or UCV). The last term Ψ remains a diagonal matrix indicating the amounts of unique variance (UV).

Classical approaches to factor analysis (like ULS or Maximum Likelihood) estimate Eq. 1 and therefore do not differentiate between common variance and explained common variance. Whenever the model does not fit perfectly, this leads to an indefinite estimate of $\Sigma_c = \Sigma - \Psi$. Specifically, since the smallest $p-r$ eigenvalues of Σ_c sum to zero (Harman 1976, p.182), some of them are negative in cases of imperfect fit.

On the other hand, Minimum Rank Factor Analysis (MRFA; ten Berge 1998; ten Berge and Kiers 1991) estimates both the Explained Common Variance (ECV) and the Unexplained Common Variance (UCV). MRFA minimizes the function

$$f_{\mathrm{MRFA}}(\psi) = \sum_{i=r+1}^{p} \lambda_i \tag{3}$$

where $\lambda_{r+1} \ldots \lambda_p$ are the $p-r$ smallest eigenvalues of Σ_c for r extracted factors. These eigenvalues correspond to ignored common factors and therefore represent the amount of the unexplained common variance. The explained common variance can be determined as the sum of the first r eigenvalues, as in classical methods like ULS and ML. The possibility of decomposition of the common variance into ECV and UCV is a valuable means for determining the number of factors to be retained, since we are able to ascertain what percentage of common variance is actually explained by the extracted factors. The ratio between unexplained and total common variance can be used as a descriptive measure of fit, which should be small enough for the factor model to be appropriate.

Besides that unique property, MRFA always produces proper communality estimates. This means that communalities remain in the interval between zero and one and that the reduced covariance matrix Σ_c remains positive semidefinite.

MRFA is not included in major statistical packages, but the authors shall deliver a DOS program on request.

Shapiro and ten Berge (2002) investigated the asymptotic bias of UCV by means of the theory of semidefinite programming. Their results are based on the following assumptions:
1. in samples, a covariance matrix is analyzed rather than a correlation matrix;
2. the variables follow the multivariate normal distribution in the population;
3. the Heywood constraint is inactive in the population;
4. the minimum rank of the population covariance matrix is not lower than the Ledermann (1937) bound, e.g., at least 3, 6 or 15 for 6, 10 or 21 variables, re-

spectively. As shown by Shapiro (1982), the Ledermann bound presents a lower bound to the minimum rank of a covariance matrix almost surely.

Two important results of Shapiro and ten Berge's study are:
1. UCV is asymptotically unbiased if the model is correct, i.e. if the number of extracted factors is equal to the minimum rank;
2. when the number of extracted factors in samples is smaller than the minimum rank, an estimate of the asymptotic bias of the UCV and the asymptotic variance of the bias is available.

The aim of this study was to investigate the empirical determinants of the bias in the unexplained common variance (UCV) and the total common variance (CV). The factors possibly influencing the bias were sample size, population minimum rank, number of extracted factors and standardizing sample covariance matrices (i.e. performing MRFA on a correlation matrix rather than on a covariance matrix). Conditions where the asymptotic theory was not valid due to small minimum rank or due to the standardization of the covariance matrix were included.

2 Method

Simulations were based on four real data sets:
1. "Big5": 10 subscales of the BFQ personality questionnaire (Bucik et al. 1997; $N = 1525$). Each subscale measures an aspect of one of the Big Five personality dimensions. Five strong factors can therefore be expected on substantive grounds – in fact, the first five factors explained almost 98% of the common variance.
2. "RT": 6 measures of speed and accuracy in three reaction time paradigms (Sočan 2000; $N = 104$). Two common factors (speed and accuracy) were expected to explain most of the common variance, and the percentage of ECV for the two-factor solution was indeed 96%.
3. "Cars": 10 items measuring attitudes towards the use of cars and its influence on environment (Steg et al. 1993; $N = 537$). The first three factors explained 88% and first four factors explained 95% of the common variance.
4. "Openness": 8 items of the Openness rating scale (Bucik et al. 1997; $N = 615$). The scale was designed to be unidimensional, and the first factor explained 73% of the common variance.

The minimum rank (*mr*) of the population covariance matrices was manipulated in the following way:
1. An eigendecomposition $\Sigma = \mathbf{K\Lambda K'}$ of the covariance matrix was performed.
2. Matrices $\mathbf{K}_{mr}$ and Λ_{mr} were formed by taking the first *mr* columns of $\mathbf{K}$ and first *mr* rows and columns of Λ, respectively.
3. The covariance matrix Σ_{mr} was composed as $\Sigma_{mr} = \mathbf{K}_{mr}\Lambda_{mr}\mathbf{K}_{mr}'$.
4. The diagonal elements of Σ_{mr} were replaced by the original variances from Σ.

The resulting matrices were taken as population matrices.

For data sets Big5, RT and Cars, three levels of sample size (N =100, 500 or 1000) were combined with three levels of minimum rank (mr) and three levels of number of extracted factors (r). Minimum rank and number of factors generally varied from 1 to the Ledermann bound (i.e. 3 for 6 variables and 6 for 10 variables). The population covariance matrix of the variables was a correlation matrix for these three data sets. In each of the 27 resulting conditions, 500 random sample matrices were constructed. The population distribution of the variables was taken to be multivariate normal.

For the Openness data set, the same three levels of N (i.e. 100, 500 and 1000) were combined with two levels of sample matrix type (covariance or correlation matrix). The population variances of the variables varied between 1.17 and 2.38. The population minimum rank was not manipulated, since only the effects of sample size and standardization were of interest here. Again, 500 random sample matrices based on the multivariate normal distribution were constructed in each of the six conditions.

3 Results

3.1 The Bias of the Proportion of the Unexplained Common Variance

The proportion of unexplained common variance within the total common variance (UCV%) is a major diagnostic measure for deciding how many factors should be retained. Therefore, we examine the bias of UCV% first.

To investigate the influence of minimum rank, number of extracted factors and sample size on the bias of UCV%, we performed a three-way analysis of variance for each of the first three data sets. Table 1 presents the effect sizes for main effects and interactions. ω^2 (a measure of the proportion of total variance explained by a certain source) was used as a measure of effect size, making possible to assess the independent contributions of each source of variation.

Table 1. ω^2 for a 3-way ANOVA

Source of variation		Data set		
		Big5	RT	Cars
Main effects	mr	.26	.32	.40
	r	.17	.05	.14
	N	.06	.01	.04
Interactions	$mr \times r$	.29	.31	.24
	$N \times mr$	.04	.07	.05
	$N \times r$	.03	.00	.02
	$N \times mr \times r$	.05	.08	.03

N, sample size; r, number of factors; mr, minimum rank.

All effects were statistically significant ($p < 0.001$), thus we do not report the F ratios. Among main effects, *mr* seems to have by far the largest influence on the bias of UCV%, although r and N explain some variance, too. Among interactions only the *mr* × r interaction seems to be worth considering, with effect size comparable to *mr*.

Tables 2 and 3 show the impact of the minimum rank of the population matrix and the number of extracted factors on UCV% at two sample sizes for the data sets Big5 and RT (results for the data set Cars exhibited the same general pattern). A very similar pattern can be observed in both data sets.

Table 2. The bias of UCV% in the Big5 data

mr	N = 100			N = 1000		
	r = 2	r = 4	r = 6	r = 2	r = 4	r = 6
2	.196	.066	.008	.078	.026	.003
4	.035	.059	.006	.015	.021	.002
6	.000	.008	.008	-.002	.000	.003

N, sample size; r, number of factors; *mr*, minimum rank.

Generally, the bias of UCV% tends to diminish as *mr*, r and N become larger. The interaction between *mr* and r is also clearly visible. For instance, when there were six factors extracted for the Big5 data, the bias was very small (less than 1%) even though the minimum rank and sample size were both small (i.e. 2 and 100, respectively). On the other hand, when only 2 factors were extracted and the population minimum rank was two (being below the Ledermann bound), the bias was considerable: even in the large sample ($N = 1000$) condition it reached almost 8%, and it was nearly 20% when the sample size was only 100. Similarly, for the RT data the bias was negligible when three factors were extracted, and was relatively large (e.g., 17% at sample size 100) when both *mr* and r were equal to one.

Table 3. The bias of UCV% in the RT data

mr	N = 100			N = 1000		
	r = 1	r = 2	r = 3	r = 1	r = 2	r = 3
1	.173	.054	.009	.064	.020	.003
2	-.034	.014	.002	-.002	.004	.001
3	-.034	.002	.002	-.003	.000	.001

N, sample size; r, number of factors; *mr*, minimum rank.

An important question that emerges here is whether the bias can be considered a serious practical problem. The only case where a user of MRFA should be seriously concerned about it is when both the population minimum rank is very small relative to the number of variables and the number of extracted factors is very small. In this case, even taking a large sample (e.g., $N = 1000$) does not reduce the bias to an acceptable level. This bias almost disappears if the number of extracted factors is augmented. Fortunately, low population minimum rank is not encountered in practice, at least when psychological data are concerned.

If the population minimum rank is at or above the Ledermann bound, the size of the bias does not seem to be a severe practical problem if the sample size is at least moderate (in our simulations 500 or 1000, respectively): in these cases the bias never reached 4% of the common variance, and was actually much smaller in most cases.

It seems to be a general tendency that the bias of UCV% is positive, so we usually underestimate the proportion of the common variance explained by a certain number of factors. Some exceptions occurred in cases of underfactoring, when the values of mr were relatively high and the values of r were low. However, the bias itself was small; it reached its lowest value (-3%) in the RT data in the $N = 100$ condition.

Table 4 shows the bias of UCV% in relation to sample size for standardized and non-standardized Openness data. In samples of size 100, the bias was relatively large compared to the bias found in the previous data sets, but it declined markedly with sample size. The bias was slightly higher when the sample data were not standardized, i.e., if the covariance sample matrix was analyzed. However, the difference was practically negligible compared to the effect of the sample size: ω^2, computed by a two-way ANOVA was 0.43 for sample size and only 0.001 for both type of the sample matrix and two-way interaction. Thus, although the standardization of the data matrix invalidates the asymptotic bias theory, it seems that the bias itself does not change much.

Table 4. The bias of UCV% in the Openness data

Type of sample data	Sample size		
	100	500	1000
standardized	.072	.019	.008
non-standardized	.081	.019	.010

3.2 The Bias of the Common Variance

Because the proportion of the common variance in the observed variance (CV%) is of less practical importance than UCV%, we shall consider only two data sets (Cars and Openness).

Table 5 presents the results of ANOVA for the Cars data. The population minimum rank still had the largest effect size, but in the second place there was sample size rather than the number of extracted factors (all effects were statistically significant, $p < 0.01$).

Table 6 shows the size of the bias in various conditions. The bias was overall positive. Contrary to the bias of UCV, the bias of CV% was close to zero only when mr was large. The nature of the $mr \times r$ interaction was different from the case of UCV%: in the $mr=1$ condition, the bias was larger when r was large rather than small. In the worst case (with the smallest sample size), the bias reached 27% of the observed variance.

Table 5. ANOVA results for CV% in the Cars data

Source of variation		ω^2
Main effects	mr	.64
	r	.02
	N	.14
Interactions	$mr \times r$	.03
	$N \times mr$	.05
	$N \times r$	.00
	$N \times mr \times r$	.00

N, sample size; r, number of factors; mr, minimum rank.

Table 6. The bias of CV% in the Cars data

mr	$N = 100$			$N = 1000$		
	$r = 1$	$r = 3$	$r = 5$	$r = 1$	$r = 3$	$r = 5$
1	.220	.083	.035	.070	.022	.003
4	.238	.087	.035	.116	.024	.002
7	.267	.098	.016	.159	.040	.001

N, sample size; r, number of factors; mr, minimum rank.

Table 7 presents the results for the Openness data. As for UCV%, the sample size had a much larger effect size than type of the sample matrix (ω^2 being 0.55 and 0.02, respectively). The bias again decreased with rising sample size, and remained at about 1-2% of the observed variance at the sample size 1000. Contrary to the bias of UCV%, the bias of CV% was somewhat larger when correlation matrices were analyzed in the samples, but the difference was small compared to the effect of sample size.

Table 7. The bias of CV% in the Openness data

Type of sample data	Sample size		
	100	500	1000
standardized	.094	.033	.022
non-standardized	.081	.019	.010

4 Conclusions

The size of the bias in MRFA largely depends on sample size, number of extracted factors and especially the minimum rank of the population covariance matrix, and its interaction with number of extracted factors. Specifically, it seems that all kinds of bias are adequately small if the population minimum rank is not lower than the Ledermann bound and if the sample is at least moderately large (e.g. 500 subjects). Fortunately, the population minimum rank can be expected to be at or above the Ledermann bound in practical situations.

The bias of UCV% tended to be positive; therefore, it seems more likely that the MRFA results will suggest extracting more factors than necessary. Not surprisingly, the bias of ECV% was negative and approaching zero with rising minimum rank, sample size and the number of extracted factors, respectively. The bias of CV% was positive, thus overestimating the proportion of explained observed variance.

Performing MRFA on correlation rather than covariance sample matrices might have only minor influence on the bias of UCV and CV, respectively.

5 References

Bucik V, Boben D, Kranjc I (1997) BFQ questionnaire and BFO rating scale for measurement of the »big five« factors of personality: Slovenian adaptation (in Slovenian). Psihološka Obzorja 6:5-34

Harman HH (1976) Modern factor analysis (3rd ed.). The University of Chicago press, Chicago

Ledermann W (1937) On the rank of the reduced correlation matrix in multiple-factor analysis. Psychom 2:85-93

Shapiro A (1982) Rank-reducibility of a symmetric matrix and sampling theory of minimum trace factor analysis. Psychom 47: 187-199

Shapiro A, Ten Berge JMF (2002) Statistical inference of minimum rank factor analysis. Psychom 67: 79-94

Sočan G (2000) Convergent and discriminant validity of measurement methods for speed of information-processing and related constructs. Unpublished M.A. thesis (in Slovenian). University of Ljubljana, Ljubljana

Steg FM, Vlek CAJ, Rooyers AJ (1993) Behavior modification to reduce automobile usage. Appreciation of the problem, readiness to change and evaluation of administrative measures: a field study (in Dutch). University of Groningen, Groningen

Ten Berge JMF (1998) Some recent developments in factor analysis and the search for proper communalities. In: Rizzi A, Vichi M, Bock H-H (eds) Advances in data science and classification. Springer, Heidelberg, pp 325-334

Ten Berge JMF, Kiers HAL (1991) A numerical approach to the approximate and the exact minimum rank of a covariance matrix. Psychom 56:309-315

A Note on the Approximate Distributions of Fit Indexes for Misspecified Structural Equation Models

Haruhiko Ogasawara

Department of Information and Management Science, Otaru University of Commerce, 3-5-21 Midori, Otaru 047-8501, Japan

Summary. Two revised formulas are presented for the asymptotic variances of the fit indexes for misspecified structural equation models. The first formula gives a form simpler than that given by Ogasawara (2001) and the second one values closer to the simulated ones than those provided by Ogasawara (2001).

Key words. Fit indexes, Asymptotic variances, Approximate distributions, Structural equation models, Model misspecification

1 Purpose

This note is to supplement the results given by the author at the 2001 international meeting of the Psychometric Society, whose corresponding full paper was published as Ogasawara (2001). In this note, two revised formulas are provided for the asymptotic variances of the fit indexes except for $F_B = \ln|\mathrm{Diag}\, S| - \ln|S|$ (for the notation, see Ogasawara, 2001).

2 A Revised Formula for the Asymptotic Variances of the Fit Indexes Using a Baseline Model

In Ogasawara (2001), the asymptotic variances of the fit indexes (Is) using a baseline model were given by the following formula:

$$\mathrm{acov}(I) = \frac{\partial I}{\partial(F,\, F_B)}\,\mathrm{acov}\{(F, F_B)'\}\,\frac{\partial I}{\partial(F,\, F_B)'}\,, \tag{1}$$

where
$$I = \frac{F_B - k_1 F - k_2}{F_B - k_0} = 1 - \frac{k_1 F + k_2 - k_0}{F_B - k_0}, \tag{2}$$

$$F = \text{tr}(\hat{\Sigma}^{-1} S) + \ln|\hat{\Sigma}| - p - \ln|S| \text{ and}$$

I	k_0	k_1	k_2
9) NFI (Bentler & Bonett, 1980)	0	1	0
10) IFI (Bollen, 1989)	df/n	1	0
11) ρ_1 (Bollen, 1986)	0	df_B/df	0
12) ρ_2 (Tucker & Lewis, 1973)	df_B/n	df_B/df	0
13) FI (Bentler, 1990; RNI, McDonald & Marsh, 1990)	df_B/n	1	$(df_B - df)/n$

(3)

(*Note*. The index numbers 9 through 13 correspond to those in Tables 1 and 2 shown later.)

where df is the degrees of freedom for the test of goodness-of-fit of a misspecified model and df_B for the baseline model.

From Eq.2 we have

$$\text{avar}(I) = \text{avar}(\frac{k_1 F + k_2 - k_0}{F_B - k_0}).$$

(4)

Let $I = X/Y$ with

$$X = k_1 F + k_2 - k_0 \text{ and } Y = F_B - k_0.$$

(5)

Then, using the Taylor expansion about the true or asymptotically expected values, x_0 and y_0, of X and Y, respectively, we have

$$\frac{X}{Y} = \frac{y_0}{x_0} + \frac{1}{y_0}(X - x_0) + o_p(n^{-1}).$$

(6)

Eq. 6 comes from the following results. First, noting Eq.3,

$$x_0 = \text{E}(k_1 F) + k_2 - k_0 = k_1 \frac{df + \lambda}{n} + k_2 - k_0 = O(n^{-1})$$

and

(7)

$$y_0 = \text{E}(F_B) - k_0 = -\ln|\text{P}_t| - k_0 = O(1),$$

where λ is the noncentrality of the misspecified model and P_t is the population or true correlation matrix of observed variables. The expanded term with respect to $Y - y_0$ is written as

$$-\frac{x_0}{y_0^2}(Y - y_0) = O_p(n^{-3/2}),$$

(8)

since $x_0 / y_0^2 = O(n^{-1})$ and $Y - y_0 = O_p(n^{-1/2})$, and consequently absorbed in $O_p(n^{-1})$ of Eq.6.

From Eq.6 we find that avar(I)=avar(X/Y) can be evaluated without considering the asymptotic variance or covariance with respect to Y (note $\text{avar}(X) = O(n^{-2})$, $\text{avar}(Y) = O(n^{-1})$ and $\text{acov}(X,Y) = O(n^{-3/2})$):

$$\text{avar}(I) = \frac{k_1^2}{y_0^2} \text{avar}(F) = \frac{k_1^2}{(\ln|P_t| + k_0)^2} \text{avar}(F), \qquad (9)$$

where k_0 can be omitted because $\ln|P_t| = O(1)$ and $k_0 = O(n^{-1})$. However, considering that $\ln|P_t|$ is negative and k_0 contributes slightly to the increase of Eq.9 with finite n, which tends to be consistent with empirical data, k_0 is kept included in Eq.9. The formula of Eq.9 is much simpler than that shown in the appendix of Ogasawara (2001) and gives a justification for the approximate distribution of I by Ogasawara (2001, (A8)).

3 Evaluation of the asymptotic variance of F

The values of F for usual models with $\text{tr}(\hat{\Sigma}^{-1} S) = p$ become

$$F = \ln|\hat{\Sigma}| - \ln|S|. \qquad (10)$$

It is known that

$$E(F) = (df + \lambda)/n \qquad (11)$$

and

$$\text{avar}(F) = (2df + 4\lambda)/n^2, \qquad (12)$$

where (11) was used in the previous section. Though these equations asymptotically hold, the empirical data of Ogasawara (2001) showed that Eq.12 was somewhat underestimated while Eq.11 was very close to the simulated values. So, we present a different evaluation of avar(F). Because $\hat{\Sigma}$ in Eq.10 is an (implicit) function of S or $s=v(S)$ (v is the vectorizing operator of the non-duplicated elements of a matrix), we have

$$\text{acov}(F) = \frac{\partial F}{\partial s'} \text{acov}(s) \frac{\partial F}{\partial s}, \qquad (13)$$

where

$$\frac{\partial F}{\partial \mathbf{s}'} = (\text{vec}\Sigma(\boldsymbol{\theta}_o)^{-1})'\{-\frac{\partial \text{vec}\hat{\Sigma}}{\partial \hat{\boldsymbol{\theta}}'}(\frac{\partial^2 F}{\partial \hat{\boldsymbol{\theta}}\partial \hat{\boldsymbol{\theta}}'})^{-1}\frac{\partial^2 F}{\partial \hat{\boldsymbol{\theta}}\partial \mathbf{s}'}\} \tag{14}$$
$$-(\text{vec}\Sigma_t^{-1})'D_p$$

with the partial derivatives being evaluated at their true values; vec is the operator vectorizing all elements of a matrix; Σ_t is the true covariance matrix for observed variables; $\boldsymbol{\theta}_0$ is the vector of fitted population parameters; $\hat{\boldsymbol{\theta}}$ is the parameter estimates by maximum likelihood; and vec $\mathbf{S} = D_p\,\mathbf{s}$. Eq.14 is based on a somewhat relaxed assumption about the degree of misspecification of a model. Instead of the slight difference of the population fitted covariance matrix and the true covariance matrix i.e., $O(n^{-1/2})$ it is temporarily assumed that the difference is $O(1)$ which yields Eq.13 ($=O(n^{-1})$) different from $O(n^{-2})$ given previously. In finite samples, Eq.13 gives values different from those by Eq.12, which seems to show larger ones as is illustrated in the next section.

4 An Illustration

Revised formulas using Eqs.9 and/or 13 are applied to the simulated data for the 8 physical variables (Harman, 1976, p.22) and the 12 psychological tests (Harman, 1976, p.401) generated by Ogasawara (2001), where misspecified exploratory factor analysis models were fitted. Tables 1 and 2 show the results corresponding to the four different methods using different formulas which include the original one. They are summarized as follows:

	Methods 1(Original)	2(Revised)	3(Revised)	4(Revised)
avar(I) by Eq.9	-	*	-	*
avar(F) by Eq.13	-	-	*	*

where an asterisk indicates that the corresponding new formula is used and a hyphen not used. In Tables 1 and 2, the fit index for a baseline model F_B is included for comparison. Indexes 1 through 8 except Index 2 (F_B) depend only on F and are irrelevant to the new formula of Eq.9. From the table we see that Method 2 give slightly smaller but almost the same values given by Method 1. This tendency is also observed for the values by Methods 3 and 4. These results show the accuracy of the formula of Eq.9. The values by Methods 3 and 4 have become larger than those by Methods 1 and 2 though still somewhat smaller than the corresponding simulated values. This shows an improvement given by the formula of Eq.13 in finite samples. From these findings, Method 3 and 4 are recommended to be used in practice.

Table 1. Results for the eight physical variables (N=305; computed from the correlation matrix of Harman, 1976, p.22; partially quoted from Ogasawara, 2001, Table 1)

	Methods Indexes	1(Original)	Theoretical 2(Revised)	SEs 3(Revised)	4(Revised)	Simulated SDs
1	F	.0552	-	.0576	-	.0602
2	F_B	.339	-	-	-	.340
3	GFI	.0122	-	.0127	-	.0130
4	AGFI	.0338	-	.0353	-	.0360
5	Abs.GFI	.0249	-	.0259	-	.0264
6	RMSEA	.0167	-	.0174	-	.0166
7	Gamma 1	.0125	-	.0130	-	.0133
8	Gamma 2	.0345	-	.0360	-	.0367
9	NFI	.00808	.00796	.00841	.00830	.00878
10	IFI	.00808	.00801	.00842	.00835	.00878
11	Rho 1	.0174	.0171	.0181	.0179	.0189
12	Rho 2	.0175	.0174	.0183	.0181	.0190
13	FI(RNI)	.00814	.00806	.00848	.00841	.00884

1) F=WML fit function, 2)F_B =Baseline fit function, 3) GFI=Goodness-of-fit index (Jöreskog & Sörbom, 1981), 4) AGFI=Adjusted GFI (Jöreskog & Sörbom, 1981), 5) Abs.GFI=Absolute GFI (McDonald, 1989), 6) RMSEA=Root mean square error of approximation (Steiger & Lind, 1980), 7) Gamma 1=$\hat{\Gamma}_1$ (Steiger, 1989), 8) Gamma 2= $\hat{\Gamma}_2$ (Steiger, 1989), 9) NFI=Normed fit index (Bentler & Bonett, 1980), 10) IFI= Incremental fit index (Bollen 1989), 11) Rho 1= ρ_1 (Bollen, 1986), 12) Rho 2= ρ_2 (Tucker & Lewis, 1973), 13) FI=Fit index (Bentler, 1990; RNI, Relative noncentrality index, McDonald & Marsh, 1990).

Table 2. Results for the twelve psychological tests (N=355; computed from the correlation matrix of Harman, 1976, p.401; partially quoted from Ogasawara, 2001, Table 2)

	Methods Indexes	1(Original)	Theoretical 2(Revised)	SEs 3(Revised)	4(Revised)	Simulated SDs
1	F	.0427	-	.0493	-	.0515
2	F_B	.347	-	-	-	.352
3	GFI	.00665	-	.00768	-	.00778
4	AGFI	.0157	-	.0182	-	.0184
5	Abs.GFI	.0202	-	.0233	-	.0232
6	RMSEA	.0110	-	.0127	-	.0101
7	Gamma 1	.00686	-	.00792	-	.00801
8	Gamma 2	.0162	-	.0187	-	.0189
9	NFI	.00799	.00780	.00917	.00900	.00923
10	IFI	.00795	.00794	.00918	.00916	.00924
11	Rho 1	.0160	.0156	.0183	.0180	.0185
12	Rho 2	.0162	.0162	.0187	.0186	.0188
13	FI(RNI)	.00810	.00808	.00934	.00932	.00940

See the footnote of Table 1.

5 References

Bentler PM (1990) Comparative fit indexes in structural models. Psychological Bulletin 107: 238-246

Bentler PM, Bonett DG (1980) Significance tests and goodness of fit in the analysis of co-variance structures. Psychological Bulletin 88: 588-606

Bollen KA (1986) Sample size and Bentler and Bonett's nonnormed fit index. Psychometrika 51: 375-377

Bollen KA (1989) A new incremental fit index for general equation models. Sociological Methods & Research 17: 303-316

Harman HH (1976) Modern factor analysis, 3rd edn. University of Chicago Press, Chicago.

Jöreskog KG, Sörbom D (1981) LISREL V: Analysis of linear structural relations by the method of maximum likelihood. International Educational Services, Chicago

McDonald RP (1989) An index of goodness-of-fit based on noncentrality. Journal of Classification 6: 97-103

McDonald RP, Marsh HW (1990) Choosing a multivariate model: Noncentrality and goodness of fit. Psychological Bulletin 107: 247-255

Ogasawara H (2001) Approximations to the distributions of fit indexes for misspecified structural equation models. Structural Equation Modeling 8: 556-574

Steiger JH (1989) EzPATH: A supplementary module for SYSTAT and SYGRAPH. SYSTAT Inc, Evanstone, IL

Steiger JH, Lind JC (1980, May) Statistically based tests for the number of common factors. Paper presented at the annual Spring Meeting of the Psychometric Society, Iowa City, IA.

Tucker LR, Lewis C (1973) A reliability coefficient for maximum likelihood factor analysis. Psychometrika 38: 1-10

Longitudinal Study of Early Chinese Linguistics Growth: Revealing Sequential Relations of Linguistic Antecedents and Consequences

Chih-Chien Yang[1], and Chih-Chiang Yang[2]

[1]Graduate School of Educational Measurement & Statistics, National Taichung Teachers College, 140 MengShin Road, Taichung 403, Taiwan. [2]Department of Banking & Risk Management, The Overseas Chinese of Technology, Taichung, Taiwan.

Summary. A longitudinal study was carried out to study various growth patterns in the early learning of the Chinese language. We investigate different developmental trajectories during early learning stages of Chinese linguistic abilities. Cognitive development of Chinese reading process, i.e., phonemic/tonic awareness and word recognition can be thus revealed. Research studies have shown that it is possible to identify subgroups with different growth patterns in the early learning of the English language using mixture modeling of latent growth trajectories. We demonstrate how various subgroups with different growth patterns can be identified successfully by using mixture latent growth curve (MLGC) models. To learn about how an early growth process relates to a later growth process will be invaluable in building developmental and learning theories that can benefit proper linguistics instructions and formatting effective intervention programs. Empirical data were collected from local elementary schools in Taiwan.
Key words. Chinese Linguistics, Latent Growth Model, Finite Mixture, Longitudinal Study

1 Introduction

Examining individual linguistic growth trajectories will benefit establishments of linguistic development theory (see e.g., Francis, Shaywitz, Stuebing, Shaywitz, & Fletcher, 1996; Wagner, Torgesen, & Rashotte, 1994; MacDonald, & Cornwall, 1995; Juel, Griffith, & Grougy, 1986). In this paper, we examine different antecedents and consequences of individual Chinese linguistic learning growth processes by using mixture latent growth curve models. We specifically investigate different forms of developmental trajectories of early learning patterns on various Chinese linguistic abilities, e.g., phonemic/tonic awareness, visual skills and word recognition.

The latent growth curve (LGC) analysis (see, e.g. Scheier, Botvin, Griffin, & Diaz, 1999; Baer, & Schmitz, 2000; Barnes, Reifman, Farrell, & Dintcheff, 2000; Mason, 2001) was popularized recently for detecting aggregated individual growth trajectories. Most of these applications used LGC analysis to show the aggregated latent growth curves of targeted populations. Instead of looking at the aggregated individual latent growth curves, finite mixture latent growth curve analysis is designed to focus on analyzing the sub-groups of different latent growth trajectories. Using the different latent growth trajectories among different sub-groups, finite mixture latent growth curve analysis can further show the heterogeneity of developmental patterns. The feature can be useful for psychological or educational diagnosis purposes.

Recent research studies have shown that it is possible to identify subgroups with different forms of growth patterns in learning of the English language by using mixture modeling of latent growth trajectories (Boscardin, & Muthén, 2000; Muthén, Khoo, Francis, & Boscardin, 1998). Studying different forms of developmental trajectories enables early identification of linguistic learning disability (Muthén, Khoo, Francis, & Boscardin, 1998). In these papers, different trajectory forms were results by analyzing antecedents and consequences of the English linguistic growth processes. For example, evidences (Boscardin, & Muthén, 2000; Muthén, Khoo, Francis, & Boscardin, 1998) showed phonemic awareness skills to be the antecedents of early reading abilities. The phonemic awareness skill is believed to be one of the most critical factors in predicting word recognition ability as well as other consequent English reading abilities.

Because of the nature of Chinese characters, it is less clear what factors can be the antecedents and their consequences during early developments of Chinese reading abilities. Moreover, producing both effective phonemic and tonic pronunciations for words, phrases, and sentences is crucial to consist understandable mandarin Chinese conversations. Therefore, results found in the research of English language learning might or might not be applied equivalently in Chinese reading developments. Neither is it clear how strong are the sequential relations between these Chinese linguistic antecedents and consequences. The topics are equally important and need to be investigated thoroughly. In this paper, we first proposed mixture latent growth curve (MLGC) models that were modified versions of Muthén, Khoo, Francis, and Boscardin's (1998) model. Our MLGC models can identify various interesting early Chinese reading abilities development paradigms. These paradigms are to be identified successfully by using a 4 class mixture model of latent growth curves.

We, specifically, demonstrate how the subgroups with different forms of Chinese linguistic learning growth patterns can be identified statistically using mixture latent growth modeling. Several interesting linguistic growth patterns that are specific to early Chinese linguistic developments and different from their peers in the English language development are outlined in our analyses.

2 Mixture Latent Growth Model

A new class of latent growth models extended the simple latent growth models and incorporated finite mixture modeling techniques to interpret the heterogeneity between different subgroups' various latent growth patterns. In other words, this class of models classified subjects into subgroups by distinguishing their different latent growth trajectories or paradigms. The models were called mixture latent growth curve (MLGC) models.

Example applications of MLGC models can be found in Muthén, Khoo, Francis and Boscardin (1998), Boscardin and Muthén (2000), Muthén, Brown, Masyn, Jo, Khoo, Yang, Wang, Kellam, Carlin, and Liao (2002), and Muthén (2002). Their papers showed the values of mixture latent growth models in outlining subgroups of English reading developments by using various pre-specified latent growth trajectories. We modified the MLGC models proposed in their papers to customize the specific features of mandarin Chinese phonemics and its graphical characters.

Mixture latent growth models have a typical structure of latent growth model using CFA frameworks and a newly added categorical latent variable (C). That is, the models combine simultaneously a typical confirmatory factor analysis with a latent class analysis. By including the categorical latent variable, mixture latent growth models can have several different growth trajectories estimated at the same time. Therefore, the heterogeneity between individuals due to different growth procedures can be modeled more appropriately. Given a latent class within a MLGC model, we assume a simple linear latent growth model is established; that is, a set of latent initial status (intercept) and linear latent growth rate (slope) factors explains the linear latent growth process for individuals. Figure 1 shows that η_1 is the latent initial status factor and η_2 is the latent growth rate factor in modeling the growth trajectories. Because of MLGC models featuring the finite mixture of different latent growth trajectories, the means of η_1 and η_2 of MLGC models can be varied across latent classes (C) respectively.

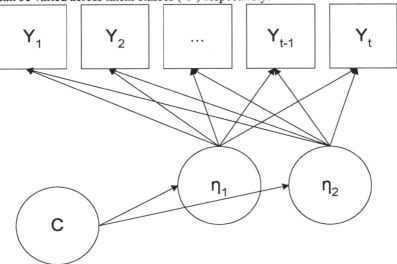

Fig. 1. Finite Mixture Latent Grwoth Curve Model

3 Chinese Linguistic Development Trajectories

To develop theories of Chinese reading development and verify them by using our models, we employed the following research design and test instruments to obtain empirical datasets. The two linguistic scales used in the paper were mandarin Chinese phonemic awareness scale and Chinese word recognition scale. Yang and Chang (2000) and Huang, Yang, and Chang (2001) developed the two instruments that were utilized by this paper. Yang and Chang (2000) and Huang, Yang, and Chang's (2001) curriculum relevant phonemic awareness scale included examinations for consonant, vowel, and combined vowel (a phoneme that needs to pronounce two vowels together) subscales. Their papers also introduced a unique subscale for tonic awareness. All these scales included sounds of both true and pseudo words as test materials.

Yang and Chang (2000) further developed a curriculum relevant word recognition scale in which different alternations of graphical features (graphemes) of true words, thus it could produce some pseudo words, were used to test subjects' word recognition abilities. These pseudo words are very similar to each other in graphical features (i.e., they have some common graphemes) and can cause distractions in visual discriminations. To answer these word recognition tests correctly, examinees needed to depend only on appropriate visual discrimination abilities and depend on no aids from phonemic information of the tested words. The authors' papers verified the scales so that they were psychometrically reliable and valid. For example, reliability Cronbach alpha's of all scales ranged from 0.65 to 0.9 and both qualitative validity (e.g., content validity) and quantitative validity (construct validity) were at satisfied levels.

Our project used the following longitudinal design and sampling procedures to collect empirical datasets. The project started in 1999 and tested subjects attending in schools of middle Taiwan, including Taichung, Changhwa, and Nantou counties. It involved four schools and twelve classes. All the sampled schools and classes represented urban and suburban school districts that made of the major school types of Taiwan. The original sample size of this study was about four hundred subjects that were divided about evenly by two cohorts. The first cohort was the first grade students in 1999 while the second cohort was all second graders in the same year. The students in this project had been tested once a semester since the fall semester of Year 1999. At the spring semester of Year 2001, they had been repeatedly tested four times.

This paper used the first cohort students to demonstrate early Chinese reading developments. The cohort had four time points of observations and time spans between any two neighboring observations were almost equal. After deleting listwisely the incomplete records, the paper used 167 samples for all analyses done in the models presented in later sections. The retaining rates were about eighty-four percents.

In our mixture latent growth curve (MLGC) models, we used both continuous and categorical latent variables to model the unobservable longitudinal structures of Chinese reading developments. A standard path diagram often seen in structural equation model research was drawn in Figure 2 to show the model setups. Observed variables $PT_1 \sim PT_4$ and $WG_1 \sim WG_4$ showed that two sets of four repeated measures for phonemic-tonic awareness and word-grapheme recognitions were in the model. The measures were obtained at even time spans and linear trends were assumed for both phonemic-tonic awareness and word-grapheme recognition developments. We selected items from Chinese phonemic-tonic awareness scale (Yang, & Chang, 2000; Huang, Yang, & Chang, 2001) in which it contained well-mixed consonants, vowels, and combined vowels items as well as tonic awareness items to assess subjects' overall phonemic-tonic awareness abilities ($PT_1 \sim PT_4$). Similarly, we also selected items from Chinese word-grapheme recognition scale (Yang, & Chang, 2000; Huang, Yang, & Chang, 2001) to assess subjects' Chinese characters recognition abilities ($WG_1 \sim WG_4$). All raw scores were recomputed by a standardized procedure to set them at a comparable scale.

The two pairs of continuous latent variables (η_{pi} - η_{ps} & η_{wi} - η_{ws}) showed intercepts and slopes of the two linear latent growth processes for phonemic-tonic awareness and word-grapheme recognition developments respectively. To model the possible heterogeneity of latent growth pattern subgroups, we added a categorical latent variable (C) to indicate that there were mixtures of heterogeneous latent growth subgroups within the subjects. In other words, instead of using a uniform latent growth trajectory for all subjects, several latent growth trajectories for different subgroups could coexist in the model. Different from Muthén, Khoo, Francis, and Boscardin's (1998) model, this MLGC model did not set predefined latent growth subgroups but it estimated them freely.

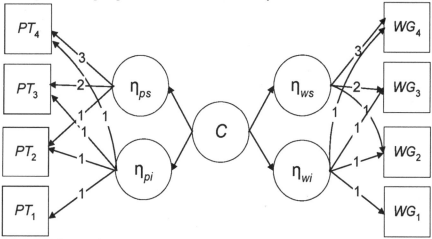

Fig. 2. Chinese Linguistic MLGC model

We used an adjusted Bayesian information criterion (ABIC; Sclove, 1987) that was derived from BIC (Schwarz, 1978) to determine the number of latent classes in our MLGC models. ABIC was shown in Yang (1998) and Yang, Muthén, and Yang (1999) to perform better in finite mixture model selections for small sample size problems than the original BIC. Indices of ABIC indicated that a model with four latent classes best fitted the dataset. A four latent classes MLGC model was thus pursued. We plotted the estimated results in Figure 3. Estimations were conducted by using the MPLUS computer software (Muthén, & Muthén, 1998) that employed a modified E-M algorithm (Dempster, Laird, & Rubin, 1977) to do the parameter estimations. Linear trends were obtained by using the estimated means of latent intercepts and slopes. Class proportions for the four different growth trajectories were listed in the legend box. The four class proportions were 6.58, 2.50, 17.08, and 73.85 percents for Class 1, Class 2, Class 3, and Class 4, respectively.

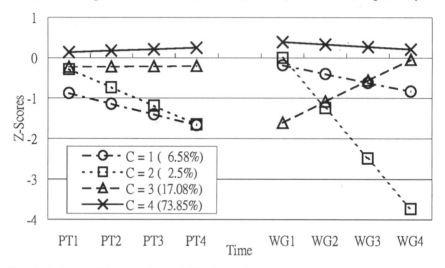

Fig. 3. Estimated Latent Growth Trajectories

We found, interestingly, that subjects in Class 4 who maintained at a high level of scores (marked by X ticks) for both phonemic awareness and word recognitions across time consisted about 73.85 percents of the whole sample. Class 3 subjects (marked by triangle ticks) whose word recognition scores, although, were with a low starting status eventually caught up with most other subjects at the time point 3 and consisted about 17 percents (17.08 %) of the samples. The two classes (Class 3 and Class 4) subjects who acquired early or developed appropriate phonemic awareness and word recognition skills should be subjects with the normal Chinese reading developments. These two classes were the majority groups that could occupy 90.93 percents of the samples.

In particular, Class 3 subjects had stayed close to the normal class of phonemic awareness developments but not for the word recognitions. This was an interesting phenomenon that was seldom seen in the reading developments of alphabetic language such as English. Subjects of this class had no troubles when they developed the phonemic awareness skills; however, they had to catch up with others' word recognition skills at a later time. The class of subjects demonstrated the different development trajectories between phonemic awareness and word recognitions. In other words, using phonemic awareness trajectories as antecedents could not effectively predict the consequences of word recognition developments in this class.

The rest two classes were interesting and worth discussions. Class 1 (marked by circle ticks) and Class 2 (marked by square ticks) subjects seemed to have troubles for developing good phonemic awareness skills and eventually deviated from the normal developments. Similarly, their word recognition scores had the going-down growth trajectory. Class 1 and Class 2 subjects might have to be placed into a risk group of reading difficulties or disabilities. The phenomena showed that phonemic awareness and word recognitions had consistent developments for these classes. That is, word recognition developments can be predictable by using phonemic awareness developing trajectories of the two classes.

To summarize, Class 4 is a normal class that has early acquired both phonemic awareness and word recognition skills. Class 1 and Class 2 are risky groups of reading difficulties or disabilities. Class 3 has a slow beginning of word recognitions but can eventually acquire the skills at a later time in the longitudinal study.

4 Conclusion

A possible paradigm of early Chinese reading development was presented by using mixture latent growth curve model in this paper. The sequential relations of Chinese reading abilities were thus examined and revealed. We also demonstrated the values of mixture latent growth model for outlining Chinese reading cognitive development subgroups. Further studies are under their ways to have more time points so that they can contribute more links between early Chinese reading abilities and its later developments such as phrase, sentence, and short story comprehensions.

References

Baer, J., & Schmitz, M.F. (2000). Latent growth curve modeling with a cohort sequential design. Social Work Research, 24, 243-248.

Barnes, G.M., Reifman, A.S., Farrell, M.P., & Dintcheff, B.A. (2000). The effects of parenting on the development of adolescent alcohol misuse: a six-wave latent growth model, Journal of Marriage and the Family, 62, 175-186.

Boscardin, K., & Muthén, B.O. (2000). Multi-Stage Analysis of Sequential Developmental Processes to Study Reading Progress: New Methodological Developments Using General Growth Mixture Modeling. Paper presented at the Annual American Educational Research Association, New Orleans, Louisiana, April 18 - 24, 2000.

Dempster, A.P., Laird, N.M., & Rubin, D.B. (1977). Maximum likelihood from incomplete data via the E-M algorithm (with discussion). Journal of the Royal Statistical Society, Ser. B., 39, 1-38.

Francis, D.J., Shaywitz, S.E., Stuebing, K.K., Shaywitz, B.A., & Fletcher, J.M. (1996). Developmental lag versus deficit models of reading disability: a longitudinal, individual growth curves analysis. Journal of Educational Psychology, 88, 3-17.

Huang, S.I., Yang, C.C., & Chang, C.C. (2001). Consequences of Teaching Language and Student Linguistic Awareness Abilities (in Chinese). Journal of National Taichung Teachers College, 15, 207-217.

Juel, C., Griffith, P.L., & Grougy, P.B. (1986). Acquisition of literacy: A longitudinal study of children in first and second grade. Journal of Educational Psychology, 78, 243-255.

MacDonald, G.W., & Cornwall, A. (1995). The relationship between phonological awareness and reading and spelling achievement eleven years later. Journal of Learning Disabilities, 28, 523-527.

Mason, W.A. (2001). Self-esteem and delinquency revisited (again): a test of Kaplan's self-derogation theory of delinquency using latent growth curve modeling. Journal of Youth and Adolescence, 30, 83-102.

Muthén, B.O. (2002). Beyond SEM: General latent variable modeling. Forthcoming in Behaviormetrika.

Muthén, B.O., Brown, C.H., Masyn, K., Jo, B., Khoo, S.T., Yang, C.C., Wang, C.P., Kellam, S., Carlin, J., & Liao, J. (2002). General growth mixture modeling for randomized preventive interventions. Forthcoming in Biostatistics.

Muthén, B.O., Khoo, S.T., Francis, D., & Boscardin, K. (1998). Analysis of reading skills development from kindergarten through first grade: an application of growth mixture modeling to sequential process, Technical report, CRESST, UCLA.

Muthén, L.K., & Muthén, B.O. (1998). Mplus user's guide, CA: Muthén. & Muthén CO.

Scheier, L.M., Botvin, G.J., Griffin, K.W., & Diaz, T. (1999). Latent growth models of drugs refusal skills and adolescent alcohol use. Journal of Alcohol and Drug Education, 44, 21-48.

Schwarz, G. (1978). Estimating the dimension of a model. The Annals of Statistics, 6, 461-464.

Sclove, L.S. (1987). Application of model-selection criteria to some problems in multivariate analysis. Psychometrika, 52, 333-343.

Wagner, R., Torgesen, J., & Rashotte, C. (1994). Development of reading-related phonological processing abilities: New evidence of bidirectional causality from a latent variable, longitudinal study, Developmental Psychology, 30, 73-87.

Yang, C.C. (1998). Finite mixture model selection with psychometrics applications. Unpublished PhD dissertation, University of California, Los Angeles, Los Angeles, CA.

Yang, C.C, & Chang, C.C. (2000). Multidimensional assessment and correlation of fundamental linguistic abilities (in Chinese). Journal of National Taichung Teachers College, 14, 81-96.

Yang, C.C., Muthén, B.O., & Yang, C.C. (1999). Finite mixture multivariate generalized linear models using Gibbs sampling and E-M algorithm, Proceedings of the National Science Council Part A: Physical Science and Engineering, 23, 695-702.

Some Cautionary Notes on Factor Loadings Estimated by Principal Component Analysis

Manabu Sato[1] and Masaaki Ito[2]

[1] Center for Foundational Arts and Sciences, Hiroshima Prefectural College of Health Sciences, 1-1, Gakuen-machi, Mihara, Hiroshima, 723-0053 JAPAN; *sato@hpc.ac.jp*

[2] Information Engineering, Graduate School of Engineering, Hiroshima University, 1-4-1, Kagamiyama, Higashi-Hiroshima, 739-8527 JAPAN; *ito@amath.hiroshima-u.ac.jp*

Summary. Factor loadings are often calculated by principal component analysis. Then, the loadings calculated with *some eigenvalues in descending order* are interpreted. In the present paper, we show that this procedure is not always an appropriate method; some such numerical examples and corresponding analytical results are presented for some six-variable two-component model.

Key words. factor analysis, factor loadings, component loadings, principal component analysis, eigenvalue

1 Introduction

Principal component analysis (PCA) is a branch of multivariate statistical analysis which is concerned with internal relationship of a set of variables. It is well known that PCA and factor analysis (FA) resemble each other but have slightly different aims (see e.g. Chap. 7 of Jolliffe(1986) and Chap. 14 of Anderson(1984)). However, PCA is very often used for the same purpose as FA. In fact, when PCA is applied, researchers calculate not only principal components but correlations between principal components and original variables (see e.g. Section 4.3.7 of Chatfield and Collins (1980)). Using the correlations, it is quite common to try to find out a latent structure. In this way, PCA is often used as a substitute for FA. Some properties between PCA and FA are investigated (see e.g. Schneeweiss, H. and Mathes, H. (1995)).

When we calculate factor loadings by PCA, we decompose a sample correlation matrix R as

$$R = Q\Theta Q' = (Q\Theta^{1/2})(Q\Theta^{1/2})' = \tilde{\Lambda}\tilde{\Lambda}' + E,$$

where Θ is a diagonal matrix with the ith largest eigenvalue of R as the ith diagonal element, Q is an orthogonal matrix such that $Q'RQ = \Theta$, $\tilde{\Lambda}$

is *the first some columns of* $Q\Theta^{1/2}$ and $E = R - \tilde{\Lambda}\tilde{\Lambda}'$ is a residual matrix. The matrix $\tilde{\Lambda}$ is named a component loading matrix (see e.g. Section 4.3.7 of Chatfield and Collins (1980)).

Researchers in many fields often adopt $\tilde{\Lambda}$, that is, component loadings calculated with *some eigenvalues in descending order*, and try to interpret their physical meanings. However, this method is not always appropriate. In the present study, we give such examples together with some analytical results.

Now we will explain an approach, the framework, and assumptions of the present problem.

(i) For population

We restrict our discussion to population cases. Because, it is very difficult to express explicitly the loadings estimated by FA for samples. If the procedure is not justified for population, we can hardly expect it to work well for samples.

(ii) For a correlation matrix

Since a correlation matrix is commonly applied instead of a variance-covariance matrix in view of the property of scale invariance, we discuss a correlation matrix.

(iii) Following an FA model

We suppose that a p-dimensional observable vector x follows an FA model

$$x = \mu + \Lambda f + u.$$

Here μ is a mean vector, Λ is a $p \times k$ $(p > k)$ population factor loading matrix of rank k, f is a common factor vector and u is an error term (see, e.g. p.6 of Lawley and Maxwell(1971)). The population variance-covariance matrix Σ of x can be written as $\Sigma = \Lambda\Lambda' + \Psi$ under the conditions that $E\{f\} = 0$, $E\{u\} = 0$, $E\{fu'\} = O$, $E\{uu'\} = \Psi$ (a diagonal matrix with unique variances as diagonal elements). Putting $D = \operatorname{diag}\Sigma$, and resetting $D^{-1/2}\Lambda \mapsto \Lambda$, $D^{-1/2}\Psi D^{-1/2} \mapsto \Psi$, we can express the population correlation matrix P as $P = \Lambda\Lambda' + \Psi$. This assumption will be natural, because when researchers want to interpret the physical meanings of $\tilde{\Lambda}$, it is assumed implicitly that an FA model holds approximately.

(iv) Uniqueness of the loading matrix

We assume that Λ satisfies the sufficient condition for uniqueness due to Anderson and Rubin(1956; Theorem 5.1). Then, we can determine a loading matrix to the true Λ uniquely up to multiplication on the right by an orthogonal matrix from P (Ihara and Kano(1986)). Therefore, our concern can be reduced to comparing $\tilde{\Lambda}$ with the true Λ.

(v) Range of the parameters

We give parameters Λ such that $\operatorname{diag}(I - \Lambda\Lambda')$ is positive definite, and set parameter $\Psi = \operatorname{diag}(I - \Lambda\Lambda')$ where I is the unit matrix.

In Section 2, some numerical examples of inappropriate cases are shown. In Section 3, analytical results corresponding to these examples are described for some six-variable two-component model.

2 Numerical Examples

To adopt component loadings in descending order of eigenvalues is not always an appropriate method. We give some such examples; the treated loading matrix is an extension of Table 6.1 in Sato(1992).

Example
    Set

$$\Lambda = (\lambda_1, \lambda_2) = \begin{pmatrix} x & 0 \\ x & 0 \\ .75 & .15 \\ .75 & .15 \\ .75 & -.15 \\ .75 & -.15 \end{pmatrix} \text{ and calculate } \tilde{\Lambda}.$$

Case 1: The second column of $\tilde{\Lambda}$ reflects λ_2.
    For example, when $x = .72$,

$$\tilde{\Lambda} = \begin{pmatrix} .777 & \mathbf{.0} & .491 & .394 \\ .777 & \mathbf{.0} & -.491 & .394 \\ .793 & \mathbf{.355} & .0 & -.193 \\ .793 & \mathbf{.355} & .0 & -.193 \\ .793 & \mathbf{-.355} & .0 & -.193 \\ .793 & \mathbf{-.355} & .0 & -.193 \end{pmatrix}.$$

Eigenvalues: 3.723   .505   .482   .460

Case 2: The third column of $\tilde{\Lambda}$ reflects λ_2.
    For example, when $x = .69$,

$$\tilde{\Lambda} = \begin{pmatrix} .754 & .512 & \mathbf{.0} & .411 \\ .754 & -.512 & \mathbf{.0} & .411 \\ .792 & .0 & \mathbf{.355} & -.196 \\ .792 & .0 & \mathbf{.355} & -.196 \\ .792 & .0 & \mathbf{-.355} & -.196 \\ .792 & .0 & \mathbf{-.355} & -.196 \end{pmatrix}.$$

Eigenvalues: 3.650   .524   .505   .491

Case 3: The fourth column of $\tilde{\Lambda}$ reflects λ_2.
    For example, when $x = .66$,

$$\tilde{\Lambda} = \begin{pmatrix} .732 & .531 & .427 & \mathbf{.0} \\ .732 & -.531 & .427 & \mathbf{.0} \\ .792 & .0 & -.197 & \mathbf{.355} \\ .792 & .0 & -.197 & \mathbf{.355} \\ .792 & .0 & -.197 & \mathbf{-.355} \\ .792 & .0 & -.197 & \mathbf{-.355} \end{pmatrix}.$$

Eigenvalues: 3.579   .564   .521   .505

When we adopt the first some columns of $\tilde{\Lambda}$ for Cases 2 and 3 and try to give physical meanings to the component loadings, we are misled. Further, even if x varies slightly, the order of the column reflecting λ_2 changes.

When we compare $\tilde{\Lambda}$ with Λ, indeterminacy of the rotation of $\tilde{\Lambda}$ need not be considered, because λ_1 and λ_2 are orthogonal.

3 Analytical Results

We analyze a six-variable two-component factor loading matrix as follows:

$$\Lambda = (\lambda_1, \lambda_2) = \begin{pmatrix} x & 0 \\ x & 0 \\ b & a \\ b & a \\ b & -a \\ b & -a \end{pmatrix}.$$

Here, from (iv) and (v) in Section 1, we assume that $0 < x < 1$, $b \neq 0$, $a > 0$ and $a^2 + b^2 < 1$. This is a generalized form of the matrix presented in Section 2.

The following lemma expresses the eigenvalues and their corresponding eigenvectors analytically.

Lemma 1. *The eigenvalues* $\varphi_1, \ldots, \varphi_6$ *of the correlation matrix*

$$P = \Lambda\Lambda' + diag(I - \Lambda\Lambda')$$

$$= \begin{pmatrix} 1 & x^2 & bx & bx & bx & bx \\ x^2 & 1 & bx & bx & bx & bx \\ bx & bx & 1 & b^2 + a^2 & b^2 - a^2 & b^2 - a^2 \\ bx & bx & b^2 + a^2 & 1 & b^2 - a^2 & b^2 - a^2 \\ bx & bx & b^2 - a^2 & b^2 - a^2 & 1 & b^2 + a^2 \\ bx & bx & b^2 - a^2 & b^2 - a^2 & b^2 + a^2 & 1 \end{pmatrix}$$

are as follows:

$\varphi_1 = 1 + (-a^2 + 3b^2 + x^2 + \sqrt{(-a^2 + 3b^2 + x^2)^2 + 4x^2(a^2 + 5b^2)})/2 > 1,$

$\varphi_2 = 1 + 3a^2 - b^2,$

$\varphi_3 = 1 - x^2 < 1,$

$\varphi_4 = 1 + (-a^2 + 3b^2 + x^2 - \sqrt{(-a^2 + 3b^2 + x^2)^2 + 4x^2(a^2 + 5b^2)})/2 < 1,$

$\varphi_5 = \varphi_6 = 1 - a^2 - b^2 < 1.$

Further, when $\varphi_1, \ldots, \varphi_4$ *are not multiple roots, the corresponding eigenvectors* $\gamma_1, \ldots, \gamma_6$ *whose lengths are not 1 are as follows:*

$$(\gamma_1 \ \gamma_2 \ \gamma_3 \ \gamma_4 \ \gamma_5 \ \gamma_6) = \begin{pmatrix} s & 0 & 1 & t & 0 & 0 \\ s & 0 & -1 & t & 0 & 0 \\ 1 & 1 & 0 & -1 & 0 & -1 \\ 1 & 1 & 0 & -1 & 0 & 1 \\ 1 & -1 & 0 & -1 & -1 & 0 \\ 1 & -1 & 0 & -1 & 1 & 0 \end{pmatrix},$$

where

$$s = \frac{x\left(a^2 + 5b^2 + x^2 + \sqrt{a^4 + 9b^4 + 26b^2 x^2 + x^4 + a^2(-6b^2 + 2x^2)}\right)}{b\left((-a^2 + 3b^2 + 3x^2 + \sqrt{a^4 + 9b^4 + 26b^2 x^2 + x^4 + a^2(-6b^2 + 2x^2)}\right)}$$

and $t = 2/s$. $\square$

The proof of this lemma is simple and will be omitted.

Note that the necessary and sufficient condition that both the denominators of s and t are never zeros is i) $b \neq 0$, ii) $x \neq 0$ and iii) $x^2 \neq a^2 + b^2$. On the other hand, if and only if $\varphi_4 \neq \varphi_5 = \varphi_6$ holds, $x^2 \neq a^2 + b^2$ is satisfied under the condition of $b \neq 0$. Therefore, i), ii) and iii) are assured by the assumptions of this lemma.

From this lemma, we see the eigenvector which affects λ_2 is γ_2. For the order of the magnitude of the corresponding eigenvalue φ_2, we have obtained the following theorem.

Theorem 1. *The order of φ_2 is determined by the following conditions.*
(1) When $|b| \leq \sqrt{3}a$, φ_2 is the first or the second eigenvalue.
(2) When $|b| > \sqrt{3}a$,
  (2-1) if $b^2 - 3a^2 < x^2$, then φ_2 is the second eigenvalue.
  (2-2) if $\dfrac{(a^2 - b^2)(3a^2 - b^2)}{a^2 + b^2} \leq x^2 \leq b^2 - 3a^2$, φ_2 is the third eigenvalue.
  (2-3) if $x^2 \leq \dfrac{(a^2 - b^2)(3a^2 - b^2)}{a^2 + b^2}$, φ_2 is the fourth eigenvalue.
(3) φ_2 is never the fifth or the sixth eigenvalue. $\square$

The proof of this theorem is simple and will be omitted.

Applying this theorem, we can examine the example shown in Section 2. Putting $a = .15$ and $b = .75$, we obtain the following results.
Case 1 occurs if $x > \sqrt{99/200} \approx .704$.
Case 2 occurs if $.675 \approx \sqrt{297/650} \leq x \leq \sqrt{99/200} \approx .704$.
Case 3 occurs if $x \leq \sqrt{297/650} \approx .675$.

4 Acknowledgements

The authors would like to thank the editors and anonymous referees for their helpful comments and suggestions. This research was partially supported by Japan Society for the Promotion of Science, Grant-in-Aid for Scientific Research under contract number (B) 11440048.

References

Anderson, T. W. (1984) An Introduction to Multivariate Statistical Analysis. 2nd ed. John Wiley & Sons, New York.

Anderson, T. W. and Rubin H. (1956) Statistical inference in factor analysis. In: Neyman, J. (ed.) Proceedings of the Third Berkeley Symposium on Mathematical Statistics and Probability, 5, 111–150, University of California, Berkeley and Los Angeles.

Chatfield, C. and Collins, A. J. (1980) Introduction to Multivariate Analysis. Chapman and Hall, London.

Ihara, M. and Kano, Y. (1986) A new estimator of the uniqueness in factor analysis. Psychometrika, 51, 563–566.

Jolliffe, I. T. (1986) Principal Component Analysis. Springer-Verlag, New York.

Lawley, D. N. and Maxwell, A. E. (1971) Factor Analysis as a Statistical Method. 2nd ed. Butterworth, London.

Sato, M. (1992) A study of an identification problem and substitute use of principal component analysis in factor analysis. Hiroshima Mathematical Journal, 22, 479–524.

Schneeweiss, H. and Mathes, H. (1995) Factor analysis and principal components. Journal of Multivariate Analysis, 55, 105–124.

Simultaneous Mean and Covariance Structure Analysis for Two Level Structural Equation Models on EQS

Peter M. Bentler[1] and Jiajuan Liang[2]

[1] University of California, Los Angeles, Department of Psychology,
   Box 951563, Los Angeles, CA 90095-1563, U.S.A.
   bentler@ucla.edu
[2] University of New Haven, School of Business,
   300 Orange Avenue, West Haven, CT 06516, U.S.A.
   jliang@newhaven.edu

Summary. This paper summarizes an internal EM type algorithm implemented in EQS software for two-level structural equation models with simultaneous mean and covariance structures. A practical example illustrates the model set for an EQS run, and gives an explanation of EQS output.

Keywords. EM algorithm, maximum likelihood, mean and covariance structure, two-level structural equation model

1 Introduction

Two-level structural equation models (SEM) have been used for analysis of data resulting from a hierarchical sampling scheme which involves latent (unobservable) variables. Typical examples include survey data from students' achievements for different courses with students nested in different schools. Various formulations of two-level SEM associated with algorithms have been proposed by a number of authors (McDonald & Goldstein 1989; Lee 1990; Muthén 1994; Raudenbush 1995; Lee & Poon 1998; Bentler & Liang 2003). By studying these existing formulations, we can arrange a general two-level SEM in the following new formulation:

$$\begin{pmatrix} z_g \\ y_{gi} \end{pmatrix} = \begin{pmatrix} z_g \\ v_g \end{pmatrix} + \begin{pmatrix} \mathbf{0} \\ v_{gi} \end{pmatrix}, \tag{1}$$

where y_{gi} ($p \times 1$) stands for an observation vector from the i-th individual (level-1 unit) nested in the g-th cluster (group or level-2 unit), e.g., the i-th student nested in the g-th school. z_g ($q \times 1$) stands for a group-level (level-2) observation, v_{gi} is a latent random variable capturing individual effects, and v_g is a latent random variable capturing cluster effects. The zero vector in Eq. (1) specifies that the group-level observation z_g has no variation among individuals nested in the same cluster. The model in Eq. (1) covers a wide range of two-level SEM including those models in the above-mentioned references.

Among the methodologies for analysis of linear two-level SEM, the maximum likelihood (ML) approach with a multivariate normality assumption plays an important role. For example, under this assumption, McDonald and Goldstein (1989) obtained the closed forms for some derivatives of the ML function and suggested using a quasi-Newton algorithm to obtain the maximum likelihood estimates (MLE) of model parameters; Muthén (1994) summarized the approximate approach called MUML; and Lee and Poon (1998) proposed an EM algorithm for full ML analysis of two-level SEM without a mean structure. Bentler and Liang (2003) generalized Lee and Poon's (1998) model and algorithm to the case of both mean and covariance structures with only one within covariance matrix. This paper generalizes the model in Bentler and Liang (2003) to the model in Eq. (1) with group-level observations $\{z_g : g = 1, \ldots, G\}$. In this paper, an ML analysis for two-level SEM is to fit Eq. (1) with the following mean and covariance structures:

$$\boldsymbol{\mu}_z(\boldsymbol{\theta}) = E(\boldsymbol{z}_g), \quad \boldsymbol{\mu}_y(\boldsymbol{\theta}) = E(\boldsymbol{y}_{gi}), \quad \boldsymbol{\Sigma}_B(\boldsymbol{\theta}) = \mathrm{cov}(\boldsymbol{v}_g),$$
$$\boldsymbol{\Sigma}_{gW}(\boldsymbol{\theta}) = \mathrm{cov}(\boldsymbol{v}_{gi}), \quad \boldsymbol{\Sigma}_{zz}(\boldsymbol{\theta}) = \mathrm{cov}(\boldsymbol{z}_g), \quad \boldsymbol{\Sigma}_{zy}(\boldsymbol{\theta}) = \mathrm{cov}(\boldsymbol{z}_g, \boldsymbol{v}_g), \tag{2}$$

where $\boldsymbol{\theta}$ $(r \times 1)$ is the parameter vector composed of all model parameters. In the structured (nontrivial or interesting) case, $r < R$ with R being the total number of means, variances and covariances in the saturated case of Eq. (1). That is,

$$R = p + q + Gp(p+1)/2 + (p+q)(p+q+1)/2. \tag{3}$$

The mean and covariance structure in Eq. (2) implies that the parameter vector uniquely determines the mean vector and the variance-covariance matrices in Eq. (1). The task for fitting Eq. (1) is to estimate $\boldsymbol{\theta}$ and to test the structured case in Eq. (2) with $r < R$ against the saturated case $r = R$. If the p-value of such a test is large enough (e.g., larger than 5%), Eq. (1) is said to fit the available data $\{\boldsymbol{y}_{gi}, \boldsymbol{z}_g\}$ well. In Section 2 we will summarize our approach for developing the EM algorithm. A practical example is illustrated in section 3 using the EQS software (Bentler 2002). Aspects of some technical derivations are outlined in Appendix A.

2 The EM Algorithm in EQS

Let $\{\boldsymbol{y}_{gi} : p \times 1, i = 1, \ldots, N_g; \boldsymbol{z}_g : q \times 1, g = 1, \ldots, G\}$ be available observations from the model in Eq. (1), where $\boldsymbol{y}_{gi}$ stands for a response vector from individual i nested in cluster g, $\boldsymbol{z}_g$ stands for a group-level observation vector from group (cluster) g. The following assumptions are imposed on Eq. (1):

A1) the individual-level latent random vectors $\{v_{gi} :\ i = 1, \ldots, N_g\}$ are i.i.d. for each fixed g and $v_{gi} \sim N_p(\mathbf{0}, \Sigma_{gW})$ for $g = 1, \ldots, G$. Σ_{gW} is positive definite and Σ_{gW} could be different from one another;

A2) the group-level latent random vectors $\{v_g :\ g = 1, \ldots, G\}$ are i.i.d. and $v_g \sim N_p(\mu_y, \Sigma_B)$ with a positive definite matrix Σ_B;

A3) $\{z_g :\ g = 1, \ldots, G\}$ are i.i.d. group-level observations and $z_g \sim N_q(\mu_z, \Sigma_{zz})$ with a positive definite matrix Σ_{zz};

A4) the random vector $(z_g', v_g')'$ $[(p + q) \times 1]$ has a joint nonsingular multivariate normal distribution and $\mathrm{cov}(z_g, v_g) = \Sigma_{zy}$;

A5) $\{z_g,\ v_g\}$ is assumed to be uncorrelated with $\{v_{gi} :\ i = 1, \ldots, N_g\}$ for each fixed g.

Let

$$
y_g = \begin{pmatrix} y_{g1} \\ \vdots \\ y_{gN_g} \end{pmatrix}, \quad u_g = \begin{pmatrix} z_g \\ y_g \end{pmatrix}, \quad x_g = \begin{pmatrix} v_g \\ u_g \end{pmatrix}, \quad X = \begin{pmatrix} x_1' \\ \vdots \\ x_G' \end{pmatrix}, \quad (4)
$$

$$
Y_{g0} = \begin{pmatrix} y_{g1}' \\ \vdots \\ y_{gN_g}' \end{pmatrix}, \quad Y = \begin{pmatrix} Y_{10} \\ \vdots \\ Y_{G0} \end{pmatrix}, \quad Z = \begin{pmatrix} z_1' \\ \vdots \\ z_G' \end{pmatrix}, \quad \bar{y}_g = \frac{1}{N_g} \sum_{i=1}^{N_g} y_{gi},
$$
$$(5)$$

and

$$
\bar{y} = \frac{1}{N} \sum_{g=1}^{G} \sum_{i=1}^{N_g} y_{gi}, \qquad \bar{z} = \frac{1}{G} \sum_{g=1}^{G} z_g, \qquad N = \sum_{g=1}^{G} N_g. \tag{6}
$$

Then x_g in Eq. (4) can be considered as a complete response vector with a missing value v_g $(p \times 1)$ and X in Eq. (4) is a matrix composed of all complete observations. Let $l(X, \theta^*)$ be the negative of twice the log-ML function computed from X with parameter vector θ arbitrarily specified at $\theta = \theta^*$. According to the principle of the EM algorithm (Dempster et al. 1977), the E-step function for computing the MLE of θ is given by the following conditional expectation

$$
M(\theta^* | \theta) = E\{l(X, \theta^*) | Z, Y, \theta\}, \tag{7}
$$

where both θ and θ^* are two arbitrarily specified values of the same model parameter vector θ. Under assumptions A1)-A5), the E-step function in Eq. (7) can be simplified as

$$
M(\theta^* | \theta) = \sum_{k=1}^{G+1} N_k \Big\{ \log |\Sigma_k(\theta^*)| + \mathrm{tr}[\Sigma_k^{-1}(\theta^*) S_k(\theta)] \Big\}, \tag{8}
$$

where

$$\Sigma_k(\theta^*) = \Sigma_{gW}(\theta^*), \quad N_k = N_g, \quad k = g = 1, \ldots, G;$$

$$\Sigma_{G+1}(\theta^*) = \widetilde{\Sigma}(\theta^*), \quad N_{G+1} = G, \tag{9}$$

$$S_k(\theta) = S_{gW}(\theta), \; k = g = 1, \ldots, G; \; S_{G+1}(\theta) = \widetilde{S}(\theta),$$

$$\widetilde{\Sigma}(\theta^*) = \begin{pmatrix} \widetilde{\Sigma}_B^* + \mu^* \mu^{*\prime} & \mu^* \\ \mu^{*\prime} & 1 \end{pmatrix}, \quad \widetilde{S}(\theta) = \begin{pmatrix} \widetilde{S}_B + dd' & d \\ d' & 1 \end{pmatrix},$$

$$d = \begin{pmatrix} \bar{z} \\ \bar{a} \end{pmatrix}, \quad \widetilde{S}_B = \begin{pmatrix} S_{zz} - \bar{z}\bar{z}' & A \\ A' & S_B - \bar{a}\bar{a}' \end{pmatrix}, \quad \widetilde{\Sigma}_B^* = \widetilde{\Sigma}_B(\theta^*), \tag{10}$$

and

$$\mu^* = \begin{pmatrix} \mu_z(\theta^*) \\ \mu_y(\theta^*) \end{pmatrix}, \quad \widetilde{\Sigma}_B^* = \begin{pmatrix} \Sigma_{zz} & \Sigma_{zy} \\ \Sigma_{yz} & \Sigma_B \end{pmatrix}\Big|_{\theta=\theta^*}, \quad \Sigma_{yz} = \Sigma_{zy}'. \tag{11}$$

The matrices $S_{gW}(\theta)$ and the terms in $\widetilde{S}(\theta)$ in Eqs. (9, 10) are given in Appendix A.

After we obtain the simple E-step function in Eq. (8), the M-step for computing the MLE of θ is to minimize Eq. (8) with respect to θ^* for each given θ iteratively until some convergence criterion has reached. Note that in Eq. (8), for each fixed θ, $M(\theta^*|\theta)$ has exactly the same form as that of the ML function from a multiple group covariance structure model and $\Sigma_k(\theta^*)$ acts as the covariance matrix from group k ($k = 1, \ldots, G+1$). The Gauss-Newton algorithm is used in EQS to optimize the multiple group ML function. Therefore, the E-step function in Eq. (8) can be minimized iteratively by calling the existing multiple group option in EQS at each iteration until the *Root Mean Square Error* (RMSE) is small enough (e.g., less than 10^{-6}). EQS can provide the default start value for θ in optimizing Eq. (8). Users can also specify their own initial value for θ in case of slow or no convergence in the iteration when analyzing two-level SEM on EQS.

By using the E-step function in Eq. (8) and calling the multiple group option in EQS, we can obtain the MLE $(\hat{\theta})$ for the structured model [$r < R$ in Eqs. (2, 3)] and the MLE $(\hat{\theta}_s)$ for the saturated model [$r = R$ in Eqs. (2, 3)] as well. The standard deviation for each component of the MLE $(\hat{\theta})$ is obtained from the asymptotic behavior of $\hat{\theta}$ in large sample case. Liang and Bentler (manuscript) proposed a fast EM gradient algorithm for the case of only one within covariance matrix and obtained the asymptotic distribution of $\hat{\theta}$, computation of the standard errors, and model chi-square.

3 An Example

A practical two-level data set is available from the National Education Longitudinal Study (NELS: 88) and the full data set (school.dat) can be downloaded from the M*plus* (Muthén & Muthén 1998) website. The data set contains measurements of some variables for schools and for 5,198 students nested in 235 schools. There are 21 columns in the data set. Here we want to study how the students' mathematical ability and their general science ability are affected by some background within and between factors. Mathematical ability was measured by four math-tests (denoted by m1-m4) and general science ability was measured by four science-tests (denoted by s1-s4). The students' scores for tests m1-m4 were collected in columns 7-10 and their scores for tests s1-s4 were collected in columns 11-14 in the data set school.dat. Two school-level (level-2) variables (denoted by Z1 and Z2) were measured and their response data were collected in columns 20-21 in the same data set. It is assumed that the test scores for m1-m4 and s1-s4 are influenced by three within (level-1) factors: a1) math-ability factor (F1); b1) science ability factor (F2); and c1) general writing ability factor (F3), and two between (level-2) factors: a2) general background factor (F1); and b2) math-background factor (F2). The two between factors are also assumed to be influenced by two between-level observable variables: minority (Z1) and school type (Z2: public and catholic schools). The within factors (F1,F3), and (F2,F3) are assumed to be correlated while F1 and F2 are assumed to be uncorrelated. The two level-2 variables Z1 and Z2 are also correlated. The EQS model for the simultaneous mean and covariance structure analysis is given in Appendix B, where the within model is given first and the between model follows. The model contains some constraints added after preliminary runs.

In this model, all within (a total of 235 schools or clusters) covariance matrices are equal, that is, $\Sigma_{gW} \equiv \Sigma_W$ in Eq. (1). A mean structure (expressed by regression on the constant unit variable V999 in EQS) is imposed on some observed variables and some latent variables (the two between factors) in the between model. Since no mean structure is assumed in the within model for v_{gi} in Eq. (1), the V999 variable can only be put in a between model when using EQS for two-level SEM analysis. As usual, some parameters of factor loadings have to be fixed (usually fixed as 1) for model identification.

The EQS output provides an optimal parameter estimate for each free parameter in the model. Here we present only the corresponding standardized solution in which all variables have been standardized to unit variance.

A) standardized solution for the within model

$$
\begin{aligned}
m1 &= V7 = .374F1 + .901F3 + .561E1, \\
m2 &= V8 = .391 * F1 + .950 * F3 + .488E2, \\
m3 &= V9 = .312 * F1 + .493 * F3 + .884E3, \\
m4 &= V10 = .224 * F1 + .544 * F3 + .866E4, \\
s1 &= V11 = .661F2 + .032 * F3 + .730E5, \\
s2 &= V12 = .382 * F1 + .463 * F2 + .160 * F3 + .747E6, \\
s3 &= V13 = .493 * F2 + .170 * F3 + .781E7, \\
s4 &= V14 = .295 * F2 + .102 * F3 + .928E8;
\end{aligned}
\tag{12}
$$

B) standardized solution for the between model

$$
\begin{aligned}
m1 &= V7 = .913F1 + .292F2 + .244E1, \\
m2 &= V8 = .916 * F1 + .350 * F2 + .112E2, \\
m3 &= V9 = .817 * F1 + .200 * F2 + .000 * V999 + .525E3, \\
m4 &= V10 = .929 * F1 + .132 * F2 + .332E4, \\
s1 &= V11 = .961 * F1 + .276E5, \\
s2 &= V12 = .914 * F1 + .114 * F2 + .377E6, \\
s3 &= V13 = .974 * F1 + .228E7, \\
s4 &= V14 = .932 * F1 + .364E8, \\
Z1 &= V20 = 1.000E20, \\
Z2 &= V21 = 1.000E21, \\
F1 &= F1 = -.700 * V20 + .015 * V21 + .708D1, \\
F2 &= F2 = -.216 * V20 - .117 * V21 + .981D2.
\end{aligned}
\tag{13}
$$

After running the program in Appendix B, the EQS output in Eqs. (12, 13) allows the following conclusions:

1) The p-value of the model chi-square is 0.26. This indicates the model in Appendix B with parameter constraints fits the data very well;

2) The standardized solution in Eq. (12) for the within model shows that the general writing ability factor (F3) has a very big influence on the four math-tests m1-m4 (the standardized coefficients are large) while it has a relatively small influence on the four science tests s1-s4 (the standardized coefficients are small). For example, the effect of F3 on the second math-test m2 is substantial (standardized beta of .950) while its effects on the four science test s1-s4 is almost negligible (from .032 to .170). The math-ability factor (F1) seems to have roughly the same moderate influence on its measured variables (m1-m4 and s2), that is, the standardized coefficients are about .3 and fairly equal in size. The influence of the science ability factor (F2) on its measured variables can be described similarly. Note that the fourth science test s4 cannot be predicted by factors F2 and F3 effectively since the residual random error (E8) already explains over 86% ($.928^2$) of the variance of s4;

3) The standardized solution in Eq. (13) for the between model shows that the general background factor (F1) explains most of the variance in its measured variables m1-m4 and s1-s4, e.g., F1 is responsible for about 95% ($.974^2$) of the variance of the third science test s3 and over 86% ($.929^2$) of the variance of the fourth math-test m4. The variance proportions explained by the math-background factor (F2) can be calculated similarly; they are much smaller than the corresponding variances explained by F1 from the standardized coefficients given in Eq. (13) (Note: variance explained is additive here, since F1, F2, and residual Es are uncorrelated). Thus at the between level, the eight tests (m1-m4 and s1-s4) are mainly influenced by the factor F1. The school-level variable Z1 (or V20, which is the minority status of schools) has a negative influence on both between factors F1 and F2. The other school-level variable Z2 (or V21, which is the school type variable, i.e., two types of schools, public=1, catholic=2) has trivial positive influence on F1 (the standardized coefficient is 0.015) and a very small negative influence on F2. The estimated measurement equation for F2 (not presented here) shows that both of the influences from Z1 and Z2 on F2 are insignificant (i.e., the two-sided t-test for the hypothesis that the coefficient is equal to zero is insignificant) at level 5%. This indicates that the math-background factor of schools is almost independent of the minority status and the types of schools;

4) The complete EQS output (not reproduced here) shows that the nonzero-correlated assumption for the pairs of factors (F1,F3), and (F2,F3) in the within model, and the nonzero-correlated assumption for the pairs of residuals (E20,E21) (i.e., the residuals for Z1 and Z2), and (E3,E21) (i.e., the residuals for m3 and Z2) in the between model are suitable because the t-test for the hypothesis that the covariance is equal to zero is significant at level 5%. Also, the correlation between D1 and D2 can be ignored. This implies that the two level-two factors F1 and F2 can be considered uncorrelated. In the between model, the mean structures on m3, s1, Z1, Z2, F1 and F2 are suitable because the individual t-tests (not shown here), evaluating the hypotheses that the various intercept and mean coefficients equal zero, are significant at level 5%.

Finally, we would like to point out a useful advantage of our model in Eqs. (1,2) and EM algorithm in EQS over alternative models and algorithms such as those used in the LISREL software (du Toit & du Toit 2001, 2002). The approach summarized here can handle both saturated and nonsaturated mean structures, while the model and Fisher scoring algorithm in the current version 8.52 of LISREL cannot handle a two-level SEM with a nonsaturated mean structure (Dr. Stephen du Toit, personal communication). A saturated mean structure implies that each of the observable variables in Eq. (1) (z_g and y_{gi}) has an individual mean parameter. A nonsaturated mean structure implies that the total number of mean parameters in Eqs. (1,2) is less than the number of observable variables. In contrast with M*plus*, EQS provides ML estimates for model parameters for both balanced and unbalanced sample designs in two-level SEM, while M*plus* provides so-called MUML estimates. These are not ML estimates with unbalanced sample designs, though MUML has performed well in practice (Hox & Maas 2001). The data set in our example has an unbalanced sample design: different schools have different number of students.

Acknowledgment. Supported by National Institute on Drug Abuse grants DA01070, DA00017, and a UNH 2002 Summer Faculty Fellowship.

References

Bentler PM (2002) EQS 6 Structural Equations Program Manual. Encino, CA: Multivariate Software. www.mvsoft.com

Bentler PM, Liang J (2003) Two-level mean and covariance structures: maximum likelihood via an EM algorithm. In: Reise S, Duan N (eds) Multilevel Modeling: Methodological Advances, Issues, and Applications, pp. 53–70. Lawrence Erlbaum Associates, Publishers. Mahwah, New Jersey

Dempster AP, Laird NM, Rubin DB (1977) Maximum likelihood from incomplete data via EM algorithm (with discussion). J Roy Statist Soc (Ser B) 39:1–38.

du Toit M, du Toit S (2001) Interactive LISREL: User's Guide. Scientific Software International, Inc.

du Toit S, du Toit M (2002) Multilevel structural equation modeling. In: de Leeuw J, Kreft I (Eds.) Handbook of Quantitative Multilevel Analysis (Chapter 13), Kluver Publications. (in press)

Hox JJ, Maas CJM (2001) The accuracy of multilevel structural equation modeling with pseudobalanced groups and small samples. Structural Equation Modeling 8:157–174.

Lee SY (1990) Multilevel analysis of structural equation models. Biometrika 77:763–772.

Lee SY, Poon WY (1998) Analysis of two-level structural equation models via EM type algorithms. Statistica Sinica 8:749–766.

McDonald RP, Goldstein H (1989) Balanced versus unbalanced designs for linear structural relations in two-level data. British J Math & Statist Psych 42:215–232.

Muthén BO (1994) Multilevel covariance structure analysis. Sociological Methods & Research 22:376–398.

Muthén LK, Muthén BO (1998) Mplus User's Guide. Los Angeles: Muthén & Muthén.

Raudenbush SW (1995) Maximum likelihood estimation for unbalanced multilevel covariance structure models via the EM algorithm. British J Math & Statist Psych 48:359–370.

Appendix A. Some Technical Derivations

Some related terms in the E-step function in Eq.(8): here we use the same notation as in Eqs. (4, 6). Let

$$U_{gW} = \frac{1}{N_g - 1}(Y_{g0}'Y_{g0} - N_g \bar{y}_g \bar{y}_g'), \quad \Sigma_g = \Sigma_{gW} + N_g \Sigma_B,$$
$$\Omega_g = \begin{pmatrix} \Sigma_{zz} & \Sigma_{zy} \\ \Sigma_{yz} & \frac{1}{N_g}\Sigma_g \end{pmatrix}, \quad b_g = \begin{pmatrix} z_g \\ \bar{y}_g \end{pmatrix}. \tag{a1}$$

By the assumptions A1)-A5) on Eq. (1), we have

$$a_g \overset{\text{def}}{=} E(v_g|z_g, y_g, \theta) = \mu_y + \Sigma_1\Omega_g^{-1}(b_g - \mu), \quad \Sigma_1 = (\Sigma_{yz}, \Sigma_B), \tag{a2}$$
$$C_g \overset{\text{def}}{=} \text{cov}(v_g|z_g, y_g, \theta) = \Sigma_B - \Sigma_1\Omega_g^{-1}\Sigma_1'.$$

Let

$$\bar{a} = \frac{1}{G}\sum_{g=1}^{G} a_g, \quad d_g = \Omega_g^{-1}(b_g - \mu), \quad \bar{d} = \frac{1}{G}\sum_{g=1}^{G} d_g,$$
$$\bar{D}_d = \frac{1}{G}\sum_{g=1}^{G} d_g d_g', \quad \bar{\Omega}^{-1} = \frac{1}{G}\sum_{g=1}^{G} \Omega_g^{-1}, \tag{a3}$$
$$A = \frac{1}{G}\sum_{g=1}^{G} z_g a_g' - \bar{z}\bar{a}', \quad S_{zz} = \frac{1}{G}Z'Z.$$

Then we have

$$a_g = \mu_y + \Sigma_1 d_g, \quad \bar{a} = \mu_y + \Sigma_1 \bar{d},$$

$$S_B = \Sigma_B + \Sigma_1(\bar{D}_d - \bar{\Omega}^{-1})\Sigma_1' + \mu_y(\Sigma_1\bar{d})' + [\mu_y(\Sigma_1\bar{d})']' + \mu_y\mu_y',$$

$$S_{gW} = U_{gW} + \Sigma_B - \Sigma_1\Omega_g^{-1}\Sigma_1' + (a_g - \bar{y}_g)(a_g - \bar{y}_g)'. \tag{a4}$$

Appendix B.   The EQS Input Program

```
/TITLE
Two-level analysis for the school data (WITHIN MODEL FIRST)
/SPECIFICATION
data='school.dat'; case =5198; variable=21; method=ml;
matrix=raw; GROUP=2; analysis=covariance; MULTILEVEL = ML; LEVEL = V19;
/LABELS
V7=m1; V8=m2; V9=m3; V10=m4; V11=s1; V12=s2; V13=s3;
V14=s4; V19=SCHOOL; V20=Z1; V21=Z2;
/EQUATIONS m1=1F1+1F3+E1;
m2=*F1+*F3+E2;
m3=*F1+*F3+E3;
m4=*F1+*F3+E4;
s1=1F2+*F3+E5;
s2=*F1+*F2+*F3+E6;
s3=*F2+*F3+E7;
s4=*F2+*F3+E8;
/VARIANCES
E1-E8=*; F1=*; F2=*; F3=*;
/COVARIANCES
F1,F2=0; F2,F3=0*; F1,F3=0*;
/CONSTRAINTS
(m2,F1)=(m3,F1)=(m4,F1)=(s2,F1);
(m2,F3)=(m4,F3);
(s2,F3)=(s3,F3)=(s4,F3);
(s2,F2)=(s3,F2)=(s4,F2);
/END

/TITLE
BETWEEN MODEL
/LABELS
V7=m1; V8=m2; V9=m3; V10=m4; V11=s1; V12=s2;
V13=s3; V14=s4; V19=SCHOOL; V20=Z1; V21=Z2;
/EQUATIONS
m1=1F1+1F2+E1;
m2=*F1+*F2+E2;
m3=*V999+*F1+*F2+E3;
m4=*F1+*F2+E4;
s1=*V999+*F1+E5; s2=*F1+*F2+E6;
s3=*F1+E7;
s4=*F1+E8;
F1=*V999+*Z1+*Z2+D1;
F2=*V999+*Z1+*Z2+D2;
Z1=*V999+E20;
Z2=*V999+E21;
/VARIANCES
E1-E8=0*; E20-E21=0*; D1-D2=*;
/COVARIANCES
D1,D2=0*; E3,E21=*0; E20,E21=0*;
/CONSTRAINTS
(s2,F1)=(s3,F1)=(s4,F1);
/tech
itr=200; con=.000001;
/END
```

On Analysis of Nonlinear Structural Equation Models

Sik Yum Lee[1] and Hong Tu Zhu[2]

[1] Department of Statistics, The Chinese University of Hong Kong, Shatin, Hong Kong
sylee@sparc2.sta.cuhk.edu.hk
[2] Medical School, Yale University, USA
htzhu@masal.med.yale.edu

Summary. The existing theory and its computer software in structural equation modeling are mainly established based on linear relationships among manifest variables and latent variables. However, models with nonlinear relationships are often encountered in social and behavioral sciences. In this article, an EM type algorithm is developed for maximum likelihood estimation of a general nonlinear structural equation model. To avoid computation of the complicated multiple integrals involved, the E-step is completed by a Metropolis-Hastings algorithm. The M-step can be completed efficiently by simple conditional maximization. Convergence is monitored by bridging sample and standard errors estimates are obtained via Louis's formula. The methodology is illustrated with a real example.

Key words. EM algorithm, Metropolis-Hastings algorithm, conditional maximization, bridge sampling.

1 Introduction

Structural equation modeling is a popular statistical method in behavioral and social sciences. The existing theory and computer software such as LIS-REL (Jöreskog and Sörbom, 1996) and EQS (Bentler, 1992) are developed based on models in which manifest variables and latent variables are related by linear functions. Recently, it is recognized that nonlinear relations among the variables are important in establishing more meaningful and correct models for some complex situations. For example, see Busemeyer and Jones (1993), Bollen and Paxton (1998), Kenny and Judd (1984), Bagozzi, Baumagartner and Yi (1992), Schumacker and Marcoulides (1998), and references therein on the importance of quadratic and interaction effects of latent factors in various applied research. Recently, useful methods that used LISREL program have been proposed to analyze some nonlinear structural equation models with quadratic and interaction terms of latent variables; see, for example, Jaccard and Wan (1995), and Jöreskog and Yang (1996), among others. The basic approach of these contributions is to include artificial products of manifest variables in the analysis to account for nonlinear relationships among variables. This approach has some practical and theoretical difficulties (see, e.g. Arminger and Muthen, 1998; Lee and Zhu, 2000). The main objective of this article is to investigate the ML estimation of a general nonlinear structural equation model.

2 ML estimation of a Nonlinear Structural Equation Model

Consider the following nonlinear structural equation model (NSEQ) with a $p \times 1$ manifest random vector $y = (y^1, \cdots, y^p)^T$:

$$y = \mu + \Lambda \xi + \epsilon, \tag{1}$$

where μ is a vector of intercepts, Λ is a $p \times q$ matrix of factor loadings, $\xi = (\xi^1, \cdots, \xi^q)^T$ is a random vector of latent factors with $q < p$, ϵ is a $p \times 1$ random vector of error measurements with distribution $N[0, \Psi]$, where Ψ is diagonal and ϵ is independent with ξ. To handle more complex situations, we partition ξ as $(\xi_{(1)}^T, \xi_{(2)}^T)^T$ and further model this latent vector via the following nonlinear structural model:

$$\xi_{(1)} = \Pi \xi_{(1)} + \Gamma H(\xi_{(2)}) + \delta, \tag{2}$$

where $\xi_{(1)}$ and $\xi_{(2)}$ are $q_1 \times 1$ and $q_2 \times 1$ latent subvectors of ξ respectively; $H(\xi_{(2)}) = (h_1(\xi_{(2)}), \cdots, h_t(\xi_{(2)}))^T$ is a $t \times 1$ non-zero vector-valued function with nonzero, linearly independent differential functions $h_1, \cdots, h_t$, and $t \geq q_2$; $\Pi(q_1 \times q_1)$ and $\Gamma(q_1 \times t)$ are matrices of regression coefficients of $\xi_{(1)}$ on $\xi_{(1)}$ and $H(\xi_{(2)})$, respectively. It is assumed that $\xi_{(2)}$ and δ are independently distributed as $N[0, \Phi]$ and $N[0, \Psi_\delta]$, respectively, where Ψ_δ is a diagonal co-variant matrix. If some $h_j(\xi_{(2)})$ are nonlinear, the distribution of the manifest random vector y is non-normal. Let $\Pi_0 = I_{q_1} - \Pi$, we assume that $|\Pi_0|$ is a non-zero constant independent of Π. The structural model in (2) is linear in parameter matrices Π and Γ, but may be nonlinear in the latent variables in $\xi_{(2)}$. Hence, nonlinear causal effects of latent variables in $\xi_{(2)}$ on latent variables in $\xi_{(1)}$ can be assessed. Let $\Lambda_\xi = (\Pi, \Gamma)$ and $G(\xi) = (\xi_{(1)}^T, H(\xi_{(2)})^T)^T$, then equation (2) can be written as $\xi_{(1)} = \Lambda_\xi G(\xi) + \delta$. To identify the model, appropriate elements in Λ and Λ_ξ are held fixed in the estimation.

Let $\mathbf{Y} = \{y_1, \cdots, y_n\}$ be the observed data matrix corresponding to a random sample obtained from a population with the NSEQ model defined in (1) and (2), $\mathbf{Z} = (\xi_1, \cdots, \xi_n)$ be the matrix of latent factors, and θ be the structural parameter vector that contains all unknown distinct parameters in μ, Λ, Λ_ξ, Φ, Ψ_δ and Ψ. The basic idea of our ML approach is to consider a data augmentation scheme in which the observed data $\mathbf{Y}$ is augmented with the matrix of latent factors $\mathbf{Z}$. Treating this as a missing data problem with hypothetical missing data $\mathbf{Z}$, ML estimate is obtained by the well-known EM algorithm (Dempster, Laird and Rubin, 1977). Let $\mathbf{X} = (\mathbf{Y}, \mathbf{Z})$ be the augmented completed-data set and $L_c(\mathbf{Y}, \mathbf{Z}|\theta) = \log p(\mathbf{X}|\theta)$ be the log-likelihood function of θ based on $\mathbf{X}$. From (1) and (2), it can be shown that $L_c(\mathbf{X}|\theta)$ is given by

$$-\frac{1}{2}\left\{(p+q)n\log(2\pi) + n\log|\Psi| + n\log|\Psi_\delta| + n\log|\Phi|\right.$$

$$-\sum_{i=1}^{n}\xi_{i(2)}^{T}\Phi^{-1}\xi_{i(2)} + \sum_{i=1}^{n}(y_i - \mu - \Lambda\xi_i)^T\Psi^{-1}(y_i - \mu - \Lambda\xi_i)$$

$$+\left.\sum_{i=1}^{n}(\xi_{i(1)} - \Lambda_\xi G(\xi_i))^T\Psi_\delta^{-1}(\xi_{i(1)} - \Lambda_\xi G(\xi_i))\right\}. \tag{3}$$

The ξ_i in (3) are not observed random variables, and they are considered as missing data. The rth iteration of a standard EM algorithm with a current value $\theta^{(r)}$ is to evaluate $Q(\theta|\theta^{(r)}) = \mathrm{E}\{L_c(\mathbf{X}|\theta)|\mathbf{Y}, \theta^{(r)}\}$, where the expectation is taken with respect to the conditional distribution of $\mathbf{Z}$ given $\mathbf{Y}$ and $\theta^{(r)}$, and then to determine $\theta^{(r+1)}$ by maximizing $Q(\theta|\theta^{(r)})$. Evaluation of the E step is rather complicated because the conditional expectation involves complex multiple integrals that are intractable. A procedure on the basis of the Metroplis-Hastings (Metropolis, et al., 1953; Hastings, 1970) algorithm is proposed here to execute this step. Since the M-step also does not have a closed form solution, $\theta^{(r+1)}$ will be obtained via a sequence of conditional maximization steps (see Meng and Rubin, 1993). Thus the proposed EM algorithm can be regarded as an Monte Carlo Expectation and Conditional Maximization (MCECM) algorithm (Wei and Tanner, 1990). As we will see, computational burden of this algorithm in solving our problem is not heavy.

It can be seen from (3) that we need to compute the conditional expectations of the following complete-data sufficient statistics $\{\xi_i, \xi_i\xi_i^T, G(\xi_i)G(\xi_i)^T, \xi_{i(1)}G(\xi_i)^T; i = 1, \cdots, n\}$ in evaluating $Q(\theta|\theta^{(r)})$ in the E-step. Owing to the generality and complexity of $G(\xi_i)$, these quantities cannot be obtained in closed form. They are approximated via a sufficiently large number of ξ_i simulated from $p(\xi_i|y_i, \theta)$, see Wei and Tanner (1990). Based on the definition of the model and assumptions, $p(\xi_i|y_i, \theta)$ is proportional to

$$\exp\left\{-\frac{1}{2}\xi_{i(2)}^T\Phi^{-1}\xi_{i(2)} - \frac{1}{2}(y_i - \mu - \Lambda\xi_i)^T\Psi_\epsilon^{-1}(y_i - \mu - \Lambda\xi_i)-\right.$$

$$\left.\frac{1}{2}(\xi_{i(1)} - \Lambda_\xi G(\xi_i))^T\Psi_\delta^{-1}(\xi_{i(1)} - \Lambda_\xi G(\xi_i))\right\}. \tag{4}$$

The Metropolis-Hastings (MH) algorithm is used to simulate observations from $p(\xi_i|y_i, \theta)$. It is a well-known Markov chain Monte Carlo method that has been widely used to simulate observations from a target density via the help of a proposal distribution from which it is easy to sample. Let $\{\xi_i^{(m)}, m = 1, \cdots, M; i = 1, \cdots, n\}$ be the random observations generated by our proposed MH algorithm from the conditional distribution $[\xi_i|y_i, \theta]$.

Conditional expectations of the complete-data sufficient statistics required to evaluate the E-step can be approximated via these random observations, for example, $E(\xi_{i(1)}G(\xi_i)^T|y_i, \theta) = M^{-1}\sum_{m=1}^{M} \xi_{i(1)}^{(m)}G(\xi_i^{(m)})^T$, and $E(\xi_{i(2)}\xi_{i(2)}^T|y_i, \theta) = M^{-1}\sum_{m=1}^{M} \xi_{i(2)}^{(m)}\xi_{i(2)}^{(m)T}$.

At the M-step, we need to maximize $Q(\theta|\theta^{(r)})$ with respect to θ. This is equivalent to solve the following system of equations:

$$\frac{\partial Q(\theta|\theta^{(r)})}{\partial\theta} = E\left\{\frac{\partial}{\partial\theta} L_c(\mathbf{X}|\theta)|\mathbf{Y}, \theta^{(r)}\right\} = 0. \tag{5}$$

This system of equations cannot be solved in closed form. Based on the idea given in Meng and Rubin (1993), the solution required in the M-step can be obtained by several computationally simpler conditional maximizations. Conditional on other parameters, the solution of each individual equation given in (5) can be obtained. For example, $\hat{\Phi} = \frac{1}{n}\sum_{i=1}^{n} E[\xi_{i(2)}\xi_{i(2)}^T|\mathbf{Y}, \theta]^T$.

An estimate of $E(\xi_i|y_i, \hat{\theta})$, which can be used as an estimate for ξ_i, can be obtained easily via the corresponding sample mean of the generated observations in $\mathbf{Z}$ from the MH algorithm at the last EM iteration:

$$\hat{E}(\xi_i|y_i, \hat{\theta}) = \hat{\xi}_i = M^{-1}\sum_{m=1}^{M} \xi_i^{(m)}.$$

Finally, the bridge sampling method (Meng and Wong, 1996) based on the likelihood ratios is used to monitor convergence of the proposed MCECM algorithm, and standard errors are computed via Louis (1980) formula.

3 An Example

A small portion of the Inter-University Consortium for Political and Social Research (ICPSR) data set collected in the project WORLD VALUES SURVEY 1981-1984 AND 1990-1993 (World Value Study Group, ICPSR Version) is analyzed in the illustrative example. Six variables in the original data set (variables 180, 96, 62, 176, 116 and 117) that are related with respondents' job, religious belief, and homelife were taken as manifest variables in $y = (y^1, \cdots, y^6)^T$. Among them, (y^1, y^2) are related to life, (y^3, y^4) are related to religious belief, and (y^5, y^6) are related to job satisfaction. After deleting cases with missing data, the sample size is 196. A nonlinear structural equation model with latent factors $\xi_{(1)} = (\xi^1)$ and $\xi_{(2)} = (\xi^2, \xi^3)$ is proposed with the following specifications: $\Pi = 0$, $H(\xi_{(2)}) = (\xi^2, \xi^3, \xi^2\xi^3)$, and

$$\Gamma^T = \begin{bmatrix} \gamma_{11} \\ \gamma_{12} \\ \gamma_{13} \end{bmatrix}, \quad \Lambda^T = \begin{bmatrix} 1.0 & \lambda_{21} & 0 & 0 & 0 & 0 \\ 0 & 0 & 1.0 & \lambda_{42} & 0 & 0 \\ 0 & 0 & 0 & 0 & 1.0 & \lambda_{63} \end{bmatrix};$$

where one's and zero's in Λ were treated as fixed parameters. In this nonlinear model, there are a total of 22 structural parameters which are unknown elements in μ and Λ, γ_{ij} in Γ, $\phi_{ij}(i \leq j)$ in Φ, diagonal elements in Ψ and ψ_δ. ML estimates of structural parameters and direct estimates of basic latent factors were obtained via the proposed MCECM algorithm. At the beginning of the MCECM algorithm, we use $M = 40$ observations obtained from the MH algorithm to approximate the conditional expectations in the E-step, then use $M = 500$ after the 45th iteration. It was found that the MCECM algorithm stabilized after about 45 iterations. To be conservative, the algorithm stopped after 60 iterations. Values of the log-likelihood ratio are shown in Figure 1 after the 8th iteration. After convergence, a total of 5000 random observations were used to calculate standard errors estimates via the Louis (1980) formula.

ML estimates of structural parameters and their standard errors estimates are reported in Table 1. From the structure of Λ, latent factors ξ^1, ξ^2 and ξ^3 can be roughly interpreted as 'life', 'religious belief' and 'job satisfaction' factors, while $\xi^2\xi^3$ represents the interaction of 'religious belief' and 'job satisfaction', From the estimate of γ_{13} and its standard error, we see that the corresponding t–value is -2.22. It seems that the interaction of 'religious belief' and 'job satisfaction' has a significant effect on 'life'. Based on the proposed approach, other nonlinear terms can also be analyzed similarly by choosing appropriate structures for Λ and $H(\xi)$.

Table 1. ML estimates and their standard errors for the ICPSR data

Parameter	EST	SD	Parameter	EST	SD
λ_{21}	0.856	0.143	ψ_{11}	0.626	0.283
λ_{42}	2.049	0.386	ψ_{22}	1.353	0.250
λ_{63}	0.795	0.139	ψ_{33}	0.674	0.307
γ_{11}	0.368	0.123	ψ_{44}	2.485	1.146
γ_{12}	0.590	0.126	ψ_{55}	1.960	0.565
γ_{13}	-0.191	0.086	ψ_{66}	4.066	0.493
μ_1	8.423	0.136	ϕ_{11}	1.780	0.449
μ_2	7.826	0.132	ϕ_{12}	-0.181	0.215
μ_3	2.350	0.147	ϕ_{22}	2.952	0.746
μ_4	5.511	0.297			
μ_5	7.551	0.169	ψ_δ	0.819	0.392
μ_6	7.357	0.180			

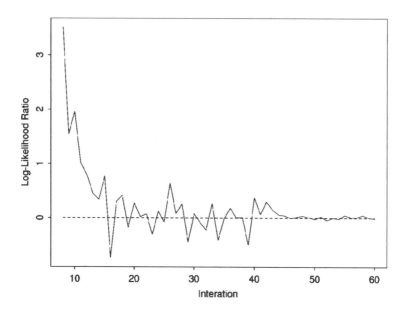

Fig. 1. ICPSR data with six manifest variables: Log-likelihood ratio versus EM iteration from the 8th iteration.

4 Discussion

Maximum likelihood estimation of linear structural equation models is traditionally based on the analysis of covariance structure framework which utilizes asymptotic properties of the sample covariance matrix obtained from observed data. Clearly, this approach cannot be applied to the more complicated nonlinear structural equation models. In this paper, ML estimation of a general nonlinear model is developed on the basis of the following useful strategy: treat latent variables as missing data and solve the problem via the EM algorithm, realizing that the complete-data likelihood is less difficult to handle. Apparently, the proposed MCECM algorithm works pretty well in our problem.

References

Arminger, G. and Muthen, B. O. (1998). A Bayesian approach to nonlinear latent variable models using the Gibbs sampler and the Metropolis-Hastings algorithm. *Psychometrika*, **63**, 271-300.

Bagozzi, R. P., Baumgartner, H. and Yi, Y. (1992). State versus action orientation and the theory of reasoned action: an application to coupon usage. *Journal of Consumer Research*, **18**, 505-517.

Bentler, P. M. (1992). EQS: *Structural Equation Program Manual*, Los Angeles, BMDP Statistical Software.

Bollen, K. A. and Paxton, P. (1998). Two-stage least squares estimation of interaction effects. In *Interaction and nonlinear effects in structural equation models*. (eds, Schumacker, R. E. and Marcoulides, G. A.), 125-151. Mahwah, N. J: Lawrence Erlbaum Associates, Publishers.

Busemeyer, J. R. and Jones, L. E. (1983). Analysis of multiplicative combination rules when the causal variables are measured with error. *Psychological Bulletin*, **93**, 549-562.

Dempster, A. P., Laird, N. M. and Rubin, D. B. (1977). Maximum likelihood from incomplete data via the EM algorithm (with discussion), *Journal of the Royal Statistical Society, Series B*, **39**, 1-38.

Hastings, W. K. (1970). Monte Carlo sampling methods using Markov chains and their application. *Biometrika*, **57**, 97-109.

Jaccard, J. and Wan, C. K. (1995). Measurement error in the analysis of interaction effects between continuous predictors using multiple regression: Multiple indicator and structural equation approaches. *Psychological Bulletin*, 117, 348-357.

Jöreskog, K. G. and Sörbom, D. (1996). LISREL 8: *Structural Equation Modeling with the SIMPLIS Command Language*. Scientific Software International: Hove and London.

Jöreskog, K. G. and Yang, F. (1996). Nonlinear structural equation models: the Kenny-Judd model with interaction effects. In *Advanced structural equation modeling techniques* (eds, G. A. Marcoulides and R. E. Schumacker), 57-88. Hillsdale, NJ: LEA.

Kenny, D. A. and Judd, C. M. (1984). Estimating the nonlinear and interactive effects of latent variables. *Psychological Bulletin*, **96**, 201-210.

Lee, S. Y. and Zhu, H. T. (2000). Statistical analysis of nonlinear structural equation models with continuous and polytomous data. *British Journal of Mathematical and Statistical Psychology*, **53**, 209-232.

Louis, T. A. (1982). Finding the observed information matrix when using EM algorithm. *Journal of the Royal Statistical Society, Series B*, **44**, 226-233.

Meng, X. L. and Rubin, D. B. (1993). Maximum likelihood estimation via the ECM algorithm: A general framework. *Biometrika*, **80**, 267-278.

Meng, X. L. and Wong, W. H. (1996). Simulating ratios of normalizing constants via a simple identity: a theoretical exploration. *Statistic Sinica* **6**, 831-860.

Metropolis, N., Rosenbluth, A. W., Rosenbluth, M. N., Teller, A. H. and Teller, E. (1953). Equations of state calculations by fast computing machine. *Journal of Chemical Physics*, **21**, 1087-1091.

Schumacker, R. E. and Marcoulides, G. A. (Eds) (1998). *Interaction and nonlinear effects in structural equation models*. Mahwah, N. J: Lawrence Erlbaum Associates, Publishers.

Wei, G. C. G. and Tanner, M. A. (1990). A Monte Carlo implementation of the EM algorithm and the Poor man's data augmentation algorithm. *Journal of the American Statistical Association*, **85**, 699-704.

WORLD VALUES SURVEY, 1981-1984, and 1990-1993. (1994). ICPSR version. Ann Arbor, MI: Institute for Social Research [producer], 1994. Ann Arbor, MI: Inter-University Consortium of Political and Social Research [distributor], 1994.

Use of SEM Programs to Precisely Measure Scale Reliability

Yutaka Kano[1] and Yukari Azuma[2]

[1] School of Human Sciences, Osaka University, Suita, Osaka 565-0871, Japan
 kano@hus.osaka-u.ac.jp
[2] School of Human Sciences, Osaka University, Suita, Osaka 565-0871, Japan
 azuma@koko15.hus.osaka-u.ac.jp

Summary. It is first pointed out that most often used reliability coefficient α and one-factor model based reliability ρ are seriously biased when unique factors are covariated. In the case, the α is no longer a lower bound of the true reliability. Use of Bollen's formula (Bollen 1980) on reliability is highly recommended. A web-based program termed "STERA" is developed which can make *stepwise* reliability analysis very easily with the help of factor analysis and structural equation modeling.

Key words. Cronbach's coefficient α, one-factor model based reliability, unique factor covariance, web-based program STERA, structural equation modeling, LM test.

1 Introduction

Reliability analysis has been discussed extensively since Cronbach (1951) proposed the famous reliability coefficient α, and the discussion recently has been made within the scope of the structural equation modeling (e.g., Raykov 2001; Hancock & Mueller, 2000; Green & Hershberger, 2000; Komaroff, 1997). A recent version of EQS (EQS6.0, Bentler 2002) can print a variety of scale reliability estimates. Although reliability analysis is an old topic, it is still given much attention.

Consider a one-factor model with possibly covariated[1] unique factors:

$$X_i = \mu_i + \lambda_i f + u_i \qquad (i = 1, \ldots, p), \tag{1}$$

where $\mu_i = E(X_i)$, λ_i being a factor loading parameter, $E(f) = E(u_i) = 0$, $V(f) = 1$, $\mathrm{Cov}(u_i, u_j) = \psi_{ij}$ and $\mathrm{Cov}(f, u_i) = 0$. Here f and u_i are called a (common) factor and a unique factor, respectively.

The scale score is defined as the total sum of X_i, i.e., $X = \sum_{i=1}^{p} X_i$. The scale reliability ρ' of X is then defined as the proportion of the true score variance to the total variance, that is,

---

[1] The term "correlated" is more often used in this context. Without a few exceptions, we use "covariated" in this paper since we mainly focus upon covariances between unique factors rather than correlations. Mathematically both of the terminologies are equivalent.

$$\rho' = \frac{V(\sum_{i=1}^{p} \lambda_i f)}{V(X)} = \frac{(\sum_{i=1}^{p} \lambda_i)^2}{(\sum_{i=1}^{p} \lambda_i)^2 + \sum_{i=1}^{p} \psi_{ii} + \sum_{i,j,i\neq j}^{p} \psi_{ij}}. \tag{2}$$

On the other hand the traditional reliability (test) theory assumes $\psi_{ij} = 0$ for $i \neq j$, so that the ρ' reduces to

$$\rho = \frac{(\sum_{i=1}^{p} \lambda_i)^2}{(\sum_{i=1}^{p} \lambda_i)^2 + \sum_{i=1}^{p} \psi_{ii}}. \tag{3}$$

The no-covariance assumption may not hold for many empirical data sets, and the recent literature focuses on effects of the unique factor covariances upon the traditional reliability measure Cronbach's α.

Bollen (1980) would be the first work that points out the importance of nonzero unique factor covariances in reliability analysis and derives the formula (2). He employed a confirmatory factor analysis model to develop a scale of political democracy, and found that the assumption of uncorrelatedness of the unique factors in the scale is inappropriate. He developed a confirmatory factor analysis model with covariated unique factors for the scale. The formula (2) is identical with Bollen's (Bollen 1980, formula (1) on page 378). Bollen's analysis (Bollen 1980, Figure A3) is reproduced in Fig.1.

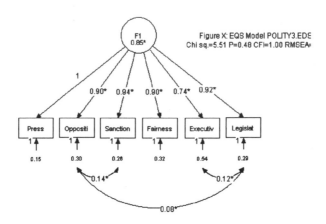

Fig. 1. Bollen's analysis: Political democracy scale

If there are many pairs of covariated unique factors, there may be additional common factors that can account for the covariances. Practitioners, then, consider that the scale is not unidimensional, extract multiple common factors and develop subscales. The problem is how to do it when there still remain covariances that can not be explained by the multiple factors, even after some subscales were developed. A typical case is where there is a common factor with only two indicators (Kano 1997) within a single (sub)scale and the factor is not interpretable or does not interest the practioners. They can then use the model (1) to estimate the reliability through the formula (2). The model could also be used when they are not interested in additional factors even if subscales are to be developed.

In this paper, we begin by illustrating how seriously covariated unique factors invalidate classical reliability coefficients α and ρ with $\psi_{ij} = 0$. In Section 3, we take Lagrange Multiplier (LM) tests to determine the pairs of unique factors to be covariated, and show a newly developed program called "STERA." We finally end with concluding remarks in Section 4.

2 Impacts of covariated unique factors

A most often used reliability coefficient in social sciences is neither ρ nor ρ' defined in (3) and (2) but Cronbach's coefficient α defined as

$$\alpha = \frac{p}{p-1} \left(\frac{\sum_{i \neq j}^{p} \mathrm{Cov}(X_i, X_j)}{V(X)} \right) \tag{4}$$

Under the assumption of a one-factor model without covariances between unique factors, it is known that $\alpha \leq \rho$, and that the equality holds when items are essentially τ-equivalent (or weakly parallel measurement), i.e., λ_i's are the same. Thus, the coefficient α is a conservative measure of the true reliability, and some researchers prefer the α because of the conservativeness. Here, a question arises as to what if the independence assumption on unique factors fails. What kind of influence is made on the ρ and α? An appealing example is provided in Fig.2.

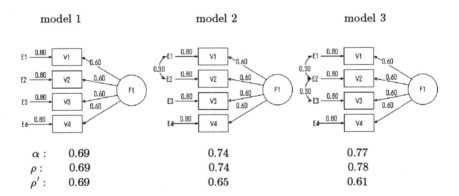

Fig. 2. Covariated unique factors and reliability coefficients

The model 1 in Fig.2 is a basic one-factor model with equal factor loadings of 0.6. The models 2 and 3 are those with unique factor covariances of 0.3

for one and two pairs of unique factors. We reported just below the path diagrams values of α, ρ and ρ' respectively defined in (4), (3) and (2). For computing ρ, we first calculated correlation matrices derived from the models and made one-factor analysis of the correlation matrices so that factor loading and unique factor variance estimates were obtained for each model.[2] The reliability was evaluated based on (3) using these estimates. Thus, the values of ρ are wrong reliability estimates that result from ignoring existing unique factor covariances.

The model 1 meets the essentially τ-equivalent assumption, and hence the α and ρ, identical with ρ', represent the true reliability as 0.69.

It is seen from the results in the models 1 and 2 that since ρ' gives the correct reliability value, α and ρ result in seriously biased estimates, and that more unique factor covariances result in more serious bias. The α coefficient is no longer a conservative estimate for the true reliability. This observation coincides with Zimmerman et. al. (1993) and Komaroff (1997). When negative covariances appear between unique factors, α and ρ underestimate the reliability. Thus, existence of unique factor covariances invalidates use of α and ρ.

It is easy to explain why such biases are made. Unique factor covariances contribute to the covariances between observed variables. The α is a monotonically increasing function of the total covariances, so positive unique factor covariances lead to a positive bias. A similar explanation can be made for ρ. When the unique factor covariances are ignored, factor loading estimates are seriously overestimated, leading to overestimation of ρ. On the other hand, when we use ρ', unique factor covariances contribute to the denominator of the formulae, and the covariances are regarded as an error. Usually the covariances of unique factors do not interest us, so the formula ρ' is reasonable.

One can examine the fit of a one-factor model employed to detect whether unique factor covariances should be introduced. A bad-fitted one-factor model may indicate existence of unique factor covariances. (Exploratory) factor analysis without model fit examination can cause an inflated or deflated reliability estimate, so it is not recommended.

3 LM approach and STERA

In the previous section, we pointed out the importance of introduction of unique factor covariances. Here, we discuss a pragmatic estimation method of the reliability based on the expression ρ' in (2). A drawback of the model (1) is nonidentifiability, so that one cannot estimate parameters. The ψ_{ij} has $p(p+1)/2$ parameters, which is the same as the number of variances and covariances of the observed variables.

---

[2] Obviously, the models are fitted very poorly.

F	Var	Factor Loading F1	FL@	ALPHA	RHO	Rho@	ALPHA 1-variable deletion	RHO 1-variable deletion	Test of Goodness-of-fit
F1	v3	0.901	0.901	0.934	0.935	0.935	0.917	0.916	X^2=38.281 df=9 P=0.000
	v2	0.895	0.895				0.919	0.917	
	v1	0.885	0.885				0.915	0.918	
	v6	0.874	0.874				0.916	0.920	
	v4	0.789	0.789				0.927	0.929	
	v5	0.686	0.686				0.939	0.939	

Fig. 3. Preliminary exploratory factor analysis

One way to estimate ψ_{ij} is to use the residual covariance matrix, that is, $\hat{\psi}_{ij} = s_{ij} - \hat{\lambda}_i \hat{\lambda}_j$ $(i \neq j)$, where s_{ij} is the sample covariance between X_i and X_j, and $\hat{\lambda}_i$ is an estimate in the usual one-factor analysis model, i.e., the model with $\psi_{ij} = 0$ $(i \neq j)$. The approach, however, does not work because $\sum_{i,j,i \neq j}^{p} \hat{\psi}_{ij}$ is almost zero almost always. Estimation process tries to minimize the residuals and in many cases, this also minimizes the sum of residuals as in regression analysis.

Here we propose that one perform Lagrange Multiplier tests for unique factor covariances sequentially, as suggested by Raykov (2001). For this, the SEM program EQS is useful (Bentler 1995). The LM option of the EQS as /LMTEST with SET= PEE; gives a list of the pairs of unique factors to be

Factor1	
Check the box if an error covariance is allowed.	
Error Covariance	Predicted Chi-square
☑ E2 , E3	18.479
☐ E4 , E1	25.922
☐ E5 , E6	30.285
☐ E4 , E2	30.554
☐ E5 , E2	30.842
☐ E6 , E3	33.542
☐ E1 , E2	35.675
☐ E4 , E3	36.362
☐ E5 , E4	37.185
☐ E6 , E2	37.443

Fig. 4. Unique factor covariances to be allowed

covariated. A covariance parameter between a statistically significant pair is released to be a free parameter, and the model is reestimated.

It is a feasible process but very tedious. In addition, one has to calculate values of ρ' by him/herself. We have developed a web-based program that can easily implement such reliability analysis. The program is called STERA (STEpwise Reliability Analysis). Any one who can access internet can use this program.

You are requested to input a sample correlation matrix, the number of variables, the number of factors, and sample size when you access the top page of the STERA.

Factor1

Reliability analysis when error covariances may be allowed				LM test for error covariance: Predicted chi-square statistic for goodness-of-fit when an error covariance is allowed	
Error Covariance Estimates					
E2 , E3 = 0.123					
Vars	Factor Loading	RHO'	Test of Goodness-of-fit	Check the box if an error covariance is allowed	
V1	0.900				
V6	0.879			Error Covariance	Predicted Chi-square
V3	0.861	0.918	χ²=21.590 df=8 P=0.006	E6 , E2	13.642
V2	0.852			E4 , E1	14.757
V4	0.813			E6 , E1	15.201
V5	0.706			E5 , E6	16.126
				E5 , E2	18.235
				E4 , E2	18.849
				E6 , E3	19.853
				E4 , E6	20.428
				E5 , E1	20.662
				E1 , E3	20.891

Fig. 5. One unique covariance is introduced

We took Bollen's political democracy data (Bollen 1980, Table 2, $n = 113$) to demonstrate the program. When you submit a job after giving necessary information, you will receive an output webpage as in Fig.3, where results of exploratory factor analysis are presented including model fit information.

When you submit a job of multiple factor analysis, the program presents reordered factor loading estimates, and reliability analysis will proceed for each factor. Factor analysis with one common factor has been made for each set of observed variables with each factor, and reliability estimates are presented based on both one-factor and multiple factor analysis results. To distinguish, estimates based on one-factor analysis are attached with the symbol "@" as in Fig.3. Since this example is a one-factor analysis, both of the results are identical with each other. Values of α and ρ are estimated as 0.934 and 0.935. The goodness-of-fit statistic indicates rejection of the model ($\chi^2 = 38.281$ df= 9, p value= 0.000).

Below the table in Fig.3, you find anther table (Fig.4) which shows which pair of the unique factors should be covariated from the statistical point of view. The table indicates a predicted chi-square statistic of the model if the unique covariance of the pair is allowed. In the example, you check a box in the pair of E2 and E3 and submit the job to get model fit information of the revised one, reliability estimates and a further analysis of unique factor covariances. Those are presented in Fig.5. The covariance is estimated as 0.123 and the reliability estimate $\hat{\rho}'$ is given as 0.918, which is a bit lower than the original one. However, again the new model receives a poor fit (p value= 0.006), so you need to introduce one more covariance. For this, you can check the box of **E6** and **E2**. You will be then noticed that you need to allow the covariance between **E5** and **E6**. If you add the covariance, then you will reach a final accepted model, where the model is fitted satisfactorily (p value= 0.480). The model is identical with Bollen's (Fig.1).

The reliability coefficient ρ' estimated based on the model in Fig.1 is 0.907, which is lower than $\hat{\rho} = 0.935$ or $\hat{\alpha} = 0.934$.

4 Concluding remarks

Many text books (e.g., Allen and Yen, 1979) on measurement theory alert that the coefficient α is nothing but a lower bound for true reliability if essential τ equivalence assumption (i.e., item homogeneity; λ_i's are the same) is violated. Less attention on the independence assumption on unique factors has been paid, as noted by Green and Hershberger (2000). We feel, however, that the independence assumption is more important than the essential τ equivalence assumption because dependency among unique factors can cause overestimation of the true reliability.

It is important to examine goodness-of-fit of a factor analysis model to detect substantial unique factor covariances. When the model receives a poor fit and unique factor covariances are considered as a possible cause, an LM test is useful to determine which pair of the unique factor be covariated.

There are many situations, already studied in the literature, which cause unique factor covariances. According to Rozeboom (1966), speeded tests can introduce covariated unique factors so that the coefficient α cannot be used. He also noted that when items on a test are administrated on a single occasion, errors among items are likely to be positively correlated. Green and Hershberger (2000) made an attempt to model error covariances in true score models. There may be a method factor that influences some of the items, so that unique factors of the items influenced can be covariated. There may be a third variable (confounding variable) that is not noticed by the researcher but can influence some of the items.

There are also situations where the error covariances are a source of reliable and repeatable variance that has a similar interpretation to that of the true scores. In the case, one could consider that the error covariances are to be added to the variance of the true scores. We have not discussed this case fully in the paper.

It is said that in the context of structural equation modeling, one should not introduce error covariances (to improve a model fit) without substantial consideration, see, e.g., Browne (1982). The LM option of EQS as default does not print results on error covariances. Thus, error covariances are allowed only if adequate reasons are given to the introduction of the covariances. We feel that in reliability analysis one should be more optimistic for introducing unique factor covariances because inflated α or inflated one-factor based ρ can prove a wrong validation of the scale constructed.

Alternative approaches could be taken to estimate reliability for a case where unique factor covariances appear. Vautier (2001) proposed an alternative way of identifying pairs of nonzero unique factor covariances in which he calls it a heuristic shifting method. A stepwise variable selection in factor analysis (Kano & Harada, 2000) could be used to select a set of variables that perfectly conforms to a factor analysis model and use the coefficient ρ.

In this paper, we have discussed a feasible procedure of precisely estimating the true reliability ρ' defined in (2) of a scale and developed an easily accessible program STERA.[3] We hope many readers will access the program to correctly evaluate reliability of scales they use.

References

Allen, M. J. & Yen, W. M. (1979). Introduction to Measurement Theory. Brooks/Cole, Monterey, CA.

Bentler, P. M.(1995, 2002): EQS Structural Equations Program Manual. Multivariate Software, Los Angeles.

Bollen, K. A. (1980): Issues in the comparative measurement of political democracy. Amer. Sociol. Rev., **45**, 370–390.

Browne, M. W.(1982) Covariance structures. In: Hawkins, D. M. (ed.), Topics in applied multivariate analysis (pp.72-141). Cambridge University Press, Cambridge.

Cronbach, L. J. (1951): Coefficient alpha and the internal structure of a test. Psychometrika, **16**, 297–334.

Green, S. B. & Hershberger, S. L. (2000): Correlated errors in true score models and their effect on coefficient alpha. Structural Equation Modeling, **7**, 251-270.

Hancock, G. & Mueller, R. (2000): Rethinking construct reliability within latent variable systems. In: Cukeck, R., Toit, D., & Söbom, D.(Eds.), Structural equation modeling: Present and future (pp.195-216). SSI, Chicago.

Kano, Y. (1997): Exploratory factor analysis with a common factor with two indicators. Behaviormetrika, **24**, 129–145.

Kano, Y. & Harada, A. (2000): Stepwise variable selection in factor analysis. Psychometrika, **65**, 7–22.

Komaroff, E. (1997): Effect of simultaneous violations of essential tau-equivalence and uncorrelated error on coefficient alpha. App. Psychol. Measurement, **21**, 337-348.

Raykov, T. (2001): Bias of Cronbach's coefficient alpha for fixed congeneric measures with correlated errors. App. Psychol. Measurement, **26**, 69–76.

Rozeboom, W. W. (1966): Foundation of the Theory of Prediction. The Dorsey Press, Homewood, IL.

Vautier, S. (2001). Assessing internal consistency reliability with the Jöreskog's Rho: New developments. (submitted)

Zimmerman, D. W., Zumbo, B. D. & Lalonde, C. (1993). Coefficient alpha as an estimate of test reliability under violation of two assumptions. Educ. Psychol. Measurement, **53**, 33-49.

---

[3] http://koko16.hus.osaka-u.ac.jp/stepwise/servlet/stera/

Estimating the Statistical Power in Small Samples by Empirical Distributions

Ab Mooijaart

Department of Psychology, Leiden University, Wassenaarseweg 52, 2333 AK, Leiden, The Netherlands

Summary. Model selection is an important issue in Structural Equation Modeling. This issue is in particular important if the sample size is small. In such a case the power may be very small, so it is hard to decide which model is the most appropriate, because alternative models may also fit the data well. There is a lot of theoretical papers on this subject, however they are almost always dealing with asymptotic theory. In cases with small samples this assumption may lead to wrong results. We will use resampling methods, like the parametric bootstrap, to investigate the empirical distribution of certain statistics. On the basis of this empirical distribution we can investigate the power of some tests, even in cases with small samples. An example will be given.

Key words. Small Samples, Type I error, Power, Parametric Bootstrap

1 Introduction

Model selection in Structural Equation Modeling is an important issue. Model selection was originally mainly based upon known statistical distributions of some test statistics. For instance, under the assumption that the observed variables are normally distributed then for large sample sizes some well-known statistics, as the X^2 statistic, are chi-square distributed. A model is selected as describing the data well if, under a type I error level of say 5%, the statistic is not larger than some critical value. However, another important issue in selection of a model is the so-called power of a test. The power of a test is the probability of rejecting a model when it is false. In practice this power is seldom investigated, however it is important to know what the power of a test is. In this paper we will be concerned with the power of some statistical tests. In particular, we concentrate on situations with small samples.

Satorra and Saris (1985) discussed the power in situations where the observed variables are normally distributed and the sample size is large. From general statistical theory it follows that when a model is not true, the corresponding test statistic is non-central χ^2 distributed and the power of the test can be computed. So the power of a test is based on the non-centrality parameter of the χ^2 distribution. How this non-centrality parameter can be estimated is discussed in their paper.

However, it turns out that in cases with large sample sizes the power of the model will always be very large, whereas with small sample sizes the power will be always very low. Therefore many other fit indices were developed. The main properties of these fit indices are that 1: they are independent of the sample size and 2: they are in different ways related to the non-centrality parameter. Examples of such proposals are Bentler and Bonnett (1980), Bollen (1989), Browne and Cudeck (1989).

A recent development in this area is the generalization of the power analysis to situations where the observed variables are non-normally distributed. Also in this case the results only hold for large sample sizes (see Satorra, 2001). Here the situation is much more complicated, because theoretically test statistics may now be mixtures of nc-χ^2 distributions. However, if the so-called Asymptotic Robustness (AR) assumption holds, the normal theory results can be applied to estimate the power. There are two problems with this approach. First, the AR assumption cannot be tested in practice, and second, higher order moments, like fourth order moments, are needed. Using higher order moments means that large samples are needed to get stable estimates of these moments.

In this paper we will concentrate on the power analysis in *small samples*. In Bentler & Yuan (1999) this problem was also tackled, however, with a different approach. They investigated how well statistics, which are developed for large samples, behave in small samples. In this paper we do not use any asymptotic statistical theory, but instead we make use of resampling methods and, in particular, we investigate the empirical distributions of some statistics. The resampling method we will use here is the parametric bootstrap method; see Bollen and Stine (1992).

For illustration purposes of our ideas we will investigate a Markov model for continuous variables.

2 The Markov Model

As an illustration we use the first order Markov model. The model equations can be written, as

$$x_j = b_{j,j-1}x_{j-1} + e_j, \quad j = 1, 2, ..., J. \tag{1}$$

The unknown parameters are the regression (transition) parameters $b_{j,j-1}$, and the variances the errors e_j. For estimating the parameters we minimize the loss function

$$f = \sum_j e_j^2 = \min.$$

Minimizing this loss function gives the following results for the unknown parameters

$$\hat{b}_{j,j-1} = \frac{s_{j,j-1}}{s_{j-1}^2} \tag{2}$$

$$var(e_j) = s_j^2 + \hat{b}_{j,j-1}^2 s_{j-1}^2 - 2\hat{b}_{j,j-1} s_{j,j-1}, \tag{3}$$

where s_j^2 and $s_{j,j-1}$ are elements of the covariance matrix $\mathbf{S}$ of the observed variables X_j. As we can see for estimation the parameters the diagonal and subdiagonal of $\mathbf{S}$ are used, only. So we use limited information from the data. This is in opposite to methods as used in, for instance, LISREL and EQS.

Remark: So far we have not assumed any statistical distribution for the variables. However, assuming the normal distribution for the observed variables and maximizing the likelihood function will give us the same estimates as in Eqs. (2) and (3).

3 The empirical distribution of the X^2 statistic

Under the normality assumption of the variables it holds for large samples that X^2 is chi square distributed, with X^2 defined as

$$X^2 = n(\log|\hat{\Sigma}| + tr(\mathbf{S}\hat{\Sigma}^{-1}) - \log(|\mathbf{S}|) - p), \tag{4}$$

where $\hat{\Sigma}$ is the estimated Σ at the optimal point. However, if the sample size is small, then even if the variables are normally distributed, X^2 is not chi square distributed.

To illustrate this point we will show an empirical distribution of an X^2 statistic. The model we use is a first order Markov model with 5 time points, sample size of 25, all b transition parameters are equal to .9 and all errors variances are equal to .64. All variables are normally distributed with means equal to 0. The empirical distribution was obtained by drawing 10,000 samples of a population with the population parameters as given above. Estimates of the parameters were obtained by Eqs. (2) and (3).

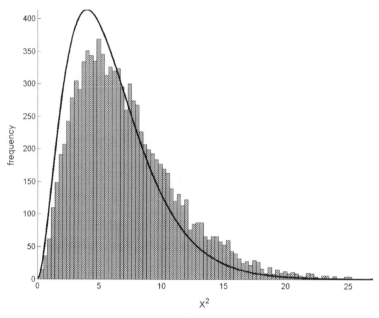

Fig.1. Empirical distribution of the X^2 **statistic**

Under the asymptotic normal theory the X^2 statistic would be chi square distributed with 6 degrees of freedom. This distribution is given in Fig. 1 by the solid line. The empirical distribution is given by the histogram in Fig. 1. We see there is a difference between the two distributions. In particular, the tail of the empirical distribution is much heavier than the tail of the chi square distribution. This fact has serious impact on model selection when it is based on the chi square distribution and, say, a type I error of 5%. In such a case the critical value under the chi square distribution is about 12.6, which gives an empirical type I error of 10.2%. So what we have a nominal type I error (α) of 5% whereas the empirical (or actual) type I error is 10.2%. So, in fact, the test is too liberal.

In the next section we will discuss a method that results in a test in which the nominal and the actual α are about the same.

4 The bootstrap method

The bootstrap approach is mostly used for investigating the stability of some estimated parameters. It is based upon repeatedly resampling from the original data. However, as was shown by Bollen and Stine (1992), this naïve bootstrapping cannot be used for finding an empirical distribution of, e.g., the empirical distribution of the X^2 statistic. The reason is that the statistical distribution of a test statistic has been computed under a specific known model. However, this 0-model will never perfectly hold for the observed data and so resampling from the data will not give the proper distribution of the test statistic. An alternative to this naïve bootstrapping is the so-called parametric or Monte Carlo bootstrap method. In this method first the model parameter are estimated from the original data and then these estimates are considered to be the population parameters. Then new samples (bootstraps) are drawn from this population (i.e. with the estimated parameters as the population parameters) and a distribution that is equal to the distribution of the original variables. Model selection is now based on the empirical distribution of the statistics from these bootstraps. The procedure can be described as follows, where we have assumed that all variables are normally distributed.

Parametric bootstrap (Monte Carlo Bootstrap) method of goodness-of-fit statistics (GFS):

- Fit the model for the original data and find $\hat{\theta}$, obtain estimates $\sigma\left(\hat{\theta}\right)$. Compute the *original* GFS.
- Draw B samples (bootstraps), with size n from estimated normal distribution with covariances $\sigma\left(\hat{\theta}\right)$.
- Fit null model for each bootstrap obtaining *empirical* distribution of the GFS.
- Sort bootstrap statistics.
- Compare *original GFS* to bootstrap GFS-distribution percentile: if larger than $(1-\alpha)B$ reject, otherwise accept the model.

5 A small study of the empirical distribution: Type I error

In this section we give the results of a small study in which the parameteric bootstrap approach is investigated. Again we assume that all the b parameters are equal to .9. Furthermore we assume that all the error standard deviations are .4, .6 or .8. The sample sizes are 20, 30, 40, or 50. This gives 12 combinations of parameters we study. For each combination of parameters and sample sizes we do a separate study. Now we suppose that there is a population with specified b (= .9) and error standard deviation (.4, .6 or .8) and we draw a sample with some specified size (20, 30, 40, or 50). This sample is called an *original sample*. For each original sample we apply the bootstrap method and decide whether we have to reject the model or not. We use a type I error of 5%, i.e., the nominal type I error. The number of bootstraps for each study is set equal to 5000. Instead of drawing just one original sample for each population, we draw 100 original samples and apply for each original sample the bootstrap method. Now we can define the empirical Type I error as the proportion (out of 100 original samples) of rejection the specified model. So the total number of model fitting is 100 x 5001 x 12 = 6,001,200.

We also compare the bootstrap method with a method in which we apply the asymptotic approach. In this situation we draw from each population, as described above, 10,000 samples and compare the critical value under the chi square distribution with the right tail surface under the empirical distribution. This is completely analogous to the example we discussed in Fig. 1. Table 1 gives the results of this approach.

Table 1. actual type I error in percentages, under asymptotic assumption; nominal type I error 5%.

	standard deviation of errors		
Sample size	.4	.6	.8
20	12.8	12.4	12.8
30	9.2	9.4	9.8
40	8.1	7.8	7.8
50	7.3	7.9	7.0

In Table 1 we see that the nominal and the actual type I errors differ a lot, which means here that we too often reject the model. If the sample size increases the nominal and the actual errors become closer to each other. Obviously, because here we are dealing with the asymptotic assumption, for larger sample sizes the actual error will approach the nominal error.

In Table 2 we see the results of the parametric bootstrap method as discussed above.

Table 2. actual type I error in percentages for bootstrap method; nominal type I error 5%.

	standard deviation of errors		
Sample size	.4	.6	.8
20	6	7	6
30	5	3	4
40	4	4	5
50	5	6	4

In Table 2 we see that the actual type I error are close to the nominal type I errors. If we take into account that the actual type I errors are based each time on 100 original samples, we know that with 95% certainty that the interval around 5% is from 1% to 9%. So, statistically we can say that in all cases the actual and the nominal type I errors are equal to each other.

Conclusion: The parametric bootstrap method gives the proper type I error level.

6 A small study of the empirical distribution: the power

In the previous section we saw that the parametric bootstrap gives a proper level of the type I error. Obviously, it does not make sense to estimate the power if the corresponding test is either liberal or conservative. Because in those cases the model will be rejected too much, which results in an overestimation of the power, or the model will be rejected too less, which gives an underestimation of the power. So, because the bootstrap method gives the proper type I error, it makes sense to compute the power by using the parametric bootstrap.

In the setup of our study we follow for a main part the same procedure as we did in investigating the type I error. However, the difference is that we suppose now that the model which is true (H_1) has transition parameters (.9, .8, .7, .6, .5)., this is the so-called variant model. The 0-model is the invariant model (H_0) in which it is supposed that all transition parameters are equal. In our study we draw 100 original samples from the population, for which the variant model holds, and we estimate the parameters and the goodness-of-fit indices under the invariant model. So we are expected to reject the model. By minimizing the same loss function as before, it is easy to prove that the invariant transition parameter, which we will denote as b, can be estimated as:

$$\hat{b} = \frac{\sum_j s_{j,j-1}}{\sum_j s_{j-1}^2}.$$

Now the empirical power is defined as the proportion of (out of 100 original samples) rejection of the H_0 model. The results are given in Table 3.

From Table 3 we see that, obviously, the power increases when the sample size increases. Furthermore, we see that if the variances of the errors become smaller the power increases, too. This is also quite clear, because in cases with small errors there is much less noise in the data than in cases with substantial error.

Table 3. empirical power in percentages for bootstrap method; nominal type I error 5%.

	standard deviation of errors		
Sample size	.4	.6	.8
20	20	13	13
30	31	17	15
40	39	32	29
50	49	35	27

7 Conclusion

In this paper we have illustrated that the parametric bootstrap method can be utilized to investigate the power of tests, even if the sample size is small. In this paper all the variables, observed variables and the error variables, are normally distributed. Studies like the one discussed in this paper can also be carried out in cases in which variables are not normally distributed.

Conclusion: In cases where statistical theory is not available, e.g. in cases with small samples and/or in cases where the variables are not normally distributed, resampling methods can be used for model selection.

References

Bentler PM, Bonett DG (1980) Significant tests and goodness-of-fit in the analysis of covariance structures. Psychological Bulletin 88:588-600

Bentler PM, Yuan KH (1999) Structural equation modeling with small samples: test statistics. Multivariate Behavioral Research 34:181-197

Bollen KA (1989) Structural equations with latent variables. Wiley, New York

Bollen KA, Stine RA (1992) Bootstrapping goodness-of-fit measures in structural equation models. Sociological Methods and Research 21:205-229

Browne MW, Cudeck R (1989) Single sample cross-validation indices for covariance structures. Multivariate Behavioral Research 24:445-455

Satorra A (2001) Goodness of fit testing of structural equation models with multiple group data and nonnormality. In Cudeck R, du Toit S, Sörbom D (eds) Structural equation modeling: present and future, a Festschrift in honor of Karl Jöreskog. Scientific Software International, Lincolnwood, pp 231-256

Satorra A, Saris WE (1985) Power of the likelihood ratio test in covariance structure analysis. Psychometrika 50:83-90

Language Selection and Social Structure Transition in Ukraine from 1959 to 1989

Masayuki Kuwata , Makoto Hayasaka , Masanori Nakagawa

Department of Human System Science, Graduate School of Decision Science & Technology, Tokyo Institute of Technology, 2-12-1 Oookayama, Meguro-ku, Tokyo, 152-8522, Japan

Summary. The purpose of this paper is to propose a method to analyze the Ukrainian People's language selections and to select the appropriate variables for this purpose. In particular, we focused on constructing the model that would capture the social transitions well. The table of contents is as follows. First, as the background of this research, the Ukrainian geographical situation with respect to its ethnic and language dispersion is described. Next, three former literary sources that deal with Soviet statistical materials concerned with Ukrainian language problems are referred to. Here we outline our former research in detail because this research shared the same data and overcame the difficulty of it. And third, this research's method is explained. Here we improved the procedure of factor analysis we had taken. Finally, this research's conclusion and its limit are shown. Consequently, this paper's method overcame our former work and revealed more appropriate social factors that could capture the social transitions than before. However it also revealed the limit of the analysis based on data that we could obtain so far.

Keywords. Soviet census, language selection, social structure transition

1 Background

Ukraine's population had increased from 41 million to 49 million during the period between 1959 and 1989 and it has had 25 provinces since 1954. Ethnic Ukrainians constitute the majority in the all provinces except for Crimea which has had ethnic Russians as an absolute majority of its population. Ukrainians and Russians occupy more than 90 % of each province except for Zakarpat province. In the western and central parts of its land, ethnic Ukrainian live densely (almost more than 90 % of each population). And ethnic Russians live more densely in the eastern and southern parts of it than others (from 10 to 30 % of each province). Almost a similar tendency was observed with respect to language affiliations. But the Russian mother tongue rate jumped twice as ethnic Russians rate in the eastern and southern part of Ukraine. Thus, former studies often pointed out that Ukrainians are dominant in the western and central parts of this land and Russians are dominant in the eastern and southern parts concerned with both ethnic compositions and language affiliations.

2 Former researches and their problems

In Ukraine, there had been some changes of language policies by the government and it was indicated by many literary sources. So-called Ukrainization (To promote the use of Ukrainian language in fields like education, publication and administration) or indigenization policy was adopted in 1920's, 1950's, and 1960's. On the other hand, Russification or Sovietization policy was adopted in 1930's and 1970's. Thus, two language policies that had quite opposite contents were adopted several times. But the trend of language selection realized gradual Russification not only in Ukraine but also in many Soviet republics. For example, the rate of people who claimed Russian as their mother tongue increased like 23%→ 27%→31%→32% from 1959 to 1989 in Ukraine. One may ascribe such gradual Russification to Soviet language polices focusing on the Sovietization in 1930's and 1970's (Solchanyk 1982). On the other hand, one may ascribe the not drastic but gradual Russificaion to the indigenization policy in 1920's, 1950's and 1960's (Pool 1978). So, it is hard to argue the efficiency of language polices of Soviet regime because both Ukrainian and Russian languages were promoted by policies. Then, an approach to grasp the language selection in relation to the other social factors was conducted by Brian D. Silver (Silver 1974, 1978). Here, including his analysis, three former literary sources and their problems are referred to for the purpose of analysis using the Soviet census data on the Ukrainian language situation. The second study is the doctoral thesis of Arel Dominique (Arel 1993). And the last is our member's research (Kuwata 2000).

2.1 Silver model

Silver's research dealt with Soviet Union as a whole. He used 1959 and 1970 Soviet census data and other limited statistical materials. He developed a multiple regression model for language selections that has mother tongue choices as a dependent variable on the one hand and has the interethnic communication, the rate of urbanization and religious belongings as independent variables. Considering the fact that those statistical materials were hard to obtain, his development was elaborate enough at that time. But his model has two problems with regard to the analysis on the Ukrainian language situation. First, his selection of those independent variables bases only on empirical explanations relying on the literatures in history. Second, those two observed variables which he called "inter-ethnic communications" and "urbanization rates" have considerable correlations (Pearson correlation coefficient is 0.79 and significant at the 0.01 level.) at least in Ukraine.

2.2 Arel's introduction of all-union censuses from 1959 to 1989

Contrary to Silver's, Dominique Arel's study revolves mainly around the Ukrainian language situation using the census data of 1959, 1970, 1979 and 1989. His contribution was that he introduced four years' census results at the provincial level within Ukraine. But his method of analysis was a mere comparison of percent data. Thereby, his research was full of description concerning the regional differences and their tendencies of transitions during the period from 1959 to 1989. He introduced the census data in details but he just followed the Silver model with respect to the explanation for the exact cause of regional differences in the long run. Hence, he ascribed the cause of mother tongue selections to "inter-ethnic communications", "urbanization rates" and "religious belongings". Having been explained in the Silver model problems, the validity for his selections of these independent variables was not confirmed concretely.

2.3 Regression model based on the latent variables (Kuwata, M. 2000)

We constituted a multiple regression model that had latent variables as independent variables and mother tongue selections as dependent variables in order to overcome the Silver model's difficulty in the analysis of Ukrainian language situation. In our former research, the model had two steps. The first step was to derive the latent variables from observed variables other than selection of mother tongue by factor analysis using the Varimax rotation. The second step was to associate the mother tongue selections with those latent variables extracted above by multiple regression analysis.

2.3.1 Data

Soviet census data of 1959, 1970, 1979 and 1989 was the main objects of the analysis. In addition to it, we also obtained data from "National economy of Ukraine" published in 1990. The latter has data collected in 1960, 1970, 1980 and 1987. Hence, there were differences between census and economical data but because of the difficulty in obtaining other statistical materials, we regarded the data synchronized with census-collected times. From these two sources, following variables were selected. Capitalized words are observed variables taken from those materials.

1. Macro data (SIZE, URB)
2. Educational level (UNIV, B_H, SP_H, H, B_H, EL, B_EL)
3. Nationality & language affiliation (UKR, RUS, L_UKR, L_RUS)
4. Economical data (KOL, SOV, PROF, GDS)
5. Birth & death rate (BIRTH, DEATH)

The variables in the first, second and third provisions were taken from censuses but the fourth and fifth ones were from "National economy of Ukraine".

The contents of variables are as follows. SIZE refers to provincial population percentage in the total population of Ukraine. URB stands for the rate of urban population in each province. UNIV refers to the rate of people who graduated from university. B_U represents the rate of people who entered into university and left before graduation. SP_H stands for the rate of people who had a special high education degree. H represents the rate of people who finished high school. B_H represents the rate of people who completed the vocational education after elementary school education. EL is the rate of people who had elementary school education and B_EL is the rate of people who did not complete the elementary school education. UKR is an ethnic Ukrainian rate and RUS is an ethnic Russian rate. L_UKR represents the rate of people who claimed Ukrainian as their mother tongue and L_RUS stands for the people who claimed Russian as their mother tongue. KOL and SOV refer to the average monthly salary of Kolkhoz and Sovkhoz labors, respectively. PROF stands for the percentages of specialists with higher education among all labors. GDS represents commercial transaction including the food service industry. BIRTH is birth rate and DEATH is death rate. In addition to it, we compiled SCND as secondary education (SCND = B_H + SP_H + H) and FIRST as first education (FIRST = B_H + EL). Further, we calculated TOB as a criterion of wealth per person (TOB = GDS / provincial population).

2.3.2 Result of the former analysis

From the results of some factor analyses, the three factors of ethnicity, social development and industrialization were extracted from 15 selected variables. As explained above, the factor scores extracted from the result of factor analysis were regressed to mother tongue selections by multiple regression analysis. This procedure revealed that the standardized partial regression coefficient of the ethnicity factor decreased in accordance with time without any exceptions, although it kept the first ranking out of three factors. To the contrary, the standardized partial regression coefficient of the industrialization factor showed the quite opposite tendency and kept the second ranking out of three factors. Thus, we assumed that industrialization played key role in citizen's language selection.

2.3.3 Problem of the former model

The procedure of our former research has a problem. The data set of factor scores, which is extracted from the factor analysis, is processed by set data composed of 1959, 1970, 1979 and 1989 data sets vertically. If there had not been any social structure transitions from 1959 to 1989, the result from the above-mentioned procedure would not have any problems. However if there had been some social structure transitions, the deduced assumption based on the factor analysis may have disregarded the structure transition (Fig. 1a).

We tried checking the result of factor analysis using the same variables in each year census data, in order to confirm this suspicion. We discovered that those variables selected from the set data were not appropriate to evaluate the same factors among respective censuses. This was due to the fact that it was impossible to

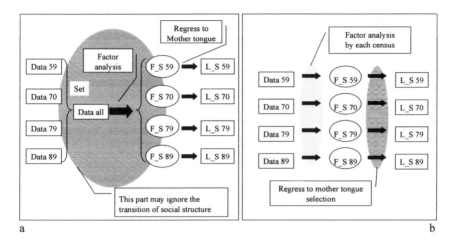

a   b

Fig. 1a, b. a Problem of our former research. **b** Method of this research.
F_S, factor score; L_S, language Selection.

extract the same factors among four years' census data using the observed variables which were derived from the set data.

3. Methods and results

Considering this vulnerable point, we took these steps as follows in order to overcome the former research. First, observed variables other than mother tongue selections were factor analyzed according to each census and the factors were extracted respectively. At this point, we tried to select the consistent observed variables, which could sustain the same factors from 1959 to 1989. Next, factor scores extracted from consistent observed variables of each census data were regressed to synchronized data sets according to mother tongue selections (Fig. 1b). These consecutive procedures enable to distill some social factors which reflect almost the same features in time series and also capture the social transitions if they occur in each factor.

As a result of revised procedure of factor analysis using the Varimax rotation, the number of selected observed variables for factor analysis decreased from 15 to 13. The change of contents was as follows.

Variables of former research: UKR, RUS, KOL, SOV, UNIV, SP_H, H, SCND, URB, GDS, PROF, SIZE, TOB, BIRTH, DEATH

Variables of this study: URK, RUS, KOL, SOV, UNIV, SCND, FIRST, URB, GDS, PROF, SIZE, BIRTH, DEATH

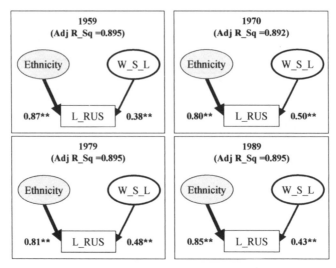

Fig. 2. Result of regression analysis.
W_S_D, wealth and social level; L_RUS, russian mother tongue rate.
*$P<0.05$, **$P<0.01$

Namely, variables SP_H, H, and TOB were deleted and the variable FIRST was added. This revised factor analysis finally extracted the three factors as ethnicity, wealth & social level, and population growth rate. (The editor suggested the use of oblique rotation such as the Promax method. However, for the sake of simplicity of the interpretation, we chose the Varimax rotation.)

The result of regression analysis toward Russian mother tongue selection is shown (Fig. 2). The population growth rate factor is removed from the regression analysis because it does not show the enough significance. From 1959 to 1970, the standardized partial regression coefficient of the ethnicity factor decreases and that of the wealth & social level factor increases. However, in contrast to the former research's result, this tendency does not continue after 1979. Rather, the ethnicity factor's standardized partial regression coefficient increases and that of the wealth & social level decreases, however not as drastically as the change of the former period. A similar trend was observed clearly in the case of the Ukrainian mother tongue selection model. We can ascribe the cause of this phenomenon to the transition of factor loadings (Table 1). Factor loadings of SIZE, PROF and GDS on ethnicity whose factor loadings on the wealth & social level show the high absolute value consistently, increase from 1959 to 1989 despite some exceptions from 1970 to 1979. This implies that the ethnicity factor absorbs the wealth & social level factor as time goes by. This point reveals a weakness of this model. Despite this problem, the revised model gives us an advantage because it grasps the social change concerned with the wealth & social level. Factor loading of FIRST on the

Table 1. Factor loadings obtained from factor analysis of each census's data

1959	Ethnicity	W_S_L	P_G_R		1970	Ethnicity	W_S_L	P_G_R
UKR	−0.885	−0.273	−0.093		UKR	−0.803	−0.384	0.322
RUS	0.870	0.319	0.052		RUS	0.825	0.427	−0.219
KOL	0.888	0.108	−0.210		KOL	0.892	0.287	0.048
SOV	0.869	0.207	−0.226		SOV	0.899	0.067	0.252
UNIV	0.592	0.447	−0.362		UNIV	0.254	0.772	0.062
SCND	0.609	0.536	−0.440		SCND	0.429	0.783	0.077
FIRST	0.310	0.460	0.147		FIRST	0.148	−0.455	−0.371
URB	0.665	0.703	−0.011		URB	0.569	0.759	−0.086
GDS	0.354	0.913	−0.004		GDS	0.385	0.831	−0.102
PROF	0.291	0.924	−0.153		PROF	0.296	0.885	−0.046
SIZE	0.048	0.959	−0.198		SIZE	0.126	0.922	0.003
BIRTH	−0.061	−0.076	0.941		BIRTH	−0.295	−0.279	−0.813
DEATH	−0.657	−0.449	−0.338		DEATH	−0.226	−0.316	0.883

1979	Ethnicity	W_S_L	P_G_R		1989	Ethnicity	W_S_L	P_G_R
UKR	−0.804	−0.378	0.238		UKR	−0.830	−0.307	0.255
RUS	0.851	0.403	−0.102		RUS	0.895	0.343	−0.118
KOL	0.900	0.266	0.206		KOL	0.850	0.393	0.142
SOV	0.788	0.323	0.405		SOV	0.712	0.326	0.388
UNIV	0.338	0.762	−0.076		UNIV	0.318	0.762	−0.119
SCND	0.537	0.747	0.001		SCND	0.555	0.675	−0.062
FIRST	−0.298	−0.708	0.163		FIRST	−0.275	−0.620	0.565
URB	0.574	0.756	0.051		URB	0.589	0.739	0.079
GDS	0.350	0.855	0.049		GDS	0.408	0.830	0.032
PROF	0.274	0.906	0.086		PROF	0.343	0.884	0.062
SIZE	0.143	0.950	0.094		SIZE	0.238	0.941	0.054
BIRTH	−0.192	−0.219	−0.928		BIRTH	−0.148	−0.344	−0.874
DEATH	−0.106	−0.231	0.952		DEATH	−0.064	−0.220	0.932

W_S_L, wealth & social level; P_G_R, population growth rate.

wealth & social level factor changes as 0.45, -0.45 and -0.70 from 1959 to 1979. This result implies that first education is more or less a positive indicator for the wealth & social level in 1959 but it gradually becomes an indicator of backwardness in the wealth & social level after 1970. On the other hand, the factor loadings of SCND and UNIV on the wealth & social level factor increase drastically from 1959 to 1970. Factor loading of second education on the wealth & social level factor decreases after 1979 but that of university sustains those high absolute values until 1989. This result shows that the role of second education in the wealth & social factor increases till 1970 and decreases after 1979. To the contrary, the role of university seldom changes in the wealth & social level after 1970. Thus, the rate of people who graduated from university was a good indicator to show the wealth & social level factor. From those results, we concluded that the procedure we had taken could capture the traces of social structural changes and could associate these social factors with citizen's language selection more rationally than former studies.

4. Discussion

First of all, we discovered the flaw of the former research. Using the set data, we disregarded the social structure change. In this paper, we confirmed this problem and devised the process of factor analysis. Factor analyses were done by each census taken time under the concept that it could take the same factors among four censuses. As a result of this procedure, three factors derived from 13 observed variables were selected and named as ethnicity, wealth & social level, and population growth rate. Multiple regression analyses which had the language affiliation as dependent variable and the ethnicity and the wealth & social level factor scores as independent variables did not show the similar results like the standardized regression coefficient of particular factor increased and that of another one decreased as time went by without any exceptions. The explanation lies in the fact that the ethnicity factor absorbed the wealth & social level factor as time went by and these factors more reflected the social transitions than the former. We concluded that it was impossible to constitute the simple model with the data we could get so far but possible to do with other data especially concerning citizens' income. The reason for the shortage of data lies in the fact that the economical data collected at the provincial level was too limited. Therefore, the method of this paper is limited in this point but it provides us the possibility to research more thoroughly with enough data. Because this method could not only get appropriate variables from some sorts of social factors but it could also capture the structure transition of each social factor.

References

Arel, D. (1993) Language and the politics of ethnicity: The case of Ukraine. University of Illinois at Urbana-Champaign, pp90-142

Kuwata, M. (2000) A method for deriving data from the Soviet censuses 1959, 1970, 1979, 1989 :The case of the Ukraine. Japanese Slavic and East European Studies 21 :7-19

Pool, J. (1978) Soviet language planning: Goals, results, options. In: Azrael R (ed) Soviet nationality policies and practices, Praeger, New York, pp 223-249

Silver, B. (1974) Social mobilization and the russification of Soviet nationalities. American political science review 68 :53-66

Silver, B. (1978) Language policy and the linguistic russifcation of Soviet nationalities. In: Azrael R (ed) Soviet nationality policies and practices, Praeger, New York, pp269-301

Solchanyk, R. (1982) Russian language and Soviet politics. Soviet Studies 34:23-42

Identifying Influential Observations for Loadings in Factor Analysis

W K Fung[1] and C W Kwan[2]

[1] Department of Statistics and Actuarial Science, The University of Hong Kong, Pokfulam Road, Hong Kong
[2] Clinical Trials Centre, The University of Hong Kong, 2/F, Block B, Nurses Quarters, Queen Mary Hospital, 102 Pokfulam Road, Hong Kong

Summary. Influence measures based on the sample influence curves for the initial and rotated loadings are discussed and some scalar influence measures based on the Cook's distance are proposed. Large values of influence measures may not necessarily imply a large influence on the factor loadings but a minor change of the variances explained leading to the change of the ordering of the factors. Therefore, the sample influence curves may, in fact, measure the difference between two different factors, instead of the change of one factor before and after an observation is omitted. The switching problem is studied by investigating the factor loadings pattern, variances explained and factor scores.

Keywords. Influential observations, Factor analysis, Factor loadings, Orthogonal rotation, Switching

1 Introduction

Factor analysis is an important and useful tool in social sciences and psychometric data analysis. For a $p \times 1$ random vector $\mathbf{x}$, a factor analysis model with q common factors is formulated as

$$\mathbf{x} - \boldsymbol{\mu} = \boldsymbol{\Lambda}\mathbf{f} + \boldsymbol{\varepsilon}, \tag{1}$$

where $\boldsymbol{\mu}$ is the mean for $\mathbf{x}$ and $\boldsymbol{\Lambda}$ is a $p \times q$ matrix of factor loadings. The unobserved common factors $\mathbf{f}$ and the residual $\boldsymbol{\varepsilon}$ are independent with zero means, $\mathrm{cov}(\mathbf{f}) = \mathbf{I}$, and $\mathrm{cov}(\boldsymbol{\varepsilon}) = \boldsymbol{\Psi}$ where $\boldsymbol{\Psi}$ is a diagonal matrix. The covariance matrix, $\boldsymbol{\Sigma}$, for $\mathbf{x}$ is therefore given as $\boldsymbol{\Sigma} = \boldsymbol{\Lambda}\boldsymbol{\Lambda}^T + \boldsymbol{\Psi}$. The maximum likelihood factor analysis is the most commonly used estimation method where the log likelihood function, up to a constant term, is given as,

$$\ell = -\frac{1}{2}n\left[\log|\boldsymbol{\Sigma}| + tr(\mathbf{S}\boldsymbol{\Sigma}^{-1})\right], \tag{2}$$

and $\mathbf{S}$ is the sample covariance matrix. The factor loadings are always of the main interest in factor analysis and for the ease of interpretation, orthogonal rotation of the factor loadings (Harman, 1972, Lawley and Maxwell, 1971) is often applied. There are three commonly used orthogonal rotation methods namely varimax, quartimax and equamax. Similar to principal component analysis where the components are ordered by the variances explained, the rotated loadings in factor analysis are usually ordered in the same way. When the influence of observations on the factor model is to be discussed, it is important to investigate the influence on the estimates of factor loadings, both before and after the rotation.

Some authors, mainly based on the unique variances, have already discussed the influence or sensitivity analysis for factor analysis. Tanaka and Odaka (1989) derived and discussed the influence curve (Hampel, 1974) for the unique variance in maximum likelihood factor. Fung and Kwan (1995) discussed the difference between the influence curves when the covariance and correlation matrices are factored. Kwan and Fung (1998) employed the local influence approach to study the effect of the perturbation of observations to the factor model. Castaño-Tostado and Tanaka (1991) discussed the influence measure based on the product of the loadings matrix and its transpose. Tanaka and Watadani (1992) discussed the influence on factor loadings in maximum likelihood factor analysis.

This paper studies the influence for the factor loadings directly, instead of the product form, based on the sample influence curve (Hampel, 1974) and illustrates a potentially misleading result due to the switching of factor loadings when an observation is deleted.

2   Influence measures

The case-deletion approach is commonly employed for the identification of influential observations. Let $\hat{\Lambda}$ and $\hat{\Lambda}_{(i)}$ be the sample estimates for the factor loadings matrix for the full data set and the reduced data set with observation i removed. The influence of the observation i is measured by the sample influence curve (interested readers may refer Hampel, 1974, and Cook and Weisberg, 1982, for details),

$$SIC_i(\Lambda) = -(n-1)\left(\hat{\Lambda}_{(i)} - \hat{\Lambda}\right), \tag{3}$$

where n is the sample size. To summarize the matrix-valued SIC into a scalar, the generalized Cook's distance (Cook and Weisberg, 1982) is used which is given as

$$C = vec(SIC)^T \mathbf{V} vec(SIC),$$

for some non-negative definite matrix $\mathbf{V}$. The observed information matrix is chosen for $\mathbf{V}$ in this paper. For the initial loadings, the information matrix is given as,

$$-\frac{\partial^2 \ell}{\partial \Lambda \partial \lambda_{ir}} = n\left[\Sigma^{-1}\left(\frac{\partial \Sigma}{\partial \lambda_{ir}} \Sigma^{-1}\mathbf{S} - \frac{\partial \Sigma}{\partial \lambda_{ir}} + \mathbf{S}\Sigma^{-1}\frac{\partial \Sigma}{\partial \lambda_{ir}} \right)\Sigma^{-1}\Lambda \right.$$

$$\left. + \left(\Sigma^{-1} - \Sigma^{-1}\mathbf{S}\Sigma^{-1}\right)A_{ir}\right], \quad i=1,\dots,p, \quad r=1,\dots,q, \tag{4}$$

where

$$\left[\frac{\partial \Sigma}{\partial \lambda_{ir}}\right] = \delta_{ik}\lambda_{lr} + \delta_{il}\lambda_{kr} \, ,$$

δ_{ij} is the Kronecker's delta and $\mathbf{A}_{ir}$ is a $p \times q$ matrix of zeros except the $i$rth position being unity. Other choice for $\mathbf{V}$ is the asymptotic covariance matrix for factor loadings in maximum likelihood factor analysis model which was given by Lawley and Maxwell (1971) and was modified by Jennrich and Thayer (1973). Tanaka and Odaka (1989) applied the same scalar measure in other context to norm the influence curves for the unique variances. The information matrix and the asymptotic covariance matrix for the rotated loadings can be estimated by $\mathbf{V}^* = \mathbf{E}^{\mathrm{T}} \mathbf{V} \mathbf{E}$, where $\mathbf{E} = \partial vec\hat{\Lambda}^* / \partial vec\hat{\Lambda}$ was derived by Archer and Jennrich (1973).

The third choice for $\mathbf{V}$ is the covariance matrix for $\hat{\Lambda}$ obtained by the jackknife method (Tukey, 1958).

3   Switching of factor loadings

A large value of the Cook's distance suggests a large influence of the observation on the factor loadings. According to the form of SIC, a large influence on the factor loadings implies a large change of the estimated factor loadings when an observation is omitted and hence the factor structure and the interpretation of the factor model is supposed to be intensively altered. In practice, however, the factor structure and the interpretation may not change, even if a large value of SIC and the corresponding Cook's distance are observed. This confusing situation is to be illustrated by a numerical example given below.

A two-factor model is applied to the data set of national track records for men (Johnson and Wichern, 1998, p 510). The data set consists of 55 observations and 8 variables. The data are standardized to have unit variances and a two-factor maximum likelihood factor analysis model is applied.

The SIC and the Cook's distance based on the observed information matrix for the initial loadings were obtained and the index plot of the Cook's distance is shown in Fig. 1(a). The most influential observation is observation 12 and followed by observation 55. Table 1 shows the estimated initial loadings for the full data set and the reduced data set when each of observations 12 and 55 is omitted. When observation 12 is removed, the loadings of the first variable on the first factor reduce substantially. When observation 55 is removed, not much change of the loadings is observed.

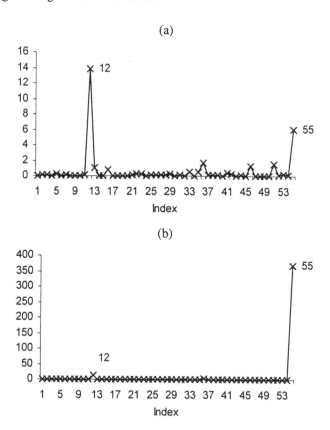

Fig. 1. Cook's distance based on the observed information matrix of the influence for (a) the initial factor loadings and (b) rotated loadings.

Table 1. Estimated initial loadings based on the full and reduced data sets with variances explained given in the last row

$\hat{\Lambda}$		$\hat{\Lambda}_{(12)}$		$\hat{\Lambda}_{(55)}$	
0.73	0.62	0.48	0.54	0.76	0.59
0.79	0.55	0.67	0.54	0.80	0.52
0.85	0.34	0.64	0.26	0.84	0.32
0.92	0.16	0.79	0.12	0.80	0.19
0.96	0.03	0.84	-0.01	0.84	0.04
0.97	-0.14	0.84	-0.19	0.88	-0.16
0.98	-0.14	0.85	-0.18	0.89	-0.15
0.92	-0.25	0.82	-0.28	0.85	-0.27
6.40	0.93	4.52	0.81	5.56	0.88

The loadings are rotated by the varimax method. Figure 1(b) shows the index plot of the Cook's distance based on the observed information matrix of the rotated loadings. The Cook's distance of observation 55 is extremely large compared with the rest. For comparison, the estimated rotated loadings for the full data set, and the reduced data sets when each of observations 12 and 55 is omitted are shown in Table 2. Let the rotated factor loadings be $\hat{\Lambda}^* = \left(\hat{\lambda}_1^*, \hat{\lambda}_2^* \right)$. Comparing the pattern of the factor loadings, it is noticed that $\hat{\lambda}_1^*$ is close to $\hat{\lambda}_{2(55)}^*$, and $\hat{\lambda}_2^*$ is close to the first factor, $\hat{\lambda}_{1(55)}^*$. This suggests that the ordering of the estimated rotated factors 1 and 2 may have been switched when observation 55 is omitted from the sample. Thus, the SIC and the Cook's distance actually compare the first (second) factor of the full data set to the second (first) factor of the reduced data set and hence, an unusually large value of Cook's distance is observed. When observation 55 is omitted, the variance explained by the second factor increases from 3.16 to 3.25 while that by the first factor decreases from 4.17 to 3.17. Therefore, when the rotated factors are ordered according to the variance explained, the factors are switched. For another influential observation, observation 12, identified for the initial factors, no such switching issue occurs.

Figure 2 (a) shows the index plot of the Cook's distance of the rotated loadings after the rearrangement of the factors such that the 'correct' pair of factors is used in evaluating the SIC. It is shown that, same as the result based on the initial loadings, observation 12 is the most influential observation while the influence measure of observation 55 is substantially reduced from 367.82 to 5.90. It is to be noted that a similar switching problem is discussed by Pack et al. (1987) in the simpler principal component analysis. The scatter plot of the Cook's distances for the initial and the rotated loadings (Figure 2 b) shows that the initial and the rotated loadings match extremely well. A very nice (nearly) rotational invariance property is observed. Experience shows that our constructed Cook's distance is (nearly) rotational invariant.

To investigate the reason for observing the switching phenomenon, we estimate the factor scores for the rotated factor model using the regression method (Figure 3). It is noticed that both observations 12 and 55 are far away from the remaining observations. The factor scores of observation 12 at both factors are large. For observation 55, only the factor score of factor 1 is large while the factor score of factor 2 is close to zero. Therefore, when observation 55 is omitted from the sample, the variance explained by factor 1 has a large drop, while that by factor 2 remains little change (increases slightly), and this leads to a swap of the two factors. However, when observation 12 is omitted, the variances explained by the two factors both drop since the two factor scores are large, and hence, the ordering of factors is retained.

Table 2. Rotated loadings estimated based on the full and reduced data sets with variances explained given in the last row

$\hat{\Lambda}^{*}$		$\hat{\Lambda}^{*}_{(12)}$		$\hat{\Lambda}^{*}_{(55)}$	
0.30	0.91	0.16	0.70	0.92	0.27
0.39	0.88	0.32	0.80	0.89	0.34
0.55	0.74	0.44	0.54	0.75	0.49
0.70	0.61	0.63	0.49	0.62	0.53
0.80	0.52	0.74	0.40	0.53	0.66
0.90	0.38	0.82	0.25	0.39	0.81
0.91	0.39	0.83	0.26	0.40	0.81
0.92	0.27	0.85	0.16	0.28	0.85
4.17	3.16	3.36	1.96	3.25	3.17

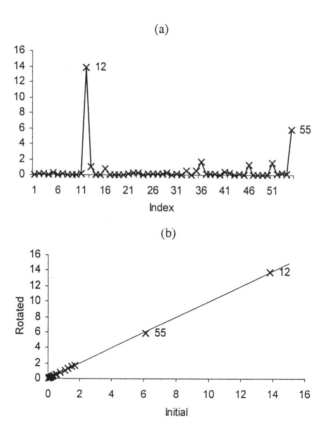

Fig. 2. (a) Index plot of Cook's distance of the rearranged rotated factor loadings and (b) the scatter plot of the Cook's distances for the initial and the rotated loadings.

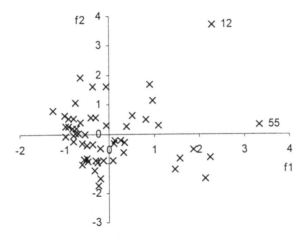

Fig. 3. Scatter plot of the factor scores.

4   Discussion

In the sensitivity analysis of factor analysis, it is natural to discuss the influence of the factor loadings which are of the main interest in the factor analysis model. However, when the SIC for the factor loadings, particularly the rotated loadings, is employed, the magnitude of the influence measure may identify some unexpected "influential observations" owing to the switching of factors. This phenomenon is more likely to happen when the rotated loadings are considered than when the initial loadings are studied, since the variances explained by the initial factors always spread more widely than that by the rotated factors. When the Cook's distance is found to be extremely large, it may not suggest that there is a substantial change of the factor loadings but the change of the variances explained by the factors in such a way that the ordering of the factors is changed as well. The magnitudes of the factor loadings, under a suitable rearrangement, may indeed do not change as large as that suggested by the influence measure. The switching of factors can be identified by comparing the Cook's distances of the initial and the rotated loadings since there is a nice rotational invariance property.

The change of the ordering of the factors may also be revealed by comparing the pattern of the factor loadings. It is based on the common situation that one factor would not change to another totally different and independent factor when an observation is omitted. This situation can be investigated by using the empirical influence curve, EIC (Hampel, 1974). The EIC has a property that the ordering of the factors is retained when an observation is omitted, and the EIC is often very close to the SIC. The identification of influential observations for factor loadings using the EIC is under investigation and the findings will be reported later.

5   Acknowledgement

The first author is partly supported by the Hong Kong RGC CERG grant 7134/98H. The authors thank the referees for helpful suggestions.

6   References

Archer, CO and Jennrich, RI (1973). Standard errors for rotated factor loadings. Psychometrika, 38, 581-592.

Castaño-Tostado, E and Tanaka, Y (1991). Sensitivity measures of influence on the loading matrix in exploratory factor analysis. Communications in Statistics - Theory and Methods, 20, 1329-1343.

Cook, RD and Weisberg S (1982). Residuals and Influence in Regression. London: Chapman and Hall.

Fung, WK and Kwan, CW (1995). Sensitivity analysis in factor analysis: Difference between using covariance and correlation matrices. Pyschometrika, 60, 607-614.

Hampel, FR (1974) The influence curve and its role in robust estimation. Journal of American Statistics Association, 69, 383-393.

Harman, HH (1967). Modern Factor Analysis. Chicago : University of Chicago Press.

Jennrich, RI and Thayer, DT, (1973). A note on lawley's formulas for standard errors in maximum likelihood factor analysis. Psychometrika, 38, 571-580.

Johnson, RA and Wichern, DW (1998) Applied Multivariate Statistical Analysis, 4th ed, London: Prentice-Hall.

Lawley, DN and Maxwell, AE (1971). Factor Analysis as a Statistical Method. London: Butterworths.

Kwan, CW and Fung, WK (1998). Assessing local influence for specific restricted likelihood: application to factor analysis. Psychometrika, 63, 35-46.

Pack, P, Jolliffe, IT and Morgan, BJT (1987). Influential observations in principal component analysis : A case study. Journal of Applied Statistics, 15, 39-50.

Tanaka, Y and Odaka, Y (1989). Sensitivity analysis in maximum likelihood factor analysis. Communications in Statistics - Theory and Methods, 18, 4067-4084.

Tanaka, Y and Watadani, Y(1992). Sensitivity analysis in covariance structure analysis with equality constraints. Communications in Statistics - Theory and Methods, 21, 1501-1515.

Effects of Self-disclosure and Self-preoccupation on Depression

Aiko Moriwaki[1], Shinji Sakamoto[2], and Yoshihiko Tanno[1]

[1] Department of Cognitive and Behavioral Sciences, Graduate School of Arts and Sciences, The University of Tokyo, 3-8-1 Komaba, Meguro-ku, Tokyo 153-8902, Japan
[2] Department of Social Psychology, Faculty of Human Relations, Otsuma Women's University, 2-7-1 Karakida, Tama-shi, Tokyo 206-8540, Japan

Summary. The purpose of the present study was to examine the causal relationship among self-disclosure, responses of recipients, and depression of self-disclosers. The effects of self-preoccupation on self-disclosure and depression were also examined. Questionnaires were administered to 120 college students twice four weeks apart. At time 1, we assessed self-preoccupation. At time 2, four weeks later, we assessed inadequate self-disclosure and negative responses of recipients between time 1 and time 2, as well as depression.

Path analysis (Structural Equation Model, SEM) among four observed variables indicated that inadequate self-disclosure of self-disclosers increases negative responses of recipients, and that these negative response of recipients increases depression of self-disclosers. Self-preoccupation increased both inadequate self-disclosure and depression. The results suggest that self-disclosure of self-disclosers and responses of recipients are important factors for depression of self-disclosers, and that self-preoccupation affects self-disclosure and depression of self-disclosers.

Keywords. Depression, Path analysis, Self-disclosure, Self-preoccupation

1 Purpose

A person may disclose his or her secrets to another person. The recipient may respond positively (for example, acceptance) or negatively (for example, refusal), which in turn may have an effect on the affective state of the self-discloser.

It is said that rates of depression are increasing. It is also said that prevention of or recovery from depression in daily life is very important (Joiner and Coyne 1999). In this context, researchers have come to focus on interpersonal effects on depression, such as effects of self-disclosure on depression. Self-disclosure is defined as "personal information verbally communicated to another person" (Chelune 1979; Cozby 1973). Is there any relationship between self-disclosure and depression?

It is often emphasized that self-disclosure positively affects self-disclosers, such that self-disclosure decreases depression (Derlega et al. 1993; Miller and Lefcourt 1983; Pennebaker 1997; Pennebaker and O'Heeron 1984; Pennebaker 1985; Pennebaker and Susman 1988). However, negative effects of self-disclosure have received little attention, and how to self-disclose and responses of recipients have been relatively ignored. Nonetheless, if we consider how to self-disclose and responses of recipients, we realize that self-disclosure will sometimes have negative effects on self-disclosers. For example, the interactional model of depression (Coyne 1976b) suggests that self-disclosure sometimes has negative effects on self-disclosers, such that inadequate self-disclosure of depressed people elicits rejection from recipients and elicits negative effects. Other previous studies also indicate negative effects, such that depressed people tend to be rejected by the other persons around them (Coyne 1976a; Gotlib and Robinson 1982; Hokanson and Butler 1992; Joiner and Barnett 1994). Reviewing and integrating these studies, Sacco (1999) presented a social-cognitive model of interpersonal processes in depression. Based upon this model, inadequate self-disclosure may elicit negative effects, such as rejection from others, and these rejections may increase depression of self-discloser, then a person with a depressed mood continue inadequate self-disclosure. This leads us to believe that self-disclosure does not always have positive effects. Furthermore, when we consider how to self-disclose and responses of recipients, self-disclosure may sometimes negatively affect depression of self-disclosers. However, the causal relationships among them, especially how to self-disclose and responses of recipients to depression have not been well examined.

The purpose of the present study was thus to examine the causal relationship among self-disclosure, responses of recipients, and depression of self-disclosers, focusing on effects of how to self-disclose, and responses of recipients on depression. It will be useful to examine these relationships for early intervention of depression. Furthermore, we examined the effects of self-preoccupation on self-disclosure and depression, because many previous studies (for example, Coyne 1976a) indicate that there are relationships between inadequate self-disclosures and self-preoccupation. Self-preoccupation is a tendency to focus more on the self and to maintain self-focused attention, and is thought to be a vulnerability factor in depression (Sakamoto 1999). People who tend to focus more on the self and to maintain self-focused attention will self-disclose inadequately or selfishly because they cannot pay enough attention to the recipients.

The hypotheses of the present study are shown in Fig. 1. The first hypothesis is that inadequate self-disclosure may be responded to negatively by recipients, which may increase depression of self-disclosers. The second hypothesis is that self-preoccupation may increase inadequate self-disclosure and thus may increase depression of self-disclosers (Sakamoto 1999).

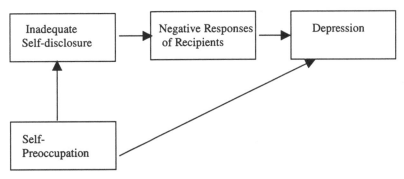

Fig. 1. A model describing the effects of inadequate self-disclosure and self-preoccupation on depression.

Fig. 1 shows that inadequate self-disclosure affects depression via negative responses of recipients. The model also shows that self-preoccupation directly affects inadequate self-disclosure and depression of self-disclosers. We examined this causal model with path analysis (Structural Equation Model, SEM) among four observed variables.

2 Method

2.1 Participants

The participants were 65 male and 55 female undergraduate students with ages ranging from18 to 22 years (Mean age=19.63 years, SD=2.78).

2.2 Timing of the Study

Questionnaires were administered to 120 college students twice four weeks apart. At time 1, we assessed self-preoccupation. At time 2, four weeks later, we assessed depression, inadequate self-disclosure and negative responses of recipients between time 1 and time 2.

2.3 Questionnaires

Self-preoccupation was measured by the Self-Preoccupation Scale (SPS). The Preoccupation Scale (Sakamoto 1998) consists of 24 items; 11 are for the Self-Preoccupation Scale (SPS), nine are for the External-Preoccupation Scale (EPS), and the remaining four are filler items. Because of the purpose of the present study, the results for external-preoccupation were not addressed.   Each item was rated on a five-point scale.   Inadequate self-disclosure and negative responses of recipients were measured on a scale of inadequate self-disclosure (Moriwaki et al. in press), including 23 items and a scale of negative responses of recipients (Moriwaki et al. in press), including 22 items.   Each item was rated on a four-point scale.   These scales have high internal consistency; the reliability coefficients of these scales were .86 and .91, respectively.   They also have been shown to have concurrent validity (Moriwaki et al. in press).   Depression was measured by the Japanese version (Fukuda and Kobayashi 1973) of the SDS (Zung 1965).   Each item was rated on a four-point scale.

3 Results

First, we investigated whether each scale of inadequate self-disclosure and responses of recipients consists of one factor, because it has not been confirmed with principal component analysis.   Table 1 and Table 2 show results of principal component analysis of these two scales; the scale of inadequate self-disclosure and the scale of responses of recipients, respectively.   Items are sorted on the descending order of component loadings.

Table 1. The result of principal component analysis of the scale of inadequate self-disclosure

Items	Component Loadings
· I talked about personal matters to a person who had no topics of common interest with me.	.86
· I talked about personal matters while having a good time at a party or playing in a group.	.86
· I talked about personal matters to a person with whom I was not so intimate.	.85
· I talked about personal matters to anybody.	.84
· I talked about personal matters in busy places.	.83
· I talked about personal matters when another purpose or task had been established and everybody had to do one thing all together.	.81
· I talked about personal matters before a group of persons.	.80
· I talked about personal matters anywhere.	.78
· I told a single matter repeatedly.	.77
· I talked about personal matters to a person when he or she was busy.	.77
· I talked about personal matters to a person whom I met for the first time.	.74
· I talked about personal matters to a person even when he or she was tired.	.73
· I talked about personal matters to a person who was not willing to listen.	.71
· I talked about personal matters one-sidedly without listening to.	.70
· I talked in circles.	.69
· I always spoke ill of others or grumbled.	.68
· I told the same story many times.	.65
· I got too excited when talking about personal matters.	.64
· I repeated the same talk.	.63
· I told the same story to a person who had heard that story many times.	.58
· The talk was biased to negative contents.	.53
· Talk content was generally negative.	.48
· Most of the talk was negative.	.44
Variance Accounted for	11.97
Proportion of Total Variance	52.04

Table 2. The result of principal component analysis of the scale of responses of recipients

Items	Component Loadings
· He or she injected another topic when I was talking.	.89
· He or she listened to me but expressed lack of interest.	.88
· He or she gave excuses not to listen to me (such as being busy).	.87
· He or she gave comments without apparent thought.	.86
· He or she replied as if the subject discussed was not his or her concern.	.85
· He or she gave curt replies.	.84
· He or she gave a vague or boring response.	.83
· He or she expressed feelings of denial or dislike.	.83
· He or she cut me short.	.80
· He or she ignored me when I was talking.	.76
· He or she listened restlessly to me.	.76
· He or she listened to me while doing something else.	.73
· He or she gave impertinent comments on the topic.	.65
· He or she pushed off.	.65
· He or she diverted the conversation.	.62
· He or she did not listen attentively to me.	.57
· He or she expressed no opinions.	.52
· He or she did not reply or comment.	.51
· He or she only kept nodding.	.43
· He or she introduced an unrelated topic.	.43
· He or she did not ask any questions.	.42
· He or she watched the clock while listening to me.	.41
Variance Accounted for	11.01
Proportion of Total Variance	50.00

Table 1 and Table 2 show that each scale consists of one factor.

All scales were shown to be highly reliable, with a Cronbach's alpha of 0.82 to 0.92. Table 3 shows correlations, means, and standard deviations (S.D.) of measured four variables.

Table 3. Correlations, Means, and Standard deviations of measured four variables

Variables	Self Preoccupation	Inadequate Self-Disclosure	Negative Responses	Depression	Means	S.D.
Self-Preoccupation Inadequate	0.82[a]	0.26**	0.06	0.39**	33.34	4.32
Self-Disclosure Negative Responses		0.86[a]	0.46**	0.10	55.43	7.04
of Recipients			0.91[a]	0.22**	58.77	10.42
Depression				0.92[a]	41.62	19.80

[a]Cronbach's alpha.   **$p<.01$

We then examined the causal relationship with path analysis using these scales.

In addition to model 1(Fig. 1), we estimated three alternative models; model 2 which adds the path from inadequate self-disclosure to depression, to model 1, model 3 which adds the path from self-preoccupation to negative responses of recipients, and model 4 which adds both the path from self-preoccupation to negative responses of recipients and the path from inadequate self-disclosure to depression, to model 1.   We compared these four models and selected one of them as the best fit.   Fit indices of the models based upon maximum likelihood methods for all parameter estimates are summarized in Table 4.

Table 4. Fit indices of four models

Model	GFI[a]	AGFI[b]	CFI[c]	RMSEA[d]	AIC[e]	CAIC[f]
model 1	0.997	0.974	1.00	0.00	-2.05	-10.40
model 2	0.994	0.970	1.00	0.02	-0.95	-5.13
model 3	0.997	0.974	1.00	0.00	-1.09	-5.27
model 4[g]	—	—	1.00	0.00	0.00	0.00

[a]Goodness-of-Fit Index.
[b]Adjusted GFI.
[c]Comparative Fit Index.
[d]Root Mean Square Error of Approximation.
[e]Akaike's Information Criterion.
[f]Consistant Akaike's Information Criterion.
[g]A saturated model.

The results of the path analysis for three alternative models indicated that parameter estimates of each additional path to model 1 were not significant and that there were almost no changes in coefficients of determination for endogenous variables.   Furthermore, from the viewpoint of AIC and CAIC values, we have concluded that model 1 is the preferred model.   Fig. 2 presents path analysis results for model 1.

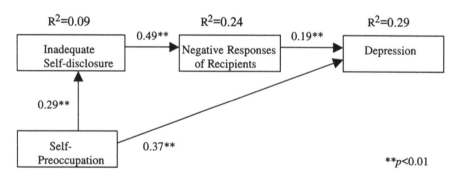

Fig. 2.   Path analysis results for model 1.   Figures attached to each path are standardized parameter estimates.

Fig. 2 indicates that inadequate self-disclosure increases negative responses of recipients, and these negative responses increase depression. Furthermore, as shown in Fig. 2, self-preoccupation increases inadequate self-disclosure and depression. Self-preoccupation has both direct effects on depression and indirect effects mediated by inadequate self-disclosure and negative responses of recipients.

4 Discussion

The purpose of the present study was to examine the causal relationship among self-disclosure, responses of recipients, and depression of self-disclosers. It also sought to examine the effects of self-preoccupation on self-disclosure and depression. We hypothesized that recipients may respond negatively to inadequate self-disclosure, which may increase depression of self-disclosers according to Sacco's (1999) model, focusing especially on effects of how to self-disclose and responses of recipients on depression. The second hypothesis was that self-preoccupation may increase inadequate self-disclosure, and may increase depression of self-disclosers. For this purpose, we examined first, unidimensionality of the scale of inadequate self-disclosure and responses of recipients. It was confirmed that each scale consists of one factor with principal component analysis. Then, we examined the causal relationship with path analysis and found that these hypotheses were supported.

The results suggest that self-disclosure and responses of recipients are important factors in depression. Inadequate self-disclosure increases depression via negative responses of recipients. Self-disclosure does not always decrease depression. It will be important to consider how we self-disclose and the responses of recipients when we self-disclose to others. The results also indicate that self-preoccupation promotes inadequate self-disclosure and depression of self-disclosers. We believe that these results may be applied to early intervention and prevention of depression in the future. Altering self-preoccupation and inadequate self-disclosure may contribute to decreasing depression.

It is important to point out at least two potential limitations to the present studies. First, although we examined effects of how to self-disclose and responses of recipients on depression, measures of responses of recipients depended upon the self-disclosers' perceptions. In the future, we must therefore examine this causal relationship with experimental design or paired data in order to exclude effects of biases of perception.

Second, we examined the relationships among these variables only with undergraduates. Therefore, future studies are needed to investigate these relationships not only in other samples (e.g., older people) but also in clinical samples.

References

Chelune GJ, Associates (1979) Self-disclosure.   San Francisco, CA.;   Jossey-Bass.

Coyne JC (1976a) Depression and the responses of others.   Journal of Abnormal Psychology 85 :186-193.

Coyne JC (1976b) Toward an interactional description of depression.   Psychiatry 39:28-40.

Cozby PC (1973) Self-disclosure: A literature review.   Psychological Bulletin 79 :73-91.

Derlega VJ, Metts S, Petronio S, Margulis ST (1993) Self-disclosure.   Newbury Park, CA; Sage.

Gotlib IH, Robinson LA (1982) Responses to depressed individuals: Discrepancies between self-report and observer-rated behavior.   Journal of Abnormal Psychology 91: 231-240.

Hokanson JE, Butler AC (1992) Cluster-Analysis of Depressed College-Students Social Behaviors.   Journal of Personality and Social Psychology 62 :273-280.

Joiner TE, Barnett J (1994) A test of Interpersonal theory of depression and adolescents using a projective technique.   Journal of Abnormal Child Psychology 22 :595-609.

Joiner T, Coyne JC (eds) (1999) The interactional Nature of Depression.   American Psychological Association, Washington, D.C

Miller RS, Lefcourt HM (1983) Social intimacy: An important moderator of stressful life events.   American Journal of Community Psychology 11:127-139.

Moriwaki A, Sakamoto S, Tanno Y (in press) Development of self-disclosure scales and response scales of recipients in college students.   The Japanese Journal of Personality.

Pennebaker JW (1985) Traumatic experience and psychomatic disease: Exploring the roles of behavioral inhibition, obsession, and confiding.   Canadian Psychology 26 :82-95.

Pennebaker JW (1997) Writing about emotional experiences as a therapeutic process.   Psychological Science 8 :162-166.

Pennebaker JW, O'Heeron RC (1984) Confiding in others and illness rate among spouses of suicide and accidental death victims.   Journal of Abnormal Psychology 93 :473-476.

Pennebaker JW, Susman JR (1988) Disclosure of traumas and psychosomatic processes.   Social Sciences and Medicine 26 :327-332.

Fukuda K, Kobayashi S (1973) A study on a Self-Rating Depression Scale. Psychiatria et Nuerologia Japonica 75 :673-679.

Sacco WP (1999) A Social-Cognitive Model of Interpersonal Processes in Depression.   In: Joiner T, Coyne JC (eds) The interactional Nature of Depression.   American Psychological Association, Washington, D.C., pp329-364.

Sakamoto S (1998) The preoccupation scale: Its development and relationship with depression scales.   Journal of Clinical Psychology 54 :645-654.

Sakamoto S (1999) A longitudinal study of the relationship of self-preoccupation with depression.   Journal of Clinical Psychology 55: 109-116.

Zung WWK (1965) A self-rating depression scale.   Archives of General Psychiatry 12: 63-70.

Part 3
IRT and Adaptive Testing

Developments in Practical Nonparametric IRT Scale Analysis

Klaas Sijtsma

Department of Methodology and Statistics, FSW, Tilburg University, P. O. Box 90153, 5000 LE Tilburg, The Netherlands *k.sijtsma@uvt.nl*

Summary The present state of nonparametric item response theory is reviewed. First, assumptions and measurement properties implied by these assumptions are discussed. Then, model-data fit methods are briefly reviewed, and quality indices for items and scales are given. Finally, three computer programs are compared with respect to their practical possibilities in the analysis of test and questionnaire data.

Keywords: goodness-of-fit methods for NIRT, NIRT software, nonparametric item response theory (NIRT), scalability coefficients

1 What is Nonparametric Item Response Theory?

Item response theory (IRT) models are used to analyze the data of N respondents on J items. The result is scales for the measurement of persons and items. A useful division is into parametric and nonparametric IRT models. The former use a particular parametric formulation for describing the data structure whereas the latter use order restrictions for this purpose; see below for more details and Boomsma et al. (2001) for an overview. This paper discusses nonparametric IRT (NIRT) models, and their practical usefulness in constructing scales.

We use the following notation. Let j be an item index, $j = 1, \ldots, J$ (test length); and let i be a person index, $i = 1, \ldots, N$ (sample size). Let X_j be the random variable for the ordered score on item j, with realization x_j; $x_j = 0, 1$ for dichotomous items, and $x_j = 0, \ldots, m$ for polytomous items with $m + 1$ ordered answer categories typical of rating scales. For respondent i, the total score on a test is denoted X_{i+} and item scores are denoted X_{ij} to express their dependence on the respondent and the item. Test score X_+ is then defined as

$$X_{i+} = \sum_{j=1}^{J} X_{ij}.$$

Let θ be the latent trait; and let $P(X_j = 1|\theta)$ be the item response function (IRF) for dichotomous items, $P(X_j = x_j|\theta)$ the category response function (CRF) for polytomous items, and $P(X_j \geq x_j|\theta)$ the item step response function (ISRF) for polytomous items.

NIRT has three classes of assumptions:

1. *Dimensionality of measurement.* For multidimensional measurement, NIRT assumes a vector $\boldsymbol{\theta} = (\theta_1, ..., \theta_T)$, and defines response probabilities as $P(X_j = 1|\boldsymbol{\theta})$, $P(X_j = x_j|\boldsymbol{\theta})$, and $P(X_j \geq x_j|\boldsymbol{\theta})$; see Holland and Rosenbaum (1986). For strictly unidimensional measurement, θ is a scalar. For essentially unidimensional measurement, $\boldsymbol{\theta}$ contains one dominant latent trait and several nuisance traits, whose influence on the response probability vanishes as $J \to \infty$; see Stout (1990). In the IRT family (and in NIRT), unidimensional (UD) models are predominant over multidimensional models. This reflects the practice of test construction where the ideal is a unidimensional test and a single test score. In this paper we assume a unidimensional θ.

2. *Relationship between items.* NIRT models assume that item scores are locally independent (LI). Let $\mathbf{X} = (X_1, \dots, X_J)$, and $\mathbf{x} = (x_1, \dots, x_J)$. Then LI means that

$$P(\mathbf{X} = \mathbf{x}|\theta) = \prod_{j=1}^{J} P(X_j = x_j|\theta).$$

A consequence of LI is that for two items, j and k, their conditional covariance, $Cov(X_j, X_k|\theta)$, equals 0.

3. *Relationship of item score and latent trait.* NIRT models are based on the general notion that the higher θ, the higher the "success" probability on an item measuring θ. This is reflected by the monotonicity (M) assumption. For dichotomous items, assumption M means that $P(X_j = 1|\theta)$ is nondecreasing in θ, and for polytomous items, that $P(X_j \geq x_j|\theta)$ is nondecreasing in θ. Nonparametric and parametric IRT models differ in the formalization of assumption M. In particular, a NIRT model imposes only order restrictions on the IRF or the ISRF; for example, for two arbitrary values θ_a and θ_b,

$$P(X_j = 1|\theta_a) \leq P(X_j = 1|\theta_b); \text{ whenever } \theta_a < \theta_b.$$

Assumptions UD, LI, and M define the NIRT model of monotone homogeneity; see Sijtsma and Molenaar (2002). A parametric IRT model defines the IRF or ISRF by choosing a specific parametric function; for example, the 3-parameter logistic model defines the IRF as

$$P(X_j = 1|\theta) = \gamma_j + (1 - \gamma_j)\frac{\exp[\alpha_j(\theta - \delta_j)]}{1 + \exp[\alpha_j(\theta - \delta_j)]}.$$

Here, γ_j, α_j, and δ_j are lower asymptote, slope, and location parameters of the IRF of item j, respectively.

2 Measurement Properties of Nonparametric IRT models

1. *Person ordering.* NIRT models for dichotomous items based on the assumptions of UD, LI, and M imply that the ordering on X_+ is stochastically the

same as the ordering on θ. This is the stochastic ordering property (Hemker et al., 1997), formalized as

$$P(\theta > c | X_+ = s) \leq P(\theta > c | X_+ = t); \text{ for all } c; \text{ and } 0 \leq s < t \leq J.$$

This property guarantees ordinal person measurement. For NIRT models for polytomous items, Hemker et al. (1997) showed that the stochastic ordering property is not implied. Van der Ark (2001) used simulated polytomous data to demonstrate that in practice for most tests and latent trait distributions the stochastic ordering property held.

2. *Item ordering.* By adding the assumption that the IRFs do not intersect to the assumptions of UD, LI, and M, we obtain the double monotonicity model. Noting that for dichotomous items $E(X_j | \theta) = P(X_j = 1 | \theta)$, for all j, and using the non-intersection of the J IRFs, it is easily seen that items can be ordered and numbered accordingly, such that

$$E(X_1 | \theta) \leq E(X_2 | \theta) \leq \ldots \leq E(X_J | \theta); \text{ for all } \theta.$$

This is an invariant item ordering; see Sijtsma and Junker (1996). For polytomous item scores, an invariant item ordering is defined in exactly the same way (Sijtsma and Hemker, 1998) as for dichotomous items, with the expectation ranging from 0 to m.

3 Investigating the Fit of Nonparametric IRT Models to Test Data

Because NIRT models are based on relatively weak assumptions, in general, their fit to data is relatively good; see Sijtsma and Molenaar (2002). Also, because of their flexibility such models provide excellent opportunities for studying item properties. The outcomes give many indications of how to improve a test or questionnaire.

For example, IRFs and ISRFs are estimated using nonparametric regression methods; see Ramsay (1991), Junker and Sijtsma (2000), and Sijtsma and Molenaar (2002). This provides the researcher with accurate information about their shape as evidenced by the data. Using, in contrast, a logistic regression or normal-ogive function would impose an S-shape on the response curves, and a model test would indicate fit or misfit of this function to the data. For the case of misfit, nonparametric regression methods tell the researcher where and how the response curves deviate from the hypothesized shape (Douglas and Cohen, 2001). For example, the estimated curves may show zero or negative discrimination for parts of the distribution of θ or suggest a bell-shape. Based on this a researcher may decide to reject the misfitting item from the test or choose a more appropriate IRT model.

Also, NIRT has given inspiration to algorithms that investigate the dimensionality of the test; see Mokken and Lewis (1982) and Stout et al. (1996).

Rather than a priori modeling a unidimensional or a multidimensional structure, these algorithms explore the dimensional structure of the data and produce a division of the items into subsets that tap different latent traits. This approach can also be used to check whether a hypothesized item subset structure is supported by the data. These methods provide useful information about the data structure and may help the researcher to decide which items to remove or which subtests to pursue further.

Next, we review some methods for investigating the fit of NIRT models to the data. The general principle is that we study observable consequences of our assumptions of UD, LI, and M.

Conditional association. The first observable consequence is conditional association (CA; see Holland and Rosenbaum, 1986). Split vector $\mathbf{X}$ into two disjoint part vectors: $\mathbf{X} = (\mathbf{Y}, \mathbf{Z})$. Define n_1 and n_2 to be nondecreasing functions in the item scores from $\mathbf{Y}$, and m to be some function of the item scores in $\mathbf{Z}$. Then UD, LI, and M imply CA,

$$Cov[n_1(\mathbf{Y}), n_2(\mathbf{Y})|m(\mathbf{Z}) = z] \geq 0, \text{ for all } z.$$

Examples of CA that clarify its meaning are the following.

1. Split $\mathbf{X}$ into three disjoint part vectors, $\mathbf{X} = (\mathbf{Y}_1, \mathbf{Y}_2, \mathbf{Z})$. For example, $\mathbf{Y}_1, \mathbf{Y}_2$ may be testlets and $\mathbf{Z}$ may be another part of an exam. Let Y_{1+}, Y_{2+}, and Z_+ be the unweighted sum scores on the three item subsets, respectively. Let $Z_{+(\text{cutoff})}$ be a cutoff score on the items in $\mathbf{Z}$, and let Z_{cutoff} be a binary pass(1)/fail(0) indicator. Then CA implies, for example,

$$Cov(Y_{1+}, Y_{2+}|Z_{\text{cutoff}} = z) \geq 0, \text{ with } z = 0 \text{ if } Z_+ < Z_{+(\text{cutoff})}; \text{ else } z = 1.$$

That is, in the subgroup of students that failed and the subgroup that passed the subexam $\mathbf{Z}$, the covariance between the two testlet scores must be nonnegative. Negative testlet covariance rejects the model of monotone homogeneity for the complete item set.

2. Ignoring a subgroup structure and studying covariances within the whole group, CA implies,

$$Cov(X_j, X_k) \geq 0, \text{ all pairs } j, k; j \neq k.$$

That is, in the whole group all $\frac{1}{2}J(J-1)$ inter-item covariances must be nonnegative. A negative covariance indicates misfit of the model of monotone homogeneity for at least one of the items involved.

3. Define a rest score based on $\mathbf{X}$ as,

$$R_{(-j,-k)} = \sum_{h \neq j,k} X_h.$$

Then CA implies that,

$$Cov[X_j, X_k | R_{(-j,-k)} = r] \geq 0, \text{ all } j, k; j \neq k; \text{ all } r = 0, 1, \ldots, J - 2.$$

That is, in the subgroup of respondents that have the same restscore r, the covariance between items j and k must be nonnegative. This special case of CA proves to be useful for investigating LI, as we discuss next.

Local independence. The previous observable covariance property is used to study a nonobservable consequence of LI; that is, $Cov(X_j, X_k | \theta) = 0$. Because θ is latent, the rest score $R_{(-j,-k)}$ is used as a proxy for θ. This is justified by a consistency result [for $J \to \infty$; see Stout (1990) for dichotomous items; and Junker (1991) for polytomous items] and the stochastic ordering property (holds for any J, but only for dichotomous items; see Hemker et al., 1997). Based on CA, we expect $Cov[X_j, X_k | R_{(-j,-k)}] \geq 0$. The reason is that, for finite J, the conditional distribution $f[\theta | R_{(-j,-k)}]$ has positive (non-zero) variance, which explains the positive covariance. It may be noted that for $J \to \infty$, this variance equals 0, due to the consistency of the restscore for the latent trait; thus, the conditional covariance then equals 0. Zhang and Stout (1999) showed that for finite J and multidimensional $\boldsymbol{\theta}$, the covariance conditional on the restscore is either negative or positive, depending on the dimensionality structure of the item set. Based on this result, Stout et al. (1996) used a genetic algorithm to find the optimal partition of a multidimensional item set into unidimensional subsets.

Monotonicity. We define another restscore as

$$R_{(-j)} = \sum_{k \neq j} X_k.$$

Like $R_{(-j,-k)}$, restscore $R_{(-j)}$ estimates θ, which is justified on the basis of the same stochastic ordering and consistency arguments. Then, $P[X_j = 1 | R_{(-j)}]$ is used to estimate $P(X_j = 1 | \theta)$. Junker (1993) showed that UD, LI, and M imply manifest monotonicity,

$$P[X_j = 1 | R_{(-j)}] \text{ non-decreasing in } R_{(-j)}; R_{(-j)} = 0, \ldots, J - 1.$$

The conditional probabilities $P[X_j = 1 | R_{(-j)} = r]$, for all r, can be used to estimate the IRF by means of nonparametric regression. This yields a discrete estimate of the IRF (see Junker and Sijtsma, 2000; Sijtsma and Molenaar, 2002) or, using kernel smoothing methods, a continuous estimate (see Douglas and Cohen, 2001; Ramsay, 1991). Deviations from manifest monotonicity are in conflict with the model of monotone homogeneity.

Intersection of IRFs. Because this paper is limited to the model of monotone homogeneity, we refer to Sijtsma and Junker (1996) for a survey of methods for investigating intersections of IRFs for the purpose of establishing invariant item ordering. They discuss methods for assessing whether pairs of IRFs intersect and whether a set of J IRFs contains intersections.

4 Quality of scales: Scalability coefficients

Because assumption M also allows IRFs to have flat or almost flat slopes, in practice a scale that satisfies the model of monotone homogeneity may not allow for accurate person ordering. Scalability coefficient H (Sijtsma and Molenaar, 2002) is used to distinguish inaccurate ordinal scales from accurate ones. For two items j and k, scalability coefficient H_{jk} is defined as,

$$H_{jk} = \frac{Cov(X_j, X_k)}{Cov(X_j, X_k)_{max}}.$$

Here, $Cov(X_j, X_k)_{max}$ is the maximum covariance given fixed marginals of a 2×2 contingency table for the frequency counts of the scores on items j and k. Also, an item scalability coefficient H_j is defined that weights all $J - 1$ $H_{jk}s$ involving item j, and a total scale H that is a weighted average of all $\frac{1}{2}J(J - 1)$ coefficients H_{jk}.

How should we interpret the H coefficient? First, the model of monotone homogeneity implies

$$0 \leq H_{jk}, H_j, H \leq 1.$$

Keeping the θ distribution and the IRFs except for IRF slopes constant, these coefficients increase as a function of the slope of the IRFs. It follows that the value of total H gives an indication of the discrimination power of a test; that is, the degree of separation of respondents (or θs) by means of the items. Thus, H is a measure of the accuracy of ordering respondents by means of total score X_+. For practical applications, $H = 0.3$ is considered to be a minimum requirement for accurately ordering persons. Total H can be used to evaluate an item set as an a priori scale, and to select items from an experimental item set into (sub)scales. An item selection algorithm that does this is part of the computer program MSP5 (Molenaar and Sijtsma, 2000).

5 Computer programs, and what they do

Finally, we briefly compare the NIRT item analysis programs MSP5 (Molenaar and Sijtsma, 2000), DETECT (Stout et al., 1996), and TestGraf98 (Ramsay, 2000). MSP5 investigates the model of monotone homogeneity through the sign of inter-item covariances, and a discrete estimate of the IRF; DETECT checks LI through inter-item covariances conditional on the restscore; and TestGraf98 uses continuous IRF estimates (Table 1, first panel). Both MSP5 and TestGraf98 allow for investigating an a priori scale (second panel; MSP5: H coefficient, reliability, information on assumption M; TestGraf98: test response function (TRF) and information function; see Ramsay, 2000). MSP5 and DETECT contain excellent algorithms for exploring the dimensionality of an item set, based on different scaling criteria; and

MSP5 also provides several statistics per scale found (second panel). MSP5 provides several methods for investigating invariant item ordering (third panel). Both MSP5 and TestGraf98 allow for scale analyses in meaningful subgroups (fourth panel). TestGraf98, in particular, provides means for investigating differential item functioning. All three programs are suited for handling polytomous items (fifth panel). TestGraf98 is predominantly a graphical item analysis program. MSP5 provides graphs for estimated IRFs/ISRFs and frequency distributions (sixth panel).

Table 1. Comparison of three programs for NIRT analysis

	Programs		
Aspects Model	MSP5	DETECT	TestGraf98
UD, LI, M	InterItemCov ≥ 0	–	–
LI	–	Dimensionality	–
M	Discrete IRF Est	–	Continuous IRF Est
A priori scale	H/Reliab; IRF info	–	TRF, InformFunc
Dimensionality	Good (M)	Very good (LI)	–
InfoPerScaleFound	H/Reliab; IRF info	–	–
InvarItemOrdering	ItemPair/Overall	–	–
Subgroups	Good	–	Good
DiffItemFunc	Modest	–	Good
Polytomous Items	+	+	+
Graphics	Few	None	Many

The three programs are complementary more than competitive. MSP5 is well suited for model-data fitting. It uses many statistics and indices for this purpose, which provide the user with a wealth of diagnostic information. Moreover, it contains an automated item selection algorithm for selecting unidimensional scales. DETECT has been designed in particular for dimensionality investigation of an item set, and accomplishes this goal excellently. It is a good alternative to factor analysis, in particular when data are dichotomous. TestGraf98 provides an unprecedented tool for the graphical analysis of response functions. It allows for the visual diagnosis of IRFs, option response curves (for multiple choice items, with one correct and several incorrect answer options, which are nominal), and category response functions (for polytomous items). Each program is a valuable tool for NIRT data analysis. Together these three programs make possible the analysis of one's test data at almost any level of granularity.

References

Boomsma A, Van Duijn MAJ, Snijders TAB (2001) Essays on Item Response Theory. Springer, New York

Douglas J, Cohen A (2001) Nonparametric item response function ICC estimation for assesssing parametric model fit. Applied Psychological Measurement 25:234–243

Hemker BT, Sijtsma K, Molenaar IW, Junker BW (1997) Stochastic ordering using the latent trait and the sum score in polytomous IRT models. Psychometrika 62:331–347

Holland PW, Rosenbaum PR (1986) Conditional association and unidimensionality in monotone latent variable models. The Annals of Statistics 14:1523–1543

Junker BW (1991) Essential independence and likelihood-based ability estimation for polytomous items. Psychometrika 56:255–278

Junker BW (1993) Conditional association, essential independence and monotone unidimensional item response models. The Annals of Statistics 21:1359–1378

Junker BW, Sijtsma K (2000) Latent and manifest monotonicity in item response models. Applied Psychological Measurement 24:65–81

Mokken RJ, Lewis C (1982) A nonparametric approach to the analysis of dichotomous item responses. Applied Psychological Measurement 6:417–430

Molenaar IW, Sijtsma K (2000) MSP5 for Windows. User's manual. iecProGAMMA, Groningen, The Netherlands

Ramsay JO (1991) Kernel smoothing approaches to nonparametric item characteristic curve estimation. Psychometrika 56:611–630

Ramsay JO (2000) TestGraf. A program for the graphical analysis of multiple choice test and questionnaire data. Department of Psychology, McGill University, Montreal, Canada

Sijtsma K, Junker BW (1996) A survey of theory and methods of invariant item ordering. British Journal of Mathematical and Statistical Psychology 49:79–105

Sijtsma K, Hemker BT (1998) Nonparametric polytomous IRT models for invariant item ordering, with results for parametric models. Psychometrika 63:183–200

Sijtsma K, Molenaar IW (2002) Introduction to nonparametric item response theory. Sage, Thousand Oaks CA

Stout WF (1990) A new item response theory modeling approach with applications to unidimensionality assessment and ability estimation. Psychometrika 55:293–325

Stout WF, Habing B, Douglas J, Kim H, Roussos L, Zhang J (1996) Conditional covariance based nonparametric multidimensionality assessment. Applied Psychological Measurement 20:331–354

Van der Ark LA (2001) Practical consequences of stochastic ordering of the latent trait under various polytomous IRT models. Tilburg University, The Netherlands

Zhang J, Stout WF (1999) The theoretical DETECT index of dimensionality and its application to approximate simple structure. Psychometrika 64:213–249

Groups of Persons and Groups of Items in Nonparametric Item Response Theory

Ivo W. Molenaar[1]

[1] University of Groningen, Joest Lewelaan 5, 9321 AL Peize, Netherlands

Summary. In standard applications of Item Response Theory (IRT), n exchangeable persons have responded to k exchangeable items. Among neither persons nor items subgroups are distinguished. This paper reviews methods and results for situations where it is meaningful to consider subgroups (of persons, of items, or both). It does so in the class of nonparametric IRT models, which is briefly explained in the first section. The main reason for such considerations is that IRT, explicitly or implicitly, not only aims to explain why certain person-item combinations have led to a positive or negative answer, but also to predict what a given person would do on other items not actually presented (test equating problems, parallel versions), and how other persons would perform on the given items (optimal test design, inference from sample to population).

Key words. nonparametric item response theory, subpopulation invariance, test dimensionality, clusters of items, Mokken models

1. Nonparametric Item Response Theory

The core concept of IRT for dichotomously scored items is the Item Response Function (IRF), which is the probability of a positive answer to a given item, viewed as a function of the latent trait value θ. Almost all IRT models assume that θ is unidimensional, that different items of one scale or test are statistically independent given θ (local independence), and that all IRFs are nondecreasing in θ. The most widely used IRT models are parametric: they also assume that all IRFs have a specific parametric form, like logistic or normal ogive, within which they differ only in location, sometimes also in slope or lower asymptote value. This allows to write down the likelihood of an observed $n \times k$ datamatrix as a function of the unknown item and person parameters, which are then estimated with their asymptotic standard errors.

Nonparametric IRT (NIRT) does not restrict IRFs to obey one parametric formula. It only assumes unidimensionality, local independence and monotonicity and thus is more flexible in fitting an IRT model to data. Some references are Mokken (1971, 1997), Holland & Rosenbaum (1986), Stout (1990), Ramsay (1991), Ellis & Junker (1997), Sijtsma (1998), Junker & Sijtsma (2000).

An important result due to Grayson (1988) states that for dichotomous items the three assumptions of NIRT allow a stochastic ordering of persons with respect to θ using the number-correct score X_+. So this quantity, which is quite generally used in scoring tests and scales, is not only the sufficient statistic for inference on θ when the Rasch model holds, but it is already sufficient for item-free ordering on θ under the far more mild NIRT assumptions.

An interesting submodel called double monotonicity imposes the additional restriction that IRFs do not intersect. Then also person-free ordering of items is possible. We return to invariant item ordering (Sijtsma & Junker, 1996) later in this paper.

Although we shall mostly discuss dichotomously scored items, we note that the NIRT models have been extended to polytomous items (Molenaar, 1997). Both cases are presented in the textbook by Sijtsma and Molenaar (2002) and for both cases procedures for estimation and model fit are available in the software package MSP5 for Windows and its manual (Molenaar & Sijtsma, 2000). For related work using ordered latent classes see Croon (1991) and Van Onna (this volume).

2. Local homogeneity, the hidden assumption

IRT is more powerful and more flexible than older measurement models because it is based on the IRF, the probability of a positive answer for a given item and a given latent trait value. In the random sampling view of IRT, an IRF value of p means that among all persons with latent trait value θ, a fraction p always give the positive answer and a fraction $1-p$ always give the negative answer. More common is the stochastic subject view (Lord & Novick, 1968, Holland, 1990) in which there is assumed to be an unobservable propensity distribution within each subject. By random fluctuations between occasions the same subject will sometimes respond positively, sometimes negatively, and it is this variation that is expressed by the probability p.

In my view it is indeed plausible in most applications that each person has a probability between 0 and 1 for a positive answer, rather than a fixed value of 1 for some persons and 0 for others. This variation between occasions is most evident when measuring attitudes and personality traits. Also in educational testing, however, it is plausible that students' concentration varies between bright and dull days. So although part of the variation may be between persons with the same θ, also a lot of variation will occur within persons between occasions.

In a fundamental paper, Ellis & Van den Wollenberg (1993) have argued that IRT interpreted with the stochastic subject view requires an additional assumption, which they call *local homogeneity*. Simply stated it says that subjects with the same latent trait value must have the same response probabilities: θ and nothing but θ is the systematic component in their response behavior. Not only does one observe a sample of persons, but each person is observed on just one occasion, and could have scored somewhat differently on another occasion. Modeling that one observes a sample of person×occasion pairs rather than just randomly chosen persons requires a careful mathematical formulation in terms of conditional probabilities. Ellis & Van den Wollenberg prove two important results. The first says that validity in a population of an IRT model including local homogeneity implies the same model with the same IRFs to hold in any subpopulation (note that a subpopulation is a selection of persons, not of person×occasion pairs). The second theorem says that adding local homogeneity to our three NIRT assumptions of unidimensionality, local independence and monotonicity implies nonnegative association between each item pair as well as experimental independence [which is local independence not given a fixed value of θ but given the selection of a person]. For both theorems the converse is also proven.

It would require too much space to explain this in more detail, or go into the other results of the cited paper. The next section about groups of persons, however, could not have been written without the concepts of local homogeneity and subpopulation invariance. These properties are often taken for granted, but actually they are important hidden assumptions.

3. Subgroups of persons

For several reasons, a psychometrician may want to distinguish subgroups of actual respondents, or subpopulations of potential respondents. It may be, for example, that not all respondents were given the same item set. Examples are parallel versions of an examination, or a quality of life questionnaire in which some items are disease specific or gender specific. A related although different situation occurs when groups with the same missing data pattern are considered during imputation (Huisman & Molenaar, 2001). Even when the same items were used for all respondents, one might be concerned whether the instrument performs similarly across groups.

Groups of respondents may differ in several aspects. If they differ in the distribution of the latent trait values, but not in the IRFs, this is usually interesting and not problematic. In NIRT with its ordering of latent trait values by total score X_+ one will probably inspect the distributions of X_+ and perhaps apply a distribution free test for the null hypothesis that group membership makes no difference.

It may happen that the overall scalability or reliability differs between subgroups. In particular, they tend to be lower in subgroups with a smaller standard deviation of θ (restriction of range). In the unlikely case of one subgroup in which all latent trait values are equal, all interitem correlations, and also the reliability, become zero due to local independence. Our instruments to detect model misfit are often sensitive to group size and latent trait distribution. For this reason small or moderate differences in model misfit are not always a reason for major concern.

Finally, it may happen that most of our IRFs appear to be invariant across groups, but one item, or a few items, show differences in IRF, like a different location and/or different fit results across groups. This is often called DIF (Differential Item Functioning). Study of DIF is rather difficult, mostly because the latent trait is unobservable, and because the number of variables that one could use for group formation is unlimited. It is recommended to restrict oneself to those grouping variables for which DIF can be expected, and for which it has negative consequences for the IRT application being considered.

Like often in psychometrics, substantive and statistical considerations should both play a role in decisions in DIF research. One might remove the offending items if they are not numerous and their removal does not damage reliability and validity. It is also feasible to view an item with DIF as being a different pseudo-item per group: say item 3 for males can then be more difficult than item 3 for females, and each gender has missing data on the pseudo-item for the other gender. Whether this is defensible and useful will be context dependent.

So far, most of our deliberations in this section were equally valid for parametric and nonparametric IRT. With exception of Shealy & Stout (1993), most DIF research has used parametric models. In the Mokken Double Monotonicity model, as incorporated in the MSP software, one may choose an integer valued grouping variable, say based on ethnicity, age or gender. One may then inspect the frequency distribution of the sumscore via tables, histograms or moments. Next one may compare the scalability H or the reliability rho as well as model assumption checks across subgroups. Finally, a special module activated as soon as a grouping variable is defined allows a graphical, descriptive and inferential comparison of the ordering of the items between groups. Group differences in item ordering (or item step ordering in the polytomous case) are an indication of DIF. Molenaar & Sijtsma (2000) give more details; the problem of empirically checking subpopulation invariance is also mentioned by Ellis & Van den Wollenberg (1993).

4. Subgroups of items and test dimensionality

Unidimensionality is a key assumption in both parametric and nonparametric IRT. A plausible alternative is multidimensionality with approximate simple structure, in other words the total test can be divided into almost unidimensional subtests. We distinguish a confirmatory and an exploratory variant; both are implemented in the MSP software..

In the former, theoretical considerations or earlier research results provide specific clues which subsets of items must be considered. One may then fit a NIRT model both to all items and to each subset .Whether it is then decided to use subscale scores or total scale scores for further analyses is again influenced by both statistical and substantive considerations.

In the exploratory variant, more often found in dimensionality analysis, there is no prior knowledge and the data alone determine how many subscales there are, and which items go into which subscale. Mokken (1971) describes a bottom up clustering procedure that begins with joining the two items, from a given item pool, that best fit together according to Loevinger's (1948) association measure H, which is the covariance divided by the maximum possible covariance given the marginals per item. Other items are added, the best ones first, until there are no more items left that satisfy the criteria of a Mokken scale, which are that all item pairs must have positive covariance (see also section 2 on the Ellis & Van den Wollenberg results) and each item must have an item H value with the remaining items that is significantly positive and exceeds a lowerbound value c, usually 0.3, that is chosen to exclude scales that are too weak to order persons reliably. Once the first scale can no more be extended, it is tried to form a second scale from the remaining items, then a third one, and so on until either no items are left or none of the remaining items can be joined. As this search procedure tends to put some items in the first scale that might fit better in a later one, the end result is extended by allowing the second and later subscales to select items from the earlier ones.

For the exact definitions and selection rules we refer to Hemker et al. (1995), Molenaar & Sijtsma (2000) and Sijtsma & Molenaar (2002). Note that there are other clustering procedures within NIRT such as DETECT (Zhang & Stout, 1999), DIMTEST (Stout, Goodwin Froelich and Gao, 2001) and HCA/CCPROX (Roussos et al., 1998), and that factor analysis may also be considered as a tool for finding the best number of clusters as well as the best assignment of items to these clusters. They differ from Mokken's automated item selection procedure in the choice of a proximity measure, in being simultaneous, or sequential in a different order, and in degree of suitability for dichotomous items. Van Abswoude (this volume) systematically compares some of these procedures.

Looking very closely, almost no scale is exactly unidimensional, unless its contents are so narrowly restricted that its applicability suffers. It is my view that IRT can also be very useful for a set of items from a somewhat heterogeneous domain, provided that the validity is safeguarded by a balanced choice of items from the subdomains within which the items could be clustered. It should be noted that the presence of such subclusters tends to lead to a slightly lower reliability and accuracy than would be obtained in the ideal local independence situation where each item provides independent information about θ.

The use of factor analysis in the search for unidimensional subscales, popular as it may be, has at least two disadvantages. First, the usual VARIMAX routine looks for orthogonal factors, whereas the most meaningful subscales tend to be positively correlated to some extent. Second, the inter-item correlation is often a poor association measure, in particular between dichotomous items of widely different popularity, and the use of tetrachoric or polychoric correlations brings its own problems, notably for small or medium sample size.

It is my view that these elegant properties make the Rasch model into the recommended choice when one can find enough items that satisfy its rather stringent restrictions. More than fifty years ago Lazarsfeld postulated his "exchangeability of indices" and Rasch his specific objectivity. Note that also in NIRT we have met person-free item measurement in the form of subpopulation invariance, invariant item ordering and absence of DIF. Also, in a truly unidimensional item pool, each subset of items should essentially order and locate all persons in the same way. This postulate of item-free person measurement remains more academic than person-free item measurement, however. One reason is that a typical data matrix has several hundreds of persons and between six and sixty items (in attitude and personality measurement even between six and sixteen).

Are persons more homogeneous than items? In the way that mental measurement is practised these seems to be an inherent belief that they are. An exception is the detection via person fit research (Emons, this volume) of a few persons with anomalous test behavior. Most researchers, however, expect people to be only different in where they stand on the latent trait. It is precisely this difference in standing that is supposed to explain the association between the items. Very little research is devoted to the issue whether the population that one wishes to consider could be split into clusters of persons between which the measurement instrument as such would function differently. In section 3 we have spoken about DIF research, which is based on splitting the person group with respect to an external variable like ethnicity or gender. Not many pages have been devoted, however, to the counterpart of the search procedure that establishes internally homogeneous and mutually different clusters of persons. Items are clustered more frequently, and more successfully, than persons are.

One possible explanation is that the social and behavioral sciences mostly deal with properties that can be defined for all persons, or at least almost all persons. Educational achievements, abilities, attitudes, personality traits: it is quite obvious to say that one person has more of such traits than the other person, and also that upon closer inspection each trait may be divided into meaningful subtraits. It is far less obvious, and also less helpful for our understanding, to say that one expects that important subgroups of persons react in a qualitatively different way to a test or scale that measures a latent trait.

Another more practical explanation is that almost all data matrices have far more persons than items. This implies that a measure of association or similarity between person pairs will often be inaccurate as an estimate of what it would be in a larger universe of items. It also implies that there are many person pairs, so the calculation of a between person association matrix will be lengthy, and the matrix will almost certainly be singular. There have been experiments with Q analysis, based on correlations, and with H^T, Loevingers H between persons. The latter is implemented in MSP for dichotomous items only. It is used there for investigating whether IRFs are non-intersecting (Sijtsma, 1998; Molenaar & Sijtsma, 2000), not for clustering persons. The weighted average of H^T between one person and all other persons is helpful in person fit research, but for this detection of a few persons with an anomalous test behavior the simple count of the number of Guttman errors performs just as well (Meijer, 1994).

Returning to the more general issue of deciding whether a given test is unidimensional, researchers will find that many interesting latent traits actually have several aspects. The requirement of validity makes it clear that a practitioner may have to compromise in order to find a scale that is good enough for practical purposes but not strictly ideal from a measure theoretic point of view.

It is precisely in this area of modest sample sizes, modest test lengths and modest ambitions that the NIRT procedures discussed here have proven their value, in dozens of applications in many different disciplines. Their likelihood based counterparts may go on to offer precision and flexibility in complicated designs and large data matrices. NIRT, however, is coming of age, as is illustrated by a growing number of books and papers, and by a special issue of Applied Psychological Measurement (Junker & Sijtsma, 2001). The plea of the APA Task Force in favor of simple models (Wilkinson and TFSI, 1999) has reinforced my conviction that parametric and nonparametric IRT both deserve a place under the sun.

References

Croon, M.A. (1991). Investigating Mokken scalability of dichotomous items by means of ordinal latent class analysis. British Journal of Mathematical and Statistical Psychology, 44, 315-331.

Ellis, J.L., & Van den Wollenberg, A.L. (1993). Local homogeneity in latent trait models. A characterization of the homogeneous monotone IRT model. Psychometrika 58, 417-429.

Ellis, J.L., & Junker, B.W. (1997). Tail-measurability in monotone latent variable models. Psychometrika, 62, 495-523.

Grayson, D.A. (1988). Two-group classification in latent trait theory: Scores with monotone likelihood ratio. Psychometrika, 53, 383-392.

Hemker, B.T., Sijtsma, K., & Molenaar, I.W. (1995). Selection of unidimensional scales from a multidimensional itembank in the polytomous Mokken IRT model. Applied Psychological Measurement, 19, 337-352.

Holland, P.W. (1990). On the sampling theory foundations of item response theory models. Psychometrika, 55, 577-601.

Holland, P.W., & Rosenbaum, P.R. (1986). Conditional association and unidimensionality in monotone latent variable models. The Annals of Statistics, 14, 1523-1543.

Huisman, M. & Molenaar, I.W. (2001). Imputation of missing scale data with item response theory. In: A. Boomsma, M.A.J. van Duijn & T.A.B. Snijders (Eds.), Essays on Item Response Theory (pp. 221-244). New York: Springer.

Junker, B.W., & Sijtsma, K. (2000). Latent and manifest monotonicity in item response models. Applied Psychological Measurement, 24, 65-81.

Junker, B.W., & Sijtsma, K. (2001). Nonparametric Item Response Theory in action: An overview of the special issue. Applied Psychological Measurement 25, 211-220.

Loevinger, J. (1948). The technique of homogeneous tests compared with some aspects of 'scale analysis' and factor analysis. Psychological Bulletin, 45, 507-530.

Lord, F.N., & Novick, M.R. (1968). Statistical theories of mental test scores. Reading (MA): Addison-Wesley.

Meijer, R.R. (1994). The number of Guttman errors as a simple and powerful person-fit statistic. Applied Psychological Measurement 18, 311-314.

Mokken, R.J. (1971). A theory and procedure of scale analysis. The Hague: Mouton/Berlin: De Gruyter.

Mokken, R.J. (1997). Nonparametric models for dichotomous responses. In W.J. van der Linden & R.K. Hambleton (Eds.), Handbook of modern item response theory (pp. 351-367). New York: Springer.

Molenaar, I.W. (1997). Nonparametric models for polytomous responses. In W.J van der Linden & R.K. Hambleton (Eds.), Handbook of modern item response theory (pp. 369-380). New York: Springer.

Molenaar, I.W. & Sijtsma, K. (2000). User's Manual MSP5 for Windows. Groningen: iec ProGAMMA.

Ramsay, J.O. (1991). Kernel smoothing approaches to nonparametric item characteristic curve estimation. Psychometrika 56, 611-630.

Roussos, L.A., Stout, W.F. & Marden, J. (1998). Using new proximity measures with hierarchical cluster analysis to detect multidimensionality. Journal of Educational Measurement, 35, 1-30.

Shealy, R.T., & Stout, W.F. (1993). An item response theory model for test bias and differential item functioning. In P.W. Holland & H. Wainer (Eds.), Differential item functioning (pp. 197 - 239). Hillsdale, NJ: Erlbaum.

Sijtsma, K. (1998). Methodology review: Nonparametric IRT approaches to the analysis of dichotomous item scores. Applied Psychological Measurement, 22, 3-32.

Sijtsma, K., & Junker, B.W. (1996). A survey of theory and methods of invariant item ordering. British Journal of Mathematical and Statistical Psychology, 49, 79-105.

Sijtsma, K., & Molenaar, I.W. (2002). Introduction to nonparametric Item Response Theory. Newbury Park (CA): Sage

Stout, W.F. (1990). A new item response theory modeling approach with applications to unidimensionality assessment and ability estimation. Psychometrika, 55, 293-325.

Stout, W.F., Goodwin Froelich, A. & Gao, F. (2001) Using resampling methods to produce an improved DIMTEST procedure. In: A. Boomsma, M.A.J. van Duijn & T.A.B. Snijders (Eds.), Essays on Item Response Theory (pp. 357-375). New York: Springer.

Wilkinson, L., & TFSI (1999). Statistical methods in psychology journals. American Psychologist 54, 594-604.

Zhang, J. & Stout, W.F. (1999). The theoretical DETECT index of dimensionality and its application to approximate simple structure. Psychometrika, 64, 213-249.

Bias of Ability Estimates Using Warm's Weighted Likelihood Estimator (WLE) in the Generalized Partial Credit Model (GPCM)

Chung Park[1] and Eiji Muraki[2]

[1] Korea Institute of Curriculum & Evaluation, 25-1 Samchung-dong, Gongro-gu, Seoul, 110-230, Korea
[2] Tohoku University, Kawauchi, Aobaku, Sendai, Miyagi-ken 980-8576, Japan

Summary. Application of IRT models to practical situations requires that parameter estimates be unbiased. Park & Swaminathan(1998) investigated the properties of maximum likelihood estimator(MLE) and Expected a posterior (EAP) estimators of ability parameters in the Generalized partial credit model (GPCM) and found that there was considerable bias of estimates in the GPCM under all conditions. Warm(1989) proposed the weighted likelihood estimator(WLE) for the 3-PL IRT model to reduce bias of MLE and showed that WLE produced less bias of estimates than ML and Bayesian estimation.

The purpose of this study is to apply WLE to the GPCM to reduce bias of estimates of ability parameters. In addition, this study investigates the properties of WLE, EAP, and ML estimates of ability parameters in the GPCM. The study shows that WLE considerably reduces the bias of estimates of ability parameters in the GPCM. WLE performs especially better than EAP and does similar to ML across all conditions. WL estimates performs better than ML estimate especially with small number of items (3 category 9 items). Conclusively, WLE could be applied to other polytomous IRT models in addition to GPCM to obtain unbiased estimates.

Key words. ability estimation, bias of estimates, polytomous IRT models, Generalized partial credit model (GPCM)

1 Introduction

Procedures based on item response theory (IRT) are widely accepted for solving many measurement problems that cannot be solved using classical test theory (CTT) procedures. Item response theory models that can deal with dichotomously scored items have been developed and are understood well. However, dichotomous IRT models restrict examinees's responses to be scored "right" or "wrong". Recently, the emphasis on performance assessment has resulted in increased interest in models for polytomously scored items, since most of the scoring rubrics for performance assessments require the scoring of examinee's responses in ordered categories.

The successful application of polytomous IRT models to practical situations depends on the availability of reasonable and well-behaved estimates of the parameters of the models. Park and Swaminathan (1998) investigated the properties of ML and EAP estimators of ability in the GPCM under various conditions such as test length, sample size, and the number of categories in each item. They found that there was considerable bias of estimates in the GPCM under all conditions.

The bias of estimates in ability parameters is undesirable in most practical situations, because the true values of the parameters in IRT models are never known and must be estimated to use ability estimates of IRT models in practical situations. Then, what we use in practical situations is the expectation of parameter estimates. Therefore the expected values of parameter estimates should be unbiased. Warm (1989) proposed the weighted likelihood estimator (WLE) for the three parameter logistic(3-PL) IRT model to reduce bias of maximum likelihood estimator (MLE) in the 3-PL IRT model and showed that WLE produced less bias of estimates than ML and Bayesian modal estimation.

The primary purpose of this research was to apply WLE for polytomous IRT models to reduce the bias of estimates of ability parameters. In addition to effectiveness of WLE, the properties of MLE, WLE, and EAP ability estimates were examined and compared with regard to their accuracy, sampling fluctuation, and bias of estimates under important conditions, such as test length and the number of categories in each item.

2 The Generalized Partial Credit Model (GPCM)

Polytomous IRT models can be classified as nominal response models and ordinal response models. The ordinal response models have important applications in performance assessment and essay scoring. Two representative ordinal polytomous IRT models are the graded response model (GRM) developed by Samejima (1969) and the generalized partial credit model (GPCM) by Muraki (1992). The GPCM is emerging as a popular model for ordinal response items because it has both advantages from the GRM and the PCM.

In the GPCM, the probability of a person with trait level responding category k ($k=1,2,...,m_j$) on the item j is defined as

$$P_{jk}(\theta) = \frac{\exp\left[\sum_{v=1}^{k} a_j(\theta - b_{jv})\right]}{\sum_{c=1}^{m_j} \exp\left[\sum_{v=1}^{c} a_j(\theta - b_{jv})\right]} , \qquad k = 1, 2, ..., m_j \qquad (1)$$

Here, a_j is the discrimination or slope parameter for item j and b_{jk}, the item category threshold parameter, is the step difficulty for the k-th step of item j.

3 Estimation Procedures for the GPCM

Maximum likelihood (ML) and Expected a posterior (EAP) estimation procedures are commonly used methods to obtain ability estimates of the GPCM. In the context of polytomous IRT ability estimation, for a test on n items with k categories, the ML estimates of ability parameter, Θ, is the value of the Θ that maximizes the likelihood function, $L(u_{jk}|\Theta)$, where

$$L(u_{jk}|\theta) = \prod_{j=1}^{n} \prod_{k=1}^{k} \left[P(u_{jk}|\theta_i) \right]^{u_{jk}} \tag{2}$$

The EAP method is to find the mean of the posterior distribution of given a response pattern $P(\Theta|U_{jk})$,

$$P(\theta|u_{jk}) = \frac{L(u_{jk}|\theta)g(\theta)}{P(u_{jk})} = \frac{L(u_{jk}|\theta)\,g(\theta)}{\int L(u_{jk}|\theta)\,g(\theta)\,d\theta} \tag{3}$$

where, $g(\Theta)$ is the prior information of the examinee's ability.
EAP has the advantage of being computationally simple than ML and can estimate all of examinees with all correct or incorrect responses.

The Warm's weighted likelihood (WL) for the GPCM is given by

$$L^*(u_{jk}|\theta) = f(\theta)L(u_{jk}|\theta) \tag{4}$$

where, $f(\Theta)$ is a square root of the test information $I(\Theta)$ and $L(u_{jk}|\Theta)$ is the likelihood of a particular response vector (U_{jk}) given Θ in Equation (2). $P(U_{jk}|\Theta)$ is the probability of a person i with ability level Θ responding category k on the item j. Thus, a weighted likelihood weighted by square root of information function, i.e., standard error of an ability estimate, WLE(Θ), is the solution of equation (5).

$$\frac{\partial}{\partial\theta}\log f(\theta) + \frac{\partial}{\partial\theta}\log L(u_{jk}|\theta) \equiv 0 \tag{5}$$

4 Design of the Study

In order to adequately investigate the properties of parameter estimates, a simulation study was conducted. A simulation study is necessary because only by using simulated data is it possible to know whether or not there are differences between true and estimated parameters with the estimation procedure for the polytomous IRT models of interest.

Three factors that can affect the parameter estimates of the GPCM were manipulated: two levels of test length (9 and 18 items), two different numbers of categories (three and five) in each item, and three estimation procedures for ability parameters (WLE, EAP, and MLE). The sample size was fixed in one size, 1000 examinees, for item calibration because the previous research (Park & Swaminathan, 1998) found that the sample size did not have an important role in estimation procedure of ability parameters.

Estimates were obtained from the generated data for each of the combinations of the factors of interest. Each condition was replicated 100 times, so that the behavior of the estimates could be studied. For each condition and each replication, item parameters were calibrated, and then ability estimates were obtained from the computer program PARSCALE version 3.2. The computer program PARSCALE version 3.2 implemented the WLE.

5 Criteria for Evaluating Adequacy of the Estimates

The criteria used to evaluate the WL, ML, and EAP estimators of the GPCM were accuracy of estimates, variance of estimates, and bias of estimates over replications. Accuracy of parameter estimates is measured by the mean squared error (MSE) between the true and estimated parameter. The smaller the MSE, the more accurate the estimates. The MSE can be separated into the variance of the estimates over replications (VAR) and Squared Bias, defined as the squared difference between the true parameter value and the mean of the estimates over replications (Gifford & Swaminathan, 1990). In addition to the above descriptive analysis, the effects of each factor on the accuracy, the variance, and the bias of the ability parameter estimates in the GPCM were determined using analysis of variance procedures. The dependent variables were the RMSE, variance, and bias of the estimates of the ability parameters.

6 Results

6.1 Bias of Estimates

The results of the ANOVA of the bias in Table 1 show that estimation procedure and number of categories have an effect on the bias of estimates of ability parameters. Test length does not have an effect on the bias of estimates of ability parameters.

Table 1. Results of ANOVA for bias

Source	Df	F value	P value
Estimation procedure	2	39.425	.000
Number of categories	1	10.117	.000
Test length	1	.436	.524

Fig. 1(b) provides that graphical description of the effect of three factors on the average bias of the ability estimates for 3 and 5 category items across estimation procedures (EAP, WLE, and ML) and test lengths (9 and 18 items). It shows that EAP procedure produces particularly larger bias than the other procedures. The average bias of estimates decreased as the number of categories in each item increased from three to five categories.

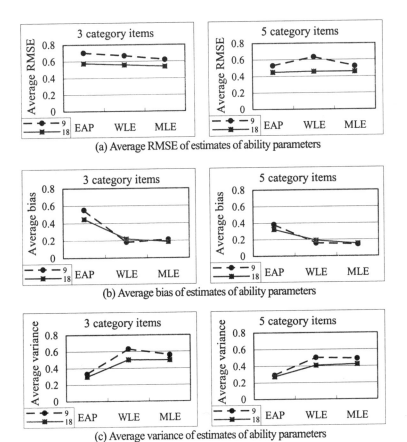

(a) Average RMSE of estimates of ability parameters

(b) Average bias of estimates of ability parameters

(c) Average variance of estimates of ability parameters

Fig. 1. Average RMSE, bias, and variance of estimates of ability parameters across estimation procedures and test lengths for 3 and 5 category items

Table 2. Bias, RMSE and variance of estimates in 3 and 5 category items

				mean	-3	-2	-1	0	1	2	3
B		3	9	EAP	-0.5516	1.4005	0.6535	0.1208	-0.1046	-0.2443	-0.3986	-0.9386
i				WLE	0.1810	0.4870	0.1507	-0.0211	-0.0543	-0.1540	-0.1464	-0.2535
a				MLE	0.2118	0.6000	0.1622	-0.0918	-0.0996	-0.1360	-0.0367	-0.3562
s		3	18	EAP	0.4472	1.0370	0.4764	0.0458	-0.1204	-0.2376	-0.4046	-0.8084
				WLE	0.2198	0.2859	0.2117	0.0025	-0.0967	-0.1997	-0.3040	-0.4383
				MLE	0.1864	0.2763	0.0870	-0.0807	-0.1148	-0.1911	-0.2353	-0.3192
		5	9	EAP	0.3840	1.1234	0.3998	0.0413	-0.0811	-0.1258	-0.2351	-0.6813
				WLE	0.1576	0.4856	0.1050	0.0032	-0.0622	-0.0774	-0.1150	-0.2545
				MLE	0.1441	0.5251	-0.0487	-0.0804	-0.0758	-0.0714	-0.0732	-0.1338
		5	18	EAP	0.3238	0.8692	0.2710	0.0092	-0.1247	-0.1694	-0.2403	-0.5827
				WLE	0.1899	0.4008	0.1279	-0.0049	-0.1169	-0.1478	-0.1880	-0.3432
				MLE	0.1519	0.3774	0.0043	-0.0374	-0.1235	-0.1448	-0.1525	-0.2234
R		3	9	EAP	0.7014	1.4156	0.7263	0.4448	0.3688	0.4395	0.5315	0.9830
M				WLE	0.6671	0.9162	0.8555	0.7287	0.3832	0.4298	0.5737	0.7914
S				MLE	0.6197	0.8010	0.6678	0.6786	0.4294	0.4421	0.5930	0.7259
E		3	18	EAP	0.5748	1.0661	0.5889	0.3697	0.2593	0.3656	0.5057	0.8684
				WLE	0.5588	0.8605	0.7016	0.4610	0.2529	0.3511	0.4989	0.7855
				MLE	0.5383	0.6963	0.6837	0.5317	0.2688	0.3539	0.5155	0.7180
		5	9	EAP	0.5281	1.1553	0.5114	0.3487	0.2546	0.3021	0.3911	0.7337
				WLE	0.5339	0.9553	0.6575	0.4247	0.2572	0.2937	0.4575	0.6913
				MLE	0.5233	0.8461	0.6697	0.5033	0.2671	0.3009	0.4114	0.6647
		5	18	EAP	0.4493	0.4338	0.4338	0.2824	0.2278	0.2428	0.3581	0.6611
				WLE	0.4582	0.5087	0.5087	0.3060	0.2251	0.2315	0.3573	0.6554
				MLE	0.4580	0.5803	0.5803	0.3250	0.2312	0.2313	0.3638	0.6526
V		3	9	EAP	0.3306	0.2064	0.3170	0.4281	0.3536	0.3654	0.3516	0.2921
a				WLE	0.6317	0.7760	0.8421	0.7284	0.3793	0.3906	0.5557	0.7497
r				MLE	0.5591	0.5305	0.6478	0.6724	0.4177	0.4207	0.5919	0.6325
i		3	18	EAP	0.2983	0.2470	0.3462	0.3669	0.2297	0.2779	0.3034	0.3172
a				WLE	0.5016	0.8117	0.6689	0.4610	0.2336	0.2888	0.3955	0.6518
n				MLE	0.4979	0.6392	0.6781	0.5255	0.2431	0.2978	0.4587	0.6432
c		5	9	EAP	0.2908	0.2698	0.3189	0.3462	0.2414	0.2746	0.3125	0.2722
e				WLE	0.5021	0.8227	0.6491	0.4247	0.2496	0.2833	0.4429	0.6428
				MLE	0.4904	0.6635	0.6679	0.4968	0.2561	0.2923	0.4048	0.6511
		5	18	EAP	0.2742	0.3558	0.3388	0.2823	0.1907	0.1739	0.2655	0.3123
				WLE	0.4090	0.8317	0.4924	0.3059	0.1923	0.1783	0.3038	0.5583
				MLE	0.4218	0.7302	0.5803	0.3228	0.1954	0.1804	0.3303	0.6133

The result of bias in Table 2 presents that EAP produces larger bias across all ability levels than the other procedures and especially larger bias at extreme ability levels (-3 and 3) than the others. WLE and ML procedures produce almost similar bias of estimates across all ability levels. However, WLE has relatively smaller bias at negatively middle ability levels (-1 and 0) than ML procedures and also shows that WLE makes smaller bias of estimates than the other procedures with small data set (3 category 9 items). It should be mentioned here that the result of ML procedure excluded examinees' responses with all correct and incorrect items, because those responses are not converge with ML procedure.

6.2 Accuracy of Estimates

The results of the ANOVA of the RMSE in Table 3 show that number of categories and test length have an effect on the RMSE of estimates of ability parameters. Estimation procedure does not have an effect on the RMSE of estimates of ability parameters.

Table 3. Results of ANOVA for Accuracy

Source	Df	F value	P value
Estimation procedure	2	2.714	.154
Number of categories	1	98.904	.000
Test length	1	55.155	.000

Fig. 1(a) exhibits that all of estimation procedures produced almost similar RMSE. The average RMSE decreased as the number of categories in each item increased. That is, the estimate of ability parameters in the GPCM is accurate as the number of categories in each item. The RMSE in Table 2 shows that EAP produces larger RMSE at extreme ability levels than the other procedures, but produced smaller RMSE at the middle level of ability.

6.3 Variance of Estimates

The results of the ANOVA of the variance of estimates in Table 4 show that estimation procedure, number of categories, and test length have an effect on the variance of estimates of ability parameters.

Table 4. Results of ANOVA for variance

Source	Df	F value	P value
Estimation procedure	2	54.661	.000
Number of categories	1	25.994	.000
Test length	1	23.241	.001

Fig. 1(c) represents that EAP procedure produces particularly smaller variance than the other procedures. The average variance of estimates decreased as the number of categories in each item increased from three to five categories. The variance of estimates in Table 2 presents that EAP produces especially smaller variance across all ability levels than the other procedures and WLE has relatively larger variance of estimates than ML, especially at the negative ability levels with small data set.

7 Summary and Conclusion

The main conclusion of this research was that Warm's WLE reduced considerably the bias of estimates of ability parameters in the GPCM. WLE performed especially better than EAP and did similar to ML. But the result of ML came form the responses without all upper and lower response examinees. WL estimates performed better than ML estimate especially with small number of items (3 category 9 items). WLE produced smaller bias than MLE at the middle levels of ability, but produced larger bias than MLE at the extreme levels of ability (-3 and 3). WL produced less bias than EAP procedure at all ability levels. Also, WL produced more accurate estimates of ability parameters than ML and EAP procedures. As Samejima (1998) pointed out, this study shows that the use of WLE decreases the bias of estimates of ability parameters in the GPCM and effectively works for all high or low response patterns. Generally, ability estimates of the GPCM with the large number of category items (5 category items) were more accurate, less bias and variance than with the small number of category items(3 category items) regardless of estimation procedures.

References

Gifford, J., & Swaminathan, H. (1990) Bias and the effect of priors in Bayesian estimation of parameters of item response models. Applied Psychological Measurement, 11, 33-44

Muraki, E. (1992) A generalized partial credit model: An application of an EM algorithm. Applied Psychological Measurement, 16, 159-176

Muraki, E., & Bock, R. D. (1997) PARSCALE 3.2: IRT based test scoring and item analysis for graded open-ended exercises and performance tasks. Chicago, IL: Scientific Software

Park, C., & Swaminathan, H. (1998, April) Accuracy of ability estimates in the generalized Partial Credit Model (GPCM). Paper presented at the annual meeting of the American Educational Research Association, San Diego, CA, 1998

Samejima, F. (1969) Estimation of latent ability using a response pattern of graded scores. Psychometrika Monograph Supplement, 34 (4, Whole No. 17)

Warm, T.A. (1989) Weighted likelihood estimation of ability in the item response theory. Psychometrika, 54, 427-450

Item Selection in Polytomous CAT

Bernard P. Veldkamp

Department of Educational Measurement and Data-Analysis, University of
Twente, P.O.Box 217, 7500 AE Enschede, The Netherlands

Summary. In polytomous CAT, items can be selected using Fisher Information,
Maximum Interval Information, or Kullback-Leibler Information. In this paper,
the different item selection criteria are described. In a simulation study the criteria
are compared for a number of item pools. The process of deciding which one to
choose is illustrated. Application of the three item selection criteria to polytomous
CAT, constrained polytomous CAT, and CAT based on multi-peaked item pools
is discussed.

Keywords. Fisher Information, Fisher Interval Information, Item selection, Kullback-Leibler Information, Polytomous CAT

1 Introduction

Computerized adaptive testing (CAT) is one of de major developments in educational measurement of the past decade. CAT stands in the long tradition of individualized testing. It can be compared with an oral exam where a computer program acts as the examiner. Like in oral exams, the difficulty of the items is
adapted to the ability of the candidate. So, the examinees do not get bored or frus-
trated due to items that are too easy or too hard. Besides, the increased flexibility
of CATs enables test developers to fullfil many of the examinee's wishes; for example shorter tests, and testing on demand.

Most research on CAT deals with dichotomously scored items. Only a few
studies deal with polytomous CAT. One of the results from these studies is that
polytomous CAT tends to need fewer items, since the items are more informative.
But still, quite a number of questions need further attention.

One of the issues in polytomous CAT is the choice of item selection criterion.
Fisher Information is commonly used, but this information measure is based on an
estimate of the ability parameter, and the ability estimate is not very stable in the
beginning of a CAT administration. Therefore, when the estimate is not close to
the true value, using Fisher's Information criterion might result in inefficient item
selection. The fact that item selection procedures may favor items with optimal
properties at wrong ability values is generally known as the attenuation paradox in
test theory (Lord and Novick, 1968, sect. 16.5). To overcome these problems
some alternative criteria have been presented in the literature. In this paper the fo-

cus is on selecting the most appropriate item selection criterion for polytomous CAT.

2 Item Selection Criteria

In the literature, three item selection criteria have been proposed for polytomous CAT. They are introduced in this section.

2.1 Maximum Fisher Information

Item selection in polytomous CAT is mainly based on Fisher Information (Dodd, De Ayala, and Koch, 1995). For a single item, Fisher's Information function is defined by:

$$I_i(\theta) = a_i^2 \left[\sum_{k=1}^m k^2 P_{ik}(\theta) - \left(\sum_{k=1}^m k P_{ik}(\theta) \right)^2 \right],$$ (1)

where m is the number of categories and $P_{ik}(\theta)$ is the probability that a candidate with ability θ will end up in category k of item i. When Fisher Information is used, the item is selected with maximum value of the information function at the estimated ability level of the examinee ($i = \arg\max_i I_i(\hat{\theta})$).

2.2 Maximum Interval Information

Veerkamp and Berger (1997) introduced an interval information criterion for dichotomous CAT to overcome the problems of Fisher Information. Instead of maximizing Fisher's information function at an ability estimate, they proposed to integrate the function over a small interval around the estimate to compensate for the uncertanty in it.

In polytomous CAT, there is an other reason to intergrate Fisher's Information function over an interval. Fisher's Information function might be multi-peaked, when items are calibrated with the GPCM (Muraki, 1993). In van Rijn, Eggen, Hemker, and Sanders (in press), it is demonstrated that a multipeaked item might contain more information for a small interval around the ability estimate than the item that contains maximum Fisher Information at the ability estimate.They propose to select the next item with a Maximum Interval Information criterion:

$$i = \arg\max_i \int_{\hat{\theta}-\delta}^{\hat{\theta}+\delta} I_i(\theta) d\theta,$$ (2)

where i is the item to be selected and δ is a small constant defining the width of the interval.

2.3 Posterior Expected Kullback-Leibler Information.

The observation that item selection based on Fisher's Information criterion might be inefficient during the first stages of a CAT was also made by Chang and Ying (1996). They propose to select items based on Kullback-Leibler Information, a global information criterion. Generally, Kullback-Leibler Information measures the distance between two likelihoods over the same parameter space (Lehmann and Casella, 1998, sect. 1.7). The purpose of CAT is to estimate the true ability of the examinee. For this purpose it is desirable to select items generating response vectors with a likelihood at the true ability differing maximally from those at any other value of the ability parameter

More precisely, Kullback-Leibler Information for a single item is defined as

$$K_i(\theta, \theta_0) \equiv \sum_{k=1}^{m} P_{ik}(\theta_0) \ln\left(\frac{P_{ik}(\theta_0)}{P_{ik}(\theta)}\right). \tag{3}$$

For a test of n items, the measure is equal to the sum of the information of the items. Because the true ability θ_0 of the examinee is unknown, and θ is unspecified, posterior expected information of θ (van der Linden, 1998) will be used. Actual item selection will be based on posterior expected Kullback-Leibler Information at the current ability estimate (Veldkamp and van der Linden, in press). Let $f(\theta \mid u_{i_1}, ..., u_{i_{k-1}})$ be the posterior density of θ after (k-1) items are administered and $\hat{\theta}^{k-1}$ the (EAP) estimate derived from this posterior. Posterior expected Kullback-Leibler Information in the response on the ith item in the pool after (k-1) items in the test is defined as

$$KL_i(\hat{\theta}^{k-1}) \equiv \int_\theta K_i(\theta \, \hat{\theta}^{k-1}) f(\theta \mid u_{i_1}, ..., u_{i_{k-1}}) d\theta. \tag{4}$$

3 How to Select a Criterion

In the previous section, three item selection criteria for polytomous CAT were introduced. The question remains, which one to choose. Due to the attenuation paradox, Maximum Interval Information and Kullback-Leibler Information seem to be preferable, at least during the early stage of a CAT. For dichotomous CAT, this statement was confirmed by the results of Chang and Ying (1996), and Berger and Veerkamp (1994). On the other hand, in van Rijn et al. (in press), no real differences in performance between Fisher Information and Maximum Interval Information were found for the polytomous case. A different argument exists that might favor Fisher Information over the others in the long run. In a frequentist framework, the asymptotic variance of the ability estimate is the reciprocal of the test information function (Lehmann, 1983, p. 465). This means that Fisher Information is proportional to the error of measurement. A third, rather pragmatic argument is that Fisher Information is easier to calculate.

Based on these arguments, it is hard to make a conclusion. During the early stages of an adaptive test, Maximum Interval Information and Kullback-Leibler information are supposed to perform better than Fisher Information. But what are these early stages? Can some general recommendation be made? And how dependent are these recommendations on the characteristics of an item pool?

In general, polytomously scored items contain more information than dichotomously scored items. As a consequense, the ability estimation will be more precise. This might explain why van Rijn et al. did not find any differences in performance between Fisher Information and Maximum Interval Information for the polytomous case, where Berger and Veerkamp did find differences for the dichotomous case. The question remains, is the difference small enough to ignore?

A first step in deciding which criteria to choose, might be to find out how much overlap in items occurs for a test. If overlap is high (above 90 percent), almost the same items have been selected by the different criteria, and not much difference in performance is expected. Looking at item overlap to select a criterion is not new. In Sympson, Weiss and Ree (see Weiss, 1982, p. 478) Fisher Information and Owen's selection criterion were compared. In a real life application, they found an overlap of approximately 85 percent of the items. If overlap is low (below 75 percent) a second step might be to check whether Maximum Interval Information and Kullback-Leibler information outperform Fisher Information. If this is not the case, no gain in performance is expected by using Maximum Interval Information or Kullback-Leibler information, and Fisher Information seems a good choice. When one of them outperforms Fisher Information, it should be applied in polytomous CAT.

4 Numerical Examples

To illustrate the process of choosing an item selection criterion, a simulation study was carried out. The effects of item pool size and the amount of information in the items were taken into account. For a number of item pools, that differed in size and in average item information, the percentage of overlapping items were recorded. In order to carry out the simulation study, an IRT model is specified first.

4.1 IRT model

In this paper, the focus is on the General Partial Credit model (GPCM) (Muraki, 1992). In the GPCM the probability of obtaining a score in category k is given by

$$P_k = \frac{\exp \sum_{v=0}^{k} a(\theta - b_v)}{\sum_{c=0}^{m} \exp \sum_{v=0}^{c} a(\theta - b_v)} \tag{5}$$

where a is the slope parameter, b_k is an item category parameter, $k=\{0,1,2,..,m\}$ is a category number, and θ represents the ability of the examinee.

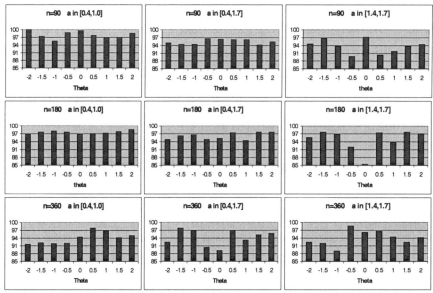

Fig. 1. For nine simulated item banks, the percentages of item overlap are shown for different theta values when different item selection criteria were used.

4.2 Simulation study

Nine GPCM item pools were simulated to compare the different item selection criteria. The item pools differed in size (90, 180 and 360 items), and the item pools differed in value of the slope parameters (a in [0.4,1.0], a in [0.4,1.7], or a in [1.4,1.7]). One third of the items in each pool consists of easy items, one third of medium difficulty items, and one third of difficult items (average category parameter in [-2,-1], in [-1,1], or in [1,2]).

To test the effect of size and average item information, the same study was carried out for all nine item pools. For several values of the ability parameter 100 examinees were simulated.

In an ordinary CAT procedure, the next item is selected by a criterion based on the estimated ability level of the examinees, and the selected item is presented to the examinee. However, because item overlap is between tests was measured, a slightly different approach was used. After every iteration of the CAT, all three item selection criteria were applied to propose the next item based on the estimated ability level. The proposed items were denoted in a file, and one of these items was presented to the examinee. In this way, we could make sure that the selection criteria were compared for identical situations. After doing the simulation study, the proposed items were compared.

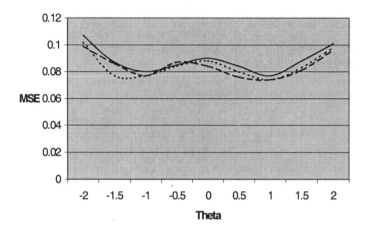

Fig. 2. MSE for polytomous CAT of 20 items when Fisher Information (line), Fisher Interval Information (dashed), or Kullback-Leibler Information (dotted) was applied.

In the simulation study, EAP-estimates were used to estimate the ability level, the number of items in the test was equal to 20, and no item exposure control methods were applied.

The results for the different item banks are shown in Figure 1. As can be seen the overlap in items is between 85 and 100 percent. For a twenty-item test this means that on average the number of non-overlapping items is less or equal to three. The result that applying different item selection criteria will only result in three different items suggests that there will not be many differences in measurement precision. However, two general trends can be distinguished in Figure 1. When the number of items in the pool increases, the percentage of overlapping items decreases. When the average discrimination of the item pool increases, the percentage of overlapping items also decreases.

To check what the effect is of the different items that were choosen by the different criteria on the measurement precision, the resulting MSEs are compared. In Figure 2, the MSEs of test assembled for the different item selection criteria are shown. Even for the item pool with minimum overlap (n=360, high slope parameters), only smal differences in measurement precision are found. After twenty items, the difference in MSE is smaller than 0.01, and no overall best or worst criterion is found.

5 Discussion

Fisher Information, Maximum Interval Information, and Kullback-Leibler Information have been applied to dichotomous CAT, and their pro's and cons have been discussed in the literature. But until now, no general recommendations about selecting one of these criteria could be given for polytomous CAT. In this study, the influences of several factors on the performance of the criteria were further investigated.

First of all, the performance of the criteria might be influenced by the quality of the items in the bank. In other words, differences between item banks might result in differences in performance. These differences can be caused by differences in the number of items in the bank, or by differences in item parameters. In a simulation study both of these factors were investigated. From the results, it can be concluded that when the number of items in an item bank increases, the differences also increase. It can also be concluded that differences in performance are higher for item banks with highly discriminating items. However, even for the largest differences in performance in this simulation study, the differences in MSE's were still small. In other words, Fisher Information does not perform much worse than the other criteria. When these results, the asymptotic properties of Fisher Information, and the complexity of calculating the selection criteria are taken into account, it is recommended to use Fisher Information for selecting the items in polytomous CAT.

However, it should be mentioned that other factors might cause differences in performance. For example, the number of items in the CAT might play a role. Fisher Information selects the item with maximum Fisher Information at the ability estimate. However, during the first few stages of a CAT, the ability estimate is not very stable in the beginning of a CAT. This might cause problems. When the estimate is not close to the true value of the ability parameter, using Fisher Information will result in inefficient item selection. In the examples above, the number of items was equal to twenty. When the number of items is smaller, for example smaller than ten, the weaknesses of Fisher Information might be demonstrated and the other criteria might outperform Fisher Information.

A second topic for further research is the use of item pools where the information of the items is multi-peaked. In van Rijn et al. (in press), it was demonstrated that Fisher Information criterion can be outperformed by Maximum Interval information criterion when Fisher's Information function is multi-peaked. The nine simulated item pools in the example above consist of single-peaked items. So, more research is needed to check for this property.

6 References

Chang H-H, Ying Z (1996) A global information approach to computerized adaptive testing. Applied Psychological Measurement 20: 213-229

Dodd BG, De Ayala RJ, Koch WR (1995) Computerized adaptive testing with polytomous items. Applied Psychological Measurement 19: 5-22

Lehmann EL (1983) Theory of point estimation. Wiley, New York

Lehmann EL, Casella G (1998) Theory of point estimation. Springer-Verlag, New York

Lord FM, Novick MR (1968) Statistical theories of mental test scores. Addison-Wesley, Reading, MA

Muraki E (1992) A generalized partial credit model: Application of an EM algorithm. Applied Psychological Measurement 19: 159-176

van der Linden WJ (1998) Bayesian item selection criteria for adaptive testing. Psychometrika 63: 201-216

van Rijn PW, Eggen TJHM, Hemker BT, Sanders PF (in press) A selection procedure for polytomous items in computerized adaptive testing. Applied Psychological Measurement

Veerkamp WJJ, Berger MPF (1997) Some new item selection criteria for adaptive testing. Journal of Educational and Behavioral Statistics 22: 203-226

Veldkamp BP, van der Linden WJ (in press) Multidimensional adaptive testing with constraints on test content. Psychometrika

Weiss DJ (1982) Improving measurement quality and efficiency with adaptive testing. Applied Psychological Measurement 4: 473-485

Bayesian Checks on Outlying Response Times in Computerized Adaptive Testing

Wim J. van der Linden

Department of Educational Measurement and Data-Analysis, University of
Twente, P.O. Box 217, 7500 AE Enschede, The Netherlands

Summary. Bayesian posterior checks for the detection of unexpected response
times in computerized adaptive testing are presented. The checks are based on a
lognormal model for response times with separate parameters for the slowness of
the examinee and the amount of time required by the item. An empirical example
in which the response times for the adaptive version of the Arithmetic Reasoning
Test in the Armed Services Vocational Aptitude Battery (ASVAB) were studied to
detect differential speeedness of the test showed that the detection rates for Bayesian checks outperformed those for classical checks convincingly, but at the cost of
slightly higher false-alarm rates. The choice between Bayesian and classical thus
basically amounts to the choice of a loss function for the Type 1 and Type 2 errors.

Key words. Computerized adaptive testing, outlier detection, posterior predictive checks, person misfit, residual analysis, response times

1 Introduction

Traditionally, the analysis of response data to check for aberrant examinee behavior on educational or psychological tests is based on the technique of residual
analysis. That is, an item response theory (IRT) model (Hambleton & Swaminathan, 1985) is fitted to the responses and tested for the goodness of its fit. If the
model shows good fit for a population of regular examinees, individual examinees
are checked for response vectors with unexpected responses. A review of several
versions of this technique for detecting aberrant examinee behavior is given in
Meijer and Sijtsma (1995).

Diagnostics based on inferences about individual responses to test items have
little statistical power though. The reason is the binary nature of the responses. For
a well-designed tests, with the difficulties of the items near the true ability of the
examinee, the possible values for the residuals tend to be close to .50 with probabilities far away from the values testing agencies are willing to accept as evidence of aberrant examinee behavior.

It seems advantageous to use response times on items rather than the responses
themselves to check for aberrant examinee behavior. In computerized adaptive
testing (CAT), the times between keystrokes is recorded automatically. Particu-

larly in high-stake testing, the assumption that these records reflect the time the examinee actually needed to process the items and produce a response is realistic. More importantly, however, response times are continuous and do not have built-in tendencies to unfavorable distributions on tests.

This paper presents a Bayesian check on unexpected response times in CAT and illustrates the use of this check for detecting differential speededness of a test among examinee. Differential speededness occurs if for some examinees the item selection algorithm capitalizes on items that require large amounts of time and the examinee runs out of time at the end of the test. In a previous study, it was discovered that this phenomenon tends to affect the more able students, because the difficulty of their items tends to increase during the test and more difficult items generally require more time (van der Linden, Scrams, & Schnipke, 1999). The illustration is based on an empirical data set from the adaptive version of a test in the Armed Services Vocational Aptitude Battery (ASVAB).

2 Lognormal Model for Response-Times

If a subject is asked to replicate a physical task a number of times, the time needed to complete the task typically shows random variation (Townsed & Ashby, 1983). Because of retention and/or learning effects, we are seldom able to replicate the experiment of an examinee producing a response to a test item. Nevertheless, it makes sense to assume a comparable process and model response times on test items as random over replications.

Distributions of response times for a population of examinees are typically skewed to the right. A common practice is to use the logarithm of the response times and model the distribution as normal. To produce an adequate model at the level of the individual examinee and item, the normal density function should have a parameterization that adequately reflects all possible sources of systematic variation at this level. In the model below, it is assumed that differences between examinees and items are both potential sources of variation, but that interaction effects can be ignored.

Let T_{ij} denote the response time by examinee $j=1,...,J$ on item $i=1,...,I$. In addition, let δ_i be a parameter for the response time required by item i and τ_j a parameter for the slowness of examinee j. The model is

$$\ln T_{ij} = \mu + \delta_i + \tau_j + \varepsilon_{ij} \tag{1}$$

with

$$\varepsilon_{ij} \sim N(o, \sigma^2), \tag{2}$$

where μ is a parameter indicating the general response time level for the population of examinees and pool of items, and ε_{ij} a normally distributed residual for item i and examinee j with mean 0 and variance σ^2. Observe that $\ln T_{ij}$ and ε_{ij} have the same variance, which is assumed to be common across items and examinees

$$\sigma_{ij}^2 = \sigma^2. \tag{3}$$

The lognormal density has been used earlier to study response times in Thissen (1983). However, his parameterization was more restrictive and included a slowness parameter defined as a function of the examinee's ability. The parameterization in (1) is discussed in Scrams and Schnipke (1997) and has been used to formulate response-time constraints to control CAT administrations for differential speededness among examinees in van der Linden, Scrams, and Schnipke (1999).

2.1 Parameter Estimation

In an adaptive testing program, it is common to calibrate the items prior to the operational stage of the test with a sample of examinees large enough to treat the estimates as the true values of the parameters. During this calibration stage, it is easy to record the responses of the examinees and estimate the parameters δ_i ($i = 1, ..., I$), μ and σ^2 in the above model simultaneously with the parameters in the IRT model. Because the model is of the analysis-of-variance type, it simplifies to scale the parameters δ and τ to have expectation zero in the population of examinees. For details of the estimation procedure, see van der Linden, Scrams, and Schnipke (1999). In the current paper, it is also assumed that these parameters have been estimated accurately enough to treat them as known parameters.

The examinee slowness parameter in (1), τ_j, is estimated during the operational stage of the test. Let the items in the adaptive test be indexed by $k=1,...,n$ and the items in the pool by $i=1,...,I$. Thus, i_k is the index of the ith item in the pool administered as the kth item in the test. A Bayesian procedure for estimating τ_j uses the posterior distribution of this parameter given the actual response times $(t_{i_1 j},...,t_{i_n j})$. It is convenient to assume a normal prior

$$\tau_j \sim N(\mu_{0j}, \sigma_{0j}^2). \tag{4}$$

Because this prior is the conjugate for the model in (1)-(2), the posterior distribution of τ_j given $(t_{i_1 j},...,t_{i_n j})$ is also normal, with mean and variance

$$E(\tau_j | t_{i_1 j},...,t_{i_n j}) = \frac{\sigma^2 \mu_{0j} + \sigma_{0j}^2 \sum_{p=1}^{n} [\ln(t_{i_p j} - \mu - \delta_{i_p})]}{\sigma^2 + n\sigma_{0j}^2} \tag{5}$$

$$Var(\tau_j | t_{i_1 j},...,t_{i_n j}) = \frac{\sigma_{0j}^2 \sigma^2}{\sigma^2 + n\sigma_{0j}^2}, \tag{6}$$

respectively.

If the examinees are exchangeable, the parameters in (11) can be chosen to be equal to the mean and variance of the empirical distribution of τ:

$$\mu_{0j} = 0, \tag{7}$$

and

$$\sigma_{0j}^2 = \sigma_\tau^2, \tag{8}$$

where σ_τ^2 denotes the empirical variance in the population of examinees. This parameter can be estimated from the sample of persons in the calibration sample and is also assumed to be known during the operational stage of the test. The posterior mean and variance are now given as

$$E(\tau_j \mid t_{i_1 j}, \ldots, t_{i_n j}) = \frac{\sigma_\tau^2 \sum_{p=1}^n [\ln(t_{i_p j} - \mu - \delta_{i_p})]}{\sigma^2 + n\sigma_\tau^2} \tag{9}$$

and

$$Var(\tau_j \mid t_{i_1 j}, \ldots, t_{i_n j}) = \frac{\sigma_\tau^2 \sigma^2}{\sigma^2 + n\sigma_\tau^2}. \tag{10}$$

In the empirical example below, the posterior mean of τ_j in (9) was used as the estimator of τ_j.

3 Posterior Predictive Checks

Outliers can be detected by checking the difference between predicted and actual response times. On the logarithmic scale in (2), the relevant quantity is the residual

$$E_{i_k j} \equiv \ln \frac{\tilde{T}_{i_k j}}{t_{i_k j}}, \tag{11}$$

where $\tilde{T}_{i_k j}$ is the predicted response time by person j on item i administered as the kth item in the test. The proposed check is a posterior predictive check on $E_{i_k j}$. In the empirical example below, the residual in (11) was calculated as a cross-validated residual, that is, with the posterior predictive density of $\tilde{T}_{i_k j}$ calculated conditional on the response times of all items administered to the examinee except the item that was checked. This practice was followed to prevent bias in the prediction due to possible corruption of the response time on the item being checked.

Let $T_{(i_k)j}$ be the random vector of response times for examinee j with item i_k omitted and $t_{(i_k)j}$ its realization. For the normal prior of τ_j with the parameters in

(7)-(8), the posterior predictive distribution of $\ln \tilde{T}_{i_k j}$ given $\mathbf{t}_{(i_k j)}$ is also normal with mean

$$E(\ln \tilde{T}_{i_k j} \mid \mathbf{t}_{(i_k)j}) = \mu + \delta_{i_k} + \frac{\sum\limits_{p=1, p \neq k}^{n} [\ln(t_{i_p j} - \mu - \delta_{i_p})]}{\sigma^2 / \sigma_\tau^2 + n - 1} \tag{12}$$

and variance

$$Var(\ln \tilde{T}_{i_k j} \mid \mathbf{t}_{(i_k)j}) = \frac{\sigma^2 + n\sigma_\tau^2}{1 + (n-1)\sigma^2 / \sigma_\tau^2}. \tag{13}$$

It thus follows that the distribution of $E_{i_k j}$ given $\mathbf{t}_{(i_k)j}$ is normal with mean

$$E(E_{i_k j} \mid \mathbf{t}_{(i_k)j}) = \mu + \delta_{i_k} - \ln t_{i_k j} + \frac{\sum\limits_{p=1, p \neq k}^{n} [\ln(t_{i_p j} - \mu - \delta_{i_p})]}{\sigma^2 / \sigma_\tau^2 + n - 1} \tag{14}$$

and variance

$$Var(E_{i_k j} \mid \mathbf{t}_{(i_k)j}) = \frac{\sigma^2 + n\sigma_\tau^2}{1 + (n-1)\sigma^2 / \sigma_\tau^2}. \tag{15}$$

This distribution fully accounts for the uncertainty inherent in the estimation of τ_j from the actual response times on the other items. Nevertheless, the density in (14)-(15) contains only known parameters and data. It thus allows us to calculate exact probabilities of exceedance for residual response times. Any residual with probability of exceedance close to zero is unlikely under the predictions from the model and should be subjected to further inspection.

4 Empirical Example

The check in (14)-(15) was used to detect differential speededness in CAT. Differential speededness of a test leads to a combination of unexpected incorrect responses and short response times toward the end of the test.

4.1 Data Set

A data set for a sample of 38,357 examinees from the CAT version of the Arithmetic Reasoning Test in the Armed Services Vocational Aptitude Battery (ASVAB) (Segall, Moreno, & Hetter, 1997) was available. The items were known to fit the 3-parameter logistic IRT model. In addition, the lognormal response time model in (1)-(2) was fitted to the data. A study of the goodness of fit of the model, in which (1)-(2) was tested against models based on the normal, gamma, and Weibull distribution, showed excellent fit (for these analyses, see Schnipke & Scrams, 1997, and van der Linden, Scrams & Schnipke, 1999). Parameters μ, δ_i ($i = 1,...,I$), σ, and σ_τ were estimated from the response times recorded for these examinees.

4.2 CAT Simulations

Adaptive tests were simulated for examinees with abilities θ=-2.0, -1.5, ...,2.0. The response times were simulated through random draws from the lognormal distribution in (1)-(2) at τ=-.6, -.3, ..., .6. The series of values for τ was chosen relative to the empirical standard deviation σ_τ for the sample of examinees (.375). For each combination of values for (θ, τ) the number of simulated examinees was equal to 500.

The estimator of θ was the EAP estimator with an uninformative prior over [-4,4]. The items were selected using the Bayesian criterion of minimum expected posterior variance (van der Linden & Pashley, 2000, sect. 3.3). For the adaptive tests a fixed-length stopping rule was simulated, and the initial estimate $\hat{\theta}$ was set equal to zero. To determine the effect of test length on the power of the checks, two different lengths were used (n = 21 and 31).

Differential speededness was simulated for the last five items in the test. The response times for these items were sampled from

$$\ln T_{ij} \sim N(\mu + \delta_i + \tau_j + L, \sigma^2), \tag{16}$$

with effect sizes L=.000, .375 or .750. The last two effect sizes were equal to one and two times the empirical standard deviation σ_τ in the sample of ASVAB examinees.

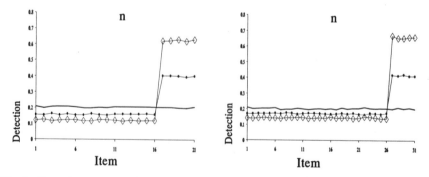

Fig. 1. Detection rates as a function of item number for n=21 (left panel) and n=31 (right panel) (diamonds: L=.750; black squares: L=.375; no marks: L=.000)

During the simulations, the checks were calculated with one-sided level of significance $\alpha = .05$, and the numbers of times the response times were flagged as outlying for the different conditions were recorded.

4.3 Results

The results for $n = 21$ and $n = 31$ are in Figure 1. The effect of the test length on the alarm rates was almost negligible but the change in effect size had a strong impact. For $L = .375$, the items that suffered from differential speededness were detected with rates approximately equal to .40 for both test lengths. For $L = .750$, the rates were over .60 ($n = 21$) and close to .70 ($n = 31$). However, these rates were obtained at the costs of false-alarm rates larger than nominal, namely .11-.15 for $L = .750$ and .375 and .20 for $L = .000$.

5 Discussion

The fact that the power of the checks was obtained at the cost of increased false alarm rates illustrates the well-known trade-off between Type 1 and Type 2 errors in statistical tests. In another study, the results for the Bayesian checks were compared with those for an approximate Gauss test, which yielded much smaller power (approximately .15 and .30 for $L=.375$ and .750, respectively) but false alarms at nominal level (van der Linden & van Krimpen-Stoop, 2003). The question which type of tests to prefer depends thus on the losses associated with the two types of error. If the purpose is to detect differential speededness, which clearly is a flaw in the design of the test for which examinees are not to be blamed, Type 1 errors should be considered as more serious than Type 2 errors, and the higher power for the Bayesian checks should be welcomed as a favorable feature.

6 References

Hambleton RK, Swaminathan H (1985) Item response theory: Principles and applications. Kluwer, Boston

Meijer RR, Sijtsma K (1995) Detection of aberrant item response patterns: A review of recent developments. Applied Measurement in Education 8: 261-272

Segall DO, Moreno KE, Hetter DH (1997) In WA. Sands, BK. Waters, JR. McBride (Eds) Computerized adaptive testing: From inquiry to operation (pp 117-130). American Psychological Association, Washington, D.C.

Schnipke DL, Scrams DJ (1997) Representing response time information in item banks (LSAC Computerized Testing Report No. 97-09). Law School Admission Council, Newtown, PA van der Linden WJ, Scrams DJ, Schnipke DL (1999) Using response-time constraints to control for speededness in computerized adaptive testing. Applied Psychological Measurement 23: 195-210

van der Linden WJ, Pashley PJ (2000) Item selection and ability estimation in adaptive testing. In WJ van der Linden, CAW Glas (Eds) Computerized adaptive testing: Theory and practice (pp. 1-25). Kluwer Academic Publishers, Norwell, MA

van der Linden, W.J., & van Krimpen-Stoop, E.M.L.A. (2003). Using response times to detect aberrant responses in computerized adaptive testing. Psychometrika, 68. In press.

Construct Comparability in International Assessments: Comparability of English and French versions of TIMSS

Kadriye Ercikan, and Kim Koh

Department of Educational & Counseling Psychology, and Special Education, Faculty of Education, University of British Columbia, Vancouver, BC V6T 1Z4, Canada

Summary. This study examined the construct comparability across the English and French versions of the TIMSS 1995 Mathematics and Science Assessments. Data from the administrations of the TIMSS in English in Canada, England and the United States, and in French in Canada and France were used. Confirmatory factor analysis (CFA), item response theory (IRT) based Linn-Harnisch differential item functioning (DIF) method and IRT item parameter correlations were conducted in assessing the construct comparability in three comparisons: Canada English-French, England-France, and US-France.

The comparisons of constructs using multi-group CFA, and IRT DIF and item parameter correlation analyses indicated that there were considerable differences as assessed by the mathematics and science tests in the US-France comparison. Further analyses need to be conducted to determine the effect of such differences on overall test score comparisons and the comparability of results from the comparison groups considered in this study as well as from all countries who participated in the TIMSS.

Key words. Construct comparability, Confirmatory factor analysis, DIF, Item Parameter Comparison, TIMSS

1 Introduction

International assessments such as the Third International Mathematics and Science Study (TIMSS) have gained considerable importance in influencing educational policy decisions in countries participating in these assessments (Ercikan, 1998). The validity of all the inferences in these assessments is critically dependent on the comparability of scores across countries. Test score comparability is closely related to the construct comparability across groups. In the context of dual- and multi-language versions of tests, construct comparability means that the factor structures being measured by the original and translated tests are invariant across different languages and cultures and the items have similar psychometric properties.

Confirmatory factor analysis (CFA) (Jöreskog, 1971) is the most widely used scale-level method for examining whether the factor structures are invariant across two or more language groups (e.g., Drasgow & Kanfer, 1985; Windle, Iwawaki,

& Lerner, 1988; Reise, Widaman, & Pugh, 1993; Marsh & Yeung, 1996; Sireci, Fitzgerald, & Xing, 1998; Gierl, Rogers, & Klinger, 1999). Reise et al. (1993), Sireci et al. (1998), and Gierl et al. (1999) have found that the CFA was useful for examining the equivalence of construct across different languages of a test, whereas the differential item functioning (DIF) detection method provided valuable information concerning the item invariance of those tests. In addition, Zumbo (in press) found that group differences that were not identified by CFA were identified by DIF methods.

The objective of this research is to examine the construct comparability assessed by the TIMSS achievement assessments using multi-group confirmatory factor analysis and item response theory (IRT) DIF methods. Differences in constructs are expected for students from different countries who take such tests in different languages. These differences can be due to curricular, linguistic and cultural differences. The study focuses on the comparability of constructs for examinees who took the tests in English versus those who took the tests in French, some of whom are from the same country and others from different countries. Even though the same versions of tests were administered in these comparisons, differing degrees of differences are expected due to curricular and cultural differences.

2 Method

2.1 Instrument

The TIMSS achievement tests consist of a pool of mathematics and science items that were matrix sampled across eight booklets. The items were divided into 26 sets and then arranged in various ways to make up eight overlapping test booklets (Martin, 1996). The examinees were administered one of eight of the test booklets (ranged from 29 to 42 items in each content area) that contained both multiple-choice and constructed-response items. The study used tests that were administered in English in the United States, England, and Canada and in French in France and Canada. The total number of items for each group ranged from 139 to 156.

2.2 Sample

Assessment data from the 1995 TIMSS (Population 2,14-year olds) on five groups, namely the Canadian English- and French-speaking students; students from England, France and the United States were used. There were approximately 3,000 to 11,000 examinees in each group.

2.3 Analyses

Construct comparability was examined separately for Mathematics and Science using multi-group confirmatory factor analysis, IRT based Linn-Harnisch DIF procedure (Linn & Harnisch, 1981) and IRT item parameter comparisons. The multi-group CFA and IRT based comparisons were conducted using LISREL 8.30 and PARDUX, respectively.

The multi-group CFA involved the testing of the full measurement invariance model in which the factor loadings and error variances were constrained to be equal across the two language groups in a unidimensional model.

In the IRT analyses multiple-choice items were calibrated using the three-parameter logistic (3PL) model (Lord, 1980) and the open-ended items were calibrated using the two-parameter partial credit (2PPC) model (Yen, 1993). The LH was used to estimate DIF. This procedure computes the observed and predicted mean response (observed and predicted p-values) and the difference between them (observed minus predicted, p_{diff}) for each item by deciles of the specified group. The predicted values are computed using the parameter estimates obtained from the entire sample, and the theta estimates (ability estimates) for the members of the specified subgroup. Based on the difference between predicted and observed p-values a Z-statistic is calculated for each decile and an average Z-statistic for the item is computed for identifying degree of DIF. A negative difference implies bias against the subgroup. An item is classified as level 3 or large DIF if the values of the differences between the observed and predicted mean is >=.10 and the absolute Z value is $|Z| >= 2.58$. If the value of the mean difference is <=.10 and $|Z| >= 2.58$, an item is classified as level 2 or moderate DIF. An item with $|Z| <= 2.58$, is classified as level 1 or negligible DIF.

3 Results

3.1 Descriptive Statistics

The differences between the mean and the standard deviation for the English- and French-speaking groups were small in all booklets in each content area. The mean differences ranged from .02 to 5.3. The reliabilities as indicated by coefficient-alpha were consistently higher for the English-speaking group in the England-France and US-France comparisons. The reliability differences ranged from .026 to .121. In the Canadian comparison, the differences in reliabilities for the two language groups were negligible.

3.2 Confirmatory Factor Analyses

The results of the confirmatory factor analyses for each of the comparisons in each content area are presented in Tables 1 and 2. Given the large number of degrees of freedom in this study, the chi-square test was not reported in assessing fit. Instead, practical fit indices such as root mean square error of approximation (RMSEA), root mean square residual (RMR), and goodness-of-fit index (GFI) were used to assess the fit of the model to the data. RMSEA values of 0.05 indicate close fit of a model to data and values of 0.08 reflect reasonable fit of a model (Reise et al., 1993). The common lower bound for the GFI is 0.90 for a good fit. These standards were used in examining the degree of the fit of the full measurement invariance model.

Table 1. Confirmatory Factor Analyses Results for Mathematics

Content Area	Comparison	Booklet	RMSEA	RMR	GFI
Mathematics	Canada E-F	1	0.021	0.083	0.92
		2	0.082	0.068	0.80
		3	0.045	0.014	0.88
		4	0.019	0.075	0.94
		5	0.084	0.098	0.61
		6	0.091	0.110	0.63
		7	0.083	0.060	0.81
		8	0.088	0.100	0.62
	Eng. - France	1	0.022	0.110	0.90
		2	0.088	0.190	0.81
		3	0.026	0.026	0.91
		4	0.087	0.110	0.74
		5	0.081	0.110	0.72
		6	0.091	0.100	0.70
		7	0.082	0.110	0.74
		8	0.019	0.100	0.92
	US-France	1	0.085	0.098	0.64
		2	0.070	0.060	0.87
		3	0.095	0.100	0.55
		4	0.081	0.066	0.83
		5	0.079	0.064	0.81
		6	0.074	0.055	0.86
		7	0.076	0.064	0.84
		8	0.092	0.100	0.56

In Table 1, the Mathematics confirmatory factor analyses results indicate that the differences between constructs assessed by the Mathematics test items were the largest for the US-France comparison. As indicated by the values of RMSEA, RMR, and GFI, three out of the eight booklets have a good fit of the model to the data in the Canada English-French comparison. Their RMSEA values ranged from 0.019 to 0.045 and the GFI values ranged from 0.88 to 0.94. Hence, the full measurement invariance model was tenable in Booklets 1, 3, and 4. The rest of the booklets have moderate fit. In the England-France comparison, three of the booklets have a good fit of the model to the data. The RMSEA values ranged from

0.019 to 0.026 and the GFI values ranged from 0.90 to 0.92. The full measurement invariance model was tenable in Booklets 1, 3, and 8. None of the booklets in the US-France comparison indicates a good fit of the model to the data. Their RMSEA values ranged from 0.070 to 0.095 and the GFI values ranged from 0.55 to 0.87. These values were below the standards of a good fit.

Table 2. Confirmatory Factor Analyses Results for Science

Content Area	Comparison	Booklet	RMSEA	RMR	GFI
Science	Canada E-F	1	0.089	0.200	0.86
		2	0.083	0.072	0.78
		3	0.077	0.070	0.82
		4	0.027	0.074	0.95
		5	0.086	0.072	0.84
		6	0.082	0.110	0.64
		7	0.091	0.060	0.66
		8	0.096	0.110	0.66
	Eng.-France	1	0.070	0.180	0.27
		2	0.077	0.110	0.74
		3	0.078	0.190	0.83
		4	0.031	0.110	0.93
		5	0.080	0.100	0.75
		6	0.085	1.250	-
		7	0.079	0.190	0.82
		8	0.080	0.100	0.77
	US-France	1	0.090	0.110	0.69
		2	0.068	0.064	0.84
		3	0.061	0.061	0.89
		4	0.087	0.073	0.72
		5	0.068	0.064	0.88
		6	0.170	0.170	-
		7	0.066	0.062	0.87
		8	0.074	0.064	0.87

The results in Table 2 indicate that the comparability of constructs assessed by the science items for the three comparisons was somewhat poorer compared to those observed for the mathematics construct comparisons. Only one booklet, that is, Booklet 4 has a good fit of the model to the data in the Canada English-French comparison (RMSEA = 0.027, GFI = 0.95) and in the England-France comparison (RMSEA = 0.031, GFI = 0.93). In the US-France comparison, none of the booklets indicates a good fit. Their RMSEA values ranged from 0.061 to 0.170 and the GFI values were ranged between 0.69 to 0.89.

3.3 IRT DIF Analyses

The results of the DIF detection procedure are summarized in Table 3. There were 22 DIF items in the English and French versions of the Mathematics items that were administered in Canada. There were larger numbers of DIF items when the French items administered in France were compared to those administered in England and the United States. These numbers were 61 for the England-France comparison and 91 for the US-France comparison. Forty-three percent of the mathematics DIF items functioned in favor of the French-speaking examinees in the Canadian comparison group, 43% in the England-France comparison, and 53% in the US-France comparison. There were 54 DIF Science items in the Canadian comparison, 54 in the England-France, and 110 in the US-France comparison. Sixty-five percent of the Science DIF items functioned in favor of the French-speaking group in the Canadian comparison, 54% in the England-France comparison, and 65% in the US-France comparison.

Table 3. Number of Mathematics and Science DIF Items

Comparisons	Pro-English		Pro-French	
	Level 2	Level 3	Level 2	Level 3
Mathematics:				
Canada E-F	11	2	8	1
Eng.-France	32	3	21	5
US-France	33	10	35	13
Science:				
Canada E-F	16	2	30	4
Eng.-France	24	1	26	3
US-France	27	11	52	20

3.4 IRT Parameter Comparisons

Table 4 presents correlations of item parameters a, b and c based on the calibrations that combined items across test booklets as well as separately for each booklet, for each comparison. The correlations between multiple-choice item parameters based on the combined calibrations indicate that the correlations of difficulty parameter b tended to be high in all three comparisons for mathematics and science, ranging between 0.68-0.87. The discrimination parameter correlations were noticeably lower, ranging between 0.27-0.45. The low a parameter correlations indicate that the relationship between what the items are assessing with the overall construct assessed by the whole test varied for some of the items in the considered comparisons. The correlations between constructed-response item parameters based on the combined calibrations indicate that the correlations of difficulty parameters β tended to be high in all three comparisons for mathematics and science, ranging between 0.65-0.94. The discrimination parameter correlations were lower than those for the difficulty parameters, for constructed-response items as well, ranging between 0.68-0.80.

Table 4. Correlation between IRT Item Parameters

Comparison	Content Area	Correlations						
		a	b	c	α	β1	β2	p
Canada E-F	Mathematics	0.454	0.865	0.366	0.749	0.938	0.699	0.959
	Science	0.296	0.808	0.339	0.670	0.934	0.531	0.911
Eng.-France	Mathematics	0.382	0.716	0.210	0.682	0.647	0.844	0.748
	Science	0.551	0.759	0.508	0.677	0.853	0.870	0.832
US-France	Mathematics	0.312	0.779	0.314	0.801	0.753	0.793	0.801
	Science	0.268	0.682	0.236	0.786	0.835	0.989	0.795

4 Summary

The comparisons of constructs using CFA, and IRT DIF and item parameter correlation analyses indicated that there were considerable differences as assessed by the mathematics and science tests in the US-France comparison. The DIF analyses indicated much larger differences between constructs assessed by the Science tests for the comparison groups. The IRT parameter comparisons indicated similarly large discrepancies between constructs as indicated by low correlations between discrimination parameters. The confirmatory factor analyses confirmed the results from the DIF and IRT analyses. In the US-France comparison, the full measurement invariance model was not tenable in all the booklets for Mathematics and Science. Hence, the constructs being assessed by the Mathematics and Science assessments in the 1995 TIMSS (Population 14-year olds) were not comparable across the English and French versions.

The differences in constructs observed in our analyses indicate that further analyses need to be conducted to determine the effect of such differences on overall test score comparisons and the comparability of results from the comparison groups considered in this study as well as from all countries who participated in the TIMSS.

References

Drasgow, F., & Kanfer, R. (1985).   Equivalence of psychological measurement in heterogeneous populations. Journal of Applied Psychology, 70, 662-680

Ercikan, K. (1998). Translation effects in international assessments. International Journal of Educational Research, 29, 543-553

Gierl, M.J., Rogers, W.T., & Klinger, D. (1999, April).   Using statistical and judgmental reviews to identify and interpret translation DIF. Paper presented at the National Council on Measurement in Education, Montréal, Quebec

Jöreskog, K.G. (1971).   Simultaneous factor analysis in several populations. Psychometrika, 36, 409-426

Linn, R. L., & Harnisch, D. L. (1981). Interactions between item content and group measurement on achievement test items. Journal of Educational Measurement, 18, 109-118

Lord, F. M. (1980). Applications of item response theory to practical testing problems. Hillsdale, NJ: Erlbaum

Marsh, H.W., & Yeung, A.S. (1996).   The distinctiveness of affects in specific school subjects: An application of confirmatory factor analysis with the National Educational Longitudinal Study of 1988. American Educational Research Journal, 3, 665-689

Martin, M. O. (1996). Third International Mathematics and Science Study: An overview. In M. O. Martin & D. L. Kelly (Eds.). Third International Mathematics and Science Study: Technical Report, Volume I, Design and Development. International Association for the Evaluation of Educational Achievement (IEA)

Reise, S.P., Widaman, K.F., & Pugh, R.H. (1993).   Confirmatory factor analysis and item response theory: two approaches for exploring measurement invariance. Psychological Bulletin, 114(3), 552-566

Sireci, S.G., Fitzgerald, C., & Xing, D. (1998, April). Adapting credentialing examinations for international uses. Laboratory of Psychometric and Evaluative Research Report, 329. University of Massachusetts, School of Education, Amherst, MA

Windle, M., Iwawaki, S., & Lerner, R.M. (1988).   Cross-cultural comparability of temperament among Japanese and American preschool children. International Journal of Psychology, 23, 547-567

Yen, W. M. (1993). Scaling performance assessments: Strategies for managing local item dependence. Journal of Educational Measurement, 30, 187-214

Zumbo, B. (in press). Does item-level DIF manifest itself in scale-level analyses?: Implications for translating language tests. Language Testing

Are the Japanese more depressed than the U.S. individuals? – An IRT-DIF study –

Noboru Iwata

Division of Health Science, University of East Asia, 2-1 Ichinomiya-Gakuencho, Shimonoseki 751-8503, Japan

Summary. This study analyzed ethnocultural differences in responses to items measuring depressive symptoms in demographically matched samples of Japanese and U.S. white collar workers (N = 368 for each). Using item response theory with a two-parameter logistic model (2PL-IRT), differential item functioning (DIF) of items comprising the Center for Epidemiologic Studies Depression Scale was assessed for Japanese and U.S. workers. The 2PL-IRT analysis revealed that the item characteristic curves (ICCs) were generally identical between (lack of) positive affect items and other negative symptom items among the U.S. workers, but not among the Japanese workers. Most of (lack of) positive affect items showed DIF between the groups: i.e., the Japanese tended to endorse such responses even at much lower depressive (latent trait) levels, as compared to the U.S. workers. Although some negative symptom items yielded significant DIF, averaged ICCs were comparable between the groups. Because of the sample-independent nature of IRT, these results provided more robust evidence to the Iwata hypothesis that Japanese respondents tend to inhibit positive affect expression.

Key Words. item response theory, differential item functioning, Center for Epidemiologic Studies Depression Scale, cross-cultural comparison

1. Introduction

Major depression is one of the most common diseases in industrialized countries, and is further estimated to be the second most debilitating disease worldwide in 2020 (Murray and Lopez 1996). Thus, the detection of depression, as well as prevention and treatment strategies, will increasingly become major health priorities in the future. The World Mental Health 2000 Initiative and the growing ethnic diversity of populations in many countries emphasize the significance of, and need for, culturally equivalent assessment methods.

The Center for Epidemiologic Studies Depression Scale (CES-D), developed in the U.S. for use in community surveys to identify those "at high-risk" for depression (Radloff 1977), is now widely used in a number of countries, including several cross-cultural studies. Ideally, scores on such a widely used measure should have equivalent meaning across race/ethnicity, cultures, and regions (Flaherty et al. 1988). That is, scale items should be free from item- and scale-level bias associated with exogenous variables such as gender, race/ethnicity, and culture.

Prior research has addressed race/ethnicity-specific response patterns to items of the CES-D (e.g. Golding et al. 1991; Iwata et al. 1989). Iwata and his colleagues (1994, 1995), for example, found Japanese to be more likely than Whites to inhibit the expression of positive affect as measured by positively-oriented (POS) items, while response patterns to negatively-oriented (NEG) items were generally comparable. However, most of these studies relied on rather simple statistical procedures such as average frequency distributions, t-tests and ANOVA. Such analytic procedures are not entirely adequate for identifying or assessing variations in response tendency. A more promising strategy is the analysis of differential item functioning ([DIF]; Holland and Thayer 1988).

DIF refers to any circumstance in which respondents, differing from one another on a certain exogenous variable (e.g. race/ethnicity), but who resemble one another on a certain latent continuum of interest (e.g. depressive symptoms), show different probabilities of endorsing an item intended to measure that latent continuum (Clauser and Mazor 1998). Of several DIF detection procedures, methods using item response theory (IRT) appear to be the most sound because of their sample-independent nature.

The present study addresses the item-level bias (or DIF) in responses to the CES-D using IRT. Particular attention is paid to difference in endorsement functioning on POS and NEG items across the groups, as an investigation of the ethno-cultural differences in the expression or inhibition of positive affect.

2. Methods

2.1 Subjects

As a secondary data analysis, responses to CES-D items in demographically matched (age, gender, education, marital status, occupation) samples of Japanese and U.S. white-collar workers ($N = 368$ for each) were used. Analysis data were selected from the following two samples. The Japanese data were obtained from a 1986 health examination survey of workers in 29 public offices in Hokkaido, Japan ($N = 2,016$). The respondents, who ranged in age from 19 to 63 years, were all full-time workers who had at least a high school education (Iwata et al. 1989). The Japanese version of the CES-D, translated and validated by Shima et al. (1985), was included in the health check questionnaire. The U.S. data were obtained from the 1974-75 Augmentation Survey of the National Health and Nutrition Examination Survey I (NHANES-IA), a national health survey for the U.S. adult population with ages 25-74 years ($N = 3,059$). The survey and charac-teristics of the sample were described elsewhere (e.g. Eaton and Kessler 1981). NHANES-IA included the CES-D.

2.2 Measure and Scoring Procedure

The CES-D is a 20-item self-administered questionnaire that assesses the frequency of depressive symptoms during the past week (Radloff 1977). The measure includes 16 NEG items, such as "I felt depressed," and four POS items, such as "I was happy." Subjects select one of four response alternatives: "Rarely or none of the time (experienced less than 1 day during the past week)," "Some or a little of the time (1-2 days)," "Occasionally or a moderate amount of the time (3-4 days)," and "Most or all of the time (5-7 days)." These are typically scored as 0, 1, 2, and 3, respectively. The four POS items are reverse-scored so that higher scores indicate greater lack of positive affect. Here, these 0-1-2-3 scores were dichotomized into 0/1 data according to 0-1-1-1 scoring for subsequent IRT analyses.

2.3 Analysis Strategy

Dichotomized responses were subjected to the 2-parameter logistic model analysis of IRT (2PL-IRT). The IRT likelihood ratio DIF detection method was used here. Firstly, the purified subset with non-DIF items was constructed as displayed in Fig. 1: (1) Screen the item candidates using Mantel-Haenszel (MH) method (Holland and Thayer 1988); (2) Select several items, and subject them to the 2PL-IRT; (3) Obtain the -2log-likelihood ratio (G^2) of that subset; (4) Constrain slope (denoted by a in Fig.1) and threshold (b) parameters to be the same across groups, and obtain the G^2; and (5) If the difference in G^2 between the constrained model and the free model is not significant, the purified subtest is confirmed.

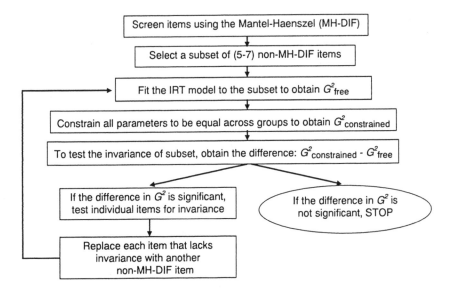

Fig. 1. Flow chart explaining the construction process of the purified (anchor) subset.

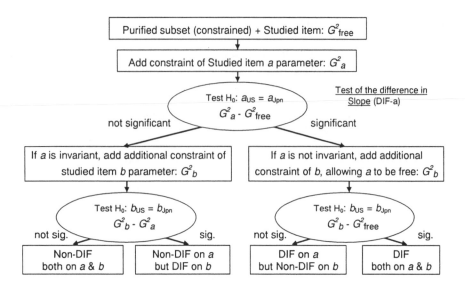

Fig. 2. Flow chart explaining the IRT likelihood ratio DIF detection method.

Second, using the purified subset mentioned above, the IRT likelihood ratio DIF detection procedure was conducted. Fig.2 shows its detailed process: (1) Construct dataset involving purified items and one studied item; (2) Test the difference in G^2 between parameter a (slope) constraint model and free model. At this execution, both parameters of purified items were constrained to be the same between the groups; (3) At the next step, parameter b (threshold) of studied item was constrained; and (4) Test the difference in G^2. Through these steps, the DIF on slope parameter and/or the DIF on threshold parameter of studied item were examined.

3. Results

3.1 DIF of Individual Items

Through an iterative process, a purified subset was constructed; it consisted of four items, #17 "Crying spells," #7 "Effort," #20 "Get going," and #15 "Unfriend-ly." Table 1 shows slope and threshold parameters of individual CES-D items for each group. The IRT-DIF results are also displayed. The items are listed along with the traditional subscales; "Depressed affect" (DEP), "Somatic & retarded ac-tivities" (SOM), "Interpersonal relations" (INT), and "Positive affect." Of NEG items, eight items showed DIF between Japanese and U.S. workers, whereas all four POS items showed DIF. The item characteristic curves (ICCs) of these DIF items revealed that the Japanese over-endorsed #6 "Depressed," #9 "Failure," but under-endorsed #18 "Sad" as compared to U.S. workers even if lower depressive level (data not shown). Similarly, of SOM items, the Japanese over-endorsed #1 'Bothered" and #2 "Appetite," but U.S. workers over-endorsed #11 "Sleep" and #20 "Get going." In contrast, the Japanese consistently and remarkably over-endorsed all POS items.

Table 1. Parameter estimates of the CES-D items for Japanese and U.S. workers

Scale/Items	Japanese		U.S. workers		DIF	
	Slope	Threshold	Slope	Threshold	Slope	Threshold
Depressed Affect						
3 Blues	2.04	1.22	2.45	1.44	ns	ns
6 Depressed	4.62	0.52	1.84	0.92	*	***
9 Failure	1.88	0.07	2.43	1.61	ns	***
10 Blues	3.94	1.85	1.54	1.44	*	ns
14 Fearful	1.65	1.58	1.56	1.43	ns	ns
17 Crying spells	1.33	3.84	2.72	2.01	purified	
18 Sad	2.16	1.46	3.61	0.74	ns	***
Somatic & Retarded Activities						
1 Bothered	2.05	0.57	1.48	1.13	ns	***
2 Appetite	0.89	1.59	0.49	4.57	ns	***
5 Trouble concentrating	2.64	0.32	2.14	0.51	ns	ns
7 Effort	1.71	0.66	1.47	0.13	purified	
11 Sleep	1.37	1.37	1.43	0.25	ns	***
13 Talked	2.02	0.56	1.34	0.23	purified	
20 Get going	2.57	1.29	2.11	0.47	ns	***
Interpersonal Relations						
15 Unfriendly	3.25	1.41	1.62	1.27	purified	
19 Dislike	2.12	1.52	2.27	1.63	ns	ns
(Lack of) Positive Affect						
4 (Not) Good	0.22	-2.70	0.43	1.79	ns	***
8 (Not) Hopeful	0.63	-2.77	0.75	0.90	ns	***
12 (Not) Happy	0.63	-2.19	1.21	0.86	*	***
16 (Not) Enjoyed	1.00	-2.00	1.20	1.39	ns	***

ns: not significant between the groups.
*, ***: significant different between the groups at $p < .05, p < .001$, respectively.
purified: items used for purified subset.

3.2 Averaged ICCs for Subscales

To make clear the overall feature of ICCs according to the subscales, slope and threshold parameters of items derived by 2PL-IRT in a same subscale were averaged for each group. Then, an ICC per subscale was drawn for visual inspection (Fig. 3). The X-axis represents the latent continuum (commonly denoted by θ) of depressive symptoms, and the Y-axis represents the probability of endorsement.

In IRT models, the probability of endorsement is estimated at each θ level, so that the difference in base rate does not have an influence on ICC.

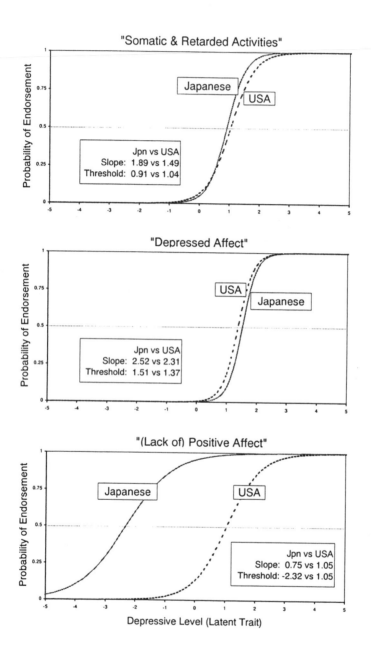

Fig. 3. Item characteristic curves (ICCs) of the CES-D subscales – on average –

Although some NEG items yielded DIF, averaged ICCs of DEP and SOM were comparable between the groups (top and middle of Fig. 3). The similar result was found for INT (data not shown). In contrast, averaged ICCs of positive affect items differed remarkably between the groups (bottom of Fig. 3); the Japanese were more likely than U.S. workers to endorse (lack of) positive affect at any given level of θ. For the Japanese, endorsement began at lower depressive level, and at the point where the U.S. endorsement starts, almost all Japanese workers already endorsed.

4. Discussion

Because of the sample-independent nature of IRT, the current results provided more robust evidence to the Iwata hypothesis that "Japanese respondents tend to suppress the expression of positive affect." With reference to our study on clinical outpatients (Iwata et al. 1998), these results might indicate that the Japanese have a tendency to suppress the expression of positive affect. This response tendency was likely to induce spuriously higher mean scores of mental health measures for the Japanese than the other (western) cultural groups (cf. Iwata et al. 1989; 1994; 1995; Iwata and Higuchi 2000). It also had a detrimental influence on psycho-metric properties of the measures (cf. Iwata and Roberts 1996; Iwata et al. 2000).

As to the reason why Japanese individuals have such a tendency, Iwata and his colleagues have discussed this fully elsewhere (e.g. Iwata et al. 1995; 2000; Iwata and Buka in press). On the other hand, Iwata and Buka (in press) revealed that North Americans, including Native Americans, might be more likely to express positive feelings as compared to South Americans. Positive feelings such as feeling good about oneself, feeling happy, and enjoying life are quite salient in mainstream American culture. Thus, it is normative for North Americans to create such feelings in daily life and to express these feelings with relatively little hesi-tation (Iwata et al. 1994; Kitayama et al. 1997). Iwata et al. (2002) also provided supportive evidence that the expression of positive affect might be over-enhanced in North American culture.

Considering similar results in earlier studies on East Asian and/or Asian im-migrants in the U.S. based on analyses using classical test theory, a common res-ponse preference may exist due to the type of item wording: i.e. POS items seem to be more likely to differ in their functioning between various ethnocultural groups. POS questions should be dealt with carefully in cross-cultural compar-isons. Moreover, it should be noted that although American samples have often been used as a reference group in most previous cross-cultural studies, they should not be necessarily suitable for the reference group. Nevertheless, the present samples did not appear to be representative of each ethnocultural population. This study therefore should be regarded as a preliminary report on this issue.

References

Clauser BE, Mazor KM (1998) Using statistical procedures to identify differential item functioning test items. Educ Measurement: Issues and Practice 17: 31-44

Eaton WW, Kessler LG (1981) Rates of symptoms of depression in a national sample. Am J Epidemiol 114: 528-538

Flaherty JA, Gaviria FM, Pathak D, Mitchell T, Wintrob R, Richman JA, Birz S (1988) Developing instruments for cross-cultural psychiatric research. J Nerv Ment Dis 176: 257-263

Golding JM, Aneshensel CS, Hough RL (1991) Responses to depression scale items among Mexican-Americans and non-Hispanic whites. J Clin Psychol 47: 61-75

Holland PW, Thayer DT, 1988. Differential item performance and the Mantel-Haenszel procedure. In: Wainer H, Baun HI. (Eds.), Test Validity. Erlbaum, Hillsdale, NJ, pp. 129-145

Iwata N, Buka S (in press) Race/ethnicity and depressive symptoms: a cross-cultural/ethnic comparison among university students in East Asia, North and South America. Soc Sci & Med

Iwata N, Higuchi HR (2000) Responses of Japanese and American university students to the STAI items that assess the presence or absence of anxiety. J Pers Assess 74: 48-62

Iwata N, Mishima N, Okabe K, Kobayashi N, Hashiguchi E, Egashira K (2000) Psychometric properties of the State-Trait Anxiety Inventory among Japanese clinical outpatients. J Clin Psychol 56: 793-806

Iwata N, Okuyama Y, Kawakami Y, Saito K (1989) Prevalence of depressive symptoms in a Japanese occupational setting: a preliminary study. Am J Public Health 79: 1486-1489

Iwata N, Roberts CR, Kawakami N (1995) Japan-U.S. comparison of responses to depression scale items among adult workers. Psychiatry Res 58: 237-245

Iwata N, Roberts RE (1996) Age differences among Japanese on the Center for Epidemiologic Studies Depression Scale: an ethnocultural perspective on somatization. Soc Sci & Med 43: 967-974

Iwata N, Saito K, Roberts RE (1994) Responses to a self-administered depression scale among younger adolescents in Japan. Psychiatry Res 53: 275-287

Iwata N, Turner RJ, Lloyd DA (2002) Race/ethnicity and depressive symptoms in community-dwelling young adults: a differential item functioning analysis. Psychiatry Res 110:281-289

Iwata N, Umesue M, Egashira K, Hiro H, Mizoue T, Mishima N, Nagata S (1998) Can positive affect items be used to assess depressive disorders in the Japanese population? Psychol Med 28: 153-158

Kitayama S, Markus HR, Matsumoto H, Norasakkunkit V (1997) Individual and collective processes in the construction of the self-enhancement in the United State and self-criticism in Japan. J Pers Soc Psychol 72: 1245-1267

Murray CJL, Lopez AD (Eds) (1996) The Global Burden of Disease: A Comprehensive Assessment of Mortality and Disability from Diseases, Injuries, and Risk Factors in 1990 and Projected to 2020. Harvard University Press, Boston.

Radloff LS (1977) The CES-D scale: A self-report depression scale for research in the general population. Appl Psychol Measure 1: 385-401

General and Specific Misfit of Nonparametric IRT-models

M.J.H. van Onna[1]

Tilburg University, Dep. Methodology and Statistics, PO Box 90153, 5000 LE Tilburg, Netherlands, *Marieke.vanOnna@kub.nl*

Summary. Model misfit in NIRT means that one or more of the items violate the assumptions of unidimensionality, local independence or monotonicity. General tests detect whether model misfit occurs. Specific item misfit tests detect which item is violating the assumptions. Two methods to detect general and item misfit are presented: the Mokken scale approach and the ordered latent class approach. The results show that the item specific Mokken approach and the ordered latent class approach detect items with decreasing or unimodal IRFs. The Mokken approach also warns for IRFs which are nearly flat.

Key words: Nonparametric Item Response Theory, Posterior predictive checks, Model misfit

1 Model violations

In nonparametric item response theory (NIRT) models three main assumptions are made. First, it is assumed that the underlying latent trait is unidimensional (UD). Second, the responses of a subject are assumed to be locally independent given the latent trait value of the subject (LI). Third, the probability of responding positively to an item (step) as a function of the latent trait value, called the item (step) response function (IRF, ISRF), is assumed to be non-decreasing in the latent trait value. This is the assumption of monotonicity (M). As can be noted, the function of the IRF is not restricted to be logistic or cumulative normal. The only requirement is that it is non-decreasing. This is the nonparametric aspect of NIRT. The Mokken monotone homogeneity model (Mokken, 1971, 1997) is characterized by these assumptions. If the assumption of non-intersecting ISRFs (NI) is added, the more restrictive Mokken double monotonicity model results. This refinement is left out of this paper, since only violations of the minimal measurement requirements are considered. Applying the assumptions to latent class models results in ordered latent class models (Van Onna, in press), which can be considered as close parametric specifications of the NIRT models.

A set of items can violate the assumptions in several ways. If UD is violated, more than one dimension is necessary to describe the latent structure of the items. LI is violated by items which show dependence, which cannot be explained completely by the latent trait. Additional dependence may be induced, for example, by the presentation format of the items. M can be violated in several ways. The IRF might be decreasing, by a non-corrected inverse wording or coding of the item. Some attitude items result in unimodal IRFs, which are better analyzed by unfolding models. An IRF which is locally decreasing, also indicates that the item is not strongly related to the latent trait.

If model misfit occurs, it has to be checked which items violate the assumptions. If most of the items violate the assumptions, a more suitable model has to be found to describe the underlying structure. If, however, only one item violates the assumptions, it is probably wiser to detect the 'bad' item and delete it, than to reject the entire model.

2 Two detection approaches

Two methods are discussed to detect either general model misfit or item misfit. The first method, Mokken scale analysis (Mokken, 1971, 1997; Sijtsma and Molenaar, 2002) is a descriptive method, which computes functions of the data and compares them to specific standard values. The ordered latent class method (Van Onna, in press) fits a semi-parametric model, using ordered latent classes instead of a continuous latent trait. The model is fitted with the Gibbs sampler. This enables posterior predictive checks for misfit.

2.1 Mokken scale analysis

The latent trait in the Mokken models is assumed to be continuous. The subjects can be stochastically ordered on the latent trait by the sum score $X_+ = \sum_j X_j$ (Hemker et al., 1997). Central in Mokken scale analysis is the scaling coefficient Loevinger's H. It indicates to what extent the items discriminate between the subjects.

H is based on pairs of items, comparing the observed and expected numbers of Guttman errors. A Guttman error is made when a 'difficult' item is positively responded to, and an 'easy' item is negatively responded to by the same person. The difficulty order of two dichotomous items j and i is determined by the proportion of correct responses. Assume, $\pi_j = P(X_j = 1) < \pi_i = P(X_i = 1)$, then the observed number of Guttman errors $F_{ij} = N \cdot P(X_j = 1, X_i = 0)$ and the expected number of Guttman errors under the null model of independent items $E_{ij} = N\pi_j(1 - \pi_i)$. The pairwise H_{ij} is equal to $1 - F_{ij}/E_{ij}$. This is equal to the ratio of the covariance between the two items and the maximum covariance given the marginal distributions: $H_{ij} = \sigma_{ij}/\max(\sigma_{ij})$. Under the assumptions of UD, LI, and M, H_{ij} is non-negative.

The H_i value at the item level is based on the item pairs in which item i is involved,

$$H_i = 1 - \frac{\sum_{j \neq i} F_{ij}}{\sum_{j \neq i} E_{ij}}, \tag{1}$$

and the scale H is defined on all pairs of items, that is,

$$H = 1 - \frac{\sum_{i<j} F_{ij}}{\sum_{i<j} E_{ij}}. \tag{2}$$

A standard minimum value of H or H_i for scalable items is 0.30. Although this index is presented for dichotomous items, an extension to polytomous items is straightforward (Molenaar, 1991).

Another index in Mokken scale analysis which can be used to detect item misfit is the $crit_i$-value of the check of monotonicity (Molenaar and Sijtsma, 2000). The check of monotonicity inspects plots of the estimated IRFs. The latent trait values are replaced by restscores, sum scores on all but the inspected item. The proportion of positive responses in each group of subjects having about the same restscore is calculated. The statistic $crit_i$ is a weighted sum of all observed violations of monotonicity of item i. When it exceeds the value of 80, serious violation of M is presumed. This index can be easily evaluated for polytomous items as well.

In the simulation studies, general model misfit was concluded when $H <$ 0.30. Item misfit was concluded when $H_i < 0.30$ or when $crit_i > 80$. This approach is a descriptive approach, because it compares descriptive statistics to standard values.

2.2 Ordered latent class models

In ordered latent class models, the latent trait is assumed to be discrete. Across the Q subsequent latent classes, the probability of responding positively to the items or the item steps, $\pi^*_{jkq} = P(X_j \geq k|q)$, is assumed to be non-decreasing. That is,

$$\pi^*_{jkq} \leq \pi^*_{jk,q+1}. \tag{3}$$

Note that the flexibility of the nonparametric definition of an IRF is maintained. However, this parameterization with class weights and class specific response probabilities opens a path to model estimation and model testing. The number of parameters, however, is usually quite large. This is a motivation to use a Bayesian estimation and model check procedure (Van Onna, in press).

After fitting the model with a fixed number of latent classes, posterior predictive checks can be performed. When a posterior predictive p-value (Gelman et al., 1995) is extreme, that is, $P_B < .025$ or $P_B > .975$, misfit of the model to the data can be inferred. This corresponds to a two-sided test with $\alpha = .05$. The model is not able to replicate data which resemble the observed data with respect to the aspect expressed by the used statistic or discrepancy function. This function is specified in several ways in this study. For general model misfit detection the log-likelihood with the saturated model, LR, the pseudo log-likelihood, PR (Van Onna, in press), and H are used. For specific item misfit detection, the statistic is specified as H_i.

The LR and the PR both involve observed and expected response frequencies. The LR discrepancy compares frequencies of full response vectors, whereas the PR focuses on bivariate response vector frequencies. Coefficient H, as in Eq. 2, focuses on bivariate tables as well, but only on the Guttman error cells. The posterior predictive approach is inferential, since it compares an aspect of the observed data with inferences on data generated according to the model.

3 Simulation studies

Several questions are to be answered by the simulation studies. First, to what extent do the two methods detect model misfit? The detection of the violation of M is considered in particular. Second, does the number of latent classes Q matter for the detection rate in ordered latent class analysis? Third, are the results different for dichotomous or polytomous items? This last question is interesting because for dichotomous items, stochastic ordering of the latent trait (SOL) in the total score X_+ holds (Hemker et al., 1997). This means that X_+ results in an ordering of subjects which reflects the ordering with respect to the latent trait, apart from measurement error. SOL X_+ does not always hold for the nonparametric models when applied to polytomous items.

3.1 Design

The cells of the design vary on three dimensions. The first dimension is the distribution of the unidimensional latent trait. The distribution of the subjects on the latent trait is either (approximately) normal or uniform. The latent trait is continuous or consists of 11 ordered latent classes, which approximates continuity to some degree. The second dimension involved is the number of subjects in a data set. It equals either 200 (small) or 2000 (large).

The third dimension describes the items. Either ten dichotomous items are generated, or five trichotomous items. In both cases, the number of item step response functions equals 10. The data are generated by conditioning on the latent trait value, using the assumption of LI. The IRFs of all items, but one, are non-decreasing. The first item has an IRF which is either strictly decreasing (M1d), decreasing only locally for low, middle or high trait values (M1l, M1m, M1h, respectively), unimodal (M1u) or flat (M1f). Or, it is increasing (M0), in which case the items fulfill all model assumptions. The assumption of M is not violated in the M1f cells, strictly speaking. However, such a 'flat' item is not useful for scaling subjects because it does not discriminate between low and high latent trait values. Therefore, detection of this kind of items is desirable. In the continuous latent trait cells, a model with logistic IRFs, the 2PL-model (dichotomous) or GRM-model (Samejima, 1969) (polytomous), is used to generate the data. In the discrete latent trait cells, class-specific response probabilities are designed by convenience.

In total four simulation studies (SS) were done. SS I and SS II have dichotomous items; SS III and SS IV have trichotomous items. SSI and SS III are generated with 11 ordered latent classes; SS II and SS IV with a continuous latent trait. The item dimension in SS III has a partly different structure than the description above, which applies to SS I, SS II and SS IV. The Msy and Msn cells have polytomous items with strong ('s') discrimination power; the Mwy and Mwn cells have polytomous items with weak ('w') discrimination power, but their ISRFs do not decrease. The property SOL X_+ holds ('y') for the generating model in the Msy and Mwy cells, it does not hold ('n') in the Msn and Mwn cells. Note that the NIRT assumptions still hold, even if SOL X_+ does not hold. The violating cells are denoted by an asterisk in Tables 1 and 2.

Ten data sets are generated in each cell of the design. For all data sets, the general model fit statistics are computed. The item specific checks are only computed for the first item of each data set. The ordered latent class models are fitted with Q equal to 3, 5, 7 or 11.

3.2 Results

In Table 1, the results of the Mokken scale analysis are shown. The number of times $H < .30$, the number of times $H_1 < .30$ and the number of times $crit_1 \geq 80$ are displayed. If an entry in the table equals 10, this means that for all simulated data sets misfit is detected in that specific cell, with that specific statistic. As one can see, no false positives are reported in the M0-cells which fulfill the assumptions. The total scale H is not functioning very well as a simple general model misfit index. It fails to report misfit (even for large samples) when one item has a decreasing or unimodal IRF and all 11 latent classes have equal class weights (SS I-M1d). It does report a misfit of badly discriminating items (SS III-Mwy,Mwn, SS II-M1f, SS IV-M1f). The item specific H_i is more sensitive to item misfit, in that it detects the decreasing, unimodal and even sometimes locally decreasing IRFs. Also, it points out badly discriminating items.

The item specific $crit_i$, which is designed to detect deviations from M, seems to be doing its job quite well, although it is also not able to detect small deviations in all cases. It shows the ambivalence in the flat IRF cells (SS II-M1f and SS IV-M1f) by not always reporting misfit of the data.

In Table 2, the results of the ordered latent class analysis with $Q = 7$ are presented. The general misfit discrepancies indicate misfit when the sample is large and/or the deviation from M is substantial. PR is sometimes more sensitive to misfit than LR or H (SS I-M1d, SS II-M1d). However, it also leads to false positives in cells where the assumptions are not violated and the items are trichotomous (SS III-Msn, SS IV-M0, SS IV-M1f). The false positives of PR cannot be explained by SOL $X+$, since in the M0 cell of SS IV SOL X_+ holds, whereas it does not hold in the Msn cells of SS III. The other general discrepancies (LR and H) do not indicate misfit of the cells

Table 1. Results of the Mokken scale analysis

Simulation Study I

	Normal						Uniform					
	$N=2000$			$N=200$			$N=2000$			$N=200$		
	H	H_1	$crit_1$	H	H_1	$crit_1$	H	H_1	$crit_1$	H	H_1	$crit_1$
M0	0	0	0	0	0	0	0	0	0	0	0	0
M1l*	0	0	0	0	0	0	0	0	1	0	0	2
M1m*	0	10	10	3	10	6	0	0	0	0	3	1
M1h*	0	0	0	0	3	0	0	0	0	0	0	0
M1u*	0	10	10	4	10	10	0	10	10	0	10	10
M1d*	10	10	10	9	10	10	0	10	10	0	10	10

Simulation Study II							Simulation Study IV						
	$N=2000$			$N=200$				$N=2000$			$N=200$		
	H	H_1	$crit_1$	H	H_1	$crit_1$		H	H_1	$crit_1$	H	H_1	$crit_1$
M0	0	0	0	0	0	0	M0	0	0	0	0	0	0
M1f	10	10	6	10	10	6	M1f	10	10	5	10	10	5
M1d*	10	10	10	10	10	10	M1d*	10	10	10	10	10	10

Simulation Study III						
	$N=2000$			$N=200$		
	H	H_1	$crit_1$	H	H_1	$crit_1$
Msy	0	0	0	0	0	0
Msn	0	0	0	0	0	0
Mwy	10	10	0	10	10	2
Mwn	10	10	0	10	10	1
M1d*	10	10	10	10	10	10

with one item with a flat IRF. The item specific inferential approach, with H_i as discrepancy function, sometimes indicates misfit of the flat IRF (SS II-M1f, SS IV-M1f).

The results presented in Table 2 are based on fitted ordered latent class models with seven latent classes. The results of five or eleven fitted latent classes were not remarkably different. However, when fitting only three latent classes, the LR discrepancy reported false positives in the M0 cells with large samples. Three latent classes seem to be too few to reflect all aspects in the data.

4 Conclusion

If one wants an overall index for misfit of a set of items, then the descriptive approach of H may fail to report decreasing or unimodal IRFs. The inferential approach with latent classes seems to be doing better. However, if one

Table 2. Results of the ordered latent class detection approach, $Q = 7$

Simulation Study I

| | Normal | | | | | | | | Uniform | | | | | | | |
| | N=2000 | | | | N=200 | | | | N=2000 | | | | N=200 | | | |
	LR	PR	H	H_1	LR	PR	H	H_1	LR	PR	H	H_1	LR	PR	H	H_1
M0	0	0	0	0	0	0	0	0	0	0	0	0	0	0	0	0
M1l*	0	0	0	0	0	0	0	0	0	0	0	0	0	0	0	0
M1m*	0	0	0	0	0	0	0	2	0	0	0	0	0	0	0	0
M1h*	0	0	0	0	0	0	0	0	0	0	0	0	0	0	0	0
M1u*	10	10	10	10	0	0	0	7	10	10	10	10	0	0	0	10
M1d*	10	10	10	10	0	5	0	10	10	10	10	10	10	10	10	10

Simulation Study II

| | N=2000 | | | | N=200 | | | |
	LR	PR	H	H_1	LR	PR	H	H_1
M0	0	0	0	0	0	0	0	0
M1f	0	0	0	5	0	0	0	3
M1d*	10	10	10	10	1	10	6	10

Simulation Study IV

| | N=2000 | | | | N=200 | | | |
	LR	PR	H	H_1	LR	PR	H	H_1
M0	1	0	0	0	0	4	0	0
M1f	3	7	0	9	0	5	0	5
M1d*	10	10	10	10	10	10	9	10

Simulation Study III

| | N=2000 | | | | N=200 | | | |
	LR	PR	H	H_1	LR	PR	H	H_1
Msy	0	0	0	0	0	0	0	0
Msn	0	0	0	0	0	7	0	0
Mwy	0	0	0	0	0	0	0	0
Mwn	0	0	0	0	0	0	0	0
M1d*	10	10	10	10	10	10	10	10

is prepared to consider an index per item, the descriptive item specific H_i and $crit_i$ indicate misfit slightly better than the inferential approach. The inferential approach and $crit_i$ are better than H_i at discerning flat IRFs from decreasing IRFs.

The behavior of H and H_i can be explained by their function as scaling coefficient. They are supposed to tell whether the item (H_i) or the total set of items (H) are fit for rank ordering subjects. If one of the items fails to order subjects, but the other nine items function well, H can still be larger than .30. If one (or more) of the IRFs is relatively flat, an observed $H_i < .30$ indicates that the item is not suited for scaling subjects. Note that an ordered latent class model can predict data which have an H value between 0 and .30. Therefore, the posterior predictive check does not have to indicate a misfit of the model to the data, while the observed H is smaller than .30.

The number of latent classes Q is not extremely relevant for the detection rate in ordered latent class analysis. Three latent classes is not enough but five or seven latent classes works just as well as 11, even when the generating latent trait is continuous. This implies that a continuous latent trait can be approximated well by a restricted number of latent classes, without loosing too much information.

The results are similar for dichotomous or polytomous items. The main difference is that especially the ordered latent class approach has more problems to detect misfit when one out of 10 items has a decreasing IRF, than if one of five items has two decreasing ISRFs. Also, the discrepancy function PR is likely to report false positives for cells with polytomous items. This is probably due to the increased sparseness of the data in the bivariate tables (3 by 3, versus 2 by 2).

Concluding, both approaches have their pros and cons. If only one overall index is requested, the proper model testing done by the ordered latent class approach is recommended. However, inspection of all items separately is better. An advantage of the Mokken approach, which might be relevant in practice, is that it has a shorter computation time, even when the detection statistics are computed for all items. This is because the time-consuming iterative model fitting of the ordered latent class model does not have to take place. Within this descriptive approach, the $crit_i$-value seems to be best fit to detect decreasing IRFs, and to discern them from flat IRFs. However, flat IRFs are not useful in a scale which intends to rank order subjects. Therefore, H and H_i are valuable as well.

References

Gelman A, Carlin JB, Stern HS, Rubin DB (1995) Bayesian data analysis. Chapman & Hall, London

Hemker BT, Sijtsma K, Molenaar IW, Junker BW (1997) Stochastic ordering using the latent trait and the sum score in polytomous IRT models. Psychometrika 62: 331–347

Mokken RJ (1971) A theory and procedure of scale analyis, with applications in political research. Mouton, The Hague

Mokken RJ (1997) Nonparametric models for polytomous responses. In: Van der Linden WJ, Hambleton RK (eds) Handbook of modern item response theory. Springer, New York, pp 369-380

Molenaar IW (1991) A weighted Loevinger H-coefficient extending Mokken scaling to multicategory items. Kwantitatieve Methoden 37: 97–117

Molenaar IW, Sijtsma K (2000) User's manual MSP5 for Windows, a program for Mokken scale analysis for polytomous items. ProGamma, Groningen

Samejima F (1969) Estimation of latent ability using a response pattern of graded scores. Psychometrika Monograph 17

Sijtsma K, Molenaar IW (2002) Introduction to nonparametric item response theory. Sage, Newbury Park CA

Van Onna MJH (in press) Bayesian estimation and model selection in ordered latent class models for polytomous items. Accepted for publication in Psychometrika

Application of IRT in Assessment of Chewing Ability

Kazuo Takeuchi

The Second Department of Prosthodontics, School of Dentistry, Aichi-Gakuin University, 2-11, Suemoridori, Chikusaku, Nagoya, 464-8651, Japan

Summary. The subjects in the three groups, who had different numbers of remaining teeth, had their masticatory abilities evaluated by using two questionnaires. The patients in the first group were edentulous and had complete dentures in both jaws. The patients of the second group were partially edentulous and had at least a partial denture. The patients of these two groups had visited a university dental clinic. The third group was made up of elderly people selected for the epidemiologic research of masticatory ability and who resided in five local towns.

The responses to the questionnaires were converted to dichotomous data and was assessed unidimensionality based on eigenvalue plots and principal factor analysis of tetrachoric correlation matrix. The items that had low discriminate power were removed after this analysis. One-parameter logistic model was applied to the remaining items and the goodness of fit between the data and the model was assessed. The difficulty parameters between the two groups showed linear relationships and significant Pearson's correlations: 0.98, 0.99 and 0.99.

These results indicated that the application of item response theory was successful to compare the chewing ability with three groups on the same scale.

Key words: Masticatory ability, Item response theory, Multiple groups, Equating

1 BACKGROUND

Rehabilitation of chewing function is one of the major concerns in dental treatments. Dentists treat patients with missing teeth by using prostheses such as dentures to recover their masticatory function. It is necessary to evaluate patient's chewing ability before and after treatments to clarify the outcomes. Asakura (1990) constructed a questionnaire to evaluate the chewing ability of edentulous patients with upper and lower complete dentures. The questionnaire was formed with 58 food items with four alternatives asking whether they could chew the foods or not. However, the scores had some limitations due to the fact that it was developed based on classical test theory. To solve these problems, Takeuchi (1998) constructed a unidimensional questionnaire to assess the chewing ability of complete denture wearers using item response theory (IRT) (Hambleton et al.1991). Furthermore, we need to clarify whether there is a significant difference of the chewing ability between outpatients with dentures and aged people who are not visiting dental clinics. If the difference is distinct, the chewing ability level of non-outpatients can be used as a barometer when treating outpatients with dentures since non-outpatients are considered to be satisfied with their masticatory abilities. Test equating method using IRT might provide the difference if the data from both subjects fit the model. However, it is not clear.

The purposes of this study were to apply IRT to evaluate the questionnaires that were developed to assess chewing ability, to examine the fitness between the data and the IRT model, and to study the possibility of comparison of the item parameters using the data from outpatients with dentures and the aged people who are not visiting dental clinics.

2   METHODS

2.1 Subjects

The subjects consisted of three groups (Table 1). The first were edentulous patients and complete denture wearers in both jaws (CD group). The second were partially edentulous patients with at least a partial denture (PD group). These two groups were outpatients who visited the dental clinic at Aichi-Gakuin University. The last were the subjects of the epidemiologic study, who were 80 or 81 years old and resided in five towns in Aichi prefecture, Japan (E group).

Table 1. Profiles of subjects

Subject groups	Numbers of subjects	Age (mean ± SD)	Numbers of remaining teeth (mean ± SD)
CD group	230	72.3 ± 8.9	0
PD group	100	66.8 ± 8.7	13.5 ± 6.3
E group	245	80 or 81	6.0 ± 7.8

2.2 Questionnaires

Two questionnaires were used in this study. One consisted of 58 food items with four alternatives for the CD and PD groups (Fig. 1). These items were made up of foods that were eaten frequently by edentulous patients with complete dentures in addition to some hard foods for the patients (Asakura 1990). The others consisted of 30 food items with three alternatives for the E group (Fig. 2). There were identical items in both questionnaires as anchor items. The subjects were asked to choose one alternative that was fit for their masticatory ability.

---

58 Food Items:
Broiled eel*, Soft white noodle*, Broiled thin pork, Apple (1cm thickness), Boiled rice with red beans*, Hard pickled radish*, Boiled egg apple, Shredded cabbage, Soaked bread in milk, Hamburger steak, Broiled salmon, Pickled Chinese cabbage*, Rice-cake cube*, Boiled prawn, Salami, Boiled radish, Raw squid*, Sponge cake, Boiled taro, Cheese, Fried onion, Steamed dumpling*, Tomato, Sliced ham, Pudding, Boiled soft seaweed*, Pear, Croquette, Boiled tangle*, Vinegared octopus*, Banana, Boiled mushroom, Steamed rice*, Sliced raw tuna*, Sliced raw turbot*, Sliced cucumber, Broiled thin beef, *Hanpeng** (Flied fish cake), Sliced bread, Omelet, Broiled chicken, *Atsuage** (Fried *Tofu*), Baguet, Lettuce, *Chikuwa** (Baked fish cake), Boiled beans, Biscuit, Boiled egg, Vienna sausage, Boiled flatfish, Boiled *Konjak**, *Uirou** (Sweet jelly of flour), *Kamaboko** (Boiled fish cake), *Tofu*, Boiled carrot, Peanuts, Vinegared shallot, Boiled potato

Alternatives:
    1) Able to chew   2) Able to chew if prepared fine or soft   3) Unable to chew
    4) Never chewed

Fig. 1. The questionnaire with 58 food items and four alternatives for the CD and PD groups (*: Japanese foods, *italic*: Japanese names)

---

30 Food Items:
Omelet, Broiled thin meat, Fried onion, *Tofu**, Shredded cabbage, Dried sardine*, Green soy beans, Apple, Sliced raw tuna*, *Karintou** (Sugar coated cookie), Beef steak, Sliced cucumber, Peanuts, Vinegared octopus*, *Kamaboko** (Boiled fish cake), Shredded burdock*, Boiled mushroom, Boiled *Konjak**, Broiled chicken, Boiled beans, Hard pickled radish*, Fried pork cutlet, Pickled Chinese cabbage*, Sliced bread, Raw carrot, Boiled rice*, Fried prawn, Biscuit, Dried cuttlefish*, Broiled salmon

Alternatives:
    1) Able to chew   2) Able to chew if prepared fine or soft   3) Unable to chew

---

Fig. 2. The questionnaire with 30 food items and three alternatives for the E group (*: Japanese foods, *italic*: Japanese names)

2.3 Analyses

The analyses proceeded in four major stages. At the first stage, all responses from the subjects in the three groups were converted to dichotomouse data with the answer "Able to chew" being 1 and the other alternatives being 0. The items, whose proportions of the answer "Able to chew" showed biased value, were removed since they might cause much error on estimation of tetrachoric correlation.

The second stage was to evaluate unidimensionality of the remaining items as a scale based on eigenvalue plots and principal factor analysis of the tetrachoric correlation using MicroFACT 1.1 (Waller 1995). The items whose principal factor solutions showed a low value were removed. These treatments were done to complete that the remaining items showed sufficient discriminations.

The third stage was to apply the one-parameter logistic model that is given by the equation (see Eq. 1). The difficultly parameters were standardized to the person ability. The items that do not fit the model based on chi-square statistics were removed. The analyses were done using RASCAL (1996).

$$P_i(\theta) = \frac{1}{1 + \exp\{-Da(\theta - b_i)\}} \tag{1}$$

where

$P_i(\theta)$ is the probability of an examinee with chewing ability θ,

a is a fixed discrimination,

b_i is the item i difficultly parameter, and

D is a scaling factor ($=1.7$).

The last stage was to assess the relationships and compare them with the parameters of the anchor items between each of the two groups.

3 RESULTS

3.1 Proportions of the Answer "Able to chew"

The items, whose proportions of the answer "Able to chew" showed biased value, were removed. The criterion for removing them was above 0.90 for the data from the CD and PD groups. The other criterion was above 0.95 for the data from the E group since it was needed for the remaining number of items. The number of items removed was 19 in the data from the CD group, 29 from the PD group and 11 from the E group. However, there was no item with proportion under 0.10.

3.2 Assessment of Unidimensionality

Unidimensionality of the items as a scale were assessed based on eigenvalue plots and principal factor analysis from the tetrachoric correlation matrix. The items with principal factor solutions above 0.70 (Although one item was above 0.69 in the CD group for clinical reasons.) were removed from the analyses after these.

The number of the remaining items was 30 in the CD group, 22 in the PD group and 19 in the E group. The eigenvalue plots from the remaining items are shown in Fig. 3. The largest eigenvalues were over ten times larger than the second largest in each group. They meant that it could assume unidimensionality in these remaining items.

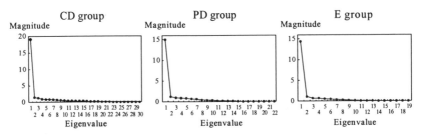

Fig. 3. Plots of the eigenvalues according to the data from the three groups

3.3 Assessment of Goodness of Fit

The model-data fits were assessed based on chi-square statistics at the 5% level of significance. Four items were removed from the later analyses for the data in CD group, two items in PD group and three items in E group at this process.

Another method, which was the fitness between observed and expected proportions of "Able to chew" answers, was applied. Nine examples in CD group are shown in Fig. 4.

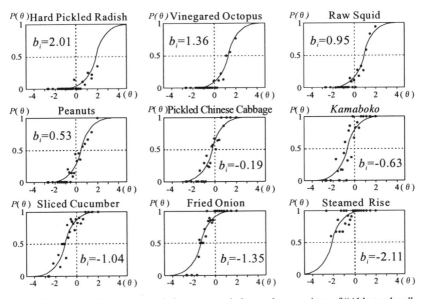

Fig. 4. Examples of item characteristic curves and observed proportions of "Able to chew" answers from the CD group.

3.4 Parameters Estimated from the Three Groups

The parameters were standardized to the chewing ability of the examinees. They were distributed between 2.01 to -2.11 estimated from the data in the CD group, 1.72 to -1.67 in the PD group and 1.05 to -1.80 in the E group. Finally, the numbers of the items that fitted to the model were 26 in the CD group, 20 in the PD group and 16 in the E group (Table 2 to 4). The discrimination parameters were fixed to 1.15 in the CD group, 1.09 in the PD group and 1.06 in the E group. Furthermore, the values of the discrimination parameters were similar together. The numbers of the corresponded items were 18 between the CD and PD groups, 9 between the CD and E groups and 9 between the PD and E groups (Fig. 5).

Table 2. 26 items which fitted to the model and their difficulty parameters b_j in the CD group (from Takeuchi. 1998, with permission)

Item	b_i	Item	b_i
Hard pickled radish*	2.01	*Kamaboko**	- 0.63
Vinegared octopus*	1.36	*Chikuwa**	- 0.65
Raw squid*	0.95	Boiled prawn	- 0.69
Pear	0.60	Lettuce	- 0.82
Peanuts	0.53	Sliced cucumber	- 1.04
Vinegared shallot*	- 0.19	Biscuit	- 1.13
Broiled thin beef	- 0.19	*Hangpeng**	- 1.22
Pickled Chinese cabbage*	- 0.19	Sliced Bread	- 1.30
Broiled chicken	- 0.24	Fried onion	- 1.32
Broiled thin pork	- 0.24	Boiled soft seaweed*	- 1.35
Boiled mushroom	- 0.32	Broiled salmon	- 1.73
Shredded cabbage	- 0.49	Boiled beans	- 1.80
Boiled *Konjak**	- 0.53	Steamed rice	- 2.11

(*: Japanese food, *italic*: Japanese name)

Table 3. 20 items which fitted to the model and their difficulty parameters b_j in the PD group

Item	b_i	Item	b_i
Hard pickled radish*	1.72	Shredded cabbage	- 0.75
Vinegared octopus*	1.13	Vinegared shallot*	- 0.87
Raw squid*	0.65	Vienna sausage	- 0.93
Peanuts	0.06	Boiled *Konjak**	- 0.93
Pear	- 0.17	*Chikuwa**	- 1.05
Broiled thin beef	- 0.65	*Kamaboko**	- 1.11
Pickled Chinese cabbage*	- 0.65	Sliced cucumber	- 1.49
Broiled chicken	- 0.65	Boiled prawn	- 1.49
Apple (1 cm thickness)	- 0.70	Lettuce	- 1.49
Boiled mushroom	- 0.70	*Hangpeng**	- 1.67

(*: Japanese food, *italic*: Japanese name)

Table 4. 16 items which fitted to the model and their difficulty parameters b_j in the E group

Item	b_i	Item	b_i
Dried cuttlefish*	1.05	Broiled chicken	- 1.29
Hard pickled radish*	0.98	Dried sardine*	- 1.57
Raw carrot	0.40	Broiled thin beef	- 1.61
Vinegared octopus*	0.17	Boiled mushroom	- 1.61
Beef steak	- 0.03	Boiled *Konjak**	- 1.75
Peanuts	- 0.52	Pickled Chinese cabbage*	- 1.75
*Karintou**	- 0.76	Shredded cabbage	- 1.80
Shredded burdock*	- 1.05	Green soy beans	- 1.80

(*: Japanese food, *italic*: Japanese name)

3.5 Relationships of the Parameters

The scatter diagrams of the difficulty parameters between each of the two groups are shown in Fig. 5. The parameters were estimated from the data that fitted to the model, and these food items finally corresponded with each of the two groups.

Linear relationships are found between the parameters of each of the two groups and large Pearson's correlation coefficients mean intense interrelations: 0.98 by 18items between the CD and PD groups, 0.99 by nine items between the CD and E groups and 0.99 by nine items between the PD and E groups.

The group, which had the highest chewing ability, was the E group. The next was the PD group and the lowest was the CD group.

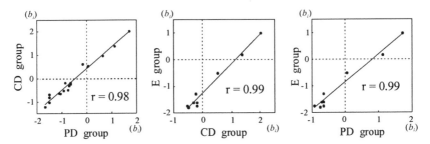

Fig. 5. Relationships of the difficulty parameters b_i between the CD, PD and E groups.

4 DISCUSSION

The one-parameter logistic model is equal to the Rasch model (1960) mathematically. This is a unidimensional IRT model and based on a restrictive assumption that all items are equally discriminating. At the same time, item discrimination should be high, if the difference of ability between persons could be discriminated clearly. To cope with these requisites, all items were sifted out based on principal factor solutions. Consequently, the remaining items showed nearly uniform and high discrimination. Furthermore, the one-parameter logistic model was practical since there were not many samples to apply to the two-parameter logistic model.

Chewing ability of human beings decreases as the number of missing teeth increases. Therefore, it was assumed that the group with the highest chewing ability should be the PD group since the PD group had more teeth than the two other groups (Table 1). However, the results suggested that the E group had the highest chewing ability. The reason for this phenomenon may be explained by the fact that outpatients as in the CD and PD groups include many patients under treatments with clinical problems. Most of the subjects in the E group showed satisfaction with their masticatory function. Hence, the level of masticatory ability in the E group may be used as a measurement to evaluate the recovery level of chewing ability when treating out patients with dentures.

Furthermore, we need to clarify the criterion-related validity of these questionnaires by using another method, as this method depends on the examinees' latent trait but not on their physical masticatory function.

5 CONCLUSION

These results meant that it was possible to compare the chewing ability with the three groups on the same scale. Thus, item response theory might be a useful tool to evaluate masticatory ability by using questionnaires.

References

Asakura Y (1990) A reliable method for evaluating the masticatory function in complete denture wearers, concerning a masticatory function evaluation chart based on food hardness. Aichi-Gakuin Daigaku Shigakkai Shi 28:1267-1285

Hambleton RK, Swaminathan H, Rogers HJ (1991) Fundamentals of item response theory. Sage, California

RASCAL (1996) RASCAL for Windows User's Guide. Assessment Systems Corporation, Minnesota

Rasch G (1960/1980) Probabilistic models for some intelligence and attainment tests. University of Chicago Press, Chicago (Original Published in 1960, Nielsen & Lydiche, Copenhagen)

Takeuchi K (1998) Construction of a scale for evaluating masticatory ability of complete denture wearers using item response theory. The Journal of the Japan Prosthodontic Society 42:961-971

Waller NG (1995) MicroFACT User's Guide. Assessment Systems Corporation, Minnesota

The Effects of the Temporal Structure and the Presentation Modality on English Listening Comprehension Test

Teruhisa Uchida, Naoko Nakaune, Kenichi Kikuchi, Shin-ichi Mayekawa, and Tomoichi Ishizuka

Research Division, The National Center for University Entrance Examinations, 2-19-23 Komaba, Meguro-ku, Tokyo 153-8501, Japan

Summary. This study examined following points concerning temporal structure and presentation modality on English listening comprehension tests. First, we investigated how temporal structure influenced the characteristics of the test items. Second, the effect of the presentation modality on the test score was examined. Finally, for improvement of the listening comprehension test, we studied the validity of equating using anchor items to compare between the test forms. Six hundred and fifty-two freshmen participated in this study. They took English listening tests consisting of 45 items. Experimental items were allocated to eight test forms, and each test form had anchor items. Each form was divided into three blocks in which the speech rate, the pause duration, and the presentation modality (character or voice) were manipulated respectively.

Results of classical and IRT (Item Response Theory) analyses were as follows: 1. Item pass rate increased and item difficulty (b) decreased, as the speech rate slowed. 2. Concerning the presentation modality of answer choices, item difficulty with the printed presentation was lower than that with the spoken presentation. 3. The difference in correct response rate according to the presentation modality was compensated in the estimated ability (θ) through the IRT equating using anchor blocks. A new type of research design using IRT to feedback score information to subjects was presented.

Key words. listening comprehension test, speech rate, presentation modality, design of experiment, Item Response Theory (IRT)

1 Issues and Purpose of This Study[1]

The policy of foreign language education in Japan is putting more importance on communication skills than reading comprehension. This paper focused on the test of English listening comprehension as measurement of such communication skills.

---

[1] Preparation of this paper was assisted by Joint project in NCUEE and Grants-in-Aid for Scientific Research 10551008 to Shin-ichi Mayekawa.

The auditory items to measure the listening comprehension have their own characteristics. For example, difference of speech rate would influence item difficulty. And we have to consider to the effect of the pause duration in the utterance as Makita (1996) pointed out. Although there were some studies concerning the effect of acoustic environment (e.g. Ishizuka et al. 1994), we had few studies investigating how the auditory items' condition, such as speech rate affected the item characteristics because of the manipulative difficulty of sound data.

Furthermore, it is necessary to examine the effect of the presentation modality on the test score. It will affect test scores systematically according to whether passages, interrogative sentences and answer choices are presented auditory or visually.

Considering these arguments, this study examined the following points. First, we investigated how temporal structure influenced the characteristics of the items. Second, the effect of the presentation modality on the test score was examined. Finally, for improvement of the listening comprehension test, we studied the validity of equating using anchor items to compare between the test forms.

2 Experimental Design and Method

2.1 Participants

Participants were 652 freshmen from University of Tokyo, Nagoya University, and Yokohama National University. They were 404 males and 248 females (average age: 19.5 years old). Half of the participants were of social science/literary major, the other half, natural science major.

2.2 Sound Materials for the Listening Comprehension Test

Items were obtained from exercises of the Society for Testing English Proficiency (STEP) Test [2] and those of Test of English for International Communication (TOEIC: Obunsha editor 1997; Sone 1998; Park D-W and Choi B-G 1998).

From the exercises of the STEP Test, two item styles, "conversation item style" and "explanation item style", were adopted. Participants listened to short English conversations and an interrogative sentence in the conversation style, and they listened to passages of one topic and an interrogative sentence in the explanation style. A total of 33 items were used for Experimental Block 1 and Experimental Block 2.

Twelve items were used as dialogic items from the exercises of TOEIC for Experimental Block 3. Dialogic items had a style such that participants chose an appropriate response from choices after a short English interrogative sentence presented by voice.

---

[2] STEP Test is measuring practical English proficiency conducted by The Society for Testing English Proficiency (STEP), Inc. in Japan.

(A) Speech-rate manipulations to produce experimental items

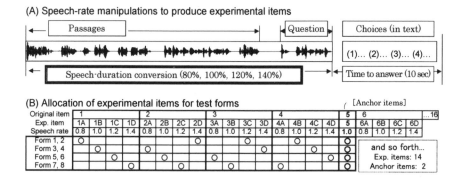

(B) Allocation of experimental items for test forms   [Anchor items]

Original item	1				2				3				4				5	6				...16
Exp. item	1A	1B	1C	1D	2A	2B	2C	2D	3A	3B	3C	3D	4A	4B	4C	4D	5	6A	6B	6C	6D	
Speech rate	0.8	1.0	1.2	1.4	0.8	1.0	1.2	1.4	0.8	1.0	1.2	1.4	0.8	1.0	1.2	1.4	1.0	0.8	1.0	1.2	1.4	
Form 1, 2	O					O					O					O	O					
Form 3, 4		O					O					O	O				O					
Form 5, 6			O					O	O					O			O					
Form 7, 8				O	O					O					O		O					

and so forth...
Exp. items: 14
Anchor items: 2

Fig. 1. Producing items and design of experiment in the Experimental Block 1.

Items for the experiment were recorded on Compact Disk Recordables (CD-Rs).

2.3 Constitution of Experimental Blocks and Test Forms

Experimental items were allocated to eight test forms, and each test form had anchor items. Each form was divided into three blocks. The details of experimental blocks and the outline of the arrangement of the items were as follows.

2.3.1 The First Experimental Block [Speech-rate Manipulation]

We used 16 original items consisting of conversation and explanation items. As shown in Fig. 1, the speech rate of passages and the interrogative sentence was manipulated in four levels as an experimental factor.

In this block, each participant answered all items. But the speech rate of each item was converted into one of four speech-rate levels. The block was arranged so that the effect of the experimental condition would be counterbalanced in each form. Furthermore, we had the anchor items such that the speech rate was not manipulated.

2.3.2 The Second Experimental Block [Pause-duration and Speech-rate Manipulations]

We used 17 original items consisting of conversation and explanation items. As shown in Fig. 2, the pause duration and the speech rate were manipulated in the passages. The speech rate had two levels, and pause duration at the end of each sentence had also two levels. As the interrogative sentence, the original sound data was used because it was a single sentence.

(A) Pause-duration and speech-rate manipulations to produce experimental items

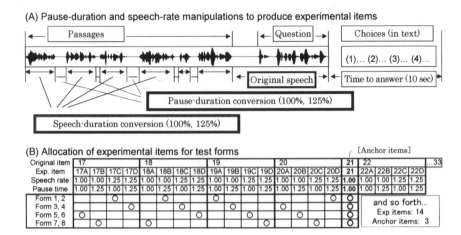

(B) Allocation of experimental items for test forms   [Anchor items]

Original item	17				18				19				20				21	22				...33
Exp. item	17A	17B	17C	17D	18A	18B	18C	18D	19A	19B	19C	19D	20A	20B	20C	20D	21	22A	22B	22C	22D	
Speech rate	1.00	1.00	1.25	1.25	1.00	1.00	1.25	1.25	1.00	1.00	1.25	1.25	1.00	1.00	1.25	1.25	1.00	1.00	1.00	1.25	1.25	
Pause time	1.00	1.25	1.00	1.25	1.00	1.25	1.00	1.25	1.00	1.25	1.00	1.25	1.00	1.25	1.00	1.25	1.00	1.00	1.25	1.00	1.25	
Form 1, 2		O			O				O					O			O	O				
Form 3, 4				O			O			O			O				O	O				
Form 5, 6	O						O				O				O		O	O				
Form 7, 8		O			O							O				O	O	O				

and so forth...
Exp items: 14
Anchor items: 3

Fig. 2. Producing items and design of experiment in the Experimental Block 2.

2.3.3 The Third Experimental Block [Presentation-modality and Speech-rate Manipulations]

We used 12 dialogic items. As shown in Fig. 3, the presentation modality of the choices was a factor between subjects. And the speech rate was manipulated in the part of the voice.

For the spoken presentation condition, speech rate of the interrogative sentence and choices were converted into four levels. In the printed presentation condition, we used items with the choices printed on the answer sheet. In this block, because the presentation modality of choices was operated, item forms were not the same. Therefore, the anchor items for all the forms were not arranged.

2.4 Procedure

Participants listened to the items from portable CD players with ear receivers, and then they chose an answer from choices. Each item was presented once.

2.5 Data Analysis

We attempted to examine the following points.
1) According to experimental factors in each block, we examined whether item difficulty and item discrimination power changed. Experimental factors were speech rate (Block 1), pause duration and speech rate (Block 2), and presentation modality of the choices and speech rate (Block 3).
2) To investigate efficiency of Item Response Theory (IRT) equating which could adjust for differences between test forms, we compared correct response rate by

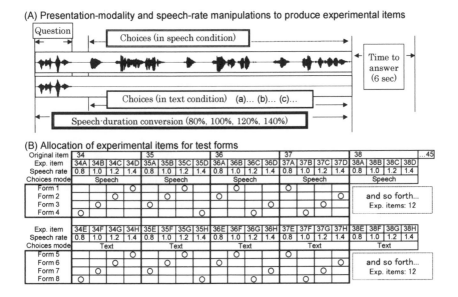

Fig. 3. Producing items and design of experiment in the Experimental Block 3.

each participant as a classical index of a participant's listening ability with esti-mated ability (θ) as an IRT one.

We excluded people with difficulty in hearing and people who had taken the same items used in this experiment. Finally, data from 591 participants were se-lected and analyzed. As item difficulty of classical test theory, we used item pass rate. Item pass rate was the rate of the participants who answered each item cor-rectly. When analyzing using IRT, we considered eight test forms to be one inte-grated form. Each experimental item was analyzed as a different item. Participants were regarded as a sample from a homogeneous group for scholastic ability, be-cause they were assigned to each test form randomly after they were stratified ac-cording to their course and university. A two-parameter logistic model was used to calculate item difficulty (b) and item discrimination power (a).

3 Results and Discussion

3.1 Results of Experimental Blocks

3.1.1 The First Experimental Block

The results of Experimental Block 1 are shown in Fig. 4. Item pass rate increased and item difficulty (b) decreased as the speech rate slowed.

We did an analysis of variance using item difficulty (b) as a dependent variable. It was thought that we could examine the characteristics of items independent of

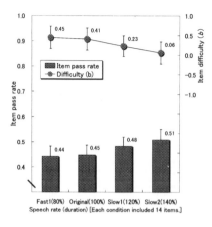

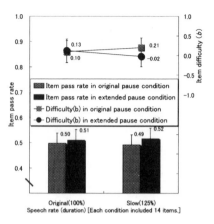

Fig. 4. Means of item pass rate and item difficulty (with S.E.) in the first experimental block.

Fig. 5. Means of item pass rate and item difficulty (with S.E.) in the second experimental block.

participants' ability through IRT (Shiba, 1991). So we examined the effects of the two factors, the speech rate and the original item. As a result, the factor of speech rate was significant ($F_{(3, 39)} = 2.99$, $p<.05$), and the factor of the original item was also highly significant ($F_{(13, 39)} = 28.21$, $p<.0001$). We also tried an ANOVA using item discrimination power (a) as a dependent variable. The speech-rate factor was not significant ($F_{(3, 39)} = 0.69$, $N.S.$). On the other hand, the factor of the original item was significant ($F_{(13, 39)} = 4.12$, $p<.001$).

3.1.2 The Second Experimental Block

As shown in Fig. 5, a conspicuous change of the item pass rate and the item difficulty (b) was not seen.

We did an analysis of variance using item difficulty (b) as a dependent variable. The model involved three factors and their interactions. The three factors were the speech rate, the pause duration and the original item. Only the factor of the original item was significant ($F_{(13, 13)} = 81.89$, $p<.0001$). We tried an ANOVA using item discrimination power (a) as a dependent variable, too. As with item difficulty (b), only the factor of the original item was significant ($F_{(13, 13)} = 6.28$, $p<.01$).

In this block, the interrogative sentence was not manipulated at all. We inferred that the manipulation of speech rate in the passage did not influence the answer because the interrogative sentence directly affected the score.

3.1.3 The Third Experimental Block

As shown in Fig. 6, item pass rate of a printed presentation was higher than that of a spoken presentation, and item difficulty (b) of a printed presentation was lower than that of a spoken presentation. On the other hand, conditions of speech rate did not have a tendency to any directions.

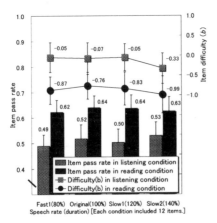

Fast1(80%) Original(100%) Slow1(120%) Slow2(140%)
Speech rate (duration) [Each condition included 12 items.]

Fig. 6. Means of item pass rate and item difficulty (with S.E.) in the third experimental block.

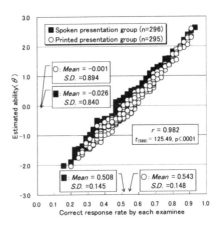

Fig. 7. Relation of correct response rate and estimated abilities among participants. (available participants: n=591)

We did an analysis of variance using item difficulty (b) as a dependent variable. We applied a model that involved the three factors and their interactions. The three factors were the presentation modality, the speech rate and the original item.

It was shown that the factor of presentation modality was highly significant ($F_{(1, 33)} = 41.35$, $p<.0001$). The factor of speech rate didn't have a significant difference, but the factor of the original item was highly significant ($F_{(11, 33)} = 37.68$, $p<.0001$). The interaction of the presentation modality and the original item was only significant ($F_{(11, 33)} = 5.61$, $p<.0001$). It was shown that the types of items influenced the degree of the change of item difficulty (b) when the presentation modality was manipulated. In the analysis with item discrimination power (a), all factors and interactions did not have a significant difference.

The results suggest that the spoken presentation of choices was more difficult than the printed presentation. This implies that the participants used the written information as a more effective cue in answering a question.

3.2 Comparison of Correct Response Rate with Estimated Ability among Participants

In Experimental Block 1 and Experimental Block 2, factors were designed as within subject factor, and the difference in conditions was counterbalanced through the blocks. However, the factor of the presentation modality was a between subject factor in the Experimental Block 3. As a result, we couldn't compare the participants' test scores with each other. We attempted a horizontal equating by IRT to estimate the participants' ability using five anchor items.

The correct response rate by each participant and estimated ability (θ) on IRT are shown in Fig. 7. Comparing the average of the correct response rate, the difference of the conditions was highly significant ($t_{(589)} = 2.91$, $p<.01$) on t-test, but in the estimated ability (θ), the difference was not seen ($t_{(589)} = 0.35$, *N.S.*). In this experiment, it was considered that the systematic difference of the participants' abilities didn't exist among test forms. It was suggested that IRT equating had a useful function such that difference in the correct response rate was compensated in estimated ability (θ).

4 General Discussion

First, we confirmed that item pass rate increased and item difficulty (b) decreased as the speech rate decreased. Second, it was found that the speech rate and pause duration didn't affect the scores, if the interrogative sentences were as they were. Third, item pass rate was higher and item difficulty was lower with written choices than with spoken choices. The results suggest that Japanese students' abilities with English inclined to those of reading and writing.

Preparation of items for a listening test needs much greater effort than that for a paper and pencil test. Therefore, it is desirable to use the existing items as effectively as possible. If we adjust item difficulty to the participants' ability by controlling speech rate, we can make good use of the existing items.

Finally, a good compensation for the difference between test forms was shown when the participants' ability was estimated by IRT. The results implied that IRT could be used to improve measurement and to provide beneficial information to participants if IRT is used with the well-designed experiment. As in our present study, using IRT with well-designed experiment is required to improve the measurement of aural communication ability and to reveal the essence of listening comprehension.

References

Ishizuka T, Ono H, Shimizu T, Suwabe M, Shirahata K (1994) An experimental study of listening comprehension test in English (in Japanese). Research Bulletin of the National Center for University Entrance Examination 23: 1-26

Makita N (1996) The effects of pausing on listening comprehension. The Bulletin of the Graduate School of Education of Waseda University Separate Vol. 5

Obunsha editor (1997) Exercises for preliminary examination in Pre-1st grade - Pre 2nd grade of the STEP (in Japanese). Obunsha, Tokyo Japan

Park D-W, Choi B-G (1998) Exercises for 520 points of TOEIC (in Japanese). Obunsha, Tokyo Japan

Shiba S (ed.) (1991) Item Response Theory –Its basic and application– (in Japanese). University of Tokyo Press, Tokyo Japan

Sone K (1998) Exercises for listening test of TOEIC (in Japanese). Obunsha, Tokyo Japan

Part 4
Testing in General

Estimating Testing Time Extension Ratios for Students with Disabilities from Item Cumulative Curves

Mamoru Fujiyoshi[1] and Akio Fujiyoshi[2]

[1] Research Division, National Center for University Entrance Examinations,
2-19-23 Komaba, Meguro-ku, Tokyo 153-8501, Japan
[2] Department of Computer and Information Sciences, Ibaraki University, 4-12-1
Nakanarusawa, Hitachi, Ibaraki 316-8511, Japan

Summary. This study was conducted to define item cumulative score ratio curves and item cumulative completion ratio curves and to propose a new method to estimate fair extension ratios of testing time for students with disabilities from these curves. The proposed method estimates extension ratios of testing time of regular tests under the time-limit method from experimentally collected test data utilizing the work-limit method. In this experiment we found that for students with visual disabilities, the present extension ratio of testing time at the National Center Test for University Admissions in Japan is fair in Mathematics and English and that in order to improve the present testing method of the National Center Test, further extension of testing time is necessary for some subjects with a large amount of reading questions, such as Japanese.

Key words: Student with disabilities, Testing time, Item cumulative curve, Subject cumulative curve, Computer-based test

1 Introduction

The purpose of this study is to develop a new estimation method of fair extension ratios of testing time for students with disabilities in the National Center Test for University Admissions. The National Center Test is the joint first stage achievement test for admissions of all national and local public universities as well as some private universities in Japan. Every year, about 600,000 students take it. As for disabled candidates, various kinds of special treatment have been administered (Fujiyoshi 1995).

The extension of testing time has been administered for disabled students according to the type and degree of their disabilities in order to eliminate the reflection of the individual's impairment on assessment of achievement level or aptitude (Fujiyoshi 1995; Laing and Farmer 1984; Willingham et al. 1988). The present extension ratio of testing time at the National Center Test is 1.3 or 1.5, and the extension ratios of the ACT Assessment and the Scholastic

Aptitude Test in the U.S. are from 1.8 to 4.8 (Bennett et al. 1985; Fujiyoshi 1995, 1997, 1999; Packer 1987; Ragosta and Wendler 1992; Willingham et al. 1988). However, the ground of the extension ratio of testing time has long been based only on experience and lacked quantitative explanations. It has been thought that multivariate or stochastic analysis cannot be used because the number of candidates with disabilities is so few. It has also been believed that defining fairness in extension ratios of testing time is delicate issue because the distributions of achievement level or aptitude for disabled students and nondisabled students might be different.

Recently, an estimation method comparing the distributions of completion time of nondisabled subjects and disabled subjects was developed (Fujiyoshi 1997; Packer 1987; Ragosta and Wendler 1992). In the estimation procedure of this method, subject cumulative completion ratio curves are employed. Another estimation method comparing the distributions of completion time weighted by score was also proposed (Fujiyoshi 1999). This method employs subject cumulative score ratio curves. Because the type and degree of disabilities of disabled students are multifarious and the number of disabled candidates is very small, it is still questionable whether the estimated extension ratios from these methods are fair.

In this study item cumulative score ratio curves and item cumulative completion ratio curves are re-defined (Fujiyoshi et al. 2001), and a new method that enables the estimation of fair extension ratios even when applied to a small number of subjects with disabilities is proposed. We also report the estimated extension ratios of testing time calculated through the method for partially sighted students who use large print test booklets and for blind students who use braille format test booklets.

2 The Definitions of Subject Cumulative Curves and Item Cumulative Curves

In this section we will mathematically re-define the two types of subject cumulative curves and the two types of item cumulative curves.

Suppose that there are n subjects ($subject_1, subject_2, \ldots, subject_n$) and m items ($item_1, item_2, \ldots, item_m$). For each $item_1, item_2, \ldots, item_m$, suppose also that the allotment of $item_j$ is $allotment_j$. Let $t_{i,j}$ be the time that $subject_i$ completed the answer of $item_j$. If $subject_i$ leaves $item_j$ unanswered, let $t_{i,j} = 0$. Let t_i be $\max\{t_{i,j} | j = 1, \ldots, m\}$. Let $c_{i,j}$ be an integer such that if $subject_i$ answered $item_j$ correctly, $c_{i,j} = 1$, otherwise $c_{i,j} = 0$. Let $total$ be $\sum_{i=1}^{n} \sum_{j=1}^{m} c_{i,j} \cdot allotment_j$.

2.1 Subject Cumulative Curves

Definition 2.1. The subject completion function for $subject_i$, SC_i is a function such that if $t < t_i$, then $SC_i(t) = 0$, otherwise $t \geq t_i$, then $SC_i(t) = 1$.

Definition 2.2. The distribution function of frequency of completed subjects FCS and the distribution function of score of completed subjects SCS are defined as follows:

$$FCS(t) = \Sigma_{i=1}^{n}(1/n) \cdot SC_i(t) \tag{1}$$

$$SCS(t) = \Sigma_{i=1}^{n}(\Sigma_{j=1}^{m} c_{i,j} \cdot allotment_j/total) \cdot SC_i(t) \tag{2}$$

Definition 2.3. A subject cumulative completion ratio curve is a set of points on a coordinate system with time t on the horizontal axis and cumulative relative frequency of completed subjects $FCS(t)$ on the vertical axis (Fujiyoshi 1997). A subject cumulative score ratio curve is a set of points on coordinate system with time t on the horizontal axis and cumulative relative score of completed subjects $SCS(t)$ on the vertical axis (Fujiyoshi 1999).

2.2 Item Cumulative Curves

Definition 2.4. The item completion function for $subject_i$ and $item_j$, $IC_{i,j}$ is a function such that if $t < t_{i,j}$, then $IC_{i,j}(t) = 0$, otherwise $t \geq t_{i,j}$, then $IC_{i,j}(t) = 1$.

Definition 2.5. The distribution function of frequency of completed items FCI and the distribution function of score of completed items SCI are defined as follows:

$$FCI(t) = \Sigma_{i=1}^{n}\Sigma_{j=1}^{m}(1/mn) \cdot IC_{i,j}(t) \tag{3}$$

$$SCI(t) = \Sigma_{i=1}^{n}\Sigma_{j=1}^{m}(c_{i,j} \cdot allotment_j/total) \cdot IC_{i,j}(t) \tag{4}$$

Definition 2.6. An item cumulative completion ratio curve is a set of points on a coordinate system with time t on the horizontal axis and cumulative relative frequency of completed items $FCI(t)$ on the vertical axis. An item cumulative score ratio curve is a set of points on coordinate system with time t on the horizontal axis and cumulative relative score of completed items $SCI(t)$ on the vertical axis (Fujiyoshi et al. 2001).

3 Experimentation on the Estimation of Testing Time Extension Ratios

3.1 Purpose

By analyzing test data acquired in this experiment, we will estimate testing time extension ratios for students with disabilities from subject cumulative completion ratio curves, subject cumulative score ratio curves, item cumulative completion ratio curves and item cumulative score ratio curves.

3.2 Method

We developed the computer-based test (CBT) to record the answering process of a conventional paper-and-pencil test (PPT) because the National Center Test is a conventional PPT which uses optical readable marking sheets (Fujiyoshi et al. 2001). Employing a pen computer (Amity SV, Mitsubishi Electric Corporation), the CBT was designed to simulate the answering process of the PPT as faithfully as possible. The PPT sheet is displayed on the computer screen, and the electronic pen replaces the pencil.

Subjects are freshmen and sophomores of four-year universities. The nondisabled group consisted of 99 students. The partially sighted group consists of 8 students who use large print test booklets. Their corrected visual acuity of common eyesight is from 0.01 to 0.1, and its median is 0.1. The blind group included 17 students who used braille format test booklets.

Nondisabled students took the CBT. On the other hand, partially sighted students were given large print test booklets and blind subjects were given braille format test booklets. The behavior of disabled students was observed by test monitors, and the answering process of disabled students was input by the monitors into the recording system used on the CBT.

The test sets were prepared from questions previously used in the National Center Test. Calculating from the quantity of exam questions, testing time required for each of the three subject was 40 minutes.

The test procedure started with issuing instructions; after that the subjects answered test questions in accordance with the work-limit method.

3.3 Results

Score Distributions: Fig. 1 is Box-and-whisker plots representing the score distributions of the three groups for Japanese, Mathematics and English. The vertical lines in the middle of the box plots indicate the medians. The '+' symbols in the boxes are the means.

The score distributions are almost similar among the three groups for each of the three subjects. Though the median of the nondisabled group is from 3 to 28 points (out of 80 points) higher than that of the partially sighted group and the blind group, there are no significant differences among the medians of the three groups for each of the three subjects according to the Mann-Whitney test.

Item Cumulative Score Ratio Curves: Firstly, we drew item cumulative score ratio curves from the experimental test data. Fig. 2 shows the curves for Japanese. The left curve made up of 'x' symbols shows the curve for the nondisabled group. The thin line is the curve of the Compound Weibull distribution function, which is used for smoothing and can be expressed by a simple formulation. The middle curve made up of '*' shows the curve for the partially sighted group. The bold line is the curve of the Compound Weibull

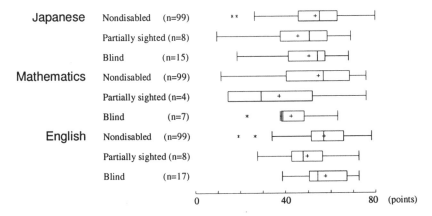

Fig. 1. Box-and-whisker plots of score distributions

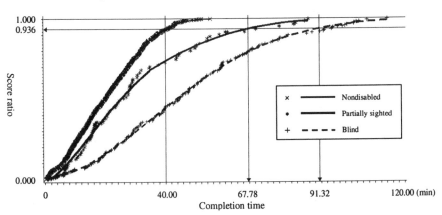

Fig. 2. Item cumulative score ratio curves for Japanese

distribution function. The right curve made up of '+' shows the curve for the blind group. The broken line is the curve of the Compound Weibull distribution function.

Author's Policy and Estimation Method: The author's policy of the estimation of extension ratio of testing time is to guarantee the partially sighted group and the blind group sufficient testing time that enables them to arrive at the same score ratio or completion ratio of the nondisabled group at the time limit of the regular tests.

Based on the Japanese curves in Fig. 2, we will show how to estimate the extension ratios of testing time from item cumulative score ratio curves. In order to formulate the estimation process of extension ratios, the curves of the compound Weibull distribution function are used instead of the item cumulative curves themselves.

We first checked the score ratio of the nondisabled group at the time limit of 40 minutes. In the case of Japanese, the score ratio to guarantee is 0.936, that is, the vertical coordinate of the intersection of the nondisabled group's curve and the vertical line of 40 minutes.

Next, we found the horizontal coordinates of the intersection of the horizontal line of 0.936 and the disabled group's curves. The completion time is 40 minutes for the nondisabled group, 67.78 minutes for the partially sighted group and 91.32 minutes for the blind group.

The estimation value of extension ratio of testing time is defined as the ratio of the completion time for the disabled group to completion time for the nondisabled group at the score ratio to guarantee. In the case of Japanese, the extension ratios of testing time are estimated to be 1.696 (67.78/40.00) for the partially sighted group and 2.284 (91.32/40.00) for the blind group.

Estimated Extension Ratios of Testing Time: We estimated the extension ratios of testing time for the disabled groups by means of the following four estimation methods:

(Method 1) Estimation from item cumulative score ratio curves: This method is explained in Section 3.3.3.

(Method 2) Estimation from item cumulative completion ratio curves: This method is obtained from Method 1 exchanging score ratio for completion ratio.

(Method 3) Estimation from subject cumulative score ratio curves: This method is obtained from Method 1 exchanging item cumulative curves for subject cumulative curves; this method was introduced in (Fujiyoshi 1999).

(Method 4) Estimation from subject cumulative completion ratio curves: This method is obtained from Method 3 exchanging score ratio for completion ratio; this method was introduced in (Fujiyoshi 1997).

Table 1 shows the score ratios (Method 1 and 3) and the completion ratios (Method 2 and 4) of the nondisabled group at 40 minutes. Table 2 shows the completion time and the extension ratios estimated from the item cumulative score ratio curves (Method 1), the item cumulative completion ratio curves (Method 2), the subject cumulative score ratio curves (Method 3) (Fujiyoshi 1999), and the subject cumulative completion ratio curves (Method 4) (Fujiyoshi 1997).

The estimated extension ratios from the four methods are similar.

Table 1. Score ratios (Method 1 and 3) and completion ratios (Method 2 and 4)

	Method 1	Method 2	Method 3	Method 4
Japanese	0.936	0.937	0.690	0.693
Mathematics	0.920	0.888	0.549	0.549
English	0.942	0.953	0.664	0.664

Table 2. Completion times and estimated extension ratios from the four methods

		Method 1		Method 2		Method 3		Method 4	
		time	ratio	time	ratio	time	ratio	time	ratio
	Nondisabled	40.00	1.000	40.00	1.000	40.00	1.000	40.00	1.000
Japanese	Partially sighted	67.78	1.696	65.24	1.629	61.53	1.538	57.14	1.428
	Blind	91.32	2.284	96.17	2.401	92.97	2.324	92.83	2.321
	Nondisabled	40.00	1.000	40.00	1.000	40.00	1.000	40.00	1.000
Mathematics	Partially sighted	68.30	1.706	82.58	2.062	51.05	1.276	59.80	1.495
	Blind	68.10	1.701	70.05	1.749	60.68	1.517	65.30	1.633
	Nondisabled	40.00	1.000	40.00	1.000	40.00	1.000	40.00	1.000
English	Partially sighted	41.95	1.049	45.33	1.133	45.31	1.133	44.36	1.116
	Blind	64.43	1.611	73.99	1.850	66.99	1.675	69.46	1.737

3.4 Discussion

We estimated extension ratios of testing time for students with disabilities from the four methods using the test data acquired in this experiment. In the National Center Test for University Admissions, the present extension ratio of testing time for all subjects has been 1.3 for partially sighted students whose corrected visual acuity of common eyesight is less than 0.15 since 1988. For blind students, the present extension ratio has been 1.5 since 1979.

The estimated extension ratios of testing time for disabled students are almost the same as the present extension ratio for Mathematics and English. However, the estimated extension ratios for Japanese are much greater than the present extension ratio.

For Mathematics, the estimated extension ratio for the partially sighted group seems much greater than the present extension ratio, 1.3. However, it is not a reliable figure because the number of subjects was too small.

4 Conclusion

We proposed methods to estimate fair extension ratios of testing time for disabled students according to author's policy of fairness from the item cumulative score ratio curves and the item cumulative completion ratio curves. It was experimentally shown that the extension ratios for disabled students in regular tests under the time-limit method can be estimated from the experimental test data under the work-limit method.

Though the estimated extension ratios from the four methods are similar, we think that the estimation method by item cumulative score ratio curves surpasses the others because of the following features in methodology:

Firstly, as item cumulative curves have more measured points than subject cumulative curves, item cumulative curves are smooth and stable even with a small number of subjects. Secondly, the estimation method by score ratio can be applied even if the score distributions of two groups are different because the estimation is made from the distributions of completion time weighted by score. Thirdly, the estimation of extension ratios of testing time is fair because sufficient testing time is guaranteed for disabled students to arrive at the same score ratio of nondisabled students at the time limit of regular tests.

This study revealed that the estimated extension ratios of testing time for Mathematics and English for students with visual disabilities are almost the same as the present extension ratios of the National Center Test. This means that the present extension ratios of testing time are fair in Mathematics and English. In order to improve the present testing method of the National Center Test, further extension of testing time is necessary for some subjects which include a large amount of reading questions, such as Japanese.

References

Bennett, R. E., Rock, D. A., and Kaplan, B. A. (1985) The Psychometric Characteristics of the SAT for Nine Handicapped Groups. ETS Research Report RR85-49, 1-70.

Fujiyoshi, M. (1995) Relationship of Type of Disability and Examination Method to Distribution of Scores of Students with Disabilities on the Joint First Stage Achievement Tests (in Japanese). Japanese Journal of Special Education, 33(2), 61-70

Fujiyoshi, M. (1997) A New Method for Estimation the Time to Be Extended for Testing Students with Visual Disabilities from the Response Time Curves (in Japanese). The National Center for University Entrance Examinations Research Bulletin, No. 27, 1-18

Fujiyoshi, M. (1999) Improvement for Estimation Method of Amount of Testing Time Extension for Students with Visual Disabilities by Means of Time-Score Ratio Curves (in Japanese). Japanese Journal of University Entrance Examination Research, No. 9, 31-37

Fujiyoshi, M., Fujiyoshi, A., Ishizuka, T. (2001) Comparability of Paper-and-Pencil Test and Computer-Based Test in Terms of Distributions of Completion Time and Score. The National Center for University Entrance Examinations Research Bulletin, No. 30, 67-82

Laing, J., Farmer, M. (1984) Use of the ACT Assessment by Examinees with Disabilities. ACT Research Report, 84, 1-35

Packer, J. (1987) SAT Testing Time for Students with Disabilities. ETS Research Report, RR-87-37, 1-25

Ragosta, M., Wendler, C. (1992) Eligibility Issues and Comparable Time Limits for Disabled and Nondisabled SAT Examinees. ETS Research Report, RR-92-35, 1-33

Willingham, W. W., Ragosta, M., Bennett, R. E., Braun, H., Rock, D. A., Powers, D. E. (1988) Testing Handicapped People. Allyn and Bacon, Inc., Massachusetts

The Effect of Clustered Objective Probability Scoring with Truncation (T-COPS) on Reliability

Tetsuhito Shizuka

Institute of Foreign Language Education and Research, Kansai University, 3-3-35, Yamate, Suita, Osaka 564-8680, Japan

Summary. Building on de Finetti (1965) and Shuford *et al.* (1966), Leclercq (1983) maintained that any method of scoring multiple-choice tests should take into account the existence of varying degrees of correctness of "correct" responses. This paper introduces Clustered Objective Probability Scoring (COPS) procedure and a modified version (T-COPS) as such methods. COPS combines 1/0 response-correctness matrices and polytomous confidence-level matrices in such a way that potentially contaminating personality factors will have no bearing on the outcome. In T-COPS, one additional step is taken at the last phase to truncate scores lower than chance level.

Five data sets produced by Japanese university students responding to several types of multiple-choice English reading tests were scored by the number-correct method, COPS, and T-COPS. The focus was the extent to which COPS and T-COPS would improve upon reliability and mean item discrimination of the original dichotomous data. The results showed that COPS indeed boosted both properties substantially, and T-COPS achieved still further improvement upon COPS. The effect of employing T-COPS on reliability was equivalent to lengthening the original dichotomously-scored test from four to five times.

Key Words. Confidence, Reliability, Item discrimination, COPS, T-COPS

1 Introduction

It is currently a common practice to score selected-response items dichotomously to produce 1/0 data sets. Not reflected in such data is different degrees of person ability involved in producing the same responses (1s or 0s) to a given item. Test-takers' responses to an item can coincide for different reasons: one may have responded correctly because he/she 'knew', 'thought' or 'guessed' it was the correct option. That is why Leclercq (1983) maintained that any method of scoring multiple-choice tests should incorporate the existence of varying degrees of correctness below the identical surface of seemingly correct responses.

Research shows people's confidence in their responses is reasonably warranted. Shizuka (2000) analyzed data produced by 150 Japanese university students responding to 50 multiple-choice sentence comprehension items and rating his/her confidence in each response on a three-point scale. The mean success probabilities in low-, medium-, and high-confidence categories were .328, .432, and .654, respectively ($F = 156.27$, $p < .01$). I have since analyzed a number of similar data sets and obtained the same result without exception: When people report levels of confidence in their responses, high-confidence answers are generally more *likely* to be correct than medium-confidence ones, which in turn are more likely to be correct than low-confidence responses.

It may follow, then, that when a person responds correctly to two items, one with high confidence and the other with low confidence, the credits for the two may justifiably differ, because the latter is likely to involve more of chance factor than the former. Traditional "confidence scoring" systems have been based on this supposition.

2 History of Confidence Scoring

So-called confidence scoring has a long history. Since Hevner (1932) investigated combining confidence and correctness in scoring true-false tests, numerous attempts have been made to extract information from below the surface of 1/0 data matrices. Some used relatively simple tariffs (Jensen 1983, Bokhorst 1986) while others depended on rather complicated formulas (de Finetti 1965, Shufford et al. 1966; Rippey 1970).

In these studies, correctness and confidence were combined in one way or another so that higher-confidence correct responses were treated more favorably than lower-confidence correct responses, while higher-confidence incorrect responses were more severely penalized than lower-confidence ones. This line of research generally reported that confidence-weighted scoring resulted in somewhat, but not much, improved reliability.

In addition to the question whether increased test-taking time would be justified by the often marginal reliability increase, a recurrent and more serious concern was that such confidence-weighted scores might be influenced by personality factors that had nothing to do with the ability in question (Jacobs 1971; Hansen 1971). For these and other reasons, academic interests in the use of confidence in scoring seem to have dwindled in recent years.

The present paper describes a scoring procedure that uses confidence information in such a way that personality factors should only have a minimal, if any, role to play, and demonstrates evidence of its impact on psychometric properties of the data.

3 Confidence-Weighted Polytomous Scoring

Let us start by confirming the effects of simple confidence-weighted scoring. Eight groups of Japanese secondary- and tertiary-level students took English reading-related multiple-choice tests. The subjects rated their confidence on a three-point scale each time they chose a preferred answer to an item. A correct response was given 5, 4, and 3 points if confidence was high, medium, and low, respectively; an incorrect response was given 0, 1, and 2 points for high, medium, and low confidence, respectively. Table 1 shows the changes in alpha and mean item-total correlation brought about by this simple polytomous scoring. Like most previous studies, alphas somewhat improved in all the data sets, and mean item discrimination slightly improved in six data sets, three of which significantly.

Table 1. Change in reliability and item-total correlation brought about by confidence-weighted polytomous scoring

Data set	n	k	Cronbach's alpha		Item-total correlation		p-level
			DICHO	POLY	DICHO	POLY	
Set 1	41	34	.751	.766	.250	.280	n.s.
Set 2	50	33	.800	.833	.300	.340	.004
Set 3	34	35	.594	.698	.150	.210	.003
Set 4	90	34	.867	.870	.380	.380	n.s.
Set 5	148	35	.779	.780	.270	.270	n.s.
Set 6	34	40	.640	.718	.170	.210	.024
Set 7	74	50	.828	.850	.272	.291	n.s.
Set 8	76	50	.762	.790	.225	.243	n.s.

n: number of subjects   k: number of items   DICHO: dichotomous scoring   POLY: polytomous scoring

4 Individual Differences

It seems true that high-confidence responses made by a *group* of persons have higher success probabilities than low-confidence responses made by the same group. It also seems reasonable that high-confidence responses made by a given person have a higher probability correct than low-confidence responses made by that same person. If we take two different persons, however, we cannot necessarily say, for example, that one person's "high-confidence" responses are more likely to be correct than the other person's "low-confidence" responses.

Let us take, for example, five persons among the subjects for Data Set 7 in Table 1. Their responses made with three confidence levels are summarized in Table 2. Each person's 50 responses were classified by perceived confidence, and their probabilities correct were computed. As expected, their responses generally follow the expected pattern: high-confidence responses in a given person tend to be more correct than medium-confidence responses by the same person, which in turn tend to be more correct than that person's low-confidence responses.

Table 2. Probabilities correct of responses made by five persons with three levels of reported confidence

	Low confidence		Medium confidence		High confidence	
	n	P-correct	n	P-correct	n	P-correct
Person 1	6	0.167	5	0.200	39	0.359
Person 2	15	0.333	23	0.304	12	0.750
Person 3	23	0.565	12	0.833	15	0.933
Person 4	23	0.348	16	0.563	11	0.545
Person 5	9	0.444	26	0.423	15	0.933

n: the number of responses in that confidence category

Despite some minor deviations from the expected pattern (e.g., the high-medium rank order is reversed for Person 4, and the medium-low rank order is reversed for two Persons 2 and 5), if we disregard medium-confidence responses, we can safely claim that high-confidence responses are more likely to be correct than low-confidence responses *within* persons. When we compare responses *between* persons, however, that no longer holds. People vary both in ability and in perception. One person's "high-confidence" response may not be as likely to be correct as another person's high-, medium-, or even low-confidence responses. For example, Person 1's high-confidence responses (p = .359) were in no way comparable to Person 3's (p = .933). In fact, Person 3's low-confidence responses (p = .565) had a much higher success rate than Person 1's high-confidence responses.

It seems, then, that credits given for correct responses made by different persons, with the same *reported* level of confidence but with different *objective* success probabilities, should justifiably differ. That is, for example, one person's high-confidence correct response may deserve more, or less, credit than another person's high-confidence response. Not all seemingly correct responses are correct to the same extent. Person 1's high-confidence responses, even when correct, should deserve much less credits than Person 3's low-confidence correct responses. Let us note that Person 1's high-confidence *correct* responses were made with the same perceived/reported confidence level as his/her high-confidence *incorrect* responses. When Person 1 perceived/reported a level of confidence that was *high* to him/her, the response was only correct about 3.6 times out of 10. Even when a response in this high-confidence category *turns out* to be correct, it should not deserve full credit because that "correct" response is perceived (or at least reported), by that person, to be *as likely to be correct as the wrong responses* in the same confidence category.

In this way, classification of responses by reported confidence level will provide us an objective clue as to the degrees to which chance factor was involved in getting the items correct.

5 Clustered Objective Probability Scoring (COPS)

5.1 The Procedure and Preliminary Results

Clustered Objective Probability Scoring (COPS) is a procedure in which the credit given to a correct response equals, or is a linearly transformed value of, the objective probability correct of the responses that particular test-taker produces in that confidence category.   For correct responses in the low-, medium-, and high-confidence categories, Person 1 will be given .167, .200, and .359 points respectively; Person 2 will get .333, .304, and .750 respectively; Person 3 will be awarded .565, .833, and .933 points respectively, and so on.   No points will be awarded or subtracted for incorrect responses irrespective of the confidence levels.

The steps to follow in COPS are as follows: for each test-taker, (1) group the responses according to the reported confidence levels; (2) compute the mean probability correct of the responses in each confidence category; and (3) use the obtained probability value as the credit for a correct response in each category.   If fractions are cumbersome to work with, the values can be linearly converted into integers by whatever method preferred by the scorer.

It should be understood that the result of COPS is not affected by the degree of optimism or pessimism of each test-taker.   For example, whether a test-taker groups responses and report his/her confidence in them as *high* or *low*, if the mean probability correct for that category is, say, .6, that will be the credit value for one correct response in that category, irrespective of its label (i.e., *high* or *low*). Therefore, a humble person will be no more penalized for humbleness than an optimistic person will be rewarded for optimism.

Table 3. Reliability and item-total correlation obtained by dichotomous scoring, polytomous, scoring, and COPS

Data	n	k	Cronbach's alpha			item-total correlation		
			DICHO	POLY	COPS	DICHO	POLY	COPS
Set 7	74	50	.828	.850	.951	.272	.291	.511
Set 8	76	50	.762	.790	.924	.225	.243	.435

Table 3 shows score reliability and mean item-total correlation obtained when COPS was applied to Data Sets 7 and 8, alongside the corresponding values for dichotomous and simple confidence-weighted polytomous scoring methods. Both alphas and mean item discriminations were substantially improved. Concerning item discrimination, F-statistics were highly significant ($p = .000$) and pair-wise comparisons revealed the only significant difference between COPS and the other two, in both sets. Hence, overall, COPS seemed quite effective for improving the psychometric property of selected-response data sets.

5.2 Identified Anomalies

To take a closer look at the nature of the procedure, it was examined whether higher COPS item scores were indeed associated with higher person abilities, using Data Set 7. First, all COPS values were multiplied by 10 and rounded, producing a matrix on an 11-point (0-10) scale. Then, for each item, persons were grouped by the COPS score they got on that item. Next, the mean ability of each group in Rasch logits (derived from the number-correct score) was computed. Here, it should be understood that, (1) unlike COPS item scores, which incorporated confidence data, the criterion Rasch logits depended solely on response correctness, and *not* at all on confidence, and that (2) the Rasch model was applied to the test scores, and *not* to the COPS data. The reason Rasch measures were used instead of number-correct scores was simply that they are known to be generally better indicators of the test-takers' abilities (Wright and Stone 1979). This was repeated for all the 90 items. Produced was an 11 (COPS scores) by 90 (items) matrix of mean person ability corresponding to each of the 11 COPS scores for each item. Figure 1 shows the results as box-plots.

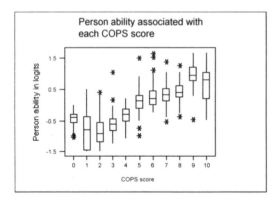

Fig. 1 Box-plots of person ability by rounded COPS scores in Data Set 7.

An expected pattern was for the mean person ability to monotonically increase as the COPS score increments. Such relationship indeed held in the range from COPS score 2 to 9, where higher COPS scores were associated with more able persons. A one-way ANOVA confirmed a significant difference among the eleven means ($F = 190.66$, $p = .000$). A simple regression model, with person ability as the predicted variable and COPS score as the predictor variable, was highly significant (p = .000) and adjusted R-squared was .575. The slope of the regression line was 0.169, indicating that when COPS score increases by 1 point, the person ability will increase by 0.169 logits on the average.

Thus, the observed pattern overall was just as expected. Nonetheless, two anomalies were identified. First, the abilities of persons associated with COPS scores 0, 1, 2, and 3 were not ranked in the expected fashion. Pair-wise comparisons revealed that the mean abilities of persons getting COPS scores 2-3 were less able than those who got COPS scores 0 or 4. This is a problem because it means that, in this ability range, more able persons are being treated less favorably by COPS than less able persons are. The other anomaly was that the mean ability of those who got COPS 9 seemed to be more able than those who got COPS 10.

5.3 Truncating COPS

One plausible account for the first anomaly would be that those who scored 1, 2, or 3 (i.e., those whose success probabilities were in .05-.14, .15-.24, and .25-.34 ranges respectively) got the items mostly by chance. That is, it is not that people who got 0 are really more able than those who got 2 or 3 but that score differences in this range do not reflect ability differences. Based on this assumption, the probability values not exceeding .34 were replaced with .00s. The other anomaly in the upper end was left as it was, since no logical explanation could be found. COPS followed by truncating the lower end of the scale in this manner will hereafter be referred to as T-COPS (that is, truncating COPS).

Table 4 Reliability and item-total correlation obtained by dichotomous scoring, COPS, and T-COPS

Data	n	k	Cronbach's alpha			Item-total correlation		
			DICHO	COPS	T-COPS	DICHO	COPS	T-COPS
Set 7	74	50	.828	.951	.960	.272	.511	.552
Set 8	76	50	.762	.924	.936	.225	.435	.472
Set 9	251	40	.834	.951	.961	.379	.585	.614
Set 10	233	40	.854	.952	.958	.425	.634	.655
Set 11	130	35	.667	.885	.901	.287	.453	.481

Data sets 9 and 10 are from Shizuka's (2000) main study

Table 4 shows reliabilities and mean item-total correlations when dichotomous scoring, COPS, and T-COPS were applied to five data sets including Sets 7 and 8. T-COPS brought out the best reliabilities and item discriminations in all the sets. Although the differences between COPS and T-COPS were not large, they did not seem like artifacts of chance because the improvements were observed constantly through the different sets. The differences between dichotomous scoring and

T-COPS were remarkable: alphas changed from .828 to .960, from .762 to .936, from .834 to .961, from 854 to .958, and from .667 to .901.   According to the Spearman-Brown formula, these improvements were equivalent to making the original tests longer by 4.99, 4.57, 4.90, 3.90, and 4.54 times respectively.

6 Conclusion

If traditional confidence scoring procedures lacked wide appeal, it was mainly because of concerns about possible contamination from personality factors, unimpressive effects on reliability, or both. COPS and T-COPS should be logically free from the influence of test-takers' personality traits and the effects on reliability and item discrimination are almost compelling. Since rating confidence levels lengthens test-taking time by only 5-6 % (Shizuka 2000), reliability improvement equivalent to lengthening the original test 3.90-4.99 times clearly justifies the additional test-taking time. Though the only setback may be the increase in scoring efforts, that should not constitute a problem if computers are available.

References

Bokhorst FD (1986) Confidence-weighting and the validity of achievement tests. Psychological Reports 59: 383-386

de Finetti B (1965) Methods of discriminating levels of partial knowledge concerning a test item. British J of Mathematical and Statistical Psychology 18: 87-123

Hansen R (1971) The influence of variables other than knowledge on probabilistic tests. J of Educational Measurement 8: 9-14

Hevner KA (1932) A method of correcting for guessing in true-false tests and empirical evidence in support of it. J of Social Psychology 3: 359-362

Jacobs SS (1971) Correlates of unwarranted confidence in responses to objective test items. J of Educational Measurement 8: 15-19

Jensen OA (1983) Increasing testing efficiency and effectiveness per item and per minute of testing time. Public Personnel Management J 12: 63-82

Leclercq D (1983) Confidence marking: Its use in testing. Evaluation in Education 6: 161-287

Rippey RM (1970) A comparison of five different scoring functions for confidence tests. J of Educational Measurement 7: 165-170

Shizuka T (2000) The validity of incorporating reading speed and response confidence in measurement of EFL reading proficiency. Doctoral dissertation The University of Reading

Shuford EH, Albert A, Massengil HE (1966) Admissible probability measurement procedures. Psychometrika 31: 125-145

Wright BD, Stone MH (1979) Best test design: Rasch measurement. MESA, Chicago

A Framework for Reusing Assessment Components

Russell G. Almond[1], Linda S. Steinberg[2], and Robert J. Mislevy[3]

[1]Center for Statistical Theory and Practice, Research Division, Educational Testing Service, MS 12-T, Princeton, NJ 08541, USA, ralmond@ets.org
[2]Center for Assessment Design and Scoring, Research Division, Educational Testing Service, MS 12-T, Princeton, NJ 08541, USA
[3]Department of Measurement, Statistics and Evaluation, School of Education, University of Maryland, 1230 Benjamin Building, College Park, MD 20742-1115, USA.

Summary. The purpose of an assessment determines a myriad of details about the delivery, presentation, and scoring of that assessment and consequently the authoring of tasks for that assessment. This paper explores the relationship between design requirements and authoring through the use of the Four Process Framework for Assessment Delivery. This ideal assessment delivery architecture describes an assessment delivery environment in terms of four processes:

– *Activity Selection*—The process which picks the next task or item;
– *Presentation*—The process which presents the item and captures the work product produced by the participant;
– *Response Processing*—The process which examines the participants response to a particular task and sets the values of observable outcome variables based on that response; and
– *Summary Scoring*—The process which is responsible for accumulating evidence across many tasks in an assessment.

This framework has proved useful in our own work in Evidence Centered Design, and is being adopted as part of the IMS Global Consortium's specification for Question and Test Interoperability.

To illustrate how changes in requirements bring about changes in design, we explore several variations on the theme of a *kanji* character reading and writing test. While varying the purpose from drill and practice to admission into a calligraphy school, the four-process framework shows how the assessment delivery must change to accommodate the new purpose.

Keywords. Computer-based testing, Computer-adaptive testing, Assessment Purpose, Assessment Design

1 Introduction

The purpose of an assessment determines many requirements for that assessment: breadth and depth of coverage of the topic; number and type of measures reported, as well as their reliability and comparability across participants; the number, nature, and mixture of tasks which are presented in the assessment; the level of security; and the delivery platform (human, computer or human–computer system). In particular, high stakes assessments whose primary purpose is selection or placement have very different requirements from low stakes assessments whose primary purpose is to support the participant's learning goals. Furthermore, targets for reliability of the measures, breadth of coverage, and authenticity of the tasks must be weighed against each other and cost. In this case, cost is measured both in terms of the effort required to author, review, calibrate, score, and equate the assessment, as well as the amount of time the participant must spend to use the assessment. These trade-offs are an important part of the art of assessment design.

In developing the Evidence Centered Design methodology, we found a need to explain how these design trade-offs would play out in delivering the assessment. To that end we produced the Four-Process Framework (Almond, Steinberg and Mislevy, 2002). This framework has proven useful for describing not only assessments designed with our own methodology, but also assessments designed using other formal or informal methods. The IMS Global Consortium's specification for Question and Test Interoperability uses this framework to organize both data describing assessments, sections, and items and result data returned from a participant's interaction with the assessment.[1] The next section presents a review of this framework.

The rest of the paper takes a single domain—reading and writing *kanji* characters—and explores what happens as we vary the purpose. Three general purposes—drill and practice for a college applicant, self-study for an adult foreign learner, and a screening exam for a calligraphy school—provide an opportunity to examine a number of design options. Furthermore, these examples show how a clear understanding of the way in which purpose affects design helps support re-use of assessment materials in new contexts with new purposes.

2 The Four-Process Architecture

Any assessment system must have (at least in some trivial form) four different processes. Figure 1 shows the four processes and the interaction among them.

---

[1] Another paper presented in Osaka by authors Almond and Smythe described the use of the Four-Process Framework in the Question and Test Interoperability specifications. We chose to include this paper in the published proceedings because most of the content of that talk can be found on-line at http://www.imsglobal.org/question/.

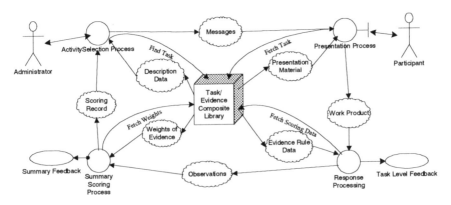

Fig. 1. *The Four Principle Processes in the Assessment Cycle*. The Activity Selection Process selects a task (or other activity) and instructs the Presentation Process to display it. When the participant has finished interacting with the item, the Presentation Process sends the results (a Work Product) to Response Processing. This process identifies key Observations about the results and passes them to the Summary Scoring Process, which updates the Scoring Model, tracking our beliefs about the participant's knowledge. All four processes add information to the Results Database. The Activity Selection then makes a decision about what to do next, based on the current beliefs about the participant.

The assessment cycle is produced by the interaction of the following four processes:
· The *Activity Selection Process* is the system responsible for selecting and sequencing tasks (or items) from the Task/Evidence Composite Library. These could be tasks with an assessment or an instructional focus, or activities related to test administration. The Activity Selection Process may use any of several different selection algorithms, or may consult the current Scoring Model (if the system is adaptive) to decide when to stop, whether to present a task with instructional or assessment focus, or which kind of task to present next to maximize information about the participant.
· The *Presentation Process* is responsible for presenting the task to the participant. As necessary, it will take details about the task from the task library. (In particular, certain kinds of presentation material (*material*) such as images, audio, or applets may be represented as external resources to be brought in with the presentation of the item.) When the participant performs the task, the Presentation Process will capture one or more Work Products from the participant. These are delivered to Response Processing for evaluation.
· *Response Processing* performs the first step in the scoring process: It identifies the essential features of the response that provide evidence about the participant's current knowledge, skills, and abilities. These are recorded as a series of Observations that are passed to the next process.
· The *Summary Scoring Process* performs the second, or summary, stage in the scoring process: It updates our beliefs about the participant's knowledge, skills, and abilities based on this evidence. As we will show below, separating the

Response Processing step from both Summary Scoring and Task Presentation is vital to supporting reuse of the task in multiple contexts.

This Four-Process Architecture can work in either a synchronous and or an asynchronous mode. In the synchronous mode, the Activity Selection Process tells the Presentation Process to start a new task after processing the results of the previous task. In this case, the messages move around the system in cycles. In the asynchronous mode, once the Presentation Process is told to start a task or series of tasks, it generates a new Work Product whenever the participant finishes an appropriate stage of the task. The Activity Selection Process is informed of the change in the Examinee Record and decides whether to let the current activities continue or to send a message to the Presentation Process requesting a new activity.

The system is capable of generating two types of feedback:

· *Task Level Feedback* is an immediate response to the participant's actions in a particular task, *independent of evidence from other tasks.* For example, the system could immediately indicate the correct answer after the response was submitted, suggest an alternative approach, or explain the underlying principle of the task if misconceptions are evident.

· *Summary Feedback* is a report about our accumulated belief based on evidence from multiple tasks concerning the participant's knowledge, skills, and abilities along the dimensions measured by the assessment. That is, it is feedback based on synthesized evidence from responses to any number of tasks. Summary Feedback can be reported to the participant, the administrator, or other interested parties.

IEEE draft standard P1484.1 (IEEE, 2001) proposes a similar architecture for assessment delivery (in the context of a more general tutoring system). However, their proposal differs from ours in one important respect: The response processing and summary scoring operations are grouped together as a single process. Because in the common case of multiple choice items, Response Processing is so simple it often gets lumped with Presentation or Summary Scoring for ease of implementation. However, as the examples below show, keeping it separate (at least conceptually) is a critical requirement for being able to re-use assessments in new contexts.

3 Theme and Variations

To illustrate the value of the four-process framework, we will follow a simple example—a *kanji* reading and writing assessment—through three different purposes—drill and practice for college application, self-study for an adult learner, and a screening exam for a calligraphy school. First, however, we must research the general features of the domain we wish to study. The Evidence Centered Design process calls this step *Domain Modeling*. The following section provides an abbreviated domain model for our *kanji* tutoring system.

3.1 Domain Description—*Kanji* Tutor

Kanji are the characters from the Chinese writing system imported into the writing of Japanese. They help give the Japanese language its distinctive look however they also present a problem for learners of the language. A college freshman is expected to know how to read and write approximately 2000 characters. Consequently, many systems for practicing reading and writing *kanji* have come about.

The first step in modeling our domain is to define the knowledge, skills, and abilities we wish to measure. A partial list of skills for our example includes the following:

· Recognizing the Meaning of the Character
· Correctly Pronouncing the Character
· Recalling the correct character(s) for a word
· Drawing the characters properly. This skill has several parts including making the right number a kind of strokes and achieving a good balance in the form of the character.

The extent to which a learner requires these skills depends on the purpose. Obviously, a calligrapher must pay more attention to aesthetic details than somebody whose goal is merely to communicate.

Closely related to the knowledge, skills, and abilities are the claims which the assessment must support. The claims under consideration include the following:

· Learner can comprehend a newspaper or technical journal article in Japanese.
· Learner can comprehend a note handwritten in Japanese.
· Learner can write an essay in Japanese.
· Learner can take dictation in Japanese.
· Learner can read aloud a passage written in Japanese.
· Learner has the potential to become a good calligrapher.

The final step in our analysis is to describe some typical tasks that might provide *evidence* that the learner has the skills about which we wish to make claims. (It is this use of "evidence" from which *Evidence Centered Design* takes its name). Some example tasks include:

· Given pronunciation and usage:
   · Recognize character (select from list of choices)
   · Write character (using paper and pencil or brush and ink).
· Given character
   · Recognize sound and/or meaning (select from list of choices)
   · Produce sound
   · Produce meaning

Obviously, some of these tasks are more expensive to design, present, and score than others, especially in a computer-based system. The choice of tasks will depend on the purpose of the assessment.

3.2 Example 1: Drill and Practice for College Applicant

The first purpose is a practice system for a college applicant living in Japan. In this instance, cost is a primary concern. Thus, expensive input capture devices or advanced speech and character recognition systems would be prohibitively expensive. As immediacy of results is more important than authentic tasks, using human raters is probably not possible. For native Japanese speakers, the recognition tasks are the primary concern; these learners will have had opportunities to practice speaking and writing elsewhere.

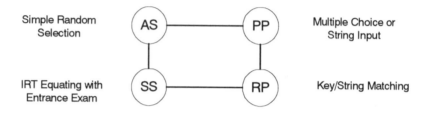

Fig. 2. Four Process Realizations for Drill and Practice System.

As cost is the primary design goal, the system is restricted in several ways. The Presentation Process is restricted to text display and text input; sound and pictures would be too expensive. By restricting the asssessment to recogintion tasks, we can use simple key matching for Response Processing (or string matching for free text input). Because the need for reliability is not high, we can use a simple random selection mechanism. Finally, we can use a summary scoring mechanism which equates the results to the National University Entrance Examination because our most important claims are about the ability to score well on that test.

3.3 Example 2: Self Study for Adult Learner

The second purpose is a practice system for an adult learner of Japanese living outside of Japan. For such a learner, practice with listening and speaking in addition to reading and writing is essential. Again, immediacy of results is important; however, the adult learner might be willing to pay a premium and assessments may include character and speech recognition systems.

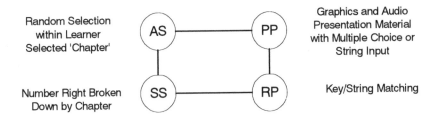

Fig. 3. Four Process Realizations for an Adult Learner

Including pictures of handwritten characters and sound clips containing samples of Japanese speech will make these tasks more authentic. In this version, to keep the costs down, we still use selection and short string inputs. As we no longer need to equate to the National Exam or across forms of the assessment, we can use a simpler number right scoring mechanism.

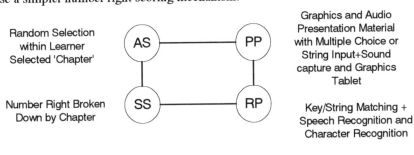

Fig. 4. Four Process Realizations for Adult Learner with Advanced Work Product Inputs.

More adanced computer systems can support more direct assessments of speaking and writing skills. Adding a combination of sound capture capability in the Presentation Process and speech recognition in the Response Processing will produce better (more authentic) assessments of pronunciation skills. Adding a combination of graphic input capability (e.g., a graphics tablet) to the Presentation Process and character recognition to Response Processing will produce better assessments of writing skills. These technologies currently exist, but we may want to make these capabilities optional for reasons of expense. We could also use human raters for the response processing, but the real-time feedback potential is probably more important than the greater authenticity. Note that keeping the Response Processing separate is important in giving us the flexibility to explore alternative response processing strategies for these constructed response tasks.

3.4 Example 3: Screening Exam for Calligraphy School

The final purpose is a screening exam for a calligraphy school. This exam has much higher stakes as the future learning path of the applicant depends on the result. For calligraphy, writing is obviously much more important than reading. Also, since aesthetic considerations are as important as legibility, we are willing to pay the costs of human raters.

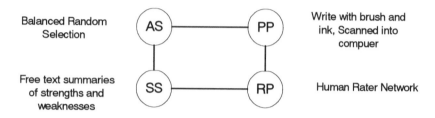

Fig. 5. Four Process Realizations for Calligraphy School Screening Exam.

Obviously this assessment emphasizes writing skills. The tasks would be based on writing in context (probably poetry). The Activity Selection process would balance across the range of contexts needed. The presention process would need to either use brush and ink (scanned into a computer for transmition to raters) or a system which emulated brush and ink very well. The Response Processing would be done by human raters (who perhaps receive their material to be graded via email). The Summary Scoring process would again be a human process, as yet another grader summarizes the reports of the individual raters.

4 Summary

These examples have explored only a few of the possibilities within the domain of reading and writing *kanji*. Still, they are adequate to show how changing the purpose of the assessment changes the delivery requirements and how the four-process framework aids in exploring the implications of those requirements.

5 References

Almond RG, Steinberg LS, Mislevy RJ (in press) A Four-Process Architecture for Assessment Delivery, with Connections to Assessment Design. JLTA.

IEEE (2001) Draft Standard for Learning Technology—Learning Technology Systems Architecture (LTSA). IEEE P1484.1/D9, 2001-11-30.

Investigating the Local Fit of Item-Score Vectors

Wilco H.M. Emons[1]

Department of Methodology, FSW, Tilburg University, P.O. Box 90153, 5000LE Tilburg, The Netherlands *w.h.m.emons@uvt.nl*

Summary. This paper discusses a nonparametric approach for testing the local fit of an item-score vector by using the person response function. Unlike most person-fit statistics, which test the fit of the *complete* pattern, the person response function indicates *which* subsets of items are misfitting. Three person-fit statistics were investigated that compare local deviations of the observed PRF from the expected PRF. A simulation study was done to compare the Type I error rates and detection rates of three person-fit statistics under varying test and item characteristics.

Keywords. Nonparametric item response theory, person-fit research, person response function.

1 Person-Fit Research

Person-fit methods are used to identify item-score vectors that do not fit a hypothesized item response theory model or deviate from the observed responses of the majority of the respondents in the sample (Meijer and Sijtsma, 2001). Such anomalous patterns may be found, for example, for respondents who copied the correct answers from a high-ability neighbor. The result is an item-score vector with unexpectedly many correct answers on difficult items. Anomalous vectors may also be found for respondents who suffered from test anxiety or fumbled and, as a result, gave unexpectedly many incorrect answers to the easy items (e.g., see Haladyna, 1994).

Most person-fit statistics test whether the *complete* vector of item scores fits; that is, they test the *global* fit of an item-score vector. For diagnostic purposes, it is interesting to know *which* subset of items shows misfit; that is, we are interested in *local* fit. For example, respondents with unusually large numbers of incorrect answers to relatively easy items may have suffered from test anxiety. In this example, only the easy items exhibit misfit.

A useful tool for investigating local fit is the person-response function (PRF; Trabin and Weiss, 1983; Lumsden, 1978). The PRF, to be defined in greater detail later on, at the individual level relates the probability of a correct answer to an item difficulty scale. The PRF can be estimated for each respondent and compared with the expected PRF under a hypothesized test model. Discrepancies between the observed and expected PRF indicate which particular items show misfit (e.g., Nering, 1998).

Recently, Sijtsma and Meijer (2001) proposed a nonparametric definition
of the PRF and presented a statistical method for testing whether local deviations of the expected shape of the PRF are significant. This paper discusses
further investigation and improvements of this approach. Two new statistics
are proposed and the usefulness of these newly proposed statistics is compared with the statistic of Sijtsma and Meijer (2001). A simulation study
was done to investigate Type I error rates and detection rates of the three
statistics under varying test and item characteristics.

2 Nonparametric Item Response Theory

Let X_j ($j = 1, \cdots, J$) denote the binary random variable for the item responses with realization x_j; $x_j = 1$ for a correct or coded answer and $x_j = 0$
otherwise; and let $\mathbf{X} = (X_1, X_2, \cdots, X_J)$ be the ordered item-score vector.
In addition, let π_j denote the proportion of persons with a 1-score on item j;
and let $\hat{\pi}_j$ be the sample estimate. We assume that the J items in the test are
ordered and numbered by increasing difficulty; that is, $\pi_1 \geq \pi_2 \geq \cdots \geq \pi_J$.

IRT models use the item response function (IRF) to relate the probability
of a correct answer to a latent trait θ, denoted by $P_j(\theta) \equiv P(X_j = 1|\theta)$.
Nonparametric IRT models are defined by order restrictions on the IRFs,
but refrain from a parametric definition of the IRF like in parametric IRT
(Sijtsma and Molenaar, 2002). In this paper, we used models defined by the
following four assumptions. First, the latent trait is unidimensional; that is, θ
is a scalar. Second, the responses are statistically independent conditional on
θ. This is the local independence assumption. Third, the IRFs are monotonely
nondecreasing in θ; that is, $P_j(\theta_a) \geq P_j(\theta_b)$ whenever $\theta_a \geq \theta_b$. Fourth, the
IRFs of the J items do not intersect. This is the assumption of an invariant
item ordering (IIO; Sijtsma and Junker, 1996), which can be formalized as
follows. For two items i and j and a fixed value θ_0, if we know that $P_i(\theta_0) >
P_j(\theta_0)$ then $P_i(\theta) \geq P_j(\theta)$ for all θ.

A NIRT model satisfying these four assumptions is Mokken (1971) double monotonicity model (DMM). It may be noted that dichotomous NIRT
models satisfying the assumptions of unidimensionality, local independence,
and monotone nondecreasing IRFs have a monotone likelihood ratio in θ
(Grayson, 1988), which implies a stochastic ordering of the θ by the number
of correct answers $X_+ = \sum_j X_j$ (Hemker, Sijtsma, Molenaar, and Junker,
1997). This result is important for practical applications, because it justifies
the use of X_+ for ordering persons on a latent trait.

3 Nonparametric Local Fit Assessment Using the PRF

3.1 The Person Response Function

The PRF relates for each person the probability of a correct answer to the item difficulty. Let S_v be the item response variable for person v, with $S_v = 1$ for a correct or coded answer and $S_v = 0$ otherwise. Furthermore, let the population item difficulty be defined by

$$1 - \pi_j = \int_\theta [1 - P_j(\theta)] dG(\theta),$$

yielding a continuous item difficulty scale with domain [0,1]. We use the sample estimate $(1-\hat{\pi}_j)$ for the item difficulty. Using $(1-\pi)$ for the population item-difficulty scale, the nonparametric PRF is defined by

$$P_v(1 - \pi) = P(S_v = 1 | 1 - \pi; \theta_v),$$

with person parameter θ_v fixed and $1 - \pi$ variable. The PRF is nonincreasing under NIRT models that have an IIO (Sijtsma and Meijer, 2001). Local deviations from this expected nonincreasingness can be used to identify particular subsets of items showing misfit. Figure 1 shows an example of three PRFs expected under NIRT models having an IIO (solid lines), and one PRF indicating misfit on relatively difficult items (dashed line).

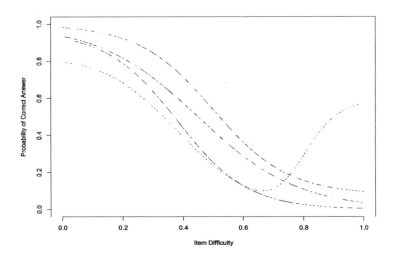

Fig. 1. Example of Three Expected PRFs and One Misfitting PRF

3.2 Estimation of the PRF

We investigated the local fit of the PRF using a discrete approximation to the PRF. Let the ordered item-score vector $\mathbf{X}$ be divided into K ordered disjoint subsets A_k $(k = 1, ..., K)$ of size m, such that A_1 contains the m easiest items, A_2 the next m easiest items, and so forth (here J is a multiple of K, but this is an arbitrary restriction). The expected proportion of correct answers to the items in A_k for person v equals $\tau_{vk} \equiv m^{-1} \sum_{j \in A_k} P_j(\theta_v)$. Given an IIO, an ordering of the items by increasing $1 - \pi$ (i.e., increasing difficulty) implies that for all θ, the minimum $P_j(\theta)$ of the items in A_k is greater than or equal to the maximum of $P_j(\theta)$ of the items in A_{k+1}. Consequently, we have that

$$m^{-1} \sum_{j \in A_k} P_j(\theta) \geq m^{-1} \sum_{j \in A_{k+1}} P_j(\theta), \text{ for all } \theta.$$

This implies that for the K item subsets and for each person v, we have that $\tau_{v1} \geq \tau_{v2} \geq \cdots \geq \tau_{vK}$. This ordering is estimated using sample fractions $\hat{\tau}_{vk} = m^{-1} \sum_{j \in A_k} X_{vj}$, with X_{vj} being the response variable for person v to item j. Local deviations of the observed ordering from the expected ordering of the $\hat{\tau}$s indicate misfit.

3.3 Testing Local Fit of the PRF

Suppose we found a local increase of the PRF for person v in the sample, manifested by $\hat{\tau}_{vk} < \hat{\tau}_{vk+1}$. To test the significance of this local increase, we need a person-fit statistic that quantifies misfit and a null distribution of the person-fit statistic under the expected response behavior. Three person-fit statistics were used: (1) sum scores on item subsets, (2) number of Guttman errors on item subsets, and (3) weighted number of Guttman errors on item subsets.

Using subset sum scores. From now on, we also use random variable notation Y_j for item scores. Let $\mathbf{Y}_e$ and $\mathbf{Y}_d$ be the ordered item-score vector of the J_e items in A_k (relatively easy items) and the J_d items in A_{k+1} (relatively difficult items), respectively. In addition, let $\mathbf{Y} = (\mathbf{Y}_e, \mathbf{Y}_d) = (Y_1, \cdots, Y_{J_Y})$ be the ordered vector of the $J_Y = J_e + J_d$ item scores for two combined subsets A_k and A_{k+1}; thus, $\mathbf{Y}$ is part vector of $\mathbf{X}$. The unweighted sum score variables based on the items from $\mathbf{Y}$, $\mathbf{Y}_e$ and $\mathbf{Y}_d$ are denoted by Y_+, Y_{+e}, and Y_{+d}, respectively.

Following Sijtsma and Meijer (2001), using subset sum scores, we test whether $Y_{+e} = y_{+e}$ is exceptionally low in comparison with $Y_{+d} = y_{+d}$ and $Y_+ = y_+$; that is, we are interested in

$$P(Y_{+e} \leq y_{+e} | J_e, J_d, y_+). \tag{1}$$

Because exact evaluation of Equation 1 is difficult under NIRT models, Sijtsma and Meijer (2001) used a null distribution that provides an upper bound for the probability in Equation 1 based on the statistical theory by Rosenbaum (1987). Using an upper bound means that the test is conservative, and deviations have to be large to be significant. Sijtsma and Meijer (2001) showed that the probability of exceedance of at most Y_{+e} correct answers can be obtained from the cumulative hypergeometric distribution. The theories of Rosenbaum (1987) and Sijtsma and Meijer (2001) were also used to derive the distribution that provides upper bounds for the significance probabilities of person-fit statistics the G and G_w.

Using the number of Guttman errors. The number of Guttman errors, denoted by G, is the number of item pairs of all unique item pairs $\{(Y_i, Y_j); i < j\}$ for which the easy item was answered incorrectly $(Y_i = 0)$ and the difficult item correctly $(Y_j = 1)$; that is,

$$G = \sum_{i=1}^{J_Y-1} \sum_{j=i+1}^{J_Y} (1 - Y_i)Y_j. \tag{2}$$

High values g of G indicate misfit (Meijer, 1986). The person-fit test evaluates whether g is exceptionally high; that is, we evaluate the probability

$$P(G \geq g|y_+, J_Y). \tag{3}$$

For statistic G, it can be shown that the Wilcoxon rank-sum distribution provides the upper bound for the significance probability of Equation 3 (see Emons, in press).

Using weighted number of Guttman errors. The weighted number of Guttman error weights the Guttman errors by the distance between the item difficulties. The idea is that a Guttman error reflects more misfit when the distance between the item difficulties is higher. The weighted number of Guttman errors is defined by

$$G_w = \sum_{i=1}^{J_Y-1} \sum_{j=i+1}^{J_Y} \omega_{ij}(1 - Y_i)Y_j, \tag{4}$$

with

$$\omega_{ij} = \frac{\pi_i(1 - \pi_j)}{\pi_j(1 - \pi_i)}.$$

High values g_ω of G_ω indicate misfit; therefore, we evaluate the probability

$$P(G_w \geq g_w|y_+, J_Y). \tag{5}$$

For statistic G_w, Emons (in press) showed that the upper bound for the significance probability of (5) can be obtained with a permutation test using bootstrap (Efron, 1993) .

4 Simulation Study

For the three person-fit statistics, we did a simulation study to compare Type I error rates with the nominal significance level to investigate the degree of conservatism. In addition, we investigated the detection rates of the three person-fit statistics to compare the relative effectiveness to detect misfitting item-score vectors.

Method. Item-score vectors were simulated using the flexible four-parameter logistic model (4PLM; Hambleton and Swaminathan, 1985), with the IRFs defined such that the assumption of an IIO was satisfied (see Sijtsma and Meijer, 2001). Misfitting item-score vectors were simulated as follows. Data were simulated for a test consisting of 40 items. All 40 item scores are simulated according to the 4PLM, but for the 5, 8, or 10 easiest items, the $P_j(\theta)$ was fixed to 0.25. Such a low $P_j(\theta)$ for easy items may be characteristic of carelessness, lack of attention, or sleeping behavior. Three different sizes of the item-score subsets were used: $J_Y = 10$ ($J_e = 5$, $J_d = 5$), $J_Y = 15$ ($J_e = 8$, $J_d = 7$), and $J_Y = 20$ ($J_e = 10$, $J_d = 10$).

The person-fit methods in this paper require an IIO. Since the assumption of an IIO of the J items may be very restrictive with respect to the data, we also studied the robustness of our person-fit methods to violations of an IIO. This was done by applying the three person-fit statistics to data simulated under a 4PLM with minor violations of an IIO.

Results. Table 1 gives the simulated Type I error rates and the detection rates at three levels of numbers of misfitting items (J_{misfit}), tested at the 5% level under the 4PLM with an IIO. The Type I error rates for the three statistics were much smaller than the expected value of 0.05; the lowest detection rates were found for Y_{+e}, meaning that this was the most conservative statistic. The least conservative statistic was G_w.

Table 1. Simulated Type I Error Rates and Detection Rates Under the 4PLM with an IIO.

	Y_{+e}			G			G_w		
	Number of items in **Y** (J_Y)								
	10	15	20	10	15	20	10	15	20
	Type I Error Rates								
	.0013	.0012	.0022	.0172	.0121	.0092	.0190	.0147	.0089
J_{misfit}	Detection Rates								
5	.2623	.1027	.0774	.3420	.1826	.0314	.3721	.2327	.0392
8	.0251	.4021	.2711	.3527	.4331	.3688	.3715	.4509	.4066
10	.0044	.1977	.4370	.2580	.3930	.4228	.2665	.4036	.4385

The detection rates of G and G_w were comparable; only small differences in favor of G_w were found. The three statistics had the highest detection rates when half of the items in **Y** were misfitting and the remaining items were fitting. Table 1 also shows decreased detection rates of Y_{+e} when J_{misfit} was relatively large compared with J_y. For example, for $J_y = 10$ and $J_{misfit} = 8$ the detection rates of Y_{+e} were .0251, whereas G and G_w yielded detection rates of .3527 and .3715, respectively.

Table 2 shows the Type I error rates and the detection rates for the simulations under the IRT model with minor violations of the IIO assumption. It can be seen that for Y_{+e} and G_w the Type I error rates and the detection rates under the 4PLM without an IIO differed from those obtained under the 4PLM with an IIO. For statistic G, however, only small deviations were found, indication that G was robust against minor violations of the IIO assumption.

Table 2. Simulated Type I Error Rates and Detection Rates Under the 4PLM with Minor Violations of an IIO.

	Y_{+e}			G			G_w		
	\multicolumn{9}{c}{Number of items in **Y** (J_Y)}								
	10	15	20	10	15	20	10	15	20
	\multicolumn{9}{c}{Type I Error Rates}								
	.0043	.0029	.0047	.0151	.0109	.0070	.0257	.0223	.0127
J_{misfit}	\multicolumn{9}{c}{Detection Rates}								
5	.1757	.0216	.0043	.3394	.1841	.0291	.2871	.1740	.0339
8	.0927	.2967	.1454	.3575	.4352	.3700	.2958	.3626	.3199
10	.0621	.2022	.3272	.2561	.4021	.4283	.1975	.3143	.3391

5 Discussion

In this paper, we investigated person-fit methods using the PRF. Compared with G and G_w, statistic Y_{+e} showed lower detection rates and was more sensitive to the ratio of numbers of fitting and misfitting items in item subsets. In addition, statistic G_w showed detection rates that were little higher than the detection rates for G, but statistic G has the advantage that the significance probability can be obtained from standard tables of the Wilcoxon distribution. In addition, statistic G was robust against mild violations of IIO. Based on the results, we recommend to use statistic G because it is easy to compute and significance probabilities can be obtained from readily available tables.

In this study, we used a discrete approximation of the PRF. As an alternative method, nonparametric and logistic regression methods can be used to estimate continuous PRFs and evaluate where and how the observed continuous PRF deviates from the expected PRF. For example, using plots of kernel smoothed PRFs the researcher can graphically inspect the shape of the PRFs and hypothesizes the cause of misfit.

References

Efron B, Tibshirani RJ (1993) An introduction to the bootstrap. Chapman & Hall New York

Emons WHM (in press) Detection and Diagnosis of Misfitting Item-Score Vectors. Unpublished Doctoral Dissertation, Tilburg University, Tilburg, The Netherlands.

Grayson DA (1988) Two group classification in latent trait theory: scores with monotone likelihood ratio. Psychometrika 53:383–392

Haladyna TM (1994) Developing and validating multiple-choice test items. Lawrence Erlbaum, New Jersey

Hambleton RK, Swaminathan H (1985) Item response theory: Principles and applications. Sage, Thousand Oaks CA

Hemker BT, Sijtsma K, Molenaar IW, Junker BW (1997) Stochastic ordering using the latent trait and the sum score in polytomous IRT models. Psychometrika 62:171–189

Lumsden J (1978) Tests are perfectly reliable. Br J math statist Psychol 31:19–26

Meijer RR (1996) The number of Guttman errors as a simple and powerful person-fit statistic. Applied Psychological Measurement 25:107–135

Meijer RR, Sijtsma K (2001) Methodology review: Evaluating person fit. Applied Psychological Measurement 25:107–135

Mokken RJ (1971) A theory and procedure of scale analysis. New York/Berlin, De Gruyter

Nering ML, Meijer RR (1998) A comparison of the person response function and the l_z statistic to person-fit measurement. Applied Psychological Measurement 22:53–69

Rosenbaum PR (1987) Probability inequalities for latent scales. Br J of math and statist Psychol 40:157–168

Sijtsma K, Junker BW (1996) A survey of theory and methods of invariant item ordering. Br J of math and statist psychol 49:97–105

Sijtsma K, Meijer RR (2001) The person response function as a tool in person-fit research. Psychometrika, 66:191–208

Sijtsma K, Molenaar IW (2002) Introduction to nonparametric item response theory. Sage, Thousand Oaks CA

Trabin TE, Weiss DJ (1983) The person response curve: fit of individuals to item response theory models. In: Weiss DJ (ed) New horizons in testing. Academic Press, New York, pp 83-108

Developing a Domain-Referenced Test given a Selection Ratio and a Cut-Off Score: An application of Item Response Theory

Soonmook Lee[1], Cheongtag Kim[2], and Myoung-So Kim[3]

[1] Department of Psychology, Sungkyunkwan University, Chongro-ku Myungryun-dong 3-ka, Seoul 110-745, Korea
[2] Department of Psychology, Seoul National University, Kwanak-ku Shinrim-dong, Seoul 151-742, Korea
[3] Department of Industrial/Organizational Psychology, Hoseo University, Asan-kun Paebang-myun, Chonan 337-795, Korea

Summary. In the present study we developed a domain-referenced test consisting of four subtests with the application of one parameter logistic model of item response theory. Some conditions are required: 10%-15% of the test takers pass the test given a cut-off score of 80% correct. Two of the four subtests satisfied the above requirements. One of the other two showed a passing ratio higher than specified. The other showed a low degree of classification consistency. In regards to validity, we attempted to secure content-related validity. Also there is an evidence of supporting construct-related validity. The correlations among the four subtests were small enough to show adequate discrimination of constructs.

Key words. domain-referenced test, item response theory, personnel selection, selection ratio, cut-off score

1. Introduction

The present study demonstrates a procedure for developing a domain-referenced test when a selection ratio and a cut-off score are given, which are usual conditions in personnel selection. There are several other names that have similar meanings to domain-referenced tests(cf. Anastasi & Urbina, 1997). When domain-referenced tests are applied in educational context where they were originated, the cut-off score is determined by considering the distribution of respondents' scores or the characteristics of items. When the domain-referenced testing is applied in personnel selection, however, the following conditions are often required: The selection ratio is predetermined and the cut-off score is given in the form of some percentages correct. The question is how to develop tests that satisfy such requirements. We applied one parameter model of item response theory(IRT) to solving this problem in developing a test, PSAT(Public Service Aptitude Test).

The purpose of PSAT is to dichotomize the test takers with a cut-off score of 80% correct measured by a composite score of four different subtests such as verbal, mathematics, situational judgement, and common sense(Central Committee of HRM-Korea, 2001). The problem is how to develop items given the selection ratio and cut-off score for the test.

2. Logic of Item Development

We will discuss two lines of logic in developing the items.

2.1 Correspondence between Ability Levels and Test Items

We need to relate the item difficulty with a certain level of test takers, called content-referencing(Mislevy & Bock, 1986). In order to do that the metric system of test-takers' ability should be in accord with that of item difficulty. While classical test theory cannot make the two metrics in accord with each other, item response theory can by relating the ability level of a certain test-taker to the difficulty level of items.

Before the IRT is applied to developing items for PSAT, one problem should be solved. Since PSAT has not been implemented yet, the distribution of the test-takers' scores is unknown. Thus we need to use a good educated guess in choosing a group of test takers whose ability level can be assumed to some degree. This group is a kind of bridge group. By fixing the location and dispersion parameters of the ability scale for the bridge group, the difficulty parameters of PSAT items can be estimated.

2.2 Relating the Cut-Off Score to Corresponding Items

In the IRT, the person parameter θ can be assumed to follow normal distribution with 0 of mean and 1 of standard deviation(e.g., Mislevy & Bock, 1986). PSAT should be designed so that 10-15% of test takers pass the test. If we assume that the ability of test takers follows the standardized normal distribution, the ability parameter values corresponding to upper 10% and 15% are $\theta_a=1.28$ and $\theta_b=1.04$, respectively from reading off the table of standardized normal distribution.

The question is how to develop items so that the last person passing the test shows 80% correct on the average. We need to develop items to which the applicants at θ_a or θ_b of ability level can provide true responses with the probability of 0.8. We would rather set the interval [0.7 0.9] instead of point estimate 0.8 as the range of probability of giving a true response to each item. We will apply one-parameter logistic model of IRT to this problem. The one-parameter logistic model can be shown as equation (1).

$$p = \frac{1}{1 + e^{-(\theta - b)}} \qquad (1)$$

In eq. (1), P stands for P(correct response$|\theta$), θ is the ability level of subjects, and b is the item difficulty. Once the values of P and θ are given as in the case of PSAT, b can be just-identified. However, if the two or three parameter model is used, the model is underidentified. Suppose we use the two parameter model, then we will have the slope parameter "a" in addition to the difficulty parameter "b", and the relationship between a and b will be obtained from the eq. (1). Neither a nor b is determined unless either one is fixed at a given value, which is not possible with our limited information. Thus, we can not use two-parameter model.

In the PSAT, P is [0.7 0.9] and θ is [1.04 1.28]. Computations of item difficulty b are followed.

$$\theta_a = 1.28, \ p = .7 \ \rightarrow b = .433$$
$$\theta_a = 1.28, \ p = .9 \ \rightarrow b = -.957$$
$$\theta_b = 1.04, \ p = .7 \ \rightarrow b = .193$$
$$\theta_b = 1.04, \ p = .9 \ \rightarrow b = -.1.157$$

The appropriate interval of item difficulties is determined as in eq. (2).

$$\text{Range of item difficulty} = [-1.157 \ 0.433] \tag{2}$$

The items resulting from the meeting of interval estimate of difficulty given in equation 2 are needed.

3. Quality of Items

3.1 Administration of tests

We developed two sets of items. The first set(test) was administered in July and the second set(test) in October to different groups. Each test was grouped into form A and form B which are parallel in their content and difficulty. Form A was administered to the test takers on the even numbered line and form B to those on the odd numbered line in the testing room. In order to link the test results administered in July and October, we constructed a bridge test including some items from the first test and the rest from the second test. We selected 20% of items from the form A of the 1st test and added them to the form B of the 2nd test. This mixture will be called a bridge test, which will be administered to a bridge group later. The numbers of participants are given in table 1.

Table 1. The number of participants

Category	first test	second test	bridge test
undergraduate students	215	366	
job incumbents*	100	54	
trainees**	220	203	
bridge group			603

*: People who are working in the government.
**: People who passed other selection test and are being trained before assignment to jobs.

3.2 Linking the scales of items

In order to put the two tests on one measurement scale we attempted to link the scales. The linking method we apply here is "equating" described in Mislevy(1992). We judged the students at E University and S University would be located at the middle level in the ability distribution of applicant population. They served as the bridge group in performing nonequivalent groups equating between form A of the first test and form A of the second test. We performed equivalent groups equating on alternate forms for each test. We administered the bridge test to the bridge group which was assigned 0 of mean and 1 of standard deviation for ability variable θ

3.3 Item Analysis

The number of items in the first and second tests are given in table 2.

Table 2. Number of Items in the Two Tests

Domains	Number of Items		Time
	1st test	2nd test	
Verbal Ability	30	30	120min
Quantitative Ability	30	30	together
Situational Judgement	30	30	120min together
Common Sense	30	50*	
Total	120 items	140 items	

* After the first test we found the length of common sense test should be increased to 50 items for the given time.

We used BILOG-MG(Zimowski, Muraki, Mislevy, & Bock, 1996) to analyze the data. The results of item analysis are shown only for the first 10 items in form A of the first test measuring verbal ability in table 3.

Table 3. Analysis and Selection of Items

	correct resp. ratio	point-biserial cor.	b*	1ˢᵗ screen	DIF	b	S.E.	lower limit	upper limit	screen by b	Chi-Sq.	prob.	model fit	Rate of items
1	0.96	0.19	-6.027	x										
2	0.74	0.22	-2.057			-1.171	0.292	-1.743	-0.599	O	8.3	0.401	V	A
3	0.73	0.28	-1.947			-1.070	0.292	-1.642	-0.498	O	6.7	0.467	V	A
4	0.75	0.29	-2.171			-1.275	0.299	-1.861	-0.689	O	1.1	0.991	V	A
5	0.77	0.44	-2.407			-1.596	0.209	-2.006	-1.186	X	11.3	0.078		B
6	0.99	0.17	-8.710	x										
7	0.34	0.34	1.290			1.893	0.279	1.346	2.440	X	7.9	0.341		
8	0.7	0.20	-1.682			-0.828	0.278	-1.373	-0.283	O	9.8	0.202	V	A
9	0.93	0.26	-5.210	x										
10	0.64	0.23	-1.188			-0.376	0.267	-0.899	0.147	O	6.8	0.564	V	A

X: discarded   O: selected   S.E.: standard error
b^*: item difficulty computed from this set of data only
 b: difficulty of items after the first and the second tests are equated.

In table 3, the column "correct response ratio" is the ratio of people who answered correct to each item. The column "point-biserial correlation" is the item-total correlation. The column "b^*" is the item difficulty computed for this set(first test, form A) of data before all the data sets are equated. The column "1ˢᵗ screen" shows the "X" marks meaning that they are inappropriate extreme items. The column "DIF" means that the items were evaluated whether they show differential functioning depending on the gender. This was examined by the option "DIF" in the BILOG-MG and no item turned out to be functioning differentially in the data above. The "b'" is the difficulty of items computed after all the data sets are equated. The 95% confidence interval for the item difficulty was obtained by subtracting and adding (1.96)•(S.E.) from and to the b. Depending on whether the interval between the lower and upper limits meets the interval estimate given in eq. (2), items are selected or discarded.

The O's in the column "screen by b" show items which difficulty levels are judged appropriate. Only for these items, goodness of fit to one parameter logistic model was tested. The results are given in the column "chi-sq", "prob.", and "model fit". If the probability that chi-square values are equal to or greater than the observed value is not extremely small, we judged the item fitting to the model and marked "V" in the column. The items that passed the screening by b and the test of model fit are rated "A" in the last column of table 3. We rated items "B" when they failed in the test of model fit, the interval estimate of the item difficulty is very close to but does not meet that of the desired level in eq. (2), or the correct response ratio, point-biserial correlation, and item difficulty b^* were not extreme enough to discard the item.

As a result of this procedure, we selected 60 items rated as "A" or "B" for each of the four domains: verbal ability, quantitative ability, situational judgement, common sense. These items comprise the developed test.

3.4 Satisfying the required conditions?

We are required that 10%-15% of the test takers get 80% correct or higher. The ratio of test takers who scored equal to or higher than 80% correct are given in Table 4.

Table 4. The % of test takers who scored 80% correct or higher

Domains	First-form A	First-form B	Second-form A	Second-form B	median
Verbal Aability	11.48 (N=183)	18.01 (N=161)	10.86 (N=221)	13.22 (N=227)	12.35
Situational Judgement	6.42 (N=187)	4.76 (N=168)	11.11 (N=216)	26.70 (N=236)	8.77
Quantative Ability	3.87 (N=181)	8.28 (N=157)	10.55 (N=218)	16.97 (N=218)	9.42
Common Sense	22.16 (N=194)	24.57 (N=175)	37.91 (N=211)	33.33 (N=216)	28.95

The medians for three domains except for common sense were close to or within the required 10%-15%, which is satisfactory.

4. Reliability and Validity of the Developed Test

4.1 Reliability

The selected items are part of the original items. Since the PSAT will be used as a domain-referenced testing, the concept of reliability is different from that in norm-referenced testing(Traub & Rowley, 1980). In the norm-referenced testing reliability is defined based on variance, but it is based on decision making in the domain-referenced testing.

The consistency of classifying test takers into pass and failure will be another index of reliability. Test takers who scored 80% correct or higher will be classified into "pass" and the rest into "failure". It is our concern whether two alternate forms produce the same classification(i.e., pass or failure). In order to check the consistency of classification we need a group of test takers who participated in both form A and B. There was none in the first test. There were some who participated in both the forms in the second test. The ratio of classification consistency for these are given in table 5.

Table 5. Ratio of Classification Consistency

	Verbal Ability	Situational Judgement	Quantitative Ability	Common Sense
N	59	45	52	57
Classification consistency	84%	60%	92%	81%

The classification consistency is somewhat low for the domain of situational judgement and reasonably high for other domains.

4.2 Validity

In a domain-referenced test, content-related validity is considered more important than any other evidence of validity, although it is difficult to quantify. We employed a strategy to improve the content validity. That is, many areas are picked up for writing texts and various types were used for asking questions.

Once the content validity is secured to some degree, we are interested in the construct-related validity and criterion-related validity. Since our present task is to develop items, we are more interested in the construct-related validity such as convergence and divergence of the four domains. The criterion-related validity will be examined in the future studies where the tests are applied to the incumbents or real applicants for government jobs.

In order to examine the divergence of the four tests, we present table 6.

Table 6. Correlations among the Four Subtests

	Verbal Ability	Situational Judgement	Quantitative Ability 3	Common Sense
Verbal Ability	1.00			
Situational Judgement	.24	1.00		
Quantitative Ability	.17	.18	1.00	
Common Sense	.21	.16	.14	1.00

Sizes of correlations in table 6 are small enough to support the divergence or discriminant validity of the four tests. It is notable to see that the correlation between verbal ability and the quantitative ability is somewhat lower compared with .4~.6 range typically found(see, Carroll, 1993). It is because only a selected group of high intelligence candidates apply for managerial jobs in government for which our tests were developed and will be used.

5. Conclusion

It is encouraging that IRT can be applied to developing a domain-referenced test given a selection ratio and cut-off score. The developed test satisfied the requirements: 10%-15% of test takers obtain a score of 80% correct. In regards to reliability three out of the four subtests showed a good degree of classification consistency. In regards to validity, we attempted to secure content-related validity and to show divergence of four tests as part of construct validity. The correlations among the four subtests were small enough to show that they are discriminated from each other.

Although the reliability of the four tests was not perfect, the tests were reliable to some degree. To improve the reliability of this type of test, it is necessary to have items converging in a given domain and to have alternate forms of parallel characteristics. In order to examine the criterion-related validity, we need to administer the developed test to the incumbents or real applicants for government jobs.

References

Anastasi, A & Urbina, S (1997) Psychological Testing(7th Ed.). Upper Saddle River, NJ: Prentice Hall.

Carroll, JB (1993) Human Cognitive Abilities: A survey of factor-analytic studies. New York, NY: Cambridge University Press.

Central Committee of HRM-Korea (2001) Request of Proposals for Developing a Public Service Aptitude Test. Seoul, Korea: Author.

Graham, D & Berquist, C (1975) An examination of criterion-referenced test characteristics in relation to assumptions about the nature of achievement variables. Paper presented at the annual meeting of the AERA, Washington.

Mislevy, RJ (1992) Linking educational assessment: Concept, issues, methods, and prospects. Princeton, NJ: Educational Testing Service.

Mislevy, RJ & Bock, RD (1986) PC-BILOG: User's Guide. Mooresville, IN: Scientific Software.

Traub, RE & Rowley, GL (1980) Reliability of test scores and decisions. Applied Psychological Measurement. 4, 517-546.

Zimowski, MF, Muraki, E, Mislevy, RJ, & Bock, RD (1996) BILOG-MG. Chicago, IL: Scientific Software.

Investigating Cross-Cultural Differences in Crying Using Manifest Invariant Item Ordering

L. Andries van der Ark[1] and Mark H. P. van Diem[2]

[1] Department of Methodology and Statistics, Tilburg University, P.O. Box 90153, 5000 LE, Tilburg, The Netherlands *a.vdark@uvt.nl*
[2] SPITS, Tilburg University, P.O. Box 90153, 5000 LE, Tilburg, The Netherlands *m.h.p.vdiem@uvt.nl*

Summary. In this paper we use *manifest invariant item ordering* to investigate cross-cultural differences in crying; that is, we distinguish several determinants of crying and compare their ordering in importance of crying eliciting behavior among different cultures. Each determinant of crying is measured by several items. Three methods are proposed which can be used to compare the orderings of the determinants: graphical devices, a concordance statistic, and a statistical test. The methods are illustrated by an empirical example.

Key words: Cross-cultural differences, crying, invariant item ordering, manifest invariant item ordering, psychological testing

1 Introduction

In this paper we discuss statistical methods for the investigation of cross-cultural differences in crying. Vingerhoets and Cornelius (1990) gave an overview of the current knowledge of crying and they provided a framework to investigate the relationships between crying and various psychological, demographical, cultural, and health-related variables. An important source of information was the Adult Crying Inventory (ACI; Vingerhoets and Cornelius, 1990, Appendix). This questionnaire contains 54 items. Each item describes a situation in which one might cry; for example, Item 20 is

Never   Always

I cry at weddings   1 2 3 4 5 6 7

The respondents were instructed to indicate how often they cry in the given situation, yielding ordinal item scores ranging from 1 (*never*) to 7 (*always*). Also, the ACI contained information about age, gender, level of education, and general crying tendencies.

The ACI was completed by 3896 respondents from 30 countries, so that the data enable the investigation of cross-cultural differences in crying. However, several reservations should be made. First, we assumed that there are no cultural differences within countries. This is disputable for multicultural countries, such as the USA and India. Second, Becht (1999) found indications that for several countries the quality of the responses was bad. Third, most important, there was no ready-made statistical method to evaluate cross-cultural differences. The ACI data have been analyzed before to find the dimensional structure of crying (Scheirs and Sijtsma, 2001), and to impute missing responses (Van Diem, 2002).

It may be noted that "cross-cultural difference in crying" has two meanings. First, it is the difference in a general tendency to cry (people in some cultures cry more often than people in other cultures). Second, it is the difference in order in which *determinants* elicit crying (e.g., in some cultures sad stories easily elicit crying and happy stories do not, while in other cultures happy stories easily elicit crying and sad stories do not). We will focus on the second meaning.

In general, we consider J items with $m+1$ ordered answer categories. The response to Item j is denoted X_j and its realization $x_j, x_j \in \{0, 1, \ldots, m\}$. The J items represent D determinants of crying. The response to Determinant d is denoted Y_d. If Determinant d is represented by a single Item j, then $Y_d = X_j$; if Determinant d is represented by a subset of items, then Y_d is the mean item score. The *attractiveness* or popularity of a determinant is defined as $E(Y_d)$ (cf. Sijtsma and Hemker, 1998, Definition). If $E(Y_c) > E(Y_d)$ then Determinant c is more attractive (elicits crying more easily) than Determinant d. A discrete variable G with K categories, generally referred to as K *groups*, is used to distinguish the K different cultures/ countries.

Using this notation, cross-cultural differences in crying can be evaluated as follows: Order and number the determinants such that for Group k,

$$E(Y_1|G = k) \leq E(Y_2|G = k) \leq \ldots \leq E(Y_D|G = k).$$

If for Group k',

$$E(Y_1|G = k') \leq E(Y_2|G = k') \leq \ldots \leq E(Y_D|G = k'), \tag{1}$$

then the determinants have the same order of attractiveness for the two groups k and k' and the hypothesis is supported that there are no cross-cultural differences in the relative importance of the determinants of crying. If Equation 1 is violated, so that the determinants do not have the same order of attractiveness for the two groups k and k', then the hypothesis is supported that there are cross-cultural differences in the relative importance of the determinants of crying.

2 Manifest Invariant Item Ordering

We formulated the hypothesis of no cultural differences in (1) such that it corresponds to *manifest invariant item ordering* (Van der Ark, 2002), which was proposed as a method to study *invariant item ordering* (IIO; Sijtsma and Hemker, 1998; Sijtsma and Junker, 1996). For a discrete variable G with

K categories, a set of items has an MIIO if the items can be ordered and numbered such that

$$E(X_1|G = k) \leq E(X_2|G = k) \leq \ldots \leq E(X_J|G = k), \text{ for } k = 1, \ldots, K. \quad (2)$$

For comparing cross-cultural differences in the determinants of crying we use MIIO, in the sense that we investigate the inequalities in (2) but replace item scores X_j by determinant scores Y_d. Although we use determinants rather than items we keep the abbreviation MIIO.

As an example, consider Table 1 where for $D = 4$ determinants and $G = 3$ groups, the numerical values of $E(Y_d)$ and $E(Y_d|G = k)$ are given. The determinants in Table 1 are ordered by $E(Y_d)$ and from the values of $E(Y_d|G = k)$ in the table, it is easily checked that MIIO is violated.

Table 1. Small data set violating MIIO

Expected value	Determinant			
	1	2	3	4
$E(Y_d|G = 1)$	0.1	0.4	0.8	1.0
$E(Y_d|G = 2)$	0.2	0.3	0.6	0.4
$E(Y_d|G = 3)$	0.3	0.5	0.4	1.0
$E(Y_d)$	0.2	0.4	0.6	0.8

2.1 Graphical Devices

Verweij, Sijtsma, and Koops (1999) studied the order of conditional expected item scores as expressed by (2). Using tables similar to Table 1 they visually investigated differences in expected item scores between boys and girls. We use graphs to facilitate a visual investigation of differences in expected item scores or determinant scores between groups. The data in Table 1 are used to construct the graphs.

In Figure 1 (left panel), the four determinants are on the horizontal axis and the values of $E(Y_d|G = k)$ are on the vertical axis. In the graph, $E(Y_1|G = k), \ldots, E(Y_4|G = k)$ are depicted and connected by line segments (for $k = 1, 2, 3$), yielding one line for each group. The dashed line connects $E(Y_1), \ldots, E(Y_4)$. A decrease indicates that for a group the order of the attractiveness of the determinants differs from the order in the total group.

Figure 1 (right panel) is slightly different. Here, the three groups are on the horizontal axis. In the graph, $E(Y_d|G = 1), \ldots, E(Y_d|G = 3)$ for all d are depicted and connected by line segments, yielding one line for each determinant. In this graph, an intersection of two lines indicates that the corresponding determinants have not the same order of attractiveness for the groups on both sides of the intersection. This graph shows that one determinant (Determinant 3, see Table 1) causes the violations of MIIO.

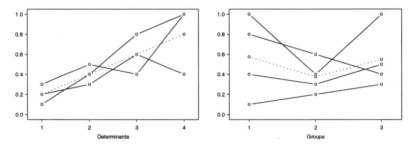

Fig. 1. Two examples of a graphical device to study MIIO

2.2 Measuring Concordance

Kendall's W (see, e.g., Siegel, 1956) can be used to summarize the degree of concordance in the ordering of the D determinants among the K groups into a single statistic. Standard software, such as SPSS can be used to compute W. Kendall's W ranges from 0 (random item ordering) to 1 (complete agreement in item ordering). Thus, high values of W indicate that MIIO holds, which means no cross-cultural differences in crying. Small values of W indicate that MIIO does not hold, supporting the hypothesis of cross-cultural differences in crying. The null hypothesis of no concordance can be tested using Friedman's statistic $Q = K(D-1)W$. Q has an approximate χ^2 distribution with $D-1$ degrees of freedom for $D \geq 7$ and Q is tabulated for $D < 7$. Unfortunately, for testing whether or not MIIO holds, the null hypothesis of complete concordance is appropriate. However, not being able to reject the null hypothesis of no concordance is a strong indication that MIIO does not hold. We advocate to use W as a heuristic device only to compare concordance in item ordering among groups. For the data in Table 1, $W = 0.78$, indicating a fairly strong concordance.

2.3 Testing Ordered Clusters

For each group k, the D determinants can be classified into $I(k)$ mutually exclusive clusters of determinants $C_1^k, \ldots, C_{I(k)}^k$, with $1 \leq I(k) \leq D$. Let Cluster C_i^k contain s determinants. The average value of the expected determinant scores in Cluster C_i^k is

$$E(C_i^k) = \frac{\sum\limits_{d \in C_i^k} E(Y_d | G = k)}{s}.$$

For each group k, *ordered clusters* are clusters of determinants, containing as few determinants as possible with restriction

$$E(C_1^k) \le E(C_2^k) \le \ldots \le E(C_{I(k)}^k).$$

In Table 1, Group $G = 1$ has four ordered clusters, each containing one determinant; Group $G = 2$ has three ordered clusters $C_1^2 = \{\text{Determinant 1}\}$, $C_2^2 = \{\text{Determinant 2}\}$, and $C_3^2 = \{\text{Determinant 3}, \text{Determinant 4}\}$; and Group $G = 3$ also has three ordered clusters $C_1^3 = \{\text{Determinant 1}\}$, $C_2^3 = \{\text{Determinant 2, Determinant 3}\}$, and $C_3^3 = \{\text{Determinant 4}\}$. Within ordered clusters MIIO is violated but between ordered clusters MIIO is not violated. MIIO cannot be rejected if the differences in expected values of the determinants within an ordered cluster are due to random fluctuation.

We need some statistic to test whether or not the difference between the largest expected determinant score and the smallest expected determinant score within the same cluster can be attributed to random fluctuation; that is, we tested

$$H_0 : \max \left[E(Y_d | G = k, d \in C_i^k) \right] = \min \left[E(Y_d | G = k, d \in C_i^k) \right] \quad (3)$$

against the alternative that the equality in (3) does not hold. For Table 1 this means testing two null hypotheses $H_0 : E(Y_2 | G = 2) = E(Y_3 | G = 2)$ and $H_0 : E(Y_3 | G = 3) = E(Y_4 | G = 3)$.

The two expected values in (3) come from the same sample. Therefore, a pairwise test is appropriate. We reported both the pairwise t-test and signed rank test (one-sided).

A possible problem is the nominal level of the Type I error rate. In other situations where multiple hypotheses are tested simultaneously it is common practice to correct for the number of hypotheses (Bonferroni correction). However, the determinants are correlated ($.23 \le r \le .65$) and this makes a Bonferroni too conservative and it may unjustly benefit the search for common cultures of crying. As a compromise we chose a linear penalty to correct for multiple hypothesis by dividing $\alpha = .05$ by the number of hypotheses tested per group.

3 Investigating Cultural Differences

Before we applied the above methods to investigate cross-cultural differences in crying, we deleted seven countries with bad quality responses (see, Becht, 1999) from the ACI data. Also, we used Mokken scale analysis (Molenaar and Sijtsma, 2000; Sijtsma and Molenaar, 2002) to select items that are fairly strongly scalable (i.e., $H > 0.4$), yielding seven scales, which we labelled *fear, threatening, and sadness* (FEAR, 23 items), *movies, tv, and books* (MOVI, 4 items), *physical pain* (PAIN, 2 items), *social crying* (SOCI, 4 items), *happiness* (HAPP, 4 items), *national pride* (NAPR, 2 items), and *beautiful experiences* (BEAU, 3 items). The remaining 11 items were not scalable and were deleted from the analyses. The seven scales were used as the determinants of crying.

Because the data analysis is meant to illustrate the methods of investigating MIIO, we restrict ourselves to the investigation of cross-cultural differences within southern European countries (Spain, Greece, Italy, and Portugal) and differences within African countries (Ghana, Kenya, and Nigeria). The expected values are given in Table 2 and the graphical representation in Figure 2, where a decrease indicates a violation of MIIO (cf. Figure 1 [right panel]). Figure 2 shows that the order of the determinants of crying is similar for the African countries; the only deviations are for Ghana, where the order is reversed for NAPR and HAPP and also for MOVI, SOCI, and FEAR. Kendall's $W = .92$, indicating a strong concordance of determinants of crying. All the southern European countries have a different ordering of the determinants. Kendall's $W = .85$, indicating a little less strong concordance of determinants of crying. For all seven countries, $W = .74$, indicating concordance in determinants of crying, yet also some cross-cultural difference between the southern European countries and the African countries.

Table 2. Determinants of crying for several countries

	NAPR	BEAU	HAPP	SOCI	PAIN	MOVI	FEAR
Spain	1.64	2.51	2.64	*2.94*	*2.70*	*3.67*	*3.28*
Greece	*1.90*	*1.80*	2.40	2.92	2.97	3.01	3.25
Italy	1.52	2.56	*2.62*	*2.45*	2.64	2.96	3.22
Portugal	*1.80*	*1.79*	2.41	2.50	*2.73*	*2.56*	*2.70*
Europe	**1.72**	**2.14**	**2.51**	**2.69**	**2.76**	**3.01**	**3.10**

	BEAU	NAPR	HAPP	MOVI	FEAR	SOCI	PAIN
Ghana	1.89	*2.66*	*2.24*	*3.12*	*2.83*	*3.09*	3.17
Kenya	1.77	2.18	2.47	3.05	*3.51*	*3.49*	4.05
Nigeria	1.98	2.34	2.45	2.81	3.15	3.17	3.58
Africa	**1.86**	**2.36**	**2.40**	**3.03**	**3.22**	**3.29**	**3.67**

	NAPR	BEAU	HAPP	SOCI	MOVI	FEAR	PAIN
Total	**2.00**	**2.02**	**2.46**	**2.96**	**3.01**	**3.15**	**3.17**

In Table 2 the numbers in italics are determinants that violated MIIO, where the target ordering is determined by the ordering of the southern European countries or the African countries. For the southern European countries there are six ordered clusters with more than one determinant and for the

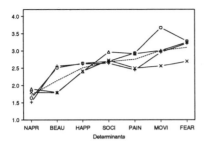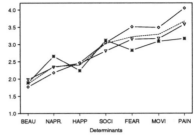

Fig. 2. Graphical display of the order of determinants of crying for four southern European countries (left panel; Spain = ○; Greece = △; Italy = +; Portugal =×) and three African countries (right panel; Ghana = *; Kenya = ◇; Nigeria = ▽)

African countries there are three ordered clusters with more than one determinant. For the southern European countries, the only violation of MIIO that could not be attributed to random fluctuation was the reversed order of MOVI and FEAR in Spain ($T = -3.18, df = 100, p = .002; Z = -2.60; p = .009$). For the African countries, the only violation of MIIO that could not be attributed to random fluctuation was the reversed order of HAPP and NAPR in Ghana ($T = -3.38, df = 102, p = .001; Z = -3.60; p = .000$). Besides these differences, the order of attractiveness within the southern European countries and within the African countries is similar. However, the assumption that the order of determinants of crying is the same for the southern European countries and the African countries is untenable. For several ordered clusters the violations of MIIO could not be attributed to random fluctuation. Also, $E(Y_d|\text{Africa}) > E(Y_d|\text{southern Europe})$ for all determinants except BEAU.

4 Discussion

In this paper we reviewed three methods for the analysis of cross-cultural differences in crying. All methods are based on the inequalities of MIIO in (2). The first two methods, visual inspection of graphs and Kendall's W are heuristic devices; the third method, testing ordered clusters, was set up as a formal method. However, several issues are unsolved. First, the tests proposed are not really suited for ordinal data; this will be a problem when the determinants have a few categories only. Second, the null hypothesis in (3) may be replaced by a more general null hypothesis where the expected determinant scores of all items in the ordered clusters are equal. Currently, these matters are under investigation. Until this is solved the method of testing ordered clusters should be treated as a heuristic device.

Nevertheless, the three methods were useful for the investigation of cross-cultural differences in crying. All three methods pointed out that within the southern European countries and within the African countries the order of attractiveness is fairly homogeneous. Moreover, the graphical devices and the testing of ordered clusters indicated where the violations of MIIO occurred.

A related topic that is investigated at this moment is the construction of scales with determinants that have an invariant ordering for all groups. The idea is to create determinants consisting of a set of items that are strongly scalable in a first step and delete the items that cause the violation of MIIO in a second step. Side conditions, such as the scalability of the items, and the number of items in a scale will be incorporated.

References

Becht MC (1999) Crying acros countries: A comparative study of the tendency and frequency of crying in 35 countries. Tilburg University, The Netherlands

Molenaar IW, Sijtsma K (2000) MSP5 for Windows [Software manual]. iec ProGAMMA, Groningen The Netherlands

Scheirs JGM, Sijtsma K (2001) The study of crying: Some methodological considerations and a comparison of methods for analyzing questionnaires. In: Vingerhoets AJJM, Cornelius RR (eds) Adult Crying. A Biopsychosocial Approach, pp 277–298 Brunner-Routledge, Hove England

Siegel S (1956) Nonparametric Statistics for the Behavioral Sciences. McGraw-Hill, New York

Sijtsma K, Hemker BT (1998) Nonparametric polytomous IRT models for invariant item ordering, with results for parametric models. Psychometrika 63:183–200

Sijtsma K, Junker BW (1996) A survey of theory and methods of invariant item ordering. Brit J Math Stat Psychol 49:79–105

Sijtsma K, Molenaar IW (2002) Introduction to Nonparametric Item Reponse Theory. Sage, Thousand Oaks CA

Van der Ark LA (2002) Investigating invariant item orderings in test data. Paper presented at the 23rd Meeting of the Society for the Multivariate Analysis in the Behavioral Sciences, Tilburg, The Netherlands.

Van Diem MHP (2002) Investigating invariant item ordering. Tilburg University, The Netherlands.

Verweij AC, Sijtsma K, Koops W (1999) An ordinal scale for transitive reasoning by means of a deductive strategy. Int J Behav Develop 23:241–264

Vingerhoets AJJM, Cornelius RR (2001) Adult Crying. A Biopsychosocial Approach. Brunner-Routledge, Hove England

Bayesian Regressions for Cross-Validation: An Application

Aye Aye Myint[1], Hidetoki Ishii[2], and Hiroshi Watanabe[3]

[1]Department of Educational Psychology, Yangon Institute of Education, Pyay Road, Kamayut Township, Yangon, Myanmar
[2]Research Division, National Center for University Entrance Examinations, 2-19-23 Komaba, Meguro-ku, Tokyo 153-8501, Japan
[3]Department of Educational Psychology, Graduate School of Education, The University of Tokyo, 7-3-1 Hongo, Bunkyo-Ku, Tokyo 113-0033, Japan

Summary. It should be noticed that the traditional correlation analysis for investigating the validity of a psychological test is often insufficient because the correlation coefficient is usually obtained by maximizing the likelihood, which is derived from the given data set. Furthermore, a simple correlation makes no sense when the criterion variable is not completely the same among the several groups of subjects. In this paper, a Bayesian cross-validation using hierarchical regression model is considered. In order to investigate the predictive effectiveness of a test, the method of deriving the cross-validity index is considered. A practical application to the Numerical Reasoning Ability Test for Myanmar high school students is also shown, which contains the scores of school subject tests as the criterion variable. Then, it is found that the cross-validity index is useful because it indicates the predictive effectiveness of the NRT to the various school subject tests.

Key words. Bayesian regression, hierarchical structure, cross-validity index

1 Introduction

It has been well recognized among the psychometricians that the statistical investigation for the validity of a psychological test is inevitably important for the practical uses of the test. It should be noted, however, that the traditional correlation analyses for the investigation are often insufficient because the correlation coefficient, so-called the validity coefficient, is usually obtained by maximizing the likelihood, which does not take into account the real world complex situation. Furthermore, a simple correlation coefficient makes no sense when the scores of school subject tests obtained from different schools should be used as the criterion variable.

With these regards, we consider a cross-validation technique using a Bayesian regression method with hierarchical structure, when the criterion variable is not identical through groups, such as schools. Recently, Bayesian hierarchical models are used in a large number of studies. In this study, we use a Bayesian hierarchical model to make a cross-validation when a common criterion measure cannot be adopted through each group.

The data of each group are divided into two parts; one is for the regression analysis, and the other is for validation. This technique is well known as the cross-validation. The usefulness and importance of the cross-validation technique has already been well known among statisticians. Then, a Bayesian method for estimating regressions in *m* groups (Lindley 1969; Jackson et al. 1971; Novick et al. 1972; Watanabe 1999) is used for the regression analysis. In the method, it is assumed that the parameters for each group are exchangeable at the identical distribution, and so regression parameters are naturally and easily estimated for each group (Gelman et al. 1995). Therefore, the cross-validation coefficients for each group could be easily estimated and integrated into a cross-validation index after the regression analysis.

As a practical application, the Bayesian cross-validation analysis is applied to the real data obtained from the newly developed Numerical Reasoning Ability Test (NRT) for Myanmar high school students. The school subjects' scores on monthly tests should be used as the criterion variable for the cross-validation. Depending on the school's situations, there are some differences in the test contents and the time and frequency of monthly test administrations among the schools and so the teacher-made tests are not the same in different schools. Accordingly, the monthly test scores of school subjects cannot be considered as a pool of data to make the conventional validation study by the traditional regression procedure. However, by taking account of measuring a common trait by the school tests of the same subject, the Bayesian regression for cross-validation mentioned above is applicable to estimate the parameters of each school and to estimate a cross-validation index (Aye 2001).

2 Bayesian Regressions for cross-validation

Let Y_{ij} denote a criterion variable of observation i in group j. The Y_{ij} do not have to be identical through groups, but have to be predicted by a common explanatory variable, for example, the scores of the school subject test obtained from different schools. Although the school subject tests are not identical through schools, the scores would be predicted by ability scores on a common trait which relates to the subject. Then, let x_{ij} denote the scores on the common trait of observation i in group j, and let the regression model be,

$$Y_{ij} = \alpha_j + \beta_j x_{ij} + e_{ij}, \quad i=1,2,...,n_j, \; j=1,2,...,m \tag{1}$$

where n_j is the number of observations in the jth group and m is the number of groups. Error e_{ij} is assumed to be mutually independent and normally distributed with mean 0 and variance σ_j^2.

To conduct the cross-validation, observations in each group should be divided into two subgroups, named as subgroup 1 and subgroup 2. Using the scores of subgroup 1 in each group, the regression parameters and error variances for each group, α_j, β_j and σ_j^2, are estimated. Lindley (1969) proposes a Bayesian method for the simultaneous estimation of regression lines in m groups, so called the Lindley equations. If both α_j and β_j have normal prior distributions and σ_j^2 has an inverted-chi-square prior distribution, the posterior modes of the parameters are simultaneously estimated by iteratively solving the equations.

The cross-validation correlation coefficients for each group are obtained as follow. On predicting the criterion variable Y from an explanatory variable X, the standard error of the prediction is obtained as $\sigma_e = \sigma_y \sqrt{1 - r^2}$, where r is the correlation coefficient between X and Y. From this fact, the cross-validation correlation coefficient for each group, which is denoted by $\hat{r}_j$, is estimated as,

$$\hat{r}_j = \text{sgn}(\hat{\beta}_j) \sqrt{1 - \frac{\hat{\sigma}_{ej}^2}{\sigma_{yj*}^2}}, \tag{2}$$

where

$$\sigma_{yj*}^2 = \frac{1}{n_j} \sum_i (y_{ij}^* - \bar{y}_j^*)^2, \tag{3}$$

$$\hat{\sigma}_{ej}^2 = \frac{1}{n_j} \sum_i (e_{ij}^* - \bar{e}_j^*)^2, \tag{4}$$

$$e_{ij}^* = y_{ij}^* - \hat{y}_{ij}^*$$
$$= y_{ij}^* - (\hat{\alpha}_j + \hat{\beta}_j x_{ij}^*), \, i = 1, 2, ..., n, \tag{5}$$

and $\text{sgn}(\hat{\beta}_j)$ indicates the sign of $\hat{\beta}_j$. Here, $\hat{\alpha}_j$ and $\hat{\beta}_j$ are the regression parameters estimated by the Bayesian method using the data set of subgroup 1. The y_{ij}^* is the test scores of observations of subgroup 2, and the $\hat{y}_{ij}^*$ is the predicted test scores by substituting the regression coefficients $\hat{\alpha}_j$ and $\hat{\beta}_j$ of subgroup 1 into the regression equations for subgroup 2.

Finally, the cross-validity index is defined by the average of $\hat{r}_j$'s. The cross-validity index could be considered to represent the integrated efficacy of prediction of the explanatory variable for the criterion variable.

3 An application procedure

In this section, an application procedure of the Bayesian cross-validation method to a practical study (Aye 2001) is shown. The results are shown in the next section. The data is obtained from 10 high schools in Union of Myanmar. The scores of monthly school subject test in each school are used as the criterion variable, and the ability scores estimated by the newly developed Numerical Reasoning Ability Test (NRT) is used as the explanatory variable. No other adequate criterion variable can be found for the newly developed test. The cross-validation procedure is as follow. Since the monthly school subject tests are developed by the high school teachers who are not so familiar with the test theory, the reliabilities and validities are considered firstly.

Procedure:

1. Standardize each monthly school subject test score by each school, that is, set the mean of a monthly test scores in a school equal to 0 and the standard deviation equal to 1. Calculate the Cronbach's alpha coefficient when several monthly tests in a school are combined, and find the most reliable set of monthly tests by each school. Then, the subject test score is composed by averaging the scores of the most reliable set of the standardized monthly school subject tests.

2. For deleting unreliable tests, the composed tests having less than 0.65 of alpha coefficients are not taken into account as the criterion variables, and are eliminated from this analysis.

3. To delete the invalid tests, the coincidence validity coefficients, that is, the correlation coefficients among certain subject test, are examined. In this case, the correlation coefficients between mathematics and natural science by each school are investigated. If the coefficient is less than 0.3, the test should not be taken into account.

4. To avoid the effect of selection, floor, and ceiling, the standard deviations of the subject test scores are checked, and if a standard deviation is too small, the test of the school is omitted.

In accordance with steps 1 to 4, the data obtained from 4 or 5 schools are selected for the cross-validation analysis. The number of students in each school and the Cronbach's alpha coefficients of monthly school subject tests are shown in **Table 1**. The procedure continues as follow:

5. So as to conduct the validation study, the NRT ability estimates are used as the explanatory variable, and the subject test scores composed in step 1 are used as the criterion variables.

Table 1. Cronbach's Alpha Coefficients within the Monthly School Subject Test and Correlation Coefficients with the Numerical Reasoning Ability Test for the Selected Schools

Subject	School Number	The Number of Students	Cronbach's Alpha Coefficients	Correlation Coefficients
Mathematics	3	58	0.84	0.18
	4	60	0.82	0.31
	5	39	0.79	0.16
	7	137	0.69	0.32
Natural Science	3	58	0.70	0.25
	4	60	0.72	0.47
	5	39	0.69	0.50
	7	137	0.79	0.34
	10	116	0.75	0.20

6. To check and omit the outliers, the method of leverage is used. After eliminating outliers, correlation coefficients between the ability estimates and the composed subject test scores are calculated.

The correlation coefficients are also shown in the last column of **Table1**. It is found that the correlation coefficients with numerical reasoning ability ranges from 0.18 to 0.50.

7. To conduct a cross-validation, subjects in each school would be randomly divided into the two subgroups, subgroup1 and subgroup 2,. The matched subset method is used to construct the random division. When considering the cross-validation between mathematics scores and the NRT ability estimates, the other remaining test scores of four school subjects, Myanmar language, natural science, social science and English, are matched and randomly divided into two subsamples.

8. The data of subgroup 1 in each school are used to obtain the Bayesian estimates of the parameters α_j, β_j, and σ_j^2. Using these estimates and the data of subgroup 2 in each school, the cross-validation correlation coefficient, $\hat{r}_j$, are estimated for each school.

9. Since these estimates may depend on the division of the data, it had better to repeat the random division and consider the distribution of estimates for each parameter. Then, by repeating the process of step 7 to step 8 for 48 times, the

distribution of $\hat{r}_j$ is obtained for each school, and the median of $\hat{r}_j$ should be adopted as a cross-validation correlation coefficient for the school.

10. Finally, the cross-validity index is defined by taking the median of the cross-validation correlation coefficient for each school. For the NRT, two cross validity indices would be obtained, that is, index with mathematics and with natural science.

4 Result

The results of the cross validation analyses with the procedures mentioned above are shown in **Table 2**. It displays the medians of the distributions of the cross-validity indices and their ranges.

It is reported that the cross-validity indices are about 0.3 for the numerical reasoning ability to mathematics and natural science. Then, it can be said that about or over the 10% of the variances in subject test scores are explained by the NRT ability estimates. We might therefore conclude that prediction effectiveness of the NRT is acceptable and satisfactory to some extent, based on the consideration that the monthly school subject test made by school teachers do not possess so high reliabilities and validities.

Table 2. Cross-validity index of the NRT to monthly school subject tests

Predictor Variables	School Subjects	Median	Range
NRT	Mathematics	0.25	0.14
	Natural Science	0.32	0.31

5 Discussion

It should be emphasized that the simple correlation coefficients are not useful to investigate the degrees of statistical validity when the school subject tests are not the same across the schools. On the other hand, the cross validity index defined in this study can be thought to be a useful index, because it indicates the integrated predictive effectiveness of a common explanatory variable to the criterion variable which is not identical through several groups.

The main advantages of the cross-validation is the following:

If a fairly high value of the cross-validation coefficient is obtained, it means that the result from one sample is similar to that from another sample. It in turn suggests the generalizability of the validity to another samples.

In addition to this fact, the Bayesian regressions for cross-validation conducted in this study contains more advantages:

1. The contents of the school subject tests whose scores are used as a criterion variable in the model can vary among the schools, and also among the semesters. If only the simple correlation coefficient is applied to each set of a criterion variable and a predictor variable under such a situation, it would be very difficult to interpret the individual results.

2. The cross-validity index developed in our study indicates the integrated predictive efficiency of a common explanatory variable to the criterion variable which is not identical through several groups but predicted by the common variable. By using the index as a cross-validity coefficient, a consistent and integrated interpretation could be conducted.

Furthermore, we show a practical application of the cross-validation method. When there is no common criterion variable or there is not a well composed measure for a criterion, the application procedure could be refered.

References

Aye Aye Myint (2001) Development of the numerical reasoning ability test and the vocabulary comprehension test for Myanmar high school students. Ph.D thesis. Graduate School of Education, University of Tokyo, Japan

Gelman A, Carlin JB, Stern HS, Rubin DB (1995) Bayesian data analysis. Chapman & Hall.

Jackson PH, Novick MR, Thayer DT (1971) Estimating regressions in m groups. Brit J Math Stat Psychol 24: 129-153

Lindley DV (1969) A Bayesian solution for some educational prediction problems: II. Res. Bulletin, Princeton, NJ: Educational Testing Service, pp 69-91

Novick MR, Jackson PH, Thayer DT, Cole NS (1972) Estimating multiple regressions in m groups: A cross-validation study. Brit J Math Stat Psychol 25: 33-50

Watanabe H (1999) Introduction to Bayesian statistics (in Japanese). Tokyo: Fukumura (in Japanese)

Validity and Truth

Denny Borsboom Jaap van Heerden Gideon J. Mellenbergh

Department of Psychology, University of Amsterdam
ml_borsboom.d@macmail.psy.uva.nl

Summary. This paper analyzes the semantics of test validity. First, a simple definition of validity is given: Test X is valid for the measurement of attribute Y, if and only if the proposition 'Scores on test X measure attribute Y' is true. We analyze the meaning of validity by examining the truth conditions of the proposition. These truth conditions depend on the interpretation of the term 'measures'. Three measurement systems that may provide such an interpretation are examined: Fundamental measurement theory, classical test theory, and latent variable theory. It is argued that the semantics of validity depend on the choice of measurement system. Because there is no logically or empirically compelling argument for or against any particular theory, the meaning of validity is to a certain extent indeterminate.

Key words: validity, truth, measurement, semantics, psychometrics

1 Introduction

Test validity is related to methodological aspects of test construction, psychometric properties of tests scores, philosophical perspectives on psychological constructs, as well as various legal and ethical issues surrounding test use. In view of the fact that validity is connected to so many questions from so many disciplines, it is no surprise that presently endorsed conceptualizations of validity (Messick, 1989) have come to cover virtually every aspect one could possibly imagine to be related to psychological testing.

If one insists on addressing all these matters by a single term, extending the scope of the validity concept in order to cover such diverse topics is not only understandable, but necessary. However, the problem with using validity as an umbrella term is that the meaning of the concept becomes clouded. And, in our view, the broadening of the validity concept in recent theoretical developments has not lead to a clear articulation of the semantics of validity. This is to say that a very basic question, namely 'what does it mean for a test to be valid' has received little attention, especially in comparison to epistemological ('how can we know that a test is valid?'), methodological ('how can we investigate whether a test is valid?'), and ethical ('when and how should we use test scores?') questions. The present paper therefore attempts to provide an overview of possible semantic interpretations of the validity concept. We explicitly do not intend the analysis to cover evidential or consequential issues; we are purely concerned with the meaning of validity.

Readers familiar with the literature on validity will note a feature of the above introduction that is dissonant with the current consensus on validity that has dominated the literature in the past two decades. The above introduction considers validity to be a characteristic of a test, not of a test score or test score interpretation. This is in sharp contrast to the currently endorsed position, which states that validity is always a feature of a test score interpretation (Messick, 1989). The reason for our diverging view on this matter is at the heart of the present analysis and the topic of the next section. We argue that validity may be viewed as a characteristic of a test, and that whether a test has the characteristic of validity depends on the truth of a given test score interpretation – namely, the interpretation that the test measures a certain attribute. This yields an exceedingly simple formulation of validity. Also, it allows for a standard type of inquiry into the semantics of validity by analyzing the following question: what makes the proposition 'Scores on test X measure attribute Y' true?

2 Defining validity in terms of truth

In the past century, the meaning of the term 'validity' has shifted from tests to test score interpretations. Originally, validity was conceived of as a characteristic of psychological tests. As Kelley (1927) put it, to ask the question of validity is to ask whether a test measures what it purports to measure. In later developments, validity was seen as a characteristic of test scores rather than of psychological tests. The reason for this may have been that validity was conceptualized in terms of the correlation between test scores and criterion scores (e.g., Lord & Novick, 1968), and the test scores, rather than the tests, are correlated with criterion scores. Still later, validity was deemed a characteristic of the test score interpretation rather than of tests or test scores, and this is the current position as expressed, for example, in Messick (1989). From an epistemological perspective, this shift of meaning is perfectly understandable. What is to be supported evidentially is not a test score, but a test score interpretation; and there is little room for argument on this point.

From a semantic perpective, however, the situation becomes slightly confused. To illustrate this, consider the following test score interpretation, which will be our working example in this paper:

IQ-scores measure intelligence.

Most psychologists and psychometricians will agree that, when we discuss the validity of test score interpretations, this is the type of test score interpretation we are concerned with. Now, there is something interesting about the above interpretation. Namely, it has the form of a proposition, and we may reasonably assume that all test score interpretations can be cast in this form. But what does it mean to say that a test score interpretation is valid, if not that the proposition that expresses this interpretation is true? That is, there seems little harm in a restatement of validity as

The test score interpretation 'IQ-scores measure intelligence' is valid, if and only if the proposition 'IQ-scores measure intelligence' is true.

Upon this restatement, however, the term 'valid' is superfluous, because its meaning has been reduced to the notion of truth. To assign the predicate 'valid' to the test score interpretation is to assign it the predicate 'true'. We now have two words for expressing the same idea.

We do not feel that much progress is being made by considering validity to be a characteristic of a test score interpretation. Not only does the concept end up doing nothing more than the concept of truth was already doing, it also seems more natural to consider validity to be a feature of a test: It was this conceptualization that made validity famous, so to speak, and it is also the way the great majority of test developers and users think about the issue. Further, we think that the argument that shifted the meaning of validity from tests to test score interpretations is erroneous. Namely, although the observation that one validates test score interpretations rather that test scores is correct, we see no reason why one would be forced to conclude from this that the term 'validity' can only meaningfully be applied to test score interpretations. Semantically, validity can be considered a characteristic of tests, rather than of test score interpretations, even though one can only validate interpretations. Namely, one can define the validity of a test in terms of the truth of a test score interpretation. That this can be done in a consistent manner is illustrated in the following definition of validity:

A test X is valid for the measurement of attribute Y, if and only if the proposition 'Scores on test X measure attribute Y' is true.

In terms of our working example, this becomes

An IQ-test is valid for the measurement of intelligence, if and only if the proposition 'IQ-scores measure intelligence' is true.

The two interesting features of this definition are a) that validity is explicitly considered to be a characteristic of the test in question, and b) that it is not at all applied to the test score interpretation: This role is taken over by the notion of truth. At the same time, the definition is not inconsistent with the idea that, in research, one validates interpretations of test scores rather than the test scores themselves. We conclude that it is not necessary to characterize validity as a property of test score interpretations, rather than of tests.

The semantics of validity are thus shifted back to where they originally came from (e.g., Kelly, 1927), and are brought in close agreement with the notion of validity that dominates the thinking of most psychologists. At the same time, however, the definition invites closer analysis; not of the concept of validity, which, as a predicate for tests, is defined in terms of the truth of a corresponding test score interpretation, but of the proposition 'IQ-scores measure intelligence'. That is, the semantics of validity can be clarified by looking at the conditions that would make the proposition true.

3 An investigation into the semantics of validity

One of the benefits of the definition above is that it makes explicit that an account of measurement is required. It is remarkable that influential treatises on validity, a concept deemed central to measurement, only superficially address theories of measurement, if at all. It seems to be tacitly assumed that it does not really matter whether one conceives of measurement from, say, a true score perspective (Lord & Novick, 1968), a latent variables perspective (Hambleton & Swaminathan, 1985), or a fundamental measurement theory perspective (Krantz, Luce, Suppes, & Tversky, 1971). As these theories conceive of the measurement process differently, however, we may expect that they assign different truth values to the proposition 'IQ-scores measure intelligence'. That is, it is likely that the semantics of validity are not independent of the measurement theory that gives the interpretation of the term 'measures'.

First, consider fundamental measurement theory. In this theory, measurement is a process of representing observed relations between objects (henceforth: persons) in a number system. Each person is assigned a number so that the relations between the assigned numbers are homomorphous with the observed relations between persons. This means that the observed relations are preserved in the numerical representation. The product of this process (i.e., the numerical assignment) is called a scale. Note that the scale is a product of human activity: it is therefore not necessary to assume, a priori, that scales exist independently of the act of measurement, and that they are somehow responsible for the observed relations. This is in contrast to, for example, latent variable models. Scales represent relations, they do not cause relations. Now, if observed relations can be represented in the number system (that is, if a homomorphism can be constructed), the resulting scale is an adequate representation by definition, and therefore measurement has succeeded. If the procedure fails, measurement has not taken place.

Let us consider our paradigm example, and interpret the proposition 'IQ-scores measure intelligence' from this perspective. As has been pointed out by Michell (1986), IQ-scores are not representations of observed relations because they involve the summation of item scores that do not form a unidimensional Guttman scale. This simply means that two people with different answer patterns may be assigned the same IQ-score. Thus, the assignment of IQ-scores does not produce a homomorphism between observed and numerical relations. Because IQ-scores are not the product of a measurement process, they cannot be properly considered measurements of anything. The proposition 'IQ-scores measure intelligence' is thus false. Moreover, from a fundamental measurement perspective, measurement is extremely rare in psychology (if it occurs at all), because very few psychological tests produce the type of consistencies required for representational theory to operate. Thus, according to this definition of measurement, most or all psychological tests are invalid.

Second, consider the measurent process from a classical test theory perspective. Classical test theory conceives of measurement in a statistical fashion. As Lord & Novick (1968, p. 20) put it, a test score is a measure of a theoretical construct if its expected value increases monotonically with that construct. At first sight, the theoretical construct could be taken to be the true score (Lord & Novick never explicitly say this, but suggest it in a number of places). Oddly enough, however, the true score is itself defined as the expected test score. Because true scores are identical to expected scores, and because any variable increases monotonically with itself, every test must measure its own true score perfectly. Therefore, if the true score on an IQ-test is considered to be identical to intelligence, the proposition 'IQ scores measure intelligence' is true by definition. This is because the proposition 'IQ-scores measure intelligence' is tranformed to 'the expected IQ-scores are monotonically related to the true scores on the IQ-test' which is vacuously true since the true scores are identical to the expected scores. Because the line of reasoning succeeds for every conceivable test, in this interpretation every psychological test is valid. However, it is only valid for its own true score. This is the price of operationalism: If the construct is equated with the true score, each distinct test defines a distinct construct, because it defines a distinct true score.

An alternative interpretation of classical test theory is that the observed scores do not measure the true scores (after all, it is rather odd to say that an expected value measures itself), but that the true scores measure something else, in the sense that they are themselves monotonically related to the theoretical construct in question. Viewing the issue in this way, the sentence 'IQ-scores measure intelligence' is true if the true scores on the test are monotonically related to intelligence. From a classical test theory perspective, this means that the theoretical construct cannot be conceived of as represented in the measurement model for the test in question, but must be viewed as an external variable. This prompts the conceptualization of validity as correlation with a criterion variable, which yields the concept of criterion validity.

Criterion validity has been extremely important to the theoretical development of the validity concept, for the following reason. Originally, the criterion was considered to be an observed variable, such as grades in college.

Because the validity question refers to measurement and not to prediction, and because IQ-scores do not attempt to measure college grades (which are, after all, observable) but intelligence, the criterion validity view was never an adequate conceptualization of test validity. What happened in response to this, is that the criterion variable was swept under the carpet of unobservability, and attained the status of a hypothetical entity. The definition of validity in terms of a statistical relation (i.e., the true score increases monotonically with the theoretical construct) was, however, retained. The measurability of the intended construct (intelligence) is thereby hypothesized a priori, and the validity of the measurements (IQ-scores) is conceptualized as a monotone relation of the true scores on the IQ-test with this hypothetically measurable attribute. In this view, validity is external to the measurement model, because in classical test theory a theoretical construct such as intelligence cannot be non-vacuously represented inside the measurement model. The proposition 'IQ-scores measure intelligence' thus becomes 'the true IQ-scores increase monotonically with a hypothetical criterion variable called intelligence'. Attempts to find 'perfect' measurements of intelligence that could function as a standard, analogeous to the standard meter in Paris, were, of course, fruitless. The type of thinking introduced by looking at intelligence as a criterion variable outside the measurement model is, however, still a very common way of thinking about test validity. That is, there is 'something out there', and the question of validity is how high the correlation between our test scores and that something is. This renders the semantics of validity dependent on two assumptions: 1) there really is something out there (intelligence), and 2) the test scores have a positive correlation with that something. If this is the case, then the proposition 'IQ-scores measure intelligence' is true. An interesting aspect of this view is that, because expected test scores will have monotonic relations to many attributes, any given test measures an indeterminate number of attributes. Thus, measures are not uniquely tied to a construct. If measurement is further reduced to correlation, everything measures everything else to a certain extent, and all tests must be valid.

The reason that classical test theory must consider theoretical constructs as external to the measurement model is that the syntactical machinery of the theory is not rich enough to represent constructs inside the model. As we have seen, the true score cannot perform this function without rendering a completely trivial account of measurement. Latent variable models (Hambleton & Swaminathan, 1985) do possess the required terminology. Such models relate the true scores on a number of items or tests to an underlying dimension. This dimension functions as a representative for the theoretical construct (to be distinguished from the function of fundamental measurement scales, which are representations of observed relations). The relation of measurement in latent variable models is rather similar to the statistical formulation of classical test theory; namely, it is conceived of in terms of a stochastic relation of the observed scores to the latent variable. However, these models do have the power to dispose of the problem that tests are valid for any attribute they are monotonically related to, because the dimensionality of the latent space can be specified in the model (this is not possible in classical test theory, except through the awkward requirement of strict parallellism). For example, in the unidimensional case, a latent variable model specifies that the true scores on each of a number of indicators are monotonically related to the same latent variable. Moreover, within such unidimensional models it is assumed that the indicators measure only this latent variable and nothing else. This implies that the indicators are independent, conditional on the latent variable. If, conditional on the latent variable, the indicators are still related to another variable (for example, group membership), the indicators are considered biased. Thus, in the unidimensional case, measurement can be seen as a monotonic relation of the expected scores with a latent variable, and only with this latent variable (in the sense that they do not systematically relate to another variable, given the latent variable). The proposition 'IQ-scores measure intelligence' thus becomes 'the expected IQ-scores increase monotonically with the latent variable intelligence, and, given the latent variable, with nothing else'. It follows that the semantics of unidimensional latent variable models do not allow indicators to be valid for more than one latent variable, in contrast to the classical test model.

This short and incomplete review of three important theories of psychological measurement shows that different definitions of the term 'measure' in the proposition 'IQ-scores measure intelligence' lead to different semantics for the validity concept. From a fundamental measurement perspective, measurement is a homomorphous mapping of observed relations into a number system; for true score theory, measurement is either a completely vacuous term, or it reduces to correlation with a possibly hypothetical criterion variable; for unidimensional latent variable theory, measurement is conceived of as an exclusive stochastic relation with a latent variable. It is not difficult to conceive of instances where the proposition 'scores on test X measure attribute Y' is assigned different truth values depending on the chosen definition of measurement. Thus, the semantics of validity cannot be considered apart from a definition of measurement, which is not altogether surprising since validity is supposed to be the central concept in measurement. Once a definition of measurement is chosen, the semantics of validity are fairly well fixed. However, the choice of a definition of measurement is not forced upon us by logical or philosophical arguments, and neither by empirical facts. Therefore, there is a degree of indeterminacy in the meaning of validity.

4 Discussion

In the present paper, we have provided a definition of validity in terms of the truth of a test score interpretation: test X is valid for the measurement of attribute Y if the proposition 'scores on test X measure attribute Y' is true. It seems to us that the benefits of formulating test validity in this way are considerable. First, defining validity in terms of truth has the advantage that it lines up nicely with pretheoretical intuitions concerning tests and test use; the consensus in the validity literature, holding that validity is a characteristic of test score interpretations instead of tests, seems not to have found its way into mainstream psychology, and understandably so. It conflicts with basic intuition which, we think, is close to, or even identical with, the definition of validity that we are suggesting here. Second, the present definition of validity clearly delineates between the semantics of validity ('what does it mean for a test to be valid?') and the evidential or epistemological problems in establishing validity ('how do we find out whether a test score interpretation is true?'). This produces a distinction between validity and validation, analogous to the distinction between truth and verification – an important distinction that, in our opinion, has often been blurred in the validity literature. It also provides a way of performing a semantic analysis of the validity concept, an undertaking of which we have reported in this paper. The analysis shows that the semantics of validity cannot be separated from the notion of measurement. Since multiple interpretations of measurement are available, none of which is logically or empirically forced upon us, the semantics of validity are to a certain extent indeterminate. Thus, the traditional question of validity, 'do IQ-scores really measure intelligence?', is not a purely factual question, although it is often presented in this way and the word 'really' invites this interpretation. The meaning of validity is fixed through a choice of measurement system that, depending on one's point of view, can either be described as arbitrary, normative, conventional, or pragmatic. After this choice is made, propositions such as 'IQ-scores measure intelligence' may be read as factual; but not before. Thus, it seems that our analysis underscores the importance of regarding validity as inherently involving norms and values, as Messick (1989) indicates. We add that this is much to our surprise.

References

1. Hambleton, R. K., Swaminathan, H. (1985): Item Response Theory: Principles and applications. Kluwer-Nijhoff, Boston
2. Kelley, T. L. (1927): Interpretation of educational measurements. Macmillan, New York
3. Krantz, D. H., Luce, R. D., Suppes, P., Tversky, A. (1971): Foundations of measurement, Vol. I. Academic Press, New York
4. Lord, F. M., Novick, M. R. (1968): Statistical theories of mental test scores. Addison-Wesley Publishing Company, Reading, MA
5. Messick, S. (1989): Validity. In Linn, L.R. (ed), Educational Measurement. American Council on Education and National Council on Measurement in Education, Washington, DC
6. Michell, J. (1986): Measurement scales and statistics: A clash of paragdigms. Psychological Bulletin, **100**, 398-407.

Part 5
Multivariate Statistical Methods

The Hierarchical Theory of Justification and Statistical Model Selection

Maarten Speekenbrink

Department of Psychology, University of Amsterdam, Roetersstraat 15, 1018 WB Amsterdam, Netherlands *mspeekenbrink@fmg.uva.nl*

Summary. This paper analyses the applicability of the hierarchical theory of justification as a normative theory of statistical model selection. The hierarchical theory prescribes a path from aim to evaluation criterion to model choice. Although the hierarchical theory has limited applicability as a normative theory due to underdetermination problems with equivalent models, it does provide an insightful framework for the area of statistical model selection.

Key words: model selection, justification, equivalence

1 Introduction

In a general sense, the problem of theory justification can be restated as problem of choice from infinitude. The number of possible (though not necessarily reasonable) explanations for a phenomenon is infinite, since it is always possible to add another explanans to a given explanation. How can one infer that a particular choice from this infinitude is the right one? One can demand that the empirical consequences of the theory match observations perfectly, but such a restriction will generally not suffice. Take for example the problem of specifying the relation between two variables by a curve. For any set of n paired observations (x, y), there exists a $(n-1)$-degree polynomial that passes through all n points, so this 'theory' would suffice. But so would a n-degree polynomial, as well as one of $(n+1)$ degree, etc. For a finite set of paired observations (x, y), there is a family of best fitting curves with infinite members and when based purely on the accuracy of description (and not the identifiability of parameters), the choice for one is arbitrary. Since science does not pride itself on arbitrary explanations, a particular choice has to be justified by an explicit and acceptable motivation. As yet, no universally valid motivation has been accepted. Without any objective criteria for justification it is quite reasonable for scientists to disagree, or at least, not irrational to do so. It is a striking aspect of science then, that scientists do often reach agreement. Since such consensus cannot be explained as the product of universal rules of scientific inference, another explanation should be offered. One of these involves the postulation of what can be called the hierarchical theory of justification (e.g. Laudan, 1984), which is also known as the theory of instrumental rationality.

1.1 The Hierarchical Theory of Justification

According to the hierarchical theory of justification, there are three interrelated levels at which, and by means of which, consensus is forged (Laudan, 1984). The factual level is the lowest in the hierarchy and concerns all descriptions and explanations of what there is in the world, formulated as hypotheses, models, theories, etc. The hierarchical theory prescribes that disagreement concerning such matters-of-fact can be resolved on a methodological level, which is one step up in the hierarchy. This level consists of rules concerning empirical support and theory comparison. The methodological rules constituting this level will not be the universal laws of scientific inference as sought by the logical positivists, but rather the inter-subjective rules that are part of specific paradigms. It is possible that scientists do not agree on the proper methodological rules. The hierarchical theory then prescribes that this disagreement on the methodological level should be resolved by moving to the highest level in the hierarchy, the axiological level, which concerns the goals and aims of science. The axiological values may resemble the Mertonian norms of science (commonality, universalism, disinterestedness and organised scepticism) but other, more specific values should be considered. More specifically, any cognitive aims in accordance to which the merits of theories are judged can be considered here. The theory allows for disagreement on the axiological level, but this disagreement must remain unresolved.

1.2 Overview

This paper analyses the applicability of the hierarchical theory of justification as a normative theory of statistical model selection. The reason for this analysis is twofold. First, the hierarchical theory of justification provides a general framework to analyse the justification of different model evaluation criteria. Second, due to its precise language, the context of statistical model selection allows for a relatively detailed analysis of the hierarchical theory itself. Since the hierarchical theory is a normative theory, in that it prescribes rational choice of method and theory given a set of axiological values, its applicability rests on restricting behaviour to a single rational course of action.

2 The Hierarchical Theory and Model Selection

The problem of statistical modelling can be stated as follows: given a set of n, k-variate observations $\mathbf{x}_i, i = 1, \dots, n$, all realisations of the environmental distribution function $F(\mathbf{x})$, find the model $g_\theta(\mathbf{x})$ which is in some sense optimal in relation to the environmental distribution that generated the observations. If $\mathcal{M}$ is the set of all k-variate distribution functions, a model $g_\theta(\mathbf{x})$ is defined as a subset of $\mathcal{M}$, with each element in $g_\theta(\mathbf{x})$ representing a fully specified model. A fitted model $g_{\hat{\theta}_n}(\mathbf{x})$ is a fully specified model of which the parameters $\hat{\theta}_n$ are fixed so as to minimise the discrepancy between the model and the observed distribution $f_n(\mathbf{x})$, as in maximum likelihood estimation. A best approximating model $g_{\hat{\theta}_F}(\mathbf{x})$ is a fully specified model of which the parameters $\hat{\theta}_F$ are fixed so as to minimise the discrepancy between the model and the environmental distribution. A model $g_\theta(\mathbf{x})$ is correctly specified if $F(\mathbf{x}) \in g_\theta(\mathbf{x})$, and otherwise misspecified. A model $g_\theta(\mathbf{x})$ is nested under model $h_\theta(\mathbf{x})$ if $g_\theta(\mathbf{x}) \subset h_\theta(\mathbf{x})$, and these models are strictly non-nested if $g_\theta(\mathbf{x}) \cap h_\theta(\mathbf{x}) = \emptyset$.

The situation considered is that of a set of proposed models $M = \{g_\theta(\mathbf{x}), h_\theta(\mathbf{x}), \ldots\}$ with the objective of choosing the element $m^\star \in M$ that optimally represents $F(\mathbf{x})$. The elements of M may be nested or non-nested and correctly specified or misspecified. The usefulness of the hierarchical theory of justification depends on the existence of a single optimal model evaluation criterion $C^\star$ given a specific stance on the axiological level, and the existence of a single model $m^\star = g_\theta(\mathbf{x})$ that is optimal in the light of the method.

2.1 The Axiological Level

An analysis of the applicability of the hierarchical theory of justification to the situation of statistical model selection naturally starts at the top level in the hierarchy: what specific values are taken into account in the evaluation of a statistical model? First, a classic distinction may be made between realist and instrumentalist aims for modelling. An optimal model $m^\star$ from a realist view is one that represents the true relations in the environmental distribution, i.e. $m^\star = F(\mathbf{x})$, while an instrumentalist aims at accurately predicting observations for particular sets of data, i.e. $m^\star = E[f_n(\mathbf{x})]$. Theoretically, an optimal model from a realist viewpoint should be optimal from an instrumentalist viewpoint, but in practise, when dealing with finite and often small samples, these aims may correspond to different choices of model. As noted in the introduction, the aim of perfect empirical fit will not lead to conclusive decisions when multiple models fit the data equally well, as well as being a 'naive empiricist' aim in disregarding measurement or sampling error. Besides the precision of a model in describing the observed data, other values should be taken into account. The two values addressed here are generality and simplicity. Although other values may enter discussions regarding the appropriateness of models, these three (precision, generality and simplicity) are commonly involved in statistical model selection and theory justification in general (e.g. Popper, 1959; and most authors in Myung, Forster & Browne, 2000). They may be taken to serve the two main axiological aims (realist and instrumentalist), which would make them methods rather than aims, but since the relation between their fulfillment and that of the higher-level aims is not entirely clear, they can be taken as aims in their own right.

Precision. Besides what can be referred to as descriptive precision, the inverse of the discrepancy between the fitted model and the observed distribution $\Delta(f_n(\mathbf{x}), g_{\hat{\theta}_n}(\mathbf{x}))$, there are other aspects of model precision. Following Linhart and Zucchini (1986), we may distinguish between a model's approximation precision and its estimation precision. A model's approximation precision is its maximum obtainable precision of representing $F(\mathbf{x})$, the inverse of the discrepancy $\Delta(F(\mathbf{x}), g_{\hat{\theta}_F}(\mathbf{x}))$ between the environmental distribution and the best approximating model. For a correctly specified model, the approximation precision clearly equals its maximum value. A model's estimation precision is the precision of the fitted model in representing the best approximating model, the inverse of the discrepancy $\Delta(g_{\hat{\theta}_n}(\mathbf{x}), g_{\hat{\theta}_F}(\mathbf{x}))$ between the fitted and best approximating model. The estimating precision thus represents a fitted model's precision in the light of sampling error and is dependent on sample size. With the types of precision distinguished here, the realist aim can now be defined as maximising approximation precision, while the instrumentalist aim is defined as maximising the expected overall precision, which effectively consists of finding an optimal balance between approximation and estimation precision. Since the environmental distribution is generally unknown, it is not straightforward to show the extent in which either aim is met, although the instrumentalist aim may be the more realistic one.

Generality. The main aspect of generality is predictive precision: the precision of a fitted model for observations that were not included in the parameter estimation. A model's maximum predictive precision equals the estimation precision defined above. A related aspect, which can be called scope, is a model's robustness to changes in the environmental distribution. This term could be operationalised as the proportion of the model-appropriate domain in which a model is expected to reach a certain level of precision. As such, it requires specification of the model-appropriate domain, or the set of environmental distributions to which the model is required to apply. This aspect of a model may be studied by simulation. While it is desirable for a fitted model to perform well under certain changes in the environmental distribution, a model that is precise in all samples to which it is fitted is regarded as too flexible and unfalsifiable. Analysis of a model's scope is obviously more involved, and usually only predictive precision is taken into account.

Simplicity. Although simplicity is arguably one of the most endorsed values in science, it is the hardest of the three values to define. It is the key element in Ockham's Razor, *plurality should not be posited without necessity'*, of which the modern interpretation usually states '*of two theories that describe the data equally well, one should prefer the simpler'*. A main problem for definitions of simplicity is language variance: for instance, a simple linear relation may be made more complex by a nonlinear transformation of one of the variables. A language invariant definition is the (incomputable) Kolmogorov complexity, where the simplicity of x is defined as the description length of the shortest binary program of a Universal Turing Machine that has x as output (Grünwald, 2000). The operationalisation of simplicity widely used for statistical models is the number of estimated parameters. The classical justification for the simplicity principle as found in works of Aristotle, Ockham, and Newton, is ontological: a simple model should be preferred because this reflects the inherent simplicity of Nature. Non-ontological justifications are for instance that simple models have a higher prior probability (Harold Jeffreys), that simple models have more empirical content since they have a higher level of falsifiability (Karl Popper), and that simple models are less cognitively demanding and therefore more effective devices for controlling nature (Ernst Mach); an overview of these ideas and their problems can be found in Bunge (1962). More recently, simplicity was justified by predictive precision (Forster and Sober, 1994), which seems to be the preferred justification for the simplicity principle in the statistical literature.

Connections. As should be clear from the preceding paragraphs, the axiological values may be dependent in their realisation. The simplicity of a model can be related to its predictive precision. For a given sample, the reliability of parameter estimates often reduces as the number of estimated parameters increases, leading to a decrease in predictive precision. In general, a model's predictive precision is a non-monotonic function of its simplicity; neither a too simple nor too complex model will lead to accurate predictions in new samples. In the presence of sampling error, descriptive precision can be negatively related to both predictive precision and simplicity, as when a model overfits the data. Note that this relation holds for a series of nested models; comparing two non-nested models, the parameter estimates in a simpler model are not necessarily more reliable, nor valid.

2.2 The Methodological Level

Due to the dependency between the axiological values, they cannot all be optimally realised and a method should establish an optimal trade-off between their realisations. Below, model evaluation criteria are classified according to the axiological values they address; since a number of indices simultaneously address multiple values, the categorisation rests on the dominant value addressed.

Criteria for Precision. A model's descriptive precision is directly observable, and a model evaluation criterion that incorporates it directly can be based on Chi-Square discrepancy $C_\chi = \sum_{i=1}^{n} (f_n(\mathbf{x}_i) - g_{\hat{\theta}}(\mathbf{x}_i))^2 / g_{\hat{\theta}}(\mathbf{x}_i)$ or the Gauss discrepancy $C_G = \sum_{i=1}^{n} (f_n(\mathbf{x}_i) - g_{\hat{\theta}}(\mathbf{x}_i))^2$. Another criterion can be defined in terms of the log-likelihood $C_L = -1/n \sum_{i=1}^{n} \log (g_{\hat{\theta}}(\mathbf{x}_i))$. In the absence of sampling error, such criteria would be good indicators of the approximation precision, but if the observed distribution is a random realisation of the environmental distribution, minimising these discrepancies will probably lead to overfitting, and a researcher should then be more interested in a model's average precision over a number of such realisations, i.e. the predictive precision.

Criteria for Generality. A natural definition predictive precision is in terms of the Kullback-Leibler distance $\Delta_{KL}(F(\mathbf{x}), g_{\hat{\theta}}(\mathbf{x}))$ between a model and the environmental distribution. A model evaluation criterion that provides an asymptotic estimate of the mean Kulback-Leibler distance of a model is the Akaike Information Criterion (Akaike, 1992[1973]), defined as $\mathcal{C}_{AIC} = -2 \sum_{i=1}^{n} \log\left(g_{\hat{\theta}_n}(\mathbf{x}_i)\right) + 2k$, where k is the number of free model parameters. The AIC is sometimes interpreted as a criterion of predictive precision, and sometimes as a criterion that penalises a model's descriptive precision with its complexity. A criterion with a similar form, although derived in a different theoretical framework, is the Bayesian Information Criterion (Schwarz, 1978), defined as $\mathcal{C}_{BIC} = -2 \sum_{i=1}^{n} \log\left(g_{\hat{\theta}_n}(\mathbf{x}_i)\right) + k \log n$. A model for which the AIC or BIC is minimal should be chosen. The difference between the AIC and the BIC is that the first selects the model of which the estimated Kullback-Leibler distance is minimal, while the latter selects the model which maximises the posterior probability of the model given the data.

Criteria for Simplicity. As previously mentioned, the AIC and BIC can be interpreted as criteria that penalise a model's fit by its complexity. The penalty term $2k$ of the AIC is a constant for a given model, while the penalty term $k \log(n)$ of the BIC is dependent on sample size, so that with increasing sample size the penalty for model complexity becomes relatively more severe. A criterion that specifically addresses a model's simplicity is the Minimum Description Length (Rissanen, 1996), which estimates the Kolmogorov Complexity by replacing algorithmic complexity with stochastic complexity (the shortest obtainable description of $\mathbf{x}$ by a model class M). The MDL takes the familiar form of a penalised likelihood and is defined as $\mathcal{C}_{MDL} = - \sum_{i=1}^{n} \log\left(g_{\hat{\theta}_n}(\mathbf{x}_i)\right) + (k/2) \log(n/2\pi) + \log \int \sqrt{|I(\theta)|} d\theta + o(1)$ (Rissanen, 1996), in which $|I(\theta)|$ is the determinant of the Fisher information matrix and $o(1)$ becomes negligible for n large. The last terms are often difficult or impossible to compute, but a reasonable practical version views stochastic complexity as a two-stage description of the data, consisting of the encoding of a model g_θ and the encoding of the data $\mathbf{x}$ using g_θ. This leads to an approximation of the MDL as $- \sum_{i=1}^{n} \log\left(g_{\hat{\theta}}(\mathbf{x}_i)\right) + (k/2) \log n$ (Grünwald, 2000), which is identical to one half of the BIC.

3 Application and Discussion

A first requirement of the hierarchical theory of justification is that a given set of evaluation criteria restricts the choice of method to one. Since all three values described here are generally endorsed, and multiple criteria address all three, this restriction either depends on (a) a single method optimally addressing all values, or (b) a correspondence between an individual's relative ranking of the aims and the relative strength with which the criteria address them. Since the optimality of the evaluation criteria depends on the correctness of the assumptions on which the criteria are based, which requires knowledge of the environmental distribution, we take (a) not to be decisively true for realistic situations. Option (b) seems viable, though. For instance, since C_{MDL} and C_{BIC} place a stronger penalty on extra parameters as the sample size increases, researchers putting more emphasis on simplicity than generality may prefer these criteria over the AIC, while researchers putting more emphasis on generality may choose the latter.

Regarding the second requirement, that a chosen criterion restricts the choice of model to one, the problem of underdetermination must be addressed. As exemplified in the introduction, multiple models may fit the data equally well, so that their choice is underdetermined by precision. Such equivalent models arise routinely, especially in the area of Structural Equation Modelling, where it has been shown that there are infinitely many equivalent models for certain model classes (Raykov & Marcoulides, 2001). Equivalent models must be distinguished by other aspects than descriptive precision and the two aims endorsed most widely are generality and simplicity. The underdetermination problem is not solved by a generality criterion defined in terms of predictive precision, since equivalent models give similar predictions for new data. If equivalent models have different numbers of parameters, they can be distinguished by a simplicity criterion, but when they have an equal number of parameters, none of the criteria given here will distinguish between them. Theoretical considerations may then have to guide model choice, which should not be taken as scientific defeat, but does mean that disagreement on the appropriate model has to be resolved on the theoretical level itself, going against the hierarchical structure of the hierarchical theory of justification.

We conclude that the hierarchical theory of justification has limited applicability as a normative model for statistical model selection, since it does not restrict choice between equivalent models. Admittedly, this conclusion is based on a specific set of axiological values and model evaluation criteria. Incorporating other axiological values, or different operationalisations thereof, may lead to different model evaluation criteria which do distinguish between otherwise equivalent models. For example, some authors argue that the definition of simplicity in terms of the number of parameters is not adequate (e.g. Bozdogan, 2000) and that the functional form of the model should also be taken into account. In the ICOMP(IFIM) criterion (Bozdogan, 2000), complexity is defined in terms of the inverse of the estimated Fisher Information matrix, of which the elements represent the (co-)variances of parameter estimates. While this criterion, as well as the proper version of the MDL criterion, might be able to distinguish between otherwise equivalent models, it is interesting to note that here it is not the simplicity of a model per se that seems to matter, but the precision of parameter estimates. This is also the main concern when applying the AIC, which amounts to choosing the model with the highest expected overall precision. Since the estimation precision will increase with sample size, it makes sense that the effect of the penalty term disappears with increasing sample size. As such, it can be argued that the simplicity aim is parasitic on the aim for reliable parameter estimates. This holds to a lesser extent for the BIC and MDL criteria, where the penalty on extra parameters becomes relatively stronger when sample size increases. As such, these criteria may be the more appropriate when simplicity per se is an aspired aim. However, it is unclear whether simplicity can be taken to serve the higher-order realist or instrumentalist aims. Taken as the maximisation of approximation precision, the realist aim is served by simplicity only under the ontological assumption that nature (the environmental distribution) is inherently simple. When the instrumentalist aim is defined as the maximisation of expected overall precision, the choice between two equivalent models performing equally well in this respect should be considered arbitrary.

References

Akaike, H. (1992[1973]). Information theory and an extension of the maximum likelihood principle. In: Kotz, S. & Johnson, K.L. (eds) Breakthroughs in statistics vol. 1, 610–624. Springer-Verlag.

Bozdogan, H. (2000). Akaike's information criterion and recent developments in information complexity. Journal of Mathematical Psychology, 44, 62–91.

Bunge, M. (1962). The complexity of simplicity. Journal of Philosophy, 59, 113–135.

Forster, M. & Sober, E. (1994). How to tell when simpler, more unified, or less ad hoc theories will provide more accurate predictions. British Journal for the Philosophy of Science, 45, 1–35.

Grünwald, P. (2000). Model selection based on minimum description length. Journal of Mathematical Psychology, 44, 133–152.

Laudan, L. (1984). Science and values. University of California Press.

Linhart, H. & Zucchini, W. (1986). Model selection. John Wiley.

Myung, I. J., Forster, M. & Browne, M. W. (2000). Special issue on model selection. Journal of Mathematical Psychology, 44, 1–231.

Popper, K. R. (1959). The logic of scientific discovery. Routledge.

Raykov, T. & Marcoulides, G. A. (2001). Can there be infinitely many models equivalent to a given covariance structure model? Structural Equation Modelling, 8, 142–149.

Rissanen, J. (1996). Fisher information and stochastic complexity. IEEE transactions on information theory, 42, 40–47.

Schwarz, G. (1978). Estimating the dimension of a model. Annals of statistics, 6, 461–464.

Robust designs for longitudinal mixed effects models

Martijn P.F. Berger, Mario J.N.M. Ouwens and Frans E.S. Tan

Department of Methodology and Statistics, University of Maastricht, P.O. Box 616, 6200 MD, Maastricht, The Netherlands

Summary. In longitudinal research studies, the allocation and selection of the number of time points will influence the variance of the estimated model parameters. Optimal designs for fixed effects models with uncorrelated errors are well documented in the statistical literature. In this paper optimal designs will be discussed for mixed effects models. Optimal designs for mixed effects models are only locally optimal, i.e. for a fixed combination of parameter values. Another problem is that optimal designs depend on the specified model. To circumvent both the local optimality problem and the dependency on the specified model, we propose to apply a maximin procedure. The results show that it is possible to find maximin designs that are highly efficient for a variety of parameter values and different models.

Key words. Linear mixed models, Optimal design, D-optimality, Maximin, Relative efficiency

1 Introduction

In psychological research longitudinal data are often obtained to investigate the pattern of change of outcome variables over time. The allocation and selection of the number of time points at which measurements are taken will influence the variance of the estimated model parameters, and the use of optimal designs for such studies will lead to the most efficient parameter estimates. Optimal designs for fixed effects regression models, with uncorrelated errors, have been studied in the statistical literature and discussed by Bunke & Bunke (1986) and Atkinson & Donev(1996), among others. Optimal designs for mixed effects regression models with and without correlated errors, have been studied more recently by Abt, Liski, Mandal & Sinka (1997), Atkins & Cheng (1999), Bischoff (1993), Mentré, Mallet & Baccar (1997) and Tan & Berger (1999), among others. Moerbeek, van Breukelen & Berger (2001) and Ouwens, Tan & Berger (2001) considered optimal designs for random effects models with covariates.

It is well known that optimal designs for one model may often not be optimal for other models. Since the correct model is usually not known in advance, it may be wise in practice to select a design which is highly efficient for alternative models. Optimal designs for longitudinal mixed effects models are locally optimal, that is, they depend heavily on combinations of parameter values. This problem can be dealt with by different approaches. In this paper, we propose a maximin approach that not only handles the local optimality problem but also takes into account the uncertainty about the best fitting model. The maximin principle has been specified in the literature by Federov (1980) and Wong (1992), and Berger, et al. (2000), among others. In this paper we propose an alternative formulation and show that highly efficient maximin designs can be found for a wide variety of parameter combinations and alternative models. These designs are referred to as robust designs. First, however, the optimal design formulation for the general linear mixed effects model will be presented.

2 Optimality and Efficiency of Designs

Linear mixed effects regression models have been described by Diggle, Liang & Zeger (1995), among others, and can be used to analyze time-structured data. This class of regression models which includes independent or dependent errors and random effects, is given by:

$$Y_j = X\beta + Zb_j + \varepsilon_j, \tag{1}$$

where the scores Y_j of subject j are modeled as a weighted linear function of the $p \times 1$ vector of fixed regression parameters β, the $q \times 1$ vector of random regression parameters b_j for each subject and the random errors ϵ_j. The design matrices X and Z are of orders $m \times p$ and $m \times q$, respectively. It is assumed that the random parameters b_j have zero mean and a variance-covariance matrix D. The random errors are normally distributed with zero mean and variance-covariance matrix Ψ. Usually the fixed parameters β are estimated by the maximum likelihood method (Diggle et al, 1994, p.63) and the random regression parameters b_j for each subject can be estimated by empirical Bayes estimators (Snijders & Bosker, 1999, p.58).

The variance of the estimated parameters $\hat{\beta}$ is a function of the variance-covariance matrix D of the random regression parameters b_j and the variance-covariance matrix Ψ of the errors, and is given by:

$$\text{Var}(\hat{\beta}) = [X'(ZDZ' + \Psi)^{-1}X]^{-1}. \tag{2}$$

Regression models for longitudinal time-structured data differ in the covariance structure Ψ of the error terms in the model. This structure may take different forms. In case of the ordinary regression analysis the error terms are independently distributed with mean zero and common error variance σ^2, i.e. $\Psi = \sigma^2 I$, where I is an identity matrix. When the responses are obtained from a series in time, the most commonly encountered correlation structure consists of correlations decreasing exponentially as the time points are located farther apart, i.e. Ψ has covariance structure with elements $\sigma^2 \rho^{\mathrm{abs}(t_i - t_{i'})}$, where t_k is the k th time point and the auto-correlation is $0 \le \rho \le 1$. Another common covariance structure is the uniform structure, i.e. $\Psi = \sigma^2 U$, where U is a correlation matrix with equal correlations ρ among the measurement errors.

As an example, consider the artificial growth data in Figure 1. Each of the lines in the figure represents a growth curve for nine different subjects. The crosses indicate the mean growth curve, which is described by a third degree polynomial.

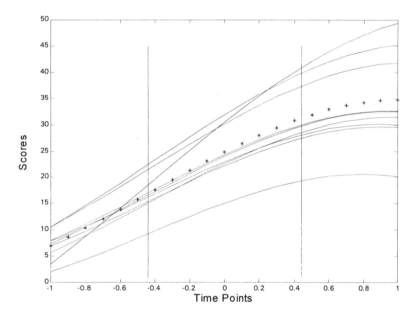

Fig. 1.   Third degree random intercept and slope model for growth data.

Without loss of generality, the time axis in Figure 1 is scaled from -1 to $+1$. The individual growth curves are described by a random intercept b_0, a random slope b_1, and a third degree polynomial with fixed parameters $\beta = [\beta_0 \ \beta_1 \ \beta_2]$ for the mean curve. The kth repeated measure for subject j is modeled as:

$$y_{jk} = \beta_0 + \beta_1 t_k + \beta_2 t_k^2 + \beta_3 t_k^3 + b_0 + b_1 t_k + \varepsilon_{jk}. \tag{3}$$

In the design stage a researcher would want to obtain data in such a way, that the parameters in $\beta = [\beta_0\ \beta_1\ \beta_2]$ are simultaneously estimated as efficiently as possible. Thus, the optimal design problem focuses on two questions, namely how may time points must be selected and what is the optimal allocation of these time points on the scale [-1 +1].

In this paper we will restrict ourselves to D-optimal designs because they are well known and have well-established properties. The main advantage is that the D-optimality criterion is invariant with respect to reparameterization. It also has a natural interpretation because it is related to the volume of the confidence ellipsoid. The mean growth curve in Figure 1 is described by a cubic polynomial model with fixed parameters and a uniform error correlation structure. The support points of the corresponding D-optimal design $\tau^* = [-1\ -0.44\ \ 0.44\ \ 1]$ are displayed in Figure 1 by the vertical lines.

A design τ^* in a design space T is Locally D-optimal if:

$$Det[Var(\hat{\beta}_{\tau*})] \leq Det[Var(\hat{\beta}_{\tau})], \tag{4}$$

for all $\tau \in T$. The relative efficiency of a design τ related to that of the D-optimal design τ^* measures the performance of such a design:

$$eff(\tau) = \left(\frac{Det\ [Var(\hat{\beta}_{\tau*})]}{Det\ [Var(\hat{\beta}_{\tau})]} \right)^{1/p} , \tag{5}$$

where p is the number of fixed polynomial parameters. This relative efficiency measure gives us an indication how many extra observations are needed to obtain maximum efficiency. For example, if $eff(\tau) = 0.9$, then $(0.9^{-1}-1)\%= 11\%$ more observations will be needed under design τ, to obtain the same efficiency as that of the D-optimal design τ^*. In other words, if design τ is used instead of the optimal design τ^*, the loss in efficiency is 11%.

3 Robustness of a Design and the Maximin Principle

The selection of an optimal design relies heavily on the selected model. Suppose that a researcher is not sure whether a linear of a quadratic polynomial will provide an adequate fit for the growth data in Figure 1. Then the D-optimal design for estimating the set of fixed parameters $\beta = [\beta_0\ \beta_1\ \beta_2]$ in a fixed effects model with a uniform covariance structure $\Psi = \sigma^2\ U$, would be the design $\tau^*_2 = [-1, 0, +1]$. (see Bunke & Bunke, 1986, p.546). The D-optimal design, however, for estimating the parameters $\beta = [\beta_0\ \beta_1]$ for the fixed effects linear model would be $\tau^*_1 = [-1, +1]$. So, the optimal design τ^*_2 with three time points is not optimal for a linear polynomial and visa versa. To answer the question which design will be highly efficient for both the linear and the quadratic model, a class of three point designs $[-1, t, 1]$, where $-1 \leq t \leq +1$, can be considered. The first and last time points -1 and $+1$, are fixed, but the second time point t may vary. The question is now for which value of t will the parameters in $\beta = [\beta_0 \ \beta_1 \ \beta_2]$ for the quadratic model, and in $\beta = [\beta_0 \ \beta_1]$ for the linear model, simultaneously be estimated as efficiently as possible?

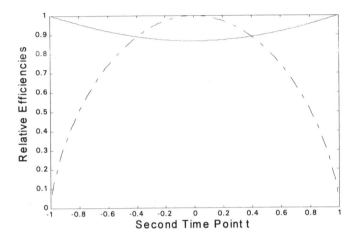

Fig 2. Relative efficiencies for a linear model (continuous line) and a quadratic model (dotted line)

In Figure 2 the relative efficiencies defined in equation (5) are plotted for the class of designs $[-1, t, 1]$. The relative efficiencies of these designs related to the D-optimal design τ^*_1 for the linear model are plotted as a continuous line, while the relative efficiencies related to the D-optimal design τ^*_2 for the quadratic model are plotted as a dotted line. The figure shows that maximum efficiency for the quadratic model is of course obtained when $t = 0$. Maximum efficiency for the linear model is, however, obtained when t approaches -1 or $+1$.

By means of the maximin principle, the most efficient design for both the linear and quadratic model can be found in two steps. For all the designs with value t, where $-1 \leq t \leq +1$, the worst case is selected, i.e. the smallest of the two relative efficiencies is selected. In the second step the maximum value of these worst cases is taken to be the maximin value MMV of the maximin design $\tau_{maximin}$. For the linear and quadratic model, the maximin designs are the designs with a value of t, where the curves cross each other. The maximin designs for both the linear and quadratic model are $\tau_{maximin} = [-1, -0.4, +1]$ and $\tau_{maximin} = [-1, +0.4, +1]$, respectively. Both designs have a MMV = 0.89. A same principle can be applied to situations with more than two alternative models.

Let the set of models be given by M, and let the space of all possible combinations of parameter values be given by Θ. Then the maximin design $\tau_{maximin}$ is the design with:

$$\text{MMV} = \max_{T} \{\min_{\Theta, M} [\textit{eff}(\tau)]\}, \tag{6}$$

where T is the design space and *eff* (τ) is the relative efficiency of τ defined in equation (5). The advantage of the maximin formulation in terms of the relative efficiency is that the MMV is a relative efficiency measure and directly indicates how well the $\tau_{maximin}$ performs. Because the smallest relative efficiency is taken over all parameter combinations and over the set of alternative models, a highly efficient maximin design will perform well for all alternative models and all combinations of parameter values. A disadvantage of the maximin design, however, is that it strongly depends on range of parameter values in Θ and on the number of different models in M. In general the MMV will decrease in value, as the range of possible parameter values increases and as the number of models in M increases.

3.1 Symmetry of maximin designs

Suppose that a design τ consists of time points in the interval [-1 +1]. Then a design -τ can be defined by multiplying all time points by -1. The two designs τ and -τ are called symmetric designs. It can be shown that for a fixed effects model the following equality holds:

$$\text{Det}[\text{Var}(\hat{\beta}_\tau)] = \text{Det}[\text{Var}(\hat{\beta}_{-\tau})]. \tag{7}$$

For mixed effects models with random intercepts and slopes the symmetry property also holds when the design τ is connected to a model with a positive covariance between the random intercepts and random slopes, and the design -τ is connected to a model with a negative covariance. Since it is difficult to find optimal designs for the models in equation (1) analytically, we used a numerical search to find these designs. This property enables us to restrict our search to half of the design space, with, for example, time points located only in the interval [0 1].

4 Some Highly Efficient Robust Designs

In this section we will present maximin designs for three often encountered research cases. The maximin designs are based on the set of models M, and on the space of all possible combinations of parameter values Θ. We will assume that the set of models contains the linear, quadratic and third degree polynomial and that the space of parameter values is $\Theta = [\sigma^2, \rho, D]$, where $\sigma^2 = 1$, $\rho \in [0, 1]$ and D may cover a wide range of values.

Case I. For this case we only have fixed parameters and we assume that we have a uniform correlation structure $\Psi = \sigma^2 U$, and that the model set contains a linear, quadratic and an third degree model. The following maximin designs are found: $\tau_{maximin} = [-1 \ -0.46 \ 0.76 \ 1]$ and $\tau_{maximin} = [-1 \ -0.76 \ 0.46 \ 1]$. The MMV = 0.84, which indicates that 19% loss of efficiency is encountered, compared to the D-optimal design.

Case II. This case is equal to Case I, except that the correlation structure Ψ has elements $\sigma^2 \rho^{abs(t_i - t_{i'})}$. The maximin designs are $\tau_{maximin} = [-1 \ -0.48 \ 0.82 \ 1]$ and $\tau_{maximin} = [-1 \ -0.82 \ 0.48 \ 1]$, respectively. The corresponding MMV= 0.76, meaning that compared to the D-optimal design, these designs have an efficiency loss of about 30%. Although these maximin designs are not very different from the maximin designs in Case 1, the loss in efficiency is larger, because the D-optimal designs are more efficient.

Case III. In this case we assume that the linear, quadratic and cubic models not only contain fixed parameters, but also random intercepts and slopes. The random effects variance-covariance matrix D is:

$$D = \begin{bmatrix} 10 & 0.2 \\ 0.2 & 1 \end{bmatrix}.$$

The correlation matrix Ψ has elements $\sigma^2 \rho^{abs(t_i - t_{i'})}$. The maximin designs are $\tau_{maximin} = [-1 \ -0.36 \ 0.22 \ 1]$ and $\tau_{maximin} = [-1 \ -0.22 \ 0.36 \ 1]$, with corresponding MMV= 0.92, which is relatively high. The loss in efficiency is about 9%.

5 Discussion and Conclusion

Researchers are often faced with the problem of designing a longitudinal study as efficiently as possible. Too many observations may lead to unnecessary high costs of data collection and not enough observations may not result in significant effects. Although, in general, the class of linear mixed effects models is adequate to analyze such data, researchers generally do not know in advance which model will give an efficient description of their longitudinal data. An optimal design depends on the specified model and on the unknown parameter values. These problems can be handled by applying a maximin procedure.

The results in this paper show that the found maximin designs remain highly efficient under different polynomial models and combinations of parameter values. The proposed methodology can easily be applied to other models and parameter values. Even if the number of models is large and a wide range of parameter values is considered, the amount of computational labor remains acceptable.

Maximin designs, however, have the disadvantage that as the number of models and the range of possible parameter values increases, the efficiency will generally decrease. Although this may be a problem in general, this disadvantage is limited in practical cases. Usually a researcher will have a fairly good notion of the set of alternative models that will fit the data best, and pilot studies may provide relative accurate estimates of the values of the parameters.

References:

Abt, M. , Liski, E .P., Mandal, N.K. & Sinha, B. K. (1997). Correlated model for linear growth: Optimal designs for slope parameter estimation and growth prediction. *Journal of Statistical Planning and Inference, 64,* 141-150.

Atkins, J.E. and Cheng, C.S. (1999). Optimal regression designs in the presence of random block effects. *Journal of Statistical Planning and Inference, 77,* 321-335.

Atkinson, A.C. & Donev, A.N. (1996). *Optimum experimental designs.* Oxford: Clarendon Press.

Berger, M.P.F., King, C.Y., and Wong, W.K. (2000). Minimax D-optimal designs for item response theory models. *Psychometrika, 65,* 377-390.

Bischoff, W. (1993). On D-optimal designs for linear models under correlated observations with an application to a linear model with multiple response. *Journal of Statistical Planning and Inference, 37,* 69-80.

Bunke, H. & Bunke O.(1986). *Statistical inference in lineair models.* New York: John Wiley.

Diggle, P.J., Liang, K.-Y.,& Zeger, S.L. (1994). *Analysis of longitudinal data.* Oxford: Clarendon Press.

Federov, V.V. (1980). Convex design theory. *Mathematische Operations Forschung und Statistics. Series Statistics, 11,* 403-413.

Mentré, F., Mallet, A. and Baccar, D. (1997). Optimal design in random effect regression models. *Biometrika, 84,* 429-442.

Moerbeek, M. Van Breukelen, G.J.P. & Berger, M.P.F. (2001). Optimal experimental designs for multilevel models with covariates. *Communications in Statistics, Theory and Methods, 30,* 12, 2683-2697.

Ouwens, J.N.M., Tan, F.E.S. & Berger, M.P.F. (2001). On the maximin designs for logistic random effects models with covariates. In B. Klein & L. Korshom (Eds.), *New trends in Statistical Modelling.* (The Proceedings of the 16th International Workshop on Statistical modelling, Odense, Denmark, pp. 321-328).

Tan, F.E.S. and Berger, M.P.F. (1999). Optimal allocation of time points for the random effects model. *Communications in Statistics, Simulation and Computation, 28,* 517-540.

Wong, W.K. (1992). A unified approach to the construction of minimax designs. *Biometrika, 79,* 611-619.

On Conditional Distribution of Sliced Inverse Regression Model

Masahiro Mizuta[1]

Center for Information and Multimedia Studies, Hokkaido University, S.11, W.5, Kita-ku, Sapporo 060-0811, Japan *mizuta@cims.hokudai.ac.jp*

Summary. In this paper, Sliced Inverse Regression (SIR) model is discussed from the viewpoint of distribution theory. Especially, we deal with conditional distribution of explanatory variables when the value of response variable is fixed.

The concept of SIR is proposed by Li (1991) and the purpose of SIR is to reduce the dimension of explanatory variables. There are many algorithms for SIR model. But, most of the algorithms cannot always derive the reasonable results for typical artificial datasets.

We show that inspection of the conditional distributions is a key to SIR algorithms. When the distribution of the explanatory variables is the normal distribution, the conditional density function for any value of response variable is divided into two parts: normal part and non-normal part. This result would be fundamental theory for development of effective SIR algorithms. It is shown that SIRpp algorithm, which was proposed for SIR model by Mizuta (1999), is more excellent than other algorithms by this theory. This fact is shown with numerical examples.

Key words. Effective dimensional reduction, SIR1, SIR2, SIRpp, projection pursuit.

1 Introduction

Multiple regression analysis is one of the fundamental methods for data analysis. Nowadays, we use not only linear regression analysis but also non-linear regression analysis. However, when the number of explanatory variables is many, we are confronted with multicollinearity, instability and huge computational cost. There are many studies on reduction of the dimension of explanatory variables space. Explanatory variable selection is one of them. The goal of explanatory variable selection is to eliminate uninformative variables. But, in the most cases, almost all explanatory variables are important to predict the response variable. PPReg (Projection Pursuit Regression) and ACE (Alternating Conditional Expectation) search several linear combinations of explanatory variables; the number of linear combinations is smaller than that of explanatory variables. So they reduce the dimension of explanatory variables.

Li (1991) proposed a new concept named Sliced Inverse Regression (SIR). The aim of SIR is also to find out a few linear combinations of explanatory variables like PPReg and ACE. PPReg and ACE assume specific models for regression, but SIR assumes generic model for regression analysis. Li (1991) developed algorithms for SIR model: SIR1, SIR2. But, these algorithms cannot always find reasonable results for all trivial artificial datasets. Mizuta (1999) proposed an algorithm for SIR model in order to overcome the defects.

We introduce the SIR model and their algorithms in the next section. In section 3 and 4, we discuss the defects of the conventional algorithms and investigate the essential structures in the SIR model with conditional distributions of explanatory variables.

2 Sliced Inverse Regression

We describe the brief introduction of SIR model and SIR algorithms and give notations.

2.1 SIR Model

SIR does not get rid of some explanatory variables themselves but may reduce the dimension of a space of explanatory variables. It is based on the model (SIR model)

$$y = f(\beta_1^T x, \beta_2^T x, \cdots, \beta_K^T x, \varepsilon), \tag{1}$$

where x is the vector of p explanatory variables, β_k $(k = 1, 2, \cdots, K)$ are unknown vectors, ε is independent of x, and f is an arbitrary unknown function on R^{K+1} (Fig.1).

The purpose of SIR is to estimate the vectors β_k when this model holds. If we get the β_k, we can reduce the dimension of x to K. Hereafter, we shall refer to any linear combination of β_k as effective dimensional reduction (e.d.r.) direction.

2.2 Conventional Algorithms

Li (1991) proposed an algorithm to find e.d.r. directions and named SIR1. The goal of SIR1 is not to find the function f, but to get the e.d.r. space, i.e. to find K vectors $\beta_1, \beta_2, \cdots, \beta_K$: e.d.r. directions. When the distribution of X is elliptically symmetric, the centered inverse regression $E[X|y] - E[X]$ are contained in the linear subspace spanned by $\beta_k^T \Sigma_{XX}$ $(k = 1, 2, \cdots, K)$, where Σ_{XX} denotes the covariance matrix of X. Here is the SIR1 algorithm to data: (y_i, x_i) $(i = 1, 2, \cdots, n)$.

<u>SIR1 algorithm</u>

1. Standardize x: $\tilde{x}_i = \hat{\Sigma}_{xx}^{-\frac{1}{2}}(x_i - \bar{x})(i = 1, 2, \cdots, n)$, where $\hat{\Sigma}_{xx}$ is the sample covariance matrix and $\bar{x}$ is the sample mean of x.

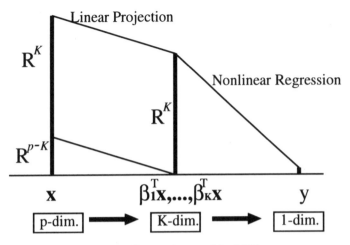

Fig. 1. Regression model of SIR

2. Divide range of y into H slices, $I_1, I_2, \cdots, I_H$; let the proportion of the y_i that falls in slice h be $\hat{p}_h$.

3. Within each slice, compute the sample mean of the $\tilde{x}_i$'s, denoted by $\hat{m}_h$ $(h = 1, 2, \cdots, H)$, so that $\hat{m}_h = \frac{1}{n\hat{p}_h} \sum_{y_i \in I_h} \tilde{x}_i$.

4. Conduct a (weighted) principal component analysis for the data $\hat{m}_h$ $(h = 1, 2, \cdots, H)$ in the following way: Form the weighted covariance matrix $\hat{V} = \sum_{h=1}^{H} \hat{p}_h \hat{m}_h \hat{m}_h^T$, then find the eigenvalues and the eigenvectors for $\hat{V}$.

5. Let the K largest eigenvectors of $\hat{V}$ be $\hat{\eta}_k$ $(k = 1, 2, \cdots, K)$.

Output $\hat{\beta}_k = \hat{\Sigma}_{xx}^{-\frac{1}{2}} \hat{\eta}_k$ $(k = 1, 2, \cdots, K)$ for estimations of e.d.r. directions.

The main idea of SIR1 is to use $E[X|y]$. $E[X|y]$ are contained in the space spanned by e.d.r. directions, but there is no guarantee that $E[X|y]$ span the space. So, Li (1991) also proposed another algorithm SIR2. SIR2 uses $Cov[X|y]$.

SIR2 algorithm

1. Same as Step 1 of SIR1 algorithm.

2. Same as Step 2 of SIR1 algorithm.

3. Within each slice, compute the sample covariance matrix $\hat{V}_h$:
$\hat{V}_h = \frac{1}{n\hat{p}_h - 1} \sum_{y_i \in I_h} (\tilde{x}_i - \hat{m}_h)(\tilde{x}_i - \hat{m}_h)^T$.

4. Compute the mean over all slice covariances:
$\bar{V} = \sum_{h=1}^{H} \hat{p}_h \hat{V}_h$.

5. Compute a variance of slice covariances:
$\hat{V} = \sum_{h=1}^{H} \hat{p}_h (\hat{V}_h - \bar{V})^2$.

6. Let the K largest eigenvectors of $\hat{V}$ be $\hat{\eta}_k$ $(k = 1, 2, \cdots, K)$.

Output $\hat{\beta}_k = \hat{\Sigma}_{xx}^{-\frac{1}{2}} \hat{\eta}_k$ $(k = 1, 2, \cdots, K)$.
There are several defects in SIR2. We deal with them in the next section.

2.3 SIRpp algorithm

Mizuta (1999) proposed an algorithm for SIR model with projection pursuit (SIRpp). The algorithm for data $(y_i, \boldsymbol{x}_i)$ $(i = 1, 2, \cdots, n)$ is as follows.

SIRpp Algorithm
  1. Same as Step 1 of SIR1 algorithm.
  2. Same as Step 2 of SIR1 algorithm.
  3. Conduct a projection pursuit in K dimensional space for each slice.
     We get H projections: $(\boldsymbol{\alpha}_1^{(h)}, \cdots, \boldsymbol{\alpha}_K^{(h)})$, $(h = 1, 2, \cdots, H)$.
  4. Let the K largest eigenvectors of $\hat{V}$ be $\hat{\eta}_k (k = 1, 2, \cdots, K)$.
     Output $\hat{\beta}_k = \hat{\Sigma}_{xx}^{-\frac{1}{2}} \hat{\eta}_k$ $(k = 1, 2, \cdots, K)$ for estimations of e.d.r. directions,
     where $\hat{V} = \sum_{h=1}^{H} w(h) \sum_{k=1}^{K} \boldsymbol{\alpha}_k^{(h)} \boldsymbol{\alpha}_k^{(h)^T}$ and $w(h)$ is a weight determined
     by the size of the slice and the projection pursuit index.

Steps 1 and 2 are the same as those of SIR1 and SIR2. The data is sphered in Step 1 and is sliced in Step 2. The H projections in Step 3 are regarded as e.d.r. directions on the coordinates of $\tilde{\boldsymbol{x}}$. We get H projections and combine them into $\hat{V}$ in Step 4; this is similar to a singular value decomposition.

3 Theoretical Aspects of SIR Model

In this section, we would like to investigate SIR model and SIR algorithms. Inspection of the conditional distributions $\boldsymbol{X}|y$ is a key to SIR model and SIR algorithms.

3.1 Conditional distribution of Explanatory variables

Because $E[\boldsymbol{X}|y]$ or $Cov[\boldsymbol{X}|y]$ are not sufficient to find e.d.r. directions, we will investigate the conditional distributions $\boldsymbol{X}|y$ themselves. We assume that the distribution of $\boldsymbol{x}$ is standard normal distribution hereafter: $\boldsymbol{x} \sim N(0, I_p)$. If not, standardize $\boldsymbol{x}$ with affine transformation. And $\boldsymbol{\beta}_i^T \boldsymbol{\beta}_j = \delta_{ij}, (i, j = 1, 2, \cdots, K)$ is supposed without loss of generality. We can choose $\boldsymbol{\beta}_i (i = K+1, \cdots, p)$ such that $\{\boldsymbol{\beta}_i\}$ $(i = 1, 2, \cdots, p)$ is an orthonormal basis for $\boldsymbol{R}^p$.

Because the distribution of $\boldsymbol{x}$ is $N(0, I_p)$, the distribution of $(\boldsymbol{\beta}_1^T \boldsymbol{x}, \cdots, \boldsymbol{\beta}_p^T \boldsymbol{x})^T$ is also $N(0, I_p)$. We put $x_i = \boldsymbol{\beta}_i^T \boldsymbol{x}$. The transformation of variable α is defined as follows:

$$\alpha(x_1, \cdots, x_p, \varepsilon) = (x_1, \cdots, x_p, y).$$

The Jacobian matrix J^{-1} is

$$J^{-1} = \frac{\partial(x_1, \cdots, x_p, y)}{\partial(x_1, \cdots, x_p, \varepsilon)} = \begin{pmatrix} 1 & \cdots & 0 & 0 \\ \vdots & \ddots & \vdots & \vdots \\ 0 & \cdots & 1 & 0 \\ * & \cdots & \cdots & \frac{\partial y}{\partial \varepsilon} \end{pmatrix},$$

where $\frac{\partial y}{\partial \varepsilon}$ is a function of $x_1, \cdots, x_k$. It is easy to derive the density function of $(\beta_1^T x, \cdots, \beta_p^T x, y)$;

$$h(\beta_1^T x, \cdots, \beta_p^T x, y) = \phi(\beta_1^T x) \cdots \phi(\beta_p^T x)\psi(\beta_1^T x, \cdots, \beta_K^T x, y),$$

where $\phi(x) = 1/\sqrt{2\pi}\exp(-x^2/2)$ and $\psi(\cdot)$ is a function of $\beta_1^T x, \cdots, \beta_K^T x, y$.
The conditional density function is

$$h(\beta_1^T x, \cdots, \beta_p^T x \mid y) = \phi(\beta_{K+1}^T x) \cdots \phi(\beta_p^T x)g(\beta_1^T x, \cdots, \beta_K^T x, y),$$

where $g(\cdot)$ is a function of $\beta_1^T x, \cdots, \beta_K^T x, y$ and is not generally normal density function. So, $h(\beta_1^T x, \cdots, \beta_p^T x \mid y)$ is divided into the normal distribution part $\phi(\beta_{K+1}^T x) \cdots \phi(\beta_p^T x)$ and the nonnormal distribution part $g(\cdot)$.

3.2 Problems of SIR1 and SIR2 Algorithms

We will examine the algorithms SIR1 and SIR2 based on the above discussions. We put $h(x_1, \cdots, x_p \mid y) = \phi(x_{K+1}) \cdots \phi(x_p)g(x_1, \cdots, x_K, y)$ for the conditional distribution.

SIR1 algorithm uses $E[X|y]$. We can get

$$E[X|y] = \left(\int x_1 g(x_1, \cdots, x_K, y)dx_1 \cdots dx_K, \cdots, \right.$$
$$\left. \int x_K g(x_1, \cdots, x_K, y)dx_1 \cdots dx_K, 0, \cdots, 0 \right)^T.$$

So, $E[X|y]$ are contained in the e.d.r. space. But sometimes $E[X|y]$ do not span e.d.r. space. For example in Li, if $(X_1, X_2) \sim N(0, I_2)$, and $Y = X_1^2$ then $E[X_1|y] = E[X_2|y] = 0$.

SIR2 algorithm uses $Cov[X|y]$;

$$Cov[X|y] = \begin{pmatrix} C_{11}(t) & 0 & \cdots & 0 \\ 0^T & 1 & \cdots & 0 \\ \vdots & \vdots & \ddots & \vdots \\ 0^T & 0 & \cdots & 1 \end{pmatrix},$$

where $C_{11}(t)$ is $k \times k$ sub-matrix. When all eigenvalues of the upper left $k \times k$ sub-matrix of $\hat{V}$ are larger than those of the lower right $(p-k) \times (p-k)$

sub-matrix, SIR2 do well. But this condition is severe for actual analysis. These problems of SIR1 and SIR2 are shown with artificial dataset in the next section.

Projection Pursuit is a good method to find out nonlinear structure. Specially, Friedman (1987) regarded the nonlinear structure as nonnormality. This is the reason why SIRpp algorithm has good performance in finding e.d.r. directions.

4 Numerical Examples

We evaluate SIR algorithms with a model of multicomponents:

$$y = \sin(x_1) + \cos(x_2) + 0 \cdot x_3 + \cdots + 0 \cdot x_{10} + \sigma \cdot \varepsilon \tag{2}$$

to generate data $n = 400$, where $\sigma = 0.5$. At first, we generate x_1, x_2, ε with N(0,1) and calculate a response variable y with (2). Eight variables $x_3, \cdots, x_{10}$ generated by N(0,1) are added to explanatory variables.

The ideal e.d.r. directions are contained in the space spanned by two vectors $(1, 0, \cdots, 0)$ and $(0, 1, \cdots, 0)$.

The squared multiple correlation coefficient between the projected variable $b^T x$ and the space B spanned by ideal e.d.r. directions;

$$R^2(b) = \max_{\beta \in B} \frac{(b^T \sum_{xx} \beta)^2}{b^T \sum_{xx} b \cdot \beta^T \sum_{xx} \beta} \tag{3}$$

is adopted as the criterion to evaluate the effectiveness of estimated e.d.r. directions. Tab.1 shows the averages and the standard deviations (in parentheses) of $R^2(\hat{\beta}_1)$ and $R^2(\hat{\beta}_2)$ of three SIR algorithms for $H = 5, 10$, and 20, after 100 replicates.

Both SIR1 and SIR2 do not find the two dimensional ideal e.d.r. space B, because $\hat{\beta}_2$ is far from B for most results of SIR1 and SIR2 ($\hat{\beta}_1$ is almost contained in B). Most of $\hat{\beta}_1$ are close to $(1, 0, 0, \cdots, 0)$ in SIR1, and $(0, 1, 0, \cdots, 0)$ in SIR2. So, SIR1 finds the asymmetric e.d.r. direction and does not find the symmetric e.d.r. direction. Conversely, SIR2 finds only the symmetric e.d.r. direction. SIRpp succeeds in detecting the both e.d.r. directions.

5 Concluding Remarks

The performance of SIRpp depends on the ability of the projection pursuit. There are many algorithms of projection pursuit. Mizuta (1999) adopted the Friedman's index (Friedman, 1987). There is some possibility of finding or constructing a better projection pursuit algorithm.

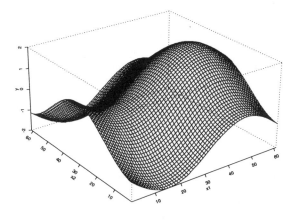

Fig. 2. 3D Plot of function f in example

Table 1. Results of SIR1, SIR2, and SIRpp

Function of asymmetric with respect to the x_1 axis
and symmetric with respect to x_2 axis. $y = \sin(x_1) + \cos(x_2) + \sigma \cdot \varepsilon$

H	SIR1		SIR2		SIRpp	
	$R^2(\hat{\beta}_1)$	$R^2(\hat{\beta}_2)$	$R^2(\hat{\beta}_1)$	$R^2(\hat{\beta}_2)$	$R^2(\hat{\beta}_1)$	$R^2(\hat{\beta}_2)$
5	.97	.12	.92	.01	.92	.88
	(.02)	(.14)	(.04)	(.10)	(.05)	(.11)
10	.97	.12	.90	.05	.88	.84
	(.02)	(.15)	(.06)	(.07)	(.08)	(.13)
20	.97	.12	.85	.05	.84	.73
	(.02)	(.14)	(.09)	(.06)	(.10)	(.22)

In most SIR methods, there is a serious restriction; the distribution of exploratory variables is elliptically symmetric distribution or normal distribution. The restriction should be removed for actual data analysis. We are constructing the new SIR method free from the restriction of the distribution of exploratory variables.

References

Friedman, J. H. (1987): Exploratory Projection Pursuit. Journal of the American Statistical Association, **82**, 249–266

Friedman, J. H. & Tukey, J. W. (1974): A Projection Pursuit Algorithm for Exploratory Data Analysis. IEEE Trans. on Computer, **c-23**, **9**, 881–890

Koyama, K., Morita, A., Mizuta, M., and Sato, Y. (1998): Projection Pursuit into Three Dimensional Space. (in Japanese) The Japanese Journal of Behaviormetrics, **25(1)**, 1–9

Li, Ker-Chau (1991): Sliced Inverse Regression for Dimension Reduction. Journal of the American Statistical Association, **86**, 316–342

Mizuta, M. (1998): A New Algorithm for Sliced Inverse Regression with Projection Pursuit. (in Japanese) Proceedings of Japan Statistical Society 1998, 158–159

Mizuta, M. (1999): Sliced Inverse Regression with Projection Pursuit., In: H. Bacelar-Nicolau, F. Costa Nicolau and J. Janssen (Eds.): Applied Stochastic Models and Data Analysis. INSTITUTO NACIONAL DE ESTATÍSTICA, 51–56

Uniqueness Properties of Three-way Component Models with Offset Terms

Henk A.L. Kiers[1]

[1]Heymans Institute (DPMG), University of Groningen, Grote Kruisstraat 2/1, 9712 TS Groningen, The Netherlands; email: h.a.l.kiers@ppsw.rug.nl.

Summary. At various places, it has been proposed to extend three-way component models by adding constant additive terms to the model. In the present paper a class of such extended three-way component models is described, and it is demonstrated in which cases such offset terms can be estimated uniquely. Procedures for fitting these models are offered elsewhere.

Key Words: Tucker3 model, CANDECOMP/PARAFAC, Additive terms

1 Introduction

Three-way component analysis is used for the analysis of three-way data that, for instance, consist of scores of a number of subjects on a number of variables, measured in a number of different situations. The aim of three-way component analysis techniques is to summarize the three sets of entities constituting the three-way data set in such a way that the main information in the data can be summarized by means of a limited number of components for each set of entities.

The two most popular three-way component analysis methods are Tucker3 analysis (Tucker, 1966, Kroonenberg & de Leeuw, 1980) and CANDECOMP/PARAFAC (Carroll and Chang, 1970; Harshman, 1970). In Tucker3 analysis, a three-way data array $\underline{\mathbf{X}}$, of order $I \times J \times K$, with scores of, say, I subjects on J variables in K situations, is described by the model

$$x_{ijk} = \sum_{p=1}^{P} \sum_{q=1}^{Q} \sum_{r=1}^{R} a_{ip} b_{jq} c_{kr} g_{pqr} + e_{ijk}, \qquad (1)$$

$i=1,...,I$, $j=1,...,J$, $k=1,...,K$; here a_{ip}, b_{jq} and c_{kr} denote the elements of $\mathbf{A}$, $\mathbf{B}$, and $\mathbf{C}$, respectively and g_{pqr} denotes the elements of core array $\underline{\mathbf{G}}$, while e_{ijk} denotes an error term associated with the description of x_{ijk}. The core efficiently describes the main relations in the data, and the component matrices $\mathbf{A}$, $\mathbf{B}$, and $\mathbf{C}$ describe how the particular subjects, variables and situations relate to their associated components. In CANDECOMP/ PARAFAC (CP), the data are described by the (simpler) model

$$x_{ijk} = \sum_{r=1}^{R} a_{ir} b_{jr} c_{kr} + e_{ijk} , \tag{2}$$

which is the special case of the Tucker3 model with $g_{pqr}=1$ if $p=q=r=1$, and $g_{pqr}=0$ otherwise (see Carroll and Chang, 1970). From now on, we will only explicitly treat the Tucker3 model, considering the CP model as a constrained version of it.

Three-way component models may apply directly to the data, but in various situations it is likely that they only fit after subtraction of so called "offset terms". For instance, in case the variables pertain to measurements on five point Likert scales, the measurement scales can be considered (at most) of interval level, which implies that addition of any constant to the scales captures the same information. Thus, the zero value in such scales is arbitrary, and it is not clear which value actually represents a neutral point with respect to which the three-way models may hold. One way of dealing with such unknown neutral points is to simply subtract the mean value from the scores on such variables, and analyze the resulting data. However, it is by no means guaranteed that the mean constitutes a relevant neutral value for the variable at hand. A more cautious approach (e.g., see Harshman & Lundy, 1984a, 1997; Kroonenberg & Heiser, 1998; van Eeuwijk & Kroonenberg, 1998) is to consider the values of the neutral points as unknowns, and estimate them along when fitting the three-way model to one's data.

In the present paper, the uniqueness properties will be studied of models of the general form

$$x_{ijk} = \sum_{p=1}^{P} \sum_{q=1}^{Q} \sum_{r=1}^{R} a_{ip} b_{jq} c_{kr} g_{pqr} + \mu_i + \mu_j + \mu_k + e_{ijk} , \tag{3}$$

where possibly one or two of the additive terms are absent. The above class of extended three-way component models contains only "singly-subscripted" offset terms. The more complex models with "doubly-subscripted" offset terms, as well as algorithms for fitting three-way models with offset terms are treated elsewhere, for instance, by Kiers (2001).

2 Three-way Component Models with Singly-Subscripted Offsets

To describe our class of extended three-way component models, we use the notation using matricized three-way arrays, described by Kiers (2000). Then the Tucker3 model is written as

$$\mathbf{X}_a = \mathbf{A}\mathbf{G}_a(\mathbf{C}' \otimes \mathbf{B}') + \mathbf{E}_a, \tag{4}$$

where X_a is the $I \times JK$ matricized version of $\underline{X}$, G_a is the $P \times QR$ matricized version of $\underline{G}$, and E_a is the $I \times JK$ matricized version of $\underline{E}$. (Remember that the CP model is considered as a constrained version of the Tucker3 model).

Using this notation, we can now easily describe the extended versions of three-way component models. We only give them for the Tucker3 model; the extended versions of the CP model are considered special cases of these. We focus on the following three extended models with singly-subscripted offset terms:

E1: $$X_a = AG_a(C' \otimes B') + 1(1' \otimes \mu_b') + E_a, \tag{5}$$

E2: $$X_a = AG_a(C' \otimes B') + 1(1' \otimes \mu_b') + 1(\mu_c' \otimes 1') + E_a, \tag{6}$$

E3 $$X_a = AG_a(C' \otimes B') + 1(1' \otimes \mu_b') + 1(\mu_c' \otimes 1') + \mu_a(1' \otimes 1') + E_a, \tag{7}$$

where 1 denotes a vector of unit elements of appropriate size, and the vectors μ_b, μ_c, and μ_a contain offset terms for mode B, mode C, and mode A, respectively. Model E1 has offset terms only for one mode, and we chose this to be the B-mode (variables), because the variables seem to be the most common source of different, unknown offset terms (e.g., when the variables pertain to rating scales with different label sets). The next model we consider is the E2 model where, in addition to offset terms for the variables, also offset terms for one other mode (arbitrarily chosen to be the C-mode) are considered. The third model, E3, contains three singly-subscripted offset terms vectors, one for each mode.

3 Uniqueness of Three-way Component Models with Singly-Subscripted Offsets

In the present section, it is described to what extent in the models with singly-subscripted offset terms, the offset terms can be estimated uniquely. This is an important property, because unique estimation of the offset terms implies that the structural part $AG_a(C' \otimes B')$ *as a whole* is estimated uniquely as well. Note that this uniqueness does not mean that the matrices A, B, C and G_a themselves are estimated uniquely. For the Tucker3 model it means that the *subspaces* for the component matrices are estimated uniquely; for the CP model, it means that the components matrices are estimated uniquely up to trivial rescalings and permutations (as in the ordinary CP model, e.g., see, Harshman and Lundy, 1984b).

For the models E2 and E3, the offset terms have a trivial indeterminacy in that addition of a scalar to one vector of offset terms can be compensated by subtracting the same scalar from a different offset term. For instance, in E2 and E3 we obtain exactly the same estimates when μ_b is replaced by $\tilde{\mu}_b = \mu_b + \alpha 1$ and μ_c is replaced by $\tilde{\mu}_c = \mu_c - \alpha 1$, with α an arbitrary constant. To avoid such trivial indeterminacies, in the models E2 and E3 we use the identification constraints $1'\mu_c=0$, and $1'\mu_c=0$ and $1'\mu_b=0$, respectively.

Given these constraints, we have the following results on uniqueness for the estimates of the offset terms in extended Tucker3 models. In all cases it is assumed that the solution is parsimonious: it is impossible to find the same representation of the data by using smaller values of P, Q, and/or R. The proofs are given in the next section.

Uniqueness of E3: Let $\{A, B, C, \underline{G}, \mu_a, \mu_b, \mu_c\}$ give a solution for the E3 model and

$$\hat{X}_a \equiv AG_a(C'\otimes B') + 1(1'\otimes\mu_b') + 1(\mu_c'\otimes1') + \mu_a(1'\otimes1'), \tag{8}$$

where μ_c and μ_b satisfy the identification constraints $1'\mu_c=0$ and $1'\mu_b=0$, and let A, B and C not contain 1 in their column spaces. Then the solutions for μ_a, μ_b and μ_c are unique. Specifically, for any alternative (parsimonious) solution $\{D, E, F, \underline{K}, v_a, v_b, v_c\}$ that yields the same data representation $\hat{X}_a$, we have $v_a = \mu_a$, $v_b = \mu_b$, $v_c = \mu_c$, $D = AS$, $E = BT$, $F = CU$, and $\underline{K}$ is related to $\underline{G}$ according to $K_a = S^{-1}G_a((U^{-1})'\otimes(T^{-1})')$, where S, T, and U are nonsingular matrices.

Uniqueness of E2: Let $\{A, B, C, \underline{G}, \mu_b, \mu_c\}$ give a solution for the E2 model, where μ_c satisfies the identification constraint $1'\mu_c=0$. Let A, B and C not contain 1 in their column spaces. Then the solutions for μ_a, μ_b and μ_c are unique. (Details similar as in the Uniqueness of E3 result are left out).

Uniqueness of E1: Let $\{A, B, C, \underline{G}, \mu_b\}$ give a solution for the E1 model, and let A and C not contain 1 in their column spaces. Then the solution for μ_b is unique. (Details similar as in the Uniqueness of E3 result are left out again).

The above results imply that, in practice, the offset terms can be estimated uniquely in all three models, provided that the trivial indeterminacy due to addition of a scalar to the offset terms is dealt with by using appropriate constraints.

4 Uniqueness Proofs

In this section, the results given in Section 3 are proven. We start by proving the uniqueness result for the E3 model. The uniqueness results for the other models can then be proven along similar lines. The E3 model (8) can be given in three forms, depending on the matricization chosen. That is, by simple cyclic permutations, from (8) we get the following B- and C-mode matricized three-way arrays (where the rows refer to the B-mode, and the C-mode entities, respectively):

$$\hat{X}_b = BG_b(A'\otimes C') + \mu_b(1'\otimes 1') + 1(1'\otimes\mu_c') + 1(\mu_a'\otimes 1'), \tag{9}$$

and

$$\hat{X}_c = CG_c(B'\otimes A') + 1(\mu_b'\otimes 1') + \mu_c(1'\otimes 1') + 1(1'\otimes\mu_a'), \tag{10}$$

where $\hat{X}_b$ has order $J{\times}KI$, G_b has order $Q{\times}RP$, $\hat{X}_c$ has order $K{\times}IJ$ and G_c has order $R{\times}PQ$.

To prove uniqueness for the E3 model, we consider an arbitrary alternative solution $\{D, E, F, \underline{K}, v_a, v_b, v_c\}$ giving the same data representation, hence for which

$$\hat{X}_a = DK_a(F'\otimes E') + 1(1'\otimes v_b') + 1(v_c'\otimes 1') + v_a(1'\otimes 1'). \tag{11}$$

Now, we have to prove that, under the assumptions mentioned with the uniqueness result for E3, this alternative solution is related to the original solution according to $v_a = \mu_a$, $v_b = \mu_b$, $v_c = \mu_c$, $D = AS$, $E = BT$, $F = CU$, and $K_a = S^{-1}G_a((U^{-1})'\otimes(T^{-1})')$, where S, T, and U are nonsingular matrices, thus showing that the offset terms are uniquely determinable. The assumptions are

(i) the solution is parsimonious: it is impossible to find the same representation of the data by using smaller values of P, Q, and/or R;

(ii) A, B, and C do not contain 1 in their column spaces.

<u>Proof of Uniqueness for E3:</u>

For later use we first note that assumption (i) implies that A, B, and C have full column rank, and that G_a, G_b, and G_c have full row rank, because otherwise, transformations of A, B, or C would exist that either make a column of A, B, or C or a row of G_a, G_b, or G_c equal to 0, which in both cases implies that a model based on a smaller value for P, Q, or R would yield the same representation of the data.

The proof can now be given as follows. From (8) and (11) it follows that

$$\begin{aligned} AG_a(C'\otimes B') + 1(1'\otimes\mu_b') + 1(\mu_c'\otimes 1') + \mu_a(1'\otimes 1') \\ = DK_a(F'\otimes E') + 1(1'\otimes v_b') + 1(v_c'\otimes 1') + v_a(1'\otimes 1'). \end{aligned} \tag{12}$$

Centering both sides of (12) across modes A and B, and denoting columnwise centered matrices by adding a superscript ^{c} to them, we get

$$A^c G_a(C'\otimes B^{c\prime}) = D^c K_a(F'\otimes E^{c\prime}), \tag{13}$$

which, expressed in different matricizations is equivalent to

$$B^c G_b(A^{c\prime}\otimes C') = E^c K_b(D^{c\prime}\otimes F') \tag{14}$$

and

$$CG_c(B^{c\prime}\otimes A^{c\prime}) = FK_c(E^{c\prime}\otimes D^{c\prime}).\tag{15}$$

Because of assumption (ii), A^c and B^c having the same (full) rank as A and B. Hence, it follows from (13) and (14) that D^c and E^c must have full rank as well, and that $D^c = A^cS$ and $E^c = B^cT$, for certain nonsingular matrices S and T. Then it follows from (15) that $F=CU$ for a certain nonsingular matrix U, and from (13) we get $K_a = S^{-1}G_a((U^{-1})^\prime\otimes(T^{-1})^\prime)$.

Fully analogously, by centering both sides of (12) across modes A and C we obtain $E=BT^*$ for a certain nonsingular matrix T^*. Now upon centering B and E it follows that $E^c=B^cT^*$, and it follows from $E^c = B^cT$ and the full rank of B^c that $T^*=T$, hence that $E=BT$. Similarly, by centering both sides of (12) across modes B and C we obtain $D=AS^*$ for a certain nonsingular matrix S^*, and upon centering A and D it follows that $D^c=A^cS^*$, hence that $S^*=S$ and $D=AS$.

As a consequence of the above results, (12) reduces to

$$\begin{aligned}AG_a(C^\prime\otimes B^\prime) + 1(1^\prime\otimes\mu_b^\prime) + 1(\mu_c^\prime\otimes1^\prime) + \mu_a(1^\prime\otimes1^\prime) = \\ ASS^{-1}G_a((U^{-1})^\prime\otimes(T^{-1})^\prime)(U^\prime C^\prime\otimes T^\prime B^\prime) + 1(1^\prime\otimes v_b^\prime) \\ + 1(v_c^\prime\otimes1^\prime) + v_a(1^\prime\otimes1^\prime)\end{aligned}\tag{16}$$

hence

$$\begin{aligned}1(1^\prime\otimes\mu_b^\prime) + 1(\mu_c^\prime\otimes1^\prime) + \mu_a(1^\prime\otimes1^\prime) = \\ 1(1^\prime\otimes v_b^\prime) + 1(v_c^\prime\otimes1^\prime) + v_a(1^\prime\otimes1^\prime).\end{aligned}\tag{17}$$

Upon centering the left- and right-hand side of (17) across mode A, we obtain $\mu_a^c(1^\prime\otimes1^\prime) = v_a^c(1^\prime\otimes1^\prime)$, hence $\mu_a^c = v_a^c$, where the superscript c denotes centering of the offset terms vectors. Similarly, centering across mode B gives $\mu_b^c = v_b^c$, and centering across mode C gives $\mu_c^c = v_c^c$. Taking into account the identification constraints that μ_b^c, v_b^c, μ_c^c, and v_c^c have zero sum, it follows that $\mu_b = v_b$ and $\mu_c = v_c$, which, combined with (17) yields $\mu_a = v_a$, which completes the proof.

Proof of Uniqueness for E2:

For this proof we simply use the proof given above, and in (17) use that $\mu_a = v_a = 0$. Now centering across C gives $\mu_c^c = v_c^c$, hence, because of the identification constraint, we have $\mu_c = v_c$. Using this, it follows at once from (17) that $\mu_b = v_b$.

Proof of Uniqueness for E1:

Now we no longer need the assumptions that B does not contain 1 in its column space, and use the following proof. From the modified versions of (8) and (11) we have

$$AG_a(C^\prime\otimes B^\prime) + 1(1^\prime\otimes\mu_b^\prime) = DK_a(F^\prime\otimes E^\prime) + 1(1^\prime\otimes v_b^\prime).\tag{18}$$

Centering both sides of (18) across modes A, we get

$$A^c G_a(C' \otimes B') = D^c K_a(F' \otimes E'),$$ (19)

from which it follows that $D^c = A^c S$, $E = BT$, $F = CU$, and $K_a = S^{-1} G_a((U^{-1})' \otimes (T^{-1})')$, for certain nonsingular matrices S, T, and U. Alternatively, centering (18) across mode C we get, in an analogous way, that $D = AS^*$, and centering both sides we get $D^c = A^c S^*$. Because A^c has full column rank, it follows that $S^* = S$, hence $D = AS$. Hence,

$$AG_a(C' \otimes B') + 1(1' \otimes \mu_b') = ASS^{-1} G_a((U^{-1})' \otimes (T^{-1})')(U'C' \otimes T'B') \\ + 1(1' \otimes v_b')$$ (20)

which implies that $1(1' \otimes \mu_b') = 1(1' \otimes v_b')$, from which it follows at once that $\mu_b = v_b$.

5 Discussion

In the present paper, it has been shown that in the extended three-way component models with singly-subscripted offset terms (see (3)), the offset terms can be estimated uniquely, provided that certain mild assumptions hold. It should be emphasized once more that this uniqueness does not imply that all model parameters will be estimated uniquely. In fact, in the extended models, the three-way component matrices have the same uniqueness properties as in the unextended counterpart models.

The extended models can be further extended by incorporating doubly- or even triply-subscripted offset terms. The latter, however, would on their own fit the data perfectly, so it makes no sense to incorporate such terms. Doubly-subscripted offset terms, like μ_{jk} could, in principle be useful. However, such terms cannot be estimated uniquely, as shown by Kiers (2001).

References

Carroll, J. D. & Chang, J.-J. (1970). Analysis of individual differences in multidimensional scaling via an N-way generalization of "Eckart-Young" decomposition, *Psychometrika, 35*, 283-319.

Harshman, R.A. (1970). Foundations of the PARAFAC procedure: models and conditions for an "explanatory" multi-mode factor analysis. University of California at Los Angeles, *UCLA Working Papers in Phonetics, 16*, 1-84.

Harshman, R.A., & Lundy, M.E. (1984a). Data preprocessing and the extended PARAFAC model. In H.G. Law, C.W. Snyder, J.A. Hattie, and R.P. McDonald (Eds.), *Research methods for multimode data analysis* (pp. 216-284). New York: Praeger.

Harshman, R.A., & Lundy, M.E. (1984b). The PARAFAC model for three-way factor analysis and multidimensional scaling. In H.G. Law, C.W. Snyder, J.A. Hattie, and R.P. McDonald (Eds.), *Research methods for multimode data analysis* (pp. 122-215). New York: Praeger.

Harshman, R.A., & Lundy, M.E. (1997). *An Extended Parafac Model Incorporating Singly-Subscripted Constants: Theory and Application.* Poster presented at the TRICAP Meeting, Lake Chelan, 1997, May.

Kiers, H.A.L. (2000). Towards a Standardized Notation and Terminology in Multiway Analysis, *Journal of Chemometrics, 14*, 105-122.

Kiers, H.A.L. (2001). *Properties of and Algorithms for Fitting Three-way Component Models with Offset Terms.* Manuscript submitted for publication.

Kroonenberg, P.M., & De Leeuw, J. (1980). Principal component analysis of three-mode data by means of alternating least squares algorithms. *Psychometrika, 45*, 69-97.

Kroonenberg, P.M. & Heiser, W.J. (1998). Parallel factor analysis with constraints on the configurations: an overview. C. Hayashi et al. (Eds.) *Data Science, Classification and Related Methods* (pp. 563-574). Tokyo: Springer-Verlag.

Tucker, L.R. (1966). Some mathematical notes on three-mode factor analysis. *Psychometrika, 31*, 279-311.

Van Eeuwijk, F.A., Kroonenberg, P.M. (1998). Multiplicative models for interaction in three-way ANOVA, with applications to plant breeding. *Biometrics*, 1315-1333.

An Assessment of Non-Monotonicity of Missing-Data Patterns for Incomplete Multivariate Data

Manabu Iwasaki[1] and Reiko Abe[2]

[1] Department of Industrial Engineering and Information Sciences, Seikei University, 3-3-1 Kichijoji-Kitamachi, Musashino, Tokyo 180-8633, Japan.
[2] Information System Development Center, Mitsubishi Electric Co Ltd, Ofuna, Kamakura, Kanagawa 247-8501, Japan

Summary. We will consider a rectangular dataset denoted by an $n \times p$ matrix $Y = \{y_{ij}\}$, in which the n rows are observational units and the p columns represent variables. In practical data analysis we often encounter the situation that some of the data are missing for some reasons. It has been argued in the literature that if the missing-data pattern is monotone then most statistical procedures become simple, and hence it would be important to assess the extent of monotonicity of the data set considered.

In this paper, we introduce an index called NMI (non-monotonicity index) which measures the extent of non-monotonicity of missing-data patterns. The NMI is analogous to an index used in the analysis of so-called S-P (student-problem) table, which was originally developed for analysis of mental test scores. This index can be used for several purposes: first, it is a key quantity to be used in converting an original dataset to a monotone or near monotone one, secondly it provides a numerical summary of the non-monotonicity of the missingness of a given dataset, thirdly it may help us to examine various response patterns in a pattern-mixture modeling.

Key Words. monotone pattern, non-monotonicity index, S-P table, test theory

1. Introduction

In practical data analysis we often encounter the situation that not all planned measurements are observed for some reasons, in which cases the data are called incomplete. After publication of the seminal paper Rubin (1976), general statistical methods for analyzing such incomplete data have been developed extensively for several decades; see Iwasaki (2002), Little and Rubin (1987), Schafer (1997), Verbeke and Molenberghs (1997, 2000) and the references therein.

Among various aspects of incomplete data analysis, the missing-data pattern plays an important role in theoretical consideration and also in numerical computation as well. If the missing-data pattern is monotone, the definition of which will be given in Section 2, we can obtain maximum likelihood estimates for population parameters without any iterative procedures, whereas if it is not monotonic we have to carry out time-consuming numerical iterations such as EM algorithms (cf. McLachlan and Krishnan, 1997). In this regard, it can be expected that the further a data set departs from the complete monotone pattern the longer time we have to spend to get required estimates. Therefore it would be important to make numerical assessment about the extent to which the data set is far from the monotone pattern.

In this article it is pointed out that our problem of assessing the non-monotonicity of an incomplete data set is closely related to the so-called Student-Problem table (S-P table) analysis introduced by Takahiro Sato, a Japanese engineer, to analyze mental test scores, see Sato (1975). We will define an index to assess the non-monotonicity in the manner analogous to an index introduced in the S-P table analysis. After the definition of monotone pattern and relevant discussion in Section2, we will briefly discuss the idea of S-P table analysis in Section 3 because it seems not well-known outside Japan. An index called non-monotonicity index (NMI) will be defined in Section 4, and then it will be shown several techniques which utilize the index. Section 5 will be devoted to conclusion and some further discussion.

2. Monotone Missing-Data Pattern

We will consider rectangular datasets or a flat file denoted by an $n \times p$ matrix $Y = \{y_{ij}\}$, in which the n rows represent observational units and the p columns represent variables recorded for those units. We consider the case that some of the observations are missing. We will give the definition of monotone pattern.

Definition 2.1. The missing-data pattern of a data matrix $Y = \{y_{ij}\}$ is said to be monotone if, whatever an element y_{ij} is missing, y_{ik} is also missing for all $k > j$.

Monotone patterns often arise in longitudinal datasets if the cause of missing is dropout only. For general multivariate datasets, however, such strict monotone pattern would be rarely observed. But, in some cases a seemingly non-monotone dataset can be made monotone or nearly so by reordering the variables and the units.

For example, we consider data sets (a-1) and (b-1) in Table 2.1, which are taken from a large dataset of physical measurements (Y1: lung capacity, Y2: chest measurement, Y3: height) for junior high school students. The dataset of (a-1), which looks non-monotone at a first glance, can be made monotone shown as (a-2) by appropriate reordering of rows and columns. On the other hand, the dataset (b-1) cannot be made monotone by such reordering. Table 2.1 (b-2) gives a near monotone set achieved by reordering. Reordering of units is almost always permissible without any loss of information of the data structure because they can be regarded as independent observations from a population. However, reordering of variables cannot be allowed for longitudinal data.

Table 2.1. Original non-monotone datasets and their reordered datasets

(a-1) Original dataset

ID	Y1	Y2	Y3
1	1850	71	136
2	2000	68	139
3	2100	72	147
4	1700	72	142
5		90	
6	2200	72	150
7	2150	77	156
8		76	
9		84	152
10		77	

(a-2) Reordered dataset

ID	Y2	Y3	Y1
1	71	136	1850
2	68	139	2000
3	72	147	2100
4	72	142	1700
6	72	150	2200
7	77	156	2150
9	84	152	
5	90		
8	76		
10	77		

(b-1) Original dataset

ID	Y1	Y2	Y3
1	1850	71	136
2	2000	68	139
3	2100	72	147
4	1700	72	142
5		90	
6	2200	72	150
7	2150		156
8		76	
9		84	152
10		77	

(b-2) Reordered dataset

ID	Y2	Y3	Y1
1	71	136	1850
2	68	139	2000
3	72	147	2100
4	72	142	1700
6	72	150	2200
7		156	2150
9	84	152	
5	90		
8	76		
10	77		

The monotone pattern has some advantages in applying statistical techniques. If the units are from a multivariate normal population, as was first shown in Anderson (1957) the procedure to obtain maximum likelihood estimates of population parameters does not use numerical iterations, see also Little and Rubin (1987). If we apply multiple imputation technique, selection of values to be imputed is much easier for monotone patterns, see for example Schafer (1997). Hence, even the original dataset is not monotone there would exist good reasons to make the dataset monotone.

In order to make the data set (b) of Table 2.1 monotone we have to delete the observed unit No. 7 from the table or impute a numerical value to the missing cell of the unit. Such decision cannot be made so easily on (b-1) but rather easier on (b-2). Therefore it is very important to make the original dataset to (near) monotone one for any analysis of such incomplete data.

For the analysis of missing-data patterns it is convenient to introduce response indicator r_{ij} such that $r_{ij} = 1$ if y_{ij} is observed and $= 0$ if y_{ij} is missing. Let m_i be the sum of the ith row of the indicator matrix $R = \{r_{ij}\}$, which is the number of observed data for ith unit, and let n_j be the sum of the jth column, the number of observed data for jth variable. The matrices of the response indicators for the datasets in Table 2.1 (a-1) and (a-2) and associated sums are given as Table 2.2 (a-1) and (a-2), respectively.

Table 2.2. Response indicator matrices

(a-1)

ID	Y1	Y2	Y3	m
1	1	1	1	3
2	1	1	1	3
3	1	1	1	3
4	1	1	1	3
5	0	1	0	1
6	1	1	1	3
7	1	1	1	3
8	0	1	0	1
9	0	1	1	2
10	0	1	0	1
n	6	10	7	23

(a-2)

ID	Y2	Y3	Y1	m
1	1	1	1	3
2	1	1	1	3
3	1	1	1	3
4	1	1	1	3
6	1	1	1	3
7	1	1	1	3
9	1	1	0	2
5	1	0	0	1
8	1	0	0	1
10	1	0	0	1
n	10	7	6	23

3. The S-P Table Analysis

The student-problem (S-P) table was originally introduced by T. Sato to analyze characteristics of the problems (test items) in an exam and the response pattern of the students (subjects) who took the exam, for details see Sato (1975). We consider the case that there are n students and p test items. Let t_{ij} be an indicator variable such that $t_{ij} = 1$ if the ith student made correct answer to the jth test item, and $t_{ij} = 0$ if he/she made wrong answer. The response pattern of the all students is shown as an $n \times p$ table (matrix) $T^* = \{t_{ij}\}$. We let m_i be the number of correct answers of the ith student and n_j be the number of students who correctly answered the jth test item. We note that m_i is the sum of the entries of the ith row and n_j is the sum of the jth column of the table T^*.

We reorder the rows and columns of T^* in the descending order of m_i and n_j, and denote the resultant table as T. This T may not be unique because there are many ties in m_i's and possibly in n_j's. Next, we draw two "curves", the S-curve and the P-curve on T. The S-curve consists of connected vertical segments which indicate m_i's for the ith row of T and the P-curve consists of connected horizontal lines which corresponds n_j's for the jth column. As an illustration, see Table 3.1 (a), (b) for the case $n = 10$ and $p = 4$ with each curve represented by dotted lines. The connected segments is not actually a curve but is called "curve" in the literature. The table of response patterns together with such curves is called the S-P table for an examination.

The curves separate the table into two areas, upper-left and lower-right parts. If the response pattern is monotone in the sense of Section 2, then the two curves coincide and the upper-left part consists of ones and the lower-right zeros. Otherwise, there exist several zeros in the upper-left part and the same number of ones in the lower-right. The number of zeros in the upper-left part gives us important information about the appropriateness of test items and also about the mental ability of students. An item with many zeros above the line may fail to assess the ability of students to be measured. In order to assess such problematic characteristics of test items and of students, an index called caution index (CI) was defined. Among several equivalent definitions the following definition is easiest to calculate:

Table 3.1. S-P tables with S-curve and with P-curve

(a) Table with the S-curve

ID	P1	P2	P3	P4	m
1	1	1	1	1	4
2	1	1	1	1	4
3	1	1	1	1	4
4	1	1	1	0	3
5	1	1	0	1	3
6	1	0	1	1	3
7	1	1	0	0	2
8	1	0	1	0	2
9	1	0	0	0	1
10	0	1	0	0	1
n	9	7	6	5	27

(b) Table with the P-curve

ID	P1	P2	P3	P4	m
1	1	1	1	1	4
2	1	1	1	1	4
3	1	1	1	1	4
4	1	1	1	0	3
5	1	1	0	1	3
6	1	0	1	1	3
7	1	1	0	0	2
8	1	0	1	0	2
9	1	0	0	0	1
10	0	1	0	0	1
n	9	7	6	5	27

Definition 3.1. A Caution Index (CI) for the ith student is defined as

$$v_i = \left(\sum_{\substack{j=1,m_i \\ t_{ij}=0}} n_j - \sum_{\substack{j=m_i+1,p \\ t_{ij}=1}} n_j \right) \bigg/ \left(\sum_{j=1,m_i} n_j - m_i \times n^* \right) \quad (i=1,\ldots,n), \tag{3.1}$$

where n^* is the average of n_j's, and the Caution Index for the jth test item is defined as

$$\xi_j = \left(\sum_{\substack{i=1,n_j \\ t_{ij}=0}} m_i - \sum_{\substack{i=n_j+1,n \\ t_{ij}=1}} m_i \right) \bigg/ \left(\sum_{i=1,n_j} m_i - n_j \times m^* \right) \quad (j=1,\ldots,p), \tag{3.2}$$

where m^* is the average of m_i's.

It can be shown that if the response pattern of the ith student is completely monotone then v_i becomes zero. The same is true for ξ_j that is if the response pattern for the jth test item is monotone then ξ_j becomes zero. Contrarily, if the response pattern is random both the indices are near one. Therefore it can be said that the indices measure the extent of unusualness of the students or the test items. The caution index may become greater than one if response pattern is unusual: for example a student who fails to answer correctly for easier test items but answers correctly for more difficult items will have large index number. For details and various uses of the indices readers should refer to Sato (1975) if he/she can read Japanese language.

4. Non-Monotone Index (NMI)

The correspondence between the missing-data pattern of Section 2 and the response pattern of S-P table in Section 3 seems obvious. Hence, it is very natural to use the caution index introduced in Section 3 as our index of non-monotonicity of missing-data patterns. The non-monotonicity indices (NMI's) v_i and ξ_j can be defined as the same manner as (3.1) and (3.2) with replacing t_{ij}'s to r_{ij}'s, the response indicator introduced in Section 2.

The NMI can be used to make original dataset monotone or near so by reordering the rows and columns as follows.
1. From the set of observations $Y = \{y_{ij}\}$ with possibly missing data, construct a matrix of corresponding response indicators $R = \{r_{ij}\}$.
2. Calculate the row sum m_i and column sums n_j of R.
3. Reorder the rows and columns in descending order of m_i and n_j.
4. Calculate the NMI's v_i and ξ_j for rows and columns.
5. For rows with the same m_i and for columns with the same n_j are to be reordered in ascending order of the NMI's. This step may require alternating reordering of rows and columns several times.

When the numbers of units and/or variables are not so large it may happen that there only exist limited number of different patterns, and then the reordering procedure may not converge. In such cases it is recommend to add small fluctuations less than one to the column sums to achieve unique convergence. This tip is just for unique convergence and will not alter the NMI's. Table 4.1 shows the NMI's for the response pattern of Table 3.1. Although the pattern of P4 column seen in Table 4.1 seems to be non-monotone, it can be made monotone by rearrangement within the rows with the same $m_j = 3$. This fact is reflected in the definition of the NMI, and the NMI of this column is actually zero as is shown in Table 4.1. Overall NMI can be defined as an arithmetic average of v_i's or ξ_j's.

Table 4.1. The NMI's for response pattern of Table 3.1

ID	P1	P2	P3	P4	m	NMI
1	1	1	1	1	4	0
2	1	1	1	1	4	0
3	1	1	1	1	4	0
4	1	1	1	0	3	0
5	1	1	0	1	3	0.571
6	1	0	1	1	3	1.143
7	1	1	0	0	2	0
8	1	0	1	0	2	0.4
9	1	0	0	0	1	0
10	0	1	0	0	1	0.036
n	9	7	6	5	27	
NMI	0	0.488	0.208	0		

Of course the NMI is not a unique device to achieve (near) monotone pattern. In fact in order to get such patterns, Iwasaki (1989) used the technique of

Hayashi's third method of quantification, which is mathematically equivalent to the correspondence analysis or dual scaling. Iwasaki's technique, however, rests on eigenvalues and vectors of the matrix considered, and hence it may take a long time to get the required results. Since recent datasets are sometimes very large or huge it is advantageous to avoid heavy computation. In this respect the NMI introduced above can be highly recommended since it calculates the row and column sums only.

5. Conclusion and Discussion

We have pointed out the similarity between missing-data patterns and response patterns of S-P table, and defined an index which assesses the non-monotonicity of the dataset. This index is very useful as a clue to make original dataset near monotone by reordering the rows and columns of the table. It also provides us a numerical value that shows the extent to which the dataset is far from the complete monotonicity.

The magnitude of the NMI would be related to the performance of estimation procedure of unknown parameters of a model postulated to the dataset. It can be expected that the greater the NMI is the larger the sampling variance of the estimates. This problem seems challenging, and will be treated in subsequent papers.

Acknowledgments

The authors are grateful to the editor and the referees for their helpful comments given on the earlier draft of the present paper.

References

Anderson TW (1957) Maximum likelihood estimates for the multivariate normal distribution when some observations are missing. J Amer Statist Assoc, 52, 200-203.

Iwasaki M (1989) Analysis of test scores by Hayashi's third method of quantification (in Japanese). Japanese J of Behaviormetrics, 16, 13-21.

Iwasaki M (2002) Foundations of incomplete data analysis (in Japanese). Economist-sha, Tokyo .

Little RJA, Rubin DB (1987) Statistical analysis with missing data. Wiley, New York.

McLachlan GJ, Krishnan T (1997) The EM algorithm and extensions. Wiley, New York.

Rubin DB (1976) Inference and missing data. Biometrika, 63, 581-592.

Sato T (1975) Construction and analysis of S-P Tables (in Japanese). Meiji Tosho, Tokyo.

Shafer JL (1997) Analysis of incomplete multivariate data. Chapman & Hall, London.

Verbeke G, Molenberghs G (1997) Linear mixed models in practice: A SAS-oriented approach. Lecture Notes in Statistics 126. Springer, New York.

Verbeke G, Molenberghs G (2000) Linear mixed models for longitudinal data. Springer, New York.

A Unified Approach to Oblique Procrustes Problems

John Gower,
Department of Statistics, The Open University, Milton Keynes, MK7 6AA, U. K.

Summary. Oblique Procrustes problems are considered that require the minimisation of $\|\mathbf{XT} - \mathbf{Y}\|$ where $\mathbf{T} = \mathbf{C}, \mathbf{C}', \mathbf{C}^{-1}$ or $(\mathbf{C}')^{-1}$ and where $\mathbf{C}$ is a matrix giving the direction cosines of oblique axes. A unified approach allows the construction of an algorithm that iteratively updates single columns of $\mathbf{C}$. The fundamental problem is to find $\mathbf{t}$ that minimizes $\|\mathbf{Xt} - \mathbf{y}\|$ for $\mathbf{t}'\mathbf{Bt} = k$. where $\mathbf{X}$, $\mathbf{B}$, $\mathbf{y}$ and k are given but their functional forms differ for different settings of $\mathbf{T}$. There is a unique minimum and an algorithm is proposed for its calculation.

Key words. Procrustes analysis, Oblique axes, Algorithms

1 Introduction

Throughout this paper, the squared norm is denoted by $\|\mathbf{A}\| = trace(\mathbf{A'A})$. A variety of oblique Procrustes problems occur in factor analysis. All require the minimization of the $\|\mathbf{XT} - \mathbf{Y}\|$ where $\mathbf{T}$ is some function of a matrix $\mathbf{C}$, whose columns give the direction cosines of the oblique axes. Because $\mathbf{C}$ is a direction cosine matrix, $diag(\mathbf{C'C}) = \mathbf{I}$. We assume that $\mathbf{X}$ and $\mathbf{Y}$ have dimension $n \times p$ and $\mathbf{T}$ and $\mathbf{C}$ $p \times p$.

Usually, the rows of $\mathbf{X}$ will refer to coordinates relative to classical orthogonal Cartesian axes and the rows of $\mathbf{Y}$ will refer to coordinates relative to one of two possible oblique axes representations – (i) the projection method for which $\mathbf{y} = \mathbf{xC}$ or (ii) the parallel axes method, based on vector-sums, for which $\mathbf{y} = \mathbf{x}(\mathbf{C}')^{-1}$. In case (i), the squared distance between two rows of $\mathbf{Y}$ is given by the metric $(\mathbf{y}_1 - \mathbf{y}_2)(\mathbf{C'C})^{-1}(\mathbf{y}_1 - \mathbf{y}_2)'$ and in case (ii) by $(\mathbf{y}_1 - \mathbf{y}_2)(\mathbf{C'C})(\mathbf{y}_1 - \mathbf{y}_2)'$. We may match $\mathbf{X}$ to $\mathbf{Y}$ in several ways but discuss only the four possibilities that depend on the two oblique axes representations and on whether or not we take into account their associated distance metrics. The simple projection match is given by choosing $\mathbf{C}$ to minimize:

$$\|\mathbf{XC} - \mathbf{Y}\| \qquad (1)$$

and for the parallel axes method to minimise:

$$\|\mathbf{X}(\mathbf{C}')^{-1} - \mathbf{Y}\|. \qquad (2)$$

In Eqs. (1) and (2) $\mathbf{X}$ is referred to rectangular Cartesian axes and we are seeking oblique axes, with directions defined by the columns of $\mathbf{C}$, in such a way that its projection, respectively parallel axes, coordinates match as well as possible the target matrix $\mathbf{Y}$. If $\mathbf{Y}$ is regarded as giving coordinates relative to the oblique axes, then both $\mathbf{Y}$ and the transformed version of $\mathbf{X}$ are in the same space, and the metrics become relevant. Then the natural least-squares criterion is to minimize:

$$trace((\mathbf{XC} - \mathbf{Y})(\mathbf{C'C})^{-1}(\mathbf{XC} - \mathbf{Y})') = \|\mathbf{X} - \mathbf{YC}^{-1}\| \qquad (3)$$

for the projection method, and:

$$trace((\mathbf{X}(\mathbf{C}')^{-1} - \mathbf{Y})\mathbf{C'C}(\mathbf{X}(\mathbf{C}')^{-1} - \mathbf{Y})') = \|\mathbf{X} - \mathbf{YC}'\| \qquad (4)$$

for the parallel axes method. Interestingly, the metrics induce an ordinary least-squares criterion but with the transformation attached to $\mathbf{Y}$ rather than to $\mathbf{X}$. For consistency of the notation of attaching the transformation to $\mathbf{X}$, we rewrite Eqs. (3) and (4) as:

$$\|\mathbf{X}\mathbf{C}^{-1} - \mathbf{Y}\| \tag{5}$$

and

$$\|\mathbf{X}\mathbf{C}' - \mathbf{Y}\| \tag{6}$$

where the roles of $\mathbf{X}$ and $\mathbf{Y}$ have been interchanged; $\mathbf{X}$ is now the target matrix.

Thus, we are concerned with $\mathbf{T} = \mathbf{C}$, $(\mathbf{C}')^{-1}$, $\mathbf{C}^{-1}$, and $\mathbf{C}'$, all subject to the constraint $diag(\mathbf{C}'\mathbf{C}) = \mathbf{I}$. For these forms of $\mathbf{T}$, we need to minimise:

$$\|\mathbf{X}\mathbf{T} - \mathbf{Y}\| + trace\{\Lambda(diag(\mathbf{C}'\mathbf{C}) - \mathbf{I})\} \tag{7}$$

where Λ is a diagonal matrix of Lagrange multipliers for the p constraints. We may differentiate Eq. (7) with respect to $\mathbf{T}$, to give the normal equations:

$$(\mathbf{X}'\mathbf{X})\mathbf{T} - \mathbf{X}'\mathbf{Y} = \Delta, \tag{8}$$

(i) where $\mathbf{T} = \mathbf{C}$ and $\Delta = \mathbf{C}\Lambda$, (ii) where $\mathbf{T} = (\mathbf{C}')^{-1}$ and $\Delta = -\mathbf{C}\Lambda\mathbf{C}'\mathbf{C}$, (iii) where $\mathbf{T} = \mathbf{C}^{-1}$ and $\Delta = -\mathbf{C}'\mathbf{C}\Lambda\mathbf{C}'$, and (iv) where $\mathbf{T} = \mathbf{C}'$ and $\Delta = \Lambda\mathbf{C}'$.

The normal equations (i) for the projection method were first given by Mosier (1939), who recognised the possibility of their solution but, lacking modern computational facilities, proposed the approximate solution of estimating $\mathbf{T} = (\mathbf{X}'\mathbf{X})^{-1}\mathbf{X}'\mathbf{Y}$ and then imposing the constraint on $\mathbf{T}$. In a well-known paper Hurley and Cattell (1962) addressed the same problem, offered the same approximate solution, did not give the normal equations but did coin the name *Procrustes Analysis*. A full analysis and algorithmic solution was given by Browne (1967).

Note that (1) may be written:

$$\|\mathbf{X}\mathbf{C} - \mathbf{Y}\| = \sum_{j=1}^{p}\|\mathbf{X}\mathbf{c}_j - \mathbf{y}_j\|$$

where $\mathbf{c}_j$ is the jth column of $\mathbf{C}$ and $\mathbf{y}_j$ is the jth column of $\mathbf{Y}$. Thus the minimum of Eq. (1) occurs when $\|\mathbf{X}\mathbf{c}_j - \mathbf{y}_j\|$ is minimum for $j = 1, 2, \ldots, p$ and we have only to solve the problem for every vector $\mathbf{c}_j$ where $\mathbf{c}_j'\mathbf{c}_j = 1$. For simplicity, we drop the suffix j and consider the minimisation of $\|\mathbf{X}\mathbf{c} - \mathbf{y}\|$ where $\mathbf{c}'\mathbf{c} = 1$.

Browne and Kristof (1969) consider minimisation in the parallel axes metric, where $\mathbf{T} = \mathbf{C}'$, seeking to solve the final of the normal equations given in Eq. (8); recall that $\mathbf{X}$ is now the target matrix. From Eq. (8)(ii) we immediately have:

$$(\mathbf{X}'\mathbf{X} - \Lambda)\mathbf{C}' = \mathbf{X}'\mathbf{Y} \tag{9}$$

whence the constraint on direction cosines gives:

$$diag[(\mathbf{X}'\mathbf{X} - \Lambda)^{-1}\mathbf{X}'\mathbf{Y}\mathbf{Y}'\mathbf{X}(\mathbf{X}'\mathbf{X} - \Lambda)^{-1}] = \mathbf{I}.$$

This gives p polynomial equations, each of degree $2p$, for the roots Λ, which Kristof and Browne (1969) solve by using the Newton-Raphson technique. Having found Λ, $\mathbf{C}$ is obtained directly from Eq. (9). Here we propose an alternative strategy that may be used for all three remaining methods. In Browne (1967), the direction of each axes is found independently of the others. As we shall see, independence no longer holds for the other problems, but given the direction of $p-1$ of the axes, we may seek the best direction of the remaining axis.

Assuming that we can find this direction, we may proceed iteratively by repeating the procedure for the other axes, each step reducing the value of the criterion. (8).

First, we show how this works in the simpler case already considered of minimising

$$\|\mathbf{XC} - \mathbf{Y}\| = trace(\mathbf{C'AC}) - 2trace(\mathbf{C'Z}) + Constant$$

where $\mathbf{A} = \mathbf{X'X}$ and $\mathbf{Z} = \mathbf{X'Y}$. We write $\mathbf{C} = (\mathbf{C_*}, \mathbf{c})$ where $\mathbf{C_*}$ represents the first $(p - 1)$ columns of $\mathbf{C}$ and $\mathbf{c}$ represents the final column giving the preferred direction to be determined conditional on a given matrix $\mathbf{C_*}$. Similarly we partition $\mathbf{Z}$ conformally to give $\mathbf{Z} = (\mathbf{Z_*}, \mathbf{z})$. We adopt this partition for simplicity and when other preferred directions are adopted we imagine them as being permuted into the final column. Substituting the partitioned form of $\mathbf{C}$ and $\mathbf{Z}$ into the criterion, shows that we have to minimise $trace(\mathbf{C'_*AC_*}) + \mathbf{c'Ac} - 2trace(\mathbf{C'_*Z_*}) - 2\mathbf{c'z}$. Differentiating with respect to $\mathbf{c}$ with the constraint $\mathbf{c'c} = 1$, gives $\mathbf{Ac} - \mathbf{z} = \lambda\mathbf{c}$, the normal equations for the projection method. Because $\mathbf{C_*}$ is not involved in this solution, as we have already seen, each column of $\mathbf{C}$ may be handled independently and p steps will be sufficient to estimate $\mathbf{C}$.

In the notation of Section 3, the solution to this problem is given by setting $\mathbf{X} = \mathbf{X}$, $\mathbf{t} = \mathbf{c}$, $\mathbf{y} = \mathbf{y}$ with constraints given by the matrix $\mathbf{B} = \mathbf{I}$ and $k = 1$. Section 3 is inspired by the solution given by Browne (1967) for the case $\mathbf{T} = \mathbf{C}$, but it differs in the following respects: (i) it deals with a more general problem, that we shall apply to other oblique axes Procrustes problems, (ii) it achieves simplifications in the algebra by using the two-sided eigen-decomposition (see e.g. Eq. (15)) rather than Browne's use of the classical spectral decomposition, available to him because of the simple form $\mathbf{B} = \mathbf{I}$, (iii) it identifies the minimum as being unique, showing that there are no local minima, leading to (iv) a simpler algorithm for computing the minimum and hence $\mathbf{c}$.

Turning to the criterion:

$$\|\mathbf{XC'} - \mathbf{Y}\| = trace(\mathbf{CAC'}) - 2trace(\mathbf{CZ}) + Constant$$

we adopt the partition $\mathbf{Z} = \begin{pmatrix} \mathbf{Z_*} \\ \mathbf{z'} \end{pmatrix}$ [now partition is by rows rather than by columns used above] and partition $\mathbf{A} = \begin{pmatrix} \mathbf{A_*} & \mathbf{a} \\ \mathbf{a'} & \alpha \end{pmatrix}$. After a little algebraic manipulation we find that the terms in $\mathbf{c}$ in the criterion may be written: $2\mathbf{c'C_*a} - 2\mathbf{c'z}$, which after differentiation with the constraint $\mathbf{c'c} = 1$ yields $\lambda\mathbf{c} = \mathbf{C_*a} - \mathbf{z}$ and therefore $\lambda^2 = \|\mathbf{C_*a} - \mathbf{z}\|$. With this setting of $\mathbf{c}$, the change in the residual sums-of-squares is $2\mathbf{c'C_*a} - 2\mathbf{c'z} = 2\lambda$, so the biggest reduction is obtained by taking the *negative* square root of λ^2. Thus, finally:

$$\mathbf{c} = \frac{\mathbf{z} - \mathbf{C_*a}}{\{(\mathbf{C_*a} - \mathbf{z})'(\mathbf{C_*a} - \mathbf{z})\}^{1/2}} \tag{10}$$

a solution that is simpler than finding the roots of a polynomial but which has the disadvantage of involving the other columns C_* of C. That the new vector c is a function of the settings in the columns of C_* implies that previously computed columns of C may need to be recomputed. Nevertheless, the use of Eq. (10) reduces the value of the criterion so its iterative use ensures convergence - see Algorithm 1; as usual, there is no guarantee that the global optimum is reached. Much depends on the initial setting of C. We may initialise by setting C to be the normalised unconstrained solution, or merely set $C = I$.

Algorithm 1

Step 1 Initialise C, compute $S_1 = \|XC'- Y\|$, set $i = 0$.
Step 2 Set $i = i \bmod(p)+1$, $S = S_1$.
Step 3 Replace the ith column of C by c_i, using Eq. (10). Compute $S_1 = \| XC'- Y\|$.
Step 4 If $S - S_1 < \varepsilon$ (threshold), exit, else go to Step 2.

The same basic strategy will be used for the other oblique criteria below but with appropriate changes to the calculation of S_1 and replacements for Eq. (10).

2 The cases $T = C^{-1}$ and $T = (C')^{-1}$

When $T = (C')^{-1}$, we are led to minimise Eq. (2) leading to the second of the normal equations Eq. (8)ii. A direct attack on this problem has been given by Gruvaeus (1970). Gruvaeus proposes an algorithm which handles constraints without appealing to Lagrange multipliers but which requires a general function minimiser. He applies his method to the oblique Procrustes problem Eq. (2) using the Fletcher and Powell function optimisation method (1963) (which requires only first derivatives) in a variant described by Jöreskog (1967).

Rather than attempting to solve the normal equations we pursue the iterative procedure discussed above. The direct approach requires the inverse $\begin{pmatrix} K \\ k' \end{pmatrix}$ of the partitioned matrix $C = (C_*, c)$. Direct multiplication $\begin{pmatrix} K \\ k \end{pmatrix}(C_*, c)$ verifies that:

$$
\left.
\begin{aligned}
K &= (C_*'C_*)^{-1}C_*'\left\{I - \frac{c'cH}{c'Hc}\right\} \\
\text{and } k &= \frac{c'H}{c'HC}
\end{aligned}
\right\}
\tag{11}
$$

where $H = I - C_*(C_*'C_*)^{-1}C_*'$ with $kk' = 1/c'Hc$.

In Eq. (11) K is a function of c and this greatly complicates the estimation of c, or equivalently k. This complication can be avoided by writing $C = QD$ where Q is orthogonal and D is an upper triangular matrix. Triangularisation is easily accomplished by pre-multiplying C by a series of p Householder transforms chosen to annihilate to zero the parts of the successive columns of C below the diagonal, yielding $Q'C = D$. These Householder transforms are functions of the successive columns of C and triangularisation is achieved in $p\text{-}1$ steps, before the final columns is used; it follows that Q is independent of c. It is easy to invert a triangular matrix.

Partitioning D we have:

$$D = \begin{pmatrix} D_* & d_* \\ & d \end{pmatrix} \text{ with inverse } G = D^{-1} = \begin{pmatrix} G_* & g_* \\ & g \end{pmatrix}$$

where D_* and G_* are both upper triangular matrices. Because $D = Q'C$, D_* is independent of c and only the final column $\begin{pmatrix} d_* \\ d \end{pmatrix} = Q'c$ is a function of c. Next we show that D^{-1} has similar properties.

From: $I = DD^{-1} = \begin{pmatrix} D_* & d_* \\ & d \end{pmatrix}\begin{pmatrix} G_* & g_* \\ & g \end{pmatrix} = \begin{pmatrix} D_*G_* & D_*g_* + gd_* \\ & gd \end{pmatrix}$,

we have that $g = 1/d$, $D_*g_* = -gd_* = -d_*/d$ and, inversely from $D^{-1}D = I$, $d = 1/g$, $G_*d_* = -dg_* = -g_*/g$. Also $D_*G_* = G_*D_* = I$, so that G_* is independent of c. Because $diag(D'D) = diag(C'QQ'C) = diag(C'C) = I$, we see that D is itself a direction cosine matrix. In particular, its final column is normalised so that:

$$d_*'d_* + d^2 = 1$$

which, through the relationships just established, may be expressed in terms of the final column of the inverse as

$$g_*'D_*'D_*g_* - g^2 = -1$$

or
$$s'Js = -1 \tag{12}$$

where $J = I - 2ee'$, e being a vector with unity in its final position (else zero) and

$$s = \begin{pmatrix} D_*g_* \\ g \end{pmatrix} = \begin{pmatrix} D_* \\ & 1 \end{pmatrix}g = Eg \tag{13}$$

so defining E.

The criterion with $T = C^{-1}$ may now be recast as follows:

$$\|XC^{-1} - Y\| = \|XGQ' - Y\| = \|XG - YQ\|;$$

only the final column, Xg, of XG involves g_* and g and hence c. Thus, denoting the final column of YQ by y, and using Eq. (13) we write:

$$Xg = XE^{-1}s, \text{ say.}$$

So we have to minimise:

$$\|XE^{-1}s - y\| \tag{14}$$

subject to the constraint Eq. (12). The solution is given in the notation of Section 3 by setting $X = XE^{-1}$, $t = s$ and $y = y$ and the constraint matrix $B = J$ with $k = -1$.

The above can be summarised in algorithmic form as in Algorithm 2. Recall that we have been concerned only in updating one column of C, which is assumed to be permuted into the final column of C. The whole process must be repeated iteratively as in Algorithm 1 but with C there replaced by C^{-1}.

A similar method is available for minimizing $\|\mathbf{X}(\mathbf{C}')^{-1} - \mathbf{Y}\|$. It turns out that now we may apply Section 3 in either of two ways:

(i) $\mathbf{X} = \mathbf{E}^{-1}$, $\mathbf{t} = \mathbf{s}$, $\mathbf{y} = \mathbf{Y}'\mathbf{x}_1/(\mathbf{x}_1'\mathbf{x}_1)$, $\mathbf{B} = \mathbf{J}$ and $k = -1$.

(ii) $\mathbf{X} = \mathbf{I}$, $\mathbf{t} = \mathbf{g}$, $\mathbf{y} = \mathbf{Y}'\mathbf{x}_1/(\mathbf{x}_1'\mathbf{x}_1)$, $\mathbf{B} = \mathbf{E}'\mathbf{J}\mathbf{E}$ (calculated from $\mathbf{C}'\mathbf{C}$ as described above), $k = -1$.

With these settings substituted for *Step 4*, algorithm 2 remains available. The required direction $\mathbf{c}$ derives from $\mathbf{s}$ or $\mathbf{g}$ through the relationships $\mathbf{s} = \mathbf{Eg} = \frac{1}{d}\begin{pmatrix} -\mathbf{d}_* \\ 1 \end{pmatrix}$, and $\mathbf{c} = \mathbf{Qd}$.

Algorithm 2

Step 1 Triangularise, i.e. Form $\mathbf{C} = \mathbf{QD}$, for $\mathbf{Q}$ orthogonal and $\mathbf{D}$ upper triangular.

Step 2 Form $\mathbf{D}^{-1}$.

Step 3 Form $\mathbf{X} = \mathbf{XE}^{-1}$, Set $\mathbf{y}$ to the final column of $\mathbf{Q}$.

Step 4 Use the algorithm 3, with $\mathbf{B} = \mathbf{J}$ and $k = -1$, to minimise $\|\mathbf{Xt} - \mathbf{y}\|$.

Step 5 From $\mathbf{s} = \frac{1}{d}\begin{pmatrix} -\mathbf{d}_* \\ 1 \end{pmatrix}$, derive $\mathbf{d}$, whence $\mathbf{c} = \mathbf{Qd}$.

---

3 A minimization problem

We study the minimum over $\mathbf{t}$ of $S = \|\mathbf{Xt} - \mathbf{y}\|$ subject to a constraint $\mathbf{t}'\mathbf{Bt} = k$, where $\mathbf{B}$ is symmetric but not necessarily definite and k is a constant. We may assume that k is either $+1$ or -1, else divide $\mathbf{B}$ by k. Note that $k = -1$ is not possible when $\mathbf{B}$ is p.s.d. and $k = +1$ is not possible when $\mathbf{B}$ is n.s.d. Minima also exist with $k = 0$; this case is not required above but we end this section with a few remarks pertaining to it.

The results are expressed in terms of the two-sided eigenvalue decomposition:

$$\mathbf{AW\Gamma} = \mathbf{BW} \tag{15}$$

which requires $\mathbf{A} = \mathbf{X}'\mathbf{X}$ to be positive definite, so we exclude the possibility that $\mathbf{X}$ has deficient rank. Because $\mathbf{A}$ is p.d. the eigenvectors may be normalised to satisfy $\mathbf{W}'\mathbf{AW} = \mathbf{I}$ and then $\mathbf{W}'\mathbf{BW} = \Gamma$ and the number of positive/negative eigenvalues of Eq. (15) is the positivity/negativity of $\mathbf{B}$. The result of minimizing the least-squares criterion may now be written:

$$(\mathbf{I} - \lambda\Gamma)\mathbf{u} = \mathbf{z} \tag{16}$$

where $\mathbf{u} = \mathbf{W}^{-1}\mathbf{t}$, $\mathbf{z} = \mathbf{W}'\mathbf{X}'\mathbf{y}$ and λ is a Lagrange multiplier. The constraint becomes:

$$\mathbf{z}'(\mathbf{I} - \lambda\Gamma)^{-1}\Gamma(\mathbf{I} - \lambda\Gamma)^{-1}\mathbf{z} = k \tag{17}$$

or, in non-matrix form:

$$f(\lambda) = \sum_{i=1}^{p} \frac{\gamma_i z_i^2}{(1 - \lambda\gamma_i)^2} - k = 0. \tag{18}$$

Thus we are concerned with the roots of Eq. (18). Suppose the eigenvalues are given in increasing order:

$$\gamma_1 < \gamma_2 < \ldots < \gamma_- < 0 < \gamma_+ < \ldots < \gamma_{p-1} < \gamma_p$$

where γ_- is the biggest negative eigenvalue and γ_+ is the smallest positive eigenvalue. A minimum of S requires that the Hessian $\mathbf{I} - \lambda\Gamma$ derived from Eq. (16) be positive definite. This is a diagonal matrix whose diagonal values are positive only for a value λ_0 of λ in the range:

$$\frac{1}{\gamma_1} < \lambda_0 < \frac{1}{\gamma_p}. \tag{19}$$

We refer to Eq. (19) as defining the permissible range for a minimum. It is straightforward to show that in this range, $f(\lambda)$ is monotone increasing and normally changes in sign (see section 3.2 for a pathological case). Thus, S has a single minimum λ_0 in the interval Eq. (19), whatever the value of k, showing that there need be no concern with local minima. Outside the range Eq. (19), S may have maxima, saddle-points etc. Thus, it is best to devise algorithms for computing λ_0 that operate only on values of λ within the range Eq. (19). Minimisation algorithms based on differentiation of $f(\lambda)$ might take one outside the safe area. Indeed, just this kind of difficulty is reported by Cramer (1974) when using the Newton-Raphson method.

The value λ_0 at the minimum is easily and safely found by bisecting in the interval (19), thus remaining in the required range throughout; this is the method recommended (see also, ten Berge (1991)). Bisection methods improve the accuracy of the root by about one bit per iteration, so three decimal figure accuracy requires about 10 iterations ($2^{10} \sim 1000$). When λ_0 has been found, it may be substituted into (16) to obtain $\mathbf{u}$, whence $\mathbf{t} = \mathbf{W}\mathbf{u}$. The value of the minimum is:

$$S_{min} = \mathbf{y}'\mathbf{y} - \mathbf{t}'(\mathbf{X}'\mathbf{y}) + \lambda_0 k.$$

When $\lambda = 0$ we have $\mathbf{t} = (\mathbf{X}'\mathbf{X})^{-1}\mathbf{X}'\mathbf{y}$ confirming that S_{min} is then the classical (multiple regression) unconstrained least-squares minimum $\mathbf{y}'[\mathbf{I} - \mathbf{X}(\mathbf{X}'\mathbf{X})^{-1}\mathbf{X}']\mathbf{y}$.

3.1 Some Special Cases

We are interested in two special cases of the above: (i) $\mathbf{B} = \mathbf{I}$ in which case we must have $k = 1$ and (ii) $\mathbf{B} = \mathbf{I} - 2\mathbf{e}\mathbf{e}'$ with $k = -1$ where $\mathbf{e}$ is a vector with a unit in its last position and zero elsewhere. Case (i) is the one discussed by Browne (1967) and subsequently by Cramer (1974) and ten Berge and Nevels (1977). Browne recommended using the Newton Raphson method for determining $\tilde{\lambda}$ but, as pointed out by Cramer, this method must be used with care. The function $f(\lambda)$ approaches the value -1 asymptotically as λ tends to $-\infty$, so that the gradient becomes very flat for large negative values of λ. Then the Newton–Raphson algorithm may take one on to the wrong branch of $f(\lambda)$ and diverge, or converge to the wrong solution. To ameliorate this situation Cramer and ten Berge and Nevels provided a good lower bound for λ_0 that guarantees convergence but it is not entirely clear that convergence is always to a global minimum if gradient methods are used. The simple bisection method avoids these difficulties but it remains efficient to confine the bisection process to a small range, so good lower bounds on λ_0 remain of interest.

When $\mathbf{B} = \mathbf{I}$, there are no negative values of γ_i so the permissible region of Eq. (19) becomes $-\infty < \lambda_0 < 1/\gamma_p$ and the bisection algorithm to find the root λ_0 of $f(\lambda) = 0$ starts with an infinite lower bound. A better lower bound for initiating the bisection process may be shown to be:

$$1/\gamma_p - z\sqrt{p} < \lambda_0 < 1/\gamma_p$$

where $z^2 = \max(z_{2i}^2/\gamma_i)$. When $\mathbf{B} = -\mathbf{I}$ and there are no positive eigenvalues, a similar argument leads to defining $-z^2 = \min(z_i^2/\gamma_i)$ and the interval:

$$1/\gamma_1 < \lambda_0 < 1/\gamma_1 + z\sqrt{p}.$$

When $\mathbf{B} = \mathbf{I} - 2\mathbf{ee}'$ there is one negative eigenvalue, γ_1, and there are no special problems unless $z_1 = 0$, when $f(\lambda)$ is always positive and there is no solution.

When there are zero values of z_i (see section 3.2) the above limits may be improved further. In the first case p may be replaced by b and in the second by $p-a+1$.

All these considerations are accommodated in Algorithm 3.

Algorithm 3

Step 1 Solve the two-sided eigenvalue problem $\mathbf{AW\Gamma} = \mathbf{BW}$, normalised so that $\mathbf{W'AW} = \mathbf{I}$.

Step 2 Determine a, where γ_a is the smallest negative eigenvalue coupled with a non-zero z_i and b, where γ_b is the biggest positive eigenvalue coupled with a non-zero z_i.

Step 3 Set $\lambda_- = 1/\gamma_a$, $\lambda_+ = 1/\gamma_b$, $\mu_- = 1/\gamma_1$, $\mu_+ = 1/\gamma_p$

Step 4 Set bounds in special cases:

If $\lambda_- > 0$ then $\mathbf{B}$ is p.s.d. Set $\lambda_- = \mu_- = 1/\gamma_b - z\sqrt{b}$ where $z^2 = \max(z_i^2/\gamma_i)$

If $\lambda_+ < 0$ then $\mathbf{B}$ is n.s.d. Set $\lambda_+ = \mu_+ = 1/\gamma_a + z\sqrt{(p-a+1)}$ where $-z^2 = \min(z_i^2/\gamma_i)$

Step 5, bisection step. Repeat:

   ① $\lambda_0 = \frac{1}{2}(\lambda_- + \lambda_+)$

   ②   if $f(\lambda_0) > 0$, set $\lambda_+ = \lambda_0$ else $\lambda_- = \lambda_0$

   ③   if $|f(\lambda_0)| > \varepsilon$, go to step ①

   Use (16) to give $\mathbf{u}$

Step 6 If $\mu_- < \lambda_0 < \mu_+$ go to step 7, else:

   If $\lambda_0 \geq \mu_+$ then (i) set $\lambda_0 = 1/\gamma_p$, (ii) set $u_p = \sqrt{-f(\lambda_0)/\gamma_p}$

   else (i) set $\lambda_0 = 1/\gamma_1$, (ii) set $u_1 = \sqrt{-f(\lambda_0)/\gamma_1}$

Step 7 Then $\mathbf{t} = \mathbf{Wu}$, $S_{\min} = \mathbf{y'y} - \mathbf{t'X'y} + \lambda_0 k$.

3.2 Zero Values of z_i

Each term of Eq. (18) pairs a value of γ_i with a value of z_i. In the above, when $z_i = 0$, then the corresponding term of Eq. (18) vanishes and may normally be disregarded. There is one pathological case, a particular instance of which was first noted by Cramer (1974) and analysed in detail by ten Berge and Nevels (1977), where more care has to be taken. This is when $z_i = 0$ pairs with γ_1 and/or γ_p and possibly with adjacent values of γ_i. Then, the asymptotes vanish (we refer to phantom asymptotes) at these values and the admissible range for λ_0 extends to:

$$\frac{1}{\gamma_a} < \lambda_0 < \frac{1}{\gamma_b} \tag{20}$$

where $z_i = 0$ pairs with $\gamma_1, \gamma_2, ..., \gamma_{a-1}$ and with $\gamma_{b+1}, \gamma_{b+2}, ..., \gamma_p$. Then it may be shown that there is a unique real minimum corresponding to one of three mutually exclusive possibilities: (i) $f(1/\gamma_p) > 0$ and $f(1/\gamma_1) < 0$, in which case the previous bisection algorithm gives λ_0, (ii) $f(1/\gamma_p) < 0$ and $f(1/\gamma_1) < 0$, in which case $\lambda_0 = 1/\gamma_p$ and (iii) $f(1/\gamma_p) > 0$ and $f(1/\gamma_1) > 0$, in which case $\lambda_0 = 1/\gamma_1$.

3.3 The Case $k = 0$.

This case has not been needed for our discussion of oblique axes but it does arise in other contexts, see e.g. ten Berge (1983) where $p = 3$, $b_{13} = b_{31} = 2$ and $b_{22} = -1$. When $k = 0$ we distinguish between the cases where $\mathbf{B}$ is semi-definite and when it is indefinite.

When $\mathbf{B}$ is semi-definite, $\mathbf{t}$ must lie in the null space of $\mathbf{B}$, assumed spanned by the (independent) columns of $\mathbf{V}$. Then $\mathbf{BV} = \mathbf{0}$ and $\mathbf{t} = \mathbf{Va}$ for some vector $\mathbf{a}$. Then, we require the minimum of $S = \|\mathbf{XVa} - \mathbf{y}\|$, which is the classical least-squares problem, with solution $\mathbf{a} = (\mathbf{V'AV})^{-1}\mathbf{V'X'y}$, whence $\mathbf{t} = \mathbf{V}(\mathbf{V'AV})^{-1}\mathbf{V'X'y}$.

When $\mathbf{B}$ is indefinite and not of full rank, the null space minimum remains available. However, there is now the possibility that $\mathbf{t}$ is not in the null space of $\mathbf{B}$. I believe that such solutions are covered by the methodology given at the beginning of section 3. To decide between the non-null space solution and, when it exists, the null space solution seems to require an examination of both to see which gives the smallest value of S.

4 References

Browne MW (1967) On oblique Procrustes rotation. Psychometrika 32 :125 - 132.

Browne MW, Kristof, W (1969) On the oblique rotation of a factor matrix to a specified pattern. Psychometrika 34 :237-248.

Cramer EM (1974) On Browne's solution for oblique Procrustes rotation. Ptka 39 :139-163.

Fletcher R, Powell MJD (1963) A rapidly convergent descent method for minimization. Computer Journal 2 :163-168.

Gruvaeus TT (1970) A general approach to Procrustes pattern rotation, Psychometrika 35 :493-505.

Hurley JR, Cattell RB (1962) The Procrustes Program: producing direct rotation to test a hypothesized factor structure. Behavioural. Science 7 :258-262.

Jöreskog KG (1967) Some contributions to maximum likelihood factor analysis. Psychometrika 23 :443-482.

Mosier CI (1939) Determinig a simple structure when loadings for certain tests are known. Psychometrika 4 :149-162.

ten Berge JMF, Nevels K (1977) A general solution for Mosier's oblique Procrustes problem. Psychometrika 42 :593-600.

ten Berge JMF (1983) A generalization of Verhelst's solution for a constrained regression problem in ALSCAL and related MDS algorithms. Psychometrika 48 :631-638.

ten Berge JMF (1991) Improved bounds for optimal intervals in weakly constrained regression problems. Psychometrika 61 :695-696.

ten Berge JMF (1996) A general solution for a class of weakly constrained linear regression problems. Psychometrika 56 :601-609

Automatic Generation of Intervention Effect Estimation Formula

Tatsuo Otsu

Department of Behavioral Science, Hokkaido University, N.10 W.7, Kita-ku, Sapporo 060-0810, Japan

Summary. Recent research on graphical modeling showed important insight on statistical causal estimation. Complicated manipulation of graphical model is required for applying these theorems. The ability of Prolog, a logic based programming language, for causal estimation on graphical models is shown. Universal pattern matching and built-in backtracking mechanism are the source of high symbolic ability of Prolog. Methods for applying Judea Pearl's inference rules on intervention effect estimation are described.

Key words: causality, graphical model, Markov property, Prolog

1 Symbolic Manipulation and Data Analysis

In various research fields, well controlled experiments are the most reliable for estimating influence relationships. Although superiority of the method is widely known, we frequently confront impossibilities of control in social/behavioral researches. Quantitatively oriented researchers in these fields have been favored statistical tools for estimating dependent structures on passively observed data. Log-linear model and structural equation model are the examples. These methods implicitly assume that the estimated structure represents the latent influence relation. An important view for criticizing the validity of causal inference was shown by Pearl (1995, 2000). Pearl's theory gives a basis for causal inference based on graphical modeling.

It is hard to cope with graphical modeling by traditional statistical analysis systems. I will show that a logic-based programming language, Prolog, is a good tool for inference about graphical models. I focus on *identifiability* detection in graphical models.

There have been some attempts to use symbolic manipulation tools for statistical analysis. The major concern of early projects was to implement automatic model diagnosis and method recommendation (Gale, 1986). There were some projects by Japanese researchers under the influence of this trend, where they used Prolog for expert system description (Nakano et al. 1990; Minami et al. 1994). The difficulty of automatic model diagnosis lies in the necessity of deep domain knowledge. Although we frequently need much domain-specific knowledge for selecting adequate models in practical problems, its implementation in a general purpose statistical system is difficult.

The second focus was on building flexible interactive statistical environment. LISP-STAT is an interactive data analysis environment build on LISP language (Tierney, 1990). Modern symbolic manipulation languages can do both interactive code interpretation and incremental compilation. These functions give attractive features for interactive data analysis. R-system (Ihaka and Gentleman, 1996) which is a GNU version of S-like system, has an internal structure similar to Scheme interpreter, a variant of LISP.

The third trend is using computer algebra system for statistical analysis. Bekker et al. (1994) made a system for identifying uniqueness of the solutions in structural equation modeling using computer algebra. Andrews and Stafford (1995) showed methods of algebraic operations for asymptotic expansion in statistical estimation.

The method in this report is in the line of the second group. There are some software systems for graphical modeling aside from traditional structural equation estimation systems. CoCo (Badsberg, 1992), BELIEF (Almond, 1995), CGGM and CGLM (Miyakawa and Haga, 1997), MIM (Edwards, 2000), and TETRAD II (Scheines et al. 1994), are the examples. CoCo was written in LIPS-STAT. BELIEF was built on Common LISP system. TETRAD II is the system based on the theory of Spirtes et al. (1993, 2001). Statistical modeling with graph structures frequently requires complicated symbol manipulations. This makes building an interactive graphical modeling system be a hard task. High symbolic manipulation ability and interactivity of Prolog have advantages to cope with these problems.

2 Markov Properties in Directed Acyclic Graphs

A graph is composed of nodes and edges. As a statistical model, nodes represent random variables, and edges represent their dependencies. Here we restrict our attention to directed acyclic graphs (DAG), which is a specific family of graphical model. Edges in a DAG are directed, and they have no cyclic structure. The formal definition is as follows.

Definition 1. (Directed Graph): A directed graph $G = (V, D)$ is a pair of nodes V and edges D between the nodes. The nodes are $V = \{v_i | i = 1, ..., n\}$, and edges are $\{e_k = (V_{i(k)}, V_{j(k)}) | V_{i(k)}, V_{j(k)} \in V, k = 1, ..., m\}$. An ordered pair (V_i, V_j) shows a directed edge from V_i to V_j.

Definition 2. (Path): A path P of a directed graph G is a sequence of nodes $(V_{i(0)}, ..., V_{i(q)})$ where either $(V_{i(k-1)}, V_{i(k)})$ or $(V_{i(k)}, V_{i(k-1)})$ is a member of D for $k = 1, ..., q$.

Definition 3. (Directed Path): A directed path P of a directed graph G is a sequence of nodes $(V_{i(0)}, ..., V_{i(q)})$ where $(V_{i(k-1)}, V_{i(k)})$ is a member of D for $k = 1, ..., q$.

Definition 4. (Cyclic Directed Path): A cyclic directed path C of a directed graph G is a directed path $(V_{i(0)}, ..., V_{i(q)})$ where $V_{i(0)} = V_{i(q)}$.

Definition 5. (Directed Acyclic Graph): A directed acyclic graph is a directed graph that has no cyclic directed path.

A DAG specifies a class of probability distributions on V. There are several definitions that relate a DAG structure to a probability class. Frydenberg (1990) defined three types of pairwise-Markov, local-Markov, and global-Markov. If the distribution class is restricted to strictly positive, these three definitions are equivalent to each other. Under this condition, the dependence relationship is called Markov property (Frydenberg, 1990; Lauritzen, 1996). Probability distributions on V that satisfy Markov property in terms of a graph G is called G-Markov.

Here we suppose that the probability is strictly positive on V. If the probability $p(V_1, ..., V_n)$ is G-Markov, it is decomposed as follows under the above condition.

$$p(V_1, ..., V_n) = \prod_i p(V_i|pa(V_i)),$$

where $pa(V_i)$ shows the parent nodes of V_i in G.

We can infer the conditional independence of a G-Markov distribution based on the topological structure of G. The following theorem shows the relationship.

Definition 6. (d-separation) (Pearl, 1995, 2000): A path P is said to be d-separated by a set of nodes Z, if and only if

1. P contains a chain $I \to M \to J$ or a fork $I \leftarrow M \to J$ such that the middle node M is in Z, or
2. P contains an inverted fork (or *collider*) $I \to M \leftarrow J$ such that the middle node M is not in Z and such that no descendant of M is in Z.

Theorem 1. *(Conditional independence in G-Markov distribution, Verma and Pearl, 1988): Suppose that three sets of nodes in DAG G, X, Y, and Z, are disjoint to each other. Tow node sets, X and Y, are conditionally independent to each other with fixed Z in any G-Markov distributions, if and only if Z d-separates X and Y in G.*

This theorem shows that d-separation essentially specifies the conditional independence in G-Markov distributions. The conditional independence property is expressed as

$$(X \perp\!\!\!\perp Y | Z)_G.$$

This notation is proposed by Dawid (1979).

3 Causality in Graphical Models

There have been been pioneering works in various fields for statistical causal estimation. Rubin (1974), Robins (1986), and Sobel(1990,1995) made important contributions. They pointed out in common that naive conditional probability of observed data is not adequate for estimating causal effect.

An important interpretation of causality for graphical modeling was proposed by Spirtes et al. (1993,2001). The core part of the theory is in the evaluation of external interventions to the system. Suppose that a variable $X = V_j$ is intervened and the value is set to be x. In this case, the intervened G-Markov distribution has the form

$$p(V_1, ..., V_{j-1}, V_{j+1}, ...|V_j = \check{x}) = \frac{p(V)}{p(V_j = x|pa(V_j))} = \prod_{i \neq j} p(V_i|pa(V_i)), \quad (1)$$

where the appeared V_js in the right-hand side are set to be x. They named this property *manipulation theorem*. This distribution is different from usual conditional distribution $p(V|V_j = x)$ except the cases where V_j is exogenous to the system. The check mark on x shows the intervention.

Pearl's research group focused on the critical aspect of graphical modeling, the validity of causal estimation (Pearl, 1995, 2000; Galles and Pearl, 1995). It gives a systematic procedure for criticizing the causal estimation based on graphical modeling. If all the variables in G are observed, every factor in the right-hand side of the formula can be estimated. Therefore we are able to estimate the probability of (1). If the observation is limited to a part of the variables, the possibility of the estimation is not trivial. Galles and Pearl (1995) showed a sufficient condition for this possibility, which seems to be very close to the necessary condition. If the intervened conditional probability $p(Y|X = \check{x}, Z)$ can be estimated from the observed probability, it is named *identifiable* (Pearl,1995). The crucial part of the theory is the following three inference rules for conditional intervened probabilities.

The following rules give rewriting admissibility of an intervened distribution. If the target distribution can be rewritten into a formula that contains observed distribution only, it is identifiable. In the following notations, $G_{\overline{X}}$ shows the DAG that is obtained by deleting all arrows into nodes in X from G. $G_{\underline{X}}$ shows the DAG that is obtained by deleting all arrows emerging from nodes in X. The variables with check mark (e.g $\check{x}$) show intervened values.

Insertion/deletion of observations

$$\text{If } (Y \perp\!\!\!\perp Z|X, W)_{G_{\overline{X}}}, \text{ then } p(y|\check{x}, z, w) = p(y|\check{x}, w). \quad (2)$$

Action/observation exchange

$$\text{If } (Y \perp\!\!\!\perp Z|X, W)_{G_{\overline{X}\underline{Z}}}, \text{ then } p(y|\check{x}, \check{z}, w) = p(y|\check{x}, z, w). \quad (3)$$

Insertion/deletion of actions

$$\text{If } (Y \perp\!\!\!\perp Z|X, W)_{G_{\overline{X}, \overline{Z(W)}}}, \text{ then } p(y|\check{x}, \check{z}, w) = p(y|\check{x}, w), \quad (4)$$

where $Z(W)$ are the nodes of Z that are not ancestors of W in $G_{\overline{X}}$.

Each condition part is sufficient for the equation. But the completeness of the rules, i.e. whether all identifiable probabilities are derived by successive application of the rules or not, is not clear (Pearl, 2000).

4 Inference on DAG by Prolog

Although Pearl's inference rules are explicitly defined, their application need complicated d-separation identification. We can use high symbolic manipulation ability of Prolog for this purpose.

There are several methods for representing a graph structure with Prolog. One standard representation is given by O'Keefe (1990). Suppose G is a DAG with four nodes $V = \{a, b, c, d\}$ and five directed edges $D = \{a \rightarrow b, a \rightarrow c, b \rightarrow c, b \rightarrow d, c \rightarrow d\}$. The Prolog representation of G is as follows.

```
[a-[b,c],b-[c,d],c-[d],d-[]]
```

In standard Prolog syntax, brackets ([and]) show list structure. The elements of the list are parent-children pairs.

The concept of variable in Prolog is very different from other programming languages. A variable of Prolog shows a symbol that can be transformed into any concrete object. The prominent characters of Prolog as practical programming language are the functions of universal pattern matching (unification) and built-in depth first search mechanism (Otsu, 2002). Using these properties, the following short code enumerates directed paths from Start to End. In standard Prolog syntax, tokens that start with upper cases show variables.

```
sg_edge(Start, End, G)  :-
            member(Start-Neib, G),
            member(End, Neib).

sdag_dpath(Start, End, G, [Start,End])  :-
            sg_edge(Start, End, G).
sdag_dpath(Start, End, G, [Start|Path1])  :-
            sg_edge(Start, Start1, G),
            sdag_dpath(Start1, End, G, Path1).
```

The first predicate sg_edge identifies the existence of an edge from Start to End in graph G, where member is a built-in predicate for testing and enumerating the members of a list. The second predicate sdag_dpath searches a directed path from Start to End, and returns the path in the fourth argument. The vertical bar in list shows CAR/CDR decomposition of LISP.

The following is an execution example, where findall is a built-in predicate for enumerating all possible solutions.

```
| ?- findall(Path,
    sdag_dpath(a,d,[a-[b,c],b-[c,d],c-[d],d-[]],Path),
       Paths).
Paths = [[a,b,d],[a,b,c,d],[a,c,d]] ?
yes
```

Iterative application of the above predicate is not the best method for identifying the reachability. The transitive closure of a graph can be obtained by $O(|V|^3)$ order computation with Warshall's algorithm (Sedgewick, 2002; O'Keefe, 1990). If we build the transitive closure of a graph, identification of the reachability is straightforward. In our cases, we must consider many graph patterns with deleted edges. Because the transitive closure construction seems to need large overhead, I did not use that.

The d-connected identification needs more complicated coding, but the basic programming strategy is the same. Prolog can enumerate d-connected paths between nodes. Nonexistence of d-connected paths ensures d-separation between the nodes. The d-separation identification enables application of the inference rules. We can take two strategies for obtaining the causal effect estimation formula. One method is starting at the target intervened distribution. Then we apply the inference rules. Another method is starting at the observed distribution and its marginals. The former method searches the restricted class of distributions that relate to the target. The latter method generates many irrelevant distributions. Here we name the former top-down search and the latter bottom-up search.

Both methods are able to generate formulas for intervention effect estimation. Although top-down search is usually far faster than bottom-up search, it may generate needlessly complex formula. The reason of this problem is non-uniqueness of the estimation formula. The following bottom-up search procedure reaches to the target distribution with minimum rewriting steps from the observed marginals. This tend to produce simple formulas.

Step 1. Put the observed marginals as initial reached distributions.

Step 2. Apply the three inference rules and the integration rule

$$p(y|w, \check{x}) = \sum_z p(y|z, w, \check{x})p(z|w, \check{x})$$

to the already reached distributions. If a new distribution is generated, stack it on the working area.

Step 3. If no new distribution is generated, then do the next step. If there are newly generated distributions, then merge them into the reached distributions. Then proceed to the step 2.

Step 4. Search for the target in the reached distributions. If it was not there, the inference rules could not generate the target. (Usually, this indicates that the target distribution is not identifiable. But its proof has not been given.)

Step 5. If the target is found in the reached distributions, then trace back the generation process for obtaining the estimation formula.

Figure 1 shows a DAG example, which is Fig. 3.8(g) in Pearl(2000). This graph has 5 observed variables and 4 unobserved variables. The Prolog representation of the graph is

```
[u1-[x,z2],u2-[x,z3],u3-[y,z2],u4-[x,y],
x-[z1],y-[],z1-[y],z2-[x,z1,z3],z3-[y]] ,
```

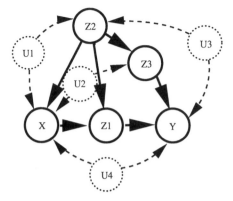

Fig. 1. A DAG example

where u1, u2, u3, and u4 are unobserved, and x, y, z1, z2, and z3 are observed variables. The bottom-up search generated the following formula in 5.3 seconds on Pentium3 500MHz PC with SICStus Prolog3.9. The obtained term is expressed as

```
sum([z2],sum([z1],sum([x],pr([y],[x,z1,z2],[])*
pr([x],[z2],[]))* pr([z1],[x,z2],[]))*pr([z2],[],[]))
```
,

where pr([y],[z],[x]) shows $p(y|z, \check{x})$. This formula means in usual notation

$$p(y|\check{x}) = \sum_{z_2}\sum_{z_1}\left\{\sum_{x'}p(y|x',z_1,z_2)p(x'|z_2)\right\}p(z_1|x,z_2)p(z_2).$$

The top-down search proved the identifiability in 0.1 seconds, but it generated a more complicated formula that contains an extra integration on z_3.

The prolog code is available from the author's site.
(http://wwwbs.let.hokudai.ac.jp/~otsu)

References

Almond,R. (1995): Graphical belief modeling. Chapman & Hall, New York

Andrews,D.F., Stafford,J.E. (2000) Symbolic Computation for Statistical Inference. Oxford University Press, New York

Bekker,P.A., Merckens,A., Wansbeek,T.J. (1994) Identification, equivalent models, and computer algebra. Academic Press, Boston

Badsberg, J. H. (1992) Model search in contingency table by CoCo. In: Dodge, Y., Whittaker, J. (eds) Computational Statistics, COMPSTAT 1992, **1**, 251–256. Neuchatel, Physica Verlag, Heidelberg

Dawid,A.P. (1979) Conditional independence in statistical theory. Journal of the Royal Statistical Society, Ser B, **41**, 1–31

Edwards,D. (2000) Introduction to Graphical Modelling 2nd ed. Springer-Verlag, Berlin Heidelberg

Frydenberg,M. (1990) The chain graph Markov property. Scandinavian Journal of Statistics, **17**, 333–353

Gale,W.A. (ed) (1986) Artificial Intelligence and Statistics. Addison-Wesley

Galles,D., Pearl,J. (1995) Testing identifiability of causal effects. In: Besnard,P., Hanks,S. (eds) Uncertainty in Artificial Intelligence, **11**, 185–95. Morgan Kaufmann

Ihaka,R., Gentleman,R. (1996) R: A language for data analysis and graphics. Journal of Computational and Graphical Statistics, **5**, 299–314

Lauritzen,S.L. (1996) Graphical Models. Clarendon, Oxford,U.K.

Minami,H., Mizuta,M., Sato,Y. (1994) Multivariate analysis support system with a hypothesis reasoning mechanism (in Japanese). Japanese Journal of Applied Statistics, **23**, 63–79

Miyakawa,M., Haga,T. (1997) Conversational data analysis system for graphical Gaussian modeling (in Japanese). Hinshitsu (Quality), **27**, 326–336

Nakano,J., Yamamoto,Y., Okada,M. (1990) Knowledge base multiple regression analysis system (in Japanese). Japanese Journal of Applied Statistics, **20**, 11–23

O'Keefe,R.A. (1990) The Craft of Prolog, MIT Press, Cambridge Massachusetts

Otsu,T. (2002) Prolog as a model search engine for data analysis. In: Nishisato,S., Baba,Y., Bozdogan,H., Kanefuji,K. (eds) Measurement and Multivariate Analysis, 289–300. Springer-Verlag, Tokyo

Pearl,J. (1995) Causal diagrams for empirical research. Biometrika, **82**, 669–710

Pearl,J. (2000) Causality; Models, Reasoning, and Inference. Cambridge U.P., Cambridge,U.K.

Robins,J.M. (1986) A new approach to causal inference in mortality studies with sustained exposure periods - Application to control of the healthy worker survivor effect. Computers and Mathematics with Applications, **14**, 923–945

Rubin,D.B. (1974) Estimating causal effects of treatments in randomized and nonrandomized studies. Journal of Educational Psychology, **66**, 688–701.

Sedgewick,R. (2002) Algorithms in C 3rd ed. Part 5 Graph Algorithms. Addison-Wesley, Boston

Sobel,M.E. (1990) Effect analysis and causation in linear structural equation models. Psychometrika, **79**, 247–253

Sobel,M.E. (1995) Causal inference in the social and behavioral sciences. In: Arminger,G. , Clogg,C.C., Sobel, M.E. (eds) Handbook of Statistical Modeling for the Social and Behavioral Sciences. Plenum Press, New York

Scheines,R., Spirtes,P., Glymour,C., Meek,C. (1994) TETRAD II: User's Manual. Lawrence Erlbaum, Hillsdale, N.J.

Spirtes,P., Glymour,C., Scheins,R. (2001) Causation, Prediction, and Search 2nd ed. MIT Press: Cambridge Massachusetts; 1st ed. (1993) Springer-Verlag, New York

Tierney,L. (1990) LISP-STAT: An Object-Oriented Environment for Statistical Computing and Dynamic Graphics. Wiley, New York

Verma,T., Pearl,J. (1988) Causal Networks: Semantics and expressiveness. In: Proceedings of the 4th Workshop on Uncertainty in Artificial Intelligence. Mountain View, CA., 352–359. Reprinted in: Shachter,R., Levitt,T.S., Kanal,L.N. (eds) Uncertainty in Artificial Intelligence, **4**, 69–76. Elsevier, Amsterdam

An Investigation of Bayes Estimation Procedures for the Two-Parameter Logistic Model

Seock-Ho Kim

Department of Educational Psychology, The University of Georgia, 325 Aderhold Hall, Athens, GA 30602-7143, U.S.A. *skim@coe.uga.edu*

Summary. The accuracy of Bayesian procedures was considered for estimation of parameters in the two-parameter logistic item response theory model. For the example data, all estimation procedures yielded comparable item and ability estimates. Simulated data sets were also analyzed using six estimation procedures for item parameters. Hierarchical Bayes estimation yielded consistently smaller root mean square differences and mean euclidean distances.

Key words. Bayesian Estimation, Gibbs sampler, hierarchical prior, item response theory, maximum likelihood estimation.

1 Introduction

Many Bayesian approaches have been proposed under item response theory (IRT) for estimating item and ability parameters. The key feature of the Bayesian approach is its reliance upon simple probability theory that provides a theoretical framework for incorporating prior information or belief into the estimation of parameters to improve accuracy of estimates.

Complete exploitation of the potential of the Bayesian estimation requires understanding of its mathematical underpinnings, particularly the role of prior distributions in estimating parameters. Since specification of priors in Bayesian analysis is a subjective matter, a number of different forms of priors have been studies in IRT. The hierarchical Bayes approach has been successfully applied to the estimation of item and ability parameters (Kim et al., 1994; Mislevy, 1986; Swaminathan & Gifford, 1985).

The method of maximum marginal likelihood can be considered as the standard estimation technique in IRT for obtaining item parameter estimates. The hierarchical Bayes estimation and Gibbs sampler (e.g., Albert, 1992) are relatively new approaches based on the Bayesian framework. All methods should yield similar item parameter estimates, when comparable priors are used and when ignorance or locally uniform priors are used. The current study was designed to evaluate this issue using the two-parameter logistic (2PL) model. The hierarchical Bayes estimation of item parameters with a two-stage hierarchical prior distribution is less well-known and, hence, presented in detail below.

2 Two-Stage Hierarchical Bayes Estimation

2.1 IRT Model and Marginalization

Consider binary responses to a test with n items by each of N examinees. For the 2PL model, the probability of a correct response has the form, $P_j(\theta_i) = 1/\{1 + \exp[-a_j(\theta_i - b_j)]\}$, where θ_i is ability and a_j and b_j are the item discrimination and difficulty parameters, respectively.

The marginal probability of obtaining the $N \times n$ response matrix Y is given by $\int p(Y|\theta, \xi)g(\theta)d\theta = p(Y|\xi) = l(\xi|Y)$, where θ is the vector of ability parameters, $g(\theta)$ is the density of θ, ξ is the vector of item parameters, and $l(\xi|Y)$ is the likelihood function. In maximum marginal likelihood estimation, the likelihood is maximized to obtain item parameter estimates (Bock & Aitkin, 1981). Since the marginal likelihood is not a probability density function, we cannot make a probabilistic statement regarding ξ. We can accomplish this by analyzing the marginal posterior distribution,

$$p(\xi|Y) \propto l(\xi|Y)p(\xi), \tag{1}$$

where $p(\xi)$ is the prior. In marginal Bayesian estimation of item parameters, the marginal posterior is maximized to obtain Bayes modal estimates of item parameters.

2.2 Hierarchical Priors

We can express $p(\xi)$ in many ways. To have flexibility in assigning priors, we may use the transformation, $\alpha_j = \log a_j$, and $\beta_j = b_j$. We assume that the vector of item parameters ξ possesses a multivariate normal distribution conditional on the respective mean vector μ_ξ and covariance matrix Σ_ξ. The complete form of the hierarchical prior is given by $p(\xi) \equiv p(\xi, \eta) = p_1(\xi|\eta)p_2(\eta)$, where the hyperparameter $\eta = \{\mu_\xi, \Sigma_\xi\}$ and the subscripts 1 and 2 denote the first stage and the second stage. If we assume the vectors of item parameters α and β are independent and $p(\beta) \propto 1$, then we can take the prior to possess a multivariate normal distribution, conditional only on the mean vector μ_{ξ_α} and the covariance matrix Σ_α. When we further assume exchangeability for all parameters, we may take $\mu_{\xi_\alpha} = \mu_\alpha I$ and $\Sigma_\alpha = \sigma_\alpha^2 I_n$, where μ_α and σ_α^2 are scalars, I is an $n \times 1$ vector of ones, and I_n is an identity matrix of order n. The first stage prior can be expressed as $p_1(\xi|\eta) = \prod_{j=1}^n p_1(\alpha_j|\mu_\alpha, \sigma_\alpha^2)$ and $\alpha_j \sim N(\mu_\alpha, \sigma_\alpha^2)$. The hierarchical Bayes approach then assigns another stage priors to the hyperparameter η. Hyperpriors for μ_α and σ_α^2 can be specified by assuming that μ_α has a noninformative uniform distribution and $\nu_\alpha \lambda_\alpha / \sigma_\alpha^2$ is distributed as $\chi_{\nu_\alpha}^2$. With the hyperhyperparameter $\eta^{(2)} = \{\nu_\alpha, \lambda_\alpha\}$, integrating out the two nuisance parameters, μ_α and σ_α^2, yields

$$p(\xi) \equiv p(\xi|\eta^{(2)}) = p(\alpha|\nu_\alpha, \lambda_\alpha) \propto \left[\sum_{j=1}^n (\alpha_j - \bar{\alpha})^2 + \nu_\alpha \lambda_\alpha\right]^{-(n+\nu_\alpha-1)/2}. \tag{2}$$

2.3 The Posterior

In the two-stage hierarchical Bayes estimation, Bayes modal estimates of item parameters are obtained by maximizing the marginal posterior, $p(\xi|Y) \propto l(\xi|Y)p(\xi|\eta^{(2)})$. The computer program and the detailed equations to implement the procedure were presented in Kim (1994). Ability parameters are estimated assuming that the item parameter estimates are true values.

3 An Example

3.1 Data and Estimation Procedures

The Law School Admission Test Section 6 (LSAT 6) data reported in Bock and Aitkin (1981) were analyzed via a computer program HBAYES (Kim, 1994) to provide hierarchical Bayes estimates of item parameters with the two-stage prior distribution (HB2). In HB2, the mean hyperparameter was assumed to have a noninformative uniform distribution and the variance hyperparameter was set to have an inverse chi-square distribution, $\nu_\alpha \lambda_\alpha / \sigma_\alpha^2 \sim \chi^2_{\nu_\alpha}$ with $\nu_\alpha = 8$ and $\lambda_\alpha = .25$.

The same LSAT 6 data were analyzed via the computer program BILOG (Mislevy & Bock, 1990). For the 2PL BILOG runs, three different estimation procedures were used: marginal Bayesian with the default prior distribution, $a_j \sim \text{lognormal}(0, .5^2)$ (MB); marginal Bayesian with the default prior distribution and the float option, $a_j \sim \text{lognormal}(\hat{\mu}_{\log a}, .5^2)$ (MBF); and maximum marginal likelihood (MML, i.e., without any prior distributions).

The LSAT6 data were also analyzed by Gibbs sampler using the computer program BUGS (Spiegelhalter et al., 1997). Gibbs sampling in BUGS works by iteratively drawing samples from the full conditional distributions of unobserved nodes using the adaptive rejection sampling algorithm. For estimation purposes, the logit, $\lambda_j \theta_i + \zeta_j$, was used instead of $a_j(\theta_i - b_j)$. To complete the specification of a full probability model in BUGS, prior distributions of the nodes should be specified. The θ_i were assumed to be independently drawn from a standard normal distribution for scaling purposes. Both informative and uninformative priors were chosen for Gibbs sampling: (1) $\lambda_j \sim N(0,1)$ with $\lambda_j > 0$ and $\zeta_j \sim N(0,100^2)$ (i.e., GSI) and (2) $\lambda_j \sim N(0,100^2)$ with $\lambda_j > 0$ and $\zeta_j \sim N(0,100^2)$ (i.e., GSU). The starting values were $\lambda_j = 1$ and $\zeta_j = 0$. The analyses of the Gelman and Rubin statistics for convergence diagnostics suggested that 5,000 iterations be burn-in and the subsequent 5,000 iterations be used for estimating. The posterior mean of the sampled values was obtained for each item parameter in the Gibbs sampler.

3.2 Item Parameter Estimates

All estimation procedures yielded similar item parameter estimates for LSAT 6. HB2 yielded a similar result as MBF in which shrinkage was toward the mean of the item discrimination estimates. On the other hand, the MB pattern shows that shrinkage was toward the prior mean.

Table 1. Average Unsigned Areas Between Estimation Methods

Method	HB2	BILOG			BUGS	
		MB	MBF	MML	GSI	GSU
HB2		0.131	0.039	0.071	0.082	0.055
MB			0.106	0.138	0.216	0.138
MBF				0.086	0.125	0.069
MML					0.079	0.047
GSI						0.095

In order to compare similarities among estimation procedures, the unsigned area (i.e., the sum of absolute differences between two item response functions over the entire ability range) was obtained for each item. The average values of the unsigned areas are presented in Table 1. HB2 and MBF yielded the smallest average unsigned areas, indicating the item parameter estimates from the two estimation procedures were quite similar. MML and GSU yielded similar sets of item parameter estimates.

3.3 Ability Estimates

There were 1,000 examinees in LSAT 6 data. Although there could be 32 possible response patterns for this five-item test, 30 patterns actually occurred. The expected a posteriori (EAP) method was applied with the item parameter estimates from HB2, MB, and MBF. The method of maximum likelihood (ML) was used under MML. The same standard normal distribution was used in all Bayes estimation procedures for the ability prior.

Table 2. Average Absolute Deviations of Ability Estimates

Method	HB2/EAP	BILOG			BUGS	
		MB/EAP	MBF/EAP	MML/ML	GSI	GSU
HB2/EAP		0.014	0.011	0.752	0.016	0.012
MB/EAP			0.007	0.755	0.026	0.021
MBF/EAP				0.759	0.020	0.021
MML/ML					0.761	0.744
GSI						0.021

The absolute deviations of ability estimates between two estimation procedures were obtained and averaged to compare similarities (see Table 2). Small values indicate more similarity. MML/ML yielded dissimilar ability estimates. The ability estimates from all Bayes procedures were quite similar.

Note that any differential effects in ability estimates were a joint function of the priors employed for item parameters and algorithm to implement estimation techniques. In Gibbs sampler the same response pattern might yield different ability estimates. Values reported in GSI and GSU columns were based on one typical estimate for the response pattern.

4 Data Simulation

Data were simulated under the following conditions: the number of examinees ($N = 100, 300$) and the number of items ($n = 15, 45$). Item response vectors were generated via the computer program GENIRV (Baker, 1982) for the 2PL model. The generating parameters for item discrimination were distributed with mean 1.046 and variance .103, and the underlying item difficulty parameters were distributed with mean 0 and variance 1. The distribution of underlying ability parameters was $N(0, 1)$. Four replications were generated for each combination of sample size and test length.

Each of the generated data sets was analyzed for HB2, MB, MBF, MML, GSI, and GSU. Point estimates of the ability parameters do not arise during the course of the HB2, MB, MBF, and MML estimation of item parameters. No discussion is presented for the estimation of ability parameters.

After applying the test characteristic curve method for metric linking, root mean square difference (RMSD), correlation between estimates and parameters, mean Euclidean distance (MED) between estimates and parameters, and bias were obtained. Bias was obtained for each item parameter across the replications.

5 Results

5.1 RMSD and Correlation Results

Item Discrimination Average RMSDs of item discrimination over four replications are reported in Table 3. As sample size increased, RMSDs decreased. Marginal RMSD means were 0.299 and 0.209 for sample sizes 100 and 300, respectively. For sample size 100, increasing the number of items did not change RMSDs except for MML. Increasing the number of items reduced the size of RMSDs for sample size 300. HB2 consistently yielded the smallest RMSDs, followed by MB and MBF. MML and GSU yielded larger RMSDs than other estimation procedures.

The average correlations between true and estimated values of item discrimination across four replications were obtained, but only trivial differences occurred among the estimation procedures. The larger the sample size, the higher the correlation in general. The median average correlations were .67 and .86 for sample sizes 100 and 300, respectively. Increasing the number of items yielded slightly higher correlations.

Table 3. RMSD for Item Discrimination and Item Difficulty

Parameter	Sample	Item	HB2	BILOG			BUGS	
				MB	MBF	MML	GSI	GSU
Discrimination	100	15	0.23	0.26	0.25	0.41	0.30	0.37
	100	45	0.23	0.26	0.25	0.35	0.30	0.37
	300	15	0.19	0.21	0.21	0.25	0.22	0.27
	300	45	0.16	0.18	0.18	0.22	0.20	0.22
Difficulty	100	15	0.31	0.31	0.31	0.33	0.34	0.32
	100	45	0.28	0.30	0.30	0.35	0.35	0.35
	300	15	0.16	0.17	0.17	0.21	0.20	0.21
	300	45	0.19	0.20	0.20	0.22	0.22	0.22

Item Difficulty Table 3 also contains the average RMSDs of item difficulty. An increase in sample size appeared to be associated with a decrease in the size of RMSDs. For sample size 100, increasing the number of items appeared to slightly decrease RMSDs except for HB2, MB, and MBF. For sample size 300, increasing the number of items resulted in larger RMSDs. The RMSDs from MML, GSI, and GSU were larger than those from other estimation procedures regardless of sample size or test length.

For each data set, all estimation procedures yielded nearly the same high correlations between estimates and parameters. The larger the sample size, the higher the correlation. The median average correlations were .95 and .98 for sample sizes 100 and 300, respectively.

5.2 MED Results

HB2 consistently yielded the smallest average MEDs, followed by MB and MBF (see Table 4). MML and GSU yielded larger MEDs then other estimation procedures. MEDs decreased as the sample size increased. Increasing the number of items slightly reduced the size of MEDs.

Table 4. MED for Both Item Discrimination and Item Difficulty

Sample	Item	HB2	BILOG			BUGS	
			MB	MBF	MML	GSI	GSU
100	15	0.34	0.36	0.36	0.45	0.40	0.44
100	45	0.32	0.34	0.34	0.42	0.40	0.44
300	15	0.22	0.23	0.23	0.27	0.26	0.28
300	45	0.21	0.23	0.23	0.26	0.25	0.27

5.3 Bias Results

Item Discrimination The bias results of item discrimination, presented in Figure 1, appear to reflect influence by a number of factors. For each test length, increasing sample size resulted in a decrease in bias values. When priors were used in Bayes estimation, positive bias values would be obtained for the smaller item discrimination parameters and negative bias values would be obtained for the relatively larger item discrimination parameters. This shrinkage effect was observed for HB2, MB, and MBF. HB2 yielded slightly more biased results especially for sample size 100. The patterns of bias from MML and GSU were very similar. The differences in bias patterns among the estimation procedures were very pronounced in sample size 100. The differences diminished as the sample size increased to 300.

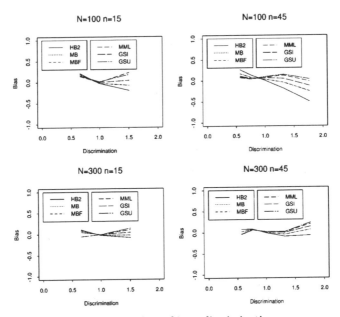

Fig. 1. Bias plots of item discrimination

Item Difficulty The bias results of item difficulty are presented in Figure 2. The bias pattern was somewhat different from that of item discrimination. For both 15- and 45-item tests, all estimation procedures yielded nearly the same pattern of essentially no bias. MML yielded relatively larger, albeit the differences might be trivial, bias in sample size 100. Sample size 300 yielded more stable results than sample size 100.

6 Discussion

Maximum likelihood approaches in IRT suffer from a number of problems, and the problems have led to interest in the development of Bayesian approaches for estimation of item and ability parameters. The role of the prior distribution is central in Bayesian analysis, and there is still a great need for efficient algorithm for parameter estimation.

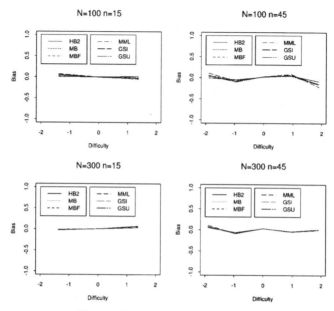

Fig. 2. Bias plots of item difficulty

References

Albert, J. H. (1992). Bayesian estimation of normal ogive item response curves using Gibbs sampling. *Journal of Educational Statistics, 17,* 251–269.

Baker, F. B. (1982). GENIRV [Computer software]. Madison, University of Wisconsin, Laboratory of Experimental Design.

Bock, R. D., & Aitkin, M. (1981). Marginal maximum likelihood estimation of item parameters: Application of an EM algorithm. *Psychometrika, 46,* 443–459.

Kim, S.-H. (1994, April). *Hierarchical Bayes estimation of item parameters.* Paper presented at the annual meeting of the AERA, New Orleans, LA.

Kim, S.-H., Cohen, A. S., Baker, F. B., Subkoviak, M. J., & Leonard, T. (1994). An investigation of hierarchical Bayes procedures in item response theory. *Psychometrika, 59,* 405–421.

Mislevy, R. J. (1986). Bayes modal estimation in item response models. *Psychometrika, 51,* 177–195.

Mislevy, R. J., & Bock, R. D. (1990). BILOG 3: Item analysis and test scoring with binary logistic models [Computer software]. Mooresville, IN: SSI.

Spiegelhalter, D. J., Thomas, A., Best, N. G., & Gilks, W. R. (1997). BUGS: Bayesian inference using Gibbs sampling (Version 0.6) [Computer software]. Cambridge, UK: University of Cambridge, Institute of Public Health, Medical Research Council Biostatistics Unit.

Swaminathan, H., & Gifford, J. A. (1985). Bayesian estimation in the two-parameter logistic model. *Psychometrika, 50,* 349–364.

Coping Strategies as Predictors of Psychological Distress among Employees in Japan

Akihito Shimazu[1], and Shoutaroh Kosugi[2]

[1]Department of Psychology, Graduate School of Education, Hiroshima University, 1-1-1 Kagamiyama, Higashi-Hiroshima, 739-8524, JAPAN

[2]Department of Psychology, School of Literature, Waseda University, 1-24-1 Toyama Shinjuku-ku Tokyo, 162-8644

Summary. The aim of this study was to examine the effects of coping with job stressor on employees' mental health. The questionnaire, which assesses job stressor, coping, and stress response, was administered to 4487 men employed in a research institute of an industrial company in Japan. Multiple logistic regression analysis was performed to evaluate the association between coping and stress response. Two of six stress response subscales (fatigue and depressive symptoms) were used as the dependent variables, and five coping subscales (proactive, escape, seeking social support, resignation, and restraint) as the independent variables. Among employees who perceived quantitative job stressor, the coping subscales which were significantly associated with fatigue were, in order of importance, "resignation" (odds ratio=1.71), "restraint" (1.54), and "proactive" (0.73) after controlling for age. Those which were significantly associated with depressive symptoms were "resignation" (1.95), "restraint" (1.73), "escape" (1.29), "seeking social support" (0.70), and "proactive" (0.47). On the other hand, among employees who perceived qualitative job stressor, those which were significantly associated with fatigue were "restraint" (1.62), "resignation" (1.41), "escape" (1.24), and "proactive" (0.76). Those which were significantly associated with depressive symptoms were "resignation" (1.95), "restraint" (1.78), "escape" (1.35), and "proactive" (0.55). These findings suggest that "resignation" and "restraint" coping with quantitative and qualitative job stressors had increasing effects on fatigue and depressive symptoms, while "proactive" coping had decreasing effect on them.

Key words. Coping, Psychological distress, Job stress, Employee, Multiple logistic regression analysis, Odds ratio, PROMAX rotation

1 Introduction

In recent years, it has been acknowledged that employees' well-being are influenced not only by work environment, but also by how employees cope with them. Among many coping research studies, there is some convergence around the notion that coping is not a trait or style treated as a personality characteristic, but a process defined as ongoing cognitive and behavioral efforts to manage stressors. From the perspective of the process theory of stress, coping changes in accordance with the situational contexts in which it is used. Therefore, which strategy one take in any given stressful encounter can be critical in determining health outcomes (Lazarus, 1993). The aim of this study was to examine effects of coping with job stressor on employees' mental health.

2 Method

2.1 Participants

Questionnaires were distributed to all men and women (n=5630) employed in a research institute of an industrial company in Japan, and were returned by 5251 employees, a response rate of 93.3 %. Missing data in one or more measures reduced this number to 4713. Almost 95 % of those who returned completed questionnaires were men. The mean age of men (36.2 years, SD=7.41) was significantly higher than that of women (30.0 years, SD=5.55)(p<.001). Furthermore, job content of men were largely different from that of women; that is, most men were engaged in research and development of new products, whereas most women were in routine office work. For the purpose of the present study, data from 226 women were excluded, and those from 4487 men were analyzed.

2.2 Measures

All data was measured by a Japanese version of the Job Stress Scale (JSS: Kosugi,2000). The JSS assesses the following four aspects chiefly related to the psychological stress model (Lazarus & Folkman,1984): job stressor, coping, stress response, and social support. Each aspect is measured by several subscales. Details of the development process and psychometric properties have been reported by Shimazu, Fuse, Taneichi, Ohashi, & Kosugi (1997) and Shimazu & Kosugi (1998). In this study, data related to job stressor, coping, and stress response were analyzed. Details of each scale used in the analyses were described below.

2.2.1 Job stressor

Job stressor was assessed by 28 items, scored on a five-point Likert scale, ranging from 'strongly disagree' (1) to 'strongly agree' (5). Factor analysis by oblique Promax rotation method yielded the following four subscales: *over-responsibility* (6 items), *role ambiguity* (6 items), *insufficiency of authority* (9 items), and *overload* (7 items). Because there were high intercorrelations among subscales (r=.72 for over-responsibility and overload, and .76 for role ambiguity and insufficiency of authority, respectively), over-responsibility and overload were integrated into '*quantitative job stressor*', and role ambiguity and insufficiency of authority into '*qualitative job stressor*', respectively in this study. The alpha coefficients of quantitative and qualitative stressor scales were .80 and .88, respectively.

2.2.2 Coping

Coping was assessed by 31 items, scored on a four-point Likert scale. Respondents were asked to identify the most distressing problem that they had experienced during the previous three months in the workplace, and then to indicate the extent to which they had used the strategy described by the particular item, ranging from 'not used at all' (1) to 'used a great deal' (4), for the respondent-identified problem. Factor analysis by oblique Promax rotation method yielded the following five subscales: *proactive* (9 items), *escape* (7 items), *seeking social support* (5 items), *resignation* (5 items), and *restraint* (5 items). The alpha coefficients of these five subscales were .86, .69, .72, .75, and .53, respectively.

2.2.3 Stress response

Stress response was assessed by 37 items, scored on a five-point Likert scale, ranging from 'strongly disagree' (1) to 'strongly agree' (5). Factor analysis by oblique Promax rotation method yielded the following six subscales: *anger* (6 items), *cardiovascular symptoms* (5 items), *interpersonal sensitivity* (7 items), *fatigue* (5 items), *irritability* (4 items), and *depressive symptoms* (10 items). In this study, fatigue and depressive symptoms were used as the indicators of psychological distress in the data analyses. The alpha coefficients of these two subscales were .80 and .91, respectively.

2.3 Analyses

Multiple logistic regression analysis was performed to evaluate the association between the risk of psychological distress (high fatigue and depression) and coping strategies. Fatigue and depression classes were used as the dependent variables, and the coping classes of five subscales as the independent variables. Participants with a fatigue scale score of 16 (equivalent to 67 percentile value) or greater were defined as high fatigue group, and those with a depressive symptoms scale score of 30 (equivalent to 67 percentile value) or greater were defined as high depression group. Median score on each coping scale was used to assign participants to two categories (Low / High). The odds ratios and its 95% confidence intervals (CIs) were calculated by using low coping categories as the reference categories. The odds ratio is the number by which we would multiply the odds of being high fatigue or depression (the probability divided by 1 minus the probability) for each one-unit increase in the independent variable. An odds ratio greater than 1 indicates that the odds of being high fatigue or depression increase when the independent variable increases; an odds ratio of less than 1 indicates that the odds of being high fatigue or depression decrease when the independent variable increases. Therefore, a high odds ratio indicates increased risk of psychological distress compared with the reference group.

The analyses mentioned above were performed separately for quantitative stressor group and qualitative stressor group, because coping is a part of the transaction between environment and person and it changes in accordance with the situational contexts in which it is used. The former group consisted of those who perceived more quantitative than qualitative stressor, while the latter consisted of those who perceived more qualitative than quantitative one. Those two groups were divided according to one's dominant perceived job stressor which was identified by comparing percentile values of the two scales (quantitative and qualitative). These statistical analyses were performed using the SAS release 6.12 for Windows.

3 Results

3.1 Quantitative stressor group

Table 1 shows the results of multiple logistic regression analysis for fatigue in quantitative stressor group. The coping subscales which were significantly associated with fatigue were, in order of importance, 'resignation', 'restraint', and 'proactive', after controlling for age. Of the three subscales, the highest odds ratio (1.71) was observed in 'resignation', and the lowest (0.73) in 'proactive'.

Table 2 shows the results of multiple logistic regression analysis for depressive symptoms in quantitative stressor group. All coping subscales had significant relationship with depressive symptoms, after controlling for age. Of the five subscales, the highest odds ratio (1.95) was observed in 'resignation', and the lowest (0.47) in 'proactive'.

3.2 Qualitative stressor group

Table 3 shows the results of multiple logistic regression analysis for fatigue in qualitative stressor group. The coping subscales which were significantly associated with fatigue were, in order of importance, 'restraint', 'resignation', 'escape', and 'proactive', after controlling for age. Of the four subscales, the highest odds ratio (1.62) was observed in 'restraint', and the lowest (0.76) in 'proactive'.

Table 4 shows the results of multiple logistic regression analysis for depressive symptoms in qualitative stressor group. The coping subscales which were significantly associated with depressive symptoms were, in order of importance, 'restraint', 'resignation', 'escape', and 'proactive', after controlling for age. Of four subscales which had significant relationship, the highest odds ratio (1.95) was observed in 'resignation', and the lowest (0.55) in 'proactive'.

Table 1 Results of multiple logistic regression analysis for *Fatigue* in *Quantitative* stressor group

Subscale of coping		High stress group proportion (%)		Odds ratio (95% confidence intervals) [a]		
proactive	Low	264/740	(35.7)	referent		
	High	419/1456	(28.8)	0.73	**	(0.59-0.89)
escape	Low	354/1229	(28.8)	referent		
	High	329/967	(34.0)	1.02		(0.84-1.25)
seeking social support	Low	333/1098	(30.3)	referent		
	High	350/1098	(31.9)	0.94		(0.78-1.15)
resignation	Low	368/1406	(26.2)	referent		
	High	315/790	(39.9)	1.71	***	(1.40-2.09)
restraint	Low	250/956	(26.2)	referent		
	High	433/1240	(34.9)	1.54	***	(1.26-1.88)

[a] adjusted for age
*** $p < .001$ ** $p < .01$ * $< .05$ † $p < .10$

Table 2　Results of multiple logistic regression analysis for _Depression_ in _Quantitative_ stressor group

Subscale of coping		High stress group proportion (%)		Odds ratio (95% confidence intervals) [a]		
proactive	Low	248/740	(33.5)	referent		
	High	271/1456	(18.6)	0.47	***	(0.37-0.58)
escape	Low	242/1229	(19.7)	referent		
	High	277/967	(28.7)	1.29	*	(1.04-1.60)
seeking social support	Low	282/1098	(25.7)	referent		
	High	237/1098	(21.6)	0.70	**	(0.57-0.87)
resignation	Low	251/1406	(17.9)	referent		
	High	268/790	(33.9)	1.95	***	(1.57-2.43)
restraint	Low	183/956	(19.1)	referent		
	High	336/1240	(27.1)	1.73	***	(1.38-2.17)

[a] adjusted for age
*** $p < .001$　** $p < .01$　* $< .05$　† $p < .10$

Table 3　Results of multiple logistic regression analysis for _Fatigue_ in _Qualitative_ stressor group

Subscale of coping		High stress group proportion (%)		Odds ratio (95% confidence intervals) [a]		
proactive	Low	437/1388	(31.5)	referent		
	High	244/868	(28.1)	0.76	*	(0.62-0.94)
escape	Low	258/1010	(25.5)	referent		
	High	423/1246	(34.0)	1.24	*	(1.02-1.52)
seeking social support	Low	355/1290	(27.5)	referent		
	High	326/966	(33.8)	1.17		(0.96-1.42)
resignation	Low	256/1044	(24.5)	referent		
	High	425/1212	(35.1)	1.41	***	(1.15-1.73)
restraint	Low	270/1096	(24.6)	referent		
	High	411/1160	(35.4)	1.62	***	(1.33-1.97)

[a] adjusted for age
*** $p < .001$　** $p < .01$　* $< .05$　† $p < .10$

Table 4   Results of multiple logistic regression analysis for *Depression* in *Qualitative* stressor group

Subscale of coping		High stress group proportion (%)		Odds ratio (95% confidence intervals) [a]		
proactive	Low	616/1388	(44.4)	referent		
	High	276/868	(31.8)	0.55	***	(0.45-0.67)
escape	Low	319/1010	(31.6)	referent		
	High	573/1246	(46.0)	1.35	**	(1.12-1.64)
seeking social support	Low	504/1290	(39.1)	referent		
	High	388/966	(40.2)	0.98		(0.81-1.19)
resignation	Low	294/1044	(28.2)	referent		
	High	598/1212	(49.3)	1.95	***	(1.61-2.36)
restraint	Low	352/1096	(32.1)	referent		
	High	540/1160	(46.6)	1.78	***	(1.48-2.16)

[a] adjusted for age

*** $p<.001$ ** $p<.01$ * $<.05$ † $p<.10$

4 Discussion

The aim of this study was to examine the association between the risk of psychological distress and coping strategies with job stressors. To evaluate the association, we adopted the multiple logistic regression analysis, not covariance structure analysis, because our chief interest is to predict the probability that a case will be classified into one as opposed to the other of the two categories of the dependent variable by the independent variables (Menard, 2002).

The findings from this study were generally consistent with previous ones (e.g. Shimazu, 1998; Lazarus, 1993) in that proactive strategies decrease psychological distress but that escape or avoidance strategies increase it. This was true whether participants perceived quantitative or qualitative job stressor. This may be because proactive effort to change the source of the problem directly reduced the risk of high fatigue and depression.

Finally, some limitations of this study may come from the cross-sectional design. Implicit in our hypotheses is the assumption that job stressor influenced coping, which is then related to stress response. However, stress response at the time of the measurement could influence the choice of coping strategies with job stressor, because examination of the causal relationship among job stressor, coping, and stress response was beyond the scope of this study.

In addition, this study did not deal with long-term outcome of a given coping strategy. Past studies showed that one group of coping strategies (problem-focused coping, proactive, seeking social support, etc) appears more adaptive than does another group (emotion-focused coping, disengagement, escape, resignation, etc) when measured cross-sectionally (e.g., Scheier, Weintraub, & Carver,1986). However, we should be careful to conclude no clear effects of the latter group on adaptation, because those two groups may have different effects on the long-term adaptation. For example, a disengagement, which in the short term interferes with active coping, may in the long term act as a breather, making the person more effective as a problem-focused coper later on (Scheier, et al., 1986). Thus, a longitudinal study would be needed for a more elaborate examination of the effects of coping strategy on long-term outcome.

References

Kosugi,S. (2000). Mental health activities in the workplace by a general checkup using the Job Stress Scale. Job Stress Research, 7, 141-150 (in Japanese).

Lazarus,R.S. (1993). Coping theory and research : Past, present, and future. Psychosomatic medicine, 55, 234-247.

Lazarus,R.S., & Folkman,S. (1984). Stress, appraisal, and coping. New York : Springer.

Menard, S. (2002). Applied logistic regression analysis (2nd ed.). California: Sage.

Scheier,M.F., Weintraub,J.K., & Carver,C.S. (1986). Coping with stress: Divergent strategies of optimists and pessimists. Journal of Personality and Social Psychology, 51, 1257-1264.

Shimazu,A., Fuse,M., Taneichi,K, Ohashi,Y., & Kosugi,S. (1997) The development of stress inventory for workers (1): With reference to stressor, stress reaction scale. Job Stress Research, 4, 41-52 (in Japanese).

Shimazu, A. (1998) A study of coping strategy for job stress. Job Stress Research, 5, 64-71 (in Japanese).

Shimazu, A., & Kosugi, S. (1998) The development of stress inventory for workers (2) With reference to coping scale. Waseda Psychological Reports, 30, 19-28 (in Japanese).

Estimating Mediated Effects with Survival Data

Jenn-Yun Tein[1], and David P. MacKinnon[2]

1. Program for Prevention Research, Arizona State University, 900 S. McAllister St., Tempe, Arizona 85287-6005, USA
2. Department of Psychology, Arizona State University, 900 S. McAllister St., Tempe, Arizona, 85287-1104, USA

Summary. Mediation analyses help identify variables in the causal sequence relating predictor variables to outcome variables. In many studies, outcomes are time until an event occurs and survival analyses are applied. This study examines the point and interval estimates of the mediated effect using two methods of survival analyses: the log-survival time and log-hazard time models. The results show that, under the condition of no censored data, the assumption that mediated effects calculated by the product of coefficients method ($\alpha\beta$) and those calculated by the difference in coefficients method ($\tau - \tau'$) are identical does apply to log-survival time survival analyses but not to log-hazard time survival analyses. The standard error of the mediated effect can be calculated with the delta formula, the second order Taylor series formula, and the unbiased formula. Consistent with ordinary least squares regression, the three formulas yield similar results. Although the log-survival time model and the log-hazard time model utilize different estimation methods, the results of the significant tests, using the ratio of $\alpha\beta$ to $se_{\alpha\beta}$, were comparable between the two methods. However, the significance tests based on the empirical standard error appear to be more conservative than those from the three analytical standard errors.

Keyword: Mediation model, survival analysis.

Introduction

In many studies, researchers are interested in identifying factors that mediate the association between selected predictors and adjustment outcomes. Mediating variables can be psychological, such as attitudes; behavioral, such as social skills; or biological, such as serum cholesterol levels. Mediation analyses have been studied extensively with normally distributed continuous dependent variables. The purpose of this project is to conduct a simulation study using survival analyses to assess point and interval estimates of mediated effects in which the dependent variable is the 'timing' or 'occurrence' of events. Survival analysis is a class of statistical methods in which the onset of occurrence is important (e.g., disease, drug use, arrests, and death) and is useful in estimating predictive models in which the occurrence of an event depends on covariates. This method has also been adapted in many fields, although its labels have varied: event history analysis (sociology), failure time analysis (engineering), and transition analysis (economics), etc.

For situations in which the dependent and mediating variables are continuous with normally distributed error terms, methods of estimating the mediated effect and standard errors for the mediated effect are available and are generally accurate (Sobel 1982; MacKinnon et al. 1995). In this study, the focus is to examine whether these standard approaches can be appropriately applied to survival analyses. For one mediator models, there are two standard statistical approaches for the point estimate of mediated effects. Mediated effects can be determined with three equations:

$$Y = \gamma_1 + \tau X + \varepsilon_1 \tag{1}$$
$$Y = \gamma_3 + \tau'X + \beta M + \varepsilon_3 \tag{2}$$
$$M = \gamma_2 + \alpha X + \varepsilon_2 \tag{3}$$

where X is the independent variable, M is the mediator, and Y is the dependent variable. In Eq. (1), the dependent variable is regressed on the independent variable. In Eq. (2), the mediating variable is included as another independent variable. In Eq. (3), the mediating variable is regressed on the independent variable. Two methods of calculating mediated effects are employed. The first (Judd and Kenny 1981), which is more often applied in epidemiology, is named the difference of coefficients method because the mediated effect is computed by taking the difference of regression coefficients associated with the independent variable in Eq. (1) and in Eq. (2), $\tau - \tau'$. The second, which is more common in the social sciences, is named the product of coefficients method since the mediated effect is calculated by the product of the two parameters, $\alpha\beta$, in Eqs. (2) and (3).

Under the assumption that the dependent variable is continuous and the residual variance follows normal distribution, the two methods, using ordinary least squares regression (OLS), yield identical estimates of mediation effect, $\alpha\beta = \tau - \tau'$ (MacKinnon et al. 1995). However, in a common hazard function model, the dependent variable (i.e., time of event occurring) has residual variance which is generally not normal but may follow a 2-parameter extreme value distribution (Weibull function), a 1-parameter extreme value distribution (exponential function), or a log-gamma distribution (gamma function) (Klein 1997; Allison 1995). It has been shown that, for mediation analyses with binary dependent variables, $\alpha\beta$ is not equal $\tau - \tau'$ (MacKinnon and Dwyer 1993). This is due to the fact that the residual variance is a constant in the logistic regression so the coefficients of τ and τ' come from equations on different scales. For a similar reason, we will examine the hypothesis whether $\tau - \tau'$ equals to $\alpha\beta$ with survival analyses.

There are several methods for computing the standard errors of a product of two random variables (Mackinnon et al. 1995): (1) first order Taylor series or the multivariate delta formula (Sobel 1982), (2) second order Taylor series formula (Mood et al. 1974), and (3) unbiased standard error formula (Goodman 1960). These methods have been applied to computing confidence intervals and testing the statistical significance of mediated effects (i.e., $z = \alpha\beta \, / \, se_{\alpha\beta}$), and the results indicate that there are no significant differences among the three analytical methods with OLS (MacKinnon et al. 1995) and they are, in general, consistent with the empirical standard errors. It is unknown whether these conclusions apply to survival analyses. Thus, we will also examine the consistency and accuracy of the three formulas for the standard errors using survival analyses.

Method

To study the mediation process with survival data, we simulated data which follow a classical mediation pathway where the relationship between the independent (X) and dependent variable (Y) was mediated by a third variable (M). The independent and mediating variables were continuous, followed a normal distribution. In this simulation, we assumed that there was no censored event, the mediating variable was time invariant, and there were no ties among the events. We simulated survival time, T_i, following a popular hazard function in social science (Weibull distribution), based on the equation (see Klein 1997),

$$Y = \log T_i = u + \tau'X_i + \beta M_i + \sigma W \qquad (4)$$

where the dependent variable Y is the log function of T_i, the time of the event for subject i. X_i and M_i are the independent and mediating variables, respectively. The residual term is the product of W, which has a 2-parameter extreme value distribution, and σ, which is the scale parameter determining the shape of the hazard rate. Like the normal distribution, the extreme-value distribution is a unimodal distribution defined on the entire real line. However, unlike the normal distribution, it is not symmetrical. We estimated the Weibull model with a log-survival time model and a log-hazard time model, the two most flexible procedures which estimate regression models with covariates and censored data. The two methods can be easily estimated with the LIFEREG and PHREG procedures in SAS® (Allison 1995). The LIFEREG procedure estimates the log-survival time of the model:

$$\log T_i = \beta_0 + \beta_1 x_{i1} + ... + \beta_k x_{ik} + \sigma \epsilon_i \qquad (5)$$

where $x_{i1} ... x_{ik}$ are the k covariates for subject i; ϵ_i is the measurement error, $\beta_0 ... \beta_k$ are the regression parameters and σ is the scale parameter. The differences between Eq. (5) and the OLS are that for Eq. (5) there is a σ before ϵ and the dependent variable is the logarithm of the dependent variable. In a linear regression model, it is typical to assume that ϵ_i has a normal distribution. However, the log-survival time model estimated here allows for non-normal distributions. Because of the possibility of a non-normal ϵ, the distribution of the variable T (which relates to the distribution of ϵ and the scale value of σ) needs to be specified for the LIFEREG procedure. The parameters are estimated with maximum likelihood.

The PHREG procedure estimates the log-hazard form of the model

$$\log h(t) = \alpha(t) + \beta'_1 x_{i1} + \dots + \beta'_k x_{ik} \qquad (6)$$

where $\alpha(t) = \log \lambda_0(t)$; $\lambda_0(t)$ is a baseline hazard function for any individual whose covariates all have values of 0. While LIFEREG estimates parametric regression models using the maximum likelihood, PHREG implements the popular Cox's proportional hazards model, a semi-parametric procedure with maximum partial likelihood. Unlike the parametric methods, the Cox's model does not require specifications of the probability distribution to represent survival time. For the Weibull model, the relationship between the parameters in Eqs. (5) and (6) can be equated as $\beta'_k = -\beta_k / \sigma$ (see Allison, 1995).

Models with log-survival time as dependent variable examine mediation processes of percent of increase or decrease in the expected survival time. Models with log-hazard time as dependent variable examine mediation processes of percent change in hazard rate. If there are no censored data, Eq. (1) can be readily estimated with OLS by simply creating the dependent variable as the logarithm of the event time (i.e., $Y = \log T_i$). This yields the best linear unbiased estimates of the β coefficients, regardless of the shape of the distribution of ϵ (Allison 1995). If ϵ is normal, the OLS estimates will also be maximum likelihood estimates and will have minimum variance among all estimates.

SAS® was used to conduct the statistical simulation. The data were generated based on Eq. (4), where X and M followed normal distribution. The current time was used as the seed for each simulation. The residual term is determined by the product of σ (the scale parameter which was set at .4) and W (the extreme value variable in which the location parameter was set at 0 and the mode scale parameter was set at .7). The parameter α was varied between .2 and .4; β was varied between .2, .4, .6, and .8; and τ was set to constant at .2. As a result, there were a total of 8 different parameter combinations. Eight different sample sizes were chosen to reflect sample sizes found in social science studies: 20, 50, 100, 200, 500, 1000, 2000, and 5000. For each simulation condition, 500 replications were conducted. As mentioned earlier, we assumed that there was no censored event, the mediating variable was time invariant, and there were no ties of the events.

Results

The simulated data based on Eq. (4) were analyzed, individually, with log-survival time model (see Eq. 5), log-hazard time model (see Eq. 6), and ordinary least square model using LIFEREG, PHREG, and REG procedures in SAS®, respectively. The sample values of the population parameters, α, β, τ, τ' are represented by a, b, t, and t'. The results of point estimates and standard errors were pooled across the 8 parameter value combinations for each of the sample sizes (i.e., 500 x 8 = 4000 estimations). Table 1 shows the average point estimate of the mediated effect using the product of coefficients method, ab, and the difference in coefficients method, t-t'. Table 1 also shows the difference of the two methods for each of the 3 statistical procedures. Under the condition with no censoring time, the estimation of ab and t-t' from the LIFEREG procedure were close to those from the REG procedure. As expected, ab and t-t' were identical from the REG procedure. However, the differences were only close to zero from the LIFEREG procedure. As mentioned earlier, path coefficients from the log-hazard form (i.e., PHREG) can be derived from those from the log-survival time (i.e., LIFEREG) by dividing the latter with the scale parameter, σ, and adding a negative sign (i.e., b' = -b/σ). The results show that |ab'| (i.e., in absolute values) from the PHREG procedure were constantly smaller than |-ab/σ|. However the discrepancy got smaller as the sample size got larger. With a sample size larger than 500, the discrepancy is beyond .01. Note that as sample size increased the estimated scale values from LIFEREG procedures increased but the estimated |ab| with the PHREG procedures decreased. The differences between ab and t-t' from the PHREG procedure were quite different; the mediation estimates for |t-t'| were consistently smaller than those for |ab|. The differences ranged from .189 to .519 and the difference decreased as the sample size got larger.

Table 2 presents the standard errors and statistical tests from the LIFEREG, PHREG, and REG procedures. The results show that within the same procedures, the standard errors, se_{ab}, from the 3 analytical solutions were similar, and when the sample size was greater than 100, the standard errors were nearly identical. In addition, the standard errors between the LIFEREG and REG procedures were comparable, although those from LIFEREG were slightly larger. Although the analytical and empirical standard errors from the REG procedure were similar, the empirical standard errors were consistently larger than the analytical standard errors from the LIFEREG, PHREG, and REG procedures. Table 2 also shows the z statistics of the mediated effect by dividing the mediated effect, ab, by its standard error ($z = ab / se_{ab}$). Although the LIFEREG, PHREG, and REG procedures utilized different estimation methods, the z scores were comparable among the three procedures with only one exception. The z scores based on the empirical standard errors were smaller than those based on the analytical standard errors for the LIFEREG and PHREG procedures.

Discussions

The purpose of this paper was to examine the point and interval estimates of mediated effects when the dependent variable pertains to time of onset for an event and survival analysis is necessary. With OLS, the mediated effect can be assessed with the difference in coefficients method, $\tau - \tau'$, or the product of coefficients methods, $\alpha\beta$, and the two yield identical results. This study first examined whether the same conclusion applies to survival analyses using log-survival time model (i.e., LIFEREG) or the log-hazard time model (i.e., PHREG). The results indicate that under the condition of no censored data and no time-variant mediators, the differences of two methods were negligible using LIFEREG procedure. An explanation of why they are not exactly the same may be that the parameters are estimated with the maximum likelihood estimator which, through iterations, finds only the optimal solutions of the model. Although the estimated τ - τ' were the same, the estimated absolute values of $\alpha\beta$ decreased as the sample size increased using the PHREG procedure. The estimated $\alpha\beta$ and τ - τ' remained similar across variations in sample size using the LIFEREG procedure. There were consistent differences between $\alpha\beta$ and τ - τ' for the log-hazard model. As a result, the use of this model could lead to different conclusions depending on whether the $\alpha\beta$ or τ - τ' method was used.

As with the OLS estimator, there were no noticeable differences in the standard errors, $se_{\alpha\beta}$, estimated by the delta formula (Sobel 1982), the second order Taylor series formula (Mood et al. 1974), and the unbiased formula (Goodman 1960) with LIFEREG and PHREG procedures. However, the empirical $se_{\alpha\beta}$ tended to be larger than those from the three analytical methods. Although the PHREG and LIFEREG procedures use different estimation methods, the estimated ratios of $\alpha\beta$ and $se_{\alpha\beta}$ (i.e., z-scores) for testing the significance of the mediation effects were comparable between the log-survival time model and the log-hazard time model. They were also similar to the z-scores with the OLS procedure, under the condition of no censored data. The empirical z-scores from the PHREG and LIFEREG procedures were consistently smaller than the analytical z scores. As a result, tests of significance based on the empirical standard errors might produce more Type II errors than the tests based on the analytical standard errors. The advantage of the PHREG and LIFEREG procedures is that they both deal with censored data. It is important in the future to examine whether the conclusions of this study apply to data that have censored data and time-invariant mediating variables.

References

Allison P (1995). Survival analysis using the SAS system: A practical guide. Gary, NC: SAS Institute Inc.

Goodman LA (1960). On the exact variance of products. Journal of the American Statistical Association 55: 708-713.

Judd CM, Kenny DA (1981). Process Analysis: Estimating mediation in treatment evaluations. Evaluation Review 5: 602-619.

Klein JP, Moeschberger ML (1997). Survival analysis: Techniques for censored and truncated data. New York: Springer-Verlag.

MacKinnon, DP, Dwyer J H (1993). Estimating mediated effects in prevention studies. Evaluation Review 17: 144-158.

MacKinnon DP, Warsi G, Dwyer JH (1995). A simulation study of mediated effect measures. Multivariate Behavioral Research 30: 41-62.

Mood A, Graybill FA, Boes DC (1974). Introduction to the theory of statistics. New York: McGraw-Hill.

Sobel ME (1982). Asymptotic confidence intervals for indirect effects in structural equation models. In Leinhardt S (ed) Sociological Methodology 192. Washington, DC: American Sociological Association, pp. 290-293.

Table 1: Testing of Mediation Effect for Hazard Function Model with Weibull Distribution : The difference between αβ and c - c'

Method[a]		Sample Size							
		20	50	100	200	500	1000	2000	5000
LIFEREG	ab	.1508	.1480	.1503	.1506	.1502	.1500	.1500	.1499
	t − t'	.1512	.1482	.1517	.1513	.1497	.1493	.1504	.1504
	ab−(t −t')	-.0003	-.0002	-.0015	-.0007	.0005	.0006	-.0004	-.0005
PHREG[b]	ab	-.5189	-.4078	-.3765	-.3563	-.3371	-.3281	-.3232	-.3192
	t − t'	.0635	-.0010	-.0314	-.0416	-.0527	-.0575	-.0628	-.0650
	ab−(t −t')	-.5825	-.4068	-.3450	-.3147	-.2844	-.2706	-.2603	-.2542
REG	ab	.1510	.1482	.1503	.1508	.1501	.1500	.1500	.1499
	t − t'	.1510	.1482	.1503	.1508	.1501	.1500	.1500	.1499
	ab−(t −t')	0	0	0	0	0	0	0	0

[a]LIFEREG: log-survival time model; PHREG: log-hazard time model; REG: ordinary lest squares model.
[b]According to LIFEREG procedures, the estimated scale values are .3381, .3950, .4251, .4432, .4622, .4710, .4784, and .4835 for sample size 20, 50, 100, 500, 1000, 2000, and 5000 respectively. Dividing the estimated mediated effect aḇ from the LIFEREG procedure by the scale parameter, and taking a negative sign of the value, the estimated mediated effect, ab, for the LIFEREG procedure should be -.4461, -.3746, -.3535, -.3398, -.3250, -.3185, -.3135, and -.3100 for sample size 20, 50, 100, 500, 1000, 2000, and 5000 respectively.

Table 2: Testing the significant Mediation Effect for Hazard Function Model with Weibull Distribution

Method	Estimator		20	50	100	200	500	1000	2000	5000
LIFEREG	Delta	se_{ab}	.1269	.0767	.0530	.0375	.0236	.0167	.0118	.0075
		z	1.1253	1.8297	2.7007	3.8478	6.1013	8.6332	12.2071	19.3016
	Taylor	se_{ab}	.1293	.0773	.0532	.0375	.0237	.0167	.0118	.0075
		z	1.1047	1.8105	2.6852	3.8360	6.0934	8.6275	12.2030	19.2991
	Unbias	se_{ab}	.1256	.0761	.0528	.0374	.0236	.0167	.0118	.0075
		z	1.1647	1.8552	2.7172	3.8599	6.1093	8.6389	12.2112	19.3043
	Sample	se_{ab}	.1353	.0827	.0570	.0403	.0263	.0193	.0259	.0091
		z	1.0599	1.6955	2.4925	3.4959	5.3518	7.3084	10.0391	15.2095
PHREG	Delta	se_{ab}	.4591	.2169	.1358	.0903	.0539	.0371	.0259	.0162
		z	-1.0264	-1.7601	-2.6300	-3.7655	-5.9968	-8.4970	-12.0319	-19.0467
	Taylor	se_{ab}	.4601	.2171	.1359	.0903	.0539	.0371	.0259	.0162
		z	-1.0234	-1.7568	-2.6271	-3.7633	-5.9952	-8.4959	-12.0310	-19.0462
	Unbias	se_{ab}	.4468	.2142	.1349	.0900	.0539	.0371	.0259	.0162
		z	-1.0833	-1.7926	-2.6514	-3.7806	-6.0063	-8.5039	-12.0367	-19.0498
	Sample	se_{ab}	.5211	.2420	.1520	.1023	.0636	.0454	.0320	.0206
		z	-.0959	-1.6094	-2.3632	-3.2863	-5.0655	-6.9524	-9.6618	-14.8986
REG	Delta	se_{ab}	.1252	.0754	.0520	.0367	.0231	.0163	.0115	.0073
		z	1.1592	1.9007	2.8007	3.9842	6.3177	8.9450	12.6606	20.0282
	Taylor	se_{ab}	.1273	.0759	.0522	.0368	.0231	.0163	.0115	.0073
		z	1.1383	1.8845	2.7887	3.9757	6.3122	8.9412	12.6579	20.0265
	Unbias	se_{ab}	.1239	.0749	.0519	.0367	.0231	.0163	.0115	.0073
		z	1.1949	1.9181	2.8131	3.9929	6.3231	8.9489	12.6634	20.0300
	Sample	se_{ab}	.1287	.0772	.0524	.0365	.0231	.0165	.0117	.0073
		z	1.1347	1.8743	2.0893	-3.9780	6.3407	8.9273	12.4368	19.9744

A Backward Induction Computational Procedure to Sequential Mastery Testing

Hans J. Vos

University of Twente, Faculty of Educational Science and Technology,
Department of Educational Measurement and Data Analysis, P.O. Box 217, 7500
AE Enschede, The Netherlands

Summary. In a sequential mastery test, the decision is to classify a student as a master, a non-master, or to continue testing and administering another random item. Sequential mastery tests are designed with the goal of maximizing the probability of making correct classification decisions (i.e., mastery and non-mastery) while at the same time minimizing test length. The purpose of this paper is to derive optimal rules for sequential mastery tests. The framework of Bayesian sequential decision theory is used; that is, optimal rules are obtained by minimizing the posterior expected losses associated with all possible decision rules at each stage of testing. The main advantage of this approach is that costs of testing can be explicitly taken into account. Techniques of backward induction (i.e., dynamic programming) are used for computing optimal rules that minimize the posterior expected loss at each stage of testing. This technique starts by considering the final stage of testing and then works backward to the first stage of testing. For given maximum number of items to be administered, it is shown how the appropriate action can be computed at each stage of testing for different number-correct score.

Key words. Sequential mastery testing, Bayesian sequential rules, Backward induction, Threshold loss, Binomial distribution

1 Introduction

In a sequential mastery test (SMT), the decision is to classify a student as a master, a non-master, or to continue testing and administering another random item. The main advantage of SMT is to provide shorter tests for students who have clearly attained a certain level of mastery (or clearly non-mastery) and longer tests for those students for whom the mastery decision is not as clear-cut. One of the earliest approaches to SMT dates back to Ferguson (1969) using Wald's (1947) well-known sequential probability ratio test (SPRT).

As indicated by Ferguson (1969), three elements must be specified in advance in applying the SPRT-framework to SMT. First, two values p_0 and p_1 on the proportion-correct metric must be specified representing points that correspond to lower and upper limits of student's (unknown) true level of functioning at which a mastery and non-mastery decision will be made, respectively. Also, these two values mark the boundaries of the small region (i.e., indifference region) where we never can be sure to take the right classification decision, and, thus, in which testing will continue. Second, two types of error acceptance α and β must be specified, reflecting the relative costs of the false positive (i.e., incorrect mastery decision) and false negative (i.e., incorrect non-mastery decision) error types. Intervals can be derived as functions of these two error rates for which mastery and non-mastery are respectively declared, and for which testing is continued (Wald 1947). Third, Ferguson (1969) specified a maximum test length in order to classify within a reasonable period of time those students for whom the decision of declaring mastery or non-mastery is not as clear-cut (i.e., truncated procedure).

A major drawback of the SPRT-framework, however, is that it does not take costs of testing into account. The purpose of this paper, therefore, is to derive optimal rules for SMT that takes costs of testing explicitly into account. The framework of Bayesian sequential decision theory (e.g., Lehmann 1959) will be used; that is, optimal rules are obtained by minimizing the posterior expected losses associated with all possible decision rules at each stage of testing. The Bayes principle assumes that prior knowledge about student's true level of functioning is available and can be characterized by a probability distribution called the prior.

2 Framework of Bayesian Sequential Decision Theory

Three basic elements can be identified in Bayesian sequential decision theory. In addition to a measurement model relating the probability of a correct response to student's true level of functioning and a loss function evaluating the total costs and benefits for each possible combination of classification outcome and true level of functioning, costs of administering one additional item must be explicitly specified in this approach. Doing so, posterior expected losses corresponding to the mastery and non-mastery decisions can now be calculated straightforward at each stage of testing. As far as the posterior expected loss corresponding to continue testing concerns, this quantity is determined by averaging the posterior expected losses corresponding to each of the possible future classification outcomes relative to observing those outcomes (i.e., the posterior predictive distributions).

Optimal rules (i.e., Bayesian sequential rules) are now obtained by minimizing the posterior expected losses (payoffs) associated with all possible decision rules at each stage of testing using techniques of backward induction (i.e., dynamic programming). This technique starts by considering the final stage of testing (where the option to continue testing is not available) and then works backward to the first stage of testing.

3 Notation

In the sequel, following Ferguson (1969), a sequential mastery test is supposed to have a maximum test length of n ($n \geq 1$). Let the observed item response at each stage k ($1 \leq k \leq n$) of testing for a randomly sampled student be denoted by a discrete random variable X_k, with realization x_k. The observed response variables $X_1, \ldots, X_k$ are assumed to be independent and identically distributed for each value of k, and take the values 0 and 1 for respectively incorrect and correct responses to item k. Furthermore, let the observed number-correct score be denoted by a discrete random variable $S_k = X_1 + \ldots + X_k$, with realization $s_k = x_1 + \ldots + x_k$ ($0 \leq s_k \leq k$).

Student's true level of functioning is unknown due to measurement and sampling error. All that is known is his/her observed number-correct score s_k. In other words, the mastery test is not a perfect indicator of student's true performance. Therefore, let student's true level of functioning be denoted by a continuous random variable T on the latent proportion-correct metric, with realization $t \in [0,1]$.

Finally, a criterion level t_c ($0 \leq t_c \leq 1$) on T is required to be specified in advance by the decision-maker using methods of standard setting (e.g., Angoff 1971). A student is considered a true non-master and true master if his/her true level of functioning t is smaller or larger than t_c, respectively.

4 Loss Function, Costs of Testing, and Measurement Model

The threshold loss function (e.g., Lewis and Sheehan 1990) is adopted as the loss structure involved. The choice of this loss function implies that the "seriousness" of all possible consequences of the decisions can be summarized by possibly different constants, one for each of the possible classification outcomes. For other frequently used loss structures, such as linear and normal-ogive loss, refer to Novick and Lindley (1979) (see also van der Linden and Vos 1996; Vos 1997).

For the sequential mastery problem, a threshold loss function can be formulated as a natural extension of the one for the fixed-length mastery problem (i.e., declaring mastery or non-mastery) at each stage k of testing as follows (see also Lewis and Sheehan 1990):

Table 1. Table for threshold loss function at stage k ($1 \leq k \leq n$) of testing

Decision	True level of functioning	
	$T \leq t_c$	$T > t_c$
Declare non-mastery	ke	$l_{01} + ke$
Declare mastery	$l_{10} + ke$	ke

The value e represents the costs of administering one random item. For the sake of simplicity, following Lewis and Sheehan (1990), these costs are assumed to be equal for each classification outcome as well as for each testing occasion. Since loss functions are measured on an interval scale (e.g., Luce and Raiffa 1957), and assuming the losses l_{00} and l_{11} corresponding to the correct classification outcomes are equal and take the smallest values, the threshold loss function in Table 1 was rescaled such that l_{00} and l_{11} were equal to zero. Hence, the losses l_{01} and l_{10} corresponding to the incorrect classification outcomes must take positive values. The ratio l_{10}/l_{01} is denoted as the loss ratio R, and refers to the relative losses for declaring mastery to a student whose true level of functioning is below t_c (i.e., false positive) and declaring non-mastery to a student whose true level of functioning exceeds t_c (i.e., false negative).

Note that no losses need to be specified in Table 1 for the option to continue testing. This is because the posterior expected loss corresponding to this option is computed at each stage k of testing as a weighted average of the posterior expected losses associated with the classification outcomes of future item administrations with weights equal to the probabilities of observing those outcomes.

The loss parameters l_{ij} $(i,j = 0,1; i \neq j)$ have to be empirically assessed, for which several methods, such as lottery methods, have been proposed in the literature (e.g., Luce and Raiffa 1957).

Following Ferguson (1969), the binomial distribution will be adopted for specifying the measurement model. Its distribution $f(s_k \mid t)$ is given at each stage k of testing by:

$$f(s_k \mid t) = \binom{k}{s_k} t^{s_k} (1-t)^{k-s_k} . \tag{1}$$

This modeling of response behavior reflects the assumption that all items have equal difficulty or are sampled at random from a large (real or imaginary) pool of items (Wilcox 1981).

5 Derivation of Bayesian Sequential Rules

In this section, it will be shown how optimal rules for SMT can be derived using the framework of Bayesian sequential decision theory. Doing so, given an observed response pattern $(x_1, ..., x_k)$, first the Bayes principle will be applied to the fixed-length mastery problem at each stage k of testing by determining which of the posterior expected losses corresponding to the two classification decisions is the smaller. Next, applying the Bayes principle again, optimal rules for the sequential mastery problem are derived at each stage k of testing by comparing this quantity with the posterior expected loss corresponding to the option to continue testing.

Let $y = 0,1, ..., k$ represent all possible values the number correct-score s_k ($0 \leq s_k \leq k$) can take after k items have been administered, it then can easily be verified from Table 1 and Eq. 1 that mastery is declared when the posterior expected loss corresponding to declaring mastery is smaller than the posterior expected loss corresponding to declaring non-mastery, or, equivalently, when s_k is such that

$$(l_{10} + ke)P(T \leq t_c \mid s_k) + (ke)P(T > t_c) <$$
$$(ke)P(T \leq t_c \mid s_k) + (l_{01} + ke)P(T > t_c \mid s_k), \tag{2}$$

and that non-mastery is declared otherwise. Rearranging terms, it can easily be verified that mastery is declared when s_k is such that

$$P(T \leq t_c \mid s_k) < 1/(1+R), \tag{3}$$

and that non-mastery is declared otherwise.

If a beta prior $B(\alpha,\beta)$ with parameters α and β ($\alpha,\beta > 0$) is assumed for T, it follows from an application of Bayes' theorem that under the assumed binomial model, the posterior distribution of T will be a member of the beta family again (the conjugacy property, see, e.g., Lehmann 1959). In fact, if the beta function $B(\alpha,\beta)$ is chosen as prior (i.e., the natural conjugate of the binomial distribution) and student's number-correct score is s_k from a test of length k, then the posterior distribution of T is $B(\alpha+s_k, k-s_k+\beta)$. Hence, it follows from the above inequality that mastery is declared when s_k is such that

$$B(\alpha + s_k, k - s_k + \beta) < 1/(1+R), \tag{4}$$

and that non-mastery is declared otherwise.

A subjective prior will be assumed in this paper; that is, prior knowledge about T is specified by subjective assessment. More specifically, the uniform distribution on the standard interval $[0,1]$ is taken as a non-informative prior, which results as a special case of the beta distribution $B(\alpha,\beta)$ for $\alpha = \beta = 1$. In other words, prior true level of functioning can take on all values between 0 and 1 with equal probability. It then follows immediately that mastery is declared when s_k is such that

$$B(1 + s_k, k - s_k + 1) < 1/(1+R), \tag{5}$$

and that non-mastery is declared otherwise. The beta distribution has been extensively tabulated (e.g., Pearson 1930).

Let $d_k(x_1, ..., x_k)$ denote the decision rule yielding the minimum of the posterior expected losses associated with the two classification decisions at stage k of testing, and let the posterior expected loss corresponding to this minimum be denoted as $V_k(x_1, ..., x_k)$. Bayesian sequential rules for SMT can now be found by using the following backward induction computational scheme: First, the Bayesian sequential rule at the final stage n of testing is computed. Since the option to continue testing is not available at this stage of testing, it follows immediately that the Bayesian sequential rule is given by $d_n(x_1, ..., x_n)$, and its corresponding posterior expected loss by $V_n(x_1, ..., x_n)$.

To compute the posterior expected loss associated with the option to continue testing at stage $(n\text{-}1)$ until stage 0, the risk $R_k(x_1, ..., x_k)$ will be introduced at each stage k $(1 \leq k \leq n)$ of testing. Let the risk at stage n be defined as $V_n(x_1, ..., x_n)$. Generally, given response pattern $(x_1, ..., x_k)$, the risk at stage $(k\text{-}1)$ is then computed inductively as a function of the risk at stage k as:

$$R_{k-1}(x_1,...,x_{k-1}) =$$
$$\min\{V_{k-1}(x_1,...,x_{k-1}),\ E[R_k(x_1,...,x_{k-1},X_k\mid x_1,...,x_{k-1}]\}. \tag{6}$$

The posterior expected loss corresponding to administering one more random item after $(k\text{-}1)$ items have been administered, $E[R_k(x_1, ..., x_{k-1}, X_k)\mid x_1, ..., x_{k-1}]$, can then be computed as the expected risk at stage k of testing as

$$E[R_k(x_1,...,x_{k-1},X_k\mid x_1,...,x_{k-1}] =$$
$$\sum_{x_k=0}^{x_k=1} R_k(x_1,...,x_k)P(X_k = x_k\mid x_1,...,x_{k-1}), \tag{7}$$

where $P(X_k = x_k\mid x_1, ..., x_{k-1})$ denotes the posterior predictive distribution of X_k at stage $(k\text{-}1)$ of testing.

The Bayesian sequential rule at stage $(k\text{-}1)$ is now given by: Administer one more random item if $E[R_k(x_1, ..., x_{k-1}, X_k)\mid x_1, ..., x_{k-1}]$ is smaller than $V_{k-1}(x_1, ..., x_{k-1})$; otherwise, decision $d_{k-1}(x_1, ..., x_{k-1})$ is taken. The Bayesian sequential rule at stage 0 denotes the decision whether or not to administer at least one random item.

6 Calculation of Posterior Predictive Distributions

As is clear from Eq. 7, the posterior predictive distribution $P(X_k = x_k\mid x_1, ..., x_{k-1})$ is needed for computing the posterior expected loss corresponding to administering one more random item at stage $(k\text{-}1)$ of testing. For the binomial distribution as measurement model and assuming the uniform distribution $B(1,1)$ as prior, Ferguson (1967, p. 319) showed that $P(X_k = 1 \mid x_1, ..., x_{k-1}) = (1+s_{k-1})/(k+1)$, and, thus, that $P(X_k = 0 \mid x_1, ..., x_{k-1}) = [1 - (1+s_{k-1})/(k+1)] = (k-s_{k-1})/(k+1)$.

7 Determination of Appropriate Action for Different Number-Correct Score

Using the general backward induction scheme discussed earlier, for a given maximum number n ($n \geq 1$) of items to be administered, a program BAYES was developed to determine the appropriate action (i.e., non-mastery, continuation, or mastery) at each stage k of testing for different number-correct score s_k. A copy from the program BAYES is available from the author upon request.

As an example, the appropriate action is depicted in Table 2 as a closed interval for a maximum of 20 items (i.e., $n = 20$). Students were considered as true masters if they knew at least 55% of the subject matter. Therefore t_c was fixed at 0.55. Furthermore, the loss corresponding to the false mastery decision was perceived

Table 2. Appropriate action calculated by stage of testing and number-correct score

| Stage of testing | Appropriate action by number-correct score | | |
	Non-mastery	Continuation	Mastery
0		0	
1		[0,1]	
2	0	[1,2]	
3	0	[1,3]	
4	[0,1]	[2,4]	
5	[0,1]	[2,4]	5
6	[0,2]	[3,5]	6
7	[0,2]	[3,5]	[6,7]
8	[0,3]	[4,6]	[7,8]
9	[0,4]	[5,7]	[8,9]
10	[0,4]	[5,7]	[8,10]
11	[0,5]	[6,8]	[9,11]
12	[0,5]	[6,8]	[9,12]
13	[0,6]	[7,9]	[10,13]
14	[0,7]	[8,9]	[10,14]
15	[0,7]	[8,10]	[11,15]
16	[0,8]	[9,10]	[11,16]
17	[0,9]	[10,11]	[12,17]
18	[0,10]	11	[12,18]
19	[0,11]		[12,19]
20	[0,12]		[13,20]

twice as large as the loss corresponding to the false non-mastery decision (i.e., $R =$ 2). On a scale in which one unit corresponded to the constant costs of administering one random item (i.e., $e = 1$), therefore, l_{10} and l_{01} were set equal to 200 and 100, respectively. These numerical values reflected the assumption that the losses corresponding to taking incorrect classification decisions were rather large relative to the costs of administering one random item.

As can be seen from Table 2, at least five random items need to be administered before mastery can be declared. However, in principle, non-mastery can be declared already after administering two random items. Of course, in practice, it can be decided to start making classification decisions only after a certain number of random items have been administered to the student. Also, generally a rather large number of items have to be answered correctly before mastery is declared. This can be accounted for the relatively large losses corresponding to false mastery decisions relative to the losses corresponding to false non-mastery decisions.

In this paper, using the framework of Bayesian sequential decision theory, optimal rules for the sequential mastery problem (non-mastery, mastery, or to continue testing) were derived. It should be emphasized, however, that the Bayes principle is especially appropriate when costs of testing can be assumed to be quite large. For instance, when testlets (i.e., blocks of parallel items) rather than single items are considered.

References

Angoff WH (1971) Scales, norms and equivalent scores. In: Thorndike RL (ed) Educational measurement, 3rd edn. Washington, American Council on Education, pp 508-600

Ferguson RL (1969) The development, implementation, and evaluation of a computer-assisted branched test for a program of individually prescribed instruction. University of Pittsburgh, Pittsburgh

Ferguson TS (1967) Mathematical statistics: a decision theoretic approach. Academic Press, New York

Lehmann EL (1959) Testing statistical hypotheses, 3rd edn. Macmillan, New York

Lewis C, Sheehan K (1990) Using Bayesian decision theory to design a computerized mastery test. Applied Psychological Measurement 14: 367-386

Luce RD, Raiffa H (1957) Games and decisions. Wiley, New York

Novick MR, Lindley DV (1979) The use of more realistic utility functions in educational applications. Journal of Educational Measurement 15: 181-191

Pearson K (1930) Tables for statisticians and biometricians. Cambridge University Press, London

van der Linden WJ, Vos HJ (1996) A compensatory approach to optimal selection with mastery scores. Psychometrika 61: 155-172

Vos HJ (1997) Simultaneous optimization of quota-restricted selection decisions with mastery scores. British Journal of Mathematical and Statistical Psychology 50: 105-125

Wald A (1947) Sequential analysis. Wiley, New York

Wilcox RR (1981) A review of the beta-binomial model and its extensions. Journal of Educational Statistics 6: 3-32

Bayes and Generalized Bayes Tests for Tree Ordered Normal Means

Nariaki Sugiura

Department of Mathematical and Physical Sciences, Faculty of Science, Japan Women's University, 2-8-1, Mejirodai, Bunkyoku, Tokyo 112-8681, Japan

Summary. For testing the equality of k means of normal populations with unit variance against tree ordered alternatives, a class of Bayes tests and generalized Bayes tests based on noninformative priors are derived. Numerical comparison of the powers of the obtained tests with those of the minimax single contrast tests and the likelihood ratio tests is shown. It is seen that Bayes tests have comparable minimum powers with the likelihood ratio tests and have larger maximum powers for given noncentrality parameters.

Keywords. Polyhedral convex cone, Corner vector, Restricted alternatives, Uniform diffuse prior, Power comparison.

1 Introduction

Let X_i have independently normal distribution $N(\mu_i, 1)$ for $i=1,2,...,k$. We wish to test the null hypotheses $H_0: \mu_1 = \mu_2 = \cdots = \mu_k$ against tree ordered alternatives H_T: $\mu_1 \leq \mu_2, \cdots, \mu_k$, where at least one inequality is strict. Sugiura(1994) has shown that the orthogonal contrasts test by Mukerjee, Robertson and Wright(1987) may be regarded as an approximate generalized Bayes test for uniform diffuse priors. We shall give in this paper a class of proper Bayes tests and then a generalized Bayes test for a diffuse prior on the corner vectors and on the faces of the polyhedral convex cones formed by H_T. Numerical study by simulation shows that generalized Bayes test giving prior on central direction in addition to corner vectors and generalized Bayes test giving prior on each face of the cone have good comparative minimum power to the likelihood ratio test and have larger maximum power for given noncentral parameter $\Delta = \sqrt{\sum_{i=1}^{k}(\mu_i - \overline{\mu})^2}$ where $\overline{\mu} = (1/k)\sum_{i=1}^{k}\mu_i$.

Abelson and Tukey(1963) was the first to give geometrical consideration for ordered alternatives and derive the maxmin single contrast test. Lindley's discussion in Bartholomew(1961) seems to be the first to argue on Bayes test for ordered alternatives. The generalized Bayes tests for loop-ordered alternatives are derived by Sugiura(1999), in which power comparison including likelihood ratio test is shown.

2 Preliminary Lemmas

We shall first prove two lemmas, which will be frequently used in the subsequent sections. Put $\mu_i=\mu+h_i$ for $i=1,\cdots,k$ with the condition $\sum_{i=1}^{k} h_i = 0$. Then the null hypotheses is expressed by $h_1=h_2=\cdots=h_k=0$. Note that tree ordered alternatives form polyhedral convex cones with apex at the origin in the parameter space $(h_1,\cdots,h_k)$ of contrasts. We shall assume in this section that alternative hypotheses are just a polyhedral convex cone with apex at the origin without specifying the form of the cone. Let a normalized contrast vector $c=(c_1,\cdots,c_k)$ be in the polyhedral convex cone so that $\sum_{i=1}^{k} c_i = 0$ and $\sum_{i=1}^{k} c_i^2 = 1$. Let t be a random variable having half normal distribution defined by

$$\frac{1}{\sigma}\sqrt{\frac{2}{\pi}}\exp[-\frac{1}{2\sigma^2}t^2] \qquad \text{for } t>0 \tag{2.1}$$

and put a prior distribution on $(h_1,\cdots,h_k)$ by $h_i=tc_i$ for $i=1,\ldots,k$. Further we assume that a prior distribution of μ is normal $N(0,\tau^2)$ both under the alternatives and the null hypotheses. It is easy to see the marginal density function under the null hypotheses is proportional to

$$f(x_1,x_2,\cdots,x_k \mid H_0) \propto \exp[-\frac{1}{2}\sum_{i=1}^{k}(x_i-\bar{x})^2 -\frac{1}{2}k\tau^2/(1+k\tau^2)]. \tag{2.2}$$

Concerning the ratio of the marginal density functions $f(x_1,x_2,\cdots,x_k \mid H_T)$ / $f(x_1,x_2,\cdots,x_k \mid H_0)$, we can prove the following two Lemmas.

Lemma 2.1. *Let $\Phi(\cdot)$ and $\phi(\cdot)$ be the distribution function and the density function of the standard normal distribution respectively. Then the inverse of a Bayes factor for a half normal prior on a vector $tc=(tc_1,\cdots,tc_k)$ and a prior on μ independently distributed as $N(0,\tau^2)$ is given by*

$$\Phi(\frac{\sigma}{\sqrt{\sigma^2+1}}\sum_{i=1}^{k}c_i x_i) \bigg/ \phi(\frac{\sigma}{\sqrt{\sigma^2+1}}\sum_{i=1}^{k}c_i x_i). \tag{2.3}$$

Proof. Note that

$$\sum_{i=1}^{k}(x_i-\mu_i)^2 = \sum_{i=1}^{k}(x_i-\bar{x})^2 + k(\bar{x}-\mu)^2 + \sum_{i=1}^{k}h_i^2 - 2\sum_{i=1}^{k}h_i(x_i-\bar{x}) \qquad (2.4)$$

$$= \sum_{i=1}^{k}(x_i-\bar{x})^2 + k(\bar{x}-\mu)^2 + t^2 - 2t\sum_{i=1}^{k}c_ix_i. \qquad (2.5)$$

Then apart from a constant factor, the marginal likelihood under alternatives is given by

$$\int_{-\infty}^{\infty}\int_{0}^{\infty}\exp[-\frac{1}{2}\sum_{i=1}^{k}(x_i-\mu_i)^2 - \frac{1}{2\tau^2}\mu^2 - \frac{1}{2\sigma^2}t^2]dtd\mu$$

$$= e^{-\frac{1}{2}\sum_{i=1}^{k}(x_i-\bar{x})^2} \int_{-\infty}^{\infty} e^{-\frac{k}{2}(\bar{x}-\mu)^2 - \frac{\mu^2}{2\tau^2}}d\mu \int_{0}^{\infty} e^{-\frac{1}{2}\{(1+\frac{1}{\sigma^2})t^2 - 2t\sum_{i=1}^{k}c_ix_i\}} dt$$

$$\propto \exp[-\frac{1}{2}\sum_{i=1}^{k}(x_i-\bar{x})^2 - \frac{1}{2}\frac{k\bar{x}^2}{k\tau^2+1}]\cdot\frac{\Phi(\frac{\sigma}{\sqrt{\sigma^2+1}}\sum_{i=1}^{k}c_ix_i)}{\phi(\frac{\sigma}{\sqrt{\sigma^2+1}}\sum_{i=1}^{k}c_ix_i)}. \qquad (2.6)$$

Taking the ratio of the marginal likelihood (2.6) to (2.2) gives the inverse of the Bayes factor (2.3).

We now consider to put half normal priors on a wedge shaped plane generated by two normalized contrast vectors $c=(c_1,\cdots,c_k)$ and $d=(d_1,\cdots,d_k)$ under alternatives, where $\sum_{i=1}^{k}c_i=0$, $\sum_{i=1}^{k}c_i^2=1$ and $\sum_{i=1}^{k}d_i=0, \sum_{i=1}^{k}d_i^2=1$.

Lemma 2.2. *Let t_1 and t_2 be two independent random variables having half normal distribution defined by (2.1). Let two normalized contrast vectors c and d lie in the alternative hypotheses of the polyhedral convex cone. For a prior t_1c+t_2d on the wedge shaped plane in the alternatives and an independent prior on μ for normal distribution $N(0,\tau^2)$ both under alternatives and the null hypotheses, the inverse of a Bayes factor is given by*

$$e^{\frac{A^2+B^2}{2}}\int_{0}^{\infty}\phi(\frac{\sqrt{1+\sigma^{-2}+\sum_{i=1}^{k}c_id_i}}{\sqrt{1+\sigma^{-2}-\sum_{i=1}^{k}c_id_i}}\ell-A)\{\Phi(\ell-B)-\Phi(-\ell-B)\}d\ell, \qquad (2.7)$$

where

$$A = \frac{\sum_{i=1}^{k}(c_i + d_i)x_i}{\sqrt{2}\sqrt{1+\sigma^{-2}+\sum_{i=1}^{k}c_id_i}} \quad , \quad B = \frac{\sum_{i=1}^{k}(c_i - d_i)x_i}{\sqrt{2}\sqrt{1+\sigma^{-2}-\sum_{i=1}^{k}c_id_i}} \quad . \tag{2.8}$$

Proof. Since $h_i = t_1 c_i + t_2 d_i$ under alternatives, we can write from (2.4)

$$\sum_{i=1}^{k}(x_i - \mu_i)^2$$

$$= \sum_{i=1}^{k}(x_i - \bar{x})^2 + k(\bar{x} - \mu)^2 + t_1^2 + t_2^2 + 2t_1 t_2 \sum_{i=1}^{k}c_id_i - 2t_1 \sum_{i=1}^{k}c_ix_i - 2t_2 \sum_{i=1}^{k}d_ix_i. \tag{2.9}$$

Then the marginal likelihood is proportional to

$$\int_{-\infty}^{\infty}\int_{0}^{\infty}\int_{0}^{\infty}\exp[-\frac{1}{2}\sum_{i=1}^{k}(x_i - \mu_i)^2 - \frac{1}{2\tau^2}\mu^2 - \frac{1}{2\sigma^2}(t_1^2 + t_2^2)]dt_1 dt_2 d\mu.$$

First integrate out with respect to μ on $(-\infty, +\infty)$ and then orthogonal transformation $t_1 = (\ell_1 + \ell_2)/\sqrt{2}$ and $t_2 = (\ell_1 - \ell_2)/\sqrt{2}$ yields

$$\propto e^{-\frac{1}{2}\sum_{i=1}^{k}(x_i - \bar{x})^2 - \frac{1}{2}\frac{k\bar{x}^2}{k\tau^2 + 1}} \int_{\ell_1 > \ell_2 > -\ell_1} e^{-\frac{1}{2}\{(1+\frac{1}{\sigma^2}+\sum_{i=1}^{k}c_id_i)\ell_1^2 + (1+\frac{1}{\sigma^2}-\sum_{i=1}^{k}c_id_i)\ell_2^2\}}$$

$$\cdot \exp[-\frac{1}{2}\{-\sqrt{2}\ell_1 \sum_{i=1}^{k}(c_i + d_i)x_i - \sqrt{2}\ell_2 \sum_{i=1}^{k}(c_i - d_i)x_i\}]d\ell_1 d\ell_2$$

$$\propto e^{-\frac{1}{2}\sum_{i=1}^{k}(x_i - \bar{x})^2 - \frac{1}{2}\frac{k\bar{x}^2}{k\tau^2 + 1}} \cdot e^{\frac{1}{2}(A^2 + B^2)} \int_{0}^{\infty}\phi(\sqrt{1+\sigma^{-2}+\sum_{i=1}^{k}c_id_i}\,\ell_1 - A)$$

$$\cdot\{\Phi(\sqrt{1+\sigma^{-2}-\sum_{i=1}^{k}c_id_i}\,\ell_1 - B) - \Phi(-\sqrt{1+\sigma^{-2}-\sum_{i=1}^{k}c_id_i}\,\ell_1 - B)\}d\ell_1. \tag{2.10}$$

Taking the ratio of the marginal likelihood to (2.2) gives the desired inverse of the Bayes factor (2.7).

3 Tree Order Alternatives

Since tree order alternatives H_T form a polyhedral convex cone with apex at the origin in the parameter space $(h_1, \cdots, h_k)$ of contrasts, Abelson and Tukey(1963) have shown that the normalized corner vectors are given by

$$v_1 = (-1, k-1, -1, \cdots, -1) / \sqrt{k(k-1)}$$

$$v_2 = (-1, -1, k-1, -1, \cdots, -1) / \sqrt{k(k-1)}$$

$$\cdots\cdots\cdots \qquad (3.1)$$

$$v_{k-1} = (-1, -1, -1, -1, \cdots, -1, k-1) / \sqrt{k(k-1)}$$

which intersect each other with equal angle $\cos^{-1}(-1/(k-1))$ larger than $\pi/2$.

We now put a prior distribution on μ with normal distribution $N(0, \tau^2)$ both under H_0 and H_T. Under H_T, choose a corner vector v_i in (3.1) with equal probability $1/(k-1)$ which we shall write

$$P(H_T = H_{T_i}) = 1/(k-1) \qquad \text{for } i=1,\ldots,k \qquad (3.2)$$

and put a prior distribution for given H_{Ti} by tv_i ($h>0$) with t having half normal distribution given by (2.1). Applying Lemma 2.1 for the corner vector v_i, we have

$$\sum_{\alpha=1}^{k} c_\alpha x_\alpha = \sqrt{k/(k-1)}(x_{i+1} - \bar{x}) \qquad (3.3)$$

and get the following class of Bayes critical regions

$$\sum_{j=1}^{k-1} \Phi(\sqrt{\frac{k}{k-1}} \frac{\sigma}{\sqrt{\sigma^2+1}} (x_{j+1} - \bar{x})) \Big/ \phi(\sqrt{\frac{k}{k-1}} \frac{\sigma}{\sqrt{\sigma^2+1}} (x_{j+1} - \bar{x})) > const. \, (3.4)$$

Let σ tend to infinity in (3.4), we get a critical region of a generalized Bayes test given in the following theorem.

THEOREM 1. *For testing the tree ordered alternatives, a critical region of a generalized Bayes test for a uniform diffuse prior on each corner vector is given by*

$$T_{B1} = \sum_{i=1}^{k-1} \Phi(\sqrt{\frac{k}{k-1}} (x_{i+1} - \bar{x})) \Big/ \phi(\sqrt{\frac{k}{k-1}} (x_{i+1} - \bar{x})) > const. \qquad (3.5)$$

Note that $\sqrt{k/(k-1)}(x_{i+1} - \bar{x})$ has $N(h_{i+1}, 1)$. The symmetry of the critical region (3.5) and the symmetry of the components between corner vectors in (3.1) imply the invariance of the powers of T_{B1} test on all corner vectors Δv_i for $i=1, \cdots, k-1$. This is a useful property for numerical calculation of powers in the next section.

When $k=2$, the tree ordered alternatives is simply a one sided alternatives $\mu_1 < \mu_2$ and the critical region (3.5) is equivalent to $x_2 - x_1 > const.$ since $\Phi(z)/\phi(z)$ is increasing with respect to z for $-\infty<z<\infty$, which yields the uniformly most powerful test.   When $k=3$, the critical region with respect to

$$a_2 = (x_2 - x_3)/\sqrt{2} \quad \text{and} \quad a_3 = \sqrt{3/2}(x_2 + x_3 - 2\bar{x}) \tag{3.6}$$

is written by

$$\frac{\Phi((\sqrt{3}a_2 + a_3)/2)}{\phi((\sqrt{3}a_2 + a_3)/2)} + \frac{\Phi((-\sqrt{3}a_2 + a_3)/2)}{\phi((-\sqrt{3}a_2 + a_3)/2)} > const. \tag{3.7}$$

The contours of the critical region (3.7) with respect to (a_2,a_3) are shown in Fig. 1(a), which are similar to that of orthogonal multiple contrast tests by Mukerjee, Robertson and Wright (1987). It is given by $\max(a_3+a_2, a_3-a_2)$, which was also obtained as an approximate generalized Bayes critical region by Sugiura(1994). It is easy to see that the sum of all normalized corner vectors is

$$v_0 = v_1 + \cdots + v_{k-1} = (-k+1, 1, \cdots, 1)/\sqrt{k(k-1)} \tag{3.8}$$

which has unit length and intersects with each corner vector by equal angle. Hence it may be called normalized central vector of polyhedral convex cone associated with H_T. Note that each corner vector intersects another corner vector with equal

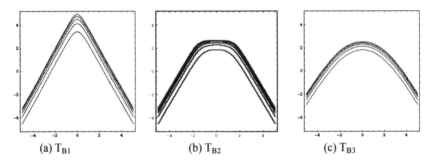

$$\text{(a) } T_{B1} \qquad\qquad \text{(b) } T_{B2} \qquad\qquad \text{(c) } T_{B3}$$

Fig. 1. Contours of the critical regions on (a_2,a_3) plane when $k=3$

angle, which is larger than $\pi/2$, we may put a positive prior on the central vector just like a corner vector to guard the power of the test along the central direction. Corresponding to a prior (3.2), we now have a uniform distribution

$$P(H_T = H_{T_i}) = 1/k \qquad \text{for } i=0,\ldots,k-1, \tag{3.9}$$

where H_{T0} stands for selecting the central vector v_0. If H_{T_0} is true, we have Bayes test by Lemma 2.1, where

$$\sum_{\alpha=1}^{k} c_\alpha x_\alpha = \sqrt{k/(k-1)}\,(-x_1 + \bar{x}).\tag{3.10}$$

The same argument as in the proof of Theorem 1 yields the Bayes critical region

$$\frac{\Phi(-\sqrt{\dfrac{k}{k-1}}\,\dfrac{\sigma}{\sqrt{1+\sigma^2}}\,(x_1-\bar{x}))}{\phi(-\sqrt{\dfrac{k}{k-1}}\,\dfrac{\sigma}{\sqrt{1+\sigma^2}}\,(x_1-\bar{x}))} + \sum_{i=2}^{k} \frac{\Phi(\sqrt{\dfrac{k}{k-1}}\,\dfrac{\sigma}{\sqrt{1+\sigma^2}}\,(x_i-\bar{x}))}{\phi(\sqrt{\dfrac{k}{k-1}}\,\dfrac{\sigma}{\sqrt{1+\sigma^2}}\,(x_i-\bar{x}))} > const.\tag{3.11}$$

The effect of putting positive prior on the central vector lies in the first term in (3.11), the argument in which has opposite sign to those of the subsequent terms. This is reasonable since $x_1 - \bar{x}$ should be small if H_0 is not true. Let σ tend to infinity. Then we get the following generalized Bayes test:

THEOREM 2. *Selecting a corner vector or the central vector equally likely and putting uniform diffuse prior on each corner vector or the central vector when it is selected, with normal distribution* $N(0,t^2)$ *on* μ, *the critical region of the generalized Bayes test is given by*

$$T_{B2} = \frac{\Phi(-\sqrt{\dfrac{k}{k-1}}\,(x_1-\bar{x}))}{\phi(-\sqrt{\dfrac{k}{k-1}}\,(x_1-\bar{x}))} + \sum_{i=2}^{k} \frac{\Phi(\sqrt{\dfrac{k}{k-1}}\,(x_i-\bar{x}))}{\phi(\sqrt{\dfrac{k}{k-1}}\,(x_i-\bar{x}))} > const.\tag{3.12}$$

By the same reason as for T_{B1} test, we can see that the powers of T_{B2} test are equal on all corner vectors Δv_i for $i=1,\cdots,k-1$.

When $k=2$, the critical region (3.12) reduces to the uniformly most powerful test $x_2-x_1 >$ const. and the generalized Bayes tests T_{B1} and T_{B2} make no difference in this case. When $k=3$, the critical region with respect to a_2 and a_3 defined by (3.6) is written by

$$\frac{\Phi(a_3)}{\phi(a_3)} + \frac{\Phi((\sqrt{3}a_2+a_3)/2)}{\phi((\sqrt{3}a_2+a_3)/2)} + \frac{\Phi((-\sqrt{3}a_2+a_3)/2)}{\phi((-\sqrt{3}a_2+a_3)/2)} > const.\tag{3.13}$$

The contours of the crtical region are shown in Fig.1(b). It is seen that the edge of the contour is made even, compared with that of T_{B1} shown in Fig.1(a).

Taking a positive prior on corner vectors of the polyhedral convex cone of H_T as is discussed in Theorems 1 and 2, is not an only way of reasonable choice. Note that each corner vector given in (3.1) intersects others with equal angle. We can give positive prior on the plane p_{ij} spanned by

$$H_{T_{ij}} : (h_1,\ldots,h_k)=t_1 v_i + t_2 v_j \qquad (3.14)$$

for every pair of (i, j) $1 \le i < j \le k$. where t_1 and t_2 are assumed to follow independently according to the half normal distribution given in (2.1) with common σ. Using the same prior on μ as in Theorems 1 and 2 and equal probability of selecting corner plane p_{ij}, we can apply Lemma 2.2 to the alternatives $H_{T_{ij}}$ in (3.14) giving,

$$A = \frac{\sqrt{k}}{\sqrt{2}\sqrt{k-2+(k-1)/\sigma^2}}(x_{i+1} + x_{j+1} - 2\bar{x})$$

$$B = \frac{\sqrt{k}}{\sqrt{2}\sqrt{k+(k-1)/\sigma^2}}(x_{i+1} - x_{j+1}) \qquad (3.15)$$

in (2.5). The inverse of a Bayes factor immediately yields the following Bayes critical region

$$\sum_{1 \le i < j \le k-1} \exp[\frac{1}{2}\frac{k}{k+(k-1)/\sigma^2}a_{ij}^2 + \frac{1}{2}\frac{k-2}{k-2+(k-1)/\sigma^2}b_{ij}^2] \int_0^\infty \{\Phi(\sqrt{\frac{1}{\sigma^2}+\frac{k}{k-1}}(\ell_1$$

$$-\frac{\sqrt{k(k-1)}}{(k-1)/\sigma^2+k}a_{ij}) - \Phi(\sqrt{\frac{1}{\sigma^2}+\frac{k}{k-1}}(-\ell_1 - \frac{\sqrt{k(k-1)}}{(k-1)/\sigma^2+k}a_{ij})\}$$

$$\phi(\sqrt{\frac{1}{\sigma^2}+\frac{k-2}{k-1}}(\ell_1 - \frac{\sqrt{(k-2)(k-1)}}{k-2+(k-1)/\sigma^2}b_{ij})d\ell_1 > const. \qquad (3.16)$$

where

$$a_{ij} = (x_{i+1} - x_{j+1})/\sqrt{2} \quad \text{and} \quad b_{ij} = (x_{i+1} + x_{j+1} - 2\bar{x})\sqrt{k/\{2(k-2)\}}. \qquad (3.17)$$

Letting σ tend to infinity and change the variable $\sqrt{k/(k-1)}\,\ell_1$ to ℓ_1, we get the following generalized Bayes critical region:

THEOREM 3. *Selecting a corner plane p_{ij} in (3.14) equal'y likely and taking uniform diffuse prior on it, a generalized Bayes critical region is given by*

$$T_{B3} = \sum_{1 \le i < j \le k-1} e^{\frac{1}{2}(a_{ij}^2 + b_{ij}^2)} \int_0^\infty \{\Phi(\ell_1 - a_{ij}) - \Phi(-\ell_1 - a_{ij})\}\phi(\sqrt{\frac{k-2}{k}}\ell_1 - b_{ij})d\ell_1 > const.$$

where a_{ij} and b_{ij} are defined by (3.17).

We note that T_{B3} is invariant under the sign change of a_{ij} and that a_{ij} and b_{ij} are independently normally distributed with unit variance and means $(h_{i+1} - h_{j+1})$ $/\sqrt{2}$ and $(h_{i+1} + h_{j+1})\sqrt{k/\{2(k-2)\}}$ respectively. Due to the symmetry and the invariance of T_{B3} and the symmetry of corner vectors we can see that the powers of T_{B3} test are equal on all corner vectors Δv_i for $i=1,\cdots,k-1$. For $k=3$, we get

$$T_{B3} = \exp[\frac{1}{2}(a_{12}^2 + b_{12}^2)]\int_0^\infty \{\Phi(\ell_1 - a_{12}) - \Phi(-\ell_1 - a_{12})\}\phi(\frac{\ell_1}{\sqrt{3}} - b_{12})d\ell_1 \quad (3.18)$$

where a_{12} and b_{12} are equal to a_2 and a_3 given by (3.6) respectively. The contours of the critical region (3.18) are shown in Fig.1(c). The curve is more smoothed near the top than those of T_{B1} and T_{B2} shown in Fig.'s1(a) and (b). Sugiura(1994) has used Fig.1(c) for approximating Bayes critical region.

4 Numerical Comparison of Powers

Abelson and Tukey(1963)'s maxmin single contrast test has the maximized minimum power $1 - \Phi(c_0 - \Delta/(k-1))$ for every corner vector and the maximum power $1 - \Phi(c_0 - \Delta)$ for the central vector for given $\Delta^2 = \sum_{i=1}^k (h_i - \bar{h})^2$, where c_0 stands for upper 100α percent point of the standard normal distribution. The powers of Abelson-Tukey's test and the likelihood ratio test in Table 2 for $k=3$ are the reproduction from Bartholomew(1962) so that comparison with the generalized Bayes test is easily seen. As Robertson, Wright and Dykstra(1988) remarked, the maximum power of the likelihood ratio test for given Δ is believed at the central vector and the minimum power at every corner vectors. When $k=3$, the central vector and corner vectors for given Δ are expressed by

$$v_0 = (-2,1,1)\Delta/\sqrt{6}, \quad v_1 = (-1,2,-1)\Delta/\sqrt{6}, \quad v_2 = (-1,-1,2)\Delta/\sqrt{6}.$$

The most convenient expressions for numerical computation of the powers of the generalized Bayes tests T_{B1} and T_{B2} are given by the formulas

$$\frac{1}{\pi\sqrt{3}}\int_{-10}^{10}\int_{-10}^{10} \exp[-\frac{2}{3}\{(x-\eta_1)^2 + (x-\eta_1)(y-\eta_2) + (y-\eta_2)^2\}]I_D(x,y)dxdy,$$

where $\eta_1 = (2h_2 - h_1)/\sqrt{6}$, $\eta_2 = (h_2 - 2h_3)/\sqrt{6}$ and $I_D(x,y)$ stands for indicator function taking value one or zero according as $(x, y) \in D$ or not. The domain D is defined by $D = \{(x,y) \mid \Phi(x)/\phi(x) + \Phi(y)/\phi(y) > 17.567\}$ for T_{B1} test and $D = \{(x,y) \mid \Phi(x)/\phi(x) + \Phi(y)/\phi(y) + \Phi(x+y)/\phi(x+y) > 28.647\}$ for T_{B2} test and the value of RHS of the inequality gives upper 5% point of each statistic calculated by numerical integration. For T_{B3} test we found that simulation is better than the direct numerical integration. By 99,999 iterations of T_{B3} given by (3.18) based on normal random numbers, the upper 5 % point is estimated by the 95000th smallest. This is repeated 5 times, giving $\{10.8678, 10.4984, 10.7488, 10.7148, 10.6362\}$ with the standard deviation 0.1227. Taking the sample mean we can estimate the upper 5% point with the estimated standard error as 10.693 ± 0.055. This is tabulated in Table 1. By the same method, other simulated 5% points of test statistics with standard error are shown in Table 1.

Table 1. Five simulated 5% points by 999999 iterations and estimated 5% points.

	$k=3$		$k=4$				
T_{B1}	17.567		T_{B1}	25.90 26.05 26.34 26.04 26.36			
				26.14 ± 0.08			
T_{B2}	28.647		T_{B2}	37.86 37.21 38.12 37.50 37.38			
T_{B3}	10.87 10.50 10.75 10.71 10.64			37.61 ± 0.15			
	10.69 ± 0.06		T_{B3}	25.82 25.99 25.85 25.81 26.42			
				25.98 ± 0.01			

Table 2. Comparison of the powers of maxmin single contrast test, likelihood ratio and the three generalized Bayes tests for given Δ and $\alpha=0.05$.

	$k=3$					$k=4$			
	$\Delta=1$	$\Delta=2$	$\Delta=3$	$\Delta=4$		$\Delta=1$	$\Delta=2$	$\Delta=3$	$\Delta=4$
A-T max(center)	.260	.639	.912	.991	A-Tmax(center)	.260	.639	.912	.991
min(corner)	.126	.260	.442	.639	min(corner)	.095	.164	.260	.378
LR max(center)	.244	.605	.857	.987	LR max(center)	.187	.489	.813	.967
min(corner)	.221	.569	.872	.983	min(corner)	.140	.416	.767	.955
T_{B1} center	.151	.365	.668	.901	T_{B1} center	.111	.235	.437	.686
corner	.176	.518	.851	.979	corner	.144	.453	.810	.969
T_{B2}center	.214	.553	.863	.981	T_{B2} center	.173	.479	.818	.970
corner	.172	.491	.827	.973	corner	.141	.428	.787	.961
T_{B3} center	.237	.594	.889	.986	T_{B3} center	.160	.396	.700	.912
corner	.162	.450	.789	.959	corner	.142	.428	.773	.955

The power of T_{B3} test is again computed by simulation with 100,000 iterations.   It is seen that (i)T_{B1} test has poor power at central direction; (ii) T_{B2} test has comparable maximum and minimum powers with LR test and may be recommended; (iii) T_{B3} test seems to have slightly less power than T_{B2} test but not always.

Acknowledgements. The author is sincerely grateful for the reviewers for pointing out many corrections and useful suggestion to improve the presentation of the paper.

References

Abelson RP, Tukey JW (1963) Efficient utilization of non-numerical information in quantitative analysis: general theory and the case of simple order. Ann Math Statist 34: 1347-1369

Bartholomew DJ (1961) A test of homogeneity of means under restricted alternatives. J Roy Statist Soc B 23: 239-281

Mukerjee H, Robertson T, Wright FT (1987) Comparison of several treatments with a control using multiple contrasts. J Amer Statist Assoc 82: 902-910

Robertson T, Wright FT, Dykstra RL (1988) Order Restricted Statistical Inference. Wiley New York.

Sugiura N (1994) Approximating Bayes critical region for testing simple and tree ordered normal means. J Statist Res 28: 1-20

Sugiura N (1999) Generalized Bayes and multiple contrasts tests for simple loop-ordered normal means. Commun Statist–Theory Meth 28(3&4): 549-580

Model Selection Criteria for Growth Curve Model with Hierachical Within-Individual Design Matrices

Yasunori Fujikoshi

Department of Mathematics, Graduate School of Science, Hiroshima University
1-3-1 Kagamiyama, Higashi-Hiroshima, 739-8526, JAPAN
fuji@math.sci.hiroshima-u.ac.jp

Summary. This paper is concerned with a selection of extended growth curve models with several hierarchical within-individual design matrices. The class of our models includes an important model whose mean structure consists of polynomial growth curves with different degrees. In general, the AIC has been proposed as an asymptotically unbiased estimator of the AIC type of risk. In this paper we study a corrected AIC which improves unbiasedness for the risk. In particular, the corrected AIC is obtained when the number of hierarchical within-individual design matrices is less than 3.

Key words. AIC, Corrected AIC, Extended Growth Curve Model, Hirachical Within-Individual Design Matrix, Maximum Likelihood Estimator

1 Introduction

This paper is concerned with a selection of extended growth curve models with several hierarchical within-individual design matrices. For an $n \times p$ random matrix Y, an extended growth curve model considered in this paper is defined by

$$Y \sim N_{n \times p}(A_1 \Theta_1 X_{(1)} + \cdots + A_k \Theta_k X_{(k)}, I_n \otimes \Sigma), \qquad (1)$$

where A_i are known $n \times r_i$ between-individual design matrices of ranks r_i, $X_{(i)}$ are known $q_i \times p$ within-individual design matrices with ranks q_i, Θ_i are unknown $r_i \times q_i$ parameter matrices, and Σ is an unknown positive definite matrix. Here it is assumed that the $X'_{(i)}s$ have a hierarchical structure such that

$$X_{(i)} = \begin{bmatrix} X_1 \\ \vdots \\ X_i \end{bmatrix}, \quad i = 1, \ldots, k, \qquad (2)$$

and $q_1 < \cdots < q_k$. The model is an extension of the growth curve model by Potthoff and Roy (1964). Note that the model includes an important one whose mean structure consists of polynomial growth curves with different degrees. The model has been studied by Srivastava and Khatri (1979), Banken (1984), Kariya (1985), von Rosen (1989, 1990), Fujikoshi and Satoh (1996), Fujikoshi, Kanda and Ohtaki (1999), etc.

For a given $\gamma = (k; q_1, \ldots, q_k)$, let the model (1) be denoted by M_γ. Note that k denotes the number of different $X'_{(i)}s$ in (1), and q_i denotes the number of the ith hierachical within-individual variables. In this paper we consider the problem of selecting a model from a set of candidate models $\{M_\gamma; \ \gamma \in \Gamma\}$, where Γ is a set of $\gamma = (k; q_1, \ldots, q_k)$ satisfying $0 \leq q_1 < q_2 < \ldots < q_k \leq p$. The AIC for a candidate model M_γ has been considered by Fujikoshi and Satoh (1996) and Fujikoshi, Kanda and Ohtaki (1999). Further, Fujikoshi and Satoh (1996) derived its correction for the case $k \leq 2$, which improves unbiasedness for AIC type of risk. The purpose of the present paper is to extend correction of the AIC, in particular, for $k = 3$. In general, a candidate model is called an overspecified model or an underspecified model according to whether it does or does not include the true model. From our result we can say that if a candidate model is an overspecified model, then its corrected AIC is an exact unbiased estimator of the AIC type of risk.

2 The AIC

The model (1) can be regarded as a submodel of

$$M : \ Y \sim N_{n \times p}(A\eta, I_n \otimes \Sigma), \tag{3}$$

where $A = [A_1, \ldots, A_k], r = r_1 + \ldots + r_k$, and η is an $r \times p$ unknown parameter matrix. We can write a model M_γ as

$$M_\gamma : \ M \ \text{and} \ \eta = \Theta X,$$

where $X = X_{(k)}$ and

$$\Theta = \begin{bmatrix} \Theta_{11} & O & \cdots & O \\ \vdots & \ddots & \ddots & \vdots \\ \vdots & & \ddots & O \\ \Theta_{k1} & \cdots & \cdots & \Theta_{kk} \end{bmatrix}.$$

We consider the problem of selecting a model from the set of candidate models defined by $\{M_\gamma; \ \gamma \in \Gamma\}$.

Let $g(Y)$ be the true density of Y, and denote the true model by M^*. It is natural to assume that under the true model M^* the rows of Y are independent, and

$$E^*[Y] = A\eta^*, \quad \text{Var}(\text{vec}(Y)) = I_n \otimes \Sigma^*, \tag{4}$$

where E^* means the expectation under the true model. Let $f(Y; \Theta, \Sigma)$ be the density function of Y under a candidate model M_γ. Further, let $\widehat{\Theta}$ and $\widehat{\Sigma}$ be the maximum likelihood estimates of Θ and Σ under M_γ. Then the AIC type of risk for M_γ is defined (see, e.g., Akaike (1973), Fujikoshi and Satoh (1996)) by

$$R_\gamma = E_Y^* E_Z^* [-2 \log f(Z; \widehat{\Theta}, \widehat{\Sigma})], \tag{5}$$

where Z is an operational $n \times p$ random matrix independent of Y. Our purpose is to choose M_γ so that R_γ is minimized. In practice we need to estimate R_γ because R_γ depends on an unknown density $g(\cdot)$. Note that R_γ can be expressed as

$$R_\gamma = E_Y^* [-2 \log f(Y; \widehat{\Theta}, \widehat{\Sigma})] + B_\gamma, \tag{6}$$

where

$$
\begin{aligned}
B_\gamma &= 2 E_Y^* E_Z^* \left[\log \frac{f(Y; \widehat{\Theta}, \widehat{\Sigma})}{f(Z; \widehat{\Theta}, \widehat{\Sigma})} \right] \\
&= -np + E^* [n \operatorname{tr} \widehat{\Sigma}^{-1} \Sigma^* \\
&\quad + \operatorname{tr} \widehat{\Sigma}^{-1} (\widehat{\Theta} X - \eta^*)' A' A (\widehat{\Theta} X - \eta^*)].
\end{aligned}
\tag{7}
$$

The AIC uses the number of independent parameters under M_γ as an estimator of B_γ which is given by

$$\tilde{b}_\gamma = 2 \left\{ \sum_{i=1}^k r_i d_i + \frac{1}{2} p(p+1) \right\}, \tag{8}$$

where $d_i = q_i - q_{i-1}, i = 1, \ldots, k$ and $q_0 = 0$. The AIC is

$$AIC_\gamma = -2 \log f(Y; \widehat{\Theta}, \widehat{\Sigma}) + \tilde{b}_\gamma. \tag{9}$$

An explicit form for the first term is given by the equation (14).

3 MLE

In this section we surmmarize the results on the MLE's $\widehat{\Theta}$ and $\widehat{\Sigma}$ of Θ and Σ under M_γ, and $-2 \log f(Y; \widehat{\Theta}, \widehat{\Sigma})$, following Fujikoshi, Kanda and Ohtaki (1999). Considering the transformation from Y to $Z = HYB$, where H and B are appropriate orthogonal matrices, we have the following canonical forms for models M and M_γ as follows. Let Z be decomposed as

$$
Z = \begin{bmatrix}
Z_{11} & \cdots & Z_{1k} & Z_{1\ell} \\
\vdots & & \vdots & \vdots \\
Z_{k1} & \cdots & Z_{kk} & Z_{k\ell} \\
Z_{\ell 1} & \cdots & Z_{\ell k} & Z_{\ell\ell}
\end{bmatrix}, \tag{10}
$$

where $Z_{ij} : r_i \times d_j$, $\ell = k + 1$, $r_\ell = n - r_1 - \cdots - r_k$ and $d_\ell = p - q_k$. It is assumed that $m = r_\ell \geq p$. Then, the model M in the term of Z is expressed as

$$M : \quad Z \sim N_{n \times p}(\mathrm{E}(Z), I_n \otimes \Omega), \tag{11}$$

where Ω is an unknown positive definite matrix and

$$E(Z) = \begin{bmatrix} \Xi & \nu \\ O & O \end{bmatrix}.$$

The model M_γ in the term of Z is expressed as

$$M_\gamma : \quad M \text{ with } \nu = 0, \text{ and } \Xi = \begin{bmatrix} \Xi_{11} & O & \cdots & O \\ \vdots & \ddots & \ddots & \vdots \\ \vdots & & \ddots & O \\ \Xi_{k1} & \cdots & \cdots & \Xi_{kk} \end{bmatrix}. \tag{12}$$

We use the following notations:

$$S = S^{(0)} = [Z_{\ell 1}, \ldots, Z_{\ell \ell}]'[Z_{\ell 1}, \ldots, Z_{\ell \ell}],$$

and for $i = 1, \ldots, k$,

$$U^{(i)} = [Z_{i1}, \ldots, Z_{i\ell}]'[Z_{i1}, \ldots, Z_{i\ell}],$$
$$S^{(i)} = S^{(0)} + U^{(1)} + \ldots + U^{(i)}$$
$$= \begin{bmatrix} S_{11}^{(i)} & \cdots & S_{1\ell}^{(i)} \\ \vdots & \ddots & \vdots \\ S_{\ell 1}^{(i)} & \cdots & S_{\ell \ell}^{(i)} \end{bmatrix},$$
$$Z_{i(1 \ldots i)} = [Z_{i1}, \ldots, Z_{ii}],$$
$$Z_{i(i+1 \ldots \ell)} = [Z_{i(i+1)}, \ldots, Z_{i\ell}],$$
$$S_{ii \cdot i+1 \ldots \ell}^{(i-1)} = S_{ii}^{(i-1)} - S_{i(i+1 \ldots \ell)}^{(i-1)} \left\{ S_{(i+1 \ldots \ell)(i+1 \ldots \ell)}^{(i-1)} \right\}^{-1} S_{(i+1 \ldots \ell)i}^{(i-1)}.$$

Similar notations are used for submatrices of Ξ, Ω, etc., partitioned in the same way. Further, let

$$\mathcal{B}_{(i+1 \ldots \ell)(1 \ldots i)} = \Omega_{(i+1 \ldots \ell)(i+1 \ldots \ell)}^{-1} \Omega_{(i+1 \ldots \ell)(1 \ldots i)}$$
$$= [\mathcal{B}_{(i+1 \ldots \ell)1}, \ldots, \mathcal{B}_{(i+1 \ldots \ell)i}], \quad (i = 1, \ldots, k).$$

Note that there exists a one-to-one correspondence between Ω and the set $\{\Omega_{11 \cdot 2 \ldots \ell}, \ldots, \Omega_{kk \cdot \ell}, \Omega_{\ell \ell}, \mathcal{B}_{(2 \ldots \ell)1}, \ldots, \mathcal{B}_{(k\ell)(k-1)}, \mathcal{B}_{\ell k}\}$.

Then it is known (see, Fujikoshi, Kanda and Ohtaki (1999)) that the MLE's of Ξ and Ω under M_γ are given as follows:

$$\widehat{\Xi}_{i(1\ldots i)} = Z_{i(1\ldots i)} - Z_{i(i+1\ldots \ell)}\widehat{B}_{(i+1\ldots \ell)(1\ldots i)},$$

$$\widehat{B}_{(i+1\ldots \ell)i} = \left\{ S^{(i-1)}_{(i+1\ldots \ell)(i+1\ldots \ell)} \right\}^{-1} S^{(i-1)}_{(i+1\ldots \ell)i},$$

$$n\widehat{\Omega}_{ii\cdot i+1\cdots \ell} = S^{(i-1)}_{ii\cdot i+1\ldots \ell}, \quad i = 1,\ldots, k,$$

$$n\widehat{\Omega}_{\ell\ell} = S^{(k)}_{\ell\ell}. \tag{13}$$

Without loss of generality we denote the density of Z under M_γ by $f(Z; \Xi, \Omega)$, using the same fuction f as in the density of Y under M_γ. Noting that

$$| \Omega | = | \Omega_{11\cdot 2\ldots \ell} | \, | \Omega_{22\cdot 3\ldots \ell} | \cdots | \Omega_{\ell\ell} |,$$

we have

$$-2\log f(Y; \widehat{\Theta}, \widehat{\Sigma})$$

$$= -2\log f(Z; \widehat{\Xi}, \widehat{\Omega})$$

$$= n\log \left\{ \left(\frac{1}{n}\right)^p | S^{(0)}_{11\cdot 2\ldots \ell} | \cdot | S^{(1)}_{22\cdot 3\ldots \ell} | \cdots | S^{(k)}_{\ell\ell} | \right\} \tag{14}$$

$$+ pn\{\log(2\pi) + 1\}.$$

4 Corrected AIC

This section is concerned with the problem of estimating the bias term B_γ in the estimation of AIC type risk R_γ. Let B_γ in (7) be decomposed as

$$B_\gamma = -np + B^{(1)}_\gamma + B^{(2)}_\gamma, \tag{15}$$

where

$$B^{(1)}_\gamma = E^*[n\mathrm{tr}\widehat{\Sigma}^{-1}\Sigma^*],$$

$$B^{(2)}_\gamma = E^*[\mathrm{tr}\widehat{\Sigma}^{-1}(\widehat{\Theta}X - \eta^*)'A'A(\widehat{\Theta}X - \eta^*)].$$

In the following we attempt to derive an explicit expression for B_γ, assuming that the true model M^* is included into a candidate model M_γ, that is

$$\mathrm{A1}: \quad M^* \subset M_\gamma, \tag{16}$$

or $g(Z) = f(Z; \Xi^*, \Omega^*)$ for some Ξ^* and Ω^*. For notational simplicity, we write Ξ^* and Ω^* as simply Ξ and Ω, respectively. Then, it is easily seen that $B^{(1)}_\gamma$ and $B^{(2)}_\gamma$ can be expressed in terms of Z as

$$B^{(1)}_\gamma = E^*[n\mathrm{tr}\widehat{\Omega}^{-1}\Omega],$$

$$B^{(2)}_\gamma = E^*[\mathrm{tr}\widehat{\Omega}^{-1}[\widehat{\Xi} - \Xi \quad O]'[\widehat{\Xi} - \Xi \quad O]].$$

Lemma 1. *Under the assumption* A1 *we can reduce* $B_\gamma^{(1)}$ *and* $B_\gamma^{(2)}$ *as*

$$B_\gamma^{(1)} = \mathrm{E}_Z^{(0)}[n\mathrm{tr}\widehat{\Omega}^{-1}],$$
$$B_\gamma^{(2)} = \mathrm{E}_Z^{(0)}[\mathrm{tr}\widehat{\Omega}^{-1}[\widehat{\Xi}\ \ O]'[\widehat{\Xi}\ \ O]],$$

respectively. Here $\mathrm{E}_Z^{(0)}$ *means the expectation with respect to* Z *when* $Z \sim N_{n\times p}(O,\ I_p \otimes I_n)$.

Proof. Put $h_1(Z) = n\mathrm{tr}\widehat{\Omega}^{-1}\Omega$ and $h_2(Z) = \mathrm{tr}\widehat{\Omega}^{-1}[\widehat{\Xi} - \Xi\ \ O]'[\widehat{\Xi} - \Xi\ \ O]$. Let F be a $p \times p$ lower triangular matrix such that $F'\Omega F = I_p$. Consider the transformation

$$\tilde{Z} = \left(Z - \begin{bmatrix} \Xi & O \\ O & O \end{bmatrix}\right) F.$$

Then we can see that

$$h_1(\tilde{Z}) = n\mathrm{tr}\widehat{\Omega}^{-1},$$
$$h_2(\tilde{Z}) = \mathrm{tr}\widehat{\Omega}^{-1}[\widehat{\Xi}\ \ O]'[\widehat{\Xi}\ \ O].$$

These imply the lemma.

Lemma 2. *Under the assumption* A1 *it holds that*

$$
\begin{aligned}
B_\gamma^{(1)} = n^2 \Bigg\{ &\sum_{i=1}^{k} \frac{d_i}{m + r_1 + \ldots + r_{i-1} - d_i - \ldots - d_\ell - 1} \\
&\times \frac{m + r_1 + \ldots + r_{i-1} - 1}{m + r_1 + \ldots + r_{i-1} - d_{i+1} - \ldots - d_\ell - 1} \\
&+ \frac{d_\ell}{m + r_1 + \ldots + r_k - d_\ell - 1} \Bigg\} \\
\equiv\ & b_\gamma^{(1)},
\end{aligned}
$$

where $m = r_\ell = n - r_1 - \ldots - r_k$ *and* $r_0 = 0$.

Proof. Note that

$$
\Omega^{-1} = \begin{bmatrix} O & O \\ O & \Omega_{(2\ldots\ell)(2\ldots\ell)}^{-1} \end{bmatrix} + \begin{bmatrix} I_{d_1} \\ -\Omega_{(2\ldots\ell)(2\ldots\ell)}^{-1}\Omega_{(2\ldots\ell)1} \end{bmatrix}
$$
$$
\times \Omega_{11\cdot2\ldots\ell}^{-1} \begin{bmatrix} I_{d_1} \\ -\Omega_{(2\ldots\ell)(2\ldots\ell)}^{-1}\Omega_{(2\ldots\ell)1} \end{bmatrix}'
$$

Applying this formula to $\Omega_{(2\ldots\ell)(2\ldots\ell)}^{-1}$ and repeating this procedure, we have

$$
\begin{aligned}
\mathrm{tr}\Omega^{-1} = \sum_{i=1}^{k} \mathrm{tr}\Omega_{ii\cdot2\ldots\ell}^{-1} \Big\{ &I_{d_i} \\
&+ \Omega_{i(i+1\ldots\ell)}\Omega_{(i+1\ldots\ell)(i+1\ldots\ell)}^{-2}\Omega_{(i+1\ldots\ell)i} \Big\} + \mathrm{tr}\Omega_{\ell\ell}^{-1}.
\end{aligned}
$$

Therefore we have

$$
\mathrm{tr}\hat{\Omega}^{-1} = n \sum_{i=1}^{k} \mathrm{tr}\{S_{ii\cdot2\ldots\ell}^{(i-1)}\}^{-1}\{I_{d_i}
$$
$$
+ S_{i(i+1\ldots\ell)}^{(i-1)}\{S_{(i+1\ldots\ell)(i+1\ldots\ell)}^{(i-1)}\}^{-2}S_{(i+1\ldots\ell)i}^{(i-1)}\} + n\mathrm{tr}\{S_{\ell\ell}^{(i-1)}\}^{-1}.
$$

Note (see, e.g. Siotani, Hayakawa and Fujikoshi (1985)) that

$$
S_{ii\cdot2\ldots\ell}^{(i-1)} \sim W_{d_i}(m + r_1 + \ldots + r_{i-1} - d_{i+1} - \ldots - d_\ell, \; I_{d_i}),
$$
$$
S_{i(i+1\ldots\ell)}\{S_{ii\cdot2\ldots\ell}^{(i-1)}\}^{-1/2} \sim N_{d_i\times(d_{i+1}+\ldots+d_\ell)}(0, \; I_{d_i(d_{i+1}+\ldots+d_\ell)}),
$$
$$
S_{(i+1\ldots\ell)(i+1\ldots\ell)} \sim W_{d_i+\ldots+d_\ell}(m + r_1 + \ldots + r_{i-1}, \; I_{d_i+\ldots+d_\ell}),
$$

and these are independent, since $S^{(i-1)} \sim W_p(m + r_1 + \ldots + r_{i-1}, \; I_p)$. Using these properties we can get the final result.

Lemma 3. *Let* $b_\gamma^{(2)}$ *be the value of* $B_\gamma^{(2)}$ *under the assumption A1 in (16). Then, for* $k = 1, 2, 3$*, it holds that*

(i) $k = 1$:

$$
b_\gamma^{(2)} = \frac{nd_1 r_1(m-1)}{(m - d_1 - d_2 - 1)(m - d_2 - 1)}. \tag{17}
$$

(ii) $k = 2$:

$$
b_\gamma^{(2)} = \frac{nd_1(r_1 + r_2)(m-1)}{(m - d_1 - d_2 - d_3 - 1)(m - d_2 - d_3 - 1)}
$$
$$
+ \frac{nd_2 r_2(m + r_1 - 1)}{(m + r_1 - d_2 - d_3 - 1)(m + r_1 - d_3 - 1)}. \tag{18}
$$

(iii) $k = 3$:

$$
b_\gamma^{(2)} = \frac{nd_1(r_1 + r_2 + r_3)(m-1)}{(m - d_1 - d_2 - d_3 - d_4 - 1)(m - d_2 - d_3 - d_4 - 1)}
$$
$$
+ \frac{nd_2(r_2 + r_3)(m + r_1 - 1)}{(m + r_1 - d_2 - d_3 - d_4 - 1)(m + r_1 - d_3 - d_4 - 1)} \tag{19}
$$
$$
+ \frac{nd_3 r_3(m + r_1 + r_2 - 1)}{(m + r_1 + r_2 - d_3 - d_4 - 1)(m + r_1 + r_2 - d_4 - 1)}.
$$

Proof. A simple expression for $\hat{\Omega}^{-1}$ can be obtained by using the recurrence relation in the proof of Lemma 2 and the expressions in (13). In order to evaluate $B_\gamma^{(2)}$ in Lemma 1 we need to have a simple expression for $\hat{\Xi}_{i(1\ldots i)}$ or more precisely for $\hat{B}_{(i+1\ldots\ell)(1\ldots i)}$. A simple expression for $\hat{B}_{(i+1\ldots\ell)i}$ is given in (13). Such a simple expression for $\hat{B}_{(i+1\ldots\ell)(1\ldots i-1)}$ can be found by using the following relations, for example, $k = 3$:

$$\mathcal{B}_{(34)1} = [\mathcal{B}_{(34)2} \quad I_{d_3+d_4}]\mathcal{B}_{(234)1},$$
$$\mathcal{B}_{42} = [\mathcal{B}_{43} \quad I_{d_4}]\mathcal{B}_{(34)2},$$
$$\mathcal{B}_{41} = [\mathcal{B}_{42} \quad \mathcal{B}_{43} \quad I_{d_4}]\mathcal{B}_{(234)1}.$$

By using these expressions we can get the Lemma 3, after computations similar to the ones of Lemma 2.

Based on Lemmas 1 and 2, we can propose a corrected AIC for model M_γ as

$$CAIC_\gamma = n\log\left\{\left(\frac{1}{n}\right)^p |S_{11\cdot2\cdots\ell}^{(0)}| \cdot |S_{22\cdot3\cdots\ell}^{(1)}| \cdots |S_{\ell\ell}^{(k)}|\right\}$$
$$+pn\{\log(2\pi) + 1\} + b_\gamma, \tag{20}$$

where

$$b_\gamma = -np + b_\gamma^{(1)} + b_\gamma^{(2)}.$$

The corrected AIC has an unbiased property such that $E[CAIC_\gamma] = R_\gamma$ under the assumption A1. The CAIC in the case $k = 2$ was given by Fujikoshi and Satoh (1996). However, the expression "$q_2(n - k_2 - 1)/n_1$" in page 646 ↓ 9 of the paper should be read as "$n^2 q_2(n - k_2 - 1)/n_1$". Simlarly the last line of page 719 of Fujikoshi, Kanda and Ohtaki (1999) should be read as

$$+\frac{(q_2 - q_1)N}{(N - p - 3)(N - p + q_2 - 3)}\left\{\frac{N(N - 2)}{N - p + q_1 - 3} + p - q_2\right\}.$$

Suppose that we are interesting in choosing the model minimizing the AIC type of risk from a set of candidate models $\{M_\gamma; \gamma \in \Gamma\}$. If a candidate model is an overspecified model with $k \leq 3$, then its CAIC is an exact unbiassed estimator for the AIC type of risk.

We applied the above results to the dental measurement data (see Potthoff and Roy (1964)), which are made on each of 11 girls and 16 boys at ages 8, 10, 12, 14 years. We analyzed by deleting two boy's measurements, since they are regarded (Lee and Geisser (1975), Sugiura (1997)) as outliers. So, $n = 11 + 14 = 25$ and $p = 4$.

Table 1. Values of AIC and CAIC

	AIC	CAIC
$M_{(1;2)}$	362	373
$M_{(1;3)}$	356	363
$M_{(2;2,3)}$	353	336

We consider three models for the dental measurement data, which are denoted by $M_{(2;q_1,q_2)}$ with $q_1 = 2$ and $q_2 = 3$. As the other possible models, we consider the models $M_{(1;2)}$ both girl's and boy's data are linear, $M_{(1;3)}$ both girl's and boy's data are quadratic. The AIC and CAIC are given in Table 1. We can see that the model $M_{(2;2,3)}$ is more appropriate, in the comparison with $M_{(1;2)}$ and $M_{(1;3)}$. This suggestion can be more clearly done in the use of CAIC.

Acknowledgment

The author would like to thank the two referees for several valuable comments and suggestions.

References

Anderson, T. W. (1984) An Introduction to Multivariate Statistical Analysis, 2nd ed. Wiley, New York

Banken, L. (1984) Eine Verallgemeinerung des GMANOVA-Models. Thesis, University of Trier, Germany

Fujikoshi, Y., Satoh, K. (1996) Estimation and model selection in an extended growth curve model. Hiroshima Math. J., 26:635–647

Fujikoshi, Y., Kanda, T., Ohtaki, M. (1999) Growth curves model with hierarchical within-individuals design matrices Ann. Inst. Statist. Math., 51:707–721

Kariya, T. (1985): Testing in the Multivariate General Linear Model. Kinokuniya, Tokyo

Lee, J.C., Geisser, S. (1975) Applications of growth curve prediction. Sankhyā Ser. A, 37:239–256

Potthoff, R.F., Roy, S.N. (1964) A generalized multivariate analysis of variance model useful especially for growth curve problems. Biometrika, 51:313–327

Siotani, M., Hayakawa, T., Fujikoshi, Y. (1985): Modern Multivariate Statistical Analysis: A Graduate Course and Handbook. American Sciences Press, INC., Columbus, Ohio, U.S.A.

Srivastava, M.S., Khatri, C.G. (1979) An Introduction to Multivariate Statistics. North-Holland, New York

Sugiura, N. (1997) Multivariate Analysis. In: Imaizumi, M., Inaba, Y., (ed) Health Statistics (in Japanese), Baifuu-kan, Tokyo, Japan, pp 22–49

von Rosen, D. Maximum likelihood estimators in multivariate linear normal models. J. Multivariate Anal. 31:187–200

Pooling Component Means: Making Sense or Folly

S. E. Ahmed

Department of Mathematics and Statistics, University of Windsor, Windsor,
Ontario Canada N9B 3P4
seahme@uwindsor.ca

Summary. This article discusses improved estimation methods for the first component mean vector μ_1 of a q-variate normal distribution when it is suspected that $\mu_1 = \mu_2$, where μ_2 is the second component mean vector. Some statistical properties of the proposed estimators are investigated. The relative dominance picture of the estimators is presented.

Key words. Pooling means, multivariate normal distribution, preliminary test and shrinkage estimation, biases and risks.

1 Introduction

The purpose of this communication is to discuss estimation techniques on how to combine component means efficiently. In combining data, the question is often asked: is the pooled estimator better than the estimator based on a single set of data. It is advantageous to pool the data if indeed the population parameters are the same or at least close to each other. A logical question then arises: "How close to each other should the parameters be?" This question is to be addressed systematically in this article. To this end, some other estimators are to be introduced. Statistical parametric estimation theory has been developed for the last four decades in two main subjects– specifically, (1) the large sample properties of the maximum likelihood estimator (MLE), and (2) shrinkage estimation problem, now referred to as the Stein-rule problem for the inadmissibility of the MLE in small samples. The large sample theory simplified the structure of the theory of parametric estimation and granted the higher order asymptotic efficiency of the MLE and its differential geometric interpretation. Antithetically, in many practical settings one may not afford the luxury of a large data set. For instance, in psychometrics, biometrics and in several engineering applications, a large sample may not be expected. As such, we are primarily interested in the estimation of parameters when there may be some *uncertainty* about the *constraints* to modify usual estimators such as maximum likelihood or unbiased estimators for increasing their efficiencies. The research led by the remarkable observation of Stein (1956), and following Stein's result, James and Stein (1961) exhibited an estimator that under squared error loss dominates the usual estimator and thus demonstrates its inadmissibility. This result means that the unbiased rule may have an inferior risk when compared to other biased estimators. This research area has received considerable attention since then and a remarkably large amount of theoretical results have been produced. Indeed, Stein-rule estimation has been evaluated as an effective procedure in small samples from a practical point of view while the theoretical research has progressed exponentially. Useful discussions on some of the implications of pretest and shrinkage estimators in parametric theory are in Ahmed *at el.* (2001), Kubokawa (1998) and Stigler (1990), among others. It may be worth mentioning that this is one of the two areas Professor Efron predicted for continuing research for the early 21st century in *RSS News of January, 1995.*

Suppose $X_j, j = 1, 2, \cdots n$, is a random sample of size n from a q-variate normal population with mean vector μ and a positive semi-definite matrix Σ. Further, we assume that q is an even integer, $q = 2p$. To facilitate the presentation of the main results, we introduce the following notation. Let $\mu_1 = (\mu_1, \mu_2, \cdots, \mu_p)'$ and $\mu_2 = (\mu_{p+1}, \mu_{p+2}, \cdots, \mu_q)'$.
Suppose a random sample of size n is taken from a q-dimensional multivariate normal distribution with mean vector μ and covariance matrix Σ, where

$$\mu = \begin{pmatrix} \mu_1 \\ \mu_2 \end{pmatrix}, \text{ and } \Sigma = \begin{pmatrix} \Sigma_{11} & \Sigma_{12} \\ \Sigma_{21} & \Sigma_{22} \end{pmatrix}.$$

Further, we assume that $\Sigma_{11} = \Sigma_{22}$. As a special case, we will also assume that the covariance matrix Σ is of the equicorrelation structure, that is, $\Sigma = \rho\sigma^2 J + (1-\rho)\sigma^2 I$, $-1/(q-1) < \rho < 1$, where J is a unit matrix, I is an identity matrix and ρ is the correlation coefficient. Under the restriction, all the measurements have the same variance and all the pairs of measurements on the same characters have the same covariance.

It is the objective to estimate μ_1, the first component mean vector when it is suspected that $\mu_1 = \mu_2$ is plausible. This information may be explicitly incorporated into the estimation procedure by modifying the parameter space. The reduction in dimensionality generally provides efficient estimators. However, in the case of an incorrect restriction, opposite conclusions will hold.

Let us consider the following examples to motivate the problem at hand.

Example 1: In many anthropological problems $x_1 = (x_1, x_2, \cdots, x_p)$ represent measurements on characters on the left side and $x_2 = (x_{p+1}, x_{p+2}, \cdots, x_q)$ represent measurements on the same characters on the right side. Further, anthropologists suspect that there is no average difference between the two sides.

Example 2: Suppose two group of psychiatrists were asked to rate each of 25 prison inmates on their rehabilitative potential using a scale from 0 to 20, the larger the rating, the greater the potential for rehabilitation. It is suspected that that there is not a significant difference between mean rating scores given by two groups of psychiatrists.

Example 3: As another example, consider the Charles Darwin's study of cross-fertilized and self-fertilized plants. In his experiment, Darwin planted a pair of seedings, one produced by cross-fertilization and the other by self-fertilization, on opposite sides of a pot to determine which grew faster. If there is no significant difference in the heights of the plants from the two methods of fertilization, then this information can be used to improve the estimation of the average height of the plant.

Ahmed and Saleh (1993) considered the problem of estimating the component mean vector μ_1 and studied the properties of the usual preliminary test and shrinkage estimators. In this communication, we propose improved versions of the preliminary test and shrinkage estimators of the first component mean vector μ_1. In summary, this article describes improved estimation strategies for the component mean vector in the presence of additional information.

After Section 2 that introduces the estimators and basic concepts, we begin in Section 3 by providing an analysis of the bias and risk of the proposed estimators. Finally, Section 5 contains some concluding remarks.

2 Improved Estimation

The unrestricted maximum likelihood estimators (UMLE) for the mean vectors are readily available as:

$$\tilde{\mu}_i = \overline{\mathbf{x}}^{(i)} = n^{-1} \sum_{j=1}^{n} \mathbf{x}_{ij}, \quad i = 1, 2. \tag{2.1}$$

On the other hand, a restricted estimator (RE) for μ_1 is obtained as

$$\hat{\mu}_1 = \frac{1}{2}(\tilde{\mu}_1 + \tilde{\mu}_2). \tag{2.2}$$

The UMLE and RE are useful estimators of μ when $\mu_1 \neq \mu_2$ and $\mu_1 = \mu_2$ respectively. As always, $\hat{\mu}_1$ quadratic risk at or near the null hypothesis is smaller at the expense of poorer performance in the remaining parameter space. Further, the performance of $\tilde{\mu}_1$ remains invariable over such departures. As such a situation arises, Ahmed and Saleh (1993) suggested a preliminary test approach to tackle the above uncertainty. The preliminary test estimator (PTE) is defined as

$$\hat{\mu}_1^P = \tilde{\mu}_1 I(T_n^2 \geq T_{n,\alpha}^2) + \hat{\mu}_1 I(T_n^2 < T_{n,\alpha}^2), \tag{2.3}$$

where $I_{(A)}$ is the indicator function of the set A and T_n^2 is the Hotelling's T_n^2-statistic defined by

$$T_n^2 = n(\tilde{\boldsymbol{\mu}}_2 - \tilde{\boldsymbol{\mu}}_1)' \mathbf{S}^{-1}(\tilde{\boldsymbol{\mu}}_2 - \tilde{\boldsymbol{\mu}}_1), \qquad \mathbf{S} = \mathbf{S}_{22} - \mathbf{S}_{21} - \mathbf{S}_{12} + \mathbf{S}_{11},$$

where $\mathbf{S}$ is the sample covariance matrix and $T_{n,\alpha}^2$ denotes the α-level critical values of the T_n^2-statistic. They also propose a shrinkage estimator (SE)

$$\hat{\boldsymbol{\mu}}_1^S = \tilde{\boldsymbol{\mu}}_1 + \frac{c}{2}(\tilde{\boldsymbol{\mu}}_2 - \tilde{\boldsymbol{\mu}}_1)(n-1)T_n^{-2}, \qquad (2.4)$$

where c is the shrinkage factor such that $0 < c < 2c^*$ with $c^* = \frac{p-2}{m+2}$, and $m = n - p$. Later we will use the optimal value of c which is c^* with $p \geq 3$.

Under certain assumptions, Ahmed and Saleh (1993) concluded that the shrinkage estimator is superior to UMLE. Notwithstanding, the drawback of SE is that it may shrink beyond the restricted estimator. Consequently, we propose a superior alternative to the shrinkage estimator by considering its positive part only. Thus, a *positive-part shrinkage estimator (PSE)* is defined as,

$$\hat{\boldsymbol{\mu}}_1^{S+} = \hat{\boldsymbol{\mu}}_1 + [1 - c(n-1)T_n^{-2}]^+(\tilde{\boldsymbol{\mu}}_1 - \hat{\boldsymbol{\mu}}_1), \quad p > 2, \qquad (2.5)$$

In the sprit of Sclove *et al.* (1972) the estimator $\hat{\boldsymbol{\mu}}_1^P$ in display (2.3) can be improved if we replace $\tilde{\boldsymbol{\mu}}_1$ by $\hat{\boldsymbol{\mu}}_1^S$ in (2.3). Hence, the *improved preliminary test estimator (IPE)* is defined as

$$\hat{\boldsymbol{\mu}}_1^{P+} = \hat{\boldsymbol{\mu}}_1^P - c(n-1)T_n^{-2}I(T_n^2 > T_{n,\alpha}^2)(\tilde{\boldsymbol{\mu}}_1 - \hat{\boldsymbol{\mu}}_1), \quad p > 2. \qquad (2.6)$$

3 Main Results

This section showcases our principal results, and provides analysis for quadratic bias and risk of the proposed estimators. The expressions for bias and proof for theorem 3.1 can be found in Ahmed (2002, *Windsor Mathematics Statistics Report, University of Windsor*).

It is noted that all the estimators are biased except $\tilde{\boldsymbol{\mu}}_1$. Further, it is seen that the graph of the bias of $\hat{\boldsymbol{\mu}}_1^S$ remains above the graph of the bias of $\hat{\boldsymbol{\mu}}_1^{S+}$ and hence $\hat{\boldsymbol{\mu}}_1^{S+}$ has an edge over $\hat{\boldsymbol{\mu}}_1^S$. On the other hand, the bias of $\hat{\boldsymbol{\mu}}_1^{P+}$ remains either above or equal to the bias of $\hat{\boldsymbol{\mu}}_1^P$ for all values of Δ, since both components of $\hat{\boldsymbol{\mu}}_1^{P+}$ are biased.

Theorem 3.1:   Let $\mathbf{W}$ be a positive semi definite weight matrix and $tr(\mathbf{A})$ be the trace of matrix $\mathbf{A}$. The quadratic risk functions of the estimators are

$$\Re(\hat{\boldsymbol{\mu}}_1^{S+}) = R(\hat{\boldsymbol{\mu}}_1^S) - \frac{1}{4}H_{p+2,m}\left(\frac{c^*m}{2(p+2)};\Delta\right)tr(\mathbf{W}\boldsymbol{\Sigma}_o) - \frac{c^*m}{4}$$

$$\mathcal{E}\left[\{(p-2)\chi_{p+2}^{-4}(\Delta) - 2\chi_{p+2}^{-2}(\Delta)\}I(c_1 \leq c^*]tr(\mathbf{W}\boldsymbol{\Sigma}_o) - \right.$$

$$\frac{c^*m}{4}\Delta_w\mathcal{E}\left[\{(p-2)\chi_{p+4}^{-4}(\Delta) - 2\chi_{p+4}^{-2}(\Delta)\}I(c_2 \leq c^*) + \right.$$

$$2\chi_{p+2}^{-2}(\Delta)I(c_1 \leq c^*)\right] + \frac{1}{4}\Delta_w\left\{2H_{p+2,m}\left(\frac{c^*m}{p+4};\Delta\right) - \right.$$

$$H_{p+4,m}\left(\frac{c^*m}{4};\Delta\right)\right\},$$

$$\Re(\hat{\boldsymbol{\mu}}_1^S) = tr(\mathbf{W}\boldsymbol{\Sigma}_o) - \frac{c^*m}{4}\mathcal{E}\left\{2\chi_{p+2}^{-2}(\Delta) - (p-2)\chi_{p+2}^{-4}(\Delta)\right\}tr(\mathbf{W}\boldsymbol{\Sigma}_o) +$$
$$\frac{1}{4}c^*m(p+2)\Delta_w\mathcal{E}\left(\chi_{p+4}^{-4}(\Delta)\right).$$

$$\Re(\hat{\boldsymbol{\mu}}_1^{P+}) = \Re(\hat{\boldsymbol{\mu}}_1^P) - \frac{c^*m}{4}\mathcal{E}\left[\left\{2\chi_{p+2}^{-2}(\Delta) - (p-2)\chi_{p+2}^{-4}(\Delta)\right\}\right.$$
$$I(c_1 > F^+)\Big]tr(\mathbf{W}\boldsymbol{\Sigma}_o) - \frac{a^*m}{4}$$
$$\Delta_w\mathcal{E}\left[\left\{2\chi_{p+4}^{-2}(\Delta) - (p-2)\chi_{p+4}^{-4}(\Delta)\right\}I(c_2 > F^+)\right.$$
$$\left. -2\chi_{p+2}^{-2}(\Delta)I(c_1 > F^+)\right],$$

$$\Re(\hat{\boldsymbol{\mu}}_1^P;\boldsymbol{\mu}_1) = \Re(\tilde{\boldsymbol{\mu}}_1;\boldsymbol{\mu}_1) - \frac{1}{2}H_{p+2,m}(F^*;\Delta)tr(\mathbf{W}\boldsymbol{\Sigma}_o) +$$
$$\frac{1}{2}\Delta_w\{2H_{p+2,m}(F^*;\Delta) - H_{p+4,m}(F^o;\Delta)\},$$

where $H_{\nu_1,\nu_2}(\cdot;\Delta)$ is the cumulative distribution function of a non-central F-distribution with (ν_1,ν_2) degrees of freedom and non-centrality parameter $\Delta = n\boldsymbol{\delta}'\boldsymbol{\Sigma}_o^{-1}\boldsymbol{\delta}$, $\boldsymbol{\Sigma}_o^{-1} = 2(\boldsymbol{\Sigma}_{11} - \boldsymbol{\Sigma}_{12})$, and

$$F^* = \frac{p}{p+2}F_{p,m}(\alpha), \quad F^o = \frac{p}{p+4}F_{p,m}(\alpha), \quad F^+ = \frac{p}{m}F_{p,m}(\alpha)$$

with $F_{\nu_1,\nu_2}(\alpha)$ the upper α-level critical value of a central F-distribution with (ν_1,ν_2) degrees of freedom, and

$$c_1 = \frac{\chi_{p+2}^2(\Delta)}{\chi_m^2}, \quad c_2 = \frac{\chi_{p+4}^2(\Delta)}{\chi_m^2}.$$

It is seen that the risk difference

$$\Re(\hat{}_1^{S+}) - \Re(\hat{}_1^S) = -\frac{1}{4}H_{p+2,m}\left(\frac{c^*m}{2(p+2)};\Delta\right) - \frac{c^*m}{4}$$
$$\mathcal{E}\left[\left\{(p-2)\chi_{p+2}^{-4}(\Delta) - 2\chi_{p+2}^{-2}(\Delta)\right\}I(c_1 \le c^*)\right]tr(\mathbf{W}\quad_o) -$$
$$\frac{c^*m}{(m+2)}\Delta_w\mathcal{E}\left[\left\{(p-2)\chi_{p+4}^{-4}(\Delta) - 2\chi_{p+4}^{-2}(\Delta)\right\}I(c_2 \le c^*) +\right.$$
$$\left. 2\chi_{p+2}^{-2}(\Delta)I(c_1 \le c^*)\right] + \frac{1}{4}\Delta_w$$
$$\left\{2H_{p+2,m}\left(\frac{c^*m}{2(p+4)};\Delta\right) - H_{p+4,m}\left(\frac{c^*m}{2(p+2)};\Delta\right)\right\}$$
$$\le 0$$

where strict inequality holds for $\Delta = 0$. Hence, we conclude that $\hat{\boldsymbol{\mu}}_1^{S+}$ dominates $\hat{\boldsymbol{\mu}}_1^S$ in entire parameter space induced by Δ. Further, Ahmed and Saleh

(1993) established that $\Re(\hat{\mu}_1^S) \leq \Re(\tilde{\mu}_1)$, $p \geq 3$. Thus, $\Re(\hat{\mu}_1^{S+}) \leq \Re(\hat{\mu}_1^S) \leq \Re(\tilde{\mu}_1)$. Hence, the positive-part Stein-rule estimator dominates the MLE. Most importantly, by definition, the coordinates of $\hat{\mu}_1^{S+}$ cannot have a different sign from the coordinates of $\tilde{\mu}_1$.

The risk difference between $\hat{\mu}_1^{P+}$ and $\hat{\mu}_1^P$ reveals that $Re(\hat{\mu}_1^{P+}) \leq \Re(\hat{\mu}_1^P) \leq 0$ where strict inequality holds for at least one Δ, which happens when $\Delta = 0$. Further, at $\Delta = 0$, $\hat{\mu}_1^{P+}$ outperforms $\tilde{\mu}_1$. For the general case, if $F_{(\alpha)} \in [0, c^*]$, then $\hat{\mu}_1^{P+}$ provides a minimax substitute for $\hat{\mu}_1^P$, since it is identical to $\hat{\mu}_1^{S+}$. Accordingly, we conclude that $\hat{\mu}_1^{P+}$ dominates the usual Stein-rule estimator $\hat{\mu}_1^S$ and therefore dominates $\tilde{\mu}_1$. In reality, $F_{(\alpha)}$ cannot be restricted to this interval and can assume any value in the interval $(0, \infty)$, so $\hat{\mu}_1^{P+}$ is no longer a superior estimator. More precisely, when $F_{(\alpha)} \in (c^*, \infty)$, $\hat{\mu}_1^{P+}$ is not superior to $\tilde{\mu}_1$ for all values of Δ. The risk function of $\hat{\mu}_1^{P+}$ crosses the risk function of $\tilde{\mu}_1$ at some point in the parameter space and then approaches the risk of $\tilde{\mu}_1$ as $\Delta \to \infty$.

4 Conclusion

The Stein-rule estimation methodologies are superior to maximum likelihood estimation. The positive-part of the shrinkage estimator performs better than the usual shrinkage estimator. By considering the positive part of $\hat{\mu}_1^S$, the resulting estimator $\hat{\mu}_1^{S+}$ removes the funny behavior of $\hat{\mu}_1^S$ when the test statistic takes values near zero, that is, it does not change the sign of the estimators. We recommend that the usual shrinkage estimator should be used as a tool for developing the positive part estimator and should not be used as an estimator in its own right. Further, the IPE risk performance is superior to that of PE.

Acknowledgements

My appreciation is due to two anonymous referees and the editors for their suggestions that were instrumental in preparing the final version of the paper. The research was partially supported by an NSERC of Canada individual research grant, as well as by a Faculty of Science, University of Windsor grant.

References

Ahmed, S. E., A. K. Gupta, S. M. Khan and C. Nicol (2001). Simultaneous estimation of several intraclass correlation coefficients. Ann. Inst. Statist. Math., **53**, 354-369.

Ahmed S. E. and E. Saleh (1993). Improved estimation for the component mean-vector. Japan Journal of Statistics, **43**, 177-195.

Bancroft, T. A. (1944). On biases in estimation due to the use of preliminary tests of significance. The Annals of Mathematical Statistics, **15**, 190-204.

James, W., and C. Stein (1961). Estimation with quadratic loss. Proceedings of the Fourth Berkeley Symposium on Mathematical Statistics and probability, (UCLA Press, Berkeley, California), 361-379.

Kubokawa, T. (1998). The Stein phenomenon in simultaneous estimation: A review. In S.E. Ahmed et al. (Eds.), Nonparametric Statistics and Related Topics (pp. 143-173). New York: Nova Science.

Judge, G. G., and M. E. Bock (1978). The statistical implication of pre-test and Stein-rule estimators in econometrics. New York:North-Holland.

Sclove, S. L., C. Morris, and R. Radhakrishnan (1972). Non-optimality of preliminary test estimators of the mean of a multivariate normal distribution. Annals of Mathematical Statistics, **43**, 1481-1490.

Stein, C. (1956). Inadmissibility of the usual estimator for the mean of a multivariate normal distribution. Proceedings of the Third Berkeley Symposium on Mathematical Statistics and Probability, Berkeley and Los Angeles, Univ. of California Press, Vol 1, 197-206.

Stigler, S. M. (1990). The 1988 Neyman Memorial Lecture: A Galtonian perspective on shrinkage estimators. Statistical Science **5**, 147-155.

Part 6
Scaling

Geometric Perspectives of Dual Scaling for Assessment of Information in Data

Shizuhiko Nishisato[1]

The Ontario Institute for Studies in Education of the University of Toronto
252 Bloor Street, Toronto, Ontario, Canada M5S 1V6
snishisato@oise.utoronto.ca

Summary. Dual scaling offers us an invaluable opportunity to have another look at the total information contained in data. This paper sheds some light on the necessity of developing a tool for full-information analysis and the potential of dual scaling as such a tool.

Key words. Linear analysis, nonlinear analysis, total information, principal hyper-space.

1 Some Fundamentals

Dual scaling has many well-known aliases, and all of them are based on singular-value decomposition of categorical data. Thus, what it does is mathematically clear, and therefore there is not much more to look at. Surprisingly, however, its understanding is much more profound than its simple mathematical structure. This paper offers a glimpse at some interesting features, which may aid to assess the amount of information contained in data.

1.1 Singular Value Decomposition

Dual scaling (abbreviated as DS hereafter), coined by Nishisato (1980), is a quantification method, with many aliases such as the method of reciprocal averages (Richardson and Kuder, 1933; Horst, 1935), simultaneous linear regressions (Hirschfeld, 1935; Lingoes, 1964), Hayashi's theory of quantification Type III (Hayashi, 1950, 1952), principal component analysis of categorical data (Torgerson, 1958), optimal scaling (Bock, 1960), analyse des correspondances (Escofier-Cordier, 1969; Benzécri and others, 1973), correspondence analysis (Hill, 1974), and homogeneity analysis (Gifi, 1990). It is based on singular-value decomposition (abbreviated as SVD hereafter)(e.g., Beltrami, 1873; Jordan, 1874; Schmidt, 1907) of categorical variables.

For DS, these categorical variables are further divided into incidence data and dominance data (Nishisato, 1993) (A) because of the two distinct objec-

---

[1]This study was supported by a grant to Shizuhiko Nishisato from the Natural Sciences and Engineering Research Council of Canada. The study was conducted and written while the author was a Visiting Professor at Kwansei Gakuin University, Nishinomiya, Japan.

tives that govern DS (Nishisato, 1996) and (B) because of two distinct metrics used, the chi-square metric for incidence data and the Euclidean metric for dominance data. Unlike the others, DS covers both types of data, the reason why Meulman (1998) called it a comprehensive framework for analysis of categorical data.

Principal component analysis (abbreviated as PCA hereafter) (Pearson, 1901; Hotelling, 1936) is also based on SVD, the main difference being in the data types, that is, DS for categorical data and PCA for continuous data. We can now see why Torgerson called DS PCA of categorical data.

1.2   Rectangular Coordinates

Suppose we consider a linear combination k of n variables, for subject i,

$$Y_{ki} = w_1 X_{1i} + w_2 X_{2i} + w_3 X_{3i} + \cdots + w_n X_{ni}, \tag{1}$$

under the condition that the sum of the squared weights is 1. We know its mathematical meaning that this linear combination is an axis going through the origin and a point with coordinates $(w_1, w_2, w_3, ..., w_n)$, along which all variates lie. In other words, *all linear combinations can be expressed as a set of scores lying on a single line (axis)*. In PCA, those weights are determined so as to make the variance of the composite scores Y_i be a maximum. This maximized variance is the eigenvalue λ and the corresponding axis is called the *principal axis*. Once we obtain n principal components, $Y_k, k = 1, 2, \cdots, n$, we can in turn express each variable as a linear combination of these orthogonal components as

$$X_{ji} = u_1 Y_{1i} + u_2 Y_{2i} + \cdots + u_n Y_{ni}, \tag{2}$$

where the sum of squared weights is 1, the same condition as for w. Thus, any variable X_j can be expressed as a linear combination of weights associated with the rectangular coordinates, and because of the very nature of linear combinations, explained above, any variable can be expressed as a single axis in multidimensional Euclidean space, going through the origin and a point with rectangular coordinates $(u_1, u_2, u_3, ..., u_n)$. And, *all the scores on a variable lie on this single axis*. The product-moment correlation is the cosine of the angle between the axes of the two variables. This is a more sensible representation of a variable than that of using generally correlated variables (e.g., mathematics and English scores) as axes.

1.3   Multidimensional Space

Pierce (1961) presented an interesting explanation of multidimensional space as follows. The area of a circle in 2-dimensional space of the radius r is πr^2, and the area of a concentric circle of the radius $0.99r$ inside it is $\pi(0.99)^2 r$, which is 98 percent of the other circle. The volume of a sphere of the radius

0.99r is 97 percent of that of the radius r. As the dimension increases to n, one can safely say that the volume of a hyper-sphere of n dimensions is proportional to r^n. Then, for a 1000-dimensional hyper-sphere, a fraction of 0.00004 of the volume lies in a sphere of 0.99r the radius! His conclusion, therefore, is that in the case of a hyper-sphere of a very high dimensionality, essentially all of the volume lies very near the surface. This is a remarkable revelation!

Consider a point P in K-dimensional space with coordinates x_{pk}, where $k=1,2,...,K$. We can identify two other fundamental properties of a hyper-space:

(1) The distance of P from the origin, d_p, is a monotonically increasing function of the number of dimensions.

$$d_p = \sqrt{\sum_{k=1}^{K} x_{pk}^2} \tag{3}$$

(2) Similarly, the distance between any two points, d_{pq} is a monotonically increasing function of the number of dimensions.

$$d_{pq} = \sqrt{\sum_{k=1}^{K} (x_{pk} - x_{qk})^2} \tag{4}$$

When we look at the graph of, for example, the first two principal components or factors, it is the general practice to identify only those clusters of closely located variables for an interpretation. Unless these two components account for nearly 100 per cent of the variance by the first two dimensions, however, we must admit that there is no guarantee that those closely located variables are indeed close to one another in a hyper-space. Only if two points are widely separated in a 2-dimensional graph, it is guaranteed that they are widely separated in a hyper-space.

1.4 Principal Hyper-Space

PCA and DS seek the coordinate systems expressed in terms of principal axes, and the space is then called principal hyper-space. This is the most economical, hence preferred, way to describe multivariate data. Its mathematics is provided by SVD, and its transformation of the data means (i) that the data themselves, whether continuous or categorical, have an exact geometric representation, as inferred from the previous section, and (ii) that the SVD offers only a special way of looking at the data, that is, in the most efficient way.

2   DS and PCA

Both DS and PCA seek the best linear combination of variables, and the total information captured by DS and PCA is defined by the sum of the eigenvalues of all possible components. However, there exists an important difference between them: DS seeks the 'best' linear combination of *categories* of n variables (e.g., items), while PCA looks for the best linear combination of n *variables*.

2.1   A Numerical Example

To see the differences between DS and PCA, let us look at a numerical example of the following six multiple-choice questions (Nishisato, 2000):

1. Rate your blood pressure.(Low, Medium, High): coded 1, 2, 3
2. Do you get migraines?(Rarely, Sometimes, Often): coded 1, 2, 3
3. What is your age group?(20-34; 35-49; 50-65): coded 1, 2, 3
4. Rate your daily level of anxiety.(Low, Medium, High): coded 1, 2, 3
5. How about your weight?(Light, Medium, Heavy): coded 1, 2, 3
6. How about your height?(Short, Medium, Tall): coded 1, 2, 3

Suppose we use the traditional Likert scores for PCA, that is, 1, 2, 3 as appropriate scores for the three categories of each question. DS uses response patterns of 1's and 0's. The two data sets from 15 subjects, one in Likert scores and the other in response patterns, are given as follows, where BP=blood pressure, Mig=migraine, Anx=anxiety, Wgt=weight and Hgt-height:

PCA Subject	BP Q1	Mig Q2	Age Q3	Anx Q4	Wgt Q5	Hgt Q6	DS Ss	Bpr 123	Mig 123	Age 123	Anx 123	Wgt 123	Hgt 123
1	1	3	1	3	1	1	1	100	001	001	001	100	100
2	1	3	1	3	2	3	2	100	001	100	001	010	001
3	3	3	3	3	1	3	3	001	001	001	001	100	001
4	3	3	3	3	1	1	4	001	001	001	001	100	100
5	2	1	2	2	3	2	5	010	100	010	010	001	010
6	2	1	2	3	3	1	6	010	100	010	001	001	100
7	2	2	2	1	1	3	7	010	010	010	100	100	001
8	1	3	1	3	1	3	8	100	001	100	001	100	001
9	2	2	2	1	1	2	9	010	010	010	100	100	010
10	1	3	2	2	1	3	10	100	001	010	010	100	001
11	2	1	1	3	2	2	11	010	100	100	001	010	010
12	2	2	3	3	2	2	12	010	010	001	001	010	010
13	3	3	3	3	3	1	13	001	001	001	001	001	100
14	1	3	1	2	1	1	14	100	001	100	010	100	100
15	3	3	3	3	1	2	15	001	001	001	001	100	010

The matrix of product-moment correlations based on the Likert scores (for PCA) and that obtained from optimal category weight from the first DS component are given as follows:

			(PCA)							(DS)			
BP	1.00						1.00						
Mig	-.06	1.00					.99	1.00					
Age	.66	.23	1.00				.60	.58	1.00				
Anx	.18	.21	.22	1.00			.47	.52	.67	1.00			
Wgt	.17	-.58	-.02	.26	1.00		.43	.39	.08	-.33	1.00		
Hgt	-.21	.10	-.30	-.23	-.31	1.00	.56	.57	.13	.19	.20	1.00	
	BP	Mig	Age	Anx	Wgt	Hgt	BP	Mig	Age	Anx	Wgt	Hgt	

Let us examine the correlation between blood pressure (abbreviated as BP hereafter) and age (r=0.66) and that between BP and migraines (r=-0.06) in the form of contingency tables.

Age	20-34	35-49	50-65	Migraine	Rarely	Sometimes	Often
High BP	0	0	4	High BP	0	0	4
Mid BP	1	4	1	Mid BP	3	3	0
Low BP	3	1	1	Low BP	0	0	5

We can understand why the two correlation coefficients are so different, the former pair is linearly related (i.e., the older one gets the higher the BP) and the latter nonlinearly (i.e., frequent migraines appear when the BP is either low or high). As far as we can see, the latter nonlinear relation is clearer (stronger) than the linear relation. This can be verified by Cramér's coefficient which captures both linear and nonlinear relations, namely, this coefficient being 0.63 for the BP and age relation and 0.71 for BP and migraines. Let us look at a graph of the first two DS solutions(Figure 1).

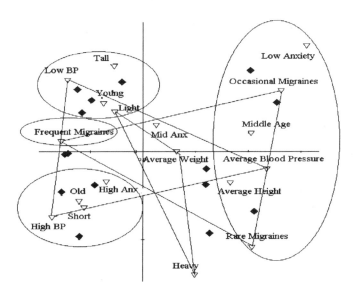

Figure 1: Dual Scaling Solutions 1 and 2

Unlike the case of linear analysis such as PCA, the three categories of each variable form a triangle, and the area of each triangle is different for a different variable. In DS, we do not look for clusters of variables, but clusters of categories. Then, the first two DS solutions can be roughly characterized as follows:

Solution 1		Solution 2	
One End	The Other End	One End	The Other End
Low BP	Medium BP	High BP	Low BP
High BP	Rare migraine	Rare migraine	Occasional migraine
Frequent migraine	Middle age	Old	Young
Old	Low anxiety	Heavy	Tall
High anxiety	Medium height	Short	
Short			

Note that "nonlinear combinations" of response categories are involved in each solution. This is so because "DS maximizes linear correlation between generally nonlinear transforms of ordered categorical variables," hence providing nonlinear PCA.

2.2   Information in Data

In contrast to the graph of DS solutions, the graph (omitted due to the limit of the space) of PCA places variables, and it is important to notice that the three response categories of each variable in the PCA graph are located on a straight line going through the origin and the coordinate of the variable (call this as axis of the variable) because as discussed earlier each variable can be expressed as a linear combination of orthogonal variables (axes). This is a stark contrast to the graph of DS. In the PCA graph, the axes of variables BP and Age are close (i.e., having a small angle), and they are almost orthogonal to the axis of variable Migraine. In PCA, the contribution of each variable is reflected on the length of the corresponding vector (i.e., how far the variable is from the origin), while in DS it is quite different from it.

The total information in data is generally given by the sum of the eigenvalues (squared singular values), but in DS a better definition than that seems to be in order. Observe in the above DS two-dimensional graph that different variables form different triangles. Noting that in the total space the triangle of a variable expands to a comparable size for all variables. In other words, each triangle in two dimensional space, for example, cannot become smaller in three-dimensional space, and so on. From the Pierce conclusion mentioned above, it is not difficult to realize that the area of each triangle increases as the dimensionality of space increases. Thus, it makes sense to define the information of an item explained by the first two, three, four dimensions, for example, to be expressed as the percentage of the area of each triangle over the corresponding triangle in the total space.

In the total space of DS, triangles of comparable sizes associated with variables float with different orientations. As the average inter-variable correlation increases, those triangles will gradually converge to a single triangle, at which point all inter-variable correlation is one. In other words, multiple-choice item data with three categories each, for example, requires two dimensions to be represented even when all inter-item correlation is 1. In this case, it should be further noted that the contributions of the two dimensions are equal, that is, 50 percent each. In other words, in the total space, each triangle has the property of a regular simplex: no matter how it is rotated, its contributions to the two dimensions are equal. When the frequencies of three categories are not equal, the triangle formed by connecting three categories is no longer regular. However, due to the use of the chi-square metric, such a non-regular triangle has the same property as the regular triangle, that is, the contributions to two dimensions are equal to 50 percent each.

If each item has four categories, in the total space the four category points form a pyramidal shape with each side being a triangle. In this case, it is clear that when the average inter-item correlation increases to one, all pyramids converge to a single pyramid, with the property that contributions of the pyramid to each of the three dimensions are equal to 33 percent. In this case, even when all inter-item correlation coefficients are one, the data require three dimensions to be fully represented.

The above discussion poses an intriguing question. What is information? The ordinary definition by the sum of eigenvalues appears inadequate. If all items are perfectly correlated, we need a single item to describe the data, rather than n items. In DS, we need a single triangle, rather than n triangles. This view tells us that when all the items are perfectly correlated, the entire data set does not have as much information as the case where items are poorly correlated. In DS, the difference is whether we can describe data by a single triangle or n triangles, the latter being the case when all items are statistically independent of one another. What this amounts to is that it is strange to use the sum of the eigenvalues as the measure of information, because the sum is independent of the inter-item correlation coefficients.

If the variable has n categories, the contribution of the variable in $n\text{-}1$ or higher dimensional space is given by the volume of the form created by connecting n points on n orthogonal axes.

Thus, by stretching our imagination to the continuous variable, where the number of categories is considered very large but finite, we can conclude that the total information in data must be expressed by the volume of a shape and not by the length of a vector.

The above conjecture can be reinforced by the fact that many key statistics associated with DS are related to the number of categories of variables. Some of the examples are given below.

The total number of dimensions required to accommodate a variable with m_j categories is at most $N_j = m_j - 1$. The total number of dimensions needed for n variables is at most $N_T = \sum_{j=1}^{n}(m_j - 1) = \sum_{j=1}^{n} m_j - n = m - n$. The sum of the squared singular values, excluding 1, is given by $\sum_{k=1}^{K} \rho_k^2 = \frac{\sum_{j=1}^{n} m_j}{n} - 1 = \overline{m} - 1$. Thus, as the number of categories of each variable increases, so does the total information in the data set. Whether this statistic provides a measure of total information is questionable as discussed in this section.

The total contribution of variable j with m_j categories can also be assessed by the squared item-total correlation, $r_{jt}{}^2$, summed over all the dimensions, as $\sum_{k=1}^{m-n} r_{jt(k)}^2 = m_j - 1$. With these expressions, all related to the number of categories of each variable, we can imagine what will happen as m_j increases to infinity, or, in practice, to the number of observations (subjects) N, assuming that m_j is less than N. This latter case is practical in the sense that for N respondents there are at most N distinct variates for each variable. An inevitable conclusion is that the total information in the data set is much more than what PCA captures, and can be expressed as the sum of the volumes of hyper-spheres associated with categories of individual variables.

The above suggestion is not for the use of dual scaling, for it will lead to an over-fitting phenomenon. Instead, the discussion is for the assessment of information contained in data. No matter how many categories we may bring in, there exists a corresponding geometric representation in hyper-space, for which we must develop a new method for extracting information in an efficient way, dimension reduction first and then scaling.

In PCA, there is only one correlation matrix, while there is a correlation matrix for each DS solution. In other words, PCA generally yields n components for n variables, while DS produces many more correlation matrices than one, each of which can be subjected to SVD to yield n components. Thus, DS can extract much more information from data than PCA. This in turn means that DS captures more information than PCA.

3   Linear versus Nonlinear Analysis

The above conclusion suggests how little information the traditional linear analysis such as PCA captures. In a general context, in which we consider both linear and nonlinear relations among variables, DS offers the sum of the eigenvalues (squared singular values) as a reasonable statistic to indicate the total information in the data. DS involves nonlinear transformations of categories of variables such that the transformed categorical variables attain maximal linear correlations. Thus, the sum of the eigenvalues of DS reflects both linear and nonlinear relations among variables. As suggested in the previous section, however, the current definition of information in terms of the sum of the eigenvalues may not be appropriate even for dual scaling.

To capture more information in continuous data than by PCA, we can use DS for continuous variables by treating distinct values of the variables as categories. However, some caution must be exercised because DS is likely to produce spurious, totally 'meaningless' results if applied to data with very large numbers of categories. It is not difficult to show that using a simple example of a continuous data set, whose structure is known, DS of discretized data into many categories can produce spurious results which are very different from the original data structure (Nishisato, 1994). Thus one must devise a reasonable way to discretize continuous variables in order for DS to tap into not only linear but also nonlinear relations among variables. It is surprising to know that there seems to be little knowledge available on optimal discretization of continuous variables.

4 Concluding Remarks

Traditionally we define the total information in data by the sum of the eigenvalues. This paper is to call attention that such a definition needs to be qualified, for example, as it is appropriate only if one is looking for the information captured by a linear model such as PCA, or both linear and nonlinear relations with dual scaling. Moving away from linear models, we used DS to find that the potential total information contained in data is much more than what PCA captures. How to capture all the information in data would involve much more work than what we know now, but at least an initial modest step forward has been taken by Nishisato and Eouanzoui (2002) and Eouanzoui and Nishsato (2002), who are investigating applications of DS to discretized continuous variables, the main focus being on discretization of continuous variables so as to extract a maximal amount of information from given data. It looks so far that this "maximal amount" can be defined only under some specific conditions. The current paper is focused on the basic question of "what is information?"

References

Beltrami, E. (1873). Sulle funzioni bilineari (On the linear functions). In G. Battagline and E. Fergola (Eds.), *Giornale di Mathematiche*, **11**, 98-106.

Benzécri, J.-P. et al. (1973). *L'Analyse des Données: II. L'Analyse des Correspondances (Data analysis II: Correspondence analysis*. Paris: Dunod

Bock, R.D. (1960). Methods and applications of optimal scaling. *The University of North Carolina Psychometric Laboratory Research Memorandum*, No.5.

Cronbach, L.J. (1951). Coefficient alpha and the internal structure of tests. *Psychometrika*, **16**, 297-334.

Eouanzoui, B. K. and Nishisato, S. (2002). Discretizing variables for dual scaling of continuous variables, II. Algorithms. *Paper presented at the Annual Meeting of the Psychometric Society*, Chapel Hill, University of North Carolina.

Escofier-Cordier, B. (1969).L analyse factorielle des correspondances. *Bureau Universitaire de Recherche Operationelle, Cahiers, Série Recherche*, **13**, 25-29.

Gifi, A. (1990). *Nonlinear multivariate analysis*. New York: Wiley.

Gower, J. C. (1966). Some distance properties of latent root and vector methods in multivariate analysis. *Biometrika, 53*, 325-328.

Greenacre, M.J. (1984). *Theory and applications of correspondence Analysis*. London: Academic Press.

Guttman, L. (1950). Chapters 3-6. In Stouffer, S.A. et al. (eds.), *Measurement and prediction*. Princeton: Princeton University Press.

Hayashi, C. (1950). On the quantification of qualitative data from the mathematico-statistical point of view. *Annals of the Institute of Statistical Mathematics*, **2**, 35-47.

Hayashi, C. (1952). On the prediction of phenomenon from qualitative data and the quantification of qualitative data from the mathematico-statistical point of view. *Annals of the Institute of Statistical Mathematics*, **3**, 69-98.

Hill, M.O. (1974). Correspondence analysis: A neglected multivariate method. *Applied Statistics*, **23**, 340-354.

Hirschfeld, H.O. (1935). A connection between correlation and contingency. *Cambridge Philosophical Society Proceedings*, **31**, 520-524.

Horst, P. (1935). Measuring complex attitudes. *Journal of Social Psychology*, **6**, 369-374.

Jordan, C. (1874). Mémoire sur les formes bilineares (Notes on bilinear forms). *Journal de Mathématiques Pures et Appliquées, Deuxiéme Série*, **19**, 35-54.

Kendall, M.G. and Stuart, A. (1961). *The Advanced Theory of Statistics*. Volume II. London: Griffin.

Likert, R. (1932). A technique for the measurement of attitudes. *Archives of Psychology*, **140**, 44-53.

Lingoes, J.C. (1964). Simultaneous linear regression: An IBM 7090 program for analyzing metric/nonmetric data. *Behavioral Science*, **9**, 87-88.

Lord,F.M. (1958). Some relations between Guttman's principal components of scale analysis and other psychometric theory. *Psychometrika*,**23**,291-296.

Meulman, J.J. (1998). Review of W.J. Krzanowski and F.H.C.Marriott, Multivariate analysis. Part I. Distributions, ordinations, and inference. London: Edward Arnold, 1994. *Journal of Classification, 15*, 297-293.

Nishisato, S. (1980). *Analysis of categorical data: Dual scaling and its applications*. Toronto: University of Toronto Press.

Nishisato, S. (1993) On quantifying different types of categorical data. *Psychometrika*, **58**, 617-629.

Nishisato, S. (1994). *Elements of dual scaling*. Hillsdale, N.J.: Lawrence Erlbaum Associates.

Nishisato, S. (1996). Gleaning in the field of dual scaling. *Psychometrika*,**61**, 559-599.

Nishisato, S. (2000). Data types and information: Beyond the current practice of data analysis. In Decker, R. and Gaul, W. (eds.), *Classification and Information Processing at the Turn of the Millennium*. Heidelberg: Springer-Verlag, 40-51.

Nishisato, S. and Eouanzoui, B.K. (2002). Discretizing variables for dual scaling of continuous variables, I. Background. *Paper presented at the Annual Meeting of the Psychometric Society*, Chapel Hill, University of North Carolina.

Pierce, J.R. (1961). *Symbols, signals and noise: The nature and process of communication*. New York" Harper and Row.

Richardson, M. and Kuder, G.F. (1933). Making a rating scale that measures. *Personnel Journal*, **12**, 36-40.

Schmidt, E. (1907). Zür Theorie der linearen und nichtlinearen Integleichungen Erster Teil. Entwicklung willkürlicher Functionen nach Syetemen vorgeschriebener. *Mathematische Annalen*, **63**, 433-476.

Torgerson, W. S. (1958). *Theory and Methods of Scaling*. New York: Wiley.

Factors which Influence Disclosure about Human Resources. An International Comparison Based on Disclosure Issued in Form 20-F and Annual Reports[1]

José G. Clavel[1], Esther Ortiz[2], Isabel Martínez[2]

[1]Departament of Quantitative Methods for the Economy, University of Murcia, Faculty of Business and Economics, 30100 Campus de Espinardo, Murcia, Spain
[2]Departament of Accounting and Finance, University of Murcia, Faculty of Business and Economics, 30100 Campus de Espinardo, Murcia, Spain

Summary. At the present moment global capital markets need an international consensus about disclosure requirements in different stock exchanges. We are now witnessing a wide range of disclosure that does not belong to the financial statements but is issued with them. Recently the US-Securities Exchange Commission (US-SEC) has adopted international disclosure standards for foreign private issuers that will become mandatory for annual reports relating to fiscal years ending on or after September 30th, 2000.

Bearing in mind all of the above, we have examined 84 Annual Reports and Forms 20-F for 1998 and 1999 of European companies listed on the New York Stock Exchange (NYSE), in order to analyse with correspondence analysis, whether the disclosure policy about human resources depends on different factors. The results obtained show that there is a wide range of variety in this disclosure and that the most important difference is the one which distinguishes between the kinds of reporting, even though factors such as firm's country of the origin shape the disclosure policy.

Key words. Disclosure, Human Resources, Harmonisation

[1] This work is part of the research project financed by the DGI: *Influencia de la diversidad contable en el análisis financiero internacional. Un estudio empírico* (SEC2000-0410) in collaboration with Analistas Financieros Internacionales and Morgan Stanley Dean Witter.

1 Introduction and Background

The rising flow of capital across borders increases the interest of securities regulators around the world to raise the level and quality of information available to investors. It is necessary to develop a set of high quality international standards that could be used in cross-border offerings and listings to improve the protection of investors.

This common goal has produced a point of meeting on securities commissions around the world involved in the International Organisation of Securities Commission's (IOSCO) effort to support a high quality of standards for incoming multinational issuers in cross-border offering and listing. This effort has been focused not only on accounting standards, but also on disclosure standards. New disclosure requirements: International Disclosure Standards (IDS) have been adopted by the US-SEC for foreign companies in September 1999 (SEC, 1999) to incorporate into Form 20-F, and they will become effective next year.

Companies worldwide expanded their annual reports to include sections on social issues. In the corporate social disclosure (CSD) the two most important areas are: employees/human resources and environment (Singh and Ahuja 1983) (Andrew et al. 1989) (Lynn 1992) (Savage 1994) (Gray et al. 1995) (Kreuze et al. 1996) (Nafez and Naser 2000). If we want to identify relationships between disclosures about human resources and other variables, we can highlight that the firms' disclosure strategy is influenced by a wide range of factors (such as industry, country, date, level of detail, among others).

Many studies have tried to establish an empirical relationship between disclosures and these variables. Many authors believe that the size is the most important variable in explaining disclosure (Cooke 1989) (Depoers 2000) (Street and Bryant 2000). It is supposed that a big firm generates more interest in disclosures than a small firm (Atiase 1987). Cavaglia et al. (2000) emphasize the importance of industry factors, because they determine important features in the disclosure.

2 Design and Methods

2.1 Hypotheses

In this research correspondence analysis is used to check the following supposition:
1. There is no significant difference in disclosure about employees between various country groups.
2. The level of disclosure about employees does not depend on the size of the companies.

3. There is no significant difference between disclosure US-SEC requirements included in Form 20-F (Item about employees) and disclosure about human resources in the domestic Annual Reports of the companies listed on the NYSE.

2.2 Sample

Whether the information revealed has been taken from Annual Reports or from Form 20-F the first condition to be included in the sample was to be listed on the New York Stock Exchange on September 19th, 1998. We have chosen NYSE-listed companies from three different European countries: Spain, United Kingdom and Germany.

Each company was contacted through their web site and a copy of its Annual Reports and Forms 20-F for 1998 and 1999 were requested. To sum up, eighty-four Annual Reports and Forms 20-F have been examined, forty-two for each year. In our sample there are 21 firms: 7 of each nationality.

The subrogate of the company's size will be total assets in 1998. We have decided to change Deutsche Mark, Pesetas and Pounds to Dollars, using the exchange rate at the end of the fiscal year 1998 in order to homogenise total assets reported in Balance Sheet. We have got two size groups: companies whose assets are above the average and companies whose assets are below the average and other two groups according to industry: financial or non-financial entities.

Table 1. List of Items searched on the reports

Group I: Required disclosure in Form 20-F	Old Form 20-F (Item 1)	Changes in number of employees in the various departments such as research and development, production, sales or administration. A description of any material country risks which are unlikely to be known or anticipated by investors and could materially affect the registrant's operations.
	New Form 20-F (Item 6)	a) Either number of employees at the end of the period
		b) or average for the period for each of the past three financial years
		c) If possible, breakdown of persons employed by main category of activity
		d) If possible, breakdown of persons employed by geographic location
		e) Any significant change in the number of employees
		f) Information regarding the relationship between management and labour unions
		g) If the company employs a significant number of temporary employees, number of temporary employees on an average during the most recent financial year
Group II: Voluntary disclosure	A. Remuneration	A1: Pensions
		A2: Stock Options
		A3: Incentives
		A4: Other non-monetary remuneration
	B. Training	B1: Relationships with Universities

	B2: Specific courses
	B3: Promotions
C. Employment conditions	C1: Flexible work schedule
	C2: Facilities, such as nursery gardens among others (creches, babysitting facilities)
	C3: Employment quality

2.3 Methodology

In order to capture disclosure practices a scoring sheet was developed, see Table 1. The eleven items of information about human resources are classified in two large groups:

• Group I: Disclosure required by the US-SEC in the Form 20-F, in the old format and in the new one.

• Group II: This group's information has been reclassified in these sub-categories: A: Remuneration, B: Training and C: Employment conditions.

The categories to score the information about employees were obtained a priori from a depth content analysis of the disclosure in Annual Reports and 20-F. The information obtained could be summarised in different contingency tables, according to the sum criteria we choose. For example, depending on the year of the report, the 21x11 total table of presence or absence of that item in the report becomes a 4x11 contingency table.

We have chosen correspondence analysis to analyse these tables not showed because space limitation. Correspondence analysis (CA herein) is a very well known exploratory method, whose primary goal is to transform a table of numerical information into a graphical display, facilitating the interpretation of this numerical information. As Greenacre (1994) pointed out, in CA the total variation in date is measured by the usual chi-squared statistic for row-column independence and it is the chi-square distance which is decomposed along the principal axes. The inertia of a table is the weighted average of the squared chi-squared distance between the column profiles and the average profile. At the end of the process, the more inertia the final solution maintains, the better it is.

The solution of CA (see Table 2) includes besides point coordinates, each contribution to the k-th axis relative to the corresponding principal inertia. These results, labelled CTR in SimCA output (the computer programme we used to do the analysis), allow us to diagnose which points have played a major role in determining the orientation of the principal axis. The second piece of information are the squared angle cosines, labelled COR in SimCa output). It allows diagnosing the position of each point and whether is well represented in the map.

Table 2. SimCA ouptut from Correspondence Analysis of disclousure according to Countries and kind of report.

Name	MAS	INR	K1	COR1	CTR1	K2	COR2	CTR2
Rows								
Sp8F20	62	113	642	659	151	-235	88	56
Sp9F20	72	97	198	84	17	-394	332	182
Sp8AR	89	64	-389	603	79	-193	149	54
Sp9AR	89	83	-477	702	119	29	3	1
Ge8F20	84	127	571	622	161	396	300	215
Ge9F20	86	123	560	635	160	354	253	176
Ge8AR	134	70	-378	785	113	87	41	17
Ge9AR	146	79	-328	573	92	148	117	52
Uk8F20	58	57	406	480	56	-357	370	120
Uk9F20	53	79	353	240	39	-362	252	113
Uk8AR	62	46	-127	64	6	79	25	6
Uk9AR	65	63	-141	59	8	-74	16	6
Columns								
Of	14	66	266	45	6	1002	633	236
a)	153	61	303	666	83	-103	78	27
b)	48	121	348	138	34	-825	777	533
c)	86	28	130	150	9	116	118	19
d)	101	22	146	284	13	87	102	13
e)	79	23	16	3	0	105	109	14
f)	74	195	851	794	317	262	75	83
g)	10	50	132	10	1	272	41	12
A	235	94	-184	243	47	-104	77	41
B	108	251	-843	880	451	81	8	12
C	91	88	-270	218	39	82	20	10

Columns labels on Table 1. Row labels: Name of the Country (Germany , United Kingdom or Spain); Year (1998 or 1999) and Report (Annual Report, or Form 20F). Example Ge9F20: Germany 1999 report Form-20F; Uk8AR: United Kingdom 1998 Anual Report.

3 Results

3.1 Differences by countries and size

The first, second and third supposition are shown not to be true. Even more, if the classical chi-squared statistic is calculate for the different contingency tables gene-

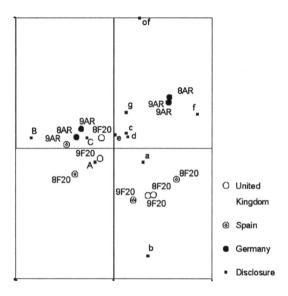

Fig. 1. Correspondence Analysis of disclosure according to Countries. Data in Table 2.

rated, hypothesis can be rejected taking a 5% level of significance. In CA analysis, always the first dimension (see Figure 1 and 2) offers a clear classification between disclosure in 20-F and Annual Report. The category relatively morecharacteristic of disclosure in 20-F is Item f: *Information regarding the relationship between management and labour unions*. On the other hand, for Annual Report the Item is B: *Training.*

Country, industry and size effect are found in the second most relevant dimension. Disclosure policy between countries (see Figure 1) could be classified in two groups: German companies in one group, and then, Spanish and British companies in the other. German companies disclose mainly required disclosure in old Form 20-F (item r1), and item g and f of the new Form 20-F containing information regarding the relationship between management and labour unions. In terms of temporal evolution, it is clear that Spanish companies have modified the content of their reports from 1998 to 1999, including more information than the one appeared in the Annual Reports more than companies from other countries.

Regarding size criteria, bigger companies are located in the low part of the map (see Figure 2), showing that their discloses contains relatively more information about the average number of employees for the period for each of the past three financial years (item g), and smaller companies tend to disclose information about any significant change in the number of employees (item e). Like in the previous analysis, the kind of report separate the columns along the horizontal axis that content 77.13% of the total inertia.

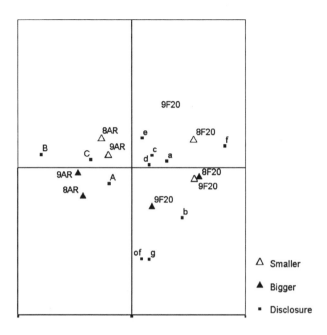

Fig. 2. Correspondence Analysis of disclosure according to Size. Data in Table 2.

3.2 Differences between 20-F: old and new and Annual Reports

Anyway, bearing in mind any of the chosen variables: country, industry, or size, it can be seen that one axis always groups the disclosure items required in 20-F (it does not matter whether it is the old or the new one) and the other items, as we have previously established. Hence, our last supposition may be rejected. In spite of the different other variables, the first dimension has always remarked differences in disclosure depending on the kind of report, whether 20-F or Annual Report.

4 Concluding Discussion

Subject to limitations that may be due to sample sizes, selection criteria, and assumptions underlying the methodology, the results presented suggest that information required by Form 20-F is essentially different from information disclosed in domestic Annual Reports. Factors like country, industry, or size shape the characteristics of disclosure. Correspondence Analysis has been showed to be an excellent technique to analysis information generated by Content Analysis.

To summarise, although the efforts to homogenize disclosure about employees have increased, there are multiple variables, which go on affecting disclosure and creating diversity. Hence the recent initiatives of different organisms will contribute to homogenise disclosure of non-financial information a bit more. This attempt aims to cope with all these features, adding this information to the financial information in order to reach a better-informed decision-making process.

5 References

Andrew BH, Gul FA, Guthrie JE, Teoh HY (1989) A note on corporate social disclosure practices in developing countries: The case of Malaysia and Singapore, BAR, Vol. 21, pp 371-376.

Atiase RK (1987) Market Implications of Predisclosure Information: Size and Exchange Effects, JAR, Vol. 25, n°1, Spring, pp 168-176.

Cavaglia S, Brightman C, Aked M (2000) The Increasing Importance of Industry Factors, FAJ, September/October, pp 41-54.

Cooke TE (1989) Voluntary corporate disclosure by Swedish companies, JIFMA, Vol. 1, n°2, pp 171-195.

Depoers F (2000) A cost-benefit study of voluntary disclosure: some empirical evidence from French listed Companies, EAR, Vol. 9, n°2, pp 245-263.

Gray R, Kouhy R, Lavers S (1995) Corporate social and environmental reporting- a review of the literature and longitudinal study of UK disclosure, AAAJ, Vol. 8, n°2, pp 47-77.

Greenacre, M (1994): "Correspondence Analysis and its Interpretation", in *Correspondence Analysis in the Social Sciences*, edited by Greenacre, M. and Blasius, J. London, Academic Press.

Kreuze JG, Newell GE, Newell SJ (1996) Environmental disclosures: What companies are reporting, MA, Jul, Vol. 78, Issue 1, pp 37-46.

Lynn M (1992) A note on corporate social disclosure in Hong Kong, BAR, Vol. 24, pp 105-110.

Nafez AB, Naser K (2000) Empirical evidence on corporate social disclosure (CSD) practices in Jordan, IJCM, Vol. 10, n°3 y4, pp 18-34.

Savage AA (1994) Corporate social disclosure practices in South Africa, social and environmental accounting. Centre for Social and Environmental Accounting Research, University of Dundee, U.K.

SEC (1999) International Disclosure Standards, Final Rule S7-3-99 available on SEC web site at http://www.sec.gov/rules/final/34-41936.htm.

Singh DR, Ahuja JM (1983) Corporate social reporting in India, IJAER, Vol. 18, pp 151-169.

Street DL, Bryant SM (2000) Disclosure Level and Compaliance with IASs: A Comparison of Companies With and Without U.S. Listings and Filings, IJA, Vol. 35, n°3, pp 305-329.

An application of rotation in correspondence analysis

Michel van de Velden[1] and Henk A. L. Kiers[2]

[1] Departament d' Economia i Empresa, Universitat Pompeu Fabra, Ramon Trias Fargas 25-27, 08005 Barcelona, Spain, *michel.vandevelden@econ.upf.es*

[2] Heymans Instituut (DPMG), Rijksuniversiteit Groningen, Grote Kruisstraat 2/1, 9712 TS Groningen, The Netherlands, *h.a.l.kiers@ppsw.rug.nl*

Summary. In correspondence analysis rows and columns of a nonnegative data matrix are depicted as points in a, usually, two dimensional plot. It is well known that the correspondence analysis solution is closely related to a biplot. In this paper we will use this close relationship to introduce simple structure rotation in correspondence analysis. By means of an application to cross-citation data we will show that, similar to the situation in principal component and factor analysis, rotation can be an important tool in improving the interpretability of the original correspondence analysis solution.

Key words: Correspondence analysis, rotation

1 Introduction

Correspondence analysis is primarily a graphical method for depicting multivariate data. It is typically applied to data summarized in a contingency table. That is, a matrix consisting of counts of co-occurrences between the categories of two categorical variables.

In correspondence analysis, the relationships between the categories of each variable, as well as the relationships between the categories of the row and column variables, are summarized by means of a, usually two-dimensional, biplot, see e.g. Greenacre (1993). Van de Velden and Kiers (2002) showed that, similar to the situation for biplots as described by Gabriel (1971), there exists rotational freedom in correspondence analysis. This rotational freedom can be employed, in a similar way as is common in principal component analysis and factor analysis, to improve the interpretability of the original correspondence analysis solution.

An important issue which is specific to rotation in correspondence analysis, concerns the scaling of the coordinates. In this paper we will not be concerned with this problem in great detail and we refer the reader to van de Velden and Kiers (2002) for a more elaborate treatment of this topic. Instead, we will illustrate the usefulness of rotation in correspondence analysis by means of an application to cross-citation data. Moreover, in contrast to the examples given by van de Velden and Kiers, we will employ a simultaneous simple structure rotation of the row and column coordinates.

2 Correspondence analysis

There exist many excellent expositions of correspondence analysis, see, e.g., Greenacre (1984, 1993) or Gifi (1990). Therefore, we will not give a complete description of the method but merely introduce some notation and provide some fundamental formulas.

Let $\mathbf{F}$ be an $n \times p$ contingency table scaled in such a way that its elements sum to one. That is, $\mathbf{1}_n'\mathbf{F}\mathbf{1}_p = 1$, where, generically, $\mathbf{1}_i$ is an $i \times 1$ vector of ones. Furthermore, let $\mathbf{r} = \mathbf{F}\mathbf{1}_p$ and $\mathbf{c} = \mathbf{F}'\mathbf{1}_n$ and define $\mathbf{D}_r$ and $\mathbf{D}_c$ as diagonal scaling matrices with as diagonal elements the elements of $\mathbf{r}$ and $\mathbf{c}$ respectively. We can then construct a matrix of standardized residuals as

$$\tilde{\mathbf{F}} = \mathbf{D}_r^{-\frac{1}{2}} \left(\mathbf{F} - \mathbf{rc}' \right) \mathbf{D}_c^{-\frac{1}{2}}. \tag{1}$$

We can express the singular value decomposition of $\tilde{\mathbf{F}}$ as

$$\tilde{\mathbf{F}} = \mathbf{U}\mathbf{\Lambda}\mathbf{V}', \tag{2}$$

where

$$\mathbf{U}'\mathbf{U} = \mathbf{V}'\mathbf{V} = \mathbf{I}_\kappa, \tag{3}$$

$\mathbf{\Lambda}$ is a diagonal matrix with singular values on the diagonal, in weakly descending order, and $\kappa \leq p \leq n$ is the rank of $\tilde{\mathbf{F}}$. The columns of the matrices $\mathbf{U}$ and $\mathbf{V}$ contain eigenvectors of $\tilde{\mathbf{F}}\tilde{\mathbf{F}}'$ and $\tilde{\mathbf{F}}'\tilde{\mathbf{F}}$ respectively.

Eckart and Young (1936) showed that a k-dimensional (with $k \leq \kappa$) least-squares approximation of $\tilde{\mathbf{F}}$ can be obtained by selecting the first k rows and columns of $\mathbf{\Lambda}$ together with the corresponding columns of $\mathbf{U}$ and $\mathbf{V}$. This least-squares approximation is of crucial importance in correspondence analysis. Coordinates for the row and column points in correspondence analysis are directly related to it in the following way. Let $0 \leq \alpha \leq 1$. (The choice of α is discussed later). Then, k-dimensional row coordinates can be obtained by selecting the first k columns of

$$\mathbf{X} = \mathbf{D}_r^{-\frac{1}{2}}\mathbf{U}\mathbf{\Lambda}^\alpha, \tag{4}$$

and, similarly, k-dimensional column coordinates by selecting the first k columns of

$$\mathbf{Y} = \mathbf{D}_c^{-\frac{1}{2}}\mathbf{V}\mathbf{\Lambda}^{1-\alpha}. \tag{5}$$

Thus, a k-dimensional least-squares approximation of $\tilde{\mathbf{F}}$ can be expressed as

$$\hat{\mathbf{F}} = \mathbf{D}_r^{\frac{1}{2}}\mathbf{X}\mathbf{Y}'\mathbf{D}_c^{\frac{1}{2}}. \tag{6}$$

From (3), (4), and (5), it immediately follows that the coordinates are scaled such that

$$\mathbf{X}'\mathbf{D}_r\mathbf{X} = \mathbf{\Lambda}^{2\alpha}, \tag{7}$$

and

$$\mathbf{Y}'\mathbf{D}_c\mathbf{Y} = \mathbf{\Lambda}^{2-2\alpha}. \tag{8}$$

From (6) it is immediately clear how closely the correspondence analysis solution is related to a biplot as introduced by Gabriel (1971).

3 Rotation of the coordinate matrices

The rotational freedom in correspondence analysis follows immediately from the biplot representation (6). Simply post-multiply $\mathbf{X}$ and $\mathbf{Y}$ by an orthogonal matrix and insert the rotated coordinate matrices in (6) to see this. Thus, depending on a particular choice of α, there are several options for rotation in correspondence analysis. Let us briefly summarize four choices of α that are common in correspondence analysis.

1. $\alpha = 0$: The column coordinates are *principal coordinates*. The row coordinates are *standard coordinates* (i.e. the weighted sum of squared coordinates is equal to 1). Distances between column points are chi-squared distances.
2. $\alpha = 1$: The row coordinates are *principal coordinates*. The column coordinates are *standard coordinates*. Distances between row points are chi-squared distances.
3. $\alpha = \frac{1}{2}$: Row and column coordinates are scaled similarly. The sum of weighted squared coordinates for each dimension is equal to the corresponding singular value. We will refer to these coordinates as symmetric coordinates.
4. $\alpha = 1$ for the row coordinates, and $\alpha = 0$ for the column coordinates: Both row and column points are in principal coordinates. By plotting both in one figure we obtain in fact an overlay of two different plots. The distances between row points are chi-squared distances, as are the distances between column points. However, nothing can be said about the distances between the row and column points.

The first and second option lead to *asymmetric* plots whereas plots associated with the third and fourth option are both referred to as *symmetric* plots. It is important to note that the first three plots satisfy the biplot relationship (6). The fourth plot is in fact an overlay of two different plots. For this plot, relationship (6) is no longer satisfied. Consequently, rotation in this fourth plot is much less straightforward than in the other cases.

As was indicated before, any orthogonal rotation can be applied to correspondence analysis coordinates satisfying the biplot relationship (6). In this paper, however, we will only be concerned with so-called simple structure rotation of the symmetrical coordinates, i.e. the coordinates obtained when $\alpha = \frac{1}{2}$. For this purpose we will use a procedure proposed by Hakstian (1976) in the context of two-battery factor analysis. The aim in his approach is to obtain a rotation matrix $\mathbf{T}$ such that both $\mathbf{XT}$ and $\mathbf{YT}$ are of simple structure (i.e. both the row and column coordinate matrices are rotated to simple structure). If we use Kaiser's varimax criterion as criterion for simple structure, we can formulate the following objective:

$$\max_{\mathbf{T}} \quad \sum_{j=1}^{k}\sum_{i=1}^{n}\left(\tilde{x}_{ij}^2 - \frac{1}{n}\sum_{l=1}^{n}\tilde{x}_{lj}^2\right)^2 + \sum_{j=1}^{k}\sum_{i=1}^{p}\left(\tilde{y}_{ij}^2 - \frac{1}{p}\sum_{l=1}^{p}\tilde{y}_{lj}^2\right)^2$$

$$s.t.\mathbf{T}'\mathbf{T} = \mathbf{T}\mathbf{T}' = \mathbf{I}_k,$$

where $\tilde{x}_{ij}$ denotes the ijth element of the $n \times k$ rotated row coordinate matrix $\mathbf{XT}$ and, similarly, $\tilde{y}_{ij}$ denotes the ijth element of the $p \times k$ rotated column coordinates matrix $\mathbf{YT}$. The rotation matrix $\mathbf{T}$ can be obtained using an iterative procedure. For more computational details we refer to Hakstian (1976). For a more detailed treatment of the various rotation options we refer the reader to van de Velden and Kiers (2002).

4 Citation data

Table 1. Contingency table of cross-citations

From — To	ECTR	JE	JAE	JF	JMR	MKS	PM
ECTR	1777	228	12	53	0	0	0
JE	1789	1283	126	172	0	0	0
JAE	636	317	104	37	0	0	0
JF	625	108	3	2723	0	0	0
JMR	68	14	0	0	1439	451	136
MKS	118	16	0	0	642	606	30
PM	7	0	0	0	48	10	1310

Table 1, taken from Wansbeek and Wedel (1999), presents figures from the Social Sciences Citation index, 1990-1996, for seven selected journals: Econometrica (*ECTR*), the Journal of Econometrics (*JE*), the Journal of Applied Econometrics (*JAE*), the Journal of Finance (*JF*), the Journal of Marketing Research (*JMR*), Marketing Science (*MKS*), Psychometrika (*PM*). The ijth element in Table 1 gives the number of citations *from* articles in journal i *to* articles in journal j. The specific order in which the rows and columns are presented immediately exposes some features of the data. For example, Wansbeek and Wedel (1999) note that there are citations *from* the marketing journals *to* the econometric journals, however, there are *no* citations *from* the econometric journals *to* the marketing journals. Besides this asymmetry, Table 1 suggests that there are two clusters of journals concerning their cross-reference patterns: an econometrics and finance cluster (*ECTR, JE, JAE, JF*), and a marketing and psychometrics cluster (*JMR, MKS, PM*).

In order to get a better understanding of the citation patterns we will analyze the data using correspondence analysis. As our main interest here concerns the relationship between the citations *to* and the citations *from* journals, we select the symmetrical biplot, i.e. $\alpha = \frac{1}{2}$.

A two-dimensional approximation of the data accounts for approximately 69% of the inertia whereas a three-dimensional approximation accounts for approximately 94%. Therefore, we will use the three-dimensional approximation and rotate the corresponding symmetrical biplot.

Table 2. Coordinates for citations *From* a journal

	Before rotation			After rotation		
ECTR	0.63	-0.05	-0.79	0.62	0.36	-0.70
JE	0.64	-0.06	-0.81	0.65	0.37	-0.73
JAE	0.64	-0.06	-0.87	0.65	0.37	-0.78
JF	0.76	-0.22	1.44	0.49	0.34	1.53
JMR	-1.25	1.19	0.15	-1.73	0.09	-0.12
MKS	-1.11	1.30	0.10	-1.68	0.27	-0.17
PM	-1.87	-2.33	-0.07	0.11	-2.99	-0.03

Table 3. Coordinates for citations *To* a journal

	Before rotation			After rotation		
ECTR	0.60	-0.04	-0.64	0.57	0.36	-0.56
JE	0.64	-0.06	-0.88	0.65	0.37	-0.79
JAE	0.66	-0.07	-1.04	0.70	0.37	-0.95
JF	0.77	-0.24	1.60	0.48	0.34	1.69
JMR	-1.26	1.31	0.17	-1.81	0.17	-0.12
MKS	-1.21	1.39	0.15	-1.83	0.27	-0.14
PM	-1.85	-2.21	-0.06	0.04	-2.88	-0.03

In Table 2 we find the 3-dimensional symmetrical coordinates, before and after rotation, for the rows of the original contingency table. That is, the coordinates for the citations *from* one journal to the other. Table 3 gives the original and rotated coordinates for the citations *to* journals. We see that in the *rotated* solution the points representing the Marketing Journals (i.e., *JMR* and *MKS*) are still separated from the econometric journals (i.e., *ECTR, JE* and *JAE*) along the first axes. However, unlike in the unrotated case, we immediately see that Psychometrika (*PM*), with respect to its cross reference pattern, is separated from both the marketing and the econometric journals. Thus, the rotated first dimension separates the marketing journals from the other journals. The second dimension, after rotation, separates the quantitative psychology journal Psychometrika from the marketing and economy journals. Finally, both before and after rotation the third dimension clearly separates the Journal of Finance from the other journals. Thus, due to the simple structure of the third dimension even before rotation, the third axis remained practically unaltered after rotation.

Figures 1 and 2 illustrate the rotation of the first two dimensions in this particular case. The amounts of explained inertia for the first two dimensions are written next to the axes. The procedure for calculating the inertias after rotation is straightforward, see van de Velden and Kiers (2002) for more details.

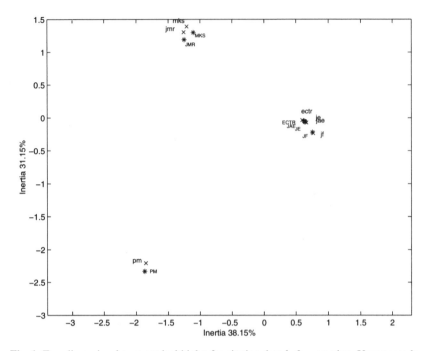

Fig. 1. Two-dimensional symmetrical biplot for citation data *before* rotation. Upper case labels indicate citations from journals. Lower case labels indicate citations to journals.

5 Concluding remarks

It is well-known that correspondence analysis is mathematically equivalent to several other methods such as dual scaling (Nishisato, 1994), homogeneity analysis (Gifi, 1990), and reciprocal averaging (Hill, 1974). Hence, mathematically, our results apply to all of these methods as well. However, it should be noted that there are important differences concerning the underlying rationales of these methods, see, for example Greenacre (1984). These differences may play a role when considering rotation.

One important issue that may arise when using a different rationale than the one employed in this paper, involves the distribution of inertia before and after rotation. It is well known that in correspondence analysis, similar to the situation in

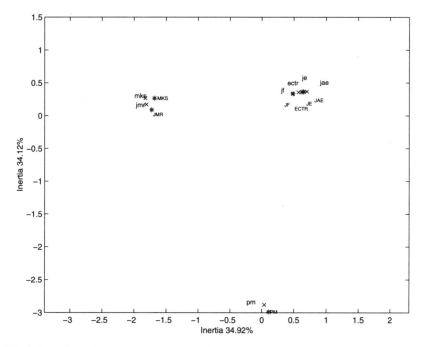

Fig. 2. Two-dimensional symmetrical biplot for citation data *after* rotation. Upper case labels indicate citations from journals . Lower case labels indicate citations to journals.

principal component analysis, the amount of explained inertia is distributed over the dimensions in a decreasing manner. That is, the first dimension accounts for a maximum of inertia, the second dimension, orthogonal to the first, accounts for a maximum of the remaining unexplained inertia etc.. Clearly, this distribution of inertia is affected by rotation. Hence, after rotation, the first dimension no longer accounts for the maximum of inertia. However, the *total* amount of explained inertia for the k-dimensional approximation is not affected by rotation. Thus, in the rotated solution the same amount of explained inertia is accounted for. As the objective in correspondence analysis is to find a low-dimensional approximation representing as much inertia as possible, the redistribution of inertia along the axes does not pose a problem. The interpretation of each separate dimension as a dimension along which a maximum of inertia is described, is after rotation no longer valid.

References

1. Eckart, C., Young, G. (1936): The approximation of one matrix by another of lower rank. Psychometrika **1**, 211-218
2. Gabriel, K.R. (1971): The biplot graphical display of matrices with applications in principal component analysis. Biometrika **58**, 453-467

3. Gifi , A. (1990): Nonlinear Multivariate Analysis. Wiley, Chichester
4. Greenacre, M.J. (1984): Theory and Applications of Correspondence Analysis. Academic Press, London
5. Greenacre, M.J. (1993): Correspondence Analysis in Practice. Academic Press, London
6. Hakstian, A.R. (1976): Two-matrix orthogonal rotation procedures. Psychometrika **41**, 267-272
7. Hill, M.O. (1974): Correspondence analysis: a neglected multivariate method. Journal of the royal statistical society, series C, **23**, 340-354
8. Kaiser, H.F. (1958): The varimax criterion for analytic rotation in factor analysis. Psychometrika **23**, 187-200
9. Nishisato, S. (1994): Elements of Dual Scaling: An Introduction to Practical Data Analysis. Lawrence Erlbaum, Hillsdale, NJ
10. Wansbeek, T., Wedel, M. (1999): Marketing and econometrics: Editors' introduction. Journal of Econometrics **89**, 1-14
11. van de Velden, M., Kiers, H.A.L. (2002): Rotation in correspondence analysis. Submitted.

Complex Difference System Models for the Analysis of Asymmetry

Naohito Chino

Department of Psychology, Aichi Gakuin University, 12 Araike, Iwasaki, Nisshin-city, Aichi, Japan

Summary. A class of complex difference system models of social interaction is discussed, which is designed to predict change in interpersonal sentiment relations in small groups over time. While most of the traditional mathematical models of social interaction deal merely with binary sentiment relations, the complex difference system models enable us to utilize intensity of sentiment. State spaces in these models are assumed to be finite-dimensional complex spaces (to be precise, Hilbert space, or indefinite metric space). Some results from simulations of a simple model are shown.

Key words: interpersonal sentiment relations, difference equation system, Hilbert space, circular hierarchy, asymmetric MDS

1 Introduction

A variety of mathematical, psychometrical, and/or social psychological models have been proposed for interpersonal relations in small groups after the late 1940's (for example, Holland & Leinhardt 1977; Katz & Procter 1959; Luce 1950; Sørensen & Hallinan 1976).

For example, Katz and Proctor (1959) suggested a discrete Markov process model to explain change in a special sociometric configuration of a group over time. Sørensen and Hallinan (1976) proposed a continuous-time, discrete-state Markov chain model for analyzing the evolution of triads over time. By contrast, Holland and Leinhardt (1977) proposed a similar model to a set of traditional binary-valued sociometric configurations. In these models each state is viewed as a snapshot or momentary observation of a stochastic process that operates dynamically in continuous-time, as Holland and Leinhardt (1977) point out.

However, there is a shortfall in these models, in that the interpersonal relation dealt with by them is, in almost all cases, *binary*. One way to overcome this defect may be to utilize asymmetric multidimensional scaling (hereafter, abbreviated as *asymmetric MDS*).

For example, *Hermitian Form Model* (HFM) proposed by Chino and Shiraiwa (1993) embeds objects in a p-dimensional complex space, given an observed similarity matrix S. The complex space may be either the *finite-dimensional complex* (f.d.c.) Hilbert space or the same dimensional complex indefinite metric space depending on the nature of the Hermitian matrix $H = \{h_{jk}\}$ constructed uniquely from the matrix S in such a way that

$$H = \{h_{jk}\} = \frac{1}{2}(S + S^t) + \frac{1}{2}i(S - S^t) = S_s + iS_{sk}. \tag{1}$$

Although HFM is a *complex* space model, observed similarity s_{jk} can be expressed only in terms of *real* parameters as follows:

$$s_{jk} \cong \sum_{l=1}^{p} \lambda_l\, s_{jk}^{(l)}, \tag{2}$$

where

$$s_{jk}^{(l)} = (\rho_{jl}\rho_{kl} + \sigma_{jl}\sigma_{kl}) - (\rho_{jl}\sigma_{kl} - \sigma_{jl}\rho_{kl}). \tag{3}$$

Here, s_{jk} is the (j, k)-element of S, and $\lambda_1, \lambda_2, \cdots, \lambda_p$ are the nonzero eigenvalues of H. The term $s_{jk}^{(l)}$ defined by (3) may be said to be a *component similarity* from object j to object k on the lth complex dimension. Moreover, ρ_{jl} and σ_{jl}, respectively, indicate the real part and the imaginary part of the complex coordinate of object j on the lth complex dimension. Therefore, if we denote it by $z_j^{(l)}$, then it is expressed as

$$z_j^{(l)} = \rho_{jl} + i\,\sigma_{jl}. \tag{4}$$

The coordinate $z_j^{(l)}$ on the lth complex plane defined above has a one-to-one correspondence with the coordinate set (ρ_{jl}, σ_{jl}) in a two-dimensional Euclidean plane.

According to the Chino-Shiraiwa theorem (Chino & Shiraiwa 1993), objects are embedded in an f.d.c. Hilbert space if H is positive (or negative) semi-definite, and otherwise in an indefinite metric space. Although Escoufier and Grorud (1980) introduce essentially the same real model as (2) using a different approach, they do not refer to these complex space properties at all.

HFM has some desirable properties from an approximation theoretical point of view. For example, the matrix decomposition utilized by HFM is thought of as a special case of the *generalized Fourier series expansion*. In fact, the decomposition of H in HFM, i.e., $H = U\Lambda U^*$, which is nothing but an eigenvalue-eigenvector decomposition of H, can be rewritten as

$$H = \sum_{k=1}^{N} \lambda_k\, G_k, \tag{5}$$

where $\lambda_1, \lambda_2, \cdots, \lambda_N$ are all the eigenvalues of H, and the rank one (Hermitian matrix) G_k is defined as $G_k = u_k u_k^*$. Here, u_k is the eigenvector associated with the eigenvalue λ_k, which is equal to the kth column of U defined above, and u_k^* is the conjugate transpose of u_k. It is easy to prove that matrices $G_1, G_2, \cdots, G_N$ constitute an *orthonormal system*, i.e., $\langle G_i, G_j \rangle = \delta_{ij}$, the Kronecker delta.

The above results clearly indicate that all the quantitative asymmetric information contained in the observed similarity matrix S can be captured economically by projecting it into "orthogonal" unidimensional complex component spaces (complex component planes) through the complexification of S defined by (1). Since any unidimensional complex plane can be identified with a two-dimensional Euclidean plane, we can seize most of the information contained in S by examining the features of configurations of objects on several two-dimensional Euclidean planes corresponding to relatively large eigenvalues of H.

2 A class of complex difference system models

Let us now remember that objects are embedded either in an f.d.c. Hilbert space or in a complex indefinite metric space depending on the feature of H according to the Chino-Shiraiwa theorem. This result suggests that we may choose these complex spaces as the state spaces of our complex difference system models discussed below depending on the nature of the data.

Let us suppose first that in *pairwise relations* the following two axioms hold:

1. *if one has a positive sentiment to the other, then one will move toward the other in a sociopsychological space,*
2. *if one has a negative sentiment to the other, then one will move away from the other in the space.*

Furthermore, we shall assume that the *state space* of a small group of size N is a *p-dimensional complex space*. This space may be either the *f.d.c. Hilbert space* or an *indefinite metric space*. Let us denote the coordinate of member j at discrete point in time n in this space by

$$z_{j,n} = (z_{j,n}^{(1)}, z_{j,n}^{(2)}, \cdots, z_{j,n}^{(p)})^t. \tag{6}$$

Finally, we shall assume that the interpersonal sentiment structure can be observed only at discrete time intervals, and that the strength of interpersonal sentiment of a member toward others at discrete time $n+1$ can be predicted by that of the sentiment at discrete time n.

Then, a simple and plausible class of models (Chino 2000) may be a *complex difference system model*, which we shall hereafter call a *simple linear model*,

$$z_{j,n+1} = z_{j,n} + \sum_{\substack{k=1 \\ k \neq j}}^{N} D_{jk,n}(z_{k,n} - z_{j,n}), \quad j = 1, 2, \cdots, N, \tag{7}$$

where $D_{jk,n} = diag\left\{w_{jk,n}^{(1)}, \cdots, w_{jk,n}^{(p)}\right\}$, and

$$w_{jk,n}^{(l)} = a_n^{(l)} r_{j,n}^{(l)} r_{k,n}^{(l)} \sin\left(\theta_{k,n}^{(l)} - \theta_{j,n}^{(l)}\right), \quad l = 1, 2, \cdots, p. \tag{8}$$

Here, the first right-hand side factor of (8), $a_n^{(l)}$, is a known constant which characterizes the speed of change in the configuration of objects on the lth complex plane in the state space at time n. We shall thus call it an *accelerator* of the structural change of the system under consideration. The second right-hand side factor, $r_{j,n}^{(l)}$, is the modulus of object j on dimension l at time n. Angles $\theta_{j,n}^{(l)}$ and $\theta_{k,n}^{(l)}$, respectively, denote usual counterclockwise oriented angles of object j and object k from the real axis in the lth complex plane at time n.

If we rewrite (7) as

$$z_{j,n+1} = \left\{ I - \sum_{k \neq j}^{N} D_{jk,n} \right\} z_{j,n} + \sum_{k \neq j}^{N} D_{jk,n} z_{k,n}, \quad j = 1, 2, \cdots, N, \tag{9}$$

then it is easy to see that each of the N equations constituting this model described by (7) is a *nonhomogeneous linear difference system* that is *nonautonomous*, or *time-variant* (for example, Elaydi 1999). Furthermore, the system described by (7) can be said to be a *multi-body problem* or *n-body problem* since (7) has N such equations corresponding to the N objects or members (Hirsch & Smale 1974).

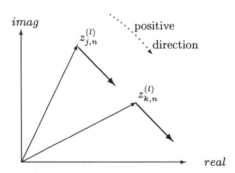

Fig. 1. Motion of two members when the positive direction of the lth complex plane is assumed to be clockwise.

Let us now consider what the simple linear model introduced above means in the simplest case, i.e., in a pairwise relation. Figure 1 illustrates this. Let this plane be the lth complex plane corresponding to a *positive* eigenvalue of H. Then, the positive direction of the configuration of members is *clockwise*, and in this case we can interpret that member j has a positive sentiment toward member k, while member k has a negative sentiment toward member j according to HFM. Notice that angles $\theta_{j,n}^{(l)}$ and $\theta_{k,n}^{(l)}$ must always be oriented counterclockwise.

As shown in this figure, the simple linear model asserts that two members will move toward the direction indicated by the thick vectors. If the positive direction of the configuration under study is *counterclockwise*, then these members will move toward the reverse direction. In any case, these motions coincide with the two axioms stated previously. Of course, these thick vectors are described by the second right-hand side of (7).

It is apparent from (8) of the simple linear model that all the members cease moving when all the configurations of members on the complex planes become either of the following three states:

1. all the members concentrate on a *point*,
2. all the members concentrate on a *line which passes through the origin*,
3. members are located on a *regular polygon* whose center is the origin.

The third state has long been known as the so-called *circular hierarchy*. However, the precise mathematical properties of this structure has not been discussed fully in the psychometric literature. However, it has already been discussed considerably in a physics literature. According to Berlin and Kac (1952), Kowaleski(1948) examines the eigenvalue problem of the so-called "*cyclic matrix*" directly. Eigenstructure of this matrix *includes* the circular hierarchy.

The cyclic matrix is defined as follows:

$$
C = \begin{pmatrix}
c_1 & c_2 & c_3 & \cdots & c_{N-1} & c_N \\
c_N & c_1 & c_2 & \cdots & c_{N-2} & c_{N-1} \\
c_{N-1} & c_N & c_1 & \cdots & c_{N-3} & c_{N-2} \\
\multicolumn{6}{c}{\dotfill} \\
c_2 & c_3 & c_4 & \cdots & c_N & c_1
\end{pmatrix}. \tag{10}
$$

Eigenvalues and eigenvectors of C are generally complex, as they discuss the solution of the direct eigenvalue-eigenvector decomposition of it. However, if we convert it into a Hermitian matrix using (3), it is relatively easy to imagine the hierarchical structure contained in this matrix.

As an example, let the order of C be 4, and let c_1, c_2, c_3, and c_4 be 1, 2, 3, and 4, respectively. Then, the eigenvalues of the Hermitian matrix corresponding to this C are 10, -4, -2, and 0. The eigenvector associated with 10 is $(.5, .5, .5, .5)^t$, and in this case four members coincide with each other. The eigenvector corresponding to -4 is of the form, $(x - iy, -y - ix, -x + iy, y + ix)^t$, and thus the four members constitute the vertices of a regular tetragon. The eigenvector corresponding to -2 is of the form, $(s + it, -s - it, s + it, -s - it)^t$, and therefore these four members constitute the two points on a line which passes through the origin.

In such a configuration of members, the simple linear model predicts that

1. members remain unchanged on the first and the third complex planes,
2. each of the members moves counterclockwise on the second complex plane, but their relative locations do not change forever.

The simple linear model described by (7) can be slightly modified by adding a threshold term, s_0, in (8) as follows:

$$w_{jk,n}^{(l)} = a_n^{(l)} r_{j,n}^{(l)} r_{k,n}^{(l)} \left\{ (\sin(\theta_{k,n}^{(l)} - \theta_{j,n}^{(l)})) - s_0 \right\}, \quad l = 1, 2, \cdots, p. \quad (11)$$

We may call this version a *threshold linear model*. Parameter, s_0, is a threshold below which no approach occurs to other members.

A more complicated model may be constructed by converting the linear term of (7) into nonlinear one as follows:

$$z_{j,n+1} = z_{j,n} + \sum_{m=1}^{r} \sum_{k \neq j}^{N} D_{jk,n}^{(m)} f^{(m)}(z_{k,n} - z_{j,n}), \quad j = 1, 2, \cdots, N, \quad (12)$$

where,

$$f^{(m)}(z_{k,n} - z_{j,n}) = \begin{pmatrix} (z_{k,n}^{(1)} - z_{j,n}^{(1)})^m \\ (z_{k,n}^{(2)} - z_{j,n}^{(2)})^m \\ \vdots \\ (z_{k,n}^{(p)} - z_{j,n}^{(p)})^m \end{pmatrix}. \quad (13)$$

Moreover, $D_{jk,n}^{(m)} = diag\left\{ w_{jk,n}^{(1,m)}, \cdots, w_{jk,n}^{(p,m)} \right\}$, and

$$w_{jk,n}^{(l,m)} = a_n^{(l,m)} r_{j,n}^{(l,m)} r_{k,n}^{(l,m)} \sin(\theta_{k,n}^{(l,m)} - \theta_{j,n}^{(l,m)}), \quad l = 1, 2, \cdots, p, \quad m = 1, 2, \cdots, r. \quad (14)$$

This model may be called a *general nonlinear model*. Of course, this model contains the simple linear model as a special case when $m = 1$.

At a glance, the general model seems to be very complicated because it includes higher power terms defined by (13). However, it can be said to be a simple model if we remember the well-known *De Moivre's Theorem*. In fact, if we put

$$z_{k,n}^{(l)} - z_{j,n}^{(l)} = r_{kj,n}^{(l)}(\cos \theta_{kj,n}^{(l)} + i \sin \theta_{kj,n}^{(l)}), \quad (15)$$

then we have, using this theorem,

$$(z_{k,n}^{(l)} - z_{j,n}^{(l)})^m = (r_{kj,n}^{(l)})^m (\cos m\theta_{kj,n}^{(l)} + i \sin m\theta_{kj,n}^{(l)}). \quad (16)$$

This means that the higher terms than $z_{k,n}^{(l)} - z_{j,n}^{(l)}$ are added to the simple linear model, and that they contribute to the change of members in the directions, $2\theta_{kj,n}^{(l)}, 3\theta_{kj,n}^{(l)}, \cdots, r\theta_{kj,n}^{(l)}$, too. It is plausible that such additional terms may explain complicated motions of members in the state space.

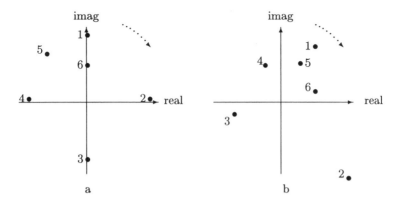

Fig. 2. Configurations of 6 members at two points in time, where the positive direction is clockwise. (**a**) initial point in time (time, n=1) (**b**) time, n=8.

Finally, it should be noticed here that we can predict the similarity matrix in the future by these models stated above using (2), (3), and (4). Moreover, we can express the similarities at a future time, say at discrete point in time $n + 1$, in another way in terms of norms in an f.d.c. Hilbert space as follows in the special case when the Hermitian matrix constructed from an observed similarity matrix at time n is positive or negative semi-definite, and this space is assumed to be invariant, at least, up to time $n + 1$:

$$s_{jk,n+1} = \frac{1}{2}(\|z_{j,n+1}\|^2 + \|z_{k,n+1}\|^2 - \|z_{j,n+1} - z_{k,n+1}\|^2)$$
$$+ \frac{1}{2}(\|z_{j,n+1}\|^2 + \|z_{k,n+1}\|^2 - \|z_{j,n+1} - iz_{k,n+1}\|^2), \quad (17)$$

where these norms defined above are induced from the Hermitian scalar product $\varphi(\zeta, \tau) \ (= \zeta \Lambda \tau^*)$ as

$$\|\zeta\| = \sqrt{\varphi(\zeta, \zeta)}. \quad (18)$$

Equation (17) is a version of the equation (42) in Chino and Shiraiwa (1993).

3 A simulation study

We have not completed to examine the mathematical properties of the models proposed in the previous section. But, it is easier to check the behavior of these systems by a numerical method. Here, we shall show a result from simulations of the simple linear model. The starting configuration is a complex unidimensional configuration obtained via HFM for the artificial similarity matrix cited in Chino (1978), which is shown in Figure 2a. Since the single nonzero eigenvalue of the Hermitian matrix constructed from the matrix was

5.25, the positive direction of this configuration is clockwise. Moreover, the value of the accelerator $a_n^{(1)}$ was set equal to 0.25.

Figure 2b is the predicted configuration of members at discrete point in time, n=8 by the model. As is apparent from this figure, every member of this group of size 6 moves clockwise as time proceeds. Furthermore, it seems that four members 1, 4, 5, and 6 gradually forms a subgroup, while member 2 becomes an isolate as time proceeds. The simulation shows, however, that after a sufficient period of time positions of members of this group converge to the respective limiting points on a line passing through the origin.

Finally, it will be necessary to develop algorithms for fitting our models to a set of longitudinal similarity matrices, $S_1, S_2, \cdots, S_m$. An easy way is to estimate all the unknown parameters of our model by a usual least squares method.

References

Berlin, T. H., Kac, M. (1952) The spherical model of a ferromagnet. The Physical Review 86:821-835

Chino, N. (1978) A graphical technique for representing the asymmetric relationships between N objects. Behaviormetrika 5:23-40

Chino, N. (2000) Complex space models for the analysis of asymmetry. Proceedings of The International Conference on Measurement and Multivariate Analysis. Vol. 1, 117-119, Banff, Canada

Chino, N., Shiraiwa, K. (1993) Geometrical structures of some non-distance models for asymmetric MDS. Behaviormetrika 20:35-47

Elaydi, S. N. (1999) An introduction to difference equations. Springer, Berlin

Escoufier, Y., Grorud, A. (1980) Analyse factorielle des matrices carrees non symetriques. In: Diday, E. et al. (Eds.) Data Analysis and Informatics. North Holland, Amsterdam,pp 263-276

Hirsch, M. W., Smale, S. (1974) Differential equations, dynamical systems, and linear algebra. Academic Press, New York

Holland, P. W., Leinhardt, S. (1977) A dynamic model for social networks. Journal of Mathematical Sociology 5:5-20

Katz, L., Proctor, C. H. (1959) The concept of configuration of interpersonal relations in a group as a time-dependent stochastic process. Psychometrika 24:317-327

Kowaleski, G. (1948) Determinantentheorie. 3rd edition. Chelsea Publishing Company, New York

Luce, R. D. (1950) Connectivity and generalized cliques in sociometric group structure. Psychometrika 15:169-190

Sφrensen, A. B., Hallinan, M. T. (1976) A stochastic model for change in group structure. Social Science Research 5:43-61

A Distance Representation of the Quasi-Symmetry Model and Related Distance Models

Mark de Rooij[1] and Willem J. Heiser[2]

[1] Department of Psychology, Leiden University *rooijm@fsw.leidenuniv.nl*
[2] Department of Psychology, Leiden University *heiser@fsw.leidenuniv.nl*

Summary. We propose a complete distance representation for the quasi-symmetry model for the analysis of square contingency tables. Complete in the sense that both interaction and main effects will be represented in a single distance model. Distances represent a departure from the maximum frequency in the contingency table. The model is explained in some detail and applied to occupational mobility data. Finally, it is compared to existing multidimensional scaling models for asymmetric tables.

Key words. Asymmetry, Contingency tables, Multidimensional scaling.

1 Square contingency tables

The analysis of square contingency tables often asks for symmetric or close to symmetric models. Basic loglinear modeling provides two models: the symmetry model and the quasi-symmetry model (see Agresti, 1990, Chapter 10). The quasi-symmetry model can be written as

$$\log(F_{ij}) = g + r_i + c_j + s_{ij}, \text{ with } s_{ij} = s_{ji}, \tag{1}$$

where g is a constant, r_i a row-effect $(i = 1, \ldots, I)$, c_j a column-effect $(j = 1, \ldots, I)$, s_{ij} the interaction effect which is symmetric, i.e. $s_{ij} = s_{ji}$, and F_{ij} is the resulting expected frequency. When we constrain the row- and column-effects to be the same, i.e. $r_i = c_i$ we obtain the symmetry model.

In the present paper we will discuss a distance representation of the quasi-symmetry model. First, the interaction effects will be transformed to Euclidean distances; second, the main effects will be rescaled to unique dimensions. The resulting model has an extremely simple interpretation in terms of distances: the smaller the distance between two categories the larger the transition frequency; the larger the distance the smaller the transition frequency. So, distances give a departure from the maximum frequency in the data.

When we have discussed our model and an application, we will discuss relationships with other distance models for asymmetric tables. The models to be discussed are the distance density model by Krumhansl (1978), the extended Euclidean model by Winsberg and Carroll (1989), the slide-vector model by Zielman and Heiser (1993), the wind model by Gower (1977), and

Table 1. Occupational Mobility data (Goodman, 1991)

	1	2	3	4	5	6	7
1	50	19	26	8	18	6	2
2	16	40	34	18	31	8	3
3	12	35	65	66	123	23	21
4	11	20	58	110	223	64	32
5	14	36	114	185	715	258	189
6	0	6	19	40	179	143	71
7	0	3	14	32	141	91	106

models by Okada and Imaizumi (1987), Weeks and Bentler (1982), and Saito (1991).

Before we discuss modeling we will show a data set here, to be used later in the application. It is an occupational mobility data set obtained from Goodman (1991), reproduced in Table 1. Both ways have seven occupational categories, here simply denoted by the numbers 1 to 7. From these data we have removed the diagonal, which is often done in the analysis of square contingency tables. The symmetry model does not fit the data ($X^2 = 50.6$, $G^2 = 54.0$, $df = 21$), but the quasi-symmetry model provides an adequate fit ($X^2 = 13.1$ and $G^2 = 15.6$ with $df = 15$).

2 Distance representation

2.1 Distance representation of the interaction

Multidimensional scaling models have been strongly developed in psychology and were initially used for the analysis of (dis)similarity judgments. Nowadays, these models have a much larger field of application. Scaling models have the virtue of a simple interpretation, since distances are encountered in every day life. In the present paper we will deal with the frequencies as similarity measures and so the distances must be a monotone decreasing function of the frequencies. In the quasi-symmetry model we will transform the interaction parameters s_{ij} to distances using the Gaussian transform (Shepard, 1958, p. 249; Nosofsky, 1985, p. 422). The model we will work with is defined by

$$\log(F_{ij}) = g + r_i + c_j - d_{ij}^2(\mathbf{X}), \tag{2}$$

where the squared distance is defined as

$$d_{ij}^2(\mathbf{X}) = \sum_{p=1}^{P} (x_{ip} - x_{jp})^2. \tag{3}$$

The $I \times P$ matrix $\mathbf{X}$ contains coordinates, x_{ip}, of the I categories on P dimensions. If $P = I - 1$ the number of parameters is the same as in the quasi-symmetry model, but of course dimensionality restrictions can be imposed. De Rooij and Heiser (submitted paper) coin model (2) the *symmetric distance association model* and present an algorithm to approximate observed frequencies (f_{ij}) with expected frequencies (F_{ij}) using a maximum likelihood function and assuming a Poisson sampling distribution.

2.2 Distance representation of the row- and column-effects

Besides the interaction, the main effects for rows and columns can also be transformed such that they can be incorporated in the distance representation. Therefore, we first make them all negative, i.e. we subtract a value from the row/column-effects such that the largest equals zero, and add these values to the constant g, that is

$$\log(F_{ij}) = g + \max_i(r_i) + \max_j(c_j)$$
$$+ r_i - \max_i(r_i)$$
$$+ c_j - \max_j(c_j)$$
$$- d_{ij}^2(\mathbf{X}). \tag{4}$$

Take the square root of the absolute values of the row parameters and denote them by u_i, i.e. $u_i = \sqrt{|(r_i - \max_i(r_i)|}$, and analogously for the column parameters to obtain v_j. We can add K unique dimensions for the rows and L unique dimensions for the columns to our graphical representation by defining $u_{ik} = u_i$ if $i = k$ otherwise $u_{ik} = 0$, and $v_{jl} = v_j$ if $j = l$ otherwise $v_{jl} = 0$. Our complete distance model can be written as

$$\log(F_{ij}) = g^*$$
$$- \sum_{k=1}^{K}(u_{ik} - u_{jk})^2$$
$$- \sum_{l=1}^{L}(v_{il} - v_{jl})^2$$
$$- \sum_{p=1}^{P}(x_{ip} - x_{jp})^2$$
$$= g^* - d_{ij}^2(\mathbf{X}; \mathbf{U}; \mathbf{V}), \tag{5}$$

where $g^* = g + \max_i(r_i) + \max_j(c_j)$ and denotes the maximum frequency from which distances are subtracted. Notice that we still have the same expected frequencies as in model (2), we just changed the identification constraints.

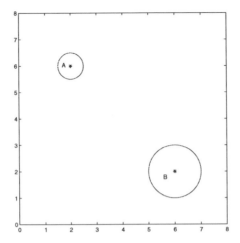

Fig. 1. Configuration with unique dimensions as circles

2.3 Graphical representation in low dimensionality

A disadvantage of the formulation as it is up to this point, is the huge number of dimensions. Suppose we have only two dimensions for the interaction, then our graphical representation has $2 + 2(I - 1)$ dimensions, and basically our graphical representation is lost. We can, however, draw the unique contributions in our two-dimensional representation and maintain the distance interpretation. If we draw circles around each point with radius u_{ik} for the point being a row category, and a circle with radius v_{jl} for the point being a column category, we obtain a novel interpretation of this distance model (see Figure 1, where only the row circle for category A is shown and the column circle for category B).

Since the model is defined in squared distances, by repeated use of Pythagoras theorem we can obtain the complete distance. This is shown in Figure 2. In the first step, we draw a radius (Bb) orthogonal to line AB (Left figure) and by Pythagoras we have that the squared length of the line Ab is equal to $AB^2 + Bb^2$. Then we repeat this (right figure) and draw the radius Aa orthogonal on Ab, the square of the length of ab is the complete distance, i.e. the deviance from the maximum frequency.

2.4 Asymmetry

In our model, each category is represented by one point and two circles, a circle for the row-effect and a circle for the column effect. The distance between two points is symmetric, i.e. $d_{ij}(\mathbf{X}) = d_{ji}(\mathbf{X})$. However, the complete distance between the two categories is not symmetric, i.e. $d_{ij}(\mathbf{X}; \mathbf{U}; \mathbf{V}) \neq d_{ji}(\mathbf{X}; \mathbf{U}; \mathbf{V})$. The asymmetry in the data is represented by the radii of the

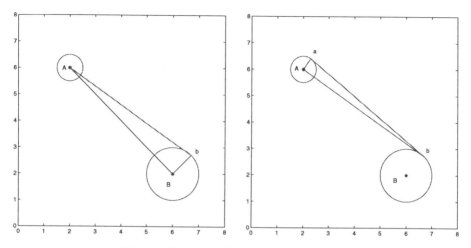

Fig. 2. Obtaining the complete distance

circles. See Figure 3 where point A has a dotted circle representing the row-effect and a solid circle representing the column-effect, for point B the row and column effect are equal, i.e. the same circle. We obtain complete distances as discussed above and we see that the complete distance from A to B (from dotted circle around A to circle around B) is smaller than the complete distance from B to A (from circle around B to solid circle around A). Since the expected frequencies are equal to the maximum frequency minus the complete distance, we have that F_{AB} is larger than F_{BA}.

2.5 Mass

The radius of the circle is inversely related to the mass of the corresponding category. So, in Figure 3, the mass of A being a row point (dotted circle) is larger than for A being a column point (solid circle). The advantage of the inverse relationship is outlined above, i.e. the advantage is having a distance representation. The disadvantage is clear and a warning is on its place. A natural interpretation of the circles in terms of mass is that the larger the circle the larger the mass. This is not true in the representation given above.

3 Application

Applying our model to the occupational mobility data we find that the two-dimensional model fits well, $X^2 = 16.0$ and $G^2 = 18.5$ with $df = 18$. The fit hardly decreases but the number of degrees of freedom increases from 15 to 18 compared to the quasi-symmetry model, so the model is more parsimonious. The graphical representation is given in Figure 4.

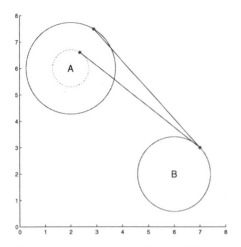

Fig. 3. Asymmetry in the graphical representation

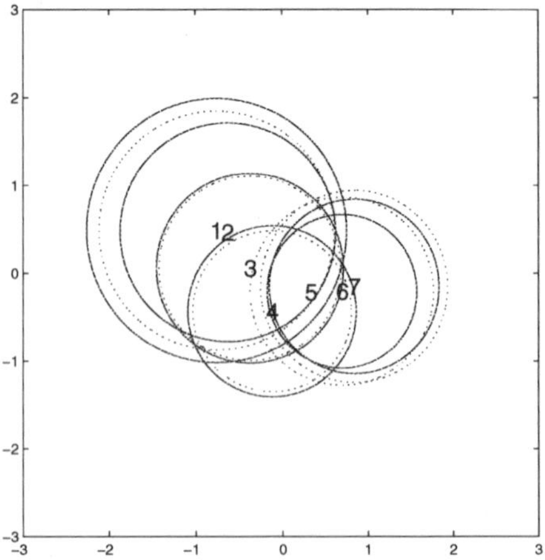

Fig. 4. Solution of occupational Mobility data

First, the points lie neatly ordered from 1 till 7. Since this was also found by Goodman (1991) using the $RC(M)$-association model, it appears to be some status ordering, where transitions occur more often between two adjacent categories than between categories far apart. The conclusion might be that going up or down the social status order goes, in general, smoothly step by step.

The unique contributions are drawn for the rows by dotted circles and for the columns by solid circles. Category 5 has for both the rows and the columns no circle, i.e. category five has largest mass by both sons and fathers. We see that the dotted and solid circles are basically the same, there is few asymmetry in the data or the masses for fathers and sons are about equal. For categories 1, 3, and 4 the solid circles are larger than the dotted circles; For categories 6 and 7 the dotted circles are larger than the solid circles. Since transitions always go from row (dotted) to column (solid) we have in general that a transition up the social status ladder occurs more frequently than a transition down the social ladder. For example, the complete distance from category 7 to 1 is larger than the complete distance from 1 to 7. So, the expected transition frequency from 1 to 7 is larger than that from 7 to 1. This is also true in the observed data.

4 Related distance models

Before comparing our model to related distance models we will first write our model in matrix terminology. Model 2 can be written as

$$\log(\mathbf{F}) = g\mathbf{1}\mathbf{1}' + \mathbf{r}\mathbf{1}' + \mathbf{1}\mathbf{c}' - \mathbf{D}^2(\mathbf{X}). \tag{6}$$

Table 2. Related distance models and their matrix expression

Model	Matrix expression
Distance Density Model	$\phi(\mathbf{\Delta}) = \mathbf{D} + w_1\mathbf{m}\mathbf{1}' + w_2\mathbf{1}\mathbf{m}'$
Extended Euclidean Model	$\phi(\mathbf{\Delta}) = \mathbf{D}^2 + \mathbf{m}\mathbf{1}' + \mathbf{1}\mathbf{m}'$
Slide-Vector Model	$\phi(\mathbf{\Delta}) = \mathbf{D}_z^2 + 2(\mathbf{X}\mathbf{z}\mathbf{1}' - \mathbf{1}\mathbf{z}'\mathbf{X}')$
	$\phi(\mathbf{\Delta}) = \mathbf{D}_z^2 + \mathbf{n}\mathbf{1}' - \mathbf{1}\mathbf{n}'$
Wind Model	$\phi(\mathbf{\Delta}) = \mathbf{D} + \mathbf{n}\mathbf{1}' - \mathbf{1}\mathbf{n}'$
Okada & Imaizumi Model	$\phi(\mathbf{\Delta}) = \mathbf{D} - \mathbf{n}\mathbf{1}' + \mathbf{1}\mathbf{n}'$
Weeks & Bentler Model	$\phi(\mathbf{\Delta}) = b\mathbf{D} + k(\mathbf{1}\mathbf{1}' - \mathbf{I}) + \mathbf{n}\mathbf{1}' - \mathbf{1}\mathbf{n}'$
Saito Model	$\phi(\mathbf{\Delta}) = \mathbf{D} + \mathbf{M} + \mathbf{n}\mathbf{1}' - \mathbf{1}\mathbf{n}'$

If we define

$$\mathbf{m} = (\mathbf{r} + \mathbf{c})/2$$
$$\mathbf{n} = (\mathbf{r} - \mathbf{c})/2, \tag{7}$$

and

$$\mathbf{M} = \mathbf{m}\mathbf{1}' + \mathbf{1}\mathbf{m}' + g\mathbf{1}\mathbf{1}'$$
$$\mathbf{N} = \mathbf{n}\mathbf{1}' - \mathbf{1}\mathbf{n}', \tag{8}$$

then $\mathbf{M}$ is symmetric and $\mathbf{N}$ is skew-symmetric. The idea to decompose the parameters of an asymmetric model into a symmetric and a skew-symmetric part was first fully exploited by Zielman and Heiser (1996).

Model 2 is then:

$$\log(\mathbf{F}) = \mathbf{M} + \mathbf{N} - \mathbf{D}^2(\mathbf{X}). \tag{9}$$

In multidimensional scaling we often work with dissimilarities to which we fit distances. The frequencies are similarity measures, and so the negation of frequencies are dissimilarities up to a constant. We can then write

$$-\log(\mathbf{F}) = \phi(\mathbf{\Delta}) = \mathbf{D}^2(\mathbf{X}) - \mathbf{M} - \mathbf{N}, \tag{10}$$

where of course the sign on $\mathbf{M}$ and $\mathbf{N}$ is arbitrary.

In Table 2 we give different distance models and their matrix expressions. The models discussed are Krumhansl's (1978) distance density model; the extended Euclidean model by Winsberg and Carroll (1989); the slide-vector model by Zielman and Heiser (1993); the wind model by Gower (1977); and models by Okada and Imaizumi (1987), Weeks and Bentler (1982, and Saito (1991). An important difference is that our model is estimated by maximizing a likelihood function where all these models are estimated by minimizing a least squares function. Comparing the models, we see that all models use either the vector $\mathbf{m}$ as defined above or the vector $\mathbf{n}$ to model skew-symmetry. Only Saito's model uses both terms. In the distance density model the asymmetry is defined by two weights, one for the rows and one for the columns.

The extended Euclidean model is a symmetric model extending the standard Euclidean part with unique dimensions. The last three models are distance models for asymmetric tables, where we have a distance part and some departure from the symmetric distance by a skew-symmetric term. Note that in the slide vector model we have $\mathbf{D}_z^2$ denoting that it is a distance matrix with a constant added to all cells. For a further discussion of these relationships see Gower (2000).

References

Agresti A (1990) Categorical data analysis. John Wiley and sons, New York

De Rooij M, Heiser WJ (2002, submitted) Graphical representations and odds ratios in a distance-association model for the analysis of cross-classified data

Goodman LA (1991) Measures, models, and graphical displays in the analysis of cross-classified data. Journal of the American Statistical Association, 86: 1085-1111

Gower JC (1977) The analysis of asymmetry and orthogonality. In: Barra JR, Brodeau F, Romer G, Van Cutsem B (eds) Recent developments in statistics. North-Holland, Amsterdam, pp 109-123

Gower JC (2000) Rank-one and rank-two departures from symmetry. Computational statistics and data analysis 33: 177-188

Krumhansl C (1978) Concerning the applicability of geometric models to similarity data: the interrelationship between similarity and spatial density. Psychological Review 85: 445-463

Nosofsky RM (1985) Overall similarity and the identification of seperable dimension stimuli: a choice model analysis. Perception and Psychophysics 38: 415-432

Okada A, Imaizumi T (1987) Nonmetric multidimensional scaling of asymmetric proximities. Behaviormetrika 21: 81-96

Saito T (1991) Analysis of asymmetric proximity matrix by a model of distance and additive terms. Behaviormetrika 29: 45-60

Shepard RN (1958) Stimulus and response generalization: deduction of the generalization gradient from a trace model. Psychological Review 65: 242-256

Weeks DG, Bentler PM (1982) Restricted multidimensional scaling models for asymmetic proximities. Psychometrika 47: 201-208

Winsberg S, Carroll JD (1989) A quasi-nonmetric method for multidimensional scaling via an extended Euclidean model. Psychometrika 54: 217-229

Zielman B, Heiser WJ (1993) The analysis of asymmetry by a slide-vector. Psychometrika 58: 101-114

Zielman B, Heiser WJ (1996) Models for asymmetric proximities. British Journal of Mathematical and Statistical Psychology 49: 127-146.

Two-Mode Three-Way Nonmetric Multidimensional Scaling with Different Directions of Asymmetry for Different Sources

Akinori Okada[1] and Tadashi Imaizumi[2]

[1] Department of Industrial Relations, School of Social Relations
Rikkyo (St. Paul's) University, 3-34-1 Nishi Ikebukuro, Toshima-ku
Tokyo, Japan 171-8501 *okada@rikkyo.ac.jp*
[2] School of Management and Information Sciences, Tama University, 4-4-1
Hijirigaoka, Tama-city, Tokyo, Japan 206-0022 *imaizumi@tama.ac.jp*

Summary. A model and an associated nonmetric algorithm of multidimensional scaling (MDS) for analyzing two-mode three-way (object×object×source) asymmetric proximities are introduced. The model and the algorithm of the present two-mode three-way asymmetric MDS were extended from those of Okada and Imaizumi (1997) which can represent differences of symmetric and asymmetric relationships among sources. But the model assumes that the directions of asymmetry are the same for all sources. The present model allows different sources to have different directions of asymmetry. The present two-mode three-way asymmetric MDS was applied to analyze the data on the international trade.

Keywords: asymmetric MDS, asymmetry weight, individual differences

1 Introduction

Two-mode three-way proximities typically consist of proximities among objects given by a set of sources. INDSCAL (Carroll and Chang, 1970) is the most widely used multidimensional scaling (MDS) procedure to analyze two-mode three-way proximities. When proximities given by each source are asymmetric, we have two-mode three-way asymmetric proximities. When two-mode three-way asymmetric proximities are analyzed by INDSCAL, asymmetry in proximity relationships among objects is regarded to be an error, because INDSCAL assumes that proximity relationships are symmetric.

Several MDS procedures for analyzing two-mode three-way asymmetric proximities were introduced (DeSarbo, Johnson, A. Manrai, L. Manrai, and Edwards, 1992; Okada and Imaizumi, 1997; Zielman, 1991; Zielman and Heiser, 1993). They can analyze two-mode three-way asymmetric proximities, and can represent differences among sources of asymmetric proximity relationships among objects. Each of them has its own characteristics. Although only the predecessor model satisfies three characteristics which seem important to two-mode three-way asymmetric MDS (Okada and Imaizumi,

1997), it assumes that the directions of asymmetry in proximity relationships among objects are the same for all sources. DeSarbo et al. (1992) and Zielman (1991) allow different directions of asymmetry among sources. Zielman and Heiser (1993) seems not to allow different directions of asymmetry among sources, because the weights for sources seem implicitly restricted to be non-negative. Even if there are more brand switches from brands j to k than from brands k to j in a market segment, there might be more brand switches from brands k to j than from brands j to k in another market segment. Directions of asymmetry need not be the same for all sources. The purpose of the present paper is to develop the model and an associated nonmetric algorithm to analyze two-mode three-way asymmetric proximities, which allow different directions of asymmetry for different sources.

2 The Model and the Algorithm

The present model consists of the common object configuration, the symmetry weights, and the asymmetry weight configuration like the predecessor model. In the common object configuration each object is represented as a point and a circle (sphere, hypersphere) centered at that point in a multidimensional Euclidean space. The common object configuration represents the relationships among objects which are common for all sources. Each source has its own symmetry weight. A symmetry weight for a source represents the salience of symmetric proximity relationships among objects for the source. Each source has a set of asymmetry weights, and is represented as a point in the asymmetry weight configuration. A set of asymmetry weights for a source represents the salience of asymmetric relationships among objects along each of the dimensions for the source.

Let x_{jt} be the coordinate of object j on dimension t, $w_i(\geq 0)$ be the symmetry weight for source i, and u_{it} be the asymmetry weight along dimension t for source i. Object j is represented as a point $(x_{j1}, x_{j2}, \cdots, x_{jp})$ and a circle of radius r_j in a p-dimensional Euclidean space. $r_j(\geq 0)$ is normalized so that the smallest radius is zero. Source i is represented as a point $(u_{i1}, u_{i2}, \cdots, u_{ip})$ in a p-dimensional space. Each source has its own configuration of objects. An object configuration for source i is derived (a) by applying the symmetry weight w_i to the configuration of points in the common object configuration in order to stretch or shrink the configuration of points uniformly, and then (b) by applying the asymmetry weight u_{it} to the radius of the circle along dimension t in order to transform a circle into an ellipse (ellipsoid, hyperellipsoid). In the predecessor model, the asymmetry weight is restricted to be nonnegative ($u_{it} \geq 0$). This is the reason why the predecessor model assumes the same direction of asymmetry for all sources. In the present model the asymmetry weight can be negative to allow different directions of asymmetry for different sources. Let s_{jki} be the observed proximity from objects j to k for source i. It is assumed that s_{jki} is monotonically decreasingly (when s_{jki}

is the similarity) or increasingly (when s_{jki} is the dissimilarity) related to m_{jki};

$$m_{jki} = d_{jki} - sign(z_{jki})|z_{jki}|^{1/2}r_j + sign(z_{kji})|z_{kji}|^{1/2}r_k, \qquad (1)$$

where d_{jki} is the distance between two points representing objects j and k in the configuration of objects for source i; $d_{jki} = w_i[\sum_{t=1}^{p}(x_{jt} - x_{kt})^2]^{1/2}$, and

$$z_{jki}^2 = w_i \sum_{t=1}^{p} sign(u_{it})(x_{jt} - x_{kt})^2 / \sum_{t'=1}^{p}[(x_{jt'} - x_{kt'})/u_{it'}]^2. \qquad (2)$$

Figure 1(a) shows objects j and k in the two-dimensional configuration of objects for source i when u_{i1} and u_{i2} are positive. Object j is represented as a point $(w_i x_{j1}, w_i x_{j2})$ and an ellipse of semiaxes $u_{i1}r_j$ and $u_{i2}r_j$, and object k is represented as a point $(w_i x_{k1}, w_i x_{k2})$ and an ellipse of semiaxes $u_{i1}r_k$ and $u_{i2}r_k$. m_{jki} is represented as an arrow from objects j to k in the left panel, and m_{kji} is represented as an arrow from objects k to j in the right panel, and

$$m_{jki} > m_{kji}.$$

Figure 1(b) shows objects j and k in the two-dimensional configuration of objects for source g when u_{g1} and u_{g2} are negative and have the same absolute values with u_{i1} and u_{i2}. Ellipses are the same as those shown in Figure 1(a), but are drawn by dotted curves instead of solid curves in Figure 1(a). m_{jkg} and m_{kjg} are represented as dotted arrows, and

$$m_{jkg} < m_{kjg}.$$

Thus sources i and g have the opposite directions of asymmetry;

$$m_{jki} > m_{kji} \text{ in Figure 1(a), and } m_{jkg} < m_{kjg} \text{ in Figure 1(b).}$$

Figure 1(c) shows objects j and k in the two-dimensional configuration of objects for source f when $u_{f1} > 0$ and $u_{f2} < 0$ and have the same absolute values with u_{i1} and u_{i2}. Ellipses become figures shaped like four leaves. m_{jkf} and m_{kjf} are represented as gray arrows. Source i and f have the same direction of asymmetry;

$$m_{jkf} > m_{kjf} \text{ in Figure 1(a), and } m_{jkf} > m_{kjf} \text{ in Figure 1(c).}$$

In the predecessor model where the asymmetry weight is restricted to be nonnegative ($u_{it} \geq 0$ and $u_{ht} \geq 0$),

$$m_{jki} > m_{kji}(m_{jki} < m_{kji}) \text{ automatically means}$$
$$m_{jkh} > m_{kjh}(m_{jkh} < m_{kjh}).$$

Thus the predecessor model presupposes that

$$\text{if } s_{jki} > s_{kji}(s_{jki} < s_{kji}), \text{ then } s_{jkh} > s_{kjh}(s_{jkh} < s_{kjh}).$$

In the present model,

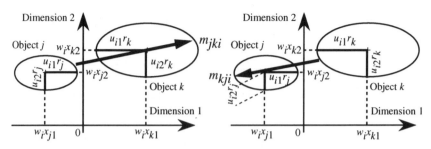

(a) m_{jki} and m_{kji} in the two-dimensional configuration of objects for souce i
$(u_{i1} > 0$ and $u_{i2} > 0)$.

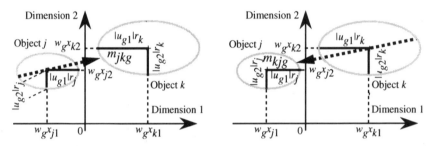

(b) m_{jkg} and m_{kjg} in the two-dimensional configuration of objects for souce g
$(u_{g1} < 0$ and $u_{g2} < 0)$.

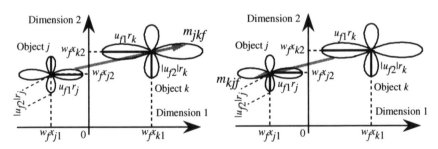

(c) m_{jkf} and m_{kjf} in the two-dimensional configuration of objects for souce f
$(u_{f1} > 0$ and $u_{f2} < 0)$.

Fig. 1. Different directions of asymmetry for different sources.

$m_{jki} > m_{kji}(m_{jki} < m_{kji})$ does not necessarily mean
$$m_{jkh} > m_{kjh}(m_{jkh} < m_{kjh}).$$

Thus,

when $s_{jki} > s_{kji}(s_{jki} < s_{kji})$, it can be $s_{jkh} > s_{kjh}$ or $s_{jkh} < s_{kjh}$.

The associated nonmetric algorithm to fit the present model to observed two-mode three-way proximities was extended from the algorithm of the predecessor which is based on Kruskal's (1964) monotone algorithm. The present algorithm is the same as that of the predecessor except for the treatment of the negative asymmetry weight. While in the algorithm of the predecessor a negative asymmetry weight is replaced by a small positive value, in the present algorithm it remains unchanged. Let there be n objects and N sources. The common object configuration, symmetry weights, and the asymmetry weight configuration which minimize the badness of fit measure S (Kruskal and Carroll, 1969);

$$S = \sqrt{\frac{1}{N} \sum_{i=1}^{N} \left[\sum_{\substack{j=1 \\ j \neq k}}^{n} \sum_{k=1}^{n} (m_{jki} - \hat{m}_{jki})^2 / \sum_{\substack{j=1 \\ j \neq k}}^{n} \sum_{k=1}^{n} (m_{jki} - \bar{m}_i)^2 \right]}, \quad (3)$$

are derived. $\hat{m}_{jki}$ is the monotone transformed s_{jki} defined by Kruskal's monotone algorithm, and $\bar{m}_i$ is the mean of m_{jki} for source i.

3 An Application

The present two-mode three-way asymmetric MDS was applied to the amount of international trade among nine countries/areas of nine commodities in 1998 (United Nations, 1999). We selected nine commodities; (1) **Food**, beverages and tobacco, (2) **Crude materials** (excluding fuels), oils, fats, (3) Mineral **fuels** and related materials, (4) **Chemicals**, (5) **Machinery** and transport equipment, (6) **Passenger road vehicles** and their parts, (7) **Other manufactures** goods, (8) **Textile** yarn and fabrics, and (9) **Clothing**: and nine countries/areas; (1) **OPEC**, (2) Former **USSR** Europe, (3) Developed economies **Europe**, (4) **Canada**, (5) **U.S.A.**, (6) **Japan**, (7) Developing economies **Africa**, (8) Developing economies **America** total, and (9) Developing economies **Asia** other. The emboldened word(s) above are used to represent each commodity or country/area hereinafter. The data consist of nine 9×9 tables where the (j, k) element of the i-th table represents the amount of export of commodity i from countries/areas j to k. We regarded the amount of trade as the similarity from the country/area of the export to the country/area of the import. The data were analyzed by the present two-mode three-way asymmetric MDS from five- through unidimensional spaces. The resulting minimized S in five- through unidimensional spaces were 0.482,

0.491, 0.519, 0.614, and 0.724. The two-dimensional result was adopted as the solution, because of the easiness of the interpretation.

The two-dimensional common object configuration is shown in Figure 2, where each country/area is represented as a point and a circle centered at that point. In the predecessor model, the larger radius suggests that the corresponding country/area has the larger tendency of exporting to the other countries/areas and the smaller tendency of importing from the other countries/areas, and the smaller radius suggests that the corresponding country/area has the smaller tendency of exporting and the larger tendency of importing. In the present model, when u_{it} is positive, the radius has the same meaning of that of the predecessor model, but when u_{it} is negative, the radius has the opposite meaning along dimension t. Africa has the largest radius. Japan has the smallest radius (the radius is zero), and is represented only by a point. Africa has the largest tendency of exporting along dimension t when u_{it} is positive, and has the smallest tendency of exporting along dimension t when u_{it} is negative. On the other hand, Japan has the smallest tendency of exporting along dimension t when u_{it} is positive, and has the largest tendency of exporting along dimension t when u_{it} is negative.

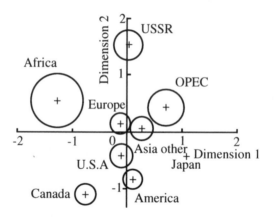

Fig. 2. Common object configuration of nine countries/areas.

Figure 3 shows the asymmetry weight configuration of the nine commodities. Each commodity is represented as a point. Fuels has positive asymmetry weights along both dimensions 1 and 2, and passenger road vehicle has negative asymmetry weights along both dimensions 1 and 2. Thus, Africa, which has the largest radius, has the largest tendency of exporting fuels, and has the smallest tendency of exporting passenger road vehicles. Japan, which has the smallest radius, has the smallest tendency of exporting fuels and has the largest tendency of exporting passenger road vehicles. Clothing has the negative asymmetry weight along dimenison 1 and the positive asymmetry weight along dimension 2. Thus Africa has the smallest tendency of exporting clothing along dimension 1, e.g., to Europe, but has the largest tendency of exporting clothing along dimension 2, e.g., to Canada. The symmetry weight were almost the same for all the nine commodities, and ranged from 0.96 to 1.04. Fuels and passenger road vehicles have the smallest symmetry weight, and thus have the largest asymmetric component or the largest trade imbalance among the nine commodities.

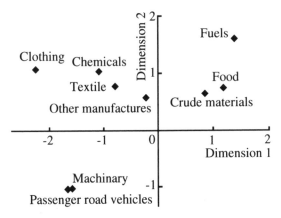

Fig. 3. Asymmetry weight configuration of nine commodities.

4 Discussion

In the present model for two-mode three-way asymmetric proximities, the negative asymmetry weight was introduced to allow different directions of asymmetry for different sources. This means that the model can deal with the larger variety of differences among sources, suggesting the larger versatility in applications. Zielman (1991) also used the negative asymmetry weight which allows different directions of asymmetry for different sources. Both Zielman (1991) and the present model use the negative asymmetry weight, which represents the salience of asymmetry along each dimension, applied to the radius. While in the present model dimensions representing the asymmetry are same as those of representing objects, in Zielman (1991) dimensions representing the asymmetry are different from those of representing objects. In the model of DeSarbo et al. (1992), the difference of the salience of two kinds of distinctive features allows different directions of asymmetry for different sources. For the proximity from objects j to k for a source, which of objects j or k is paid more attention, varies from one source to another, that leads to different directions of asymmetry for different sources.

When asymmetry weight u_{it} is negative, we have to reverse the interpretation of the meaning of radii of circles in the common object configuration along dimension t for source i. Thus, the result with the smaller number of negative asymmetry weights seems to be desirable. When we transform a solution by subtracting each radius from the largest radius; $r_j = r_{max} - r_j$, and by reversing the sign of all asymmetry weights; $u_{it} = -u_{it}$, the obtained result with the transformed radii and with asymmetry weighs having reversed sign has the same S value with the original result. It might be preferable to obtain the solution by assigning a condition of minimizing the number of negative asymmetry weights.

Figure 1 (c) shows m_{jkf} and m_{kjf}, where source f has the positive $(u_{f1} > 0)$ and the negative asymmetry weights $(u_{f2} < 0)$. The radius has two different meanings. The larger radius means that the similarity from the corresponding object to the other objects is larger along dimension 1, and is smaller along dimension 2. In Figure 1 (c) $m_{jkf} > m_{kjf}$, which coincide with Figure 1 (a) $(m_{jki} > m_{kji})$. The line connecting two points representing objects j and k forms a small angle with dimension 1. Thus m_{jkf} and m_{kjf} are influenced more by dimension 1 than by dimension 2. This is the reason why $m_{jkf} > m_{kjf}$. The smaller the line forms the angle with dimension 2, the more dimension 2 influences m_{jkf} and m_{kjf}.

Acknowledgment

The authors would like to express their gratitude to two anonymous referees for their helpful reviews.

References

Caroll, J.D., Chang, J.J. (1970): Analysis of individual differences in multidimensional scaling via an N-way generalization of 'Eckart-Young' decomposition. Psychometrika, **35**, 283–319

DeSarbo, W.S., Johnson, M.D., Manrai, A.K., Manrai, L.A., Edwards. E.A. (1992): TSCALE: A new multidimensional scaling procedure based on Tversky's contrast model. Psychometrika, **57**, 43–69

Kruskal, J.B. (1964). Nonmetric multidimensional scaling: A numerical method. Psychometrika, **29**, 115–129

Kruskal, J.B., Carroll, J.D. (1969): Geometric models and badness-of-fit measures. In: Krishnaiah, P.K. (ed) Multivariate analysis. Academic Press, New York

Okada, A., Imaizumi, T. (1997): Asymmetric multidimensional scaling of two-mode three-way proximities. Journal of Classification, **14**, 195–224

United Nations. (1999): 1998 international trade statistics vol. 2: Trade by commodity. United Nations, New York

Zielman, B. (1991): Three-way scaling of asymmetric proximities. Research Report RR91-01, Department of Data Theory, University of Leiden, The Netherlands

Zielman, B., Heiser, W.J. (1993): Analysis of asymmetry by a slide vector. Psychometrika, **58**, 101–114

A Latent Variable Model
for Multidimensional Unfolding

Kohei Adachi

Department of Psychology, Koshien University, 10-1, Momijigaoka, Takarazuka, Hyogo
665-0006, Japan

Summary. In multidimensional unfolding technique, preference data are fitted to
the distances between the points associated with subjects and stimuli, but the joint
estimation of subject and stimulus points is statistically undesirable. To avoid this
difficulty, we propose a latent variable model for metric unfolding, in which
subject points are regarded as normally-distributed random variables, whereas
stimulus ones are treated as unknown fixed parameters. Marginal likelihood,
defined by integrating out subject points, is maximized over stimulus point
parameters, using an EM algorithm. After stimulus points are obtained, subject
points are given by Bayes posterior means. The proposed method recovered true
points well in a simulation study and showed better fitting to real data than factor
analysis. Finally, its relations to other unfolding methods are discussed.

Key words. Multidimensional scaling, Unfolding, Latent variable models,
Marginal likelihood, Factor Analysis

1 Introduction

Multidimensional unfolding technique is used for analyzing an n-subjects by m-
stimuli matrix $\mathbf{X}=(x_{ij})$ of preference data, with the purpose of representing the
subjects and stimuli as points in a low-dimensional space. We use $\mathbf{f}_i$ for the
coordinates of the point of subject i and $\mathbf{a}_j$ for those of stimulus j, where both
vectors are of K-dimensional. These coordinates are estimated in such a way that
the distance between $\mathbf{f}_i$ and $\mathbf{a}_j$ becomes the shorter for the larger preference x_{ij}
(Borg and Groenen, 1997; Coombs, 1964; Heiser, 1981).

In standard unfolding technique, both $\mathbf{f}_i$ and $\mathbf{a}_j$ are estimated jointly. Here, we
should note that $\mathbf{f}_i$ are incidental parameters in contrast to $\mathbf{a}_j$ being structural
parameters: the number of $\mathbf{f}_i$ to be estimated increases with n (the number of
observations), whereas that of $\mathbf{a}_j$ remains unchanged. In general, when a model
has incidental parameters, estimates of structural parameters are biased even for

larger n (Neyman and Scott, 1948). That is, if we have more observations, we must calculate more $\mathbf{f}_i$, but the accuracy in estimating $\mathbf{a}_j$ is not improved.

Such difficulties can be avoided by treating incidental parameters as latent variables and integrating out them to define a loss function to be optimized over structural parameters. This latent variable approach is popular in some psychometric methods such as factor analysis (e.g., Yanai et al., 1990) and is also used in unfolding analysis of binary data (Andrich, 1988; Hoijtink, 1991; Takane; 1998), item choice data (Takane, 1996) and ranking data (Hojo, 1997). In this paper, we consider quantitative data to propose a latent variable model for metric unfolding.

2 Model and Parameter Estimation

We relate preference data x_{ij} to inter-point distances, using

$$x_{ij} = c - b\left\|\mathbf{f}_i - \mathbf{a}_j\right\| + e_{ij}, \tag{1}$$

with $\left\|\bullet\right\|$ the Euclidean norm (not squared). Here, $\mathbf{a}_j$, b and c are unknown fixed parameters, while $\mathbf{f}_i$ and e_{ij} are random variables. Subject coordinates $\mathbf{f}_i$ are assumed to follow the standard normal distribution independently over i:

$$\mathbf{f}_i \sim N_K(\mathbf{0}, \mathbf{I}) \tag{2}$$

(as factor scores in factor analysis) with $\mathbf{0}$ the vector of zeros and $\mathbf{I}$ the identity matrix. Errors e_{ij} are assumed to be distributed normally independently over i and j, with

$$e_{ij} \sim N(0, \sigma_j^2) . \tag{3}$$

We suppose the independence between $\mathbf{f}_i$ and e_{ij}. The density of data vector $\mathbf{x}_i = [x_{i1},\ldots,x_{im}]'$ conditional on $\mathbf{f}_i$ and a parameter set $\Theta = \{\mathbf{a}_1,\ldots,\mathbf{a}_m, b, c, \sigma_1^2,\ldots,\sigma_m^2\}$ is written as

$$p(\mathbf{x}_i|\mathbf{f}_i, \Theta) = \prod_{j=1}^{m} (2\pi\sigma_j^2)^{-1/2} \exp\left\{-\frac{1}{2\sigma_j^2}(x_{ij} - c + b\left\|\mathbf{f}_i - \mathbf{a}_j\right\|)^2\right\}. \tag{4}$$

Integrating out $\mathbf{f}_i$ we have marginal density $p(\mathbf{x}_i|\Theta) = \int p(\mathbf{x}_i|\mathbf{f}_i, \Theta) p(\mathbf{f}_i) d\mathbf{f}_i$ with $p(\mathbf{f}_i)$ the density of $\mathbf{f}_i$ given in (2). In practice, $p(\mathbf{x}_i|\Theta)$ is approximated, by substituting discrete points $\mathbf{f}_q^*$ $(q = 1,\cdots,Q)$ for continuous $\mathbf{f}_i$;

$$p(\mathbf{x}_i|\Theta) = \sum_{q=1}^{Q} p(\mathbf{x}_i|\mathbf{f}_q^*, \Theta) p^*(\mathbf{f}_q^*) \tag{5}$$

with $p^*(\mathbf{f}_q^*) = p(\mathbf{f}_q^*)/\sum_{r=1}^{Q} p(\mathbf{f}_r^*)$. Using (5), the marginal likelihood of Θ for a data set $\mathbf{X}=[\mathbf{x}_1,...,\mathbf{x}_n]'$ is given by

$$L(\Theta|\mathbf{X}) = \prod_{i=1}^{n} p(\mathbf{x}_i|\Theta) = \prod_{i=1}^{n} \left\{ \sum_{q=1}^{Q} p(\mathbf{x}_i|\mathbf{f}_q^*,\Theta)p^*(\mathbf{f}_q^*) \right\}, \tag{6}$$

which is maximized over Θ.

After $\hat{\Theta}$ (the estimate of Θ) is obtained, Bayes posterior mean

$$\hat{\mathbf{f}}_i = \sum_{q=1}^{Q} \mathbf{f}_q^* p\left(\mathbf{f}_q^*|\mathbf{x}_i,\hat{\Theta}\right) \tag{7}$$

gives the estimate of the coordinates for subject i ($=1,...,n$), where

$$p(\mathbf{f}_q^*|\mathbf{x}_i,\Theta) = \frac{p(\mathbf{x}_i|\mathbf{f}_q^*,\Theta)p^*(\mathbf{f}_q^*)}{\sum_{r=1}^{Q} p(\mathbf{x}_i|\mathbf{f}_r^*,\Theta)p^*(\mathbf{f}_r^*)}. \tag{8}$$

We use $Q = 9^K$ and set $\mathbf{f}_q^*$ ($q = 1,...,9^K$) at $[f(s_1),..., f(s_k),..., f(s_K)]'$ with s_k $=1,...,9$. Here, $f(s_k)$ is the center of each of the nine intervals into which $[-4, 4]$ are equally partitioned, with $f(1) = -3.556$, $f(2) = -2.667$, ..., $f(9) = 3.556$.

A generalized EM algorithm (McLachlan and Krishnan, 1997) is used to maximize (6), i.e., to obtain $\hat{\Theta}$, in which E and M steps are alternately iterated to update Θ until the increase of $L(\Theta|\mathbf{X})$ by the update becomes negligible. In the E-step of the $(t+1)$th iteration, $h_{iq} = p(\mathbf{f}_q^*|\mathbf{x}_i,\Theta^{(t)})$ is calculated, with $\Theta^{(t)}$ the Θ given at the tth iteration. In the subsequent M-step, the $\Theta^{(t+1)}$ satisfying $l(\Theta^{(t+1)}) \geq l(\Theta^{(t)})$ is obtained, where $l(\Theta) = \sum_{i=1}^{n} \sum_{q=1}^{Q} h_{iq} \log p(\mathbf{x}_i|\mathbf{f}_q^*,\Theta)p^*(\mathbf{f}_q^*)$. That is, we first find the b_j and c maximizing $l(\Theta)$ for given a_j and σ_j^2, next find the σ_j^2 maximizing $l(\Theta)$ for given a_j, b_j and c, and finally use Heiser's (1991) generalized majorization method to obtain the a_j increasing $l(\Theta)$ for given b_j, c and σ_j^2. This method is detailed also in De Soete and Heiser (1993).

3 Simulation

We performed simulation using artificial data synthesized in the following procedures. First, with $K=2$ and $m=9$, we chose true values of parameters a_j, b, c and σ_j^2 (see Fig. 1 and Table 1). Next, we sampled subject points $\mathbf{f}_i$ and data $\mathbf{x}_i$ ($i = 1,...,n$) according to (1) to (3) with $n = 50$, 100, or 200. For each n we had 15 data-sets ($\mathbf{X}$'s), which were analyzed by the proposed method. Since its solutions have indeterminacy on orthogonal rotation, $\hat{\mathbf{f}}_i$ and $\hat{\mathbf{a}}_i$ were rotated by the Procrustes method so that $\hat{\mathbf{a}}_i$ are matched with true $\mathbf{a}_j$ as closely as possible.

For each data-set $\mathbf{X}$, we assessed the recovery of stimulus points by NSE(a) $= v_{\mathbf{a}}^{-1}\sum_j \left\|\hat{\mathbf{a}}_j - \mathbf{a}_j\right\|^2$ (a Normalized sum of Squared Errors) and the recovery of subject points by NSE(f)$= v_{\mathbf{f}}^{-1}\sum_i \left\|\hat{\mathbf{f}}_i - \mathbf{f}_i\right\|^2$, where $v_{\mathbf{a}} = \sum_j \left\|\mathbf{a}_j - m^{-1}\sum_g \mathbf{a}_g\right\|^2$ and $v_{\mathbf{f}}$ $= \sum_i \left\|\mathbf{f}_i - n^{-1}\sum_h \mathbf{f}_h\right\|^2$. For each n, Fig. 1 shows $\mathbf{a}_j$ and the $\hat{\mathbf{a}}_j$ for the $\mathbf{X}$ yielding the median NSE(a) among 15 $\mathbf{X}$'s, and Fig. 2 shows the $\mathbf{f}_i$ and $\hat{\mathbf{f}}_i$ for the $\mathbf{X}$ giving the median NSE(f). The recovery of b, c and σ_j^2 was assessed by the absolute-value of the difference between true and estimated values. Table 1 describes the estimate corresponding to the median of 15 absolute differences. In Fig. 1, Fig. 2, and Table 1, we find that (except for a few results in Table 1) recovery is the better for the larger n. However, even for small n (= 50), the recovery is not bad: for example, in Fig. 1, each estimated point is closer to the corresponding true one than the other estimated points.

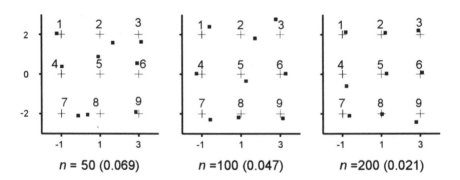

n = 50 (0.069)   n =100 (0.047)   n =200 (0.021)

Fig. 1. Configurations of true and estimated stimulus points indicated by crosses and squares, respectively, with NSE(a) in parentheses.

Table 1. True b, c and σ_j^2, and their estimates

True values	Estimates			True values	Estimates		
	$n=50$	$n=100$	$n=200$		$n=50$	$n=100$	$n=200$
$b=1.5$	1.621	1.579	1.441	$\sigma_5^2=7.0$	6.414	6.888	6.572
$c=10.0$	9.877	10.107	10.151	$\sigma_6^2=1.0$	1.348	0.893	0.914
$\sigma_1^2=3.0$	2.716	3.260	3.139	$\sigma_7^2=4.0$	3.511	4.297	4.238
$\sigma_2^2=9.0$	8.351	8.681	9.244	$\sigma_8^2=8.0$	8.340	7.627	8.203
$\sigma_3^2=2.0$	1.609	2.204	2.049	$\sigma_9^2=5.0$	5.436	4.760	5.321
$\sigma_4^2=6.0$	6.511	6.464	5.867				

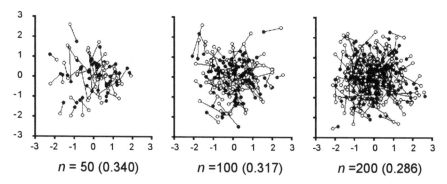

Fig. 2. Estimated subject points (filled circles) connected to the corresponding true ones (blank circles) by lines, with NSE(**f**) in parentheses.

4 Comparison with Factor Analysis

The proposed unfolding model (1) is related to the FA (factor analysis) model

$$x_{ij} = c_j + \mathbf{f}_i' \widetilde{\mathbf{a}}_j + e_{ij}. \tag{9}$$

That is, we have the latter, substituting inner product $\mathbf{f}_i' \mathbf{a}_j$ for negative distance $-\|\mathbf{f}_i - \mathbf{a}_j\|$ and c_j for c in the former, without changing the distributional assumptions in section 2 (Yanai et al., 1990).

To compare the proposed method with FA (maximum likelihood FA), we applied both methods to the data of the preference for five stimuli (items), which had been rated by 70 subjects (students at a faculty of the humanities in a Japanese university) using integers of zero to ten. The items are M (mathematics), N (natural sciences), E (English), J (Japanese), and S (social Sciences).

The resulting AIC, which is an index of the badness-of-fit of a model (Akaike, 1987), was shown in Table 2. There, we find the proposed unfolding and FA models with $K=2$ fit the data better than the saturated model in which only the normality of data, i.e., $\mathbf{x}_i \sim N_m(\mu, \Sigma)$, is assumed. Further, the proposed unfolding

Table 2. AIC of models for item preference data with the effective number of parameters in parentheses.

K^*	Unfolding	Factor analysis	Saturated model
1	1688.5 (12)	1687.4 (15)	
2	1680.2 (16)	1685.4 (19)	1687.4 (20)
3	1686.1 (19)	not defined[**]	

[*] Dimensionality or the number of factors; [**] FA model with $K \geq 3$ cannot be defined.

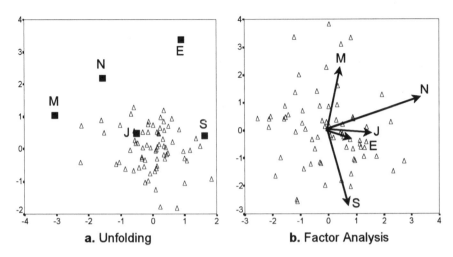

Fig. 3a, b. Solutions of unfolding and FA with K=2, for item preference data

with K=2 is found to fit better than FA, i.e., to fit the data best among the models considered.

Fig. 3a and b show the configurations of the estimates for K =2. We first note the configuration of the proposed unfolding in Fig. 3a. Its horizontal dimension seems to differentiate scientific items (N and M) from human studies (S and E). The lower area (around **0**) has many subject points in contrast to the upper area, showing that the vertical dimension differentiates preferred items from disliked ones: J and S are preferred, while the others are not. This observation is congruous to that the preference ratings averaged over subjects were 7.2, 6.3, 4.7, 3.9, and 3.5 for J, S, N, M, and E, respectively. Next, we note Fig. 3b in which factor score $\mathbf{f}_i$ and loading $\widetilde{\mathbf{a}}_j$ are represented as a point and a vector, respectively, so that $\mathbf{f}_i'\widetilde{\mathbf{a}}_j$ expresses preference. There, we cannot distinguish preferred items from disliked ones, since the averaged preference for each stimulus is represented by the stimulus-specific additive constant c_j in (9) and thus does not appear in the configuration of $\mathbf{f}_i'\widetilde{\mathbf{a}}_j$. Relationships between subjects and stimuli seem to be easier to grasp in Fig.3a than in b, because the former is identical to familiar usual maps in that every entity is plotted as a point.

5 Related unfolding methods

In this paper, we proposed a latent variable method for metric unfolding, which was found useful in the simulation and the application to real data.

A key idea in latent variable unfolding is to treat subject point f_i as a normally-distributed variable. Such a normality assumption has also been used in the WIP (wandering ideal point) model developed by De Soete, Carroll, and DeSarbo (1986). In the WIP model, data is supposed to be observed repeatedly for each subject, and the point f_{ir} for subject i on occasion r is assumed to follow the normal distribution with f_i its mean vector. That is, *occasional* subject point f_{ir} is treated as a variable, but *average* subject point f_i is dealt with as a fixed (unknown) parameter, which differs from f_i in our method.

In order to obtain point coordinates, latent variable unfolding uses the following two-steps procedure.

1. Stimulus points are estimated by maximizing marginal likelihood.
2. Subject points are estimated a posteriori, for given stimulus points.

Step 2 is regarded as a kind of external unfolding (Carroll, 1972) in that subject points are obtained after stimulus ones were determined. However, external unfolding differs from latent variable unfolding in the following point. In the latter, both stimulus and subject points are estimated from a single data-set X, whereas subject points are obtained from a data-set after stimulus ones are determined using another data-set or prior information in usual external unfolding.

References

Akaike H (1987) Factor analysis and AIC. Psychometrika 52: 317-332.

Andrich D (1988) The application of an unfolding model of the PIRT type to the measurement of attitude. Applied Psychological Measurement 12: 33-51

Borg I, Groenen P (1997) Modern multidimensional scaling: theory and applications. Springer, Berlin Heidelberg New York

Carroll JD (1972) Individual differences and multidimensional scaling. In: Shepard RN, Romney AK, Nerlove SB (eds) Multidimensional scaling, Vol. 1. Seminar Press, New York, pp.105-155

Coombs CH (1964) A theory of data. Wiley, New York

De Soete G, Carroll JD, DeSarbo WS (1986) The wandering ideal point model: a probabilistic multidimensional unfolding model for paired comparison data. Journal of Mathematical Psychology 30: 28-41.

De Soete G, Heiser WJ (1993) A latent class unfolding model for analyzing single stimulus preference ratings. Psychometrika 58: 545-565

Heiser WJ (1981) Unfolding analysis of proximity data. Unpublished doctoral dissertation, University of Leiden, The Netherlands

Heiser WJ (1991) A generalized majorization method for least squares multidimensional scaling of pseudodistances that may be negative. Psychometrika 56: 7-27

Hoijtink H (1991) A latent trait model for dichotomous choice data. Psychometrika 55: 641-656

Hojo H (1997) A marginalization model for the multidimensional unfolding analysis of ranking data. Japanese Psychological Research 39: 33-42

McLachlan GJ, Krishnan T (1997) The EM algorithm and extensions. Wiley, New York

Neyman J, Scott EL (1948) Consistent estimates based on partially consistent observations. Econometrika 16: 1-32

Takane Y (1996) An item response model for multidimensional analysis of multiple-choice data. Behaviormetrika 23: 153-167

Takane Y (1998) Choice model analysis of the "pick any/n" data. Japanese Psychological Research 40: 31-39

Yanai H, Shigemasu K, Mayekawa S, Ichikawa M (1990) Factor analysis: theory and methods (Inshi bunseki – sono riron to houhou) Asakura Shoten, Tokyo (in Japanese)

Monte Carlo Simulation in Three-Way Unfolding: Assessing the Combined Effect of Sparseness and Variation of the Cell Frequencies

Laurence E. Frank, Mark de Rooij, Willem J. Heiser

Psychometrics and Research Methodology, Department of Psychology, Leiden University, P.O. Box 9555, 2300 RB Leiden, The Netherlands

Summary. The usual methods for simulation studies in multidimensional scaling proved to be inadequate to create artificial data that match the required experimental conditions of this study. Therefore, a method was developed to model the degree of variability of the cell frequencies by manipulating the variability of the cell probabilities that control the sampling process in simulation. The creation of precise levels of sparseness and variability in the simulated data was necessary in order to evaluate the performance of recently developed triadic distance models for the analysis of asymmetric three-way proximity data (De Rooij and Heiser, 2000). One of the interesting features of these models resides in the additional possibilities they offer in comparison to log-linear models. Theoretically, triadic distance models can be used to analyze large tables with sparse cells as long as there is enough variation in the cell frequencies. This statement on the interaction between degree of sparseness and variability in the cell frequencies was verified by Monte Carlo simulation for two models: the slide-1 model and the unfolding model. Even with a substantial amount of sparseness and very little variability of the cell frequencies, both models perform satisfactorily.

Key words. Asymmetry, Monte Carlo simulation, Slide-vector, Triadic distances, Unfolding

1 Introduction

A recent development in multidimensional scaling combines the issue of asymmetry with triadic distances. De Rooij and Heiser (2000) proposed several triadic distance models for the analysis of asymmetric three-way proximity data. Such data occur, for example, when one categorical variable is measured at three time points. The data can be arranged in a three-way contingency table with every way corresponding to a time point. In the case of transition frequency data, each cell f_{ijk} of the table represents the number of transitions from category i to category j to category k, where $i, j, k = 1, \ldots, K$. The proximity data become asymmetric when the number of transitions between three categories in a particular order is not the same as the number of transitions between the same three categories in a different order.

Because the models of De Rooij and Heiser (2000) have been developed very recently, only little information is available on their performance. One of the interesting features of the models resides in the additional possibilities they offer in comparison to log-linear models. Analysis by the triadic distance models concentrates at the structure of the interaction on the category level, which is not the main objective in log-linear analysis that operates predominantly at the variable level. In theory, the models can be used to analyze large tables with sparse cells, as long as there is enough variation in the cell frequencies. This statement on the interaction between degree of sparseness and variability in the cell frequencies will be verified by Monte Carlo simulation. Frequency tables will be sampled from the multinomial distribution, aiming at an evaluation of the performance of the models under specific data conditions: a combination of different degrees of sparseness and variability of the cell frequencies. Sampling from the multinomial distribution requires explicit specification of the cell probabilities to create the desired data conditions, considering the fact that it has no parameter for variability. To the best of the authors' knowledge, there has been no Monte Carlo study in which the simultaneous effect of sparseness and variability of the cell frequencies on the solution of a multidimensional scaling model or a log-linear model has been evaluated.

2 Monte Carlo Design

The two experimental factors of the present study are sparseness and variability of the cell frequencies. To explore the effect of the two factors and their interaction on the fit of the slide-1 model and the unfolding model, simulated data sets are used matching the conditions of the experimental design. For each combination of the two factors, such a data set is created serving as a population from which Monte Carlo samples are drawn. In the present study, 100 samples are drawn from each population to be sure that a potentially significant main effect or interaction effect will be detected. The Monte Carlo samples are 4×4×4 tables with transition frequencies of total sample size equal to $n = 3000$. Sparseness is defined as the proportion of cells with observed frequencies equal to zero and comes in five levels: 0.0, 0.16, 0.31, 0.47 and 0.63. The variability of the cell frequencies is expressed by the coefficient of variation (CV) and has the following three levels in the samples (to be explained later): low (0.14), medium (0.73) and high (1.18).

Optimal population solutions were obtained for the slide-1 model and the unfolding model (in two dimensions) by performing 50 random starts. Next, each Monte Carlo sample was analyzed by the slide-1 model and the unfolding model (in two dimensions), using the starting values that produced the best fit on the populations. Prior to analysis the transition frequencies were transformed to dissimilarities using the inverse Gaussian transform ($\delta_{ijk}^2 = -\log p_{ijk}$), where the p_{ijk} were bounded from zero by some small number. For each model the zero cell frequencies were weighted in two different ways: weight 1.0 includes the zero cells in the analyses and weight 0.0 excludes them from the analyses. Furthermore, the configuration of each sample was compared to the population configuration by means of the coefficient of congruence. The results were evaluated by comparing the mean and standard deviation of the replications in each experimental condition. The interaction between the degree of sparseness and cell frequency variation was quantitatively assessed by factorial analysis of variance.

2.1 Generating the Data: a New Sampling Scheme

In order to evaluate the performance of the slide-1 model and the unfolding model, artificial data were created that match the experimental conditions and, at the same time, reflect the properties of the data used by De Rooij and Heiser (2000) to illustrate their models, that is, 4×4×4 tables with asymmetric transition frequencies.

A way to create a frequency table is to sample from a multinomial distribution, a procedure commonly applied in simulation studies on log-linear models (see, e.g., Koehler, 1986). The frequencies can be seen as resulting from a multinomial distribution with m classes (representing the total number of cells in the frequency table) and parameters p_1 to p_m representing the probability of each cell. Using this procedure, it is however not possible to obtain frequency tables with different variability levels, since the multinomial distribution lacks a parameter for variability. The method of error perturbed distances is not suitable for our study because, in practice, it is not possible to create precise levels of sparseness and variability by manipulating distances between points in a configuration. Sampling frequencies from the normal distribution that has a parameter for variability is not an option either, because with increasing variance levels, negative numbers can result from the sampling process.

The solution proposed in this study was inspired by the design of a study on log-linear models by Koehler (1986). This author demonstrated that the asymptotic chi-squared approximation for the Pearson X^2 can be inaccurate for sparse tables containing both very small and moderately large expected frequencies. He arrived at this conclusion by testing the hypothesis of homogeneity on contingency tables of size 2×k×k with different marginal probabilities. In one case, the marginal probabilities were equal, while in another case they were substantially different from each other, for example .25 and .75. The large difference between the marginal probabilities results in expected frequencies that are either very small or very large. The simultaneous presence of very small and very large frequencies in turn increases the variability between the cell frequencies. The approach used in the present study is based on that idea. However, the constraints are applied to the cell probabilities of each population matrix, rather than to the marginal probabilities.

The population data sets are 4×4×4 tables and consequently each population has 64 cells that are to be described by probabilities. The 5 levels of sparseness are not difficult to achieve: for each sparseness condition a fixed number of the 64 probabilities are set to zero. It is much less straightforward to produce data sets matching the three levels of variation of the cell frequencies, given a certain level of sparseness. This requires manipulation of the values of the population cell probabilities in such a way that the frequency samples drawn from the populations satisfy the required levels of variation. The coexistence of smaller and larger probabilities in the population data sets leads to the occurrence of both small and larger frequencies in the samples and consequently the variation of the cell frequencies increases. Using this principle, three levels of variation were created in the following way. The variation between the observations in the cells will be extremely small when all cells have the same frequency. Therefore, the lowest level of variation was achieved by allocating equal probabilities to all cells. A medium level of variation results when half of the cell probabilities sum up to .30 and the other half to .70. Allowing a larger discrepancy in the population probability matrix, like .05 and .95 creates the highest level of variation used in the present study.

The three levels of variation were obtained by manipulating the probabilities of the nonzero cells only. As suggested by De Rooij & Heiser (2000), the amount of variation of the cell frequencies is crucial for the behavior of sparse tables. More precisely, it is the variability of the nonzero cell frequencies that is important here, because the nonzero cells should compensate for the presumable effect that is produced by the zero cells. Measuring the variability of the nonzero cell frequencies in the context of our design has the following consequence. Data with different proportions of zero cells and, as a result, different proportions of nonzero cells necessitate the use of a variability measure that does not depend on the number of nonzero cells. The coefficient of variation expresses variability as proportion of the mean for variables that have a fixed and meaningful zero point and is therefore more suitable to measure variability under experimental conditions that produce different magnitudes of mean.

Because the number of nonzero cell probabilities that must sum up to a certain p-value changes according to the proportion of sparseness, the probabilities of each cell must be chosen in such a way that the same value for the CV is achieved at each level of sparseness. For example, the 24 nonzero cell probabilities in case of sparseness level .63 should yield the same CV-value as the 44 nonzero cell probabilities of sparseness level .31. This objective is achieved in the following way. If, for example, there are 24 nonzero cells and the desired probability for half of the cells equals $p = .30$, the constant c is the result of solving the following equation:

$$c + 2c + 3c + 4c + (...) + 12c = .30 \tag{1}$$

$$c = \frac{.30}{78} = 0.00385 .$$

The resulting 12 probabilities are different, but the interval between the probabilities remains constant (= 0.00385). The final equation to calculate the constant c for every desired probability and every possible number of cells becomes:

$$c = \frac{p}{\frac{m(m+1)}{2}}, \tag{2}$$

in which p refers to the desired probability (.30, .70, or .05, .95) and m is the number of nonzero cells that sum up to the probability value p. The effect of this operation is that it divides the probability area into m sections of different size, which is an adequate representation of asymmetric three-way proximity data.

The population probabilities matching each of the 15 experimental conditions were created by using Eq. 2. Note that in the lowest variation condition, all nonzero cells have equal probability. Evidently, this situation does not satisfactorily represent asymmetric three-way proximity data. However, the sampling process itself introduces variability among the cell frequencies: the lowest level of CV in the samples is equal to 0.14, opposed to 0.0 in the population. Consequently, in order to create the lowest possible condition of variation in the samples, the population probabilities in the lowest CV condition are all equal.

The population probabilities were not assigned to the cells of the data matrices in a random way, but by reproducing the pattern of the Swedish politics data (De Rooij and Heiser, 2000; Upton, 1978). The pattern was imitated by assigning rank numbers to the cells with transition frequencies of the original data. Next, the population probabilities were allocated to the cells of the 4×4×4 tables in accordance with the pattern of the rank numbers. In order to imitate the trend present in the original data even better, the zero frequencies were allocated to the same cells as the original data and higher levels of sparseness were created by allocating zero probability to cells with the lowest rank numbers.

2.2 Dependent Variable

Analysis by the triadic distance models (De Rooij and Heiser, 2000) results in a simultaneous representation of symmetry and asymmetry in a low-dimensional configuration. There are several ways to represent symmetry and asymmetry concurrently. It can be achieved by a three-way unfolding model (Eq. 3), where a co-ordinate matrix is estimated for each way, such that the triadic distances between the points of each way represent the dissimilarities as well as possible:

$$d_{ijk}^2(\mathbf{X};\mathbf{Y};\mathbf{Z}) = d_{ij}^2(\mathbf{X};\mathbf{Y}) + d_{jk}^2(\mathbf{Y};\mathbf{Z}) + d_{ik}^2(\mathbf{X};\mathbf{Z}). \tag{3}$$

Another possibility is to use the slide-vector model, a restricted unfolding model where $\mathbf{Y}=\mathbf{X}-\mathbf{1u}'$ and $\mathbf{Z}=\mathbf{Y}-\mathbf{1v}'$. In this model, the symmetric part is represented by distances in Euclidean space. The asymmetric part is represented by a uniform shift in one direction imposed on the symmetric distances (De Rooij and Heiser, 2000; Zielman and Heiser, 1993). Different kinds of asymmetry can be modeled if one assumes that the asymmetry is the same for both ways, i.e. $\mathbf{u}=\mathbf{v}$ (slide-1 model), or if $\mathbf{u}$ does not equal $\mathbf{v}$ (slide-2 model), see De Rooij and Heiser (2000).

In order to evaluate which model yields the best description of the data, the different models are compared by means of a stress value,

$$\sigma^2(\hat{\mathbf{X}};\hat{\mathbf{Y}};\hat{\mathbf{Z}}) = \sum_{ijk} w_{ijk}\delta_{ijk}^2 - \sum_{ijk} w_{ijk}d_{ijk}^2(\hat{\mathbf{X}};\hat{\mathbf{Y}};\hat{\mathbf{Z}}), \tag{4}$$

and the percentage dispersion accounted for (%DAF), which is analogous to the diagnostic *variance accounted for* in regression analysis,

$$\%DAF = 100 \times \frac{\sum_{ijk} w_{ijk}d_{ijk}^2(\hat{\mathbf{X}};\hat{\mathbf{Y}};\hat{\mathbf{Z}})}{SSQ_\delta}, \tag{5}$$

where the δ_{ijk}^2 represent the given three-way dissimilarities, the $d_{ijk}^2(\hat{\mathbf{X}};\hat{\mathbf{Y}};\hat{\mathbf{Z}})$ represent the estimated triadic distances, the w_{ijk} are predefined weights, and SSQ_δ corresponds to the weighted sum of squares of the dissimilarities. The effect of the two experimental factors and their interaction on the slide-1 model and the unfolding model was evaluated by the %DAF-value (Eq. 5), which serves as the outcome variable of the design.

3. Results and Discussion

The extent to which the Monte Carlo samples reflect the situation in the populations, was evaluated by comparing the population %DAF-values with the mean of the samples in each experimental condition. All mean %DAF-values are almost equal to the population values. The mean values of the coefficient of congruence, computed between the population distances and the sample distances, range from 0.99 to 1.0 and the standard deviations range from 0.0 to 0.003, showing a very strong geometrical similarity between the configuration of each sample and the corresponding population.

Since the results for the slide-1 model and the unfolding model are almost similar, only the results of the slide-1 model are displayed graphically. Figure 1 shows the means of the %DAF-values for each of the 100 Monte Carlo replications in each combination of sparseness and variation. In general, the slide-1 model performs well in all experimental conditions as can be deduced from the means of the %DAF-values that range from 95.08 to 99.95 and the corresponding standard deviations with range [0.01, 0.61]. Furthermore, Figure 1 shows the effect of the interaction between the degree of sparseness and the variation of the cell frequencies on the %DAF-values. In the zero cells *included* condition (top of Figure 1), the mean %DAF-values increase monotonically with increasing levels of variation, for each sparseness condition. In the 0% sparseness condition however, the %DAF-values decrease with increasing levels of variation, but the %DAF-values remain higher than in the other sparseness conditions. In the zero cells *excluded* condition (bottom of Figure 1), the mean %DAF-values are higher than in the zero cells *included* condition and, not surprisingly, they show the same pattern as the 0% sparseness condition of the zero cells included condition.

The results of the analysis of variance for the slide-1 model (for the zero cells included condition as well as the zero cells excluded condition) show that all main effects and interaction effects are statistically significant at an alpha level of .001.

In the zero cells *in*cluded condition, the main effect of sparseness has $F(4, 1485) =$ 41996.82 with $p = .000$, $\eta^2 = 0.99$ and CV has $F(2, 1485) = 3914.84$ with $p = .000$, $\eta^2 = 0.84$. The interaction of sparseness and CV has $F(8, 1485) = 3601.05$ with $p = .000$ and $\eta^2 = 0.95$. In the zero cells *ex*cluded condition, the main effects have the following values. Sparseness: $F(4, 1485) = 92.86$, $p = .000$, $\eta^2 = 0.20$; CV: $F(2, 1485) = 9365.74$, $p = .000$, $\eta^2 = 0.93$; interaction between sparseness and CV: $F(8, 1485) = 40.08$, $p = .000$, $\eta^2 = 0.18$.

The ANOVA-results for the unfolding model in the zero cells *in*cluded condition are as follows. Sparseness: $F(4, 1485) = 18331.85$, $p = .000$, $\eta^2 = 0.98$; CV: $F(2, 1485) = 4029.82$, $p = .000$, $\eta^2 = 0.84$; interaction: $F(8, 1485) = 2234.55$, $p = .000$, $\eta^2 = 0.92$. The zero cells *ex*cluded condition has the following results. Sparseness: $F(4, 1485) = 225.94$, $p = .000$, $\eta^2 = 0.38$; CV: $F(2, 1485) = 5768.81$, $p = .000$, $\eta^2 = 0.89$; interaction: $F(8, 1485) = 113.32$, $p = .000$, $\eta^2 = 0.38$.

The ANOVA results together with the pattern of the means in Figure 1 confirm that the variability of the cell frequencies has a positive, compensating effect on the %DAF-values when sparseness is considerable and the zero cells are included in the analysis. At the same time, these results validate the hypothesis that the slide-1 model and the unfolding model can analyze sparse frequency tables as long as there is enough variation in the cell frequencies. It should be noted that in some of the experimental conditions heterogeneous variances and deviations from the normal distribution occur in the %DAF-values. Therefore, the ANOVA results should be interpreted with some caution, although the power level is high enough to detect significant effects in all experimental conditions.

The use of simulated data is inevitable to assess the performance of newly developed methods. We proposed a method that allows for sampling from the multinomial distribution concomitant with manipulation of the variability of the cell frequencies. The method is flexible, precise and easy to use. Although in this study, only three levels of variation of the cell frequencies are used, unlimited number of levels of variation can be created. Moreover, it can be used for frequency tables of any size and in many different situations where the simulation of frequency tables is required. In the present situation, the variability of the cell frequencies was combined with the factor sparseness. It should be noted that this specific combination of factors introduces some limitations on the maximum possible variability levels. In the highest condition of variation, which was created by the division .05/.95, both large and very small probabilities are present. Due to the sampling process, these very small probabilities sporadically result in no observation, which increases the proportion of zero cells in the frequency table. A more strict division, e.g. .01/.99, would have enhanced this effect. Therefore, the highest possible variation level that could be reproduced without causing alterations in the proportion of zero cells equals 1.18. Despite the fact that the presence of the sparseness factor limits the possible levels of the coefficient of variation, we believe that the method proposed in this study offers more control on the data characteristics, which represents an improvement in the simulation of real life data.

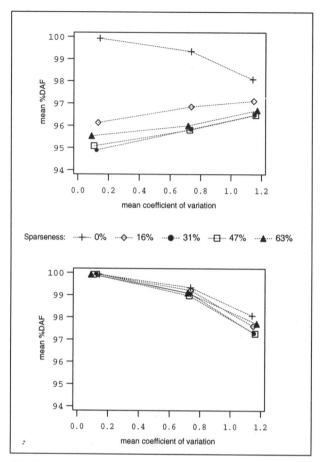

Fig. 1. Mean %DAF-values for Monte Carlo replications under the experimental conditions. Top: slide-1 model, zero cells included. Bottom: slide-1 model, zero cells excluded.

References

De Rooij M, Heiser WJ (2000) Triadic distance models for the analysis of asymmetric three-way proximity data. British Journal of Mathematical and Statistical Psychology 53: 99-119

Heiser WJ, Bennani M (1997) Triadic distance models: Axiomatization and least squares representation. Journal of Mathematical Psychology 41: 189-206

Koehler KJ (1986) Goodness-of-fit tests for log-linear models in sparse contingency tables. Journal of the American Statistical Association 81: 483-493

Upton GJG (1978) The analysis of cross-tabulated data. Chichester: Wiley

Zielman B, Heiser WJ (1993) Analysis of asymmetry by a slide-vector. Psychometrika 58 (1): 101-114

ON THURSTONE'S MODEL FOR PAIRED COMPARISONS AND RANKING DATA

Albert Maydeu-Olivares

Dept. of Psychology. University of Barcelona. Paseo Valle de Hebrón, 171. 08035 Barcelona (Spain).

Summary. We investigate by means of a simulation study whether standard structural equation modeling techniques are suitable for estimating an unrestricted Thurstonian model to: (a) multiple judgment paired comparisons data, and (b) ranking data. We point out that Thurstone's (1927) original model is not a proper model for multiple judgment paired comparisons data as it assigns zero probability to all intransitive paired comparisons patterns. To fit multiple judgment paired comparisons data one must employ Takane's (1987) extension of Thurstone's original model, or alternatively, a Thurstonian correlation structure model, which we introduce. We found that for some models as few as 100 observations suffice to obtain accurate parameter estimates, standard errors and goodness of fit tests when 7 stimuli are modeled (21 binary variables). For other models, however, sample sizes of 1000 observations are needed. All in all, the procedure investigated appears to be an attractive choice to estimate these models.

Keywords: limited information, comparative data, random utility models.

1. Introduction

In 1927 Thurstone suggested a class of models for fitting paired comparison data that has been highly influential in the literature (see Bock & Jones, 1968). In 1931 Thurstone suggested his model could also be suitable for ranking data (after rankings are transformed into paired comparisons). Thurstone's model is simply a multivariate normal density with an structured mean vector and covariance matrix that has been dichotomized. Thus, it is somewhat natural to consider its estimation using existing procedures for structural equation modeling for dichotomous variables (Muthén, 1978, 1993).

In this paper we investigate how well an unrestricted Thurstonian model for paired comparisons and ranking data can be estimated using structural equation modeling procedures for dichotomous variables. To do so, we first introduce Thurstone's original model using matrix notation. Using this notation, it is easy to see that Thurstone's original model is a proper model for ranking data but it is not a proper model for multiple judgment paired comparisons data. Next, we introduce two modifications of Thurstone's model that address this problem. We conclude our presentation with some simulation results to illustrate the performance of structural equation modeling procedures to estimate these models.

2. Thurstone's model

Thurstone (1927) introduced a model for paired comparisons characterized by three assumptions:
1. Whenever a pair of stimuli is presented to a subject it elicits a continuous preference (utility function, or in Thurstone's terminology, *discriminal process*) for each stimulus.
2. The stimulus whose value is larger at the moment of the comparison will be preferred by the subject.
3. These unobserved preferences are normally distributed in the population.

We assume each individual from a random sample responds to all possible $\tilde{n} = \dfrac{n(n-1)}{2}$ paired comparisons, where n denotes the number of stimuli being compared. This has been termed *multiple judgment sampling procedure* (Bock & Jones, 1968). Thus, we obtain a $\tilde{n}$-dimensional vector of binary variables $\mathbf{y}$ from each respondent such that

$$y_{i,j} = \begin{cases} 1 & \text{if object } i \text{ is chosen} \\ 0 & \text{if object } j \text{ is chosen} \end{cases} \tag{1}$$

for all pairs $\{i, j\}$. Then, letting $\mathbf{t}$ denote the n-dimensional vector of continuous preferences in Thurstone's model such that $\mathbf{t} \sim N(\mu_t, \Sigma_t)$, we write

$$\mathbf{y}^* = \mathbf{A}\,\mathbf{t}, \tag{2}$$

where $\mathbf{A}$ is a $\tilde{n} \times n$ design matrix where each column corresponds to one of the stimuli, and each row to one of the paired comparisons. For example, when $n = 4$, $\mathbf{A}$ is

$$\mathbf{A} = \begin{bmatrix} 1 & -1 & 0 & 0 \\ 1 & 0 & -1 & 0 \\ 1 & 0 & 0 & -1 \\ 0 & 1 & -1 & 0 \\ 0 & 1 & 0 & -1 \\ 0 & 0 & 1 & -1 \end{bmatrix}. \tag{3}$$

Finally,

$$
y_{i,j} = \begin{cases} 1 & \text{if } y_{i,j}^* \geq 0 \\ 0 & \text{if } y_{i,j}^* < 0 \end{cases} \tag{4}
$$

These equations describe in matrix notation Thurstone's (1927) model applied to multiple judgment sampling paired comparisons data. To analyze ranking data, Thurstone (1931) suggested transforming each ranking pattern into a vector of $\tilde{n}$ binary variables using

$$
y_{i,j} = \begin{cases} 1 & \text{if object } i \text{ is ranked above object } j \\ 0 & \text{if object } i \text{ is ranked below object } j \end{cases} \tag{5}
$$

and applying his model for paired comparisons data to these data.

Under Thurstone's model the probability of any paired comparisons pattern is

$$
\Pr\left(\bigcap_{i,j} y_{i,j} \right) = \int_{\mathbf{R}} \cdots \int \phi_{\tilde{n}}\left(\mathbf{y}^* : \boldsymbol{\mu}_{y^*}, \boldsymbol{\Sigma}_{y^*} \right) d\mathbf{y}^* \tag{6}
$$

$$
\boldsymbol{\mu}_{y^*} = \mathbf{A}\boldsymbol{\mu}_t \qquad\qquad \boldsymbol{\Sigma}_{y^*} = \mathbf{A}\boldsymbol{\Sigma}_t\mathbf{A}' \tag{7}
$$

where $\phi_{\tilde{n}}(\bullet)$ denotes a $\tilde{n}$-variate normal density function and $\mathbf{R}$ is the multidimensional rectangular region formed by the product of intervals

$$
R_{i,j} = \begin{cases} (0,\infty) & \text{if } y_{i,j} = 1 \\ (-\infty,0) & \text{if } y_{i,j} = 0 \end{cases}. \tag{8}
$$

We can perform a change of variable of integration in (6) and standardize $\mathbf{y}^*$ using

$$
\mathbf{z}^* = \mathbf{D}\left(\mathbf{y}^* - \boldsymbol{\mu}_{y^*} \right) \qquad\qquad \mathbf{D} = \left(\text{Diag}\left(\boldsymbol{\Sigma}_{y^*} \right) \right)^{-\frac{1}{2}}. \tag{9}
$$

As a result, $\boldsymbol{\mu}_{z^*} = \mathbf{0}$ and

$$
\boldsymbol{\tau} = -\mathbf{D}\boldsymbol{\mu}_{y^*} = -\mathbf{D}\mathbf{A}\boldsymbol{\mu}_t \qquad\qquad \mathbf{P}_{z^*} = \mathbf{D}\boldsymbol{\Sigma}_{y^*}\mathbf{D} = \mathbf{D}\left(\mathbf{A}\boldsymbol{\Sigma}_t\mathbf{A}' \right)\mathbf{D} \tag{10}
$$

where $\boldsymbol{\tau}$ denotes a vector of thresholds $\tau_{i,j}$, and the off-diagonal elements of $\mathbf{P}_{z^*}$ are tetrachoric correlations. As a result, (6), can be equivalently rewritten as

$$
\Pr\left(\bigcap_{i,j} y_{i,j} \right) = \int_{\check{\mathbf{R}}} \cdots \int \phi_{\tilde{n}}\left(\mathbf{z}^* : \mathbf{0}, \mathbf{P}_{z^*} \right) d\mathbf{z}^* \tag{11}
$$

where $\check{\mathbf{R}}$ is now a multidimensional rectangular region formed by the product of intervals

$$\tilde{R}_{i,j} = \begin{cases} \left(\tau_{i,j}, \infty\right) & \text{if} \quad y_{i,j} = 1 \\ \left(-\infty, \tau_{i,j}\right) & \text{if} \quad y_{i,j} = 0 \end{cases}. \tag{12}$$

Equations (10), (11), and (12) define in fact a class of models as μ_t and Σ_t can be restricted in various ways. Takane (1987) provides an excellent overview of restricted Thurstonian models. Here we shall concentrate on the *unrestricted* Thurstonian model, a model where only minimal identification restrictions are imposed on μ_t and Σ_t.

A very interesting feature of Thurstone's original model is that since $\mathbf{A}$ is of rank $n - 1$, Σ_y has rank $n - 1$. As a result, Thurstone's model assigns zero probabilities to all the $2^{\tilde{n}} - n!$ intransitive paired comparisons patterns (those patterns that do not correspond to ranking patterns). Thus, Thurstone's model is not a plausible model for multiple judgment paired comparisons data, but it may be a suitable model for ranking data (Maydeu-Olivares, 1999).

3. Thurstonian models appropriate for multiple judgment paired comparisons

We now describe two different solutions to the problem of specifying a Thurstonian model that assigns non-zero probabilities to all $2^{\tilde{n}}$ binary patterns.

3.1 The Thurstone-Takane model

Takane (1987) proposed adding a random error to each paired comparison so that $\mathbf{y}^* = \mathbf{A}\,\mathbf{t} + \mathbf{e}$. Furthermore, he assumed that

$$\begin{pmatrix} \mathbf{t} \\ \mathbf{e} \end{pmatrix} \sim N\left(\begin{pmatrix} \mu_t \\ \mathbf{0} \end{pmatrix}, \begin{pmatrix} \Sigma_t & \mathbf{0} \\ \mathbf{0} & \Omega^2 \end{pmatrix}\right) \tag{13}$$

where Ω^2 is a diagonal matrix with elements $\omega_{i,j}^2$.

Under this model, the probability of any paired comparisons pattern is given also by (6) and (8) but now $\mu_{y^*} = \mathbf{A}\mu_t$ and $\Sigma_{y^*} = \mathbf{A}\Sigma_t\mathbf{A}' + \Omega^2$. Furthermore, performing the change of variable of integration (9), we can write these pattern probabilities as (11) and (12) where instead of (10) we have

$$\tau = -\mathbf{D}\mathbf{A}\mu_t \qquad\qquad \mathbf{P}_{z^*} = \mathbf{D}\left(\mathbf{A}\Sigma_t\mathbf{A}' + \Omega^2\right)\mathbf{D} \tag{14}$$

Takane (1987) also proposed an interesting special case of this model in which it is assumed that $\Omega^2 = \omega^2\mathbf{I}$.

3.2 Thurstonian correlation structure models

The Thurstone and Thurstone-Takane models are mean and covariance structure models in the sense that they impose constraints on the mean vector and covariance matrix of y^*. However, as only the binary choices are observed, the covariance matrix of y^* can only be estimated from a correlation matrix. Moreover, to estimate the parameters of these models one must resort to pre and post-multiply the covariance structure by the inverse of a diagonal matrix of model-based standard deviations. This results in complex non-linear restrictions on the thresholds and tetrachoric correlations.

An alternative solution to the problem of specifying a proper model for multiple judgment paired comparison data within a Thurstonian framework is to specify restrictions on the means and correlations of y^* while leaving the structure for the variances of y^* unspecified. Now, the mean and covariance structures for y^* implied by Thurstone's model are $\mu_{y^*} = A\mu_t$ and $\Sigma_{y^*} = A\Sigma_t A'$. Thus, we shall assume $\mu_{y^*} = A\mu_t$. Also, by parsimony we shall assume $P_{y^*} = \text{Off}\left(A\Sigma_t A'\right)$, where Off($\bullet$) denotes the restrictions imposed on the off-diagonal elements of a correlation matrix. That is, we assume that the restrictions on the correlations among y^* have the same functional form as the restrictions of Thurstone's model on the covariances among y^*. Then, the probability of any paired comparisons pattern under this Thurstonian mean and correlation structure model is

$$\Pr\left(\bigcap_{l=1}^{\tilde{n}} y_l\right) = \int_R \cdots \int \phi_{\tilde{n}}\left(y^* : \mu_{y^*}, P_{y^*}\right) dy^* \tag{15}$$

with limits of integration (8). These pattern probabilities are unchanged when we transform y^* using $z^* = y^* - \mu_{y^*}$. As a result, $\mu_{z^*} = 0$ and

$$\tau = -A\mu_t \qquad\qquad P_{z^*} = \text{Off}\left(A\Sigma_t A'\right) \tag{16}$$

where now the pattern probabilities are given by (11), (12) and (16).

This model is more restrictive than the Thurstone-Takane model. However, unlike (14), the restrictions in (16) are linear.

4. Limited information estimation and testing

We shall now discuss minimal identification restrictions for the models just described. These minimal identification restrictions yield unrestricted models.

Given the comparative nature of the data, in all cases it is necessary to set the location of the elements of μ_t and the location of the elements in each of the rows (columns) of Σ_t. Arbitrarily, we set $\mu_n = 0$ and $\Sigma_t = P_t$ (a matrix with ones along its diagonal). In addition, in the Thurstonian ranking model it is necessary to fix one of the elements of P_t (Dansie, 1986). Arbitrarily, we set $\rho_{n,n-1} = 0$. Also, in the Thurstone-Takane model, if Ω^2 is assumed to be diagonal it is necessary to set the location for its elements; arbitrarily we set $\omega_{\tilde{n}}^2 = 1$. Alternatively, if $\Omega^2 = \omega^2 I$ is assumed, we impose the constraint $\omega^2 = 1$.

Now, we collect the observed paired comparisons patterns in a $\tilde{n}$-way binary contingency table. We have seen that the models under consideration assume that the contingency table arises by dichotomizing a $\tilde{n}$-dimensional multivariate standard normal density according to a set of thresholds while imposing constraints - given by Eq. (10), (14), and (16)- on the thresholds and tetrachoric correlations. Muthén (1978, 1993) has proposed well established methods for estimating dichotomized multivariate normal structural models from the univariate and bivariate marginals of the contingency table. Here, we investigate whether Muthén's (1993) approach is suitable for these type of models by means of a simulation study.

In this estimation procedure, first each threshold is estimated separately from the univariate marginals of the contingency table via. Then, each of the tetrachoric correlations of the contingency table is estimated separately from the bivariate marginals of the contingency table given the estimated thresholds. Finally, the model parameters are estimated from the estimated thresholds and tetrachoric correlations using an unweighted least squares (ULS) function. His method yields asymptotically correct standard errors and tests of the structural restrictions imposed by the model on the thresholds and tetrachoric correlations. The latter are obtained by adjusting the minimum of the ULS fitting function by its mean (T_s) or by its mean and variance (T_a). Recently, Maydeu-Olivares (2001) has proposed a similar adjustment to the sum of squared residuals to the univariate and bivariate margins of the table, which gives us a limited information test of the overall restrictions imposed by the model on the contingency table. The degrees of freedom available for testing when fitting paired comparisons models is $r = \dfrac{\tilde{n}(\tilde{n}+1)}{2} - q$, where q is the number of model parameters. When fitting ranking data it is necessary to adjust for the number of redundancies among the univariate and bivariate marginals which arise from having $2^{\tilde{n}} - n!$ structural empty cells in the contingency table. The number of degrees of freedom in this case is

$$r = \frac{\tilde{n}(\tilde{n}+1)}{2} - \sum_{x=2}^{n-1}\binom{x}{2} - q \quad \text{(Maydeu-Olivares, 1999)}.$$

We provide in Table 1 the simulation results obtained in estimating a model for 7 stimuli. Hence $\tilde{n} = 21$ binary variables were modeled. Sample size was 500. The true parameters were

$$\mu_t = (0.5, 0, -0.5, 0, 0.5, -0.5, 0)', \rho_t = (0.8, 0.7, 0.6, 0.8, 0.7, 0.6, \cdots, 0.8, 0.7, 0.6)'$$

where ρ_t denotes the elements below the diagonal in P_t. In the Thurstone-Takane model where Ω^2 was assumed to be diagonal, we used as true values $\Omega^2 = \mathbf{I}$. 1000 replications were used for each of the three models estimated.

In this table we point out the largest relative bias (in %) observed in the parameter estimates and standard errors. We also provide the empirical rejection rates for the test statistics at $\alpha = 0.05$. They should be as close as possible to 0.05. Finally, we also provide the value of D_{KS}, the Kolmogorov-Smirnov one-sample test. The null hypothesis of a chi-square distribution for the empirical distribution of the test statistic is rejected at $\alpha = 0.05$ if $D_{KS} > 1.35$.

As can be seen in this table, for this particular choice of true generating values and sample size:
1. The performance of the tests statistics considered depends on the model. In all cases the mean and variance adjusted test statistics of overall restrictions matched well its reference chi-square distribution as indicated by D_{KS}.
2. Accurate parameter estimates and standard errors (largest relative bias $< |10|$%) were obtained for all models but for the Thurstone-Takane model when Ω^2 is assumed to be diagonal.

Table 1. Simulation results

model	maximum relative bias (%)						D_{KS} statistic (RR at $\alpha = 0.05$)			
	par. estimates			standard errors			structur. tests		overall tests	
	μ_t	P_t	Ω^2	μ_t	P_t	Ω^2	T_s	T_a	T_s	T_a
(A) Thurstone's	<1	<1	-	-3	-4	-	3.9 (13.9)	2.3 (4.2)	7.9 (26.3)	1.2 (6.4)
(B) TT, Ω^2 diagonal	2	-5	29	-8	-17	22	1.0 (5.5)	1.8 (2.2)	7.8 (23.0)	0.8 (5.6)
(C) TT, $\Omega^2 = \omega^2 I$	1	-1	-	-5	4	-	1.2 (6.1)	2.1 (2.4)	8.5 (25.2)	0.9 (5.0)
(D) correlation struct.	<1	<1	-	-1	-6	-	2.2 (9.4)	2.2 (3.8)	7.8 (24.6)	1.1 (4.3)

In Thurstone's model we fixed $\rho_{7,6} = .6$ (the true value) to calculate relative bias
Thurstone's model was fitted to ranking data, the other three models to paired comparisons
TT, Thurstone-Takane model; RR, rejection rate in %, should be close to 0.05.

Additional simulation studies with these true generating values reveal that accurate parameter estimates, standard errors and goodness of fit tests can be obtained for model (B) with 1000 observations, with model (A) with 300 observations, and with models (C) and (D) with as few as 100 observations.

5. Discussion and conclusions

Classical estimation procedures for Thurstonian models (e.g., Bock & Jones, 1968) estimate the model parameters using only the univariate means of the binary variables. These procedures are clearly unsatisfactory because:

1. The sample means are not independent. Standard errors and tests of the goodness of fit of the model computed under an independence assumption will be incorrect.

2. Unrestricted Thurstonian models and many restricted models are not identified from univariate information only. However, any Thurstonian model can be identified as soon as bivariate information is employed.

We have shown that using univariate and bivariate information it is possible to obtain accurate parameter estimates, standard errors and tests of goodness of fit to Thurstonian models for paired comparisons and ranking data with very small samples, even in large models. We have also pointed out that Thurstone's original model is suitable for ranking data, but that it is not a proper model for multiple judgment paired comparisons data. We have discussed two classes of classes of Thurstonian models suitable for these data: a correlation structure model, and a covariance structure model (the Thurstone-Takane model). These two models are not equivalent because the Thurstone-Takane model is not scale invariant. Although the choice between a Thurstonian covariance vs. a correlation structure model should be substantively motivated, it is also important to consider model fit and estimation issues in choosing between these models.

References

Bock, R.D. & Jones, L.V. (1968). *The measurement and prediction of judgment and choice*. San Francisco: Holden-Day.

Dansie, B.R. (1986) Normal order statistics as permutation probability models. *Applied Statistics, 35*, 269-275.

Maydeu-Olivares, A. (1999). Thurstonian modeling of ranking data via mean and covariance structure analysis. *Psychometrika, 64*, 325-340.

Maydeu-Olivares, A. (2001). Limited information estimation and testing of Thurstonian models for paired comparison data under multiple judgment sampling. *Psychometrika, 66*, 209-228.

Muthén, B. (1978). Contributions to factor analysis of dichotomous variables. *Psychometrika, 43*, 551-560.

Muthén, B. (1993). Goodness of fit with categorical and other non normal variables. In K.A. Bollen & J.S. Long [Eds.] *Testing structural equation models* (pp. 205-234). Newbury Park, CA: Sage.

Takane, Y. (1987). Analysis of covariance structures and probabilistic binary choice data. *Communication and Cognition, 20*, 45-62.

Thurstone, L.L. (1927). A law of comparative judgment. *Psychological Review, 79*, 281-299.

Thurstone, L.L. (1931). Rank order as a psychological method. *Journal of Experimental Psychology, 14*, 187-201.

Two kinds of space in psychophysics

Tarow Indow

Department of Cognitive Sciences, University of California, Irvine, CA 92697 U.S.A.

Summary. Colors can be represented as points in a 3-D space. We have various color spaces and each is a means to specify colors according to a specified principle. We are not necessarily obliged to regard that all aspects of the spatial representation are meaningfully related to perceptual properties of colors. In psychophysics, we have a space that is not a means of representation. It is visual space (VS) that one perceives in front of the self. It is a perceptual reality as the final product of a long series of processes starting from retinal image of the physical space (X). In spite of that VS is based on multiple glances, it is stable and structured in accordance with the condition of X. Hence, it is a challenging problem to make explicit its geometrical properties under various conditions of X. Studies of the author on the two above-mentioned spaces will be summarized. Psychophysical scaling and construction of formal models will play fundamental roles.

Key words: Color system, visual space, scaling, multidimensional mapping

1 Visual Space and Color

The first step of the series of processes to produce *Visual space* (VS) is the retinal image of the *physical space* (X), which is formed according to physical laws. The next process is the excitation of physiological processes in the retina that are finally conveyed to the brain. The last process is our awareness of VS according to which we can guide our movement in X. VS as a total entity extends around the *self* in three directions. The self is the percept of our *body* as a physical organism. This awareness is mainly due to proprioceptive stimulation in the body. When we say "P appears far to the right direction", for instance, the distance and direction are meant from the self as the origin of VS. In other words, the process underlying VS is of multiple sources and must be extended over a wide area in the brain. It is a process integrated over time also. Nevertheless, VS supported by this process is experienced as a united stable entity in which many percepts are geometrically embedded. In the neighborhood of the self, geometrical patterns we see in VS are isomorphic to the stimulus pattern in X. Otherwise, we cannot move around in X. Beyond this range, however, how a perceptual pattern is related to the stimulus pattern in X is complex and dynamic. Since we cannot see an infinite distance in VS, a physical stimulus sufficiently far away in X appears at a finite distance from the self in VS. Since we cannot see the void, we always see a surface at the end of line of sight. In this sense, VS is closed and continuous at the boundary. The surface always has a color, chromatic or achoromatic. The sky appears as a vault, bluish when it is fine and grayish when it is cloudy. The form of the retinal image and spectrum of light respectively determine the structure and color of a percept in VS.

2 Systems of Surface Color

The number of colors we can discriminate one from another is about 7 million. Hence, to identify each color, we have a few options than representing colors as points in a space. According to the principle by which colors are allocated, we have various *color spaces*. Color can appear in various modes. Herein it suffices to mention only two modes, *aperture color* and *surface (object) color*. The former is the color we see in a small hole. The aperture appears to be filled by the color floating in the air. The latter is the color we see on the surface of a percept located somewhere in VS. We can touch a surface color. In the case of aperture color, we feel as if our finger penetrates into the color. An exceptional case that an extended surface appears in the aperture color mode is the blue sky.

Correspondence between color and spectrum $P(\lambda)$ of light is one to (indefinitely) many. By psychophysical experiments to establish a matching between two light stimuli in a small opening, the Commission Internationale de l'Eclairage (CIE) has succeeded to define a 3-D space in which all spectra $P(\lambda)$ yielding a color under the standard observing condition are specified by a point (x, y, Y). Modern color reproduction technology, such as color TV, is based on this system. The reflected light from a physical object in X and the light coming from its image on a TV monitor are not the same in $P(\lambda)$, but these are close when converted in (x, y, Y). We can uniquely define an aperture color as a point and the region of colors around it that are indiscriminable from that color. But, as to two distinct points, this system does not specify how the two colors are perceptually different to each other. In this sense, this is a topological space but not a metric space to represent color difference. We have color spaces of a different type in which surface colors are allocated as points in accordance with their perceptual relationships. Often, these are called color-order-systems. The systems most often used are the Munsell system, the OSA-Uniform Color Scale, German DIN-system and Swedish Natural Color System (NCS). Only the Munsell system will be discussed below. This has been constructed entirely based on human assessments on perceptual attributes of surface colors.

We can specify a color as (H, V/C) by comparing it with the Munsell solid, standard color chips arranged according to cylindrical coordinates (Fig.1 D), where the vertical axis in the center represents lightness V, polar angle and distance represent hue H and saturation C. The standard chips have been selected so

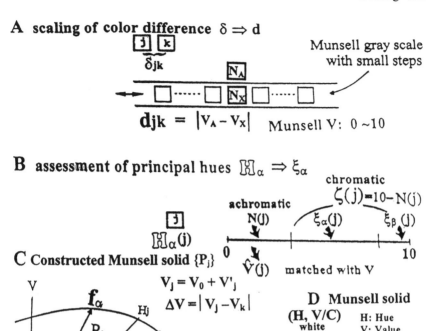

A scaling of color difference $\delta \Rightarrow d$

δ_{jk}

Munsell gray scale with small steps

$d_{jk} = |V_A - V_X|$ Munsell V: 0 ~10

B assessment of principal hues $\mathbb{H}_\alpha \Rightarrow \xi_\alpha$

chromatic

achromatic

$\zeta(j) = 10 - N(j)$

$N(j)$ $\xi_\alpha(j)$ $\xi_\beta(j)$

$\mathbb{H}_\alpha(j)$

$\hat{V}(j)$ matched with V

C Constructed Munsell solid $\{P_j\}$

$V_j = V_0 + V'_j$

$\Delta V = |V_j - V_k|$

(H, C)-plan at V_0

$d_{jk}(H, C)$

D Munsell solid
(H, V/C)

H: Hue
V: Value
C: Chroma

white

7/8

6/12 6/10

5/12

4/13 4/12

5YR

10R

5RP

black 5R 10RP

Fig. 1. Testing the Structure of Munsell Color Solid

that chips neighboring along respective axes represent the same magnitude of uni-attribute color difference. In the stage of construction, no due attention has been paid to equating units for the three attributes and to multi-attribute color differences. Namely, Fig.1 D is a schematic spatial representation of colors. In order for making the solid to be more than that, we must find the way to relate the distance $\hat{d}_{jk}$ between any two points P_j (H_j V_j/C_j) and P_k (H_k V_k/C_k) to difference δ_{jk} we see between the two colors. Over forty years, the author has been concerned with this problem (Table 1 in Indow 1988a).

The perceptual color difference δ_{jk} is a *latent variable* in the sense that no other person than the subject can experience it. The method of converting δ_{jk} to an observable variable d_{jk} is shown in Fig.1 A. The subject is asked to select such a pair of grays (N_A, N_x) that the difference matches δ_{jk} in size. The Munsell gray series ranging from black (V=0) to white (V=10) is a most well established equal-appearing interval scale. In the figure, N_A is fixed and the series below is Munsell grays with a small step, e.g., 0.4V. The subject moves this part to select one N_X by comparing (N_A, N_X) with a presented pair of colors (j, k) under the same illumination and on the same background. The matching is repeated with different N_A's, and the mean difference $|V_A-V_X|$ over repetitions and subjects is defined as the scale value d_{jk} for δ_{jk}. Thus is obtained a matrix of differences between N colors (d_{jk}), N×N. In experiments after 1980, N is larger than 100 (Indow 1988a). The assessment is limited to such (j, k) in which the quantity-type experience δ_{jk} is felt real, because if two colors are too different, e.g., (saturated red and green), they are simply entirely different. Hence, $d_{jk} < 4.0V$ and the matrix (d_{jk}) has a number of vacant cells.

A color j appears to be reddish, yellowish, etc., with various degree of saturation. A procedure to scale these *latent variables* is shown in Fig.1 B. The subject is asked first to divide a line segment of length 10 into two parts, $N(j)$, and $\zeta(j)$, in accordance with the degrees of grayness and chromaticness in the color. Then, $\zeta(j)$ is divided further into $\xi_\alpha(j)$ according to the degrees of principal hues α. In the Munsell system, R(red), Y(yellow), G(green), B(blue), and P(purple) are taken as principal hues. For a color j, only one or two hue components are sufficient to describe its chromaticness, e.g., R and Y for an orange color. Means over repetitions and subjects are defined as $N(j)$ and $\xi_\alpha(j)$, each has the possibility of varying from 0 to 10. Thus is obtained a matrix of absolute principal hue components $(\xi_\alpha(j))$, $5 \times N$ (Indow, 1999a).

Through a number of experiments, various sets of (d_{jk}) and $(\xi_\alpha(j))$ were obtained and it became apparent by the use of various forms of multidimensional mapping that we can define in a 3-D space a configuration of N points $\{P_j\}$ that has the following properties (Fig.1 C). 1) Euclidean distances $\hat{d}_{jk}$ between P_j and P_k numerically reproduce d_{jk} with the accuracy that the root-mean-squares (RMS) of $(d_{jk} - \hat{d}_{jk})$ is 0.2 ~ 0.3 V (Indow 1988a). Notice that discrimination threshold of lightness is about 0.15V. 2) Radial vectors $\mathbf{f}_\alpha$, α = R, Y, G, B, P, can be defined in a plane orthogonal to the axis V so that data $\xi_\alpha(j)$ is a power function of coordinate $\hat{\xi}_\alpha(j)$ of P_j on $\mathbf{f}_\alpha$. Munsell H and C are represented in this plane. An interesting finding is that the most representative blue in Munsell notation, 5B, is not exactly the color that subjects call blue, and purple P is not indispensable.

Thus, $\{P_j\}$ in Fig.1 C is a means to represent d_{jk} and the global structure of Munsell solid in a 3-D manifold with locally Euclidean metric. In $\{P_j\}$, there is a geometrical structure between $\hat{d}_{jk}$ and $(\Delta V, \Delta \hat{\xi}_\alpha, \Delta \hat{\xi}_\beta$, the angle between $\mathbf{f}_\alpha$, and $\mathbf{f}_\beta)$.

The possibility was pursued that the generation of $\hat{d}_{jk}$ and hence δ_{jk} is represented by this geometrical structure, but the result was not very satisfactory. I am inclined to regard $\{P_j\}$ as a means for giving a spatial representation for (d_{jk}) and

{$\mathbf{f}_\alpha$} only. In order to understand the mechanism by which δ_{jk} is generated, it seems to be more productive to relate d_{jk} with ($\Delta V, \Delta \hat{\xi}_\alpha, \Delta \hat{\xi}_\beta$) in a different way from the geometrical structure visible in Fig.1 C (1999b).

3 Geometrical Figures in Visual Space

We can ask the subject to adjust a configuration of stimulus points {Q_j} in an m-dimensional physical space X^m so as to yield the visual pattern {P_j} in the VS^m that satisfies a specified perceptual property. In an experiment shown in Fig.2 C (Indow 1982), all Q's (small black points) were presented in the horizontal plane at the eye-level ($\theta = 0$). The surface of table and the walls around it was covered with white sheets and the eyes of subject were at an edge of the table. Hence, what the subject saw was a configuration of points in VS^2 with no spatial framework. Two Q_1's at the furthest end were fixed and other Q's were movable. The series of black dots, including Q_1's, appear straight and parallel in VS^2. The series are called *P-alley*. Each pair of white dots, including Q_1's, appears in VS^2 being separated with the same distance. These series of Q_j's are called *D-alley*. Each series of Q_j's, j = 2 to 6, appears straight and frontoparallel. This series is sometimes called a horopter and denoted as *H-curve*. That P- and D-alleys do not coincide has been known since the beginning of the last century. Luneburg proposed in 1947 an idea that visual patterns in this subspace VS^2 are governed by hyperbolic geometry. For the reason to be stated below, he regarded VS as a Riemannian space R of constant curvature K. Then, that D-alley is outside of P-alley implies that K < 0.

A hyperbolic space can be depicted on a sheet of paper (Fig.2 B). This is a representation given by Poincare and will be called Euclidean map (EM^3) (Indow 1979). In Fig.2 B, broken circle presents the location that corresponds to Q's at infinity in X. As pointed out in 1, however, all radial distances in VS are finite and the dotted circle represents the boundary of a finite VS. Luneburg defined all curves for P- and D-alleys and H-curves within this semi-circle in EM^2 of $\vartheta = 0$, and using a set of mapping functions (below Fig.2 A,B), he projected the respective curves into X^2. These curves have only two free individual parameters, K in EM and σ to relate radial distance ρ_0 in EM to convergence angle γ. Fig.2 C is {Q_i} of a subject who participated in this type of experiment for the first time and all curves with the estimated parameter values fit the results very well. Values of K and σ under various conditions with many subjects are given in Table 1 of Indow and Watanabe (1984). It was also shown in this article that the discrepancy between P- and D-alley is not an artifact of the experimental procedure. I extended the Luneburg's model in two ways. One is to define P-and D-alleys in a perceptual plane appearing frontoparallel and the other is to make mapping relation between EM^3 and X^3 more flexible.

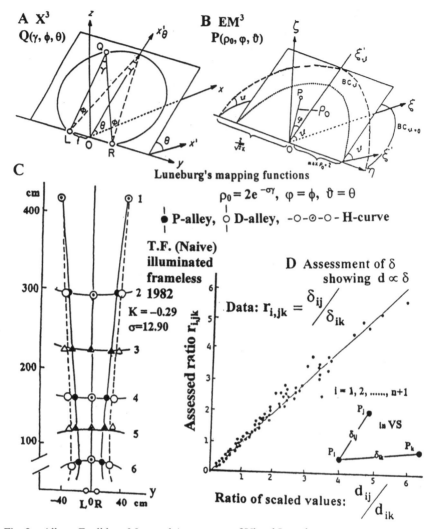

Fig. 2. Alleys, Euclidean Map, and Assessment of Visual Length.

Parallel lines we usually perceive are on a frontoparallel plane in VS and these run either horizontally or vertically. Hence, equations for a frontoparallel plane and P-and D-alleys on it were developed in EM³, and experiments were performed to adjust $\{Q_j\}$ to appear frontoparallel and to appear horizontally parallel or equidistant. The result was conclusive. The P-and D-alleys of 4m long at a distance of about 3m in X³ coincided with each other (Indow 1988b, Indow, Watanabe 1988). Let us call a frontoparallel sub-space in VS as *H-plane* and a subspace extending forward from the self as *D-plane*. If we regard VS³ as a R³ of constant K,

$K = 0$ in H-plane and $K < 0$ in D-plane. This conclusion does not change even if we analyze the results $\{Q_i\}$ without using the Luneburg's mapping functions.

We can ask the subject to assess lengths of perceived line segments. It is particularly easy when two segments start from the same point as shown in Fig.2 D. The subject can give a number $r_{i,jk}$, the ratio between perceived distances δ_{ij} and δ_{ik}, provided the ratio is not too extreme. From a matrix $\{r_{i,jk}\}$, scaled value d_{jk} for δ_{jk} can be determined with a common unit. Fig.2 D shows an example how ratio of scaled values numerically reproduces assessed ratio of δ's. Always the subject is capable of assigning ratios consistently. If we have a scaled distance matrix (d_{jk}) with $\{Q_j\}$, an experimentally obtained configuration of alleys, then we can map $\{Q_j\}$ into EM^3 as $\{P_j\}$ so that inter-point distance $\hat{d}_{jk}$ is proportional to data d_{jk} and we can fit the theoretical curves to the respective series of P_j. In this mapping, we need a value of K only. It was found that the value of K that gives the best fit is negative in D-plane and zero in H-plane (Indow 1982; Indow and Watanabe 1988). In so far as we use the Luneburg's mapping functions, we cannot go beyond a "fremeless" space, because the correspondence between $\{Q_j\}$ and $\{P_j\}$ is sensitive to the structure of framework in VS, e.g., the wall. This is the reason that all alley experiments have been conducted with configuration of light points Q's in the dark or small objects Q's in a frameless space under illumination (Fig.2 C). If we use (d_{jk}), we are free from this constraint. The mapping between VS and X varies according to the general structure of X. If the entire retina is exposed to homogeneous light of sufficiently low intensity, the generated VS has no structure and it is simply a mist of light (Ganzfeld). When some image is formed on the retina, a structured VS is generated and its structure is determined by the general pattern of image. It is my intention to make explicit the intrinsic structure of VS that is generated under a fixed condition of X.

The matrix (d_{jk}) provides us one more important information. All P's on a P-alley are collinear in VS. For P_i, P_{i+1}, P_{i+2}, it was found that $d_{i,i+3} = d_{i,i+1} + d_{i+1,i+2}$ (Fig.13 in Indow 1991). Since d is proportional to δ (Fig. 2 D), we can say that the latent variable δ behaves as a real metric and VS is a metric space. This is a confirmation of a basic postulate of Luneburg. Most studies of visual perception are concerned with local phenomena and take it for granted that VS in that region is Euclidean. If VS is a metric space and locally Euclidean, it means that VS is a Riemannian space R. The value of Gaussian total curvature K in R can vary from region to region. It is called the Helmholtz-Lie problem to conclude that the physical space X must have a constant K because a physical object can move from one position to another without changing its size (free mobility). As to VS, the free-mobility condition is subtler, because we have to deal with the invariance of a perceived figure. In order to keep the size of a figure moving away from the self in VS, the size of its physical counterpart in X must be appropriately adjusted according to distance. In an H-plane or in a D-plane, we can adjust the length of a variable line so as to match the length of a standard line, no matter where the two are located and how the two are oriented. This fact implies that K is constant within the respective planes. The sign of K cannot be specified by the free mobility condition. From the discrepancy of P-alley being inside D-alleys (Fig.2 C), we can conclude that $K < 0$ in the D-plane of $\theta = 0$. From the coincidence between P- and D-alleys in the H-plane, $K = 0$. In fact, this is the space on which ancient mathematicians drew figures.

That $K = 0$ in H-plane and $K < 0$ in D-plane matches our daily experience. Strictly speaking, congruence of and similarity between two figures is possible only in the plane of $K = 0$. Congruence is possible if K is constant but similarity is not possible unless $K = 0$. We can see similarity between the original figure in a H-plane at a distance and its picture at our hand (another H-plane). Although we may be able to establish congruence in a D-plane, it may not be possible to have proportionality both in lengths and angles between two figures when these are different in size and in distance from the self in VS (Indow 1999c). Since a figure cannot directly move from an H-plane to a D-plane, it is not contradictory that two planes have different sign of K.

The largest VS that we can have is the outdoor scene in which the horizon is visible. The horizon always appears at the eye-level in VS. However, how far the sky and horizon appear depends upon what physical object is visible in a given direction (Indow 1997). This fact was demonstrated in an experiment using stars as Q_j. The perceived shape of the night sky, $\{P_j\}$ constructed from (d_{jk}), changed in accordance with what were visible in each direction (Indow, 1991).

References

Indow, T. (1979) Alleys in visual space. J Math Psych 19 : 221- 258.

Indow, T. (1982) An approach to geometry of visual space with no a priori mapping functions: Multidimensional mapping according to Riemannian metrics. J Math Psych. 26 : 204-236.

Indow, T. (1988a) Multidimensional studies of Munsell color solid. Psych. Rev 95 : 456-470.

Indow, T. (1988b) Alleys on an apparent frontoparallel plane. J Math .Psych, 32: 259-284.

Indow, T. (1991) A critical review of Luneburg's model with regard to global structure of visual space. Psych Rev 98: 430-453.

Indow, T. (1997) Hyperbolic representation of global structure of visual space. J Math Psych 41 : 89-98.

Indow, T. (1999a) Predictions based on Munsell notation. II. Principal hue components. Color Res and Appl 24 : 19-32.

Indow, T. (1999b) Principal hue curves and color differences. Color Res and Appl 24 : 266-279.

Indow, T. (1999c) Global structure of visual space as a united entity. Math Soc Sci : 38, 377-392.

Indow, T. Watanabe, T. (1984) Parallel- and distance- alleys with moving points in the horizontal plane. Perception and Psychophysics 35 :144 -154.

Indow, T. Watanabe, T. (1988) Alleys on an extensive apparent frontoparallel plane: A second experiment. Perception 17 : 647-666.

A Variable Variance Model: A Critical Formulation of Fechner's Problem

Yasuharu Okamoto[1]

Department of Psychology, Japan Women's University, 1-1-1 Nishi Ikuta, Tama-ku, Kawasaki 214-8565, Japan

Summary. Fechner's original formulation of the logarithmic law has been criticized because of the replacement of differences by differentials in its derivation. In a revised formulation, Dzhafarow and Colonius (1999) introduced differentials and integration in their model, in which psychophysical distances are calculated by integration. But their model does not explicitly treat Weber's function and the variability of the variance of sensation intensity. Weber's function is one of the important constituents of psychophysics. Variability of the variance of sensation intensity plays a crucial role in psychophysical laws, as shown in this paper. These two factors were explicitly introduced into a new formulation of Fechner's problem by Okamoto (1993, e.g.), using Thurstonian model and a psychometric function. In the current paper, Okamoto's model is first introduced and then some special cases of the model are presented. Then the criticism against the logarithmic law is examined in reference to the variability of the variance of sensation intensity.

Key words. ' Power law, logarithmic law, discrimination, Weber's function, Ekman's law

1 Introduction

Fechner's problem is concerned with the scaling of sensation, especially based on discrimination data. Minimum differences between stimulus intensities that can be discriminated are called just noticeable differences abbreviated as JNDs. JNDs are thought to be constant over the range of the subjective sensation scale. So, it might be expected that the sensation scale could be obtained by the JND as a unit. Furthermore, replacing differences called JNDs by differentials and using Weber's law, we get a differential equation which leads to the logarithmic law. But, this process of derivation has problems, as pointed out, for example, by Luce and Ed-

---

[1] I would like to thank Professor Shizuhiko Nishisato for his detailed comments on earlier versions.

wards (1958). This conceptual difficulty can be resolved in the framework called the revised Fechner problem, as formulated by Luce and Galanter (1963, p.210):

$$u[s + \Delta(s,\pi)] - u(s) = g(\pi) \tag{1}$$

where, s represents physical intensity, u the corresponding sensory intensity, $\Delta(s,\pi)$ JND for discrimination probability π, and $g(\pi)$ the corresponding constant value of differences in the sensory scale u.

In the framework of the revised Fechner problem, JND can be any small value, which is determined by discrimination probability π. This arbitrariness of the size of JND allows the use of differential equation and can be used to justify the type of approach, adopted by Dzhafarov and Colonius[2] (1999), that is, essentially Thurstonian as is shown below:

Rewrite Eq. (1) as

$$\pi = g^{-1}\{u[s + \Delta(s,\pi)] - u(s)\}$$

Following the Dzhafarov-Colonius notation (1999), change the symbols π, u, s and Δ to p, ϕ, x and w, respectively, so that

$$p = g^{-1}\{\phi[x + w(x,p)] - \phi(x)\}. \tag{2}$$

The fact that this equation is essentially Thurstonian becomes apparent, when we set g^{-1} as follows,

$$g^{-1}(z) = \int_{-\infty}^{z} N(x)dx,$$

where $N(x)$ represents the standard normal distribution.

In this case, Eq.(2) becomes

$$p = \int_{-\infty}^{\phi[x + w(x,p)] - \phi(x)} N(t)dt. \tag{2'}$$

The above equation is the well-known Case V of Thurstone's model (1927).

From Eq. (2'), it follows that

$$dp \propto d\phi.$$

Integrating both sides of this equation, we obtain

$$G(a,b) = \phi(b) - \phi(a) \propto \int_{a}^{b} dp,$$

where $G(a,b)$ gives a sensory scale with the origin at the point corresponding to the physical intensity a.

The above derivation may appear intuitional, and perhaps a more rigorous one than that may be obtained by following Dzhafarov and Colonius (1999):

Rewrite Eq. (2) as

---

[2] In 1995, Colonius sent me a comment on Okamoto (1995).

$$\gamma_x(y) = h\{\phi(y) - \phi(x)\},\tag{3}$$

where

$$h = g^{-1}, \quad y = x + w(x, p) \quad \text{and} \quad \gamma_x(y) = p$$

This change of notation is based on Dzhafarov and Colonius (1999).

Differentiating the above equation by y, we obtain

$$\frac{d}{dy}\gamma_x(y) = \frac{dh}{d\phi} \cdot \frac{d\phi}{dy} = h'[\phi(y) - \phi(x)] \cdot (d\phi/dy).$$

As a special case, set

$$y = x \quad \text{and} \quad F(x) = \frac{d}{dy}\gamma_x(y)\Big|_{y=x},$$

And then we obtain

$$F(x) = h'(0) \cdot (d\phi/dx).$$

Hence,

$$\phi(b) - \phi(a) = (1/h'(0)) \cdot \int_a^b F(x)dx.$$

By a suitable choice of the scale unit, that is., replacing scale $h'(0) \cdot \phi$ by ϕ, we obtain

$$G(a,b) = \phi(b) - \phi(a) = \int_a^b F(x)dx\tag{4}$$

Eq.(4) is the same as presented by Dzhafarov and Colonius (1999, p.248), who also used the following expression

$$G(a,b) = \int_a^b d\gamma_x(x).\tag{4'}$$

There are, however, some problems with the Dzhafarov-Colonius model (1999):

(a) The assumption that the variances of sensation are constant is clear, when we consider their model in terms of Thurstone's Case V model, Eq. (2'). The equally–often–noticed–difference problem (Luce and Galanter, 1963, p.211) also presupposes the constant variance assumption. In fact, Luce and Galanter (1963, p.216) suggest that this problem has a solution if and only if the variances of the sensation differences are constant. But, Falmagne (1985, p.144 – 145) shows that in Thurstone's Case III, the equally-often-noticed-difference problem has a solution not only under the constant variance assumption but also under the linearly variable variance condition with the mean. In the latter case, the difference is calculated over the scale constructed as logarithmic transformation of the original sensory scale (Falmagne, 1985, p. 136).

(b) The relation between the above equation and Weber's law is not clear. Weber's law is one of the relations essential in psychophysics.

2 Assumption of the Constant Variance in Sensation

Validity of the assumption that the variance of sensation is constant is doubtful.
As counter examples against this constant variance assumption, we can cite (a)
Ekman's law and (b) asymmetrical ROC curve.
(a) Ekman's law

Stevens (1975, p.235) concludes that the Fechner-Thurstone assumption that
the variability in psychological units is constant along the psychological continuum is adequate for metathetic continua (e.g., pitch), but not for prothetic
continua (e.g., loudness), and propose that the principle of linear growth of
subjective variability should be called Ekman's law.
(b) Asymmetrical ROC Curve

Green and Swets (1966, e.g. p.95) proposed the following relation:

$$\Delta m / \Delta \sigma = 4 .$$

Choosing the unit and origin of the scale such that
$$\sigma_N = 1.0, \quad \mu_N = 0.0 ,$$

we have

$$\mu_S = \mu_N + \Delta m = \Delta m$$

$$\sigma_S = \sigma_N + \Delta \sigma = \sigma_N + (1/4)\Delta m = 1 + (1/4)\mu_S$$

That is, the variance is not constant, for it is a linear function of μ_S

3 Variable Variance Models

Okamoto (1993, 1995, e.g.) proposed models, which allow variances of sensation
to vary. The models are based on two main relations, Thurstonian modeling (Eq.
5) and psychometric function (Eq. 6). Thurstonian modeling represents the relation between discrimination probability and psychological intensities.

$$P(X_2 > X_1) = \int_{-\infty}^{(\psi(S_2) - \psi(S_1))/\sqrt{\sigma(S_2)^2 + \sigma(S_1)^2 - 2r\sigma(S_1)\sigma(S_2)} + o(\psi(S_2) - \psi(S_1))} \phi_0(x) \cdot dx \qquad (5)$$

In Eq. (5), X_1 and X_2 are two random variables, which represent the sensations
invoked by the two physical intensities, S_1 and S_2. $\psi(S_1)$ and $\psi(S_2)$ are
means of X_1 and X_2, and $\sigma^2(S_1)$ and $\sigma^2(S_2)$ variances of X_1 and X_2.
r represents the correlation coefficient between X_1 and X_2. o(little oh)-
notation (e.g. Apostol, 1974) is introduced, because the equation is required to
hold asymptotically at the point, where the discrimination probability is 0.5.

The psychometric function represents the relation between discrimination probability and physical intensities.

$$P(X_2 > X_1) = \int_{-\infty}^{k(S_1) \cdot \frac{S_2 - S_1}{S_1} + o(S_2 - S_1)} \phi_0(x) \cdot dx \tag{6}$$

In the above formulas, Eqs. (5) and (6), the assumption that $\phi_0(x)$ is the standard normal distribution is not essential. Eqs. (5) and (6) may take the following general forms with some technical constraints, Eqs. (7) and (8),

$$\mathrm{Pr}ob(X_2 > X_1) = T\left\{ \frac{\psi(S_2) - \psi(S_1)}{[\sigma^2(S_1) + \sigma^2(S_2) - 2r\sigma(S_1)\sigma(S_2)]^{1/2}} \right\} \tag{7}$$

$$\mathrm{Pr}ob(X_2 > X_1) = W\left(\frac{1}{k(S_1)} \cdot \frac{S_2 - S_1}{S_1} \right) \tag{8}$$

From Eqs. (5) and (6), we have

$$\frac{\psi(S_2) - \psi(S_1)}{[\sigma^2(S_1) + \sigma^2(S_2) - 2r\sigma(S_1)\sigma(S_2)]^{1/2}} + o[\psi(S_2) - \psi(S_1)] = \frac{1}{k(S_1)} \cdot \frac{S_2 - S_1}{S_1} + o(S_2 - S_1)$$

Replacing S_1 and S_2 with x and y, we have

$$\frac{\psi(y) - \psi(x)}{[\sigma^2(x) + \sigma^2(y) - 2r\sigma(x)\sigma(y)]^{1/2}} + o[\psi(y) - \psi(x)] = \frac{1}{k(x)} \cdot \frac{y - x}{x} + o(y - x)$$

As y approaches x, the above equation becomes Eq. (9).

$$\frac{d\psi}{dx} = \frac{\sigma(x) \cdot \sqrt{2(1 - r)}}{k(x) \cdot x} \tag{9}$$

Eq. (9) represents interrelation among physical intensity x, sensory (psychological) intensity ψ, the variance of sensation $\sigma^2(x)$, and Weber's function $k(x)$. That $k(x)$ represents Weber's function can be shown as follows:
Put

$$0.75 = \int_{-\infty}^{z_{0.75}} \phi_0(t)dt = \int_{-\infty}^{\frac{1}{k(x)} \cdot \frac{x_{0.75} - x}{x}} \phi_0(t)dt \ .$$

Then, we have

$$k(x) \approx (1/z_{0.75}) \cdot \{(x_{0.75} - x)/x\}.$$

Because $(x_{0.75} - x)/x$ is Weber's fraction for discrimination probability 0.75

and $1/z_{0.75}$ is constant, we see that $k(x)$ is Weber's function, ignoring constant term $1/z_{0.75}$.

4 Special Cases of The Variable Variance Model

By specifying functions $\sigma(x)$ and $k(x)$, we have the following cases:.

(a) Logarithmic Law:

Let

$k(x) = c = const$:   Weber's Law,

$\sigma(x) = c_1 = const$:   Constant variance, where equal differences in the sensory scale produce the same discrimination probability,

then we have

$$d\psi/dx = \left\{ c_1 \cdot \sqrt{2(1-r)} \right\} / (c \cdot x).$$

Let

$$\alpha = \left\{ c_1 \cdot \sqrt{2(1-r)} \right\} / c = const,$$

then we have

$$d\psi/dx = \alpha \cdot (1/x)$$

$$\psi = \alpha \cdot \log x + \beta, \quad \beta : \text{some constant.}$$

(b) Power Law:

Let

$k(x) = c = const$:   Weber's Law,

$\sigma(x) = \alpha \cdot \psi(x)$:   Ekman's Law,

then we have

$$d\psi/dx = \left\{ \alpha \cdot \psi(x) \cdot \sqrt{2(1-r)} \right\} / (c \cdot x)$$

Let

$$\beta = \left\{ \alpha \cdot \sqrt{2(1-r)} \right\} / c = const,$$

then we have

$$d\psi/dx = \beta \cdot \left\{ \psi(x)/x \right\},$$

$$\log \psi = \beta \cdot \log x + \gamma, \quad \gamma : \text{some constant,}$$

$$\psi = e^{\gamma} \cdot x^{\beta} = a \cdot x^{\beta}, \quad \text{where } a = e^{\gamma}.$$

(c) Near-miss to Weber's Law:

Let

$k(x) = \alpha \cdot x^{\gamma}$:   Near-miss to Weber's Law,

$\sigma(x) = \beta \cdot x^{\delta}$:   Including cases of constant variance ($\delta = 0$) and Ekman's law,

then we have

$$\frac{d\psi}{dx} = \frac{\beta x^{\delta} \cdot \sqrt{2(1-r)}}{\alpha x^{\gamma} \cdot x} = \frac{\beta \cdot \sqrt{2(1-r)}}{\alpha} \cdot x^{\delta - \gamma - 1}$$

Hence, we obtain

$$\psi = \frac{\beta \cdot \sqrt{2(1-r)}}{\alpha} \cdot \frac{1}{\delta - \gamma} \cdot x^{\delta - \gamma} + b, \quad b : \text{some constant}$$

$$= a \cdot x^{c} + b,$$

where $a = \left\{\beta \cdot \sqrt{2(1-r)}\right\} \Big/ \left\{\alpha(\delta - \gamma)\right\}$, b and $c = \delta - \gamma$ are constants

5 Discussion

The variable variance model Eq. (9) is for scales based on discrimination data. As for this kind of scales, Fechner's logarithmic law is well known. Against the logarithmic law, Stevens proposed a power law. The power law is based on direct methods. Stevens (1936) says that the same number of JNDs do not yield equal differences in loudness. But, this criticism is valid only in the case of the constant variance of sensation, and the constant variance assumption is doubtful because Ekman's law or asymmetric ROC curve do not follow from this assumption.

Moreover, validity of the power law, which is based on direct methods, is criticized as follows:

(a) Psychological/experimental validity of the method of fractionation is questioned by the experimental result of Garner (1954). He shows that fractionation was strongly affected by the range from which the stimuli were sampled.

(b) The power law itself can be produced by a non-sensory process. Baird's (1997) Number Preference Model produces a power law.

(c) Direct methods, on which the power law stands, are based on the assumption that the subject can judge the ratio of sensory magnitudes. But, Laming (1997) proposes that the judgment by the subject is ordinal and categorical even in the direct method.

The above criticisms (a) – (c) show that the validity of the power law has not been established. More empirical study on direct methods is needed before we meaningfully compare the two types of scales, the scale based on direct methods and the other on discrimination probability.

6 REFERENCES

Apostol,T.M. (1974). *Mathematical analysis, 2nd ed.* Massachusetts: Addison-Wesley Publishing Company.
Baird,J.C. (1997). *Sensation and judgment: Complementarity theory of psychophysics.* Mahwah: Lawrence Erlbaum Associates, Publishers.
Dzhafarov,E.N. and Colonius,H. (1999). Fechnerian metrics in unidimensional and multidimensional stimulus spaces. *Psychonomic Bulletin & Review*, 6, 239 – 268.
Falmagne,J.-C. (1985). *Elements of psychophysical theory.* Oxford: Oxford University Press.
Garner,W.R. (1954). Context effects and the validity of loudness scales. *Journal of Experimental Psychology*, 48, 218 – 224.
Green,D.M. and Swets,J.A. (1966). *Signal detection theory and psychophysics.* New York: John Wiley and Sons,Inc.
Laming,D. (1997). *The measurement of sensation.* Oxford: Oxford University Press.
Luce,R.D. and Edwards,W. (1958). The derivation of subjective scales from just noticeable differences. *Psychological Review*, 65, 222 – 237.
Luce,R.D. and Galanter,E. (1963). Discrimination. In R.D.Luce, R.R.Bush and E.Galanter (Eds.), *Handbook of mathematical psychology*: Vol. 1. (pp. 191 – 243). New York: John Wiley and Sons, Inc.
Okamoto,Y.(1993). *Just-noticeable difference and sensation scale.* Poster session presented at the annual meeting of the Japanese Psychonomic Society, Tokyo, Japan. (Summary of the presentation, The Japanese Journal of Psychonomic Science, 1993, 12, 60, in Japanese.)
Okamoto,Y.(1995). *Psychophysical scales and discriminability.* Unpublished manuscript.
Stevens,S.S. (1936). A scale for the measurement of a psychological magnitude: Loudness. *Psychological Review*, 43, 405 – 416.
Stevens,S.S. (1975). *Psychophysics: Introduction to its perceptual, neural, and social prospects.* New York: John Wiley & Sons.
Thurstone,L.L. (1927). A law of comparative judgment. *Psychological Review*, 34, 273 – 286.

An Application of a Multiplicative Utility for Non-commutative Joint Receipts to Portfolio Choice

Yutaka Matsushita

Izumi Research Institute, Shimizu Corporation, Fukoku-Seimei Building, 2-2-2, Uchisaiwai-Cho, Chiyoda-Ku, Tokyo 100-0011, Japan (yutaka@ori.shimz.co.jp)

Summary. The concept of joint receipt is useful for some decision problems, such as portfolio choice. The aim of this paper is to apply a multiplicative utility for non-commutative joint receipts to a concrete decision problem in which the non-commutativity plays an important role. First, postulations are introduced in portfolio choice so that the joint receipt operation can be non-commutative. Secondly, measurement methods of the multiplicative utility are developed according to prospect theory (Kahneman and Tversky 1979). Finally, it is shown that the multiplicative utility and its compound utility can explain preferences in a decision problem in Tversky and Kahneman (1981, 1986).

Key words. Joint receipt, Non-commutativity, Multiplicative utility, Risk aversion, Risk seeking

1 Introduction

The joint receipt of lotteries means that one receives two or more lotteries at once, and it is expressed by an operation joining several lotteries. Therefore it will be effective for describing combinations of uncertain alternatives, such as portfolios. Several utility models were already proposed to represent preferences over joint receipts of lotteries: Luce (1995) developed a utility function for commutative joint receipts of lotteries; Matsushita has formulated a multiplicative utility for non-commutative joint receipts.

This paper, taking a decision problem in Tversky and Kahneman (1981, 1986) as an example, considers an application of the multiplicative utility to this decision problem. Postulations are prepared to make the joint receipt operation non-commutative and to make the multiplicative utility practical. More precisely, it is assumed that two lotteries (a gain lottery and a loss lottery) in each joint receipt are evaluated according to different standards of decision, one of which is averse to risk and the other of which inclines us to seek risk. As a result, the multiplicative utility becomes the multiplication of two linear utilities that correspond to these types of standards of decision.

The main result is that two sorts of measurement methods of the multiplicative utility are proposed. One method sets each linear utility concave or convex according as the standard of decision is risk averse or risk seeking. The other method, following the idea of weighting functions (Kahneman and Tversky 1979), underweights or overweights probabilities for winning consequences according as the standard of decision is risk averse or risk seeking. Based on these measurement methods, this paper shows that the multiplicative utility and a compound of this utility and an operator can explain preferences in the above decision problem. Here the compound utility expresses a variation of each joint receipt.

2 Concepts and Notations

Let $\succsim$ be a binary relation on a nonempty set A. As usual, strict preference $\succ$ denotes the asymmetric part of $\succsim$ and indifference $\sim$ the symmetric part. The binary relation $\succsim$ on A is a *weak order* if it is connected ($a \succsim b$ or $b \succsim a$ for all $a, b \in A$) and transitive ($a \succsim b$ and $b \succsim c \Rightarrow a \succsim c$ for all $a, b, c \in A$). A real-valued function u on a weakly ordered set A is *order-preserving* if it satisfies the condition $a \succsim b \Leftrightarrow u(a) \geq u(b)$ for all $a, b \in A$. A *utility function* on $(A, \succsim)$ is an order-preserving function that is a homomorphism for an algebra structure on A.

Let $X = \{x_1,\ldots,x_n\}$ be a finite set of prizes, where n is a positive integer, and assume X is nonempty. A *lottery* is a probability distribution $p = (x_1, p_1; x_2, p_2; \ldots; x_n, p_n)$ assigning probability p_i to prize x_i for all $i = 1,\ldots,n$ ($\sum_{i=1}^{n} p_i = 1$, $p_i \geq 0$). A *degenerate lottery* is a lottery p such that $p(x_i) = 1$ for some $x_i \in X$, denoted by $1_{\{x_i\}}$. Every lottery p is expressed as a convex combination $\sum_{i=1}^{n} p_i 1_{\{x_i\}}$ of the $1_{\{x_i\}}$. Let P be the set of all lotteries. Clearly P is a nonempty convex set. Let $\succsim$ be a binary relation on P. In this paper, $(P, \succsim)$ is supposed to satisfy the axioms of the von Nuemann-Morgenstern theory (Fishburn 1988), (hence $\succsim$ is a weak order), and the term *linear utility* is used to denote a utility function on $(P, \succsim)$ that is linear in the convexity operation.

A *joint receipt operation* $\oplus$ is an operation joining two or more lotteries such that $p \oplus q$, where p and q are lotteries, means that one receives both p and q. A typical example is the combination of securities in portfolio choice. P^c is the set of all entities that are inductively defined from elements of P using $\oplus$ finitely many times. Clearly the joint receipt operation $\oplus$ is a binary operation on P^c. Assume P^c is endowed with a weak order $\succsim$. The associativity and commutativity of $\oplus$ are written in the weak sense: for all $p, q, r \in P^c$,

Associativity of $\oplus$: $(p \oplus q) \oplus r \sim p \oplus (q \oplus r)$.

Commutativity of $\oplus$: $p \oplus q \sim q \oplus p$.

Although neither commutativity nor associativity has been examined empirically for joint receipts of lotteries, we will suppose henceforth that $\oplus$ is weakly associative on P^c for mathematical expediency. Moreover, if $\oplus$ is weakly commutative, then elements of P^c are said to be *commutative joint receipts*, otherwise elements are said to be *non-commutative joint receipts*.

3 A Utility Function for Non-commutative Joint Receipts

Throughout the rest of the paper we shall use $\oplus$ only for the non-commutative joint receipt operation.

Let k be a positive integer, and let $K = \{1,...,k\}$. Let $P^{(k)} = \{p_1 \oplus \cdots \oplus p_k \mid p_1 \in P,$ $...,p_k \in P\}$. The set P^c equals the union of $P^{(k)}$ over all $k = 1, 2, 3, \ldots$. Let $\succsim_K$ be the restriction to $P^{(k)}$ of $\succsim$ on P^c. So $\succsim_K$ is a weak order on $P^{(k)}$. For each $i = 1,...,k$ let u_i be a linear utility on a weakly ordered set $(P, \succsim_i)$.

In this paper, we concentrate our attention on a utility function on $(P^{(k)}, \succsim_K)$ that is of the multiplicative form

$$U_K(p_1 \oplus \cdots \oplus p_k) = u_1(p_1) \cdots u_k(p_k). \tag{1}$$

Here each linear utility u_i is unique up to multiplication by a positive real number (not a positive affine transformation).

As is easily seen, the order-preserving and multiplicative properties of U_K imply a monotonicity axiom of $\oplus$. Other axioms (weak multilinearity of $\oplus$ etc.) are necessary for the formulation of Eq. (1). However, this paper does not discuss how the multiplicative utility is formulated any more because for this we need knowledge of multilinear algebra. Instead, assuming the existence of the multiplicative representation (Eq. (1)) of $(P^{(k)}, \succsim_K)$, this paper considers application of this utility function. See the Appendix for a brief comment on the reason for adopting the multiplicative form as a utility function on $(P^{(k)}, \succsim_K)$.

In the following section we write U and $\succsim$ instead of U_K and $\succsim_K$ because only the case where $k = 2$ (hence $K = \{1, 2\}$) is considered.

4 Measurement of Multiplicative Utility and its Application

4.1 A Decision Problem and Postulations

We prepare a decision problem in Tversky and Kahneman (1981, 1986), which was used to explain a certain type of framing effect.

Example 1. Subjects were asked to make two choices (one between gain lotteries and one between loss lotteries), with the understanding that the two selected options would be played out independently and simultaneously:

$$p = (\$ 240, 1.00) \quad \text{vs.} \quad q = (\$ 1000, 0.25; \$ 0, 0.75)$$

$$r = (-\$ 750, 1.00) \quad \text{vs.} \quad s = (\$ 0, 0.25; -\$ 1000, 0.75).$$

About 84% of subjects chose p over q, and 87% chose s over r. Because the subjects considered the two decisions simultaneously, they had in effect to choose one joint receipt from the set $\{p \oplus r, p \oplus s, q \oplus r, q \oplus s\}$. The most common pattern (i.e. $p \oplus s$) was chosen by 73 % of subjects, while the least popular pattern (i.e. $q \oplus r$) was chosen by only 3 % of subjects.

We can express the above majority choices as $p \succ_1 q$ and $s \succ_2 r$, where $\succsim_1$ and $\succsim_2$ are preference relations on gain lotteries and on loss lotteries, respectively. The majority preference for the two joint receipts can be written $p \oplus s \succ q \oplus r$.

Because the decision problem in Example 1 is considered henceforth, we may restrict all joint receipts in this paper to ones consisting of gain lotteries and loss lotteries (so that no lotteries with mixed consequences (gains and losses) are contained in joint receipts). Moreover, we acknowledge the following postulations:

P1. One of the two lotteries in each joint receipt is evaluated based on a decision standard averse to risk, and the other is evaluated based on a decision standard seeking risk. For simplicity, two lotteries are aligned as follows: the first is evaluated based on a risk reluctant standard and the second based on a risk seeking standard.

P2. Gain lotteries and loss lotteries are compared separately, and then their joint receipts are evaluated.

The former part of P1 says that different types of decision standards are prepared for lotteries, and the latter part of P1 is a mere rule for convenience. The former part will be rational for portfolio choice because portfolios tend to be made up of various types of lotteries with the lotteries evaluated separately according to the extent of risk. It is difficult to integrate options without computational aids in portfolio choice (Tversky and Kahneman 1981, p. 455). Actual meanings of the two postulations are as follows. First, P1 makes joint receipts non-commutative. Secondly, P2 allows us to give positive utilities both to gain lotteries and to loss lotteries. Indeed, the multiplicative utility representation causes the following problem: $0 > u_1(p) > u_1(q)$ and $0 > u_2(s) > u_2(r)$ imply $U(q \oplus r) > U(p \oplus s)$. But P2 prevents the occurrence of this problem.

Note that a pair of majority choices $p \succ_1 q$, $s \succ_2 r$ in Example 1 is a common pattern: choices involving gains are usually risk averse, and choices involving losses are often risk seeking. So it is natural that gain lotteries (respectively, loss lotteries) should be compared based on a risk reluctant standard (respectively, a risk seeking standard). However, we will compare these lotteries based on these two types of standards in Section 4.3. Henceforth let $\succ_1$ and $\succ_2$ be a risk averse preference relation on P and a risk seeking preference relation on P, respectively.

4.2 Concavity and Convexity of Utility and Preference Structure

In this subsection, risk aversion and risk seeking are associated with the concavity and convexity of utility functions, respectively (Kahneman and Tversky 1979). The measurement method proposed below is hypothetical.

Let u_1 and u_2 be linear utilities that represent $\succsim_1$ and $\succsim_2$, respectively. So u_1 is a concave utility function and u_2 is a convex one. The utilities of lotteries p, q, r, s may be given as follows:

$$(u_1(p), u_2(s)) = (0.5, 0.5), \tag{2}$$

$$(u_1(q), u_2(r)) = (0.25, 0.2). \tag{3}$$

Recall that P2 guarantees positive utilities for also loss lotteries. Taking into account the fact that utility functions tend to be steeper for losses than for gains, we make the range of u_i ($i = 1, 2$) for losses twice as great as the range of u_i ($i = 1, 2$) for gains. For example,

$$u_1(0) = 0.0 \text{ and } u_1(1000) = 1.0 \quad \text{for gains,}$$

$$u_2(-1000) = 0.0 \text{ and } u_2(0) = 2.0 \quad \text{for losses.}$$

From the linearity property, we obtain

$$u_2(s) = 0.25 \times u_2(0) + 0.75 \times u_2(-1000) = 0.5,$$

$$u_1(q) = 0.25 \times u_1(1000) + 0.75 \times u_1(0) = 0.25.$$

The utilities of 240 and -750 (i.e. $u_1(p)$ and $u_2(r)$) are determined according to concavity and convexity, as in Eqs. (2) and (3). Figure 1 shows this measurement.

Using these results, we explain the majority preference ($p \oplus s \succ q \oplus r$) in Example 1. For this it suffices to think that subjects compared p with q based on $\succsim_1$ and compared r with s based on $\succsim_2$. Substituting the values in Eqs. (2) and (3) into the multiplicative utility (Eq. (1)) yields

$$u_1(p)u_2(s) = 0.5 \times 0.5 > 0.25 \times 0.2 = u_1(q)u_2(r).$$

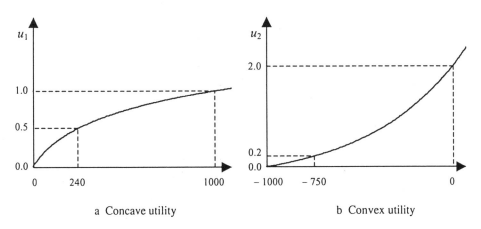

a Concave utility   b Convex utility

Fig. 1a. A concave utility function is used to represent a risk averse preference relation.
b. A convex utility function is used to represent a risk seeking preference relation.

This implies $p \oplus s \succ q \oplus r$. For the converse preference, we think that subjects compared r with s based on $\succsim_1$ and compared p with q based on $\succsim_2$. A similar procedure gives the inequality implying $r \oplus q \succ s \oplus p$. However, it may be unnatural that loss lotteries (respectively, gain lotteries) should be compared according to the risk reluctant standard (respectively, the risk seeking standard). In the next subsection, we will again consider this preference from another point of view.

4.3 A Variation of Each Joint Receipt and Preference Structure

Apart from the concavity and convexity of utility functions, we consider a clear measurement method of utility with the help of the idea of weighting functions (Kahneman and Tversky 1979). (This is also hypothetical.) When evaluating the utility of q in the context of risk averse choices (respectively, risk seeking choices), a decision maker may think that a consequence \$ 0 can be obtain with probability more than 0.75 (respectively, \$ 1000 with probability more than 0.25). A similar thing is assumed to hold with the evaluation of the utility of s. That is, the decision maker underweights or overweights probabilities for winning consequences according as he or she evaluates lotteries in the context of risk averse choices or in the context of risk seeking choices. For example,

Risk aversion	Risk seeking
$q \mapsto q_1 = (\$ 1000, 0.1; \$ 0, 0.9)$	$q \mapsto q_2 = (\$ 1000, 0.5; \$ 0, 0.5)$
$s \mapsto s_1 = (\$ 0, 0.1; -\$ 1000, 0.9)$	$s \mapsto s_2 = (\$ 0, 0.5; -\$ 1000, 0.5)$

Let π_j ($j = 1, 2$) be a transformation on P such that $\sum_{i=1}^n \pi_j(p_i) = 1$ for all $p \in P$ and $\pi_j(1_{\{x_i\}}) = 1_{\{x_i\}}$ for all degenerate lotteries. Here the indices $j = 1$ and 2 denote the risk averse evaluation and the risk seeking evaluation mentioned above, respectively. Then we can write $q_j = \pi_j(q)$ and $s_j = \pi_j(s)$. Let u be a linear utility on P such that it is concave for gains and convex for losses, and set

$$u_j = u \circ \pi_j \quad \text{for each } j = 1, 2.$$

Thus u_1 (respectively, u_2) is a utility function that corresponds to the risk averse (respectively, risk seeing) evaluation. They are linear in the convexity operation.

By this measurement, the utilities of lotteries may be as follows:

$$\begin{pmatrix} u_1(p) & u_1(s) \\ u_2(p) & u_2(s) \end{pmatrix} = \begin{pmatrix} 0.5 & 0.2 \\ 0.5 & 1.0 \end{pmatrix}, \tag{4}$$

$$\begin{pmatrix} u_1(r) & u_1(q) \\ u_2(r) & u_2(q) \end{pmatrix} = \begin{pmatrix} 0.2 & 0.1 \\ 0.2 & 0.5 \end{pmatrix}. \tag{5}$$

Because two utilities are needed for each lottery in the next paragraph, we express them as the matrix expression. (The non-diagonal entries are produced by the alternation of the risk averse evaluation and the risk seeking evaluation.) The linearity property determines $u_i(s)$ and $u_i(q)$ ($i = 1, 2$) as in the previous subsection. Again, P2 makes utilities of loss lotteries positive.

We shall consider the preference structure of a decision maker who chooses $r \oplus q$ over $p \oplus s$ in the context of variation. Indeed, a person may pay attention to a variation of each joint receipt; that is, he or she is anxious about a variation caused by changes of decision standards in evaluating lotteries in each joint receipt.

For this purpose we define a quantity by

$$A_2(p \oplus s) = 1/2 \, (p \oplus s - s \oplus p).$$

More precisely, A_2 is an operator on a vector space into which $P^{(2)}$ is transformed, and the subtraction is that of the vector space (see the Appendix). Let $p \oplus s$ be a joint receipt with lotteries aligned desirably in the sense that $U(p \oplus s) > U(s \oplus p)$. Then $s \oplus p$ is a joint receipt with lotteries aligned inversely. Restrict the multiplicative utility U to the set $A_2(P^{(2)})$ of all such quantities,

$$U(A_2(p \oplus s)) = 1/2 \, \{u_1(p)u_2(s) - u_1(s)u_2(p)\}.$$

Clearly U represents the restriction to $A_2(P^{(2)})$ of the weak order $\succsim$ on $P^{(2)}$. Taking into account the form of $U \circ A_2$, we can regard this compound function as a utility function expressing a variation of each non-commutative joint receipt, which is caused by the alternation of decision standards. Therefore it is proper to make the following rule: the smaller $U(A_2(p \oplus s))$, the more preferable is $p \oplus s$. Let $\succsim'$ denote this preference relation, i.e. $r \oplus q \succsim' p \oplus s \Leftrightarrow U(A_2(p \oplus s)) \geq U(A_2(r \oplus q))$. Substituting the values of Eqs. (4) and (5) into the formula of $U \circ A_2$ yields the inequality

$$2U(A_2(p \oplus s)) = 0.5 \times 1.0 - 0.2 \times 0.5$$

$$> 0.2 \times 0.5 - 0.1 \times 0.2 = 2U(A_2(r \oplus q)).$$

Hence we obtain $r \oplus q \succ' p \oplus s$. This procedure seems to be more rational for portfolio choice because this compound utility function $U \circ A_2$ may be interpreted as a psychological version of variance and covariance.

5 Conclusions

This paper considered an application of the multiplicative utility for non-commutative joint receipts to a decision problem in which the non-commutativity plays an important role. The introduced postulations (P1 and P2) seem to be proper for portfolio choice. Also, the measurement method of the multiplicative utility based on the idea of weighting functions will be useful for portfolio choice. We have at least two further studies. The first is to consider preferences over portfolios consisting of more than two lotteries. Classifying a lot of lotteries into proper groups (e.g. asset allocation), we can decrease the number of lotteries in portfolios (up to five). Indeed, it will be difficult to evaluate portfolios consisting of a great many lotteries correctly. The second study is to propose a multi-criteria decision model (based on a linear utility for commutative joint receipts and the multiplicative utility for non-commutative joint receipts) for portfolio choice, as Markowitz's (1991) mean-variance-criterion model. In this case, it is important to grasp the relationship between commutative joint receipts and non-commutative joint receipts.

References

Fishburn PC (1988) Nonlinear preference and utility theory. Johns Hopkins University Press, Balitimore

Kahneman D, Tversky A (1979) Prospect theory: an analysis of decision under risk. Econometrica 47: 263-291

Luce RD (1995) Joint receipt and certainty equivalents of gambles. Journal of Mathematical Psychology 39: 73-81.

Markowitz HM (1991) Portfolio selection (2nd edition). Blackwell

Tversky A, Kahneman D (1981) The framing of decisions and the psychology of choice. Science 211: 453-458.

Tversky A, Kahneman D (1986) Rational choice and the framing of decisions. In: Hogarth RM, Reder MW (eds) Rational choice. University of Chicago Press, Chicago, pp 67-94.

Appendix

This appendix compensates the definition of the operator $\mathcal{A}_2$ and accounts for adopting the multiplicative form (Eq. (1)) as a utility function on $P^{(2)}$.

By introducing addition and scalar multiplication on $(P^{(2)}, \oplus, \succsim)$, we can transform the space $P^{(2)}$ into a weakly ordered vector space, (which is a straightforward generalization of the totally ordered vector space). Thus subtraction can be defined for elements of $P^{(2)}$, and hence the operator $\mathcal{A}_2$ can be also defined for elements of $P^{(2)}$. Note here that the non-commutative joint receipt operation $\oplus$ is assumed to be an operation that gives a kind of multiplicative structure on P^c, (i.e. $\oplus$ is similar to tensor multiplication). The above addition may be interpreted as the commutative joint receipt operation $\hat{+}$. As a result, P^c is transformed into a vector space with the commutative and non-commutative joint receipt operations. Accordingly, the utility function U on $P^{(2)}$ is a homomorphism for the additive structure on $(P^{(2)}, \hat{+})$, and also a homomorphism for the multiplicative structure on $(P^{(2)}, \oplus)$. The former requires the equation $U(x \hat{+} y) = U(x) + U(y)$ for all $x, y \in P^{(2)}$, and the latter requires the multiplicative form (Eq. (1)).

Multidimensional Scaling of Computer-generated Abstract Forms

Tadasu Oyama[1], Hisao Miyano[2] , and Hiroshi Yamada[1]

[1]Department of Psychology, Nihon University, 3-25-40 Sakurajosui, Setagaya-ku, Tokyo, 156-8550, Japan
[2] Department of Cognitive and Information Science, Chiba University, 1-33 Yayoi-cho, Inage-ku, Chiba, 265-8522, Japan

Summary. We tried to find perceptual attributes of perceived forms and to construct a "perceived-form space" like a perceived-color space, applying a nonmetric individual-differences multidimensional scaling (MDS) technique. Three experiments were conducted on computer-generated abstract forms, varying the frequency and amplitude of sinusoidal or chopping wave superimposed on a circle and the random modulation in the local frequency and amplitude of the waveform. The results of MDS indicated consistently three dimensions, complexity, regularity and curvedness, corresponding to the frequency, the smallness of the random modulation, and the curvature of the waveform, respectively, with high squared Rs. The results of Semantic Differential were highly correlated with the results of MDS.

Keywords. MDS, form perception, perceptual attributes, computer-generated forms, Semantic Differential

1 Introduction

Perceptual attributes or dimensions of colors have long been established, as Hue, Brightness, and Saturation, and reconfirmed with multidimensional scaling (e.g. Indow and Kanazawa, 1960). However, only a few studies have been conducted on perceptual attributes of forms. Some investigators have tried to find perceptual attributes, applying multidimesional scaling on Attneave and Arnoult (1956) type random polygons (Behman and Brown, 1968; Kikuchi, 1971; Zusne, 1970).

We tried to find perceptual attributes of perceived forms and to construct a "perceived-form space" like a perceived-color space, applying a nonmetric individual-differences multidimensional scaling technique included in the SAS MDS procedure, to Yamada and Oyama (1996) type computer-generated   forms, which had been found useful as stimulus-forms for perceptual and cognitive studies, e.g. figural symbolism (Oyama, Yamada, and Iwasawa, 1998) and visual memory (Wada, Yamada, and Oyama, 2000) .

2 General Method

2.1 STIMULUS-FORMS

The original stimulus-form consists of five cycles of sinusoidal waveform superimposed on a circle as shown in Fig.1 a. From this original form, many variations were generated. The frequency and amplitude of waveforms were varied. The curved lines were changed into the straight lines in a half of them. Random modulations were introduced in the local frequency and amplitude of the waveform in some forms. See Appendix for more details.

2.2 PROCEDURE

Undergraduate students participated in experiments individually. The subject was shown a set of cards, on each of which a form was printed.   In the first trial, one

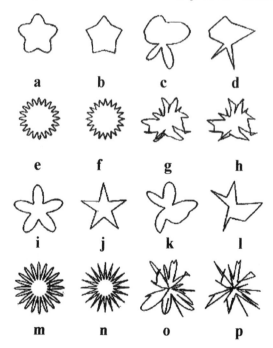

Fig. 1. Computer-generated stimulus-forms used in Experiment 1.

form was randomly selected as the standard. The subject was asked to place other forms on a table in order of their perceived similarities to the standard form. The standard form was changed one-by-one in successive trials, until every form was used as the standard once.

After that, the subject was asked to rate the same 16 stimulus-forms on 11 Semantic Differential scales shown in Table 1 (Oyama et al., 1998).

3 Experiment 1

In Experiment 1, a set of 8 curved and 8 straight-line forms shown in Fig.1 were used.   34 subjects (18 males and 16 females) participated in the experiment.   A 3-dimensional solution shown in Fig.2 was obtained (Stress1= 0.136 ; R^2 =0.828). The obtained dimensions represented "Complexity", "Regularity", and "Curvedness".   "Complexity" corresponded to the frequency of the waveform of the stimuli, "Regularity" to the smallness of random modulation, and "Curvedness"   to the stimulus curvature,   while the amplitude of   the stimulus

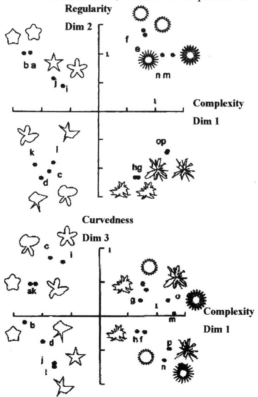

Fig. 2 Three-dimensional MDS solution obtained in Experiment 1.

Table 1.   The regressions of Semantic Differential scales to the MDS dimensions of forms.

Factor	Dimension SD Scale	1 (Complexity)	2 (Regularity)	3 (Curvedness)	R^2
	Good—Bad	-0.478	0.885	-0.057	0.904
Evaluation	Favorite—Unfavorite.	-0.404	0.708	-0.024	0.779
	Beautiful—Ugly	-0.439	1.196	-0.208	0.874
	Dynamic—Static	0.293	-0.480	-0.839	0.904
Activity	Noisy—Quiet	0.336	-0.431	-1.031	0.879
	Showy—Sober	0.338	-0.566	-0.605	0.701
	Bright—Dark	-0.154	0.686	-0.146	0.721
Lightness	Light—Heavy	-0.396	0.239	-0.221	0.400
	Cheerful—Gloomy	-0.003	-0.216	0.280	0.194
	Sharp—Blunt	0.428	0.035	-1.220	0.915
Sharpness	Tense—Loose	1.176	-0.394	-0.584	0.844

waveforms did not show any strong effect. No rotation was made in our study.

The result of each semantic scale was compared with the obtained MDS dimensions. Ten of the 11 scales showed high regressions to some of MDS dimensions, as shown in Table 1.

4 EXPERIMENT 2

In Experiment 2, two sets of stimulus-forms, 12 curved forms and 12 straight-line forms, were used. Four stimuli of each set were selected from the stimuli used in Experiment 1; typical Simple-Regular (i, j), Simple-Irregular (k, l), Complex-Regular (m, n), and Complex- Irregular (o, p) stimuli.   The other 8 new stimulus-forms had intermediate complexities (frequencies of waveform) and/or intermediate irregularities (ranges of random modulation).   Each set of stimulus-forms, curved and straight-line, was presented to 40 subjects (20 males and 20 females) individually in a separate session and the experimental result was analyzed separately.   A 2-dimensional solution for each set revealed two dimensions, "Complexity" and "Regularity" again (Stress1=0.116, 0.116; R^2=0.921, 0.921) as shown in Fig. 3.   In the obtained 2-dimensional "perceived-form space" for each stimulus set, the new 8 stimulus-forms with intermediate complexities   and/or   irregularities   were located in the positions well interpolated between the old four forms. This result indicated that the MDS is useful for to find the detailed inside structure of the "perceived-form space".

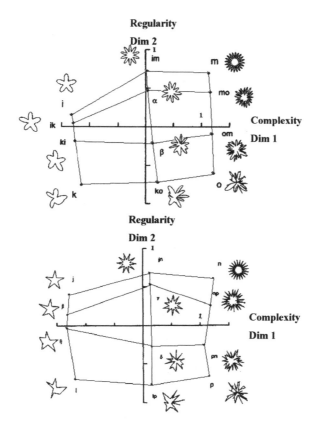

Fig. 3. Two-dimensional MDS solutions obtained for curved stimulus-forms and straight stimulus-forms in Experiment 2. The grids show equal-waveform-frequency or equal-range-of-random-modulation contours.

5 EXPERIMENT 3

In Experiment 3, a set of 16 stimulus-forms, 4 curved forms and 4 straight-line forms selected from the stimulus set of Experiment 1 (i-p) and 8 Attneave and Arnoult (1956) type random polygons (4 to 16 sided) (a1-a8) were used. 39 subjects (17 males and 22 females) participated in the experiment. A 4-dimensional solution was obtained (Stress1 = 0.104; R^2 = 0.902) as shown in Fig. 4. The obtained dimensions represented "Balance", "Complexity", "Regularity", and "Curvedness". In "Balance" dimension, all Yamada and Oyama type forms had positive values while all Atteave and Arnoult type polygons were negative. The 2nd, 3rd, and 4th dimensions corresponded to the 1st, 2nd, and 3rd dimensions in Experiment 1, respectively. In these three dimensions, the two

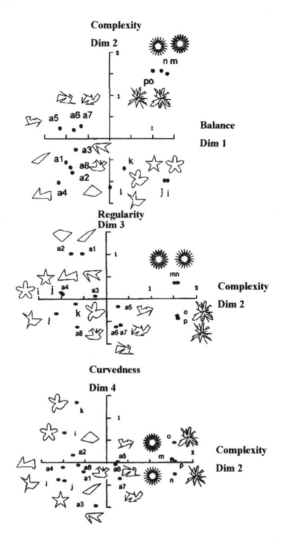

Fig. 4. Four-dimensional MDS solution for 8 Yamada-Oyama type forms and 8 Attneave-Arnoult type forms.

types of stimulus-forms were mixed in their locations.

6 Conclusion

Three perceptual dimensions, "Complexity", "Regularity", and "Curvedness" were found consistently with nonmetric individual-differences MDS analyses in three experiments. "Complexity" corresponded to the frequency of the waveform in the Yamada and Oyama type computer-generated forms, "Regularity" to the smallness of random modulation, and "Curvedness" to the stimulus curvature of these forms. Not only large variations in the frequency and random modulation, but also medium variations were reflected appropriately in locations in the obtained MDS space.

Acknowledgement We are most grateful to Masami Watanabe, Yuki Motobayashi, and Yuji Wada for their assistance.

7 References

Attneave, F. & Arnoult, M. D. (1956) The quantitative study of shape and pattern recognition. Psychological Bulletin, 53, 452-471.

Behman, B. W. & Brown, D. R. (1968) Multidimensional scaling of forms : A psychophysical analysis. Perception & Psychophysics, 4, 19-25.

Indow, T., & Kanazawa, K. (1960) Multidimensional mapping of Munsell colors varying in hue, chroma, and values. Journal of Experimental Psychology, 59 , 330-336.

Kikuchi, T. (1971) A comparison of similarity space and semantic space of random shapes. Japanese Psychological Research, 13, 183-191.

Oyama, T.,Yamada, H.& Iwasawa, H.(1998) Synesthetic tendencies as the basis of sensory symbolism : A review of a series of experiments by means of semantic differential. Psychologia , 41, 203-215.

Wada, Y. Yamada, H., & Oyama, T. (2000) Studies on form cognition (6). Effect of the meaningfulness of forms on visual memory. Japanese Journal of Psychonomic Science, 19, 47-48.

Yamada, H. & Oyama, T. (1996) Studies on form cognition (1). Quantitative control of stimulus-forms. Japanese Journal of Psychonomic Science, 15, 61.

Zusne, L. (1970) Visual perception of forms. New York: Academic Press.

8 Appendix: Algorithm of Form Construction

8.1 General

We developed an algorithm for generating figures which varies from very simple regular geometric forms to very complex irregular forms in terms of a small number of variables. The basic thought is that any form of figures could be represented by a set of feature points and straight and/or curved lines which connect between them. Therefore, our algorithm determine the number of feature points and their positions at first, and then how they are connected by straight lines or curved lines. The way of positioning a set of feature points includes two steps. The initial step is to determine the positions of feature points according to the composite functions of a circle and a sinusoidal wave. The second step is to displace them in stochastically random way. After positioning feature points, they are connected by straight lines or Hermite interpolation curves.

8.2 Initial positioning of feature points

First, a set of feature points are positioned along with a composite function expressing a circle with a certain size and a sinusoidal wave with certain cycles and amplitudes. To reduce the number of variables, the size of the circle to be used here is fixed at the radius of 100 pixels. The cycles and the amplitudes of a sinusoidal wave are variables. One cycle of the unit sinusoidal wave is defined as the circumference of the circle. The unit of the amplitude is the same as that of the radius. Following the composition, the positions of feature points are determined in terms of the positions of the flexion points of the composite curved lines, in other words, the positions at 1/4 and 3/4 phases of each cycle in the sinusoidal wave.

8.3 Displacement of feature points

Initial positions of feature points are displaced in a stochastically random way. Two independent variable are used. The first one is the amount of displacement in the direction of radiation and the second one is in the direction of the circumference; in other words, the vertical and the horizontal directions on the coordinates of the composed sinusoidal wave. Those amounts vary randomly and independently at each feature point within a given range as a function of uniform random number generation. We call them as vertical and horizontal distortions, respectively.

8.4 Interpolation between feature points

The target figure will be obtained from interpolating between adjacent feature points by straight or curved lines. Interpolation curves are generated with the Hermite interpolation method which can make an approximation of sinusoidal waves.

8.5 Deforming the obtained figures

The following rules of deformation are applied, if necessary, to the obtained figures. 1) Affine transformation: the ratio between the height and width of the whole figure can be changed. 2) Rotation of orientation: the whole figure can be rotated around the origin of the coordinates of whole figure.

Part 7
Classification Method

Time Allocation Modeling for Weekend Travel in Tokyo, Using Combined Utility Maximization and Activity Choice Approaches

Irwan Prasetyo[1], Hirosato Yoshino[1], Daisuke Fukuda[1] and Tetsuo Yai[1]

[1]Department of Civil Engineering, Tokyo Institute of Technology, 2-12-1 O-okayama, Meguro-ku, Tokyo 152-8552, Japan

Summary. Travel time saving benefit is conventionally expressed as a function of wages due to increase in production time. In Japan, value of time saving is considered higher during weekends than on weekdays. The primary reason for this is that people have limited time in the weekend to allocate for activities that are not normally done on a weekday, in particular, recreational activities with family. Explaining the higher value of weekend time saving with the conventional logic of increased production time is rather difficult. So this research proposes a new method that incorporates individual life style priority to explain the phenomenon. The objective of this research is to develop a weekend time allocation model using revealed preference (RP) method with weekend time allocation data and stated preference (SP) method with individual activity extension choice data. The underpinning theories are the psychological theory of needs from Maslow (1970), the utility maximization of consumer theory, and discrete choice models. The resulting model is a combination of two approaches: the utility maximization (using RP data) and activity choice by marginal utility (using SP data).

Keywords. Time Allocation, Activity Extension, Utility Maximization, Choice

1 Introduction and Research Objectives

The value of travel time saving in Japan is considered higher during holidays than on weekdays. The current guideline for value of time for passenger car in weekday is 3,360 yen/vehicle/hour, and 5,040 yen/vehicle/hour for weekends. The primary reason for a higher value of weekend time is that people have limited time in the weekend to spend for activities that are difficult to do on a weekday, in particular recreational activities with family.

The situation also has been explained in terms of weekend wages, accommodation charge, vehicle occupation rates, which are all higher than in the weekdays. Nevertheless, it is still difficult to explain this theoretically. In order to better explain this phenomenon, it seems that there is a need to analyze it from a different perspective instead of relying only on monetary approach.

Several questions or considerations are raised in this research. When economists consider the double producer-consumer role of households, e.g. in Becker (1965) and DeSerpa (1971), question can be raised, like: What would the household think of itself? Do households consider time an input for production or consumption? It is difficult to observe if someone really likes and enjoys working; while the economists may look at it as an act of production, the person may think that it is a consumption act with time as an input, thereby maximizing say, his mental utility. In light of these premises, the objectives of this research are firstly, to explore time saving impact on time allocation from the consumer's point of view. Secondly, this research would like to propose representative model of time allocation considering both the revealed and stated preference of individuals.

2 The Time Allocation Model Framework

The model consists of two types of approaches: the utility maximization and the activity choice model. These approaches use the same form of utility of activity, which is defined as follows.

2.1 Utility of Activity

The researches of Kraan (1995), Kitamura and Supernak (1997), Yamamoto and Kitamura (1999) that dealt with modeling the utility of activity as a function of time are highly useful and served as a starting point for this research. The focus of this research is to work in more detail on the coefficients of the utility function. The proposed utility function is as follows:

$$Max \ U_n = \sum_i \gamma_i \ln(t_{ni} + 1) + \mu \ln(q_n) + \xi \ln(z_n), \tag{1}$$

subject to

$$c_z z_n + \sum_i c_{ui} t_{ni} + G_n \leq R_n \quad \text{and} \quad q_n + \sum_i t_{ni} + T_n \leq H_n. \tag{2}$$

As shown in Eq. (1), the total utility (U_n) of individual n is a function of time spent on activity i (t_{ni}), the time spent for mandatory activities (q_n) and amount of composite goods consumed (z_n). The corresponding parameters are γ_i, μ, and ξ respectively. The activities are classified into six categories $i = 1$ to 6, based on needs. The categories are (1) physical care, (2) homemaking/comfort, (3) family care, (4) work, (5) socialization, and (6) pleasure, based on Maslow's psychological theory applied to a daily context. The constraints for maximizing U_n are income or maximum budget (R_n) and total available time (H_n). These constraints are defined in Eq. (2) where c_z is the unit price of composite goods consumed, c_{ui} is the unit cost for doing activity i (market price), G_n is the total cost of travel and T_n is the total travel time. Having defined the utility function, the first approach in the model is explained in the following section.

2.2 Utility Maximization Using Revealed Preference (RP) Data

The main concept of the approach is that the individual will try to maximize his utility by allocating time for each type of activity. Using the Lagrange method to find the solution of maximization of Eq. (1), with the constraints of Eq. (2) we got:

$$l_n = \sum_i \gamma_i \ln(t_{ni}+1) + \mu \ln(q_n) + \xi \ln(z_n)$$
$$+ \lambda_{nB}\left(R_n - c_z z_n - \sum_i c_{ui}t_{ni} - G_n\right) + \lambda_{nT}\left(H_n - q_n - \sum_i t_{ni} - T_n\right). \tag{3}$$

And the solution will be:

$$\frac{\gamma_i}{t_{ni}+1} = \frac{\mu}{q_n} + \frac{c_{ui}\xi}{c_z z_n} \quad \text{if } t_{ni} > 0 \quad \text{and} \quad \frac{\gamma_i}{t_{ni}+1} \le \frac{\mu}{q_n} + \frac{c_{ui}\xi}{c_z z_n} \quad \text{if } t_{ni} = 0. \tag{4}$$

Since coefficients γ_i, μ, and ξ are nonnegative, then the coefficients can be expressed as follows:

$$\gamma_i = \exp(A_i X_{ni} + \varepsilon_{ni}), \qquad \mu = \exp(BY_n), \qquad \xi = \exp(CY_n). \tag{5}$$

A_i, is vector of alternative specific parameters, and the B, C are parameter vectors. X_{ni} is an activity attribute vectors of priority of needs (scale 1-6) and other individual attributes, Y_n is individual attribute vectors and ε_{ni} is the error term. Substituting the Eq.(5) to Eq.(4) and arranging ε_{ni} as the dependent variable then function for ε_{ni} becomes:

$$\varepsilon_{ni} = \ln(t_{ni}+1) + \ln\left(\frac{\exp(BY_n - A_i X_{ni})}{q_n} + \frac{c_{ui}\exp(CY_n - A_i X_{ni})}{c_z z_n}\right) \quad \text{for } t_{ni} > 0,$$

$$\varepsilon_{ni} \le \ln(t_{ni}+1) + \ln\left(\frac{\exp(BY_n - A_i X_{ni})}{q_n} + \frac{c_{ui}\exp(CY_n - A_i X_{ni})}{c_z z_n}\right) \quad \text{for } t_{ni} = 0. \tag{6}$$

Assuming the error term ε_{ni} follows the normal distribution with zero mean and variance σ^2, then function of log likelihood can be represented using a Tobit Censored Regression model (Maddala 1985) as in Eq. (7). L_{Tni} is the likelihood function of individual n, ϕ is standard normal probability density function, and Φ is standard cumulative normal distribution function. For the estimation purpose, the log likelihood function LL_T, which is the sum of all the individual log likelihood, with parameter A_i, B, C, and σ which are assumed to maximize the log likelihood, is described in Eq. (8).

The ideal situation of utility maximization is that individual with time constraint could allocate time for all activities with equal satisfaction, which means that the marginal utility of all activities are equal. However, in reality there are significant constraints like budget. Because of this, individual might be forced to reduce the time allocation for some activities. This means that marginal utility for some activities might still not be equalized to reach the maximum utility.

$$
L_{T_{ni}} = \begin{cases} \dfrac{1}{\sigma}\phi\left[\dfrac{1}{\sigma}\left\{\ln\left(t_{ni}+1\right)+\ln\left(\dfrac{\exp\left(BY_n-A_iX_{ni}\right)}{q_n}+\dfrac{c_{ui}\exp\left(CY_n-A_iX_{ni}\right)}{c_zz_n}\right)\right\}\right] & \text{if } t_{ni}>0, \\[4mm] \Phi\left[\dfrac{1}{\sigma}\ln\left(\dfrac{\exp\left(BY_n-A_iX_{ni}\right)}{q_n}+\dfrac{c_{ui}\exp\left(CY_n-A_iX_{ni}\right)}{c_zz_n}\right)\right] & \text{if } t_{ni}=0. \end{cases}
$$
(7)

$$
LL_T = \sum_n \sum_i \ln\left(L_{T_{ni}}\right).
$$
(8)

2.3 The Activity Choice Model using Stated Preference (SP) Data

The second approach for supporting the situation of difference in marginal utility is to adopt an additional model, that takes into account the situation whether an individual has reached equal marginal utility for each type of activity or not. This situation can be captured by asking them directly whether they are satisfied or not with the time allocation of the particular activity engagement. If he is not satisfied with the time provided, then it means that the existing time allocation is not fully satisfactory to the individual. If extra time can be obtained, hypothetically an individual will choose an activity expansion/engagement that has the highest marginal utility. The marginal utility of the time of Activity i is represented in equation as a function of t_i as follows.

$$
\frac{\partial U_n}{\partial t_{ni}} = \frac{\gamma_i}{t_{ni}+1} = \frac{1}{t_{ni}+1}\exp\left(A_iX_{ni}+\varepsilon_{ni}\right).
$$
(9)

Using natural logarithm, the previous equation becomes:

$$
\ln\left[\frac{\partial U_n}{\partial t_{ni}}\right] = A_iX_{ni} - \ln(t_{ni}+1) + \varepsilon_{ni} = V_{ni} + \varepsilon_{ni},
$$
(10)

where V_i as the observable part of marginal utility of Activity i.

Since error term ε_{ni} is assumed to follow the normal distribution with zero mean and variance σ^2, (same as stated in the utility maximization approach), then the Multinomial Probit model (Daganzo 1979) is formulated as follows:

$$P_{ni} = \int_{\varepsilon_{n1}=-\infty}^{\varepsilon_{ni}-V_{ni}-V_{n1}} \cdots \int_{\varepsilon_{nm}=-\infty}^{\varepsilon_{ni}-V_{ni}-V_{nm}} \phi\left(\varepsilon_n\right) d\varepsilon_{nm} \cdots d\varepsilon_{n1}, \tag{11}$$

$$\phi\left(\varepsilon_n\right) \equiv \frac{1}{\left(\sqrt{2\pi}\right)^m |\Omega|^{1/2}} \exp\left[-\frac{1}{2}\varepsilon_n{'}\left(\Omega\right)^{-1}\varepsilon_n\right], \tag{12}$$

$$\varepsilon_n \equiv \left(\varepsilon_{n1}, \ldots, \varepsilon_{nm}\right), \tag{13}$$

where P_{ni} is the probability of individual n extending activity type i, Ω is the variance-covariance matrix of error term, and m is the total number of choice alternatives.

The log likelihood function for the probit model is defined by LL_P as:

$$LL_p = \sum_n \sum_i \delta_{ni} \ln\left(P_{ni}\right), \tag{14}$$

where $\delta_{ni} = 1$ when the alternative has been chosen and $\delta_{ni} = 0$ otherwise.

The A_i and σ are unknown parameters that make the log likelihood (LL_p) function reach maximum and the LL_p is basically the sum of all the individual log likelihood function.

The activity choice model uses data obtained from the SP method. The SP Method is used in describing and predicting individual preference and choice for not-yet-existing (hypothetical) situation and there is no consideration of constraints. The SP approach is known to contain more biases then RP data. Since using the model based on SP data alone tends to overestimate the projection of the result, it is deemed necessary to propose some alternative method that could reduce this bias.

2.5 Combining The Utility Maximization and Activity Choice Model

As previously explained, the activity choice approach tends to overestimate the individual's behavior of time allocation of needs. To correct this, the idea is to combine both the utility maximization and the activity choice model and use them simultaneously. The way of combining is to define a new log likelihood function, which is basically the sum of log likelihood functions from each model since they share the same error term, and parameters. The new combined equation is written in Eq. (15).

$$LL = LL_T + LL_P. \tag{15}$$

LL is the total log likelihood and is the sum of the log likelihood from utility maximization model and activity choice model. This combined modeling process is that constitutes the time allocation model proposed in this research.

3 Estimation of the Model Using Data From Survey in Tokyo

3.1 Data Structure

A survey was conducted at a toll road near the Tokyo Bay Area on one weekend of November 2000. From the total sample of 266 working commuters that have family with children there are usable data of 169 samples for the estimation of the model.

The RP data consists of:

(1) Average time allocation in weekday,

(2) Time allocation in that particular weekend,

(3) General life style priority by making rank/score order of their six needs type,

(4) The level of needs satisfaction (scale 1-5) in weekly time allocation, and the SP data contains,

(5) The activity extension choice, answering in hypothetical situation "If the travel time to your destination is reduced by one hour, what type of activity you want to extend?", and

(6) The individual attribute data such as sex, age, income, education, family member, age of the youngest child etc.

The empirical data analysis shows that the rank of top priority of needs for the individual life style are family care (35.0%), followed by physical care (30.1%), pleasure (17.3%), working (12.0%), homemaking (3.0%) and lastly socialization (2.6%). In the level of satisfaction in weekly time allocating, for the needs of work, family and socialization, around 75% of the individuals have no complaints, but for pleasure and physical care needs there are more than 25% and 50% respectively stating that they are not satisfied. This situation will be a concern especially regarding the application of the utility maximization model. The SP data shows that around 33.4% of the respondents chose to engage in or extend family care activities with the extra time, while 25.5% chose pleasure, and another 22.8% for physical care. All of this data is utilized in the following estimation process, with the RP data applied to the utility maximization part and the SP data applied to the activity choice part.

3.2 The Estimation Results

In this estimation exercise the choices will be the three types of classification taking into account the most prominent needs in the weekend that is Family Activity, and Personal Pleasure Activity, while the rest is classified as Other Activity. The estimation is using the GAUSS Programming Language environment with the application of three types of methods of Multinomial Probit (SP Method) and Tobit Censored Regression (RP Method), and Combination of Probit and Tobit (Combined Method). The result of the estimation is shown in the Table 1.

Table 1. The Estimation Result using SP, RP and Combined Method

		SP METHOD	RP METHOD	COMBINED METHOD
	3 Choices of Extension: · Family Activity (FA) · Pleasure Activity (PA) · Other Activity (OA)	Multi-nomial Probit (MNP)	Tobit Censored Regression	MNP & Tobit Censored Regression
			Estimates of A_i	
1	X_1=Priority of Family (specific for FA)	1.7489 *(7.27)*	0.8101 *(6.06)*	1.3573 *(7.11)*
2	X_2=Age of Youngest Child (specific for FA)	-0.3717 *(-6.40)*	-0.1821 *(-5.02)*	-0.3320 *(-6.67)*
3	X_1=Priority of Pleasure (specific for PA)	0.9637 *(3.59)*	0.4515 *(2.57)*	0.7150 *(3.08)*
4	X_2=Sex (specific for PA)	-0.5086 *(-0.47)*	-0.2123 *(-0.34)*	-0.7596 *(-0.891)*
5	X_1=Priority of Physical Care (specific for OA)	-0.2212 *(-0.77)*	-0.0903 *(-0.48)*	-0.2205 *(-0.91)*
6	X_2=Age (specific for OA)	0.0413 *(1.10)*	0.0158 *(0.71)*	0.0196 *(0.66)*
			Estimates of B_i and C_i	
7	Y_1=Income level [1-7] (for CY)		0.1020 *(0.79)*	0.3659 *(1.89)*
8	Y_2=Satisfaction Level of Physical Care (for BY)		1.1555 *(3.789)*	1.6088 *(4.73)*
9	σ=Variance of error term	4.0140 (assumed)	4.0140 *(21.15)*	6.1869 *(19.92)*
	Initial Likelihood with σ = 4.0140	-416.18	-954.78	-1370.96
	Final Likelihood	-345.90	-917.10	-1226.73
	Likelihood ratio	0.17	0.03	0.11
	Number of Samples		169	

Note: t statistics in italic bracket.
Assumption: c_{ui} / c_{zn} for PA=0.06, FA=0.04, OA=0.05 respectively.

The table shows that the values of parameter A_i in RP Method and Combined Method for priorities of family and pleasure have large and significant positive influence to the utility of respective type of activity. Also the t-statistics and the likelihood ratio for the Combined Method are higher than RP Method alone reflecting better model performance for the Combined Method. This means that accommodating the difference in marginal utility as demonstrated in the Combined Method is proven useful for parameter estimation.

4 Conclusions

The conclusions of this paper are as follows.

(1) Using this time allocation model, given the parameters and individual attributes, the individual time allocation can be predicted. Furthermore, the change of time allocation as a result of time saving can also be calculated.

(2) The combination of two approaches is proven to improve the performance of parameter estimation.

(3) Level of priority of need as shown by the result of estimation has a significant part-worth in the respective type of utility of activity. Thus, individual priority basically influences how he or she allocates time for each activity.

(4) Generally, income and satisfaction of physical care will increase the utility of all activities.

(5) The part-worths of priorities of family and pleasure with respect to the total utility in weekend are relatively high. This implies that extending the activity time for family activity and pleasure is significant in maximizing total utility.

(6) Although the model still needs continuous improvement and development, our examples have shed some directions on the features that this model will have.

5 References

Antonides G (1996) Psychology in Economics and Business. Kluwer, Boston

Becker GS (1965) A Theory of The Allocation of Time. Economic Journal 75: 493-517

Bhat C, Koppelman FS (1999) A Retrospective and Prospective Survey of Time-use Research. Transportation 26: 119-139

Chapin Jr F (1974) Human Activity Pattern in The City: Things People Do in Time and Space. John Wiley and Sons, New York

Daganzo, CF (1979) Multinomial Probit. Academic Press, New York

DeSerpa AC (1971) A Theory of The Economics of Time. Economic Journal 81: 828-845

Kitamura R, Supernak J (1997) Temporal Utility Profiles of Activities and Travel: Some Empirical Evidence. In: Stopher PR, Lee-Goselin M (eds) Understanding Travel Behavior in an Era of Change. Pergamon, Oxford, pp 339-350

Kraan M (1995) Modeling Activity Patterns with Respect to Limited Time and Money Budget. In: Hensher D, King J, Oum T (eds) World Transport Research: Proceeding of 7th World Conference on Transport Research Vol 1. Pergamon, Oxford, pp 151-163

Maddala GS (1985) Limited-Dependent and Qualitative Variables in Econometrics. Cambridge University Press, Cambridge

Maslow, AH (1970) Motivation and Personality. Harper & Row, New York

Solomon I, Ben-Akiva M (1983) The Use of The Life-style Concept in Travel Demand Models. Environment and Planning A 15: 623-638

Yamamoto T, Kitamura R (1999) An Analysis of Time Allocation to In-Home and Out-of-Home Discretionary Activities across Working Days and Non-Working Days. Transportation 26: 211-230

Cluster Instability as a Result of Data Input Order

Willem A. van der Kloot[1], Samantha Bouwmeester[2], and Willem J. Heiser[1]

[1]Psychometrics and Research Methodology, Department of Psychology, Leiden University, PO Box 9555, 2300 RB Leiden, The Netherlands
[2]Faculty of Social Sciences, Tilburg University, PO Box 90153, 5000 LE Tilburg, The Netherlands

Summary. Under certain conditions, hierarchical cluster analysis will produce different solutions when the input order of the data to be clustered is permuted. Such instability may occur if there are ties in the proximities used for clustering, and if the input order of some of the tied objects is reversed. This vulnerability to input order has important consequences for the interpretation of results. With some exceptions, this problem has hardly been discussed in the literature and is not generally known among the typical users of cluster analysis. In this paper we give three examples that demonstrate the permutation instability of cluster analysis, and we propose a procedure to select an optimal solution among non-unique clusterings. Finally, we present an application of the proposed method.

Key words. cluster analysis, instability, non-uniqueness

1 Non-uniqueness of cluster solutions

Although different methods of cluster analysis may, and generally will, give different clusterings, it is not obvious that one and the same method may yield different results when the input data are sorted in different orders. Of course, such a form of instability would be highly undesirable. Unfortunately, there is evidence (e.g. Backeljau et al., 1996, 2000; Bouwmeester, 2000; Hart, 1983; Morgan & Ray, 1995) that such anomalies (a) indeed do occur, and (b) are the results of ties in the distance measures that are used for joining objects and clusters.

This phenomenon has also been acknowledged by, for instance, Wishart (2000) who warned that "clustering procedures are notoriously sensitive to the case order " (p. 2) and by Podani (1997) who asserted that "*it has long been known* [italics added] that … [several] hierarchical agglomerative procedures are *not* permutation invariant" (p. 154). We doubt, however, that this notoriety is as pervasive as the word suggests. A literature search revealed no more than a handful of articles on the effects of input order instability of ordination results (Backeljau et al., 1996, 2000; Gordon, 1999; Hart, 1983; Jain & Dubes, 1988; Morgan & Ray, 1995; Oksanen and Minchin, 1997; Podani, 1997; Sibson, 1971; Tausch,

Charlet, Weixelman, & Zamudio, 1995). Therefore, we surmise that the circle of scientists who are knowledgeable with this issue must be rather restricted.

Among the sources cited above is an article by Sibson (1971), who proved that the single linkage or nearest neighbor method is the only cluster method that is well defined when confronted with tied dissimilarities and that other cluster methods can produce arbitrary results when data are tied. His article is probably the first one that pointed this out. However, the fact that there are only very few citations of this article supports our contention that if the data order instability problem has *long* been known, it certainly is *not widely* known.

1.1 Some examples of data order instability

The most general formulation of any agglomerative hierarchical clustering algorithm is as follows: (a) let all objects to be clustered be separate one-element clusters; (b) compute all distances among the clusters; (c) join the two clusters that have the smallest distance into one cluster; (d) compute all intercluster distances (i.e. the relevant fusion coefficients), (e) join the two clusters with minimum distance (i.e. optimal value for fusion), and so on, until all objects are in one final cluster. Obviously, whenever two or more pairs of clusters have the same minimum distance or optimal fusion coefficient, the algorithm cannot 'decide' which two clusters should be joined at that particular stage. However, most computer programs have been programmed to proceed in such cases one way or the other, apparently by joining clusters on the bases of their location in computer memory. Below we will present a number of examples in which the data order instability of cluster analysis is clearly demonstrated.

Table 1. Interpoint dissimilarities of six objects: Example 1

	A	B	C	D	E	F
A	0	25	18	115	102	60
B	25	0	18	90	76	34
C	18	18	0	101	89	44
D	115	90	101	0	17	60
E	102	76	89	17	0	50
F	60	34	44	60	50	0

1.1.1 Example 1

Consider the matrix of interpoint dissimilarities (δ) of Table 1. Cluster analysis by SPSS' complete linkage method (furthest neighbor method) may yield the four different dendrograms represented in Figure 1. In these dendrograms there are two differences that catch the eye: in the left dendrograms A is joined to the cluster of B and C, while in the rightmost trees B is joined to A and C. This happens because both δ_{BC} and δ_{AC} have the value 18 and because there is no compelling reason for either merging B and C or A and C first. The differences between

the two solutions solely depend on the order in which the data have been submitted to the analysis, in particular on the different orders of A, B and C.
The second difference concerns object F, which is merged with cluster {A, B, C} in the upper two dendrograms and with {D, E} in the lower trees. This happens because $\delta_{F\{DE\}} = \delta_{FD}$ and $\delta_{F\{ABC\}} = \delta_{FA}$ are tied (both are equal to 60). The difference between the upper and the lower two solutions is much more important for the interpretation of the clusters, because the two-cluster structures of the upper and lower solutions are substantially different. Again, this difference depends on the input order, particularly of the placement of F among the rest of the objects.

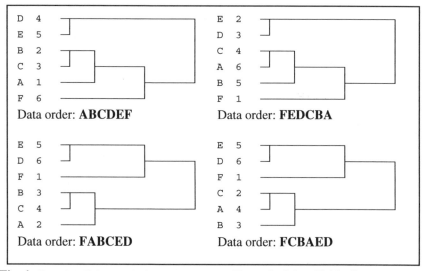

Fig. 1. Complete linkage solutions of the data of Example 1 (see Table 1)

Table 2. Dissimilarities among six objects: Example 2

	A	B	C	D	E	F
A	0	25	17	115	102	64
B	25	0	19	90	76	38
C	17	19	0	101	89	48
D	115	90	101	0	22	51
E	102	76	89	22	0	49
F	64	38	48	51	49	0

1.1.2 Example 2

With regard to Example 1, one could argue that it is obvious that more than one solution is possible because simple inspection of the dissimilarity matrix shows that four values are tied. However, in the following example (see Table 2) there are no ties at all in the data matrix, yet two different dendrograms can be obtained by permuting the order in which the data are entered into the analysis.

These dendrograms are displayed in Figure 2. In the left solution F is merged with A, B and C, whereas in the right tree F is merged with D and E. Note that these different solutions emerge because in the average between group linkage method $\delta_{F\{ABC\}} = (\delta_{FA} + \delta_{FB} + \delta_{FC})/3 = 55$ is tied to $\delta_{F\{DE\}} = (\delta_{FD} + \delta_{FE})/2$. These ties are not visible in the dissimilarity matrix but arise during the clustering process. The crucial condition is that at some stage in the process the relevant fusion coefficients are tied.

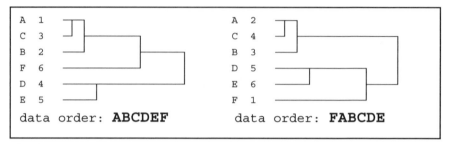

Fig. 2. Average between group linkage dendrograms for two different data input orders of Example 2 (see Table 2)

1.1.3 Example 3

A special position is taken by the method of single linkage (nearest neighbor linkage). At every stage of the clustering process, single linkage looks for the smallest between cluster dissimilarity and subsequently merges the corresponding clusters. After merging two clusters, the distance of the newly formed cluster to all the other ones is set equal to the smallest dissimilarity between any of the elements of the new cluster and any of the elements of the other ones. Therefore, as Sibson (1971) has pointed out, merging in single linkage does not change the distances between the clusters that are relevant for fusion. When there are two sets of clusters whose distances are equal and smallest, single linkage proceeds by merging one of the two sets first, directly followed by merging the other sets. Sets of clusters with tied and smallest distances are always merged immediately after one another, however, the sequence in which the two sets are merged may vary. Thus, when there are ties in the distances, data order permutations will result in different *sequences* in which the clusters are formed, even in the single linkage method. This is demonstrated by the data of Table 3.

Table 3. Dissimilarities between six points: Example 3

	A	B	C	D	E	F
A	0	10	30	30	30	50
B	10	0	40	30	30	30
C	30	40	0	10	30	30
D	30	30	10	0	30	60
E	30	30	30	30	0	10
F	50	30	30	60	10	0

All analyses by means of single linkage clustering yield the dendrogram depicted in Figure 3. This dendrogram clearly shows that there are three equidistant clusters in the data. However, entering the data in different orders may result in eighteen different sequences. Therefore, if one were to select automatically the two-cluster solution, one could end up with three different constellations: {{A, B, C, D}{E, F}}, {{A, B, E, F}{C, D}}, or {{A,B}{C, D, E, F}}.

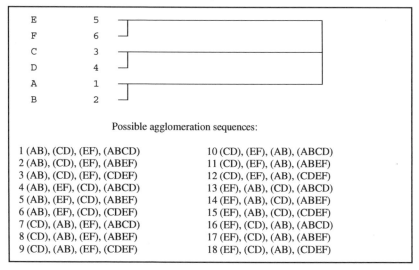

E	5
F	6
C	3
D	4
A	1
B	2

Possible agglomeration sequences:

1 (AB), (CD), (EF), (ABCD)	10 (CD), (EF), (AB), (ABCD)
2 (AB), (CD), (EF), (ABEF)	11 (CD), (EF), (AB), (ABEF)
3 (AB), (CD), (EF), (CDEF)	12 (CD), (EF), (AB), (CDEF)
4 (AB), (EF), (CD), (ABCD)	13 (EF), (AB), (CD), (ABCD)
5 (AB), (EF), (CD), (ABEF)	14 (EF), (AB), (CD), (ABEF)
6 (AB), (EF), (CD), (CDEF)	15 (EF), (AB), (CD), (CDEF)
7 (CD), (AB), (EF), (ABCD)	16 (EF), (CD), (AB), (ABCD)
8 (CD), (AB), (EF), (ABEF)	17 (EF), (CD), (AB), (ABEF)
9 (CD), (AB), (EF), (CDEF)	18 (EF), (CD), (AB), (CDEF)

Fig. 3. Dendrogram of Example 3 found by single linkage clustering plus the list of 18 sequences in which the tree can be obtained by permuting the data matrix

1.2 Approaches to data order instability

Presently there seem to be three ways to deal with data order instability. The most frequent approach is just to ignore the fact that tied dissimilarities can lead to multiple solutions. This is the default of the cluster modules in SPSS and many other statistical analysis packages (cf. Backeljau et al., 1996). Some programs issue a warning in their output or contain at least a cautionary remark in their User Guide (e.g. Wishart, 1999). Two other approaches consist of performing repeated cluster analyses under (random) permutations of the rows or columns of the input matrix. If the permutations produce different solutions, one could either report and interpret all separate trees (cf. Backeljau et al., 1996) or one could select the cluster solution that emerges as the most frequent one (Wishart, 2000). Although the latter approach has the advantage of yielding one tree, it is not certain that this most frequent solution indeed is the *best* one for the data at hand.

1.3 Goodness of fit

A suitable method to choose among two or more cluster solutions of the same data can be based on the *goodness of fit*. That is, we want to keep that particular cluster solution that yields the best description of the data. A straightforward measure of goodness (or rather: *bad*ness) of fit (Hartigan, 1967), is the sum of squared differences $SSDIF = \sum_i\sum_{j>i} (\delta_{ij} - d_{ij})^2$ between the dissimilarities δ_{ij} in the data matrix and the cophenetic distances d_{ij} (cf. Everitt, 1993) in the cluster solution. After running cluster analyses on many random permutations of the input order, one can use *SSDIF* to decide which solution is best. This approach is similar to the strategy used in multidimensional scaling of using a large number of random initial configurations in order to increase the probability of finding the solution with global minimum stress (cf. Borg & Groenen, 1997).

We have computed the *SSDIF*-values of the various solutions of our earlier examples. In the first two examples, the solutions in which F is joined to the cluster $\{A, B, C\}$ have lower *SSDIF*-values than the solutions in which F is merged with $\{D, E\}$ (Example 1: 11418.0 *vs.* 17963.0; Example 2: 4374.88 *vs.* 5410.0). The *SSDIF* of the tree in Example 3 is 1400.00.

Example 1 and 2 thus show that SSDIF is useful for finding the best solution among a set of possible dendrograms. In the remainder of this chapter we will illustrate this strategy on a set of empirical data of a psychological study.

2 Method

2.1 Subjects and material

The data consist of the scores of 115 patients on the eight subscales of the Dutch version of the SCL90 symptom checklist (Arrindell & Ettema, 1986). The patients had been referred to the pain clinic of a general hospital. They had to complete the SCL-90 questionnaire as a part of the intake procedure. The SCL-90 subscales measure eight different forms of psychopathological complaints (e.g. agoraphobia, anxiety, depression, and hostility). In a previous study (Flik, Van der Kloot, Koers, & Huisman, 2001), these data were analyzed by a k-means cluster analysis, which yielded one cluster ($n = 91$) of 'normal' patients and a second cluster ($n = 24$) of patients with appreciable pathology. These two clusters could almost perfectly be discriminated by means of linear discriminant analysis. The means and standard deviations of the clusters coincided almost completely with the norms of a 'normal' and a 'psychiatric' population, respectively.

2.2 Analysis

Of the data matrix of 115 rows by 8 columns 100 copies were created by random permutation of the rows. The resulting matrices were submitted to SPSS' median method hierarchical cluster analysis using squared Euclidean distances among the patients. For each solution cophenetic distances among the patients were computed, which were used to obtain values of the goodness-of-fit measure *SSDIF*.

3 Results

Below we have summarized our results in terms of the two-cluster solutions. Among the 100 solutions we found seven different two-cluster solutions. The frequencies of these solutions, the numbers of patients in the clusters, and the minimum and maximum *SSDIF*-values are listed in Table 4. Note that among each type of two-cluster solutions there may be several different sequences in which the patients are fused, that is, each type may have different dendrograms and correspondingly may have different fit values. Table 4 shows that one of the Type 4 solutions has the smallest *SSDIF*-value, and is therefore the two-cluster solution that we would prefer as the solution to be reported and interpreted.

Table 4. Summary of two-cluster solutions

Type of solution	first occur-rence	frequen-cy	patients in largest cluster	patients in smallest cluster	Minimum value of *SSDIF*	Maximum value of *SSDIF*
1	1	27	114	1	1818.84	1818.88
2	2	8	103	12	914.00	914.53
3	6	12	109	6	3937.49	3943.22
4	7	10	107	8	854.88	871.78
5	8	8	102	13	1154.75	1155.57
6	12	32	114	1	1178.26	1746.14
7	21	3	98	17	1605.29	1605.67

4 Conclusion and discussion

We have shown that ties in the distances that are used for merging clusters can lead to several non-unique clusterings, when the objects to be clustered are arranged in different orders. Ties may be visible in the original dissimilarity matrix, in which case the problem can be recognized rather easily. However, ties may also emerge hiddenly during the agglomeration process, as new intercluster distances are computed after every step at which two clusters have been merged.

As the input order of data usually is arbitrary, there is no *a priori* reason for choosing one solution over the other. Therefore, we have proposed to use the sum of squared differences between the original dissimilarities and the cophenetic distances (*SSDIF*) as a measure of fit. This value can be used to determine the solution that is the optimal representation of the original dissimilarities. Ideally, one could try and find the optimal solution by straightforwardly minimizing *SSDIF*. However, as finding the tree with minimal *SSDIF* is a *NP-*

hard problem (cf. Gordon, 1999) this is only possible for relatively small trees (i.e. with no more than approximately 20 objects). Since most cluster applications concern much larger data sets, direct optimization is not feasible. Therefore, our method, which consists of selecting the best tree among a set of trees obtained from a (large) number of random permutations of the input order, appears to be a suitable alternative.

References

Arrindel WA, Ettema JHM (1986) *Klachtenlijst (SCL-90)*. Swets & Zeitlinger, Lisse

Backeljau T, De Bruyn L, De Wolf H, Jordaens K, Van Dongen S, Winnepenninckx B. (1996) Multiple UPGMA and neighbour joining trees and the performance of some computer packages. Molecular Biology and Evolution 13: 309-313

Backeljau T, Breugelmans K, De Wolf H, Geenen S, Harrier LA, Jordaens K, Van Riel K, Winnepenninckx B. (2000) Software dependent phenetic relationships of non-nodulating African species of Acacia. Plant Systematics and Evolution 220: 139-146

Borg I, Groenen P (1997) Modern multidimensional scaling. Springer, New York

Bouwmeester S. (2000) Tekstbestudering [Study methods of texts]. Unpublished Masters Thesis, Leiden University, Department of Psychology

Hartigan JA (1967) Representation of similarity matrices by trees. Journal of the American Statistical Association 62: 1140-1158

Everitt BS (1993) Cluster analysis. Third edition. Arnold, London

Flik C, Van der Kloot WA, Koers H, & Huisman M. (2001) Multidisciplinair pijnteam: mode of model? [Multidisciplinary pain team: fashion or model?]. Tijdschrift voor Psychiatrie 43: 71-81

Gordon AD (199) Classification (Second edition). Chapman & Hall/CRC, London.

Hart G (1983) The occurrence of multiple UPGMA phenograms. In: Felsenstein J. (ed.) Numerical taxonomy. Springer, Berlin, pp. 254-258

Jain AK, Dubes RC (1988) Algorithms for clustering data. Prentice Hall, Englewood Cliffs, NJ

Morgan BJT, Ray APG (1995) Non-uniqueness and inversions in cluster analysis. Journal of Applied Statistics 44: 117-134

Oksanen J., Minchin PR (1997) Instability of ordination results under changes in input data order. Journal of Vegetation Science 8: 447-454

Podani J (1997) On the sensitivity of ordination and classification methods to variation in the input order of data. Journal of Vegetation Science 8: 153-156

Sibson R (1971) Some observations on a paper by Lance and Williams. The Computer Journal 14: 56-57

Tausch RJ, Charlet DA, Weixelman DA, Zamudio DC (1995) Patterns of ordination and classification instability resulting from changes in input data order. Journal of Vegetation Science: 897-902

Wishart D. (1999) ClustanGraphics Primer: A guide to cluster analysis.Clustan Limited, Edinburgh, Scotland

Wishart D. (2000) FocalPoint Clustering user guide. Clustan Ltd, Edinburgh, Scotland

A Connectionist Model of Phonological Working Memory[1]

Shogo Makioka

Department of Human Sciences, Osaka Women's University, 2-1 Daisen-cho, Sakai 590-0035, Japan

Summary. We propose a connectionist model that can learn the pronunciation of words by imitation. The model "hears" the pronunciation of words (sequences of phonemes) and develops a static internal representation of phonology. It then tries to reproduce the pronunciation from the internal representation. We trained the model to imitate the pronunciation of 3,684 English monosyllabic words. After 15 million training trials, the network achieved a 99.2% correct response. To simulate the process of the serial recall of words or nonwords, we added a subsystem called a temporary maintenance module. This module preserves the phonological internal representation by using a Hebbian one-shot algorithm to transform the activation pattern to a connection pattern. The model could reproduce the effect of the phonotactic probability on a serial recall task done by human children. The result of the simulation implies that our model can explain the effect of long-term memory on the phonological working memory.

Key words: working memory, phonological loop, connectionist model

1 Introduction

Baddeley (1986) proposed a model of working memory that consists of three parts: the phonological loop, the visuo-spatial sketchpad, and the central executive. Recently, Baddeley, Gathercole, and Papagno (1998) proposed that the phonological loop should be regarded as a language learning device. Their claim is based on the following findings.

1) The performance of nonword repetition at age 3-8 is positively correlated with the amount of vocabulary knowledge (e.g. Gathercole & Adams, 1993).

2) Gathercole, Willis, Emslie, and Baddeley (1992) investigated the performance of nonword repetition and vocabulary knowledge of the same child successively. They found that nonword repetition at age 4 was significantly correlated with the amount of vocabulary at age 5, whereas vocabulary at age 4 was not a significant predictor of the nonword repetition score at age 5. This means that the

---

[1] This work was supported by Grant JSPS-RFTF99P01401 from the Japan Society for the Promotion of Science.

capacity of the phonological loop (measured through the nonword repetition task) affects the speed of vocabulary acquisition.

3) Nonword repetition is easier when the stimulus is more "wordlike." Gathercole, Frankish, Pickering, and Peaker (1999) investigated the effect of phonotactic probability on serial recall. Children of 7 and 8 years were tested on their serial recall of monosyllabic words and nonwords varying in phonotactic frequencies. Nonword recall showed superior accuracy for high-probability over low-probability nonwords. This result suggests that maintenance of verbal information in the phonological loop is affected by long-term memory.

Although Baddeley et al. (1998) presented a descriptive model, no simulation model that can explain all three findings has been proposed. We have constructed a connectionist model that can replicate the effect of long-term memory on the phonological loop and believe that this model will also be able to explain the other two findings.

2 The Model

A native speaker of a language can repeat a novel word if its pronunciation obeys the phonotactic rules of the language. For example, when an English speaker hears the nonword "bip", he or she can easily repeat the word. The listener does not have to repeat phonemes or syllables one by one but can instantly imitate the pronunciation of the entire word. This implies that human speakers can temporarily maintain the phoneme sequence contained in the word (Fig. 1).

We propose a connectionist model that can learn the pronunciation of words by imitation. The model "hears" the pronunciation of words (sequences of phonemes), develops an internal representation of phonology, and then tries to reproduce the pronunciation from the internal representation. At first, the model has no knowledge of phonology and cannot repeat the words correctly. As it learns the pronunciation of many words by imitation, it becomes able to repeat them properly. We assumed that the internal representation of phonology is static. The information on pronunciation is represented by the static activation pattern of the units. If the representation is static, it is easy to preserve the knowledge of the

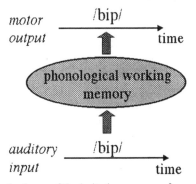

Fig. 1. General scheme of the imitation process of a novel word pronunciation.

phonology in the form of synaptic weights among the units. We suggest that the transformation from a sequence of phonemes to the static representation corresponds to the process of chunking. The model is called Echo Net because it simply learns to reproduce the words it has heard (Fig. 2).

The output of the phonological route returns to the input layer and forms a closed loop. Thus, the model can repeat the dynamic pattern of the input phoneme sequences over and over again. This rehearsal process facilitates the learning of the semantic route. We suggest that human children learn the pronunciation and meaning of words by a similar process, and that this is the reason why children with a high phonological loop capacity can acquire vocabulary knowledge faster than others.

The model can only rehearse one word at a time so far, but a human child can maintain a list of words and recall them in the presented order. Therefore, we have added a subsystem called a temporary maintenance module. This module preserves the internal representation by using a Hebbian one-shot algorithm to transform the activation pattern into a connection pattern. This enables Echo Net to handle the next input pattern while preserving the information regarding earlier input patterns.

3 Simulations

3.1 Network Architecture

Input units represent phonological features of English (based on Chomsky & Halle, 1968). If a phoneme contains one of the features, the activation of the corresponding unit is set to 1. If the phoneme does not have the feature, the activation of the unit is set to 0. To represent termination of the word, the neutral activation value of 0.5 is fed to all of the input units.

We assume that speech perception and production share the same representation; that is, output representation is identical to input representation. We consider this assumption reasonable, since an infant must acquire the equivalence of ones' own speech and others' speech. In an earlier stage of development, he or she must learn that "ba" uttered by others falls into the same category as "ba" uttered by themselves.

Phonological input module This module learns to transform the input phoneme sequence into a static phonological representation. As shown in Fig. 2, it consists of two simple recurrent networks (SRNs; Elman, 1990). The networks are trained to output the input pattern at t-1. The module learns to reproduce past input, rather than predict future input, to make the learning converge. If the network learns to output the next input pattern, its prediction cannot be perfect because more than one phoneme can follow the same phoneme sequence (e.g., "cat", "cap"). Thus the learning will not converge. On the contrary, if the network learns

580   Shogo Makioka

Echo Net

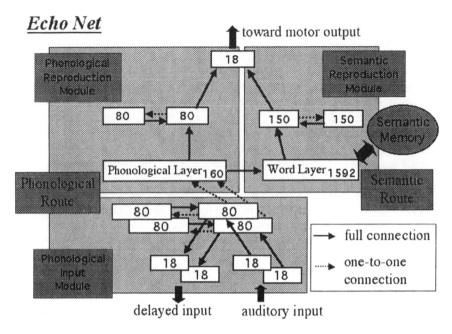

Fig. 2. Architecture of the model.

to output past input, its learning will surely converge because the network has already been given the information to output. When the network outputs the past input, the mixture of the current and past inputs is represented in the hidden layer. Thus, the phonological input module develops the internal representation of the sequence of the input patterns; i.e., English phonology. After the termination pattern is input, the activation pattern of the two hidden layers is copied to the phonological layer. Then, the phonological reproduction module begins to reproduce the phoneme sequence.

In the early stage of learning, one of the networks learns to reproduce the first CV string of the words (cycles < 1,000,000). The other network then starts to learn to reproduce the pronunciation of the whole word. We used two networks because the information regarding the head of the word tended to diminish after many phonemes were input. Because the first network processes only the first CV string, it can preserve the information regarding the head of the word.

Phonological reproduction module This module is also an SRN. It learns to reproduce the same phoneme sequence from the static activation pattern in the phonological layer. The architecture of this module is almost the same as that of Dell, Juliano, and Govindjee's (1993) model of speech errors.

Semantic reproduction module This module is also an SRN. It is trained to transform the representation of words to the phoneme sequence. For simplicity, we use purely local coding for the word representation; that is, each word is represented by a single unit in the word layer. (The mapping from the phonological layer to the word layer has not been implemented yet.)

Temporary maintenance module This module preserves the activation pattern of the phonological or word layer in the form of a connection pattern. This is realized through the Hebbian one-shot learning algorithm. Although this module works on both routes, here we will explain its relationship to the phonological route. As shown in Fig. 3, the module consists of the maintenance layer and the connections to the phonological layer from that layer. The units in the maintenance layer are activated by top-down input. The learning is conducted in the following way. When the termination pattern is input, one of the maintenance units is activated (the activation value is one). The rest of the maintenance units are turned off (the activation value is zero). The module then learns according to a standard Hebb rule as shown below.

$$\Delta w_{ji} = a_i m_j$$

a_i : activation of the phonological units

m_j : activation of the maintenance units

Δw_{ji} : change in the connection weight between the two layers

After the weight pattern is updated by the above rule, the weight vector from the activated maintenance unit to the phonological layer becomes identical to the activation vector of the phonological layer. Then the activation of the phonological layer is automatically reset to 0. When the previously activated maintenance unit is turned on, the same activation pattern is reconstructed in the phonological layer. This means that the maintenance unit acts as the address of the activation patterns in the phonological layer.

Use of a Hebb rule in a model of short-term memory is not a new idea. The unique point of this model is its use of top-down input. By activating the maintenance unit through top-down feedback, the activation pattern of the phonological layer can be "copied" to the connection pattern and preserved. Because the feedback signal comes to a single unit at a time, the memorized patterns become orthogonal to each other. This means that there is no need to standardize the activation value in the phonological layer, unlike in other models. We believe that this

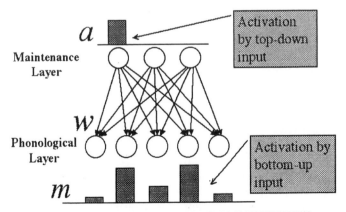

Fig. 3. Learning mechanism of the temporary maintenance module.

top-down maintenance mechanism can be regarded as a general model of intentional learning by the central executive of working memory.

3.2 Stimulus

The input/output pattern was constructed based on the database CELEX English Version 2.5. This database contains 160,596 word forms and their frequencies. We extracted 3,684 monosyllabic words whose frequency was above 10 and transformed them into input vectors. These words included many homophones, and 1,592 of the words had a unique pronunciation. Discrimination between homophones was assumed to be realized by using contextual information in the semantic memory.

3.3 Learning Procedure

Phonological route The input patterns were presented randomly to the network, and the number of presentations of each word was proportional to the logarithm of the word frequency. The two modules were trained simultaneously. The learning was done using a backpropagation algorithm (Rumelhart, Hinton, Williams; 1986). The training of the phonological input module was terminated after three million trials, and the phonological reproduction module continued learning for 15 million trials. The learning coefficient of the phonological input module was 0.005, and that of the phonological reproduction module was 0.01. The momentum term was 0.4 in both modules.

Semantic route The learning of the semantic route was assumed to proceed in parallel with that of the phonological route. However, the training was conducted independently because of limited computing resources. The stimulus presentation order was completely random, and the learning was conducted by a backpropagation algorithm. The learning coefficient was 0.001, and the momentum term was 0.4. Seven million learning trials were conducted.

3.4 Results

Phonological route The output pattern of the network was regarded as correct if it was closer in Euclidian distance to the desired phoneme than to any other phonemes. After learning, the phonological route achieved a 99.2% correct response for the entire training set. We then examined the performance for the stimuli used by Gathercole et al. (1999), who used four types of stimuli: words (e.g. "hip," "tin"), high- phonotactic-probability nonwords (e.g. "bip," "rin"), low-probability nonwords (e.g. "beng," "rol"), and very low-probability nonwords (e.g. "bez," "rog"). These stimuli were transformed to the input vector and presented to the network. The performance of the model was fairly good (words: 100%, high-probability nonwords: 96%, low-probability nonwords: 100%, very low-probability nonwords: 93%). Although the network did not have any experience of nonword repetition, it could repeat most of the nonwords.

Next, we examined the serial-recall performance. In the study of Gathercole et al. (1999), four words/nonwords were sequentially presented to a child in a session, and the child was asked to recall them in the correct order. In the same way, we presented four stimuli to the network in turn, and the temporary maintenance module preserved the activation pattern in the phonological layer. After the last item had been input, the activation value of each unit was reset to zero. The maintenance units were then activated one by one, and the network recalled the input patterns. To produce errors, we added Gaussian random noise to the weight pattern between the maintenance layer and the phonological layer. The noise level was adjusted to attain the same correct rate as in the Gathercole et al. (1999) experiment for very low-phonotactic-probability nonwords (33%). If the network could achieve a performance for the other types of stimuli that was similar to that in the experiment using children as subjects, we would be able to conclude that the network replicated the effect of long-term memory on working memory. The variance of Gaussian random noise was 0.034, and the mean value of the noise was 0.

One hundred test trials with different random noise were conducted for each type of stimuli, and the results are shown in Fig. 4. For the nonwords, the network performance (black squares) was similar to that of children (white circles). However, the correct rate for the words was much lower than the human data. We think this was because the children used semantic knowledge in their recall process. Thus, we have to examine the effect of the semantic route on the network's performance.

Semantic route The correct reproduction rate of the semantic reproduction module for the entire training set was 97.5%. To examine the effect of the semantic route on the word condition, we presented the word stimuli to the semantic reproduction module and ran the serial recall simulation with the temporary maintenance module. We assumed that the phonological route and the semantic route ran

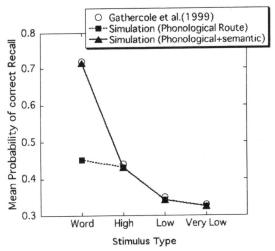

Fig. 4. Simulation results.

independently. Therefore, we obtained the correct recall rate for the word stimuli by computing the inclusive OR of the correct response of both modules. As in the recall by the phonological route, Gaussian random noise was added to the weight pattern between the maintenance layer and the semantic layer. We adjusted the variance of the noise to attain similar performance as that for the word stimuli. The variance of noise for the semantic route was 0.013. As shown in Fig. 4, we could obtain a correct recall rate that was similar to the earlier data (black triangles).

3.5 Discussion

Now we return to the relationship between the capacity of the phonological working memory and the speed of vocabulary acquisition. In our model, two factors determine the memory capacity: quality of the phonological representation and the noise level in the temporary maintenance module. If the phonological representation is not well developed, the phonological route makes errors when it repeats words and cannot maintain the information regarding word pronunciation. Also, if the noise level in the temporary maintenance module is too high, the network cannot maintain more than one word at a time. As mentioned, we assume that the maintenance of the phoneme sequence in the phonological route facilitates the learning of the semantic route. If the network had better phonological representation and a low-noise maintenance module, it would be able to acquire the vocabulary faster. We are planning to run simulations to examine these factors.

References

Baddeley AD (1986) Working Memory. Clarendon Press, Oxford

Baddeley AD, Gathercole SE, and Papagno C (1998) The phonological loop as a language learning device. Psych Rev 105:158-173

Chomsky N, Halle M (1968) The sound pattern of English. MIT Press, Cambridge

Dell GS, Juliano C Govindjee, A (1993) Structure and content in language production: A theory of frame constraints in phonological speech errors. Cog Sci 17:149-195

Elman J (1990) Finding structure in time. Cog Sci 14:179-211

Gathercole SE, Willis C, Emsile H, Baddeley AD (1992) Phonological memory and vocabulary development during the early school years: A longitudinal study. Devel Psych 28:887-898

Gathercole SE, Adams A (1993) Phonological working memory in very young children. Devel Psych, 29:770-778

Gathercole SE, Frankish CR, Pickering SJ, Peaker S (1999) Phonotactic influences on short-term memory. J Exp Psych: Learning, Memory, and Cognition 25:84-95

Rumelhart DE, Hinton GE, Williams RJ (1986) Learning internal representations by error propagation. In: Rumelhart DE McClelland JL (eds) Parallel distributed processing: Explorations in the microstructure of cognition Vol.1. MIT Press, Cambridge, pp 318-364

Brain Mapping Data: Classification, Principal Components and Multidimensional Scaling

Keith J. Worsley

Department of Mathematics and Statistics, McGill University 805 ouest, rue Sherbrooke, Montreal, Québec, Canada H3A 2K6

Summary. Brain mapping data consists of 3D images of brain function (blood flow or blood oxygenation dependent response), or brain anatomy (MRI images), repeated under different experimental conditions and over different subjects. We can regard the image values, sampled at up to 500,000 voxels, as a very high dimensional multivariate observation, but a better approach is to model them as a continuous function or random field. The result of the statistical analysis is an image of test statistics, and our main interest is how to deal with them. We use a topological quantity, the Euler characteristic of the excursion set of a random field, as a tool to test for localised changes. The data is highly non-isotropic, that is, the effective smoothness is not constant across the image, so the usual random field theory does not apply. We propose a solution that warps the data to isotropy using local multidimensional scaling. Recent theoretical work has shown that the subsequent corrections to the random field theory can be done without actually doing the warping (Taylor and Adler, 2002). We shall apply these methods to a set of 151 brain images from the Human Brain Mapping data base.

Key words. Brain mapping, Classification, Principal components, Multidimensional scaling, Random fields, Euler characteristic.

1 Brain mapping data and Classification

Brain mapping data consists of 3D images of brain function, measured either by blood flow (positron emission tomography: PET) or blood oxygenation dependent response (functional magnetic resonance imaging: fMRI), or brain structure measured by anatomical MRI. These images are repeated under different experimental conditions and over different subjects. The statistical problem is to find those brain regions that are related to the external covariates. Our first example is brain structure. Recent studies have shown that brain structures can change size or shape in response to disease; a recent

586 Keith J. Worsley

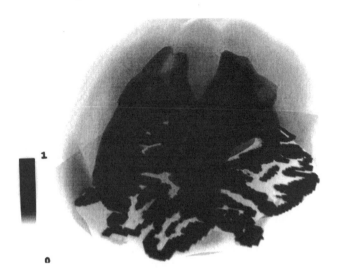

Figure 1: The first type of data is a binary classification of grey matter Shown here is one slice for a single subject, superimposed on a transparent rendering of the cortex.

study found that the sub-genual pre-frontal cortex was half the size in hereditary depressives (*Time* magazine, May 5, 1997, p. 43). This region was pinpointed because a previous PET study had shown a decrease in blood flow. However in many cases researchers do not know where to look, and so we propose to scan the entire brain for localised shape changes. Shape change has been traditionally analysed using landmarks, but these are very hard to define for the brain. Instead, three types of data on structural change are now available for a set of 151 brain images from the Human Brain Mapping data base.

The first is a classification of the image into points that are inside the structure (1) and outside (0) using a simple neural network classifier (Figure 1). After smoothing, we use the binomial likelihood to fit a logistic regression to relate structure density to explanatory variables, in this case a difference between females and males. The result is a 3D image of T statistics for detecting shape change encoded by the explanatory variables of the linear model.

The second is the coordinates of the surface of the structure, found by shrinking a triangular mesh to the outer surface (Figure 2). We treat the surface normal displacements as univariate Gaussian data and fit a linear model in the explanatory variables as before. The result is a 2D image of T statistics on the surface, a 2D manifold embedded in 3D.

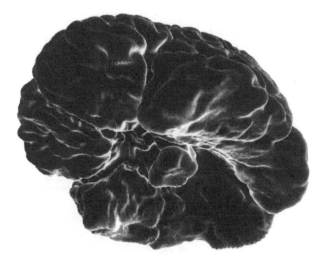

Figure 2: The second type of data is the coordinates of the outer cortical surface found by shrinking a triangular mesh to the outer cortical surface, here shown for a single subject.

The third is the 3D vector of displacements required to warp the structure to an atlas standard, shown as small vectors (Figure 3). We treat this as multivariate Gaussian data, and we use multivariate regression to detect the effect of the explanatory variables. The result is a 3D image of Hotelling's T^2 statistics at each point in space (Cao and Worsley, 1999a).

2   Random Field Theory

The result of the above statistical analyses is a random field of test statistics, and our main interest is how to deal with them. Clearly thresholding these test statistic images at the usual uncorrected $P < 0.05$ critical value results in far too many false positive differences. We shall show how to correct for this 'multiple testing' problem using random field theory. We could regard the image values, sampled at up to 500,000 voxels, as a very high dimensional multivariate observation, but a better approach is to model them as a continuous function or random field.

We use a topological quantity, the *Euler characteristic* (EC) of the excursion set of a random field, as a tool to detect localised changes (Adler, 1981; Worsley, 1994, 1995). The excursion set is the set of points in the search region (here the brain) where the value exceeds a given threshold. The EC counts the number of isolated components in the excursion set, minus the

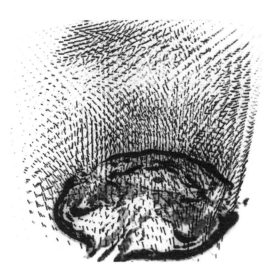

Figure 3: The third type of data are the deformations required to warp the brain of a single subject to an atlas standard, here shown as small vectors.

number of holes. As the threshold becomes high, the excursion set becomes smaller and the holes tend to disappear, so that the EC counts the number of isolated components, each of which contains just one local maximum. At even higher thresholds, near the global maximum, the EC takes the value 1 if the global maximum is above the threshold, and 0 otherwise. Thus at very high thresholds, the EC becomes an indicator function for the presence of the global maximum above the threshold. It immediately follows that the the expected EC is an accurate approximation to the P-value of the global maximum. The beauty of using the EC is that its expectation can be found *exactly* for all thresholds and search regions of any shape or size. Moreover, Adler (2000) has recently shown that it is an extremely accurate approximation to the P-value of the global maximum.

3   Multidimensional Scaling

The above theory rests on the assumption that the data is isotropic, that is, the spatial correlation function is identical at all points. This is definitely not the cases for our data: the effective smoothness is not constant across the image. We propose a solution that warps the data to isotropy using local multidimensional scaling (MDS). Recent theoretical work has shown that the subsequent corrections to the random field theory can be done without actually doing the warping (Taylor and Adler, 2002).

Figure 4: The cortical surface after local MDS to make the random field isotropic The edges of the triangular mesh are inversely proportional to the FWHM of the smoothing kernel.

We only illustrate the multidimensional scaling for the second data set on cortical surface displacements. The effective smoothness is conveniently measured by the FWHM, the Full Width at Half Maximum (FWHM) of a Gaussian kernel used to smooth white noise. It is estimated by $\sqrt{4\log 2/\mathrm{Var}(\dot{u})}$, where u is the normalised residual from the linear model and dot is spatial derivative. To see this, take the 1D case. Suppose that we can write the error component of the data as $e = k \star w$, where k is a smoothing kernel, ϵ is a white noise process, and $\star$ is convolution. Then $\lambda = \mathrm{Var}(\dot{e})/\mathrm{Var}(e) = \dot{k} \star \dot{k}/k \star k$. For the Gaussian shaped kernel $k(x) \propto \exp(-(x/\sigma)^2/2)$, then $\lambda = 1/(2\sigma^2)$. The FWHM of a Gaussian kernel is a multiple of its standard deviation: $\sqrt{8\log 2}\sigma$. Equating these, and replacing e by normalised residuals, gives the above estimator.

We apply local MDS by making the edge lengths of the triangular mesh inversely proportional to the estimated FWHM. Note that this is a local metric MDS, in which we only try to match distances between neighbouring points. After 4000 iterations of a simple algorithm that re-positions each point in turn relative to its neighbours, the result is a shrinking of the occipital lobe (which had high smoothness) and an expansion of basal areas (which had low smoothness). The FWHM on the transformed surface is fairly constant over the entire brain, so that the T statistic image on the new surface is now isotropic (Figure 4). Applying random field theory, the threshold for controlling the false positive rate to $P = 0.05$ is 4.57, which suggests significant changes in the basal regions on the original brain surface.

Figure 5: The cortical surface after global MDS, equivalent to a PCA of the surface coordinates The result is a very highly convoluted surface.

4   Principal Components Analysis

For comparison, we also tried a global MDS in which we try to match distances between all pairs of points on the mesh, not just neighbouring points as above. This is equivalent to a Principal Components Analysis of the subjects × mesh points (151 × 40, 962) matrix of normalised residuals u. The eigen vector corresponding to the largest eigen value is the classical MDS solution for the coordinates of the mesh points. The result, explaining 32.5% of the variability, is a highly convoluted, self-intersecting surface that bears little resemblance to the original cortical surface (Figure 5).

We are also interested in detecting pairs of regions of the brain that show functional connectivity, measured by high correlation between PET or fMRI measurements. Here the data consists of a sequence of 3D images taken either on the same subject (over time) or on different subjects, and we wish to find pairs of points that are highly correlated. Previous analyses have either looked for correlations between a small set of pre-selected points, or betwenn one pre-selected point and all others in the image (Friston *et al.*, 1997; Gitelman *et al.*, 2002; Gonalves *et al.*, 2001; Grady *et al.*, 2001; Strother *et al.*, 2002). In our approach we consider correlations between *all* pairs of points, to create a 6D 'image', and once again we use random field theory to detect high correlations (Cao and Worsley, 1999b). A set of 6 Positron Emission Tomography images measuring cerebral blood flow were taken on each of 8 subjects during a vigilance task. The significant correlations (P¡0.05) are between the ends of the rods in Figure 6.

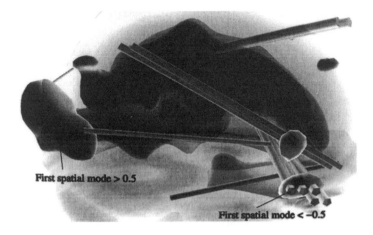

Figure 6: Functional connectivity detected by regions that are highly correlated (ends of rods) Also shown is the first component (first spatial mode) of a PCA analysis of the same data.

An alternative method for this is a Principal Components Analysis of the images × lattice points matrix to reveal patterns of points that vary together. This method is better at detecting large regions of covarying points, whereas the method above is better at picking up isolated local regions that have highly correlated values. The first temporal component indicated an increasing time trend. The first spatial component is shown in Figure 6 thresholded at 0.5 and -0.5. These coincide nicely with highly correlated voxels at the ends of the rods. The high (> 0.5) regions in the visual cortex show where cerebral blood flow increased over time, whereas the low (< 0.5) regions show where it decreased. The latter actually come from an artery outside the brain that supplies blood to the jaw muscles; the explanation for the decreased blood flow was that the subjects were initially nervous and clenched their jaws, then they relaxed over time, decreasing the blood flow.

5 Conclusion

Brain mapping data is a fascinating source of interesting statistical problems that should be a great stimulus to the field of psychometrics. As this paper shows, many classical methods such as classification, principal components, and multidimensional scaling, find new uses in the context of images. For example, principal components themselves become images, and multidimensional scaling can be constrained by local spatial distances rather than all possible distances. Moreover, some fascinating ideas from integral geometry and differential topology, such as the Euler characteristic, play a key role in inference about images of test statistics. Their are many hurdles to overcome before we can analyse this strange and unfamiliar data, such as its sheer size, unusual format, and the need for specialized software. But once crossed, the rewards for research in psychometrics should be worth it.

References

Adler RJ (1981) *The Geometry of Random Fields* Wiley, New York

Adler RJ (2000) On excursion sets, tube formulae, and maxima of random fields (Invited Paper) *Annals of Applied Probability,* **10**:1-74

Cao J, Worsley KJ (1999a) The detection of local shape changes via the geometry of Hotelling's T^2 fields *Annals of Statistics* **27**:925-942

Cao J, Worsley KJ (1999b) The geometry of correlation fields, with an application to functional connectivity of the brain *Annals of Applied Probability,* **9**:1021-1057

Friston KJ, Buechel C, Fink GR, Morris J, Rolls E, Dolan, RJ (1997) Psychophysiological and modulatory interactions in neuroimaging *NeuroImage,* **6**:218-229

Gitelman DR, Parrish TB, Friston KJ, Mesulam MM (2002) Functional anatomy of visual search: regional segregations within the frontal eye fields and effective connectivity of the superior colliculus *NeuroImage,* **15**:970-982

Gonalves MS, Hall DA, Johnsrude IS, Haggard, MP (2001) Can meaningful effective connectivities be obtained between auditory cortical regions? *NeuroImage,* **14**:1353-1360

Grady CL, McIntosh AR, Deig S, Craik, FIM (2001) An examination of the effects of stimulus type, encoding task, and functional connectivity on the role of right prefrontal cortex in recognition memory *NeuroImage,* **14**:556-57

Strother SC, MacFarlane AC, Morris P, Anderson J, Clark, CR, Egan, GF (2002) Abnormal functional connectivity in posttraumatic stress disorder *NeuroImage,* **15**:661-674

Taylor JE, Adler RJ (2002) Euler characteristics for Gaussian fields on manifolds *Annals of Probability,* accepted

Worsley KJ (1994) Local maxima and the expected Euler characteristic of excursion sets of χ^2, F and t fields *Advances in Applied Probability,* **26**:13-42

Worsley KJ (1995) Boundary corrections for the expected Euler characteristic of excursion sets of random fields, with an application to astrophysics *Advances in Applied Probability,* **27**:943-959

Human Decision Making Model by Boolean Approach and Fuzzy Reasoning

Yasunari Kono[1] and Toshiyuki Yamashita[2]

[1]Applied Sociology, Graduate School of Social Relations, Rikkyo University, 3-34-1 Nishi Ikebukuro, Toshima, Tokyo 171-8501, Japan
[2]Graduate School of Engineering, Tokyo Metropolitan Institute of Technology, 6-6 Asahigaoka, Hino Tokyo 191-0065, Japan

Summary. Constructing fuzzy rules for fuzzy reasoning models is relatively difficult although fuzzy reasoning has been used for human decision making models. Boolean approach is proper for seeking and formulizing patterns of unanticipated as well as expected relationships between the combinations of causal conditions because of the results expressed by minimized algebraic equations.

This paper proposes a new method using Boolean approach as a complementary tool to build the fuzzy rules for a fuzzy reasoning model. The effectiveness of Boolean approach for some fuzzy reasoning model is demonstrated by using the data on a human decision making.

Key words. Boolean approach, fuzzy reasoning, decision making

1 Introduction

Yamashita and Furusawa (2000) propose a career decision making model based on fuzzy reasoning to develop a support system for high school students' choosing their careers. The fuzzy rules of the model are based on the results from a factor analysis of the questionnaire data concerning career motives. Their study reveals the difficulty in constructing the fuzzy rules for the fuzzy reasoning model while it becomes clear that the prediction of the model can provide valuable information for the teacher who is engaged in guidance counseling. Hence, it is significant to develop an effective method to construct the fuzzy rules for the model.

Boolean approach developed by Ragin (1987) as a case-oriented comparative method has been applied to various topics in the field of social sciences for case studies. Several causal conditions often unite in specific configurations to produce particular qualitative outcomes in most of social phenomena. Boolean approach seems to be proper for seeking and formulizing patterns of unanticipated as well as expected relationships between the combinations of causal conditions because of the results expressed by minimized algebraic equations (Kono, 1999).

This paper proposes a new method building fuzzy rules by Boolean approach, and illustrates the efficiency of the method by using the data from Yamashita and Furusawa (2000).

2 Boolean Approach and Fuzzy Reasoning

Boolean approach and fuzzy reasoning construct a model for human decision making. These two methods have been used completely different purposes or fields. This model clearly reveals the characteristics of each method.

2.1 Boolean approach

Boolean approach uses dichotomous data basically. The data have the form of a truth table, in which the columns represent causal variables and the rows represent individuals. Each causal variable may take the values 0 or 1 for an individual. 0 is equivalent to a lower-case letter and 1 to an upper-case letter in the column of the causal variable. The cutoff method codes the outputs when the ratio of each row is not 100 percent, and re-codes them by percentage of 1 or 0 of R in each row case.

Table 1 demonstrates an example of a 75 percent cutoff value. The second, third, fourth and eighth rows' outputs in this table are coded 1 since these ratios are over 75 percent.

Table 1. Example of a truth table

Causal variable			Minterm	Occurrence	Output	Numbers of $R=1$	Ratio
X	Y	Z					
0	0	0	xyz	10	**0**	1	10%
0	0	1	xyZ	1	**1**	1	100%
0	1	0	xYz	5	**1**	4	80%
0	1	1	xYZ	8	**1**	7	88%
1	0	0	Xyz	2	**0**	0	0%
1	0	1	XyZ	1	**0**	0	0%
1	1	0	XYz	5	**0**	1	20%
1	1	1	XYZ	3	**1**	3	100%
				35	Total	17	

QCA (Drass & Ragin, 1986) which is a computer program for Boolean approach produces the results, and finds a minimized equation by Quine-McClusky algorithm (Quine, 1952). The equation is found according to a truth table after setting cutoff value. QCA calculates the minimized equation of the 75 percent cutoff for **Table 1** as follows:

$$R = xY + xZ + YZ,\tag{1}$$

where xY, xZ, and YZ are conjunctions, or logical products. Disjunction or logical sum is denoted by "+."

2.2 Fuzzy reasoning model

Fuzzy reasoning model usually takes the form as follows:

Rule 1	:	A	and b	and C	$\Rightarrow$	R_1
Rule 2	:	A	and b	and c	$\Rightarrow$	R_2
			$\cdot \quad \cdot \quad \cdot$			
Rule n	:	a	and B	and c	$\Rightarrow$	R_n
Fact	:	a_0	b_0	c_0		
Conclusion	:					R'

where A, a, B, b and C, c in the antecedent part are fuzzy sets, and R_i, i=1, 2,..., n, in the consequent part are also fuzzy sets. a_0, b_0 and c_0 are inputs to the fuzzy reasoning model.

The result of Rule i (i=1, 2, ..., n) is calculated by

$$\mu_{R_i'}(z) = \mu_A(a_0) \wedge \mu_B(b_0) \wedge \mu_C(c_0) \wedge \mu_{R_i}(z),\tag{2}$$

and the combined conclusion of the rules is given as

$$\mu_{R'}(z) = \mu_{R_1'}(z) \vee \mu_{R_2'}(z) \vee ... \vee \mu_{R_n'}(z).\tag{3}$$

2.3 The Construction of Fuzzy rules by Boolean Approach

Boolean approach is quite effective to identify the configurations of causal conditions. However, Boolean approach requires binary variables, or each variable takes the values of 0 or 1 for a case or an individual. This is a problem to directly apply Boolean approach to the modeling of human decision making because people often have a vague sense of their own motives when choosing and deciding on their behavior. Moreover, each career motive which has a degree of strength is a fuzzy set. Fuzzy reasoning is suitable for capturing and modeling the fuzziness in human decision making although there is no objective method for constructing fuzzy rules for a fuzzy reasoning model.

This paper develops a new method in which Boolean approach can be used as a complementary tool to build the fuzzy rules for a fuzzy reasoning model.

3 Applications

This research uses the data collected from a questionnaire survey to 138 third year students attending a high school for women (Yamashita & Furusawa, 2000). Question 1 describes 26 items concerning career motives. The students rate these items by the fuzzy rating method. On the right side of each item is a 48-mm horizontal line with the left end labeled "weak" and the right end labeled "strong." Each student makes a mark on the horizontal line according to how much influence is exerted by the item when she makes a career choice after graduation from high school. This kind of fuzzy rating method is called point estimation method (Chameau & Santamarina, 1987). The rated values by the fuzzy ratings are transformed into values ranging from 0 to 1 after the survey. Factor analysis is done for 26 items, and the five factors with eigenvalues over 1.0 are identified. Varimax rotation is then performed for the five factors.

Table 2 shows the results, and the items with an absolute factor loading of greater than 0.47 are combined and framed.

Table 2. Factor loading

Item	Factor1 Motive to receive a higher education	Factor2 Moratorium motive	Factor3 Motive to be free and independent	Factor4 Motive to enjoy life	Factor5 Motive based on scholastic ability
26.Need for future career	**0.83**	-0.07	0.07	0.07	-0.06
25.Wants to obtain qualifications and licenses	**0.81**	-0.21	-0.02	-0.06	0.06
5.Is advantageous for future career	**0.78**	-0.14	0.03	-0.10	-0.04
18.Wants to learn special knowledge and techniques	**0.73**	-0.10	-0.24	-0.16	-0.19
11.Wants to fulfill possibilities	**0.52**	-0.01	0.14	-0.42	-0.42
13.Yearns for something	**0.47**	-0.01	0.14	-0.41	-0.19
24.Wants to fully demonstrate self	**0.47**	0.09	0.11	-0.44	-0.41
3.Does not want to go out into the world	0.23	**-0.81**	-0.05	-0.14	0.03
19.Does not want to work	0.29	**-0.77**	-0.04	-0.08	-0.09
20.Other people will go	-0.09	**-0.66**	0.25	0.07	-0.33
17.Wantd to play around	-0.03	**-0.66**	0.14	-0.39	-0.02
4.Current fashion	0.12	**-0.62**	0.42	0.06	-0.25
14.Wants free time	0.02	**-0.51**	0.14	**-0.56**	-0.13
8.Wants to make money and to spend it freely	-0.30	-0.06	**0.73**	-0.16	0.09
23.To set parent's heart to rest	0.13	-0.02	**0.72**	-0.18	0.04
6.Wants to be respected	0.25	-0.35	**0.61**	-0.02	-0.14
9.Wants to become independent	0.35	0.17	**0.57**	-0.23	-0.21
22.It is advantageous to marry	0.10	-0.33	**0.56**	-0.17	-0.06
7.Because it is recommended by teachers	-0.09	-0.24	**0.56**	0.14	-0.38
21.Does not want to continue further study	-0.36	-0.11	**0.53**	-0.25	0.22
1.Because it is recommended by parents	-0.01	-0.42	**0.50**	0.34	-0.06
2.To solve family economic problem	-0.23	-0.19	**0.48**	0.07	-0.33
12.Wants to be able to associate with many people	0.22	0.00	0.09	**-0.76**	-0.02
16.Wants to enjoy life	0.14	-0.31	0.10	**-0.74**	-0.04
15.Because of insufficient scholastic ability	0.07	-0.32	0.04	-0.15	**-0.62**
10.Wants to continue to study	0.44	-0.24	-0.05	-0.08	**-0.60**
Eigenvalue	4.11	3.63	3.55	2.58	1.75
Contribution ratio (%)	15.79	13.98	13.66	9.92	6.75
Cumulative contribution ratio (%)	15.79	29.76	43.42	53.34	60.09

The first, second, third, fourth, and fifth factors are labeled "motive to receive a higher education," "moratorium motive," "motive to be free and independent," "motive to enjoy life," and "motive based on insufficient scholastic ability," respectively. The fifth factor is excluded from this study because it is considered to be more related to a selection of school than to a choice among types of careers.

Truth tables for Boolean approach used in this research are made on the basis of these factors as follows:

- A: Motive to receive a higher education
- B: Moratorium motive
- C: Motive to be free and independent
- D: Motive to enjoy life.

It is assumed that a truth value is coded to 1 when the average rated value for each student across the items included in each factor is greater than or equal to 0.5 and that the truth value is coded to 0 when the average rated value is less than 0.5. Both the disjunctive canonical forms and the minimized algebraic equations are acquired from the truth tables.

Table 3. Truth table

Causal variable				Minterm	Occurrence	Output P_1	Actual choice Going on to a school of higher grade		Output P_2	Actual choice Finding an employment	
A	B	C	D								
0	0	0	0	abcd	28	0	4	14%	1	24	86%
0	0	0	1	abcD	10	0	0	0%	1	10	100%
0	0	1	1	abCD	5	0	0	0%	1	5	100%
0	1	0	0	aBcd	3	0	2	67%	0	1	33%
0	1	0	1	aBcD	1	1	1	100%	0	0	0%
0	1	1	1	aBCD	2	1	2	100%	0	0	0%
1	0	0	0	Abcd	28	1	27	96%	0	1	4%
1	0	0	1	AbcD	30	1	23	77%	0	7	23%
1	0	1	1	AbCD	5	0	2	40%	0	3	60%
1	1	0	0	ABcd	2	1	2	100%	0	0	0%
1	1	0	1	ABcD	16	1	14	88%	0	2	13%
1	1	1	1	ABCD	8	0	4	50%	0	4	50%

QCA minimizes Equation 4 as for "going on to a school of higher grade" in **Table 3** to Equation 5 as follows:

$$P_1 = aBcD + aBCD + Abcd + AbcD + ABcd + ABcD \tag{4}$$

$$P_1 = aBD + Ac. \tag{5}$$

Equation 5 signifies that the students who desire to go on to a school of higher grade are divided into two subgroups. One is a type of person who has a weak motive to receive a higher education (a) and a strong moratorium motive (B) and a strong motive to enjoy life (D). The other is a kind of person who has a strong motive to receive a higher education (A) and a weak motive to be free and independent (c).

QCA also minimizes Equation 6 as for "finding employment" in **Table 3** to Equation 7 as follows:

$$P_2 = abcd + abcD + abCD \tag{6}$$

$$P_2 = abc + abD. \tag{7}$$

Equation 7 expresses that the students who desire to find employment are divided into two subgroups. Both have a weak motive to receive a higher education (a) and a weak moratorium motive (b) commonly. In addition to two motives, one type of student has a weak motive to be free and independent (c), and the other has a strong motive to enjoy life (D).

The fuzzy reasoning model for career decision making is built based on the outputs of Boolean approach. Figure 1 represents the rule of fuzzy reasoning the using Mamdami's method (Mamdami, 1974).

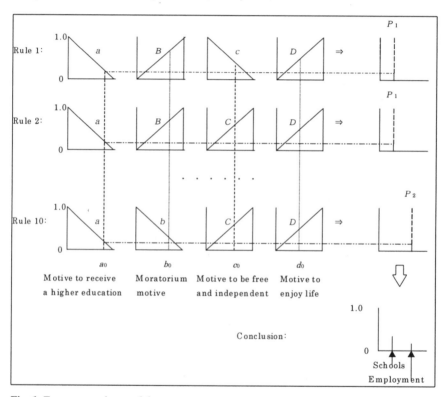

Fig. 1. Fuzzy reasoning model

For example, a, B, c, and D in the antecedent part are fuzzy sets of career motives for Rule 1, and P_1 and P_2 in the consequent part are fuzzy sets of desired careers; P_1 is a desire to go on to a school of higher grade, and P_2 is a desire to find employment. The average rated values for each student on the items included in the four factors are used as such input values as a_0, b_0, c_0, and d_0. The abscissas indicate the intensity of each motive, and the ordinates indicate the grade of membership for each career motive. The membership functions shape triangular because of the simple treatment. A triangle with an apex on the right is used as a membership function when a motive has a strong influence on a student's career choice. A triangle with an apex on the left is used as a membership function when a motive doesn't have a strong influence on a student's career choice. For example, Rule 1 means if the "motive to receive a higher education" is weak, and the "moratorium motive" is strong, and "motive to be free and independent" is weak, and the "motive to enjoy life" is strong, then the desired career is to go on to schools of higher grade.

Mamdani's method computes the conclusion. The career with higher grade of membership is assumed as the career predicted by the model. "Going on to a school of higher grade" is predicted in this figure

4 Discussions

Table 4 indicates the relationship between the careers actually chosen by the students and the careers predicted by the fuzzy reasoning model.

Table 4. Actually chosen careers and results from the fuzzy reasoning model

		Actual choice		Total
		Going on to a school of higher grade	Finding employment	
Fuzzy reasoning	Going on to a school of higher grade	76	18	94
	Finding an employment	4	40	44
Total		80	58	138

The model predicts the actual choice in 76 of 80 (95%) students who decide to go on to a school of higher grade and in 40 out of 58 (67%) students who decide to find employment. The model is thus able to predict the actually chosen careers in 118 out of 138 students (85.5%). The results indicate that the fuzzy reasoning model obtained by applying Boolean approach to constructing fuzzy rules enables to predict career choices with high accuracy.

Table 5 shows the relationship between the careers actually chosen by the students and the careers predicted by discriminant analysis using average rating values on the items included in the four factors.

Table 5. Actually chosen careers and results from discriminant analysis

		Actual choice		Total
		Going on to a school of higher grade	Finding employment	
Discriminant analysis	Going on to a school of higher grade	**73**	12	85
	Finding an employment	7	**46**	53
Total		80	58	138

Discriminant analysis predicts the actual choice in 73 out of 80 (91.3%) students who decide to go on to a school of higher grade, and in 46 out of 58 (79.3%) students who decide to find employment. Discriminant analysis predicts the actually chosen careers in 119 out of 138 students (86.2%).

The results indicate that the fuzzy reasoning model predicts career choices with the same accuracy as discriminant analysis. Moreover, the fuzzy reasoning model is superior to discriminant analysis in presenting the rules, which is helpful to interpret the results.

This research uses Boolean approach to build the fuzzy reasoning model. The model constructed by using Boolean approach predicts career choices with high accuracy. Fuzzy theory approach and Boolean approach should be developed to the hybrid approaches in future though they are complementally used in this paper.

References

Chameau, J-L. & Santamarina, J. C. (1987). Membership function I: Comparing methods of measurement, International Journal of Approximate Reasoning, 1, 287-301.

Drass, K. and Ragin, C. C. (1986). QCA: A microcomputer package for qualitative comparative analysis of social data. Center for urban affairs and policy research, Northwestern University.

Kono, Y. (1999). A design for contradictory terms in Boolean approach: Head and tail analysis. Unpublished master's thesis, Rikkyo University, Tokyo.

Mamdami, E. H. (1974). Application of fuzzy algorithm for control of a simple dynamic plant, Proceedings of IEEE, 121, 1585-1588.

Quine, W. V. (1952). The Problem of Simplifying Truth Functions. American Mathematics Monthly, October, 1952, 59, 521-531

Ragin, C. C. (1987). The comparative method: Moving beyond qualitative and quantitative strategies. Berkeley: The University of California Press.

Yamashita, T. & Furusawa, T. (2000). Modeling of career decision making by fuzzy reasoning. Japan Journal of Educational Technology, 24(Suppl.), 103-108.

A New Model of Rating Scale Method Considering Context Effects Based on Fuzzy Logic and its Application for a Psychological Response to the Acoustic Noise

Yuichi Kato[1], Takahiro Imaoka[1] and Shizuma Yamaguchi[2]

[1]Interdisciplinary Faculty of Science and Engineering, Shimane University, 1060 Nishikawatu-cho, Matsue City, Shimane 690-8504, Japan

[2]Faculty of Engineering, Yamaguchi University, 2557 Tokiwadai, Ube City, Yamaguchi 755-8611, Japan

Summary. The rating scale method and/or the method of successive categories are widely used for rating objects using the successive categories. This paper points out several problems with the conventional method and studies the rating problems from the viewpoint that the rating conducts can be regarded as a kind of fuzzy and subjective logical judging process. The fuzziness and the subjectivity are derived from the meaning of rating words and the difference of feeling to the stimulus. The quality and the structure of the judging process, especially the context effect are clearly discussed in Fuzzy Theory. These studies are developed into a dynamic rating system in order to rate the acoustic noise in time series. The validity of the studies and the usefulness of the system are experimentally confirmed by applying it to the noise rating problem and by clarifying the criterion of judgment and the context effect.

Key words. Fuzzy logic, Successive categories, Acoustic noise, Fuzzy proposition

1 The Conventional Model and its Problems

The outline of the conventional rating scale model is shown in Fig.1. The model consists mainly of three assumptions (Guilford,1954):(1)A stimulus S_i in the stimulus continuum is projected on the psychological continuum. (2)The psychological continuum is divided into several categories expressed by words. For example, F1:"very calm", F2:"quite calm", F3:"slightly calm", F4:"medium", F5:"slightly noisy", F6:"quite noisy" F7:"very noisy" are specified in order to rate the acoustic noise. These categories have crisp boundaries on the continuum even if their boundaries fluctuate in terms of probabilities. (3)The response of stimulus is based on the stochastic process and has usually Gaussian distribution.

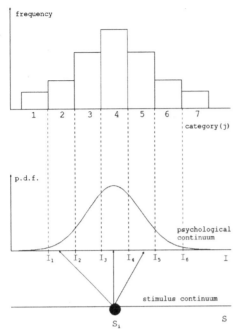

Fig. 1. The outline of the rating scale model.

However, several problems arise when we use the model. One of them is whether the meanings of the words like "very calm", "quite calm" and so on can be clearly defined or not. Meanings of words also seem to highly depend on the subject who is rating the stimulus. Another problem is how the stochastic process is specified. These problems give us important clues to study more about the model.

2 The Logical Model of Rating

When we are asked to rate a stimulus using the specified categories, we will judge which category is best suited for the given stimulus. In the process, we seem to be unconsciously thinking the proposition(P6) that the given acoustic noise(O) is, for instance, quite noisy(F6). One subjectively judges its impression based on ones' truth value. That is, P6:"O is F6", is judged to be true in degree of μ_{F6} . If we find the physical quantities $\{l_1, l_2,...\}$ to affect μ_{F6} effectively, μ_{F6} can be concretely specified as $\mu_{F6}(l_1, l_2,...)$. However, one can not crisply specify the border of the truth values between "true(1)" and "false(0)" because of the vagueness of meanings of F6. Accordingly, the range of $\mu_{F6}(l_1, l_2,...)$ is in the unit interval [0,1] and $\mu_{F6}(l_1, l_2,...)$ is the so-called fuzzy truth value function (Klir et al 1995). Corresponding to the presented stimulus, one will eventually choose the j-th category Fj of a high degree of truth value from seven ones.

The proposition P6 includes two words of different qualities. One is a linguistic hedge of "quite(τ_6)". The other is an adjective word of "noisy(T)". The linguistic hedge modifies the adjective. Accordingly, the proposition P6 is arranged as GP6: "(O is T) is τ_6 ", using the general form of a fuzzy proposition (Zadeh, 1972).

Generally, the linguistic hedges like "very", "quite", "slightly" and so on are used in our daily life to rate the degree of the stimulus. On the other hand, the adjectives like "noisy" or "calm" are used to represent the quality of the stimulus and are directly combined with the physical quantities $\{l_1, l_2,...\}$. Accordingly, the truth value of the proposition(PT): "O is T", is given by $\mu_T(l_1,l_2,...)$. The truth value of GP6 is given by $\tau_6(\mu_T(l_1,l_2,...))$, which is called to be quantified by τ_6.

The context effects by the change of the stimulus domain(Namba et al, 1968) are caused in PT since $\mu_T(l_1,l_2,...)$ is directly combined with the physical quantities $\{l_1,l_2,...\}$ and strongly influenced by the change. On the other hand, $\tau_i(s)$ (i=1,...,7) is hardly influenced by the change since they are only quantifiers and have nothing to do with the physical quantities. As the results, $\mu_{Fi}(l_1,l_2,...)$ $(=\tau_i(\mu_T(l_1,l_2,...)))$ is influenced by the context effects derived from $\mu_T(l_1,l_2,...)$.

The main differences and relationships between the conventional model and the proposed one are shown in Table 1.

Table 1. Differences and relationship between conventional model and the propoed one.

	The conventional model	The proposed model
Process	A stochastic process	A logical judging process
Range of rating	Psychological continuum I	Truth value space[0, 1]
Categories	Crisp categories on I	Fuzzy categories on [0, 1]

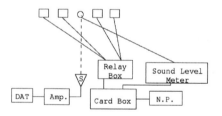

Fig.2. Experimental situation of measurring psychological experiment.○:Sound level meter, □:Subject.

3 Rating Acoustic Noise

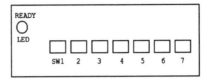

Fig.3. Button swich box

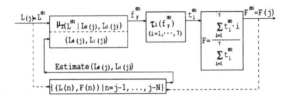

Fig.4. Dynamic rating system for the acoustic noise

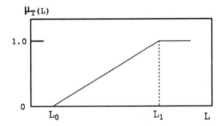

Fig.5. Fuzzy truth value function $\mu_T(L \mid L_0, L_1)$

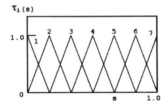

Fig.6. Fuzzy truth value function $\tau_i(s)$

3.1 Experimental Situation

Figure 2 shows an experimental situation of rating the acoustic noise. The noise recorded in DAT in advance was presented through an amplifier Amp. and a speaker S to subjects. The noise was the white one and its amplitude was changed randomly in the domain [r1, r2] [dB(A)] every 5[s]. The duration time was 300[s]. Each subject had the button switch box shown in Fig.3 and rated the noise at the second when the READY LED(see Fig. 3) was on for 1 [s], using the switch assigning the impression Fi(i=1,...,7). The note type personal computer N.P. in Fig.2 saved measured data.

3.2 Specification of Practical Rating System

The logical rating model studied in 2 was implemented as a dynamic rating system for the acoustic noise shown in Fig. 4. Here, the noise level $L(j)$ represents physical quantities $\{l_1, l_2, ...\}$ and μ_T was given as a S-type logical function shown in Fig.5, where L_0 and L_1 were parameters specifying the function. The shape implies that one feels noisier as the noise level gets higher. τ_i was a triangular one shown in Fig.6. The shape implies the equal distance between categories. The output F was calculated by the so-called non-fuzzy procedure and parameters in μ_T were estimated by the following criterion using the past N samples:

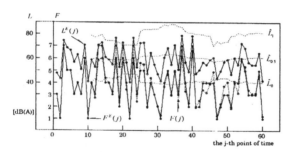

(a) Estimated $(\hat{L}_0, \hat{L}_1)$ and $\hat{L}_{0.5}$ and prediction of F

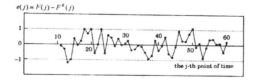

(b) Prediction errors

Fig.7. Results of experimental studies(Subject A)

$$l_F = \max_{(L_0, L_1)} \sum_j \log[\tau_i(\mu_T(L(j) \mid L_0, L_1))]\big|_{i=F(j)}. \qquad (1)$$

Equation 1 is a kind of maximum likelihood method although it estimates the logical function.

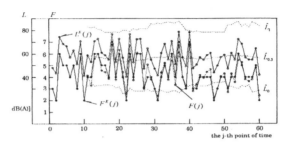

(a) Estimated ($\hat{L}_0, \hat{L}_1$) and $\hat{L}_{0.5}$ and prediction of F

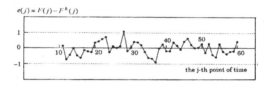

(b) Prediction errors

Fig.8. Results of experimental studies(Subject B)

3.3 Results of Experimental Studies and Differences between Subjects

Figure 7(a) shows results of Subject A where $L^E(j)$ ($\in [40, 80][\text{dB(A)}]$) is the presented noise level, $F^E(j)$ ($\in \{1,2, ...,7\}$) is a measured impression and $F(j)(\in [1, 7])$ is an calculated output of the proposed system in Fig.4 at the j-th time point. The calculation starts from the eleventh time point since the first ten data are consumed for the estimation of μ_T. Errors between the measured and calculated values are almost within one rank(see Fig.7(b)) and their correlation is 0.94. The proposed system seems to work properly. Moreover, the proposed system can estimate the judgment level: L_0, L_1 and $L_{0.5}$ which is the center of judgment, is from 40 to 46, from 70 to 80 and about 60 [dB(A)] respectively.

In the same way, Fig.8 shows results of Subject B. Compared with Subject A, B's dynamic range is wider and his calmness level is quite low (see his L_0 and $L_{0.5}$). The proposed system can clearly show the differences between subjects.

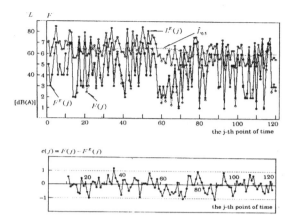

Fig.9. Studies for context effect (Subject A) in Case(a)

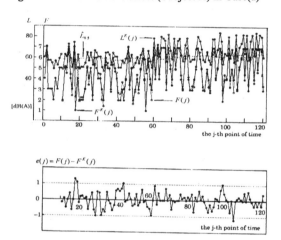

Fig. 10. Studies for context effect (Subject A) in Case(b)

3.4 Studies on Context Effect

In order to examine the context effect by the change of the stimulus domain, the following two experiments were conducted: Case(a): $L^E(j) \in$ [55,85][dB(A)] (j =1,...,60), $L^E(j) \in$ [45, 75] [dB(A)] (j = 61,..,120), Case(b): $L^E(j) \in$ [45,75] [dB(A)] (j =1,...,60), $L^E(j) \in$ [55, 85][dB(A)] (j = 61,...,120). That is, the stimulus domain was changed between the former and the latter of the experiment and the total duration time was 600[s]. The result of both cases is shown in Fig.9 and Fig.10 respectively. In Fig.9 (Case(a)), the proposed system clearly shows the shift of the $L_{0.5}$ from 64 or 65 to 60[dB(A)] at the past 60-th time point. In the same way, Fig.10 (Case(b)) shows the result of the reverse pattern of the change. The center level of judgment $L_{0.5}$ moves from 59 to 63 or 64 [dB(A)] with errors almost within 1 rank. The proposed system clearly captured the context effect.

4 Conclusion

This paper has studied the followings:
1. A new model of rating scale method based on fuzzy logic has been proposed and has clearly discussed the differences between the proposed and the conventional one.
2. The new model has been developed into a dynamic rating system and has been applied to the problem of rating the acoustic noise.
3. The system has represented the structure and the criterion of judgment($\mu_T (L \mid L_0, L_1)$) besides predicting psychological outputs.
4. The proposed system has been useful to show the difference of features among subjects.
5. The system has reasonably explained the context effect caused by the change of the stimulus domain and has been adaptive to such changes.

Up to now, various kinds of rating models have been proposed. However, the conventional models seem to have difficulty getting the results shown in this paper. The reason seems to start from the model based on the stochastic process (cf. 1). They have not explained the meanings of rating words which are vague and highly dependent on subjectivity. This paper has studied these problems of conventional models using Fuzzy Theory.

Reference

Guilford, J.P.(1994) Psychometric Methods. McGraw-Hill. NewYork,Toronto London, pp.223-262. Klir,G.J.,& Yuan, B. (1995) Fuzzy sets and fuzzy logic Theory and Applications. Prentice Hall, New Jersey.

Namba, S., Nakamura, T.,& Kuwano,S.(1968). Context Effects in Loudness Judgment. Jap. of J. Psychol, 39, 191-199.

Namba, S., Kuwano, S., & Nakamura, T..(1978). Rating of Road Traffic Noise using the Method of Continuous Judgment by Category. Journal of the Acoustical Society of Japan, 34, pp.29-34.

Zadeh, L.A.. (1972). A Fuzzy-Set-Theoretic Interpretation of Linguistic Hedges. Journal of Cybernetics, 2, pp.4-34.

Subtype Classification of Social Anxiety in Japanese Undergraduates

Ibuki Mohri, and Yoshihiko Tanno

Department of Cognitive and Behavioral Science, Graduate School of Arts and Sciences, The University of Tokyo, 3-8-1 Komaba, Meguro-ku, Tokyo 153-8902, Japan

Summary. Previous studies have revealed two subtypes of social phobia, the generalized subtype and the non-generalized subtype. These subtypes have been reported mainly in Western countries. The purpose of the present study was to investigate the subtypes of social anxiety in Japan. Eight hundred forty-one Japanese undergraduate students completed the Social Anxiety Scale by Social Situations (SASSS). Ward's cluster analysis on five subscales of SASSS revealed five clusters. These clusters were labeled (1) non-anxiety group, (2) average social anxiety group, (3) silence anxiety group, (4) presentation/speech anxiety group, and (5) generalized social anxiety group. The last three clusters were subtypes of social anxiety in Japan. The presentation/speech anxiety group may correspond to the non-generalized subtype, and the generalized social anxiety group may correspond to the generalized subtype. The silence anxiety group has not been reported in Western countries. It was presumed that the presence of the silence anxiety group is specific to Japan.

Keywords. Social anxiety, Social phobia, Subtype, Classification, Taijin kyofu-sho

1 Introduction

Research has revealed that there are two subtypes of social phobia, the generalized subtype and the non-generalized subtype (Gelernter et al. 1992, Heimberg et al 1990). DSM-IV (American Psychiatric Association 1994) described the generalized subtype of social phobia, in which an individual fears most social situations. Persons with non-generalized social phobia typically fear "performance" situations such as public speaking, although the non-generalized subtype is not defined in DSM-IV. Persons with generalized social phobia are more anxious and more depressed than persons with non-generalized social phobia (Gelernter et al. 1992). These subtypes have been primarily reported for social anxiety and social phobia of people in Western countries (e.g., US, Canada, Germany). Little is known about the subtypes of social anxiety in Japan.

A common social phobia in Japan is Taijin-kyoufu-sho (TKS), which is almost nonexistent in Western countries. TKS is characterized by a two-stage structure of fear. The first stage is a fear of offending others through the expression of certain imagined shortcomings within oneself (e.g., one's body, body parts, or bodily functions).   The next stage is a fear of being considered disgusting by others because of having offended them.   The former fear was emphasized when TKS was introduced in Western countries.   TKS has long been considered to be a culture-bound phobia in Japan.   Reported cases of TKS in Japan are of a higher frequency than those in Western countries.

The social situations that evoke TKS are different from those for social phobia. Silence in social interactions and social interactions with others who are not close are important factors in TKS.   These situations have not been the focus of social phobia and social anxiety research in Western countries.   The subtypes in Japan may be found to differ from those in Western countries if the subtypes are classified from the standpoint of social situations.   The purpose of the present study was to classify the subtypes of social anxiety in Japan.

2 Method

2.1 Participants

Eight hundred forty-one Japanese undergraduates voluntarily participated in the present study.   Twenty-eight participants with outliers[1] were excluded.   The data of 803 undergraduates (634 men, 169 women) with a mean age of 18.9 years (SD=1.0) were subject to analyses.   The participants who completed a supplementary questionnaire about their personal history of suffering from social anxiety were 262 undergraduates in 803.

2.2 Questionnaires

The Social Anxiety Scale by Social Situations (SASSS, Mohri and Tanno 2001) assesses the subjective aspects of social anxiety in five social situations.   SASSS contains 30 items, each of which is rated on a five-point scale. The items were generated based on the results of an open-ended questionnaire distributed to Japanese undergraduates (Mohri and Tanno 2001).   SASSS has five subscales, (1) presentation/speech anxiety, (2) distanced anxiety, (3) heterosocial anxiety, (4) silence anxiety, and (5) authoritative anxiety.   The subscales possess a high level of Cronbach's alpha of .86 to .92, and a high test-retest reliability of .76 to .89 (Mohri and Tanno 2001).   The items, Cronbach's alpha and test-retest reliability of these five sub scales are given in Appendix.   The subscales correlated well with the established measures of social anxiety and trait anxiety (Mohri and Tanno 2001). SASSS is a reliable and valid measure of social anxiety and is the first scale that measures social anxiety caused by silence in social interactions and social interactions with others who are not close.

---

[1] Ward's method is very sensitive to outliers (Milligan 1980).   Thus, five-subscale scores of the Social Anxiety Scale by Social Situations that exceeded 2.5 standard deviations from each mean score were considered to be outliers.

In addition, 262 participants were asked to choose the most suitable answer from among the following choices: (1) I have never suffered from social anxiety, (2) I suffer from social anxiety at present, (3) I have suffered from social anxiety in the past, but at present I don't suffer from it very much.

2.3 Cluster Analyses

We used Ward's hierarchical agglomerative cluster analysis to establish the initial clusters (Ward 1963). Ward's method is a minimum variance technique that identifies the number of clusters by finding groupings that have the smallest ratio for within group variance to between group variance. The squared euclidian distance was used as the similarity measure. This procedure is used frequently in behavioral sciences because of its high interpretability (Borgen and Barnett 1987).

The five-subscale rating scores of SASSS were first subjected to a hierarchical cluster analysis. The cluster solution was analyzed based on Z scores, with a mean of 0 and standard deviation of 1. A combination of a subjective inspection of the dendrogram structure and the interpretability of clusters was used to select the optimal cluster solution.

Statistical Analysis System (SAS) Release 6.12 was used to perform all statistical analyses.

3 Results

A five-cluster solution was obtained using Ward's cluster analysis. Social anxiety situation profiles based on SASSS scores were shown in Figure 1. Cluster 1 was labeled the "non-anxiety group" because all SASSS subscale scores were under the average. Cluster 2 was labeled the "average social anxiety group" because all SASSS subscale scores were near average. Cluster 3 was labeled the "silence anxiety group" because the silence anxiety score was the highest among all clusters. Cluster 4 was labeled the "presentation/speech anxiety group" because the presentation/speech anxiety score was the highest among all clusters. Cluster 5 was labeled the "generalized social anxiety group" because all SASSS subscale scores were higher than average.

Mean scores of SASSS subscales for each cluster were shown in Table 1. The mean scores in all clusters were compared using one-way analyses of the variance (ANOVA). These ANOVAs of SASSS subscales, presentation/ speech anxiety, silence anxiety, distanced anxiety, heterosocial anxiety, and authoritative anxiety, revealed a significant main effect for the clusters ($F_{(4, 798)}= 245.84, p < .001$; $F_{(4, 798)}= 286.85, p < .001$; $F_{(4, 798)}= 335.11, p < .001$; $F_{(4, 798)}= 245.94, p < .001$; $F_{(4, 798)}= 236.26, p < .001$; respectively). The results of Tukey's honestly significant difference (HSD) test with an alpha level of .01 were indicated in Table 1. For example, HSD test of presentation/speech anxiety indicated that clusters 4 and 5 exhibited the highest score among all clusters ($p < .01$). Clusters 2 and 3 had higher scores than cluster 1. There was no significant difference between clusters 2 and 3.

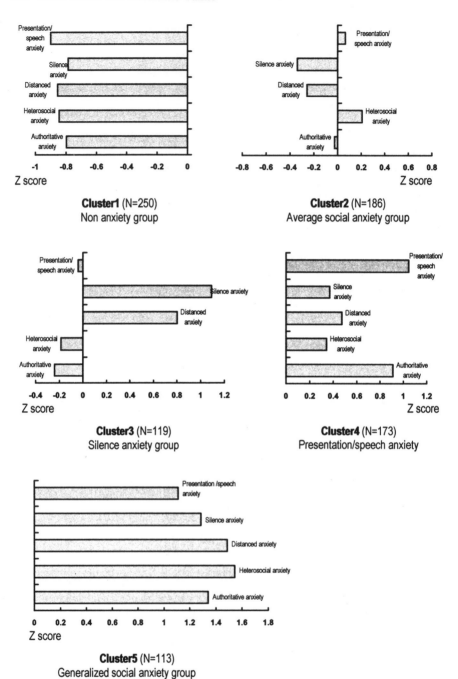

Fig. 1. Average z-score of SASSS subscales per cluster.

Table 1. Mean scores on the subscales of SASSS for each cluster.

	Cluster 1 Non-anxiety group, n=265	Cluster 2 Average social anxiety group, n=223	Cluster 3 Silence anxiety group, n=101	Cluster 4 Presentation/ speech anxiety group, n=109	Cluster 5 Generalized social anxiety, n=105
Presentation/ speech anxiety	13.2^a	20.5^b	19.7^b	27.9^c	28.4^c
Silence anxiety	8.8^a	10.8^b	17.5^d	14.1^c	18.4^d
Distanced anxiety	11.2^a	15.1^b	21.9^d	19.8^c	26.3^e
Heterosocial anxiety	7.2^a	12.2^c	10.3^b	12.9^c	18.6^d
Authoritative anxiety	5.0^a	7.4^b	6.7^b	10.2^c	11.6^d

Means in the same row that share letter superscripts differed at $P < 0.01$.

Table 2 shows the personal histories of suffering from social anxiety. The distributions of the histories differed significantly among the five clusters ($x^2(8)=64.61$, p<.01). The residual analyses of cluster 1 demonstrated that the frequency of "never" was significantly higher than the predicted value and that the frequency of "at present" was significantly lower than the predicted value. The frequency of "never" in clusters 4 and 5 was significantly lower than the predicted value, and the frequency of "at present" in those clusters was significantly higher than the predicted value.

Table 2. Personal histories of suffering from social anxiety

	Cluster 1 Non-anxiety group	Cluster 2 Average social anxiety group	Cluster 3 Silence anxiety group	Cluster 4 Presentation / speech anxiety group	Cluster 5 Generalized social anxiety	Total
Never	55	30	13	9	5	112
	21.0 %	11.5 %	5.0 %	3.4 %	1.9 %	42.7 %
	(5.37**)	(0.39)	(-1.42)	(-2.69**)	(-3.54**)	
At present	7	26	20	27	24	104
	2.7 %	9.9 %	7.6 %	10.3 %	9.2 %	40.0 %
	(-6.96**)	(-0.17)	(1.45)	(4.09**)	(3.95**)	
In the past	20	11	7	3	5	46
	7.6 %	4.2 %	2.3 %	1.1 %	1.9 %	17.6 %
	(1.96)	(-0.28)	(-0.01)	(-1.76)	(-0.47)	
Total	82	67	40	39	34	262
	31.3 %	25.6 %	15.3 %	14.9 %	13.0 %	100.0 %

Data in the upper row are frequencies.
Numbers in parentheses are residuals.
Two hundred sixty-two students in 803 attended to this questionnaire.
** $P < 0.01$

4 Discussion

The primary objective of the present study was to classify the subtypes of social anxiety in Japan.   The hierarchical procedure revealed five clusters, (1) non-anxiety group, (2) average social anxiety group, (3) silence anxiety group, (4) presentation/speech anxiety group, and (5) generalized social anxiety group.   The non-anxiety group and the average social anxiety group did not exhibit high SASSS subscale scores.   There were three subtypes of social anxiety in Japan, the silence anxiety group, presentation/speech anxiety group, and generalized social anxiety group.

The presentation/speech anxiety group may correspond to the non-generalized subtype, and the generalized social anxiety group may correspond to the generalized subtype.   The silence anxiety group has not been reported in Western countries.   This group is characterized by a significant level of silence anxiety and distanced anxiety.   These social situations have been the focus of TKS research in Japan.   It is presumed that the presence of the silence anxiety group is specific to Japan.

More research is necessary to resolve two questions.   The first question is about the differences among the subtypes of social anxiety in Japan.   Persons with generalized social phobia usually exhibit more anxiety and depression than persons with non-generalized social phobia (Heimberg et al. 1990).   The second is a question regarding the samples.   The participants in the present study were non-clinical undergraduates; it remains unresolved whether the same subtypes can be obtained in clinical samples in Japan.

References

American Psychiatric Association (1994) Diagnostic and statistical manual of mental disorders. Fourth Edition. American Psychiatric Association, Washington, D.C.

Borgen, F. H. & Barnett, D. C. (1987) Applying cluster analysis in counseling psychology research. Journal of Counseling Psychology 34: 456-468

Gelernter, C. S., Uhde, T. W., Cimbolic, P., Arnkoff, D. B., Vittone, B. J., Tancer, M. E., & Bartko, J.J. (1991) Cognitive-behavioral and pharmacological treatments of social phobia. A controlled study. Archives of General Psychiatry 48: 938-945

Heimberg, R. G., Hope, D. A.., Dodge, C. S., & Becker, R. E. (1990) DSM-III-R subtypes of social phobia: comparison of generalized social phobics and public speaking phobics. Journal of Nervous and Mental Disease 178: 172-179

Milligan, G. W. (1980) An examination of the effects of six types of error perturbation on fifteen clustering algorithms. Psychometrika 45: 325-342

Mohri, I., and Tannno, Y., (2001) Development and Validation of the Social Anxiety Scale by Social Situations (in Japanese). Japanese Journal of Health Psychology 14: 23-31

Ward, J. H. (1963) Hierarchical grouping to optimize an objective function. Journal of the American Statistical Association 58: 236-244

Appendix

Items on the Social Anxiety Scale by Social Situations

Presentation/speech anxiety (Cronbach's alpha is .92, test-retest reliability is .89)

1. My nervousness about speaking in public seems greater than that which others might experience.
2. I fear giving my opinions in a meeting.
9. I get nervous when I perform or do something in public.
12. I get very tense when I read a manuscript aloud in front of a large number of people.
13. I get more uneasy than I imagine others might when I make a proposal or suggestion at a meeting.
18. I get more uneasy than I imagine others might whenever I have to introduce myself before a large number of people.
23. I'm afraid of making a presentation before a large audience.
24. I get very tense when I'm asked my opinion during a meeting.

Distanced anxiety (Cronbach's alpha is .89, test-retest reliability is .81)

5. I fear a one-on-one situation with a new or passing friend of the same sex.
6. I experience more tension when I run across a very uncongenial person of the same sex than I imagine others would in the same situation.
15. I get nervous when I run across a passing acquaintance of the same sex.
16. I get more uneasy than I imagine others might when a person of the same sex whom I dislike approaches and talks to me.
21. I experience more tension when I am with an acquaintance of the same sex than I imagine others would in the same situation.
22. I get very tense when I chat with someone of the same sex that is completely incompatible with me.
25. I get more uneasy than I imagine others might when I chat with a stranger.
28. I get very tense when I talk to a friend of the same sex who is not close to me.

Heterosocial anxiety (Cronbach's alpha is .87, test-retest reliability is .84)

4. I get very tense when I run into an acquaintance of the opposite sex.
11. I feel nervous when I am with a person of the opposite sex I care for.
14. I get more tense than I imagine others might when I try to talk to an attractive person of the opposite sex.
20. I'm afraid of talking with a passing acquaintance of the opposite sex.
27. I get more uneasy than I imagine others might in a one-on-one situation with a person of the opposite sex.

Silence anxiety (Cronbach's alpha is .86, test-retest reliability is .83)

7. I feel nervous when there are frequent silent pauses during a conversation.

8.   I fear becoming unable to participate in the conversation when the subject changes.
17. I feel nervous when I am left out of the conversation.
29. I experience more tension when the conversation gets dull than I imagine others would in the same situation.
30. I experience more tension when I am left out of the conversation than I imagine others would in the same situation.

Authoritative anxiety (Cronbach's alpha is .86, test-retest reliability is .76)

3.   I get more uneasy than I imagine others might when I am with someone in authority (teacher, boss, etc.) than I imagine others would in the same situation.
10. I experience more tension when someone in authority (teacher, boss, etc.) talks to me than I imagine others would in the same situation.
19. I feel nervous when I am alone with a person considered my senior or superior (teacher, boss, etc.).
26. I fear meeting a person considered my senior or superior (teacher, boss, etc.).

Instructions to participants

"Please read each item and decide the degree to which the statement is characteristic or true of you.   Then circle the number between "1" and "5" on the scale by the side of each item."

Not at all	Slightly	Moderately	Very	Extremely
1	2	3	4	5

Another Aspect of Psychometrics; Survey Meta-data Description by XML

Daisuke Saito and Tatsuo Otsu

Hokkaido University Department of Behavioral System Science, Japan
saito@bs.let.hokudai.ac.jp, otsu@let.hokudai.ac.jp

Summary. Descriptions of metadata have been separately maintained from the body of data in survey research. Metadata are usually described on papers or electrical texts that can not be handled by systematic way. One reason for this problem is the lack of methods for organizing documents. Markup languages can support convenient description of documents. This feature attracts attentions of the researchers in this field. Especially markup descriptions for code-books bring the following advantages for survey research.

- A standardized definition of the document structures gives a common format, and enables uniform handling.
- The code-book that is described in markup language can represent relevance and references in the data.
- It makes automatic computing easy.

A project in ICPSR, Data Documentation Initiative (DDI), proposed a standard schema for code-books. The major concern of DDI is in the description of bibliographical aspect of survey data. It is similar to library indexes. A potential of DDI code-books is not limited to this aspect. There is larger availability for data analysis. Here after, we call DDI code-books as simply "DDI". DDI is described in XML (eXtensible Markup Language). XML is a markup language suitable for the use on Internet, and beginning to spread as an international standard. Moreover, various related technologies are developed for XML.

In this paper, we introduce the system for displaying DDI. This is a displaying system for DDI with XSL. Using this system, we can get selected view of DDI.

Key words: Metadata, DDI, XML, XSL, XSLT, Style sheet

1 What is XSL ?

XSL (eXtensible Style Language) is a language for controlling the display of XML. XSL is generally called "style sheet". The most popular purpose of XSL is displaying XML documents. XSL displays XML documents with web browsers, and add visible formats. XSL is a kind of translator for XML. XSL translates XML documents into other types of documents such as HTML. XML documents themselves do not have any visible formats. But translated XML documents with XSL have various visible formats, and can display by web browsers.

2 DDI with XSL

Visualization using XSL is possible about XML code-books. But, it will be almost meaningless that we add information on character colors or character sizes. Because functions of XSL are not only ornamenting, but also performing a more expansive display.

XSL is a language developed for browsing XML documents on WWW. XSL is a specification of language for translating XML into other formats. With this function of XSL, we made a system for displaying contents of DDI.

We used Internet Explorer 5.5 and MSXML3.0 on Microsoft Windows2000. MSXML3.0 is an additional software, which add parsing functions for XML to Internet Explorer.

3 XSL Library

We created a XSL library for displaying DDI documents with web browsers. By using this library, the following functions are able to realize.

- Extraction of information
- Formatted display
- Browsing with WWW technology.

—— Fig. 1. XSL example 1 ——

```
01:<?xml version="1.0" encoding="Shift_JIS"?>
02:<xsl:stylesheet version="1.0"
03:xmlns:xsl="http://www.w3.org/TR/WD-xsl" xml:lang="en">
04:<xsl:template match="/">
05:   <html lang="en">
06:   <head><title>Tabulation Sample</title></head>
07:    <body>
08:    <xsl:apply-templates select="codeBook/dataDscr/var" />
09:   </body>
10:  </html></xsl:template>
11:<xsl:template match="codeBook/dataDscr/var">
12:  <h2 align="center">Variable ID: <font color="#FF3333">
13:      <xsl:value-of select="@ID" /></font></h2>
14:  <h3>Question ID: <font color="#0066CC">
15:      <xsl:value-of select="qstn" /></font></h3>
16:  <table align="center" border="0"><tr bgcolor="#00CC66">
17:      <xsl:for-each select="catgry/labl">
18:      <th><xsl:value-of /></th>
19:      </xsl:for-each></tr><tr bgcolor="#99FF99">
20:      <xsl:for-each select="catgry/catStat">
21:      <td><center><xsl:value-of /></center></td>
22:      </xsl:for-each></tr></table><br/>
23:</xsl:template></xsl:stylesheet>
```

We created some style sheets which must be useful for efficient display of DDI. Fig.1 shows an example. Although this example is simple, all the foundations of our library are included. This style sheet extracts the part of variables information in DDI, that is surrounded by <var> and </var>. The information of every variable can be displayed as a table. Each line means as follows.

1. From line 05 to 10, there are HTML bodies.
2. Line 05, beginning of HTML forms definition.
3. Line 08, search items of "Variables Description" in DDI that are surrounded by <var> and </var>. (line 08)
4. From line 11 to 23, there are definitions of the process of XSL translation. These lines generate HTML codes.
5. Line 11, define processes for variables information ("Variables Description") in DDI.
6. From line 12 to 22, these are XSL command to extract and display element values under "Variables Description" which is one part of DDI.
7. Line 13, display contents of the ID attribute value in "Variables Description".
8. Line 15, display contents of QSTN attributes values.
9. From 17 to 19, select label information of variables and display as a table format.
10. From 20 to 22, select statistical information of variables and display as a table.

Fig.2 shows an output of this. The based XML code-book of this example is "United States Congressional Survey, 1975 (ICPSR 7377)" that is published by ICPSR and DDI. You will find this in DDIs' web site.

Next, see Fig.3. This is another example of our XSL library, and an output is Fig. 4. The based XML code-book of this is also "ICPSR 7377". We designed this XSL to extract bibliographical information from DDI as something like top page of a code-book.

1. From line 05 to 08, there are HTML bodies.
2. Line 05, beginning of HTML form definition.
3. Line 07, this line refers to other lines from 10 to 19. The command "apply-templates" calls "template" of line 10.
4. From line 10 to 20, define processes to extract and display information of title (titl), producer, copyright, or date of production (prodDate) from DDI code-books.

Fig. 2. and Fig 4. are both translated from the same code-book, but they presented different information. We were able to change only presentation of code-books without changing the original. This is the availability of our XSL library.

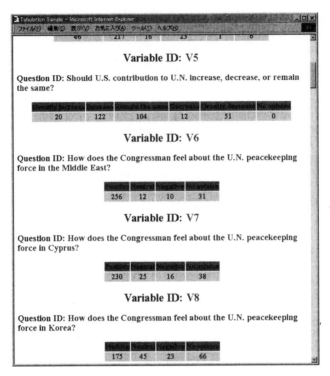

Fig. 2. Output example 1

— Fig. 3. XSL example 2 —

```
01:<?xml version="1.0" encoding="Shift_JIS"?>
02:<xsl:stylesheet version="1.0"
03:xmlns:xsl="http://www.w3.org/TR/WD-xsl" xml:lang="en">
04:<xsl:template match="/">
05    <html lang="en">
06:   <head><title>DDI Codebook</title></head>
07:      <body><xsl:apply-templates select="codeBook/docDscr"/>
08:   </body></html>
09:</xsl:template>
10:<xsl:template match="codeBook/docDscr">
11:   <h2 align="center">
12:      <xsl:value-of select="citation/titlStmt/titl"/></h2>
13:   <h3 align="center">
14:      <xsl:value-of select="citation/prodStmt/producer"/></h3>
15:   <h4 align="center">
16:      <xsl:value-of select="citation/prodStmt/copyright"/></h4>
17:   <h4 align="center">
18:      <xsl:value-of select="citation/prodStmt/prodDate"/></h4>
19:   <div><xsl:value-of select="guide"/></div>
20:</xsl:template>
```

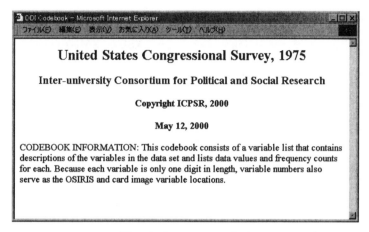

Fig. 4. Output example 2

Following functions are included in our XSL library.

- Presenting bibliographical information.
- Listing questions' IDs.
- Listing questionnaires.
- Listing variables' IDs.
- Listing variable names.
- Listing answers of questions.

Using these functions, we made 12 style sheets, and all of our XSL library is exhibited in our homepage.

http://wwwbs.let.hokudai.ac.jp/~saito/

4 Function of XSL and XSLT

XSL has functions to change an XML document into another one that has different structure. The specification of this conversion function is standardized and defined as XSLT (XSL Transformations). XML documents will obtain following various profits with XSLT.

- By changing the form definition (DTD and schema) of XML, two or more structures can be expressed from one document.
- Elements of code-books which you need can be extracted from an XML document.
- Two or more XML documents can be synthesized as a new XML document.

In section 3, we showed an XSL usage example on XML code-books. This also shows usefulness of information extraction and conversion.

We have developed and proposed that use XSL on XML code-books, and we are going to offer some more useful software. The one is the further fullness of the XSL library, and improvement of its user interface. And we are working to utilize XSL functions for information extraction and structure conversion. We are planing to realize automatic generation of statistical software codes such as SAS, SPSS, S-Plus, or R from DDI code-books..

5 Reference Research about XSL

"DandD Project" by the Shibata laboratory of Keio University is mentioned as similar research. DandD is also supporting the display of the XML code-book by XSL, and we can browse it in their homepage. Our purpose is to equip display functions at least to the extension of DandD. The style sheet of DandD is also excellent. The structure of a code-book can be displayed. Both of an explanation and numerical values can be displayed about each of variables.

References

DandD Project, Data Science Division, Keio University (in Japanese), http://www.stat.math.keio.ac.jp/

Data Documentation Initiative, http://www.icpsr.umich.edu/DDI/

Data Documentation Initiative (2000): Electronic Preservation of Data Documentation: Complementary SGML and Image Capture, DDI Final Report to NSF, http://www.icpsr.umich.edu/DDI/PAPERS/final.pdf

Ryssevik, J (2000): Bazaar Style Metadata in the Age of the Web - An 'Open Source' Approach To Metadata Development, UN/ECE Work Session on Statistical Metadata, Working paper No.4, http://www.icpsr.umich.edu/DDI/PAPERS/bazaar.pdf

World Wide Web Consortium (W3C) (1999): XSL Transformations (XSLT) Version 1.0, http://www.w3.org/TR/1999/REC-xslt-19991116

World Wide Web Consortium (W3C) (2000) Extensible markup language (XML) 1.0, 2nd edn, http://www.w3.org/TR/2000/REC-xml-20001006

World Wide Web Consortium (W3C) (2001): Extensible Stylesheet Language (XSL) Version 1.0, http://www.w3.org/TR/2001/REC-xsl-20011015

Some Alternative Clustering Methods for Mokken Scale Analysis

A.A.H. van Abswoude[1], and J. K. Vermunt[2]

[1] Department of Methodology and Statistics, Tilburg University, P.O. Box 90153, Tilburg, The Netherlands *A.A.H.vanAbswoude@kub.nl*
[2] Department of Methodology and Statistics, Tilburg University, P.O. Box 90153, Tilburg, The Netherlands *J.K.Vermunt@kub.nl*

Summary. In this paper three methods for finding the dimensionality of a data matrix - sequential clustering, hierarchical clustering, and non-hierarchical clustering - are discussed. For each method different measures are suggested to find one or more sets of dichotomous items that satisfy the conditions of a Mokken scale (Mokken, 1971). It is illustrated that non-hierarchical clustering resolves some problems associated with sequential and hierarchical clustering in finding the true dimensionality.

Key words. multidimensionality, item clustering algorithms, nonparametric item response theory.

1 Introduction

In measurement and scaling it is important to measure one single latent trait at one time. Otherwise, unless the exact relationship between the latent variables can be modelled, it will be difficult to assign meaningful scores to subjects. In practice, however, researchers are often confronted with data matrices having multiple latent traits. For example, a test that measures *crying* may contain items on sub-traits such as *distress*, *sadness*, and *joy*.

Mokken scale analysis (MSA; Mokken, 1971) may be used to find sets of items that form a single unidimensional scale. The MSA-software, MSP (Molenaar and Sijtsma, 2000), uses a sequential clustering algorithm to find sets of items (clusters) that satisfy the conditions of a Mokken scale. A drawback of this algorithm is, however, that it may not yield the *optimal solution*; that is, the solution that maximizes a certain objective function. If the objective function is correct, the optimal solution should reflect the true dimensionality of the data matrix. A practical implication of using the sequential algorithm is that the user may obtain a set of items that measures more than one trait.

In this paper, we present two new clustering methods for MSA, hierarchical and non-hierarchical clustering, which may do a better job in finding the optimal solution. In the following sections, we describe how the clustering methods work and discuss how the MSA conditions can be imposed within each of these methods so that solutions may reflect the true dimensionality and satisfy the MSA conditions. In addition, the ability of the methods in finding the optimal solution will be illustrated by means of three small generated examples.

2 Nonparametric IRT Framework

In nonparametric item response theory (IRT) it is assumed that a single underlying latent trait (θ) governs the responses on a set of items (unidimensionality, UD). Further it is assumed that given any value of θ the responses of an individual on a set of items are statistically independent (local independence, LI). Lastly, it is assumed that there is a monotonely nondecreasing relationship between the probability of answering an item correctly and θ (monotonicity, M). A set of items that satisfy UD, LI and M are denoted as monotone homogeneous (MH; Mokken, 1971). The monotone homogeneity model allows the measurement of θ by means of the total test scores of individuals (Grayson, 1988). The total test score is defined by $X_+ = \sum X_i$, with X_i denoting an individual's score on item i ($i = 1, ..., I$). Within the nonparametric IRT framework, the response probability given θ, known as the item response function (IRF), does not need to have a particular shape such as the logistic as long as the items are MH.

Mokken scale analysis, which is a nonparametric IRT method for scale analysis, uses Loevinger's coefficient of homogeneity to quantify the strength of the association within the responses to a pair of items. Let items i and j be two binary items having item scores 0 or 1. Let π_i represent the probability of answering item i correctly, and π_{ij} the probability of answering both item i and j correctly. Items are ordered such that $\pi_i > \pi_j$, $\forall i > j$. The pairwise scalability coefficient H_{ij} for items i and j is defined as

$$H_{ij} = \frac{\pi_{ij} - \pi_i \pi_j}{\pi_i(1 - \pi_j)}. \tag{1}$$

This equals the covariance between items i and j divided by the maximum covariance given the marginal score distributions of items i and j (Mokken, 1971; Molenaar and Sijtsma, 2000). The H_i for item i can be written as

$$H_i = \frac{\sum_{j \neq i}(\pi_{ij} - \pi_i \pi_j)}{\sum_{j \neq i} \pi_i(1 - \pi_j)} = \frac{\sum_{j \neq i} \pi_i(1 - \pi_j)H_{ij}}{\sum_{j \neq i} \pi_i(1 - \pi_j)} \tag{2}$$

as in Mokken (1971, p.150). The scale H is defined as

$$H = \frac{\sum_i \sum_{j \neq i}(\pi_{ij} - \pi_i \pi_j)}{\sum_i \sum_{j \neq i} \pi_i(1 - \pi_j)} = \frac{\sum_i \sum_{j \neq i} \pi_i(1 - \pi_j)H_{ij}}{\sum_i \sum_{j \neq i} \pi_i(1 - \pi_j)}. \tag{3}$$

For more information about the theoretical basis and the sampling distribution of the H coefficient we refer the reader to Mokken (1971) or Molenaar and Sijtsma (2000).

A set of I items is called a *Mokken Scale* (Mokken, 1971, p.184) if all items satisfy the following two conditions,

Condition 1 $\mathrm{cov}(X_i, X_j) > 0$, for all $i \neq j$, and

Condition 2 $H_i \geq c$, for all i, where c is a user-defined constant between 0 and 1.

From the MH model follows that $\mathrm{cov}(X_i, X_j) \geq 0$ (Holland and Rosenbaum, 1986), but the converse does not hold. The second condition serves the practical purpose of only including items into a scale that sufficiently discriminate. Also, when c is sufficiently high -in practice, $c = 0.3$ is used- a single latent trait will be measured.

Below, we present three types of clustering procedures (i.e., sequential clustering, hierarchical clustering, and non-hierarchical clustering) for finding the dimensionality of a data matrix using the H coefficient as a measure of association. Each method uses H_{ij}, π_i, and π_j as input data; and each must satisfy the two conditions of a Mokken scale. In the next sections, we describe how these conditions can be imposed, as well as what the limitations of these methods are when searching for the dimensionality of a set of items.

3 Sequential Clustering

Sequential clustering takes the following stepwise course. In the first step (Step 1), we search for the two items that form the start set for the first scale. This is the item pair with the highest significantly positive H_{ij} (Equation 1) that satisfies Conditions 1 and 2. In the next step (Step 2), items are added one at the time to this start set. More precisely, this is the item with the highest H_i with the previously selected items (Equation 2) that satisfies Conditions 1 and 2. This process of adding items with the highest H_i continues until no item remains. When this happens the first scale has been formed. As long as scalable items remain, subsequent scales may be formed by repeating Steps 1 and 2 using the remaining items. The procedure terminates when no scalable items are left.

The sequential procedure works quite well when one is interested in finding only one single Mokken scale, for example when a data matrix measures one dominant latent trait, and possibly one or more nuisance latent traits. When searching for multiple Mokken scales in a multi-trait context, however, the sequential nature of the procedure may yield suboptimal solutions: the solution that overall yields the highest H_i is not obtained. The reason that suboptimal solutions may be obtained is that sequential clustering forms the clusters one at the time. As a result, some items may be collected in Cluster 1 (clustering clustering continues until scaling criteria are no longer satisfied), although H_i may have been higher when joined with items in Cluster 2.

4 Hierarchical Clustering

Agglomerative hierarchical clustering (Everitt et al., 2001) seems to be a useful alternative because it can yield multiple clusters simultaneously, where sequential clustering could not. Starting point of a HCA is a data matrix containing proximities between items i and j. The proximities in our case are based on the H coefficient and will be discussed in more detail later on. At each hierarchical step, the two clusters with the highest proximity are joined. This means that at any hierarchical step two single items may be joined to form one new cluster, a single item may be joined with an existing cluster of items, or two clusters may be joined into a single larger cluster. This process continues until some previously defined criterion is met or until all items are in one single cluster.

In the following methods, four types of proximities may be used to form Mokken scales. The first three methods can be reproduced using the H_{ij}-matrix in combination with standard clustering procedures of most statistical packages, including SPSS, SAS, and BMDP. For the fourth method dedicated software was written in PASCAL. Before we present the proximities, however, first we need some notation. Let k and l represent two clusters, let I_k represent the number of items in cluster k, I_l represent the number of items in cluster l, and let H_{kl} represent the proximity between clusters k and l.

In *complete linkage* the proximity between clusters k and l is defined as,

$$H_{kl}^{complete} = \min(H_{ij}), \text{ where } i \in k \text{ and } j \in l.$$

This method joins the two clusters for which the lowest H_{ij} of the two clusters is maximized. This definition of proximity is intuitively attractive because it produces scales for which the $\min(H_{ij})$ satisfies some minimal requirement.

Average linkage defines the proximity between clusters as

$$H_{kl}^{average} = \frac{\sum_{i \in k} \sum_{j \in l} H_{ij}}{I_k I_l}.$$

As can be seen, $H_{kl}^{average}$ is the unweighted average of the bivariate H_{ij} *between* the items in cluster k and the items in cluster l. This measure can be viewed as a proxy for the average H_i in a cluster.

Within-groups linkage defines the proximity of two clusters k and l as the unweighted average of the H_{ij} of all items *within* k and l; that is,

$$H_{kl}^{within} = \frac{\sum_{i \in k \cup l} \sum_{j \neq i} H_{ij}}{(I_k + I_l)(I_k + I_l - 1)}.$$

This proximity can be seen as a proxy for H as defined in Equation 3.

The fourth method, *scale linkage* uses the scale H (Equation 3) of the possible new cluster that is obtained by joining two clusters as proximity measure. Written in terms of clusters k and l the proximity in scale linkage is defined as,

$$H_{kl}^{scale} = \frac{\sum_{i \in k \cup l} \sum_{j \neq i} \pi_i (1 - \pi_j) H_{ij}}{\sum_{i \in k \cup l} \sum_{j \neq i} \pi_i (1 - \pi_j)}.$$

Different from sequential clustering is that, unless a stopping rule is used, the HCA will continue clustering until all items are joined into one large cluster. For instance, the Mokken scaling conditions (especially, Condition 2) can be used to terminate the clustering process. In that case, clustering stops when the conditions are no longer satisfied. Alternative methods to decide when to stop the HCA can also be proposed, but are beyond the scope of this paper. In this paper we used the Mokken scale conditions as stopping rule.

Unfortunately, hierarchical clustering may also yield suboptimal solutions because clusters that have been formed in previous steps remain intact in subsequent steps. More precisely, a set of items that was clustered at an earlier stage may not be homogeneous with respect to items that were added later.

5 Non-Hierarchical Clustering

Non-hierarchical clustering refers to a class of algorithms where multiple clusters are formed simultaneously and single units within an object (i.e., items) can be moved from one cluster to another. The method uses a criterion, which is based on the H coefficient, to evaluate the quality of a K-cluster solution at partition $\mathcal{P}_t$ for iteration t.

Let $\delta_{ik}(\mathcal{P}_t) = 1$ if $i \in k$ (where $k = 1, ..., K$), and $\delta_{ik}(\mathcal{P}_t) = 0$ if $i \notin k$ at $\mathcal{P}_t$. In addition, let $H_{i|k}$ be matrix reflecting the conditional homogeneity of each item i with respect to the items in each cluster k. A criterion for evaluating the quality of a K-cluster solution at partition $\mathcal{P}_t$ may, for instance, be

$$\text{Crt } 1(\mathcal{P}_t) = I^{-1} \sum_{i=1}^{I} \sum_{k=1}^{K} \delta_{ik}(\mathcal{P}_t) H_{i|k}. \tag{4}$$

The goal of the non-hierarchical clustering procedure is to search for that partition that maximizes Crt 1; that is, we intend to join each item into the cluster such that the highest H_i is obtained for all items.

In this paper, we use a k-means type algorithm to assign items to clusters. This clustering method begins with an initial configuration ($t = 0$) in which I items are randomly assigned to K clusters, and the quality of $\mathcal{P}_0$ is evaluated using Crt $1(\mathcal{P}_0)$. In each iteration step, one item i may be moved to another cluster k and Crt $1(\mathcal{P}_1)$ is evaluated. Different rules may be used to move an item i to another cluster k. For example, we could move the item to that cluster for which the improvement in $H_{i|k}$ is the best. In the subsequent iterations this evaluating and maximizing of Crt $1(\mathcal{P}_t)$ is continued until the criterion can no longer be improved.

This procedure can be further refined by adding a random component to the process of assigning items to clusters, thereby reducing the probability of ending up in a local maximum: a stochastic process could be used for the assignment of items to clusters. This means that in the first iterations, Crt 1 may deteriorate from one iteration to the next (e.g., an item is moved to a cluster for which $H_{i|k}$ is not the highest). For later iterations improvements of Crt 1 are more likely. This random element in the composition of clusters is important because it may yield combinations of items that otherwise would not have been found.

Other criteria could also be used in this context. The following criterion was formulated for finding the partition having the highest H_{ij} within clusters. We adapted Zhang and Stout's statistic for this purpose, which is aimed at finding clusters of items that are locally independent (Zhang and Stout, 1999). Let $\delta_{ijk}(\mathcal{P}_t) = 1$ when items i and j are joined into cluster k at $\mathcal{P}_t$, and -1 otherwise. Then, Crt $2(\mathcal{P}_t)$ is defined as

$$\text{Crt } 2(\mathcal{P}_t) = \frac{2}{I(I-1)} \sum_{1 \leq i < j \leq I} \delta_{ijk}(\mathcal{P}_t) H_{ij}.$$

Criterion Crt 2 can also be maximized using the k-means type procedure which was presented before. In the simulation study, however, we limit ourselves to finding the dimensionality using the k-means type algorithm based on Crt 1 (i.e., without the proposed refinements).

6 Simulation study

The performance of the three general procedures (i.e., sequential, hierarchical, and non-hierarchical clustering) using their specific definitions of dimensionality is shown for three small generated item pools. We used the multidimensional extension of the 2-parameter logistic item response theory model (M2-PLM; e.g., Reckase, 1985) to generate 1000 item responses on three sets of items. Even though the data were generated, the used item parameter values are representative for true test data.

Item pool 1 consists of 6 items, $X_1 - X_6$, and two latent traits, θ_1 and θ_2. Items X_1 and X_2 are strongly related to θ_1, X_3 is weakly related to θ_1 and strongly related to θ_2, and $X_4 - X_6$ are moderately related to θ_2 but not related to θ_1.

Item pool 2 consists of 10 items, and three latent traits, $\theta_1 - \theta_3$. Items $X_1 - X_5$ are moderately related to θ_1, X_5 and X_6 are moderately related to θ_2, and $X_6 - X_{10}$ are moderately related to θ_3. The second latent trait, θ_2, has the function of a nuisance trait: that is, it is included in order to make the detection of the items measuring θ_1 and θ_3 more difficult.

Item pool 3 consists of 20 items, and two latent traits θ_1 and θ_2. Items $X_1 - X_{10}$ are strongly related to θ_1, items $X_{11} - X_{20}$ are strongly related to θ_2 and weakly related to θ_2.

The latent traits in the presented item pools are assumed to be uncorrelated. We evaluated the performance of the methods as to whether the results are optimal. Notation $[K : I_1; I_2; ...; I_K]$ is used to reflect the structure of an item pool, where K equals the number of clusters and $I_k(k = 1, ..., K)$ equals the number of items in each cluster. The optimal solution of Item pool 1 using $c = 0.3$ in Criterion 2 is $[2 : 2; 4]$; that is, items $X_1 - X_2$ are in Cluster 1 and $X_3 - X_6$ in Cluster 2. We look at two optimal solutions for Item pool 2: $[2 : 5; 5]$ using $c = 0.2$ in Condition 2 (i.e., $X_1 - X_5$ and $X_6 - X_{10}$); and $[3 : 4; 2; 4]$ using $c = 0.3$ in Condition 2 (i.e., $X_1 - X_4$, $X_5 - X_6$, and $X_7 - X_{10}$). The different values of c reflect two possible ways of defining a Mokken scale: one is moderately strict ($c = 0.3$) and one is less strict ($c = 0.2$). The optimal solution for Item pool 3 using $c = 0.3$ is $[2:10;10]$.

We used the default settings for MSP (Molenaar and Sijtsma, 2000) and HCA. For the k-means method we used the version portrayed in combination with Crt 1.

7 Results

Tabel 1 shows the optimal solution and the dimensionality results obtained with sequential clustering, hierarchical clustering, and non-hierarchical clustering. The first column gives the method used for clustering, the other columns give the results for item pools 1, 2 and 3.

Table 1. Number of clusters and number of items per cluster using sequential clustering, four hierarchical clustering methods and non-hierarchical clustering for three generated item pools

Method	Item pool 1	Item pool 2	Item pool 3
Optimal solution	[2: 2;4]	[2: 5;5], [3: 4;2;4]	[2: 10;10]
Sequential	[2: 3;3]	[2: 5;5], [3: 4;2;4]	[2: 6;14]
Complete linkage	[2: 2;4]	[2: 6;4], [3: 4;2;4]	[2: 10;10]
Average linkage	[2: 2;4]	[2: 6;4], [3: 4;2;4]	[2: 10;10]
Within-groups linkage	[2: 2;4]	[2: 5;5], [3: 1;4;5]	[2: 10;10]
Scale linkage	[2: 2;4]	[2: 5;5], [3: 1;4;5]	[2: 10;10]
Simple + Crt 1	[2: 2;4]	[2: 5;5], [3: 4;2;4]	[2: 10;10]

For item pool 1, all methods, except sequential clustering, yielded the predefined optimal solution. The reason that the first cluster, obtained with sequential clustering, contained one extra item was that this item still satisfied the scaling criteria for the first cluster, although it measures θ_2. Forming multiple clusters simultaneously (i.e., hierarchical and non-hierarchical clustering) was sufficient to find the optimal solution.

In item pool 2, both the $K = 2$ and the $K = 3$ results are presented for each method. Sequential clustering yielded the correct dimensionality for both $K = 2$ and $K = 3$. With the hierarchical procedures either the $K = 2$ or the $K = 3$ solution was correct. One may note that with a hierarchical procedure it is not possible that both the $K = 2$ and the $K = 3$ solution are optimal because the $K = 2$ solution is obtained by combining the two clusters of the $K = 3$ solution. The non-hierarchical method yielded two optimal solutions because clusters are formed simultaneously and individual items are assigned to the clusters they fit best.

In Table 1 one can see that the results of item pool 1 and 3 are similar, except that in item pool 3 an entire subset of four items (in stead of one single item) was incorrectly classified when using the sequential method. The results of item pool 3 illustrate that the mechanisms that were responsible for the results of item pool 1 and 2 may also be active in somewhat larger data matrices. Naturally, the examples can be extended to even more items.

8 Conclusion

Three types of clustering methods for finding the dimensionality of a set of items were presented in this paper. Each method was adapted to yield clusters that satisfy the Mokken scale conditions. As illustrated, non-hierarchical clustering resolves the problems associated with sequential and hierarchical clustering.

The non-hierarchical clustering algorithm we used in the simulation study may yield local maxima. Introducing randomness in the assignment of items to clusters may be the remedy for this problem that deserves further study.

References

Everitt BS, Landau S, Leese M (2001) Cluster Analysis. Arnold/Oxford University Press, London New York

Grayson DA (1988) Two-group classification in latent trait theory: Scores with monotone likelihood ratio. Psychometrika 53:383–392

Holland PW, Rosenbaum PR (1986) Conditional association and unidimensionality in monotone latent variable models. The Annals of Statistics 14:1523–1543

Mokken RJ (1971) A theory and procedure of scale analysis: With applications in political research. De Gruyter, Berlin

Molenaar IW, Sijtsma K (2000) Users manual MSP5 for Windows. A program for Mokken scale analysis for polytomous items [Software manual]. Iec ProGamma, Groningen, The Netherlands

Reckase MD (1985) The difficulty of test items that measure more than one ability. Applied Psychological Measurement 15:401–412

Zhang J, Stout WF (1999) Conditional covariance structure of generalized compensatory multidimensional items. Psychometrika 64:129–152

Knowledge-based Cascade-correlation: Varying the Size and Shape of Relevant Prior Knowledge

Thomas R. Shultz[1] and Francois Rivest[2]

[1]Department of Psychology and School of Computer Science, McGill University, Montreal, Quebec, Canada H3A 1B1
[2]School of Computer Science, McGill University, Montreal, Quebec, Canada H3A 1B1

Summary. Artificial neural networks typically ignore the role of knowledge in learning by starting from random connection weights. A new algorithm, knowledge-based cascade-correlation (KBCC), finds, adapts, and uses its relevant knowledge to speed learning. We demonstrate its performance on small, clear problems involving decisions about whether a two-dimensional input falls within a nonlinear distribution of a particular size, shape, and location. Relevance of prior knowledge to a new, target problem was implemented by systematic variations in the width of the distribution space. The more relevant the prior inexact knowledge was, the more likely that KBCC recruited it for solution of the target problem and the faster that new learning was.

Key words. Knowledge-based learning, transfer, cascade-correlation

1 Knowledge and Learning

Most learning in neural networks is done without the influence of previous knowledge, starting with random connection weights. In sharp contrast, when people learn, they make extensive use of their existing knowledge (Pazzani, 1991; Wisniewski, 1995). Learning with prior knowledge is responsible for the ease and speed with which people learn new material, and for occasional interference effects.

Cascade-correlation (CC) is a generative learning algorithm that learns not only by adjusting weights, but also by recruiting new hidden units into the network as needed in order to reduce error (Fahlman and Lebiere 1990). CC is faster than learning by the standard neural learning algorithm known as back-propagation (BP) and makes a better fit to a variety of psychological data on cognitive development than does BP (Buckingham and Shultz 2000).

In extending CC we devised a new algorithm, knowledge-based cascade-correlation (KBCC), that allows previously-learned source networks to compete with each other and with single hidden units for recruitment into a target network.

KBCC treats its existing networks like untrained single units, by training weights to the inputs of source networks to increase the correlations of their outputs with the target network's error (Shultz and Rivest 2001). The best correlating candidate recruit is installed into the target network, and the other candidates are discarded. Output weights from the new recruit are then adjusted to integrate it into a solution of the target problem. Previous work with KBCC has shown that it effectively recruits and uses its knowledge to speed learning. Preliminary experiments involved learning whether a pair of Cartesian coordinate inputs were or were not within a particular geometric shape. Source networks varied in terms of translation or rotation of a target geometric shape. Generally, the more relevant the source knowledge was, the more likely it was recruited and the more it speeded up learning of a target problem (Shultz and Rivest 2000a 2001). In this paper we describe a test of KBCC networks on similar problems in which the size of the geometric shape is varied.

2 General Method

The input space was a square centered at the origin with sides of length 2. Target outputs specified that the output should be 0.5 if the input point was inside of the shape and -0.5 if the point was outside of the shape. Networks were trained with a set of 225 patterns forming a regular 15 x 15 grid covering the input space including the boundary. We designed two different experiments to assess the impact of source knowledge on the learning of a target task. First we varied the relevance of a single source of knowledge to determine whether KBCC would learn faster if it had source knowledge that was more relevant. In a second experiment, to determine whether KBCC would find and use more relevant source knowledge, there were two sources of knowledge that varied in relevance to a new target problem. In both experiments, knowledge relevance was varied by differences in the width or shape of the two-dimensional geometric figures. The target figure in the second phase of knowledge-guided learning was a rectangle as were the figures in several of the knowledge conditions. Rectangles were always centered at (0, 0) in the input space and always had a height of 22/14. Twenty networks were run in each condition of each experiment.

3 One Source of Knowledge

3.1 Method

In this experiment, several knowledge conditions varied the width of the source rectangle. Because scaling the width up vs. down did not produce the same results, we included conditions with either narrow or wide target rectangles. The various conditions, which also included irrelevant source knowledge in the form of a circle and no knowledge at all, are described in Table 1.

Table 1

Single-source Knowledge Conditions

Condition	Description	Relation to target large rectangle	Relation to target small rectangle
Narrow rectangle	Rectangle of width 6/14	Far relevant	Exact
Medium rectangle	Rectangle of width 14/14	Near relevant	Near relevant
Wide rectangle	Rectangle of width 22/14	Exact	Far relevant
Circle	Center at (0, 0), radius 0.5	Irrelevant	Irrelevant
None	No knowledge	None	None

3.2 Results

A factorial ANOVA of the epochs required to learn when the narrow rectangle was the target yielded a main effect of knowledge condition, $F(4, 95) = 103$, $p < .0001$. Figure 1 shows the mean epochs to learn the target problem, with standard deviation bars and homogeneous subsets that were based on the LSD post hoc comparison method. Examination of the means indicates that relevant knowledge, regardless of distance from the target, enabled faster learning than did irrelevant knowledge and no knowledge at all. This suggests that scaling down in width from a wider source is not much affected by the amount of scaling. The relatively few epochs required in target learning demonstrates that scaling down in width is fairly easy for these networks to learn.

A factorial ANOVA of the epochs required to learn when the wide rectangle was the target also produced a main effect of knowledge condition, $F(4, 95) = 74$, $p < .0001$, but with a different pattern of means. Figure 2 shows the mean epochs to learn, with standard deviation bars and homogeneous subsets, based on the LSD post hoc comparison method. Exact knowledge produced the fastest learning, followed by near relevant knowledge, far relevant knowledge, and finally by no knowledge and irrelevant knowledge. Thus, scaling up in width became more difficult with the amount of scaling that was required. In these conditions, irrelevant knowledge did not speed up learning, as compared to the no-knowledge control. Examination of source-learning results confirmed that narrow rectangles were easier to learn than wide rectangles, in terms of both the number of hidden units recruited and epochs to learn.

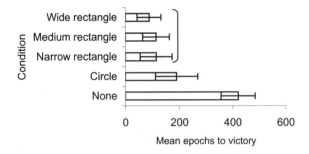

Fig. 1. Mean epochs to victory in the target phase of the narrow rectangle condition, with standard deviation bars and homogeneous subsets (adapted from Shultz and Rivest 2001, by Taylor & Francis Ltd. http://www.tandf.co.uk/journals, with permission).

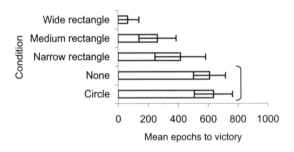

Fig. 2. Mean epochs to victory in the target phase of the wide rectangle condition, with standard deviation bars and homogeneous subsets (adapted from Shultz and Rivest 2001, published by Taylor & Francis Ltd. http://www.tandf.co.uk/journals, with permission).

Figure 3 shows output activation diagrams for networks learning a narrow target rectangle, recruiting near relevant directly connected source knowledge. In such diagrams (Figures 3 and 4), darker points represent inputs inside the target shape and lighter points represent inputs outside of the target shape. A white background indicates test inputs classified as being inside the target shape, a black background indicates test inputs classified as being outside the target shape, and a gray background indicates test inputs whose classification is uncertain. These backgrounds are somewhat irregular because they are produced by testing the network on a fine grid of 220 x 220 input patterns. Whether learning a narrow or wide target, there was a strong resemblance between the shape of the source knowledge and the shape of the final solution. Interestingly, networks learned to classify all patterns as being outside of the target class during the first output phase. Because only 33 of the 225 training patterns fall within the target class when the target is a narrow rectangle, the best initial guess without nonlinear hidden units is that patterns fall outside the target class.

a   b

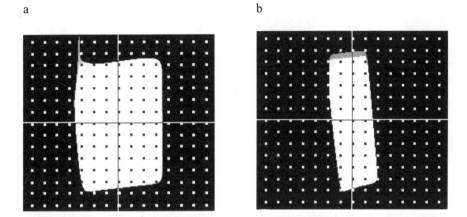

Fig. 3a, b. Output activation diagrams for a network learning a narrow rectangle. **a** Near relevant source knowledge. **b** Final target solution at the end of the second output phase after recruiting this source knowledge.

In contrast, when learning a wide target rectangle, networks do the opposite; that is, they learn to classify all patterns as being inside of the target class during the first output phase. Because the majority of the training patterns (121 out of 225) fall within the target class when the target is a wide rectangle, the best initial guess without nonlinear hidden units is that patterns fall inside the target class. Figure 4 shows output activation diagrams for networks learning a wide target rectangle with near relevant source knowledge. Figure 4b shows classification of all patterns as being inside of the target class by the end of the first output phase.

Network error during target learning, whether scaling down to a narrow rectangle or scaling up to a wide rectangle, involves patterns near the four corners of the target rectangle. These corners are regions of the intersecting hyperplanes that the network is learning. When scaling down to a narrow target rectangle, recruitment of a source network sharpens these corners, making target learning quite fast. When scaling up to a wide target rectangle, recruitment of a source network smoothes these corners, thereby prolonging target learning by resharpening the corners. When scaling up to a wide rectangle, the amount of corner smoothing and eventual resharpening increases with the degree of scaling. Because no additional corner sharpening is required when scaling down to a narrow rectangle, learning speed is relatively fast and does not vary with the degree of scaling. This explains why scaling down in width is faster to learn than scaling up in width.

a   b

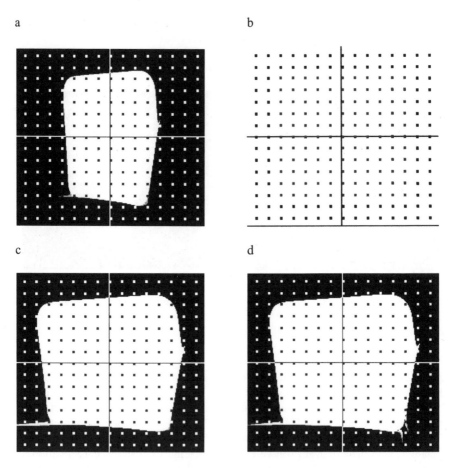

c   d

Fig. 4a, b, c, d. Output activation diagrams for a network learning a wide rectangle. **a** Near relevant source knowledge. Target solutions at the end of the first (**b**), second (**c**), and third and final (**d**) output phases.

4 Two Sources of Knowledge

In this experiment, networks first learned two source tasks of different relevance to the target task. The various source knowledge conditions, their relations to the target, and the mean times each network was recruited during input phases are presented in Table 2. The descriptions of the shapes associated with each condition were provided in Table 1. The two means in each row of Table 2 were compared with a t-test for paired samples. Exact knowledge was preferred over both relevant, $p < .005$, and irrelevant, $p < .005$, knowledge. Relevant knowledge was preferred over irrelevant knowledge only when scaling down to a narrower target rectangle, $p < .001$. The large number of recruited networks in the relevant vs. irrelevant, scaling-up condition reflects the relative difficulty of learning in this condition. The longer that learning continued, the more recruits were required.

The results of this two-source experiment fit with the analysis of the one-source experiment. Exact source knowledge was preferred over inexact source knowledge because exact knowledge made a nearly perfect match to the target problem. When scaling down to a narrow rectangle, relevant inexact source knowledge was preferred over irrelevant source knowledge because the recruitment sharpened the critical corners of the target figure, which was rectangular just like the relevant sources. In contrast, when scaling up to a wide rectangle, there was no advantage for relevant source knowledge because recruiting smoothed the critical target corners thus requiring additional resharpening through further learning.

Table 2

Dual-source Knowledge Conditions and Mean Networks Recruited (adapted from Shultz and Rivest 2001, published by Taylor & Francis, Ltd. http://www.tandf.co.uk/journals, with permission)

Source knowledge	Relation to target	Mean networks recruited		
		Narrow rectangle	Wide rectangle	Circle
Target: Narrow rectangle				
Narrow & wide rectangles	Exact vs. Relevant	1.05	0.60	n/a
Narrow rectangle, circle	Exact vs. Irrelevant	1.00	n/a	0.45
Wide rectangle, circle	Relevant vs. Irrelevant	n/a	1.50	0.45
Target: Wide rectangle				
Wide & narrow rectangles	Exact vs. Relevant	0.15	1.20	n/a
Wide rectangle, circle	Exact vs. Irrelevant	n/a	1.05	0.0
Narrow rectangle, circle	Relevant vs. Irrelevant	2.65	n/a	3.40

5 Discussion

As in previous work, the present results demonstrate that KBCC is able to find, adapt, and use its existing knowledge in the learning of a new problem, shortening the learning time. The more relevant the source knowledge is, the more likely it will be recruited for solution of a target problem and the faster that new learning will be. The fact that these results hold for a wide variety of input transformations (translation, rotation, and here, width changes) underscores the robustness of KBCC in finding knowledge along different dimensions of relevance to the target problem.

KBCC is similar in spirit to recent neural-network research on transfer, multitask learning, lifelong learning, knowledge insertion, modularity, and input recoding. However, unlike many of these other techniques, for which both the inputs and outputs of the source and target task must match precisely, KBCC can recruit any sort of differentiable function to use in a new task. The inputs and outputs of KBCC source networks can be arranged in different orders and frequencies and employ different coding techniques than in the target task. This wider range of recruitment objects offers considerably more power and flexibility than other knowledge-based learning systems provide. A direct comparison to multitask learning showed that KBCC was faster and more effective (Shultz and Rivest 2000b). KBCC has also been effective in large-scale, realistic domains such as vowel recognition (Rivest and Shultz 2002) and DNA segmentation (Thivierge and Shultz 2002).

References

Buckingham D, Shultz TR (2000) The developmental course of distance, time, and velocity concepts: A generative connectionist model. J Cog & Dev 1: 305-345

Fahlman SE, Lebiere C (1990) The cascade-correlation learning architecture. In: Touretzky DS (ed) Advances in neural information processing systems 2. Morgan Kaufmann, Los Altos CA, pp 524-532

Pazzani MJ (1991) Influence of prior knowledge on concept acquisition: Experimental and computational results. J Expt Psych: Learning, Mem, & Cog 17: 416-432

Rivest F, Shultz TR (2002) Application of knowledge-based cascade-correlation to vowel recognition. IEEE Internat World Congr on Comp Intell, pp. 53-58

Shultz TR., Rivest F (2000a) Knowledge-based cascade-correlation. Internat Joint Conf on Neural Networks Vol V. IEEE Computer Society Press, Los Alamitos CA, pp 641-646

Shultz TR, Rivest F (2000b) Using knowledge to speed learning: A comparison of knowledge-based cascade-correlation and multi-task learning. Seventeenth Internat Conf on Machine Learning. Morgan Kaufmann, San Francisco, pp 871-878

Shultz TR, Rivest, F (2001) Knowledge-based cascade-correlation: Using knowledge to speed learning. Connect Sci 13: 43-72

Thivierge JP, Shultz TR (2002) Finding relevant knowledge: KBCC applied to DNA splice-junction determination. IEEE Internat World Congr on Comp Intell, pp. 1401-1405

Wisniewski EJ (1995) Prior knowledge and functionally relevant features in concept learning. J Expt Psych: Learning, Mem, & Cog 21: 449-468

Part 8

Independent Component Analysis and Principal Component Analysis

A PCA for interval-valued data based on midpoints and radii

Francesco Palumbo[1] and Carlo N. Lauro[2]

[1] Dip. di Istituzioni Economiche e Finanziarie - Università di Macerata
   Via Crescimbeni, 14 - I-62100 Macerata, Italy
   palumbo@unimc.it
[2] Dip. di Matematica e Statistica - Università Federico II
   Complesso Universitario di Monte S. Angelo, I-80126 Napoli, Italy
   carlo.lauro@unina.it

Summary. In this paper, we propose a new approach to Principal Component Analysis, for interval-valued data. On the basis of the interval arithmetic we show that any continuous interval can be expressed in terms of a *midpoint* (location) and of a *radius* (variation). Moving from this result, we propose a well suited factorial analysis, which exploits this characteristic of interval data. Both the location and variation information are represented on maps.

Key words: Interval Data; Principal Components, Graphical Representations

1 Introduction

In real life there are many kinds of phenomena that are better described by interval bounds than by single-valued variables. In fact, intervals take into account the location as well as the variation of the phenomena. Many application fields might take advantage of statistical interval data analysis; among these, we mention: behavioral analysis, weather conditions analysis and forecast, statistical quality control, analysis of financial data.

Nowadays, thanks to the recent developments of the databases technology and of the computers storage capabilities, in many fields, large amounts of data are registered either continuously (e.g. process quality control) or at any event realization (e.g. financial transactions). In these cases, rather than analyzing such punctual data, it is more appropriate to study *variation* and *variability* of phenomena that are better described by interval-valued data. An interval-valued variable $I[X] \subset \mathbb{R}$ is represented by a series of sets of values delimited by ordered couples of bounds referred to as *minimum* and *maximum*: $I[X] = \{I[x]_1, I[x]_2, \ldots, I[x]_N\}$, where $I[x]_i \equiv [\underline{x_i}, \overline{x_i}] \; \forall i \in [1, \ldots, N]$ and $\underline{x_i} \leq \overline{x_i}$.

In the present paper, we focus our interest to the case when N statistical units are described by p interval-valued variables and we develop a special Principal Component Analysis (PCA) aiming at synthesizing, comparing and representing the complexity of interval multivariate data. Some methods for the interval-data statistical treatment were already proposed in the context of fuzzy variables analysis. However, a great upsurge of contributions on the factorial methods for complex data structure came in Symbolic Data Analysis (SDA) context over the last few years (Cazes et al., 1997; Lauro and Palumbo, 2000). Symbolic Data Analysis (Bock and Diday, 1999) paradigm consists in describing statistical units by complex data structures; interval-valued variables are one of them. The most relevant aspect in SDA is given by the interpretation capability of results.

The above mentioned papers share the same approach: a suitable coding (vertices coding) is used to define data structures to be handled with classical algorithms. Vertices coding implies all the possible min/max combinations to yield a new data matrix having $N \times 2^p$ rows and p columns. In spite of their simplicity, these methods are affected by two undesirable aspects: the analysis is optimized with respect to the vertices rather than the statistical units as a whole; the number of vertices tends to be very large as p increases.

In order to avoid the explosion of the number of rows and the difficulties in referring the vertices to the original statistical units in the treatment and the interpretation, we propose a methodology for interval-valued data that preservers a consistency in the trilogy: numerical representation, treatment and interpretation.

2 Interval arithmetic and statistics

In this section we briefly introduce some basic notations from Interval Algebra (Alefeld and Herzerberger, 1983; Neumaier, 1990) and their implications to statistics. Interval Algebra aims at numerical problems solving when data are imprecise; this implies that each data is identified by a couple of values. The generic interval $I[x]_i$ can also be expressed by the couple $\{x_i^c, x_i^r\}$ which is a biunivocal relationship, where: $x_i^c = \frac{1}{2}(\overline{x_i} + \underline{x_i})$ and $x_i^r = \frac{1}{2}(\overline{x_i} - \underline{x_i})$.

Definition 2.1 *Equal intervals:*
Let $I[x]_i$ and $I[x]_{i'}$ be two generic intervals in $\mathbb{R}$.
If $I[x]_i = I[x]_{i'} \longrightarrow \{\underline{x_i} = \underline{x_{i'}}; \overline{x_i} = \overline{x_{i'}}\}$.

Definition 2.2 *Tiny intervals:*
Let $I[x] \subset \mathbb{R}$, if $\overline{x} = \underline{x}$, $I[x]$ is said **a tiny interval**.

In the following, we are going to define some basic operators in the interval algebra. Any generic operator $\Diamond$ in interval algebra must satisfy the following condition. Let $I[x]_i$ and $I[x]_{i'}$ be two bounded intervals in $\mathbb{R}$, given any x_i

and $x_{i'}$ belonging to $I[x]_i$ and to $I[x]_{i'}$, respectively, if: $I[x]_j = I[x]_i \Diamond I[x]_{i'}$ then:

$$x_i \Diamond x_{i'} = x_j \in I[x]_j, \forall (x_i, x_{i'}).$$

Definition 2.3 *Sum of Intervals:*
Let $I[x]_i \subset \mathbb{R}$ and $I[x]_{i'} \subset \mathbb{R}$ be two generic intervals, then:
$$I[x]_j = I[x]_i + I[x]_{i'} \longrightarrow I[x]_j = [(\underline{x_i} + \underline{x_{i'}}), (\overline{x_i} + \overline{x_{i'}})].$$

Notice that the definition 2.3 can also be written in the midpoint (or center) and radius notation: $I[x]_j = \{(x_i^c + x_{i'}^c), (x_i^r + x_{i'}^r)\}$. In the interval algebra the difference between two generic intervals $(I[x]_i, I[x]_{i'}) \subset \mathbb{R}$ is given by: $I[x]_i - I[x]_{i'} = I[X] \equiv [(\underline{x_i} - \overline{x_{i'}}), (\overline{x_i} - \underline{x_{i'}})]$.

Definition 2.4 *Product of Intervals:*
Let $I[x]_i \subset \mathbb{R}$ and $I[x]_{i'} \subset \mathbb{R}$ be two generic intervals, then:
$I[x]_j = I[x]_i * I[x]_{i'} \longrightarrow I[x]_j = [\underline{x_j}, \overline{x_j}]$, where:
$\underline{x_j} = \min\{(\underline{x_i} * \underline{x_{i'}}), (\underline{x_i} * \overline{x_{i'}}), (\overline{x_i} * \underline{x_{i'}}), (\overline{x_i} * \overline{x_{i'}})\}$ and
$\overline{x_j} = \max\{(\underline{x_i} * \underline{x_{i'}}), (\underline{x_i} * \overline{x_{i'}}), (\overline{x_i} * \underline{x_{i'}}), (\overline{x_i} * \overline{x_{i'}})\}$.

The definition 2.4 also holds for the ratio between two generic intervals and can be generalized to the case in which one interval is a *Tiny* one. Let us assume that $I[x]_{i'} = [\underline{x_{i'}}, \overline{x_{i'}}]$ with $\underline{x_{i'}} = \overline{x_{i'}} > 0$, the operation $I[x]_i/I[x]_{i'}$ is given by the interval:

$$I[x]_j = \left[\frac{\underline{x_i}}{x_{i'}}, \frac{\overline{x_i}}{x_{i'}}\right],$$

where $x_{i'} = \overline{x_{i'}} = \underline{x_{i'}}$ and $x_{i'} > 0$.
The above statements allow defining the *mean* interval $I[\bar{x}]$.

Definition 2.5 *Mean interval:*
Let us define the mean interval $I[\bar{x}]$ as:

$$I[\bar{x}] = \frac{1}{N} \sum_i I[x]_i,$$

where $I[x]_i \subset \mathbb{R} \ \forall i \in \{1, \dots, N\}$.

Definition 2.6 *Distance between intervals:*

$$d(I[x]_i, I[x]_{i'}) = |x_i^c - x_{i'}^c| + |x_i^r - x_{i'}^r|$$

The following properties hold:
1) $d(I[x]_i, I[x]_{i'}) = \begin{cases} > 0 & \text{if } I[x]_i \neq I[x]_{i'} \\ 0 & \text{if } I[x]_i = I[x]_{i'} \end{cases}$
2) $d(I[x]_i, I[x]_{i'}) = d(I[x]_{i'}, I[x]_i)$
3) $d(I[x]_i, I[x]_{i'}) \leq d(I[x]_i, I[x]_j) + d(I[x]_j, I[x]_{i'})$

Taking into account definition 2.6, the following property can be verified. Let $\{I[x]_1, \dots, I[x]_N\}$ be a set of finite intervals, so that $I[x]_i \subset \mathbb{R} \ \forall i \in \{1, \dots, N\}$ and $I[\bar{x}]$ is their corresponding mean interval, then: $\sum_{i=1}^N [(x_i^c - \bar{x}^c) + (x_i^r - \bar{x}^r)] = 0$.

In addition, given any generic constant interval $I[c] \subset \mathbb{R}$, it can also be easily proved that the quantity $\sum_{i=1}^{N} d^2 \left(I[x]_i, I[c] \right)$ is minimized *iff* $I[c] \equiv I[\bar{x}]$.

Definition 2.7 introduces the notation of *scalar variance* for interval-valued data. As shown above, in Interval Algebra the definition of distance is not the same as the definition of difference in $\mathbb{R}$; we believe the distance was closer to the concept of deviation. So we define the deviance as the sum of squared distances with respect to the mean interval.

Definition 2.7 *Variance for interval-valued data:*
Given a set of N real bounded intervals $I[x]_i$ $(i \in [1, \ldots, N])$, we denote with $I[\bar{x}]$ the mean interval and with σ^2 the scalar variance, defined as:

$$\sigma^2 = \frac{1}{N} \sum_{i=1}^{N} d^2 (I[x]_i, I[\bar{x}])$$

The variance definition given in 2.7 can also be written according to the following formula:

$$\sigma^2 = \frac{1}{N} \sum_{i=1}^{N} \left(|x_i^c - \bar{x}^c| + |x_i^r - \bar{x}^r| \right)^2. \tag{1}$$

With a little algebra we obtain:

$$\sigma^2 = \frac{1}{N} \left[\sum_{i=1}^{N} (x_i^c - \bar{x}^c)^2 + \sum_{i=1}^{N} (x_i^r - \bar{x}^r)^2 + 2 \sum_{i=1}^{N} |x_i^c - \bar{x}^c| |x_i^r - \bar{x}^r| \right] \tag{2}$$

The expression in (2) affirms that the variance for interval-valued data can be decomposed into three components: variance among midpoints, variance among *radii* and twice the connection between midpoints and *radii*, given by $\gamma = \sum_{i=1}^{N} |x_i^c - \bar{x}^c| |x_i^r - \bar{x}^r| \geq 0$. Values of γ near to 0 indicate that there is no connection between *variability* and *variation*, otherwise there exists a relation between x_i^c and x_i^r. However, since γ takes only positive values, it is not capable to differentiate between inverse or direct relation.

The remarked properties in definition 2.6 indicate that the distance between intervals can be generalized to the Euclidean distance in the space $\mathbb{R}^p$.

2.1 Matrices of Intervals

We denote the generic interval matrix as $I[\mathbf{X}]$ having $2p$ columns and N rows, where p represents the number of variables and N the number of statistical units. The generic row vector $(1 \times 2p)$ will be denoted as $I[\mathbf{x}]_i$ (with $i \in (1, \ldots, N)$), whereas the generic column sub-matrix, referring to a single interval-valued variable, is indicated as $I[\mathbf{x}]_j$ having N rows and 2 columns (with $j \in (1, \ldots, p)$). Notice that, differently from single-valued variables, from a geometric point of view, the representation of a generic row vector of the matrix $I[\mathbf{X}]$ varies according to p. In case of $p = 1$, $I[\mathbf{x}]_i \subset \mathbb{R}^1$ represents a segment, a rectangle if $p = 2$, a parallelepiped or a parallelotope in case of $p = 3$ and $p > 3$, respectively.

Let us return to the distance definition 2.6. This distance in $\mathbb{R}$ is a metric distance so that, without loss of generality, it can be generalized to $\mathbb{R}^p$, $\forall p$. The distance between $I[\mathbf{x}]_i$ and $I[\mathbf{x}]_{i'}$ is defined by:

$$d(I[\mathbf{x}]_i, I[\mathbf{x}]_{i'}) = \sqrt{\sum_{j=1}^p d^2(I[\mathbf{x}]_{ij}, I[\mathbf{x}]_{i'j})}. \tag{3}$$

Let us consider the interval-valued data matrix $I[\mathbf{X}]$, having N rows and p variables. Moreover, we assume that interval variables in $I[\mathbf{X}]$ have been centered with respect to their mean interval $I[\bar{x}]_j$, with $j \in (1, \ldots, p)$.

On the basis of the above definitions, the matrix can be written in terms of midpoints and *radii*: $I[\mathbf{X}] \equiv \{\mathbf{X}^c, \mathbf{X}^r\}$. The global variance-covariance matrix is given by the following formula:

$$\mathbf{V}_X = \left\{ \frac{1}{N}(\mathbf{X}'^c\mathbf{X}^c) + \frac{1}{N}(\mathbf{X}'^r\mathbf{X}^r) + \frac{1}{N}\left[|\mathbf{X}'^c\mathbf{X}^r| + |\mathbf{X}'^r\mathbf{X}^c|\right] \right\}, \tag{4}$$

where $\mathbf{V}_X$ is a $p \times p$ symmetric matrix.

3 Midpoints-Midranges PCA

PCA on interval-valued data can be resolved in terms of *midranges, midpoints* and *inter-connection* between midpoints and midranges.

The variance decomposition for interval-valued data (4) suggests facing the PCA problem singly; the terms $(\mathbf{X}'^c\mathbf{X}^c)$ and $(\mathbf{X}'^r\mathbf{X}^r)$ are two standard *var-cov* matrices computed on single-valued data. Two independent PCA's could be singly exploited on these two matrices that do not cover the whole variance. We propose a solution that takes into account the residual variance $(|\mathbf{X}'^c\mathbf{X}^r| + |\mathbf{X}'^r\mathbf{X}^c|)$ and, at the same time, allows getting a logical graphical representation of the statistical units as a whole.

3.1 Standardization

Moving from (4), we define the *Standard Deviation* for interval-valued variables. Let σ_j^2 be the generic diagonal term of the matrix $\mathbf{V}_X$, then: $\sigma_j = \sqrt{\sigma_j^2}$ is the standard deviation of $I[\mathbf{x}]_j$ and the square diagonal $p \times p$ matrix $\boldsymbol{\Sigma}$ has the generic term σ_j. The standardized interval matrix: $I[\mathbf{Z}] \equiv \{\mathbf{X}^c\boldsymbol{\Sigma}^{-1}, \mathbf{X}^r\boldsymbol{\Sigma}^{-1}\}$, assuming $I[\mathbf{X}]$ to be centered.

Let us denote the correlation matrix by $\mathbf{R}^2$:

$$\mathbf{R}^2 = [(\mathbf{Z}'^c\mathbf{Z}^c) + (\mathbf{Z}'^r\mathbf{Z}^r) + |\mathbf{Z}'^c\mathbf{Z}^r| + |\mathbf{Z}'^r\mathbf{Z}^c|], \tag{5}$$

where $(\mathbf{Z}'^c\mathbf{Z}^r)$ and $(\mathbf{Z}'^r\mathbf{Z}^c)$ have the same diagonal elements. A noteworthy aspect is given by the decomposition of the total inertia. In fact, $\mathrm{tr}(\mathbf{R}^2) = p$ and we observe that the quantity $\mathrm{tr}(\mathbf{Z}'^c\mathbf{Z}^c)$ and the quantity $\mathrm{tr}(\mathbf{Z}'^r\mathbf{Z}^r)$ are the partial contribution to the total inertia given by midpoints and midranges, respectively. A residual inertia is given by $2\mathrm{tr}(\mathbf{Z}'^c\mathbf{Z}^r)$.

3.2 Midpoints analysis

We consider first partial analysis based on the matrix of centers (or midpoints) values. This is a classical PCA on the interval midpoints whose solutions are given by the following eigensystem:

$$\mathbf{X}^c \mathbf{\Sigma}^{-1} \mathbf{u}_m^c = \lambda_m^c \mathbf{u}_m^c, \tag{6}$$

where $\mathbf{u}_m^c$ and λ_m^c are defined under the usual orthonormality constraints.

3.3 Midranges analysis

Similarly to the PCA on midpoints, we solve the following eigensystem to get the midranges PCA solutions:

$$\mathbf{X}^r \mathbf{\Sigma}^{-1} \mathbf{u}_m^r = \lambda_m^r \mathbf{u}_m^r, \tag{7}$$

with the same orthonormality constraints on λ_m^c and $\mathbf{u}_m^c$ in eq. (6). Both midpoints and midranges PCA admit an independent representation. Of course, they have different meanings and outline different aspects. The quantity $\sum_m (\lambda_m^c + \lambda_m^r) \leq p$ but it does not include the whole variability because the residual inertia, given by the midranges-radii interconnection, has not yet been taken into account.

3.4 Global analysis and graphical representations

Hereinafter, we propose a reconstruction formula that takes into account the three components of the variance (2). The interval bounds over the Principal Components (PC's) are derived from the midpoints and midranges coordinates, if PC's of midranges are superimposed on the PC's of midpoints. This can be achieved if midranges are rotated proportionally to their connections with midpoints. A *Procrustes* rotation (Gower, 1975) algorithm maximizing the connection between midpoints and *radii* represents a possible and logical solution. The *radii* rotation problem requires the definition of the rotation matrix $\mathbf{A}$ that satisfies the following condition:

$$
\begin{aligned}
R'^2 &= \min_{\mathbf{A}} \left(\mathrm{tr} \left((\mathbf{X}^c - \mathbf{X}^r \mathbf{A})(\mathbf{X}^c - \mathbf{X}^r \mathbf{A})' \right) \right) \\
&= \mathrm{tr}(\mathbf{X}^c \mathbf{X}'^c) + \mathrm{tr}(\mathbf{X}^r \mathbf{X}'^r) - 2 \max_{\mathbf{A}} (\mathrm{tr}(\mathbf{X}'^c \mathbf{X}^r \mathbf{A}))
\end{aligned} \tag{8}
$$

The solution of (8) can be expressed in terms of singular values decomposition:

$$\mathbf{X}'^c \mathbf{X}^r = \mathbf{P} \mathbf{\Lambda}^{cr} \mathbf{Q}', \tag{9}$$

so that $\mathbf{A} = \mathbf{Q} \mathbf{P}'$. We refer to Mardia et. al (1979) for an exhaustive demonstration.

The rotated *radii* coordinates are represented on the midpoints PC's as supplementary points. Let $\mathbf{x}_i^c$ be the generic row vector of the $\mathbf{X}^c$ matrix and $\psi_{i\alpha}^c = \mathbf{x}_i^c \mathbf{u}_\alpha^c$ its corresponding coordinate on the αth axis. The interval-described statistical units reconstruction on the same axis is given by the rotated *radii* on $\mathbf{u}_\alpha^r$. In mathematical notation: $\check{\psi}_{i\alpha}^r = \mathbf{x}_i^r \mathbf{u}_\alpha^r \mathbf{a}_i$, being $\mathbf{a}_i$ a vector from $\mathbf{A}$. The interval projection is obtained as:

$$I[\psi]_{i\alpha} = [(\psi_{i\alpha}^c - \check{\psi}_{i\alpha}^r), (\psi_{i\alpha}^c + \check{\psi}_{i\alpha}^r)] \tag{10}$$

Like in single-valued PCA, also in interval-valued variables PCA, it is possible to define some indicators that are related to interval contribution.

Measures of explanatory power can be defined with respect to the partial analyses (midpoints and *radii*) as well as with respect to the global analysis. Let us remind that the variability associated to each dimension is expressed by its related eigenvalue.

The proportion of variability associated to the first dimension is given by:

$$In_1 = \frac{\lambda_1^c + \lambda_1^r + \lambda_1^{cr}}{\mathrm{tr}(\boldsymbol{\Lambda}^c + \boldsymbol{\Lambda}^r + \boldsymbol{\Lambda}^{cr})}. \tag{11}$$

Where λ_1^c and λ_1^r represent the first eigenvalues related to the midranges and *radii*, respectively. They express a partial information; in fact, the whole first PC information implies the computation of the eigenvalue λ_1^{cr}. It is possible to determine all the partial contributions, by combining the elements in expression (11). For example, the variability of the first midranges dimension with respect to the total inertia is $In_1^c = (\lambda_1^c / \mathrm{tr}(\boldsymbol{\Lambda}^c + \boldsymbol{\Lambda}^r + \boldsymbol{\Lambda}^{cr}))$.

3.5 Example

The analysis we have proposed so far has been run on the Ichino's oils data set (Lauro and Palumbo, 2000), which is a widely used interval-valued variables data set. Table 1 shows the single partial results of the three eigenproblems

Table 1. Eigenvalues and percentages of inertia

Midpoints			Midranges			Rotation		
Eig.	%	% Cum.	Eig.	%	% Cum.	Eig.	%	% Cum.
2.359	81.2	81.2	0.252	99.8	99.8	0.634	66.8	66.8
0.332	11.4	92.7	0.008	0.1	99.9	0.280	29.6	96.4
0.182	6.3	98.9	0.003	0.1	100.0	0.033	3.6	100.0
0.031	1.1	100.0	0.002	0.0	100.0	0.008	0.0	100.0

to be faced with the PCA for interval-valued data. Taking into account that total inertia is equal to p, starting from table 1, any partial contribution to the whole analysis can be determined.

Figure 1 allows a global interpretation of the results. The rectangles position with respect to the first two latent factors can be easily interpreted in terms of midpoints variability. The correlation, measured in terms of angles between the PC's and the unitary axes, helps to give an interpretation of the PC's. Sizes and shapes of rectangles represent the variation within each statistical unit. In this case the interpretation is not so intuitive and does require the representation of *radii*. With respect to the total inertia, the factorial plan in figure 1 expresses the percentages of inertia for the three variability components in the interval-valued data analysis: *Midpoints*= $[(2.359+0.332)/4]*100 = 67.2\%$, *Midranges*= $[(0.252+0.008)/4]*100 = 6.5\%$ and the *Rotation*= $[(0.634 + 0.280)/4] * 100 = 22.8\%$.

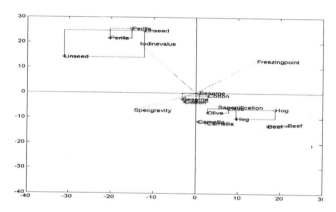

Fig. 1. Representation of the rotated *radii* over midranges PC's

Acknowledgments: The paper was financially supported by PRIN2000 grant *Analisi Simbolica e Data Mining* and by University of Macerata grant (2000) *Metodi statistici per l'analisi di variabili ad intervallo in campo economico e finanziario.*

References

Alefeld G, Herzerberger J (1983) Introduction to Interval computation. Academic Press, New York.

Bock HH, Diday E, eds. (1999) Analysis of Symbolic Data. Springr Verlag, Hiedelberg.

Cazes P, Chouakria A, Diday E, Schektman Y (1997) Extension de l'analyse en composantes principales à des données de type intervalle. Revue de Statistique Appliquée XIV(3):5–24.

Gower JC (1975) Generalized Procrustes analysis. Psychom. 40:33–51.

Lauro CN, Palumbo F (2000) Principal component analysis of interval data: A symbolic data analysis approach. Comp. Stat. 15(1):73–87.

Mardia KV, Kent JT, Bibby JM (1979) Multivariate Analysis. Academic Press, London, pp 416-417.

Neumaier A (1990) Interval methods for systems of Equations. Cambridge University Press, Cambridge.

Independent Component Analysis for Non-Normal Factor Analysis

Aapo Hyvärinen[1] and Yutaka Kano[2]

[1] Neural Networks Research Centre, Helsinki University of Technology, Finland
[2] School of Human Sciences, Osaka University, Japan

Summary. Independent component analysis (ICA) was developed in the signal processing and neural computation communities. Its original purpose was to solve what is called the blind source separation problem: when linear mixtures of some original source signals are observed, the goal is to recover the source signals, using minimum assumptions on the mixing matrix (i.e. blindly). This leads to a linear model that is very similar to the one used in *factor analysis*. What makes ICA fundamentally different from conventional factor analysis is that the source signals are assumed to be *non-Gaussian*, in addition to the basic assumption of their independence. In fact, this implies that the model can be uniquely estimated from the data, using supplementary information that is not contained in the covariance matrix. Interestingly, a very close connection can be found with *projection pursuit*: The basic form of the ICA model can be estimated by finding the projections that are maximally non-Gaussian, which is the goal of projection pursuit as well. On the other hand, the dimension of the observed data vector is often first reduced by principal component analysis, in which case ICA can be viewed as a method of determining the *factor rotation* using the non-Gaussianity of the factors.

Keywords: Factor analysis, independent component analysis, projection pursuit, factor rotation, non-normality

1 Introduction

Independent Component analysis (ICA) is a multivariate linear latent variable model. In its formulation, it is very closely related to factor analysis (see e.g., Lawley and Maxwell, 1971) which was developed mainly by social scientists. Its actual estimation methods, on the other hand, are very similar to projection pursuit, developed by statisticians (see e.g., Huber, 1985). The key difference between ICA and ordinary factor analysis is that the latent factors are assumed to be *non-Gaussian*, i.e. to have non-normal distributions. This seemingly small difference in the model definition leads to huge differences in the estimation procedure and the applications of the model. In fact, non-normality allows us to *separate* several linearly mixed independent latent *signals*, and also to *uniquely determine the factor rotation* without traditional factor rotation methods such as varimax. The purpose of this paper is to introduce ICA to a reader that is already familiar with factor analysis as it is usually applied in the social sciences.

The history of ICA goes back to the early 80's when Hérault, Jutten and Ans (Hérault and Ans, 1984; Jutten and Hérault, 1991) considered a problem in computational neuroscience: How is it possible that when neural fibres carry signals that are mixtures of some underlying source signals, the central nervous system is able to recover (separate) those source signals. A small group of researchers, mainly French, developed the basic idea further in a signal processing context. Possibly the first principled estimation method for ICA was proposed by Cardoso (1989), and Comon (1994) laid the theoretical foundation in his fundamental paper showing that the model was identifiable in the sense that everybody had hoped for. After 1995, ICA was enthusiastically received by people working on neural networks and computational neuroscience due to the work by Bell and Sejnowski (1995), who developed an improved algorithm for ICA estimation, and Olshausen and Field (1996), who showed explicit connections between ICA and models of the visual processing in the brain.

The basic definition of ICA is surprisingly simple. Let $x_1, x_2, ..., x_n$ denote n observed random variables. These are modelled as a linear transformation of n latent variables $s_1, s_2, ..., s_n$:

$$x_i = \sum_{j=1}^{n} a_{ij} s_j, \text{ for } i = 1, 2, ..., n. \tag{1}$$

The a_{ij} are constant unknown parameters to be estimated, not unlike factor loadings. We make the following assumptions on the latent variables or independent components s_i:

1. The s_i are mutually (statistically) independent.
2. The s_i are non-Gaussian, i.e. have non-normal distributions.

The linear mixing model in Eq. (1) is not terribly different from an ordinary factor analysis model. One difference is that there are no separate noise variables or specific factors in this model. However, the number of the factors is quite large, in fact, equal to the number of observed variables. Thus, we could think that the common and specific factors, as well as noise are just all grouped together in the s_i.[1]

Assumption 1 is not unlike the one usually made in factor analysis in the case of maximum likelihood estimation. If the s_i follow a joint Gaussian distribution, independence follows from the conventional assumption of uncorrelatedness. This is a special property of the normal distribution, however, and we shall see below that in the case of non-Gaussian variables, uncorrelatedness does *not* at all imply independence.

---

[1] Denoting the number of common factors be k, the total number of latent factors including specific ones becomes $n + k$ in ordinary factor analysis. This is always larger than the maximum number of independent components in ICA, which is n. However, if n is large and k is small, the difference may not be very important.

So, what really distinguishes the ICA model from ordinary factor analysis is the second assumption of non-Gaussianity. In fact, a possibly more illuminating name for ICA would be *non-Gaussian factor analysis*. Due to non-Gaussianity, both the estimation theory and practical results of ICA are very different from those obtained by ordinary factor analysis.

In the next section, we will first show how ICA is able to do "blind source separation", something that ordinary factor analys is not able to do. In section 3 we will discuss why this is so, why non-Gaussianity is so important, and how ICA can be interpreted as a factor rotation. Section 4 discusses basic statistical criteria that can be used to estimate the ICA model, and shows the intimate connection between ICA and projection pursuit. Finally, Section 5 concludes the paper.

2 Blind Source Separation

To see the drastic effect of the assumption of non-Gaussianity, let us consider a problem that has inspired a large part of ICA research, called blind source separation. Imagine that you are in a room where a number of people (say, three) are speaking simultaneously. You also have three microphones, which you hold in different locations. The microphones give you three recorded time signals, which we could denote by $x_1(t), x_2(t)$ and $x_3(t)$, with x_1, x_2 and x_3 the amplitudes, and t the time index. Each of these recorded signals is a weighted sum of the speech signals ("sources") emitted by the three speakers, which we denote by $s_1(t), s_2(t)$, and $s_3(t)$. We could express this as a linear equation which is just like Eq. (1), where the a_{ij} with $i, j = 1, ..., 3$ are some parameters that depend on the distances of the microphones from the speakers. The goal in blind source separation is to estimate the original speech signals $s_1(t), s_2(t)$, and $s_3(t)$, using only the recorded signals $x_i(t)$.

As an illustration, consider the waveforms in Fig. 1. The original speech signals could look something like those on the left, and the mixed signals could look like those in the middle. The problem is to recover the "source" signals using only the mixed data.

One approach to solving this problem would be to use some information on the statistical properties of the signals $s_i(t)$ to estimate both the a_{ij} and the $s_i(t)$. Let us assume that $s_1(t), s_2(t)$, and $s_3(t)$ are, at each time instant t, statistically independent. If the s_i are non-Gaussian as well, we see that we have in fact all the assumptions of the ICA model! Independent component analysis can thus be used to estimate the a_{ij}, and this allows us to separate the three original signals from their mixtures. This is called "blind" source separation because hardly any information on the sources was used, only the very weak assumptions on statistical independence and non-Gaussianity.

Figure 1, on the right, gives the three signals estimated by ICA. As can be seen, these are very close to the original source signals on the left (the signs of some of the signals are reversed, but this has no significance.)

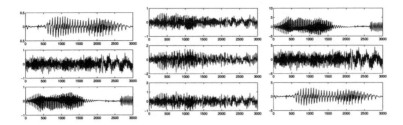

Fig. 1. Left: The original audio signals. Middle: The observed mixtures of the original signals. Right: The estimates of the original signals, obtained by ICA.

3 ICA vs. Factor Analysis

Factor analysis does not separate sources It is important to note that ordinary factor analysis cannot separate source signals as described in the preceding section. This is because factor analysis, or related techniques such as principal component analysis, can only estimate the factors up to a rotation. But in the preceding source separation example, we had three source signals, that is, three factors, and also three observed variables. If one is able to estimate the factors (source signals) only up to a rotation, that means that one is not really able to estimate them at all, since most orthogonal rotations mix the source signals just as badly as the original mixing.

It may be very surprising that the original sources or independent components can be recovered at all. Indeed, the proof that this is possible was presented only relatively recently (Comon, 1994), and it certainly does surprise many people hearing it for the first time. In the following, we will try to explain intuitively why the non-Gaussianity assumption enables the estimation of the model.

Illustration of why ICA is possible To illustrate the ICA model in statistical terms, consider two independent components that have uniform distributions The joint density of s_1 and s_2 is then uniform on a square, which is illustrated in Fig. 2, on the left.

Now, assume that the mixing matrix $\mathbf{A}$ is orthogonal. Basically, we make this assumption here because we consider the problem of estimating an orthogonal factor rotation (see below). Mixing these variables, we obtain the observed data $\mathbf{x}$ as shown in Fig. 2, in the middle. The mixed data has a uniform distribution on a rotated square. Actually, from Fig. 2 you can see an intuitive way of estimating $\mathbf{A}$: The *edges* of the square are in the directions of the columns of $\mathbf{A}$. This means that we could, in principle, estimate the ICA model by first estimating the joint density of x_1 and x_2, and then locating the edges. So, intuitively we see that the problem can be solved, in this special case.

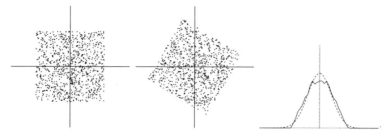

Fig. 2. Left: The joint distribution of the independent components s_1 and s_2 with uniform distributions. Middle: The joint distribution of the observed (orthogonal) mixtures x_1 and x_2. Right: The marginal distribution of a mixture.

Why Gaussian variables are no good On the other hand, we can illustrate why Gaussian variables are not allowed. Assume that the joint distribution of s_1 and s_2 is Gaussian. Using the classic formula of transforming densities we get the joint density of the mixtures x_1 and x_2 as

$$p(x_1, x_2) = \frac{1}{2\pi} \exp(-\frac{\|\mathbf{A}^T \mathbf{x}\|^2}{2})|\det \mathbf{A}^T| = \frac{1}{2\pi} \exp(-\frac{\|\mathbf{x}\|^2}{2}) \qquad (2)$$

where the latter equality comes from the orthogonality of $\mathbf{A}$ (again, we consider an orthogonal factor rotation). Thus we see that the orthogonal mixing matrix does not change the density, since it does not appear in this equation at all. This means that there is no information in the observations of x_1 and x_2 that could be used to estimate $\mathbf{A}$.

This phenomenon is related to the property that uncorrelated jointly Gaussian variables are necessarily independent. Thus, the information on the independence of the components does not get us any further than uncorrelatedness. Thus, in the case of Gaussian independent components, we can only estimate the ICA model up to an orthogonal transformation, which is in fact what ordinary factor analysis does.

ICA as factor rotation In classic factor analysis, the fact that Gaussian variables leave the orthogonal transformation undetermined is well known. Many methods have been developed to determine the "factor rotation", i.e. to find a suitable orthogonal transformation. However, none of the conventional methods try to determine the rotation so that the the blind source separation problem would be solved, that is, so that the matrix $\mathbf{A}$ of factor loadings would be properly estimated. The only exception seems to be the work by Mooijaart (1985), who employed the estimation of generalized least squares using third-order moments in addition to the second-order moments to propose a new estimation procedure in factor analysis for non-normal distributions.

Conventional factor rotations use criteria that are very different from non-normality, typically related to an easy interpretation of the factor structure.

Often in social sciences, the investigators expect there to be a relatively small number of latent factors, each of which has its indicators. That is, the indicator variables of a given factor are largely loaded on that factor, but almost unrelated with the other factors. Mathematically speaking, each row of the factor loadings matrix $\mathbf{A}$ has only one salient loading. Many rotation methods have been proposed to achieve this. However, there seems no theoretical background that justify the use of such methods.

ICA has no rotation problem, since the matrix $\mathbf{A}$ can be estimated almost completely, up to trivial scale indeterminacies. In fact, in many cases, before application of ICA, the dimension of the data is first reduced by PCA or factor analysis. ICA then gives an orthogonal rotation of the factors. Especially in that case, ICA can be seen as a factor rotation which is determined by the search for the *true factors* that really are independent.

4 Principles of ICA Estimation

"Non-Gaussian is independent"

Intuitively speaking, the key to estimating the ICA model is non-Gaussianity. The starting point here the Central Limit Theorem that says that the distribution of a sum of independent random variables tends toward a Gaussian distribution, under certain conditions. Thus, a sum of two independent random variables usually has a distribution that is closer to Gaussian than any of the two original random variables. This is illustrated in Fig. 2, on the right, where the density of a mixture is shown: it is closer to the Gaussian distribution than the uniform density is.

To estimate one of the independent components, we consider a linear combination of the x_i; let us denote this by $y = \mathbf{w}^T \mathbf{x} = \sum_i w_i x_i$, where $\mathbf{w}$ is a vector to be determined. Let us make a change of variables, defining $\mathbf{z} = \mathbf{A}^T \mathbf{w}$. Thus, y is a linear combination of the factors s_i according to Eq. (1), with weights given by z_i. Since a sum of even two independent random variables is typically more Gaussian than the original variables, $\mathbf{z}^T \mathbf{s}$ is more Gaussian than any of the s_i and becomes least Gaussian when it in fact equals one of the s_i. Therefore, we could take as $\mathbf{w}$ a vector that locally *maximizes the non-Gaussianity* of $\mathbf{w}^T \mathbf{x}$! Such a vector would necessarily correspond to a $\mathbf{z}$ which has only one nonzero component, which means that $\mathbf{w}^T \mathbf{x} = \mathbf{z}^T \mathbf{s}$ equals one of the independent components. Our approach here is rather heuristic, but it can be shown rigorously that this is a valid approach (Delfosse and Loubaton, 1995; Hyvärinen et al., 2001)

To estimate several independent components, we need to maximize the non-Gaussianities of several projections defined by vectors $\mathbf{w}_1, ..., \mathbf{w}_n$. To prevent different vectors from converging to the same maxima, it is enough to *decorrelate* the outputs $\mathbf{w}_1^T \mathbf{x}, ..., \mathbf{w}_n^T \mathbf{x}$. That is, the optimization is done under a constraint of uncorrelatedness of the $\mathbf{w}_i^T\mathbf{x}$. In the case of a factor rotation, this simply means that the rotation is orthogonal.

Our approach to ICA makes explicit the connection between ICA and *projection pursuit*. In basic projection pursuit, we try to find directions such that the projections of the data in those directions have interesting distributions, i.e., display some structure. It has been argued that the Gaussian distribution is the least interesting one, and that the most interesting directions are those that show the least Gaussian distribution. This is exactly what we do to estimate the ICA model. This also gives an interesting interpretation of what ICA is doing when the data was not generated as a sum of independent variables. Conversely, ICA gives a very illuminating characterization of projection pursuit. Typically, projection pursuit has been reported to find latent clusters and nonlinear relations, but the independence property has not been discussed at all.

Measures of non-Gaussianity

To use non-Gaussianity in ICA estimation, we must have a quantitative measure of non-Gaussianity of a random variable, say y, assumed here centred.

A classical measure of non-Gaussianity is *kurtosis*, defined as

$$\text{kurt}(y) = E\{y^4\} - 3(E\{y^2\})^2. \tag{3}$$

Kurtosis is basically a normalized version of the fourth moment $E\{y^4\}$. For a Gaussian y, kurtosis is zero, and for most (but not quite all) non-Gaussian random variables, kurtosis is non-zero. Kurtosis, or rather its absolute value, has been widely used as a measure of non-Gaussianity in ICA and related fields. The main reason is its simplicity, both computational and theoretical.

However, in practice an important problem with kurtosis is that it can be very sensitive to outliers (Huber, 1985). Hyvärinen (1999) proposed a class of *robust non-Gaussianity measures*, inspired by an information-theoretic measure of non-Gaussianity, called negentropy. These measures J take the form

$$J(y) \propto [E\{G(y)\} - E\{G(\nu)\}]^2 \tag{4}$$

for some non-quadratic function G. In particular, choosing G that does not grow too fast, one obtains more robust estimators. For example, one could take $G_1(u) = \log\cosh u$, which is basically a smoother version of the absolute value, not unlike the Huber function (Huber, 1985). A very fast algorithm, called FastICA, for actually performing the optimization was proposed by Hyvärinen (1999).

Another popular approach for estimating the ICA model is *maximum likelihood estimation*. Interestingly, one can show that principles of maximum non-Gaussianity and maximum likelihood estimation are very closely connected. If the nonquadratic function G in Eq.(4) is chosen as the logarithm of the density function of the independent components (separately for each component if they have different distributions) the methods are approximately equivalent (Hyvärinen et al., 2001). For non-Gaussian components, the log-density is nonquadratic, so we see again that it is important to use information not contained in the covariance matrix.

5 Conclusion

ICA is a recently developed method for decomposing multivariate data into independent factors. The emphasis is on finding a factor rotation that gives factors that are as independent as possible. In the general case where the factors have non-normal distributions, the covariance matrix contains only a part of the information on independence, and independence is a much stronger property than mere uncorrelatedness. It can be shown that ICA is closely related to projection pursuit: the most independent factor rotation can be found by finding the most non-Gaussian projections.

References

Bell, A. and Sejnowski, T. (1995). An information-maximization approach to blind separation and blind deconvolution. Neural Computation, 7:1129–1159.

Cardoso, J.-F. (1989). Source separation using higher order moments. In Proc. IEEE Int. Conf. on Acoustics, Speech and Signal Processing (ICASSP'89), pages 2109–2112, Glasgow, UK.

Comon, P. (1994). Independent component analysis—a new concept? Signal Processing, 36:287–314.

Delfosse, N. and Loubaton, P. (1995). Adaptive blind separation of independent sources: a deflation approach. Signal Processing, 45:59–83.

Hérault, J. and Ans, B. (1984). Circuits neuronaux à synapses modifiables: décodage de messages composites par apprentissage non supervisé. Comptes.-Rendus de l'Académie des Sciences, 299(III-13):525–528.

Huber, P. (1985). Projection pursuit. The Annals of Statistics, 13(2):435–475.

Hyvärinen, A. (1999). Fast and robust fixed-point algorithms for independent component analysis. IEEE Trans. on Neural Networks, 10(3):626–634.

Hyvärinen, A., Karhunen, J., and Oja, E. (2001). Independent Component Analysis. Wiley Interscience.

Jutten, C. and Hérault, J. (1991). Blind separation of sources, part I: An adaptive algorithm based on neuromimetic architecture. Signal Processing, 24:1–10.

Lawley, D. and Maxwell, A. (1971). Factor Analysis as a Statistical Method. London: Butterworths.

Mooijaart, A. (1985). Factor analysis for non-normal variables. Psychometrica, 50:323–342.

Olshausen, B. A. and Field, D. J. (1996). Emergence of simple-cell receptive field properties by learning a sparse code for natural images. Nature, 381:607–609.

Self-Organizing Method for Robust Blind Source Separation by β-Divergence

Mihoko Minami

The Institute of Statistical Mathematics/The Graduate University for Advanced Studies, 4-6-7 Minami-Azabu, Minato-ku, Tokyo 106-8729, Japan

Summary. Blind source separation is the problem to recover original independent signals when their linear mixtures are observed. Various methods for estimating a recovering matrix have been proposed and applied to data in many fields. Many of these methods have the same type of estimating functions which can be derived through the framework of the maximum likelihood estimation method. This type of estimating functions are unbiased, but the estimators are often too sensitive to outliers and the existence of a few outliers might change the estimate drastically. We propose a robust blind source separation method based on the β-divergence (Minami & Eguchi, 2002). The estimator is equipped with self-organizing mechanism and gives smaller weights to possible outliers.

Key words. B-robust, Estimating function, Outliers, Quasi β-likelihood

1 Introduction

Blind source separation is the problem of recovering the original independent signals when only their linear mixtures are observed. Let $s(t) = (s_1(t), s_2(t), ..., s_m(t))^T, t = 1, ..., n$ be a vector of m source signals whose components are independent of each other. We cannot observe original signals directly, but observe $x(t)$ linearly transformed by

$$x(t) = As(t), \quad t = 1, 2, ..., n$$

where A is a non-singular unknown matrix of size m. Our problem is to estimate recovering matrix W such that elements of Wx are independent of each other (cf. Hyvärinen, 1999b). Let us denote the recovered signals by $y = (y_1, ..., y_m)^T, y_i = w_i x$ where w_i is the i th row vector of W for $i = 1, ..., m$. If W is properly obtained, y is equal to s except for an arbitrary scaling of each signal component and permutation of indices. Distributions of original signals are unknown although specific density functions might be used to define loss functions or to derive estimating equations.

Suppose now that the marginal density of recovered signal y_i is q_i for $i = 1, .., m$. If components of y are independent of each other, the joint density of y is $\prod_{i=1}^{m} q_i(y_i)$ and the joint density of x is $|\det(W)| \prod_{i=1}^{m} q_i(w_i x)$ since $y = Wx$. Now we let $r(x, W) = |\det(W)| \prod_{i=1}^{m} q_i(w_i x)$. We want to find an estimate by minimizing a certain divergence between the joint density $f(x)$ and $r(x, W)$. However, we do not know any form of distributions of signals. Thus, for estimation we replace q_i by some specific density functions p_i for $i = 1, ..., m$. We note that even though we use specific density function p_i for estimation, theoretical investigation should be done under the model with unknown density q_i.

2 Methods by Kullback-Leibler divergence

The Kullback-Leibler divergence $D_{\mathrm{KL}}((f, r(\cdot, W))$ takes a non-negative value and is equal to zero if and only if W transforms x to $y = Wx$ such that $y_1, ..., y_m$ are independent of each other. An empirical version of the Kullback-Leibler divergence is given by replacing unknown q_i with p_i:

$$\widehat{D}_{\mathrm{KL}}(W) = \frac{1}{n} \sum_{t=1}^{n} \log \frac{f(x(t))}{|\det(W)| \prod_{i=1}^{m} p_i(y_i(t))}, \tag{1}$$

where $y_i(t) = w_i x(t)$. Define the estimate for W by the minimizer of $\widehat{D}_{\mathrm{KL}}(W)$, or equivalently, the maximizer of the following quasi log-likelihood function:

$$L_{\mathrm{QL}}(W) = \frac{1}{n} \sum_{t=1}^{n} l(x(t), W) \tag{2}$$

where

$$l(x, W) = \log|\det(W)| + \sum_{i=1}^{m} \log(p_i(y_i)). \tag{3}$$

We employ the term 'quasi log-likelihood' for the above function following Pham & Garat (1997) since we use functions $p_i (i = 1, ..., k)$ without assuming that they are density functions of recovered signals or are close to them, thus, it is not the real 'log-likelihood'.

2.1 Estimating function

The estimating function $F(x, W)$ is the derivative of $l(x, w)$:

$$F(x, W) = \frac{\partial l(x, W)}{\partial W} = \left(I_m - h(y)y^T\right) W^{-T} \tag{4}$$

where

$$h(y) = (h_1(y_1), ..., h_m(y_m))^T \quad \text{and} \quad h_i(y_i) = -\frac{d \log p_i(y_i)}{dy_i} = -\frac{p_i'(y_i)}{p_i(y_i)},$$

and the estimate is the solution of the estimating equation:

$$\frac{1}{n} \sum_{t=1}^{n} F(x(t), W) = 0.$$

Many of the existing estimators have the same type of estimating functions except for their diagonal terms. These include Jutten & Herault (1991)'s heuristic approach, entropy maximization (Bell & Sejnowski, 1995), minimizing cross cumulants (Cardoso & Souloumiac, 1993), and approximation of mutual information by Gram-Charlier expansion and the natural gradient approach (Amari, Cichocki & Yang, 1996). This type of estimating functions are shown to be unbiased provided means of original signals are zeros (Amari & Cardoso, 1997).

2.2 B-robustness

What is B-robustness The robustness of a maximum likelihood type estimator (M-estimator) is investigated based on its influence function (Hampel, Ronchetti, Rousseeuw and Stahel, 1986). We can view an M-estimator as a functional of a distribution G defined by

$$T[G] = \underset{\theta}{\operatorname{argmax}} \left\{ \int \Omega(\theta; x) dG(x) \right\}$$

where θ denotes a parameter vector to be estimated and $\Omega(\theta; x)$ is the objective function like the quasi log-likelihood function $l(x, W)$ in our context. The influence function for the estimator at x under distribution G is defined as

$$IF(x; G) = \lim_{h \to +0} \left\{ \left(T[(1 - h)G + h\Delta_x] - T[G] \right) / h \right\}$$

where Δ_x is the probability measure which puts mass 1 at the point x. The influence function measures the asymptotic bias caused by contamination at the point x and an estimator is said to be B-robust (the B comes from "bias") if its influence function is a bounded function of x. For M-estimators, it holds

$$IF(x; G) = M(\omega, G)^{-1} \omega(x; T[G])$$

where $\omega(x; \theta)$ is the estimating function,

$$\omega(x; \theta) = \frac{\partial \Omega(x; \theta)}{\partial \theta} \quad \text{and} \quad M(\omega, G) = - \int \left[\frac{\partial \omega(x; \theta)}{\partial \theta} \right]_{\theta = T[G]} dG(x).$$

Matrix $M(\omega, G)$ does not depend on x, thus, the B-robustness is equivalent to the boundedness of the estimating function for the M-estimator.

Methods based on K-L divergence are not B-robust Any estimator with an estimating function in the form (4) is not B-robust no matter what functions are used for $h_1, ..., h_m$. An off-diagonal element of $\left(I_m - h(y)y^T\right)$ is $-h_j(y_j)y_k$ with $j \neq k$ and is not bounded as a function of y_k for given y_j, thus, is not bounded as an m-variate function. The fixed-Point Algorithms are not also B-robust as discussed in Hyvärinen (1999a).

3 New estimator based on the β-divergence

Robust statistical procedures have been developed for many statistical models. There is much literature Hampel et al (1986). We propose a robust estimation method based on the β-divergence. Moreover, we do not assume that the means of the signals are zeros and explicitly employ shift parameters instead of the conventional way so that the estimation is performed in a unified way. The proposing estimator has unbiased estimating functions even though we use some density function p_i instead of the unknown underlying density. Moreover, it is B-robust unlike other existing estimators.

3.1 β-divergence

Let us define the β-divergence between two density functions with respect to some carrier measure ν as:

$$
D_\beta(g, f) = \begin{cases} \dfrac{1}{\beta} \int \left(g^\beta(x) - f^\beta(x)\right) g(x) \, d\nu(x) \\ \qquad - \dfrac{1}{\beta+1} \int \left(g^{\beta+1}(x) - f^{\beta+1}(x)\right) d\nu(x) & \text{for } \beta > 0 \quad (5) \\ \int \left(\log g(x) - \log f(x)\right) g(x) \, d\nu(x) & \text{for } \beta = 0. \end{cases}
$$

Since

$$
D_\beta(g, f) = \int \left\{ \int_{f(x)}^{g(x)} (g(x) - z) z^{\beta-1} dz \right\} d\nu(x),
$$

$D_\beta(g, f)$ is nonnegative and equal to 0 if and only if $g = f$ almost everywhere with respect to ν. When $\beta = 0$, the β-divergence is reduced to the Kullback-Leibler divergence.

The β-divergence (Eguchi & Kano, 2001) is related to the density power divergence $d_\beta(g, f)$ proposed by Basu, Harris, Hjort and Jones (1998) as $D_\beta(g, f) = (1 + \beta)d_\beta(g, f)$ and the same estimator is induced from these divergences. See Basu et al. for properties of the estimator in the framework of parametric statistical models.

3.2 Estimator based on the β-divergence

The β-divergence between the density of a recovered signal vector and the product of marginal densities, if they were known, would attain the minimum value, zero, if and only if recovered signals are independent of each other.

Let $r_0(x, W, \mu) = |\det(W)| \prod_{i=1}^{m} p_i(w_i x - \mu_i)$ where p_i for $i = 1, ..., m$ are specific functions we choose and $\mu = (\mu_1, ..., \mu_m)^T$ is a vector of shift parameters. We consider an estimating procedure based on the β-divergence $\hat{D}_\beta(\tilde{r}, r_0(\cdot, W, \mu))$ between the empirical distribution $\tilde{r}$ of x and $r_0(x, W, \mu)$ instead of unknown $r(x, W)$. Its opposite is equal up to the constant to the following quasi β-likelihood function:

$$
L_\beta(W, \mu) = \begin{cases} \dfrac{1}{n}\dfrac{1}{\beta}\displaystyle\sum_{t=1}^{n} r_0^\beta(x(t), W, \mu) - b_\beta(W) - \dfrac{1-\beta}{\beta} & \text{for} \quad 0 < \beta < 1 \\ \dfrac{1}{n}\displaystyle\sum_{t=1}^{n} \log\left(r_0(x(t), W, \mu)\right) & \text{for} \quad \beta = 0, \end{cases}
\tag{6}
$$

where

$$
b_\beta(W) = \frac{1}{\beta+1}\int r_0^{\beta+1}(x, W, \mu)dx = \frac{|\det(W)|^\beta}{\beta+1} \prod_{i=1}^{m}\int p_i^{\beta+1}(z)dz.
$$

Note that $b_\beta(W)$ is a function only of W and its computation might require numerical integration. However, $b_\beta(W)$ does only have an effect on scaling of recovered signals and it can be approximated or substituted by some constant in practice. In our experiments, estimation worked well even when we set $b_\beta(W) = 0$. We define the maximizer of (??) as our estimate $\hat{W}$ and $\hat{\mu}$.

3.3 Unbiasedness of Estimating Functions

The estimating functions of the proposed estimator are

$$
F_1(x, W, \mu) = r_0^\beta(x, W, \mu)\left(I_m - h(Wx - \mu)(Wx)^T\right)W^{-T} - \beta\, b_\beta(W)W^{-T},
$$
$$
F_2(x, W, \mu) = r_0^\beta(x, W, \mu)\, h(Wx - \mu).
$$

Let W_0 be a matrix that transforms x to $y = W_0 x$ such that components of y are independent of each other. For a matrix W_0, let diagonal matrix Λ^* and vector μ^* be the minimizer of $D_\beta(r(x, W_0), r_0(x, \Lambda W_0, \mu))$ regarding as a function of Λ and μ. Further, let $W^* = \Lambda^* W_0$. Then, we have

$$
E\left[F_1(x, W^*, \mu^*)\right]W^{*T} = 0 \quad \text{and} \quad E\left[F_2(x, W^*, \mu^*)\right] = 0,
$$

thus, estimating functions for the proposed estimator is unbiased.

3.4 B-robustness

Suppose that W is non-singular and the negative of the Hessian matrix is positive definite at (W, μ). Then, the influence functions are bounded if and only if the estimating functions are bounded. Let us denote $z_i = w_i x - \mu_i$ for $i = 1, ..., m$. The (j, k) th element of $F_1(x, W, \mu)W^T$ is factorized as

$$\left(F_1(x, W, \mu)W^T\right)_{jk}$$

$$= \begin{cases} -\left(\prod_{i \neq j,k} p_i^\beta(z_i)\right)\left(p_j^\beta(z_j)h_j(z_j)p_k^\beta(z_k)z_k + p_j^\beta(z_j)h_j(z_j)p_k^\beta(z_k)\mu_k\right) \\ \qquad\qquad\qquad\qquad\qquad\qquad\qquad\qquad\qquad \text{for} \quad j \neq k \\[2ex] \left(\prod_{i \neq j} p_i^\beta(z_i)\right)\left(p_j^\beta(z_j) - p_j^\beta(z_j)h_j(z_j)z_j\right) \qquad \text{for} \quad j = k \end{cases}$$

and the j th element of $F_2(x, W, \mu)$ is factorized as

$$F_2(x, W, \mu)_j = -\left(\prod_{i \neq j} p_i^\beta(z_i)\right)\left(p_j^\beta(z_j)h_j(z_j)\right).$$

Thus, estimating functions are bounded if

$$p_i^\beta(z), \quad p_i^\beta(z)h_i(z), \quad p_i^\beta(z)h_i(z)z \quad \text{and} \quad p_i^\beta(z)z \quad \text{for } i = 1, ..., m$$

are bounded functions of z. The first three functions can be made bounded by the choice of p_i for $\beta \geq 0$. However, $p_i^\beta(z)z$ cannot be bounded if $\beta = 0$. For $\beta > 0$, $p_i^\beta(z)z$ is bounded if $p_i(z)/\exp(-|z|^\alpha)$ for some $\alpha > 0$ is bounded. Most density functions commonly used for p_i including $p_i(z) = c_1 \exp(-c_2 z^4)$ and $p_i(z) = c_2/\cosh(z)$ satisfy this condition.

3.5 Asymptotic Stability

Our estimator is defined as the maximizer of the quasi β-likelihood function (6). In subsection 3.3, we discussed unbiasedness of estimating functions. However, the solution of estimating equations is a (local) maxima if and only if the negative Hessian matrix of the quasi β-likelihood function is positive definite. Also, an on-line learning algorithm is stable only when the expected negative Hessian matrix is positive definite. We now give the necessary and sufficient conditions for the expected negative Hessian matrix of the quasi β-likelihood function (6) to be positive definite.

The necessary and sufficient condition for the negative of the expected Hessian matrix at W^* and μ^* to be positive definite is as follows:

$$1 + \beta - c_\beta(1 - \beta) + m_i - k_i(r_i - \nu_i)^2 > 0 \tag{7}$$

$$k_i > 0 \tag{8}$$

$$\sigma_i^2 \sigma_j^2 k_i k_j > (1 - \beta)^2 (1 - c_\beta)^2 \tag{9}$$

for all i, j $(i \neq j)$ where

$$z_i^* = w_i^* x - \mu_i^*$$

$$\nu_i = \mathrm{E}\left[p_i^\beta(z_i^*) z_j^*\right] / \mathrm{E}\left[p_i^\beta(z_i^*)\right]$$

$$r_i = \mathrm{E}\left[p_i^\beta(z_i^*)(h_i'(z_i^*) - \beta h_i^2(z_i^*)) z_i^*\right] / \mathrm{E}\left[p_i^\beta(z_i^*)(h_i'(z_i^*) - \beta h_i^2(z_i^*))\right]$$

$$\sigma_i^2 = \mathrm{E}\left[p_i^\beta(z_i^*)(z_i^* - \nu_i)^2\right] / \mathrm{E}\left[p_i^\beta(z_i^*)\right]$$

$$k_i = \mathrm{E}\left[[p_i^\beta(z_i^*)(h_i'(z_i^*) - \beta h_i^2(z_i^*))]\right] / \mathrm{E}\left[p_i^\beta(z_i^*)\right] \qquad \text{and}$$

$$m_i = \mathrm{E}\left[p_i^\beta(z_i^*)(h_i'(z_i^*) - \beta h_i^2(z_i^*))(z_j^* - \nu_i)^2\right] / \mathrm{E}\left[p_i^\beta(z_i^*)\right].$$

3.6 Computational algorithm

The estimation of the mixing matrix for blind source separation is performed off-line in some situations and on-line in others. Here we consider both of on-line and off-line computational algorithms.

Off-line algorithm When all observations are available for estimation, it is a simple optimization problem which finds the maximum of the objective function (6).

On-line algorithm On-line algorithms might be preferable if there is a possibility that the mixing matrix is gradually changing. The natural gradient approach (Amari, 1998) can be applicable for our procedure with a following modification:

$$\widehat{W}_{t+1} = \widehat{W}_t +$$

$$\eta_t \left\{ \left|\det(\widehat{W}_t)\right|^\beta \left(\prod_{i=1}^m p_i^\beta(\widehat{w}_{it}\, x - \widehat{\mu}_{it})\right) \left(I_m - h(\widehat{W}_t\, x - \widehat{\mu}_t) x^T \widehat{W}_t^T\right) \right.$$

$$\left. - \frac{\beta}{1+\beta} \left|\det(\widehat{W}_t)\right|^\beta \int q_0^{\beta+1}(z)dz \right\} \widehat{W}_t$$

$$\widehat{\mu}_{t+1} = \widehat{\mu}_t + \xi_t\, C_t^{-1} h(\widehat{W}_t\, x - \widehat{\mu}_t)$$

where η_t, ξ_t and δ_t are learning rates, ϵ is a small positive value and

$$C_t = \mathrm{diag}\,(c_{1t}, c_{2t}, ..., c_{mt})$$

$$c_{it} = \max\,(\epsilon, e_{it})$$

$$e_{it} = (1 - \delta_t)c_{it-1} + \delta_t \left| \det(\widehat{W_t}) \right|^\beta \left(\prod_{i=1}^m p_i^\beta (\widehat{\boldsymbol{w}}_{it} \, \boldsymbol{x} - \widehat{\mu}_{it}) \right)$$
$$\times \left(h_i'(\widehat{\boldsymbol{w}}_{it} \, \boldsymbol{x} - \widehat{\mu}_{it}) - \beta h_i(\widehat{\boldsymbol{w}}_{it} \, \boldsymbol{x} - \widehat{\mu}_{it})^2 \right)$$

for $i = 1, ..., m$.

Matrix C_t is an estimate for the sub-block of the expected negative Hessian matrix corresponding to μ and is maintained to be positive definite so that $C_t^{-1} \boldsymbol{h}(\widehat{W}_t \, \boldsymbol{x} - \widehat{\mu}_t)$ is always an ascent direction of the objective function.

4 Conclusion

We proposed a robust blind source separation method. The method is based on the β-divergence and includes shift parameters explicitly instead of assuming that original signals have zero means. The proposed estimator has unbiased estimating functions and is B-robust. We also stated the necessary and sufficient conditions for asymptotic stability. For details and simulation results, see Minami and Eguchi (2002).

References

Amari, S., Cardoso, J. F. (1997): Blind source separation — Semi-parametric statistical approach. IEEE Trans. on Signal Processing, **45**, 2692–2700

Amari, S., Chichocki, A., Yang, H.H. (1996): A new learning algorithm for blind source separation. In: Advances in Neural Information Processing 8, 757–763 MIT Press, Cambridge, MA.

Basu, A., Harris, I.R., Hjort, N.L. & Jones, M.C. (1998). Robust and efficient estimation by minimizing a density power divergence. Biometrika, **85**, 549–559

Bell, A.J., Sejnowski, T.J. (1995): An information-maximization approach to blind separation and blind deconvolution. Neural Computation, **7**, 1129–1159

Cardoso, J.F. & Souloumiac, A. (1993): Blind beamforming for non-Gaussian signals. Proc. IEEE, **140**, 362–370

Eguchi, S., Kano, Y. (2001): Robustifying maximum likelihood estimation. Research Memorandum 802, The Institute of Statistical Mathematics

Hampel, F.R., Ronchetti, E.M., Rousseeuw, P.J. & Stahel, W.A. (1986): Robust Statistics. Wiley, New York

Hyvärinen, A (1999a): Fast and robust fixed-point algorithms for independent component analysis. IEEE Trans. on Neural Network, **10**(3), 626–634

Hyvärinen, A (1999b): Survay on Independent Component Analysis. Neural Computing Surveys, **2**, 94–128

Jutten, C., Herault, J. (1991): Blind separation of sources, Part I: An adaptive algorithm based on neuromimetic architecture. Signal Processing, **24**, 1–20

Minami, M. and Eguchi, S. (2002): Robust Blind Source Separation by β-Divergence. Neural Computation, **14**, 1859–1886

Pham, D.T., Garat, P. (1997): Blind Separation of Mixture of Independent Sources Through a Quasi-Maximum likelihood Approach. IEEE Trans. on Signal Processing, **45**(7), 1712–1725

Examination of Independence in Independent Component Analysis

Shohei Shimizu[1] and Yutaka Kano[2]

[1] School of Human Sciences, Osaka University, Suita, Osaka 565-0871, Japan
shimizu@hus.osaka-u.ac.jp
[2] School of Human Sciences, Osaka University, Suita, Osaka 565-0871, Japan
kano@hus.osaka-u.ac.jp

Summary. Independent component analysis (ICA) is a statistical method of iden-tifying independent latent factors. Many procedures for the estimation problem have been developed. Most of them identify *most* non-normal factors, instead of inde-pendent factors. Intuitively speaking, this is because the central limit theory tells that the sum of more independent variables gets closer to a normal variable. How-ever, this intuitive interpretation holds only if latent factors are independent. If the independent assumption is violated, ICA identifies most non-normal factors, but not independent, like projection pursuit. It has not been discussed fully whether estimated factors are really independent or not. This is because ICA has been devel-oped in the field of signal processing and in many cases there one can make sure of the independent assumption easily by considering data generation process. In social sciences, it is difficult to know beforehand whether latent factors are really indepen-dent or not. Recently applications to neuroscience have increased and applications to psychology or economics have started to increase (Kiviluoto, 1998). Thus, it has become an important problem to examine if estimated factors are independently distributed. In this paper, we propose some statistics that are based on the idea of generalized least squares to examine independence of estimated factors.

Keywords: Independent component analysis, social science, independence, non-normality

1 Introduction

One of main objectives in multivariate data analysis is to find a comprehensive representation in a lower dimensional space. Principal component analysis, factor analysis (FA), and projection pursuit have been often used especially in social sciences. On the other hand, ICA is not often used in social sciences because there are some problems in its applications to social sciences. A problem is that one cannot usually know beforehand whether latent variables are independent or not in the field of social science research, unlike in signal processing. In this paper, we discuss how to examine independence of latent factors and propose some test statistics.

The well-known FA model for an m-dimensional observed vector $\mathbf{x}$ is defined as

$$\mathbf{x} = A\mathbf{s} + \epsilon, \tag{1}$$

where A is an $m \times n$ unknown constant matrix of factor loadings, $\mathbf{s}$ is an n-dimensional common factor with $V(\mathbf{s}) = I_n$ and ϵ is a noise vector. It is assumed that $\mathbf{s}$ and all the elements of ϵ are independent of one another. If the components of $\mathbf{s}$ are non-normally but independently distributed,[1] this model is said to be the noisy ICA or Independent FA (Attias, 1998). If one further assumes that $\epsilon = \mathbf{0}$, (1) is said to be the noise-free ICA(Comon, 1994). The goal of ICA is to estimate the mixing matrix A and to recover $\mathbf{s}$ from $\mathbf{x}$. In social science researches, however, it is more important to interpret $\hat{A}$ than to recover the latent signals $\mathbf{s}$ unlike in the area of signal processing.

Since the ICA was proposed in the field of Engineering disciplines around 1990, many procedures for the estimation problem have been developed, some of which are based on maximization of kurtosis or negentropy (e.g., Comon 1994; Hyärinen et al., 1997). In psychometrics, Mooijaart(1985) employed the generalized least squares (GLS) approach to estimate parameters in the noisy ICA, that is,

$$T_{AB} = \min_{\theta} \left(\begin{bmatrix} \mathbf{m}_2 \\ \mathbf{m}_3 \end{bmatrix} - \begin{bmatrix} \sigma_2(\theta) \\ \sigma_3(\theta) \end{bmatrix} \right)^T U \left(\begin{bmatrix} \mathbf{m}_2 \\ \mathbf{m}_3 \end{bmatrix} - \begin{bmatrix} \sigma_2(\theta) \\ \sigma_3(\theta) \end{bmatrix} \right) \tag{2}$$

where $\mathbf{m}_2$ and $\mathbf{m}_3$ are the vectorized second- and third-order cross-products, $\sigma_2(\theta) = E(\mathbf{m}_2)$, and $\sigma_3(\theta) = E(\mathbf{m}_3)$. The parameter θ consists of the model parameters including A. The weight matrix U is the inverse of a consistent estimate of the variance-covariance matrix of second- and third-order cross-products. Mooijaart(1985) showed the parameters are estimable if the third-order cross-products of the elements of $\mathbf{s}$ are distinct among one another.

The GLS approach by Mooijaart can be generalized. Let $\mathbf{x}_1, \cdots, \mathbf{x}_N$ be a sample from the ICA model, and let $\mathbf{h}(\mathbf{x})$ be an integrable vector-valued function. For simplicity, the norm $\mathbf{y}^T U \mathbf{y}$ of a vector $\mathbf{y}$ associated with a nonnegative definite matrix U is expressed as $\|\mathbf{y}\|_U^2$. We consider the following objective function to perform ICA:

$$T_0 = \min \left\| \bar{\mathbf{h}} - E_\mathbf{s}(\mathbf{h}(\mathbf{x})) \right\|_U^2, \tag{3}$$

where $\bar{\mathbf{h}}$ is the empirical mean vector defined as $\frac{1}{N} \sum_i \mathbf{h}(\mathbf{x}_i)$ and $E_\mathbf{s}(\cdot)$ denotes expectation under the assumption that the components of $\mathbf{s}$ be mutually independent. Note that $\mathbf{h}(\mathbf{x})$ is not quadratic.

ICA based on maximization of non-normality identifies independent factors only when latent factors are independent. This assumption is realistic in the field of signal processing. However, in social sciences, it is doubtful because prior information about independence of latent factors is hardly obtained. Thus, it is necessary to examine independence of estimated factors and

---

[1] We assume in this article that the distribution of $\mathbf{s}$ is unknown except being non-normal and asymmetric.

discriminate most non-normal and independent factors from most non-normal but dependent factors. Whether latent factors are independent will critically influence interpretation of ICA estimation results. Research on evaluation of independence has just recently started in ICA. For example, Murata(1999) used empirical characteristic functions to test the independence assumption. The residual T_{AB} could be used to test the independence assumption while Mooijaart(1985) mentioned nothing about it. The residual T_{AB} is thought to be a measure of distance between the data and ICA model, that is, how well the independence assumption fits the data.

2 Noise-free ICA by GLS

We apply a least squares method to Noise-free ICA using Mooijaart's approach. Here the expectations of random vectors are assumed to be zero. Minimizing residuals, that is, letting the expectations of the third-order cross-products under independence assumption as close as possible to the corresponding empirical means, we have[2]

$$\min \left\| \frac{1}{N} \sum_i (\mathbf{x}_i \otimes \mathbf{x}_i \otimes \mathbf{x}_i) - E_\mathbf{s}[A\mathbf{s} \otimes A\mathbf{s} \otimes A\mathbf{s}] \right\|_U^2 . \tag{4}$$

More generally we have

$$\min \left\| \frac{1}{N} \sum_i G(\mathbf{x}_i) - E_\mathbf{s}[G(A\mathbf{s})] \right\|_U^2 \tag{5}$$

where G is any function but not quadratic.

In the LS approach, large residuals can be considered as badness of fit of the ICA model, which would imply violation of independence assumption. In contrast, almost no information on independence is obtained from the method of maximizing non-normality. Thus, the LS approach that gives information on independence of latent factors will be useful in interpreting ICA results, in social sciences.

3 Some statistics to examine independence

In this section, we shall suggest several statistics for examining the independence assumption of the latent components $\mathbf{s}$ through testing the Noise-free ICA model. In many cases, it is intractable to directly minimize a generalized

---

[2] The Kronecker product $A \otimes B$ of matrices A and B is defined as a partitioned matrix with (i, j)th block equal to $a_{ij}B$.

least squares criteria in (4). Instead, we shall explore an alternative way of constructing test statistics.

Let us make the singular value decomposition of $\Gamma = V(\mathbf{x} \otimes \mathbf{x} \otimes \mathbf{x})$ as[3]

$$\Gamma = P \begin{bmatrix} \Lambda_1 & O \\ O & O \end{bmatrix} P^T, \tag{6}$$

where Λ_1 is a diagonal matrix of positive singular (or eigen) values, and P is an orthogonal matrix. When $m = 6$ and $n = 2$, we have that four distinct third-order cross-products namely s_1^3, $s_1^2 s_2$, $s_1 s_2^2$, s_2^3, and hence $rank(\Gamma) = 4$.

Let γ be a parameter vector of A and non-zero elements of $E(\mathbf{s} \otimes \mathbf{s} \otimes \mathbf{s})$ and define

$$J = \frac{\partial (A \otimes A \otimes A) E(\mathbf{s} \otimes \mathbf{s} \otimes \mathbf{s})}{\partial \gamma^T}$$

Let

$$M = \Gamma^- - \Gamma^- J (J^T \Gamma^- J)^- J^T \Gamma^-, \tag{7}$$

where Γ^- denotes a (nonnegative definite) g-inverse matrix of Γ. Typically, we can take as Γ^-

$$\Gamma_1^- = P \begin{bmatrix} \Lambda_1^{-1} & O \\ O & O \end{bmatrix} P^T \quad \text{or} \quad \Gamma_2^- = P \begin{bmatrix} \Lambda_1^{-1} & O \\ O & I \end{bmatrix} P^T. \tag{8}$$

Note that Γ_1^- is a reflexive g-inverse matrix. If we take all the g-inverse matrix in (7) as reflexive, we have that ΓM is idemponent. Note that ΓM is not idemponent when $\Gamma^- = \Gamma_2^-$.

Define

$$T = N \left\| \frac{1}{N} \sum_i (\mathbf{x}_i \otimes \mathbf{x}_i \otimes \mathbf{x}_i) - E_{\mathbf{s}}[A\mathbf{s} \widehat{\otimes A} \mathbf{s} \otimes A\mathbf{s}] \right\|_M^2, \tag{9}$$

where $E[A\mathbf{s} \otimes A\mathbf{s} \otimes A\mathbf{s}]$ is replaced with some well-behaved estimator $\hat{\gamma}$[4]. Assume that $\sqrt{N}(\hat{\gamma} - \gamma) = O_p(1)$. Taking M with Γ_1^-, we expect that the statistic T can be approximated to a chi-square variate with degrees $\text{tr}[\Gamma M]$ of freedom with $\Gamma^- = \Gamma_1^-$. We label the statistic as T_1. If we use M with Γ_2^- in (9), the resultant statistic is termed as T_2.

We shall prove the chi-square approximation to T_1. Let us define $\bar{\mathbf{m}}_3 = \frac{1}{N} \sum_i (\mathbf{x}_i \otimes \mathbf{x}_i \otimes \mathbf{x}_i)$ and $\mathbf{m}_3(\hat{\gamma}) = E[A\mathbf{s} \widehat{\otimes A} \mathbf{s} \otimes A\mathbf{s}]$. Assuming $\sqrt{N}(\hat{\gamma} - \gamma) = O_p(1)$, by Taylor expansion we have that $\mathbf{m}_3(\hat{\gamma}) - \mathbf{m}_3(\gamma) = J(\hat{\gamma} - \gamma) + o_p(\frac{1}{\sqrt{N}})$. Using this expansion, we have

---

[3] $V(\mathbf{x})$ means the variance-covariance matrix of $\mathbf{x}$.

[4] Some of noise-free ICA algorithms (e.g., Comon, 1994; Hyvärinen et al., 1997) may be used to estimate $E_s[A\mathbf{s} \otimes A\mathbf{s} \otimes A\mathbf{s}]$.

$$\sqrt{N}[\bar{\mathbf{m}}_3 - \mathbf{m}_3(\hat{\gamma})] = \sqrt{N}[\bar{\mathbf{m}}_3 - \mathbf{m}_3(\gamma) + (\mathbf{m}_3(\hat{\gamma}) - \mathbf{m}_3(\gamma))]$$
$$= \sqrt{N}(\bar{\mathbf{m}}_3 - \mathbf{m}_3(\gamma)) + J\sqrt{N}(\hat{\gamma} - \gamma) + o_p(1). \quad (10)$$

Letting $\mathbf{c} = \sqrt{N}(\bar{\mathbf{m}}_3 - \mathbf{m}_3(\gamma)) + J\sqrt{N}(\hat{\gamma} - \gamma)$, and taking into account that $\sqrt{N}(\bar{\mathbf{m}}_3 - \mathbf{m}_3(\gamma)) \rightarrow N(\mathbf{0}, \Gamma)$ and that $MJ = O$, we have

$$T_1 = \mathbf{c}^T M \mathbf{c} \quad (11)$$
$$= \mathbf{c}^T[\Gamma_1^- - \Gamma_1^- J(J^T \Gamma_1^- J)^- J^T \Gamma_1^-]\mathbf{c} + o_p(1)$$
$$= N[\bar{\mathbf{m}}_3 - \mathbf{m}_3(\gamma)]^T[\Gamma_1^- - \Gamma_1^- J(J^T \Gamma_1^- J)^- J^T \Gamma_1^-][\bar{\mathbf{m}}_3 - \mathbf{m}_3(\gamma)] + o_p(1)$$
$$\rightarrow \chi^2(\text{tr}[\Gamma M]). \quad (12)$$

Theoretically, T_2 is not distributed as a χ^2 distribution because ΓM is not idempotent. Browne(1982) has suggested this type of test statistic.

4 Relation with Hyvärinen's FastICA

Hyvärinen's FastICA (Hyärinen et al., 1997) and the LS approach described in the previous section are closely related. Considering $\mathbf{w}_i^T \mathbf{x}$, a linear combination of observed vector $\mathbf{x}$, FastICA maximized the distance between $G(\mathbf{w}_i^T \mathbf{x})$ and $G(z_i)$, where z_i is normally distributed. That is,

$$\max_{\mathbf{w}_i} \left\| \frac{1}{N} \sum_{k=1}^m G(\mathbf{w}_i^T \mathbf{x}_k) - E[G(z_i)] \right\|^2. \quad (13)$$

The LS approach minimizes the distance between $G(\mathbf{w}_i^T \mathbf{x})$ and $G(s_i)$:

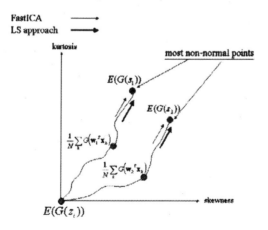

Fig. 1. Latent factors are independent. Note in this figure N is constant but enough large and only $\mathbf{w}_i$ is updated.

$$\min_{\mathbf{w}_i} \left\| \frac{1}{N} \sum_{k=1}^{m} G(\mathbf{w}_i^T \mathbf{x}_k) - E[G(s_i)] \right\|^2, \tag{14}$$

where $s_1, \cdots, s_n$ are independently distributed.[5]

We illustrate the relation between Hyvärinen's FastICA and LS approach in Fig.1, where we took

$$G(z_i) = \begin{bmatrix} \mathrm{skew}(z_i) \\ \mathrm{kurt}(z_i) \end{bmatrix}$$

as an example. If latent factors are independent, both FastICA and the LS approach will extract the same independent factors. This is because the individual latent factors are maximally non-normal. On the other hand, if the independent assumption is violated, most non-normal factors are not necessarily identical with the latent factors, and FastICA and the LS approach may result in different estimated factors. The both approaches are not able to make $G(\mathbf{w}_i^T \mathbf{x})$ enough close to $G(s_i)$ when no ICA model can be assumed. An important difference is that the LS approach gives how violated the independent assumption is. The test statistics T discussed in Section 3 measures the distance between the data and a noise-free ICA model.

5 Simulation results

We conducted a small simulation experiment to study empirical performance of our least squares test statistics T_1 and T_2 developed in Section 4. We took $m = 6$, $n = 2$ and $N = 1000$. We generated 1000 data sets of sample size $N = 1000$ for each of the independence and dependence conditions on $\mathbf{s}$. In the independence condition, we employ two independent χ^2 distributions with degrees 8 and 2 of freedom for $\mathbf{s}$; while in the dependence condition, for $\mathbf{s}$ we employ a two-dimensional distribution on a epicycloid in R^2, which are defined as $s_1 = (a + b)\cos(\theta) - b\cos(\frac{a+b}{b}\theta)$, $s_2 = (a + b)\sin\theta - b\sin(\frac{a+b}{b}\theta)$, where θ varies from 1 to 1000 and a value of a is a priori chosen randomly from 2 to 5 for each data set and b is constantly equal to 3. Note that the distribution is asymmetric for any values of a and b taken here.

For each of the data sets, we calculated T_1 and T_2 using $\hat{A}$ and $\hat{\mathbf{s}}$ estimated by FastICA. Although T_1 theoretically follows a chi-square distribution, the

---

[5] In (14), the number of squares to be minimized is too small compared to the number of parameters. So in our approach, we alternatively use the criterion below

$$\min_{A} \left\| \frac{1}{N} \sum_{i} G(\mathbf{x}_i) - E_{\mathbf{s}}[G(As)] \right\|^2_{\Gamma^-}.$$

result of simulation unexpectedly showed that the values of T_1 were almost zero. This may be because $tr[\Gamma_1 M]$ is very small. On the other hand, T_2 does not get in that situation because Γ_2 is a full rank matrix, unlike Γ_1.

Results are provided in Table 1. In case of independent latent factors, the mean of T_2 over 1000 replications is 29.41, while in case of non-independent latent factors, the mean of T_2 over 1000 replications is 176.11. Thus, a larger value of T_2 could indicate violation of the independent assumption.

Table 1. Simulation results

	Independent assumption holds	Independent assumption is violated
The mean of T_1	-1.28×10^{-18}	6.25×10^{-15}
The mean of T_2	29.41	176.11

The empirical density function of T_2, shown in Fig.2, *looks* a χ^2 distribution, but the sample variance 2584.15 is much larger than twice of the sample mean 29.4.[6]

We leave it open as a future problem to give a reasonable critical value of T_2 to perform a statistical test.

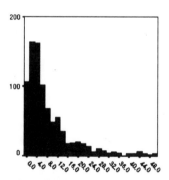

Fig. 2. The vertical axis denotes frequency and the horizontal axis intervals of T_2. In this histogram T_2 greater than 50.0, about 100 statistics out of 1000, are not shown.

6 Conclusion

In conclusion, the following points were made.

---

[6] If we truncate the distribution greater than 12, about upper 35% point, the variance 8.03 is close to twice of the mean 4.06.

1. In social sciences, interpretation of $\hat{A}$ will be more important than recovery of s. Knowing whether latent factors are independent will be useful in interpreting $\hat{A}$. Thus, it is necessary to examine the independence assumption especially for applications of ICA to social sciences.
2. Using the LS approach, large residuals indicate badness of fit of ICA model.
3. Theoretically the statistic T_1 approximates to a chi-square variate with degrees $\text{tr}[\Gamma M]$ of freedom with Γ_1^- under independence assumption. If the latent structure $\mathbf{x} = A\mathbf{s}$ is true, a large value of T implies violation of the independence assumption.
4. The simulation result conducted in Section 5 indicates that neither T_1 nor T_2 follows any chi-square distribution. It is, however, observed that the mean of T_2 under independence is much smaller than that under dependence. Thus, T_2 could be used to discriminate between independent factors and dependent factors.

Our approach uses third-order cross-products and requires that the distributions of latent factors be asymmetric. So our approach can not be applied to data with symmetric latent factors. It is possible to develop LS approach that uses fourth-order cross-products as well as third-order cross-products .

This research is the first attempt to explore possibility of examining ICA models or independence assumption of latent factors $\mathbf{s}$ using generalized least squares. Clearly more simulation studies and applications to empirical data are needed. As noted, it is important to give a reasonable cutoff value of T_2. Further research on these issues will appear soon.

References

Attias, H. (1998). Independent factor analysis. Neural Computation, **11**, 803–851.

Browne, M. W.(1982). Covariance structures. In: Hawkins, D. M. (ed.), Topics in applied multivariate analysis (pp.72-141). Cambridge University Press, Cambridge.

Comon, P. (1994). Independent component analysis, A new concept? Signal Processing, **36**, 287–314.

Hyvärinen, A. and Oja, E.(1997). A fast fixed-point algorithm for independent component analysis. Neural Computation, **9(2)**, 1483–1492.

Kiviluoto, K. and Oja, E. (1998). Independent component analysis for parallel financial time series. In Proc. Int. Conf. on Neural Information Processing (ICONIP'98). 323–342.

Mooijaart, A.(1985). Factor analysis for non-normal variables. Psychometrika, **50**, 323–342.

Murata, N.(1999). Properties of empirical characteristic function and its application to test for independence and independence component analysis. Workshop on Information-Based Induction Sciences.

Neural Coding by Temporal and Spatial Correlations

Allan Kardec Barros, Andrzej Cichocki, Noboru Ohnishi

[1] Universidade Federal do Maranhão, Brazil, *akbarros@ieee.org*.
[2] RIKEN, Japan.
[3] Nagoya University, Japan.

Summary. Redundancy reduction as a form of neural coding has been since the early sixties a topic of large research interest. A number of strategies has been proposed, but the one which is attracting most attention recently assumes that this coding is carried out so that the output signals are mutually independent. In this work we go one step further and suggest an algorithm that separates also non-orthogonal signals (i.e., "dependent" signals). The resulting algorithm is very simple, as it is computationally economic and based on second order statistics that, as it is well know, is more robust to errors than higher order statistics, moreover, the permutation/scaling problem (Comon, 1994) is avoided. The framework is given with a biological background, as we avocate throughout the manuscript that the algorithm fits well the single neuron and redundancy reduction doctrine, but it can be used as well in other applications such as biomedical engineering and telecommunications.

Key words. Neural coding, independent component analysis, correlation, neuron.

1 Introduction

The way neurons code information has been an issue of fundamental interest in the study of nervous system function. Recently, Nierenberg *et. al* (Nirenberg et. al, 2001) found that retinal ganglion cells behave independently from one another. This result agrees with the single neuron doctrine of Barlow (Barlow,1961), who suggested that neurons code information by redundancy reduction at their outputs. This reasoning was used by many researchers in the field of *blind source separation* (BSS), mainly through the recent approach called independent component analysis (ICA). Given that a linear mixture of source signals is observed, ICA attempts to extract those sources assuming that they are *mutually independent*. The codification, in neurons, would occur by assuming those sources to be basis functions which, through linear combinations, would code a given object. For example, a given image can be a result of a composition of different other 2-D basis functions which, on the other hand, could be added and weighted to result in a second image. Exploiting this statistical independence principle, Olshausen and Field (Olshausen and Field,1996) related the independent components of natural images to wavelet-like receptive fields found in cells of the visual cortex.

Their algorithm, however, works only given all the inputs at the same time, resembling population coding.

In this work, we focus on similar direction, although we aim to provide a more realistic algorithm, in the sense that, we avoid the permutation and scaling problem which is well known by the BSS community (Comon,1994). Besides this, the algorithm have a number of biological characteristics, one of which is that we extend the source separation framework also to deal with *non-orthogonal* signals (Daugman, 1990). In other words, we drop the assumption of statistical independence among the sources, although we suggest a strategy for decreasing redundancy, in the sense that the output signals should have minimal cross-correlation. Therefore, in order to differentiate it from ICA, we call this type of approach as *dependent component analysis* (DCA). As a result of this approach, we can also have sparseness at the output.

Some algorithms have been proposed in the literature that uses a fixed-point type of learning (Hyvarinen and Oja, 1997, Barros and Cichocki, 2001), extracting one signal at each time, a characteristic that we believe fits in the concept of the single neuron doctrine. The one proposed here follows this idea, the difference being that, given the required *a priori* information, it extracts the basis function straightforwardly in *one sweep* through the data. This is carried out through an internal reference input that, as a hypotheses, we assume the neuron to own, as shown in the model shown in Fig. 1. Biologically speaking, this reference input may be a pattern which belonged to the neuron previously, due either to adaptation to environment or to genetic characteristic.

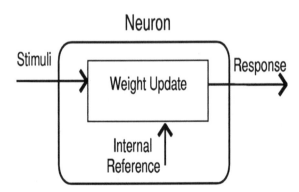

Fig. 1. Proposed model for the neuron which includes an internal reference (or pattern).

2 Source Separation by DCA

Consider n basis functions $\mathbf{s} = [s_1, s_2, .., s_n]^T$ composing a signal $\mathbf{x}$ through the following linear combination,

$$\mathbf{x} = \mathbf{As}, \qquad (1)$$

where $\mathbf{A}$ is an $n \times n$ invertible matrix. Our purpose here is to find a linear combination of the elements of $\mathbf{x}$ which yields at the output the elements of $\mathbf{s}$.

We make the following assumptions:

1. The basis functions have a diagonal zero-lag cross-correlation matrix, $E[\mathbf{s}(t)\mathbf{s}^T(t)]$. It is important to emphasize that the elements of $\mathbf{s}$ can be mutually non-orthogonal though[1].
2. There exist an available reference signal, ϕ_i, correlated to the i-th element of $\mathbf{s}$ such that $E[\mathbf{s}\phi_i] = \beta\mathbf{e}_i$, where β is a scalar and $\mathbf{e}_i = [e_1, e_2, \ldots, e_n]$ is a canonical basis vector, i.e., $e_i = \pm 1$ and $e_l = 0$, $\forall l \neq i$.

Because we want to extract, separately, each basis function, say s_i, given a reference signal, ϕ_i, we can use a simple processing unit described as $y = \mathbf{w}^T\mathbf{x}$, where y is the output signal and $\mathbf{w}$ is the weight vector. Then, let us first define the following error,

$$\varepsilon = y - \phi_i. \qquad (2)$$

We carry out the minimization of the mean squared error $\xi(\mathbf{w}) = E[\varepsilon^2]$. From (2), and dropping the index k for convenience, we find,

$$\xi(\mathbf{w}) = \mathbf{w}^T E[\mathbf{xx}^T]\mathbf{w} - 2E[\phi_i\mathbf{w}^T\mathbf{x}] + E[\phi_i^2]. \qquad (3)$$

This cost function achieves minimum when its gradient reaches zero in relation to $\mathbf{w}$. Thus, taking into account that $y = \mathbf{w}^T\mathbf{x}$, we find,

$$\frac{\partial \xi(\mathbf{w})}{\partial \mathbf{w}} = 2E[\mathbf{xx}^T]\mathbf{w} - 2E[\phi_i\mathbf{x}] = \mathbf{0}. \qquad (4)$$

This equation leads to the following algorithm,

$$\mathbf{w} = E[\mathbf{xx}^T]^{-1}E[\phi_i\mathbf{x}], \qquad (5)$$

Without loss of generality, we can assume that the mixed vector has been prewhitened so that $E[\mathbf{xx}^T] = \mathbf{I}$, with this, (5) leads to the learning rule,

$$\mathbf{w} = E[\mathbf{x}\phi_i]. \qquad (6)$$

---

[1] Notice that two random process $s_i(\tau_1)$ and $s_j(\tau_2)$ are called orthogonal if $E[s_i(\tau_1)s_j(\tau_2)]=0$, for every τ_1 and τ_2 (Papoulis, 1991).

Some remarks are in order here. Firstly, if we multiply both sides of (6) by $\mathbf{A}^T$, we find,

$$\mathbf{A}^T\mathbf{w} = \mathbf{A}^T\mathbf{A}E[\mathbf{s}\phi_i]. \tag{7}$$

Moreover, as we assumed that the mixed vector has been prewhitened, we shall have,

$$E[\mathbf{x}\mathbf{x}^T] = \mathbf{A}E[\mathbf{s}\mathbf{s}^T]\mathbf{A}^T = \mathbf{I} \Rightarrow \mathbf{A}^T\mathbf{A} = E[\mathbf{s}\mathbf{s}^T]^{-1} \tag{8}$$

which we can see, by assumption 1, that $\mathbf{A}^T\mathbf{A}$ is a diagonal matrix, whose diagonal elements, due to the inverse in (8), are inversely proportional to the variance of the equivalent elements of $\mathbf{s}$. Thus, by substituting (7) into (8) and the result into (1), we find that $\mathbf{A}^T\mathbf{w}\mathbf{s}$ is the i-th basis function, scaled by its own energy $E[s_i^2]$. From this, we conclude that the algorithm finds the correct basis function, which is the i-th, besides, we have the information regarding the scale.

A second remark is that this algorithm generalizes the one proposed by Barros and Cichocki (Barros and Cichocki, 2001), where the reference was given by $\phi_i(k) = y(k - \tau)$. Indeed, in this case, the algorithm can work in a framework where the temporal correlations can be used in the codification scheme.

3 Results

We carried out simulations to test the validity of the proposed separation algorithm. Here we show one where we mixed two different source signals: one signal was a periodic square wave and another was a sum of three sine waves, one of which had its frequency equal to the first harmonic of the square wave, as we can see in Fig. 2. We mixed randomly the source signals and used as reference a sine wave with frequency at the fundamental of the square wave, to extract it. In all the cases the proposed separation algorithm worked efficiently.

In a second example, we applied the algorithm to natural scene grayscale images. We used five images of 512x512 pixels from which we extracted 20 patches of 24x24 pixels. We then used different images as reference inputs, including sine waves, square waves and "oriented" waves, where some pixels were black and other white. One example is shown in Fig. 3, where we moved a white line to the right in a black background. It is not difficult to imagine, for example, that a reference signal generated using the *a priori* information on the temporal correlations of the desired signal can be used as well.

Notice that, in this case, the extracted basis functions resembles the reference inputs, but with some differences. One of which is that the lines are no longer continuous, and sometimes, evenly only a point appeared, as indicated by the arrow. Another aspect is that, from the analysis of two neighboring

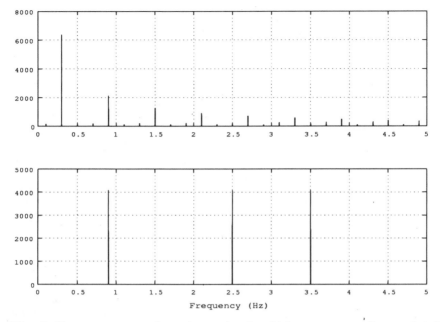

Fig. 2. Power spectrum of two input signals which are temporarily correlated. Notice the spectral overlap of the first harmonic of the top signal with the first frequency of the signal below.

neurons, one responded more strongly than the other, as we would expect to what actually happens at the biological level.

4 Discussion

There are some interesting points that can be brought to our attention from this work. Firstly, we shall remember that we developed this work following the single neuron doctrine along with the redundancy reduction concept proposed by Barlow in the early sixties (Barlow, 1961). Thus, we proposed that only one neuron was active at each time, and this neuron was modeled as having an internal reference input. Besides, this neuron activated obeying a principle of redundancy reduction carried out by the minimization of an error between the stimuli and the internal reference.

In an important contribution, Comon (Comon,1994) showed that, if we use the blind source separation framework, the output shall be the vector **s** possibly re-scaled and permuted. We do not believe that the neuron is carrying out its task in a probabilistic as this one is, but rather, in a deterministic way. Thus, although we do not have a theory at the moment of how it would be occurring at cellular level, we believe that the reference input approach

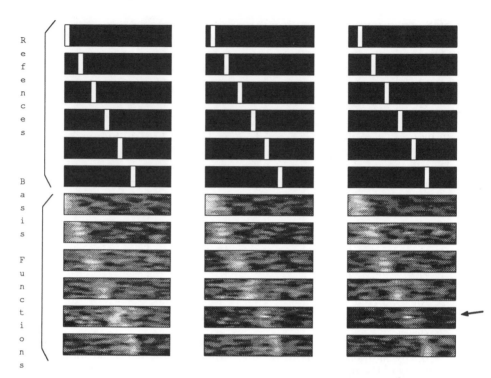

Fig. 3. Reference inputs and equivalent extracted basis functions. Notice that the basis functions are not all continuous, some are splitted into two. The arrow indicates one basis function which was sensitive only to part of the reference input.

appears as an interesting solution to this problem, as it avoids both the permutation and scaling problem.

As we can see from the simulation results, the proposed algorithm worked efficiently in two difficult cases where the source signals overlapped in time and frequency. Moreover, it is worth to emphasize that this algorithm, contrary to the ones proposed in the literature, reaches convergence in one shot through the data. And, importantly, we do not lose the sparseness avocated by Olshausen and Field (Olshausen,1996) as an important characteristic of the receptive fields. Indeed, we can have a overcomplete and mutually non-orthogonal outputs with this algorithm.

On the other hand, extracting signals from a corrupted environment has been an old issue in statistical signal processing, with different approaches which evolved together with machines computational power. In this context, different statistical tools were used. Firstly, second order statistics (SOS) by the estimation of correlations, and after, higher order statistics (HOS), involving for example the estimation of skewness and kurtosis, were proposed. However, the calculation of HOS moments are more sensitive to data size then

SOS. Thus, our algorithm shows also this advantage, since it needs only the calculation of a second order moment. Since nature, by evolution, has been clever enough to optimize the survival of the being, we believe that it is most likely that, if any is used, second order statistics are being implemented biologically.

We also believe that it can be useful in other cases of neural coding such as auditory one. But this algorithm can be as well applied to, for example, in biomedical signal processing especially in EEG/MEG, e.g., in some experiments with event related potentials (ERP), where the timing is controlled. Equally, the proposed algorithm can be used in speech/audio and telecommunication applications.

References

1. Amari S. , Cichocki, A. Yang, H. H. "A new learning algorithm for blind signal separation", *Advances in Neural Information Processing Systems*, 8, MIT press, 1996.
2. Amari, S. and Cichocki,A.: Adaptive blind signal processing - neural network approaches, *Proceedings IEEE* (invited paper), Vol.86, No.10, Oct. 1998, pp. 2026-2048.
3. Baram, Y. and Roth, Z. "Density shaping by neural networks with application to classification, estimation and forecasting," *CIS report no. 9420*, Center for Intelligent systems, Technion Israel, 1994.
4. Barlow, H. B. ,"Possible principles underlying the transformations of sensory messages" *Sensory Communication*, W. Rosenblith, e., pp. 217-234. MIT Press, Cambridge, MA, 1961.
5. Barlow, H. B. "Unsupervised learning," *Neural Computation*, 1, 295 - 311, 1989.
6. Barros, A. K. and Cichocki, A. "Extraction of specific signals with temporal structure" *Neural Computation*, to appear.
7. Bell, A.J. and Sejnowski, T. J., "An information-maximization approach to blind separation and blind deconvolution" *Neural Computation*, 7, pp. 1129 - 1159, 1995.
8. Cardoso, J-F. . "Equivariant adaptive source separation," *IEEE Trans. Signal Process.*, SP-44, pp.3017 - 3030, 1996.
9. Cichocki, A. and Moszczynski, L. "A new learning algorithm for for blind separation of sources," *Electronics Letters*, vol. 28, No.21,1992, pp.1986-1987.
10. Comon, P."Independent component analysis, a new concept?" *Signal Processing*, 24, pp. 287 - 314, 1994.
11. Deco, G. and Brauer, W. "Nonlinear higher-order statistical decorrelation by volume-conserving neural architectures,". In: Computational Neuroscience, Schwartz E, ed., MIT Press. pp. 403-423. 1990.
12. Daugman, J.G. ,"An information-theoretic view of analog representation in striate cortex," *Neural Computation*, 1, 295 - 311, 1989.
13. Hyvarinen, A. and Oja, E. "A fast fixed-point algorithm for independent component analysis". *Neural Computation* (9), 1483 - 1492, 1997.
14. Olshausen, B.A., Field, D.J. "Emergence of simple-cell receptive field properties by learning a sparse code for natural images". *Nature*, 381: 607-609, 1996.

15. Jutten, C. and Hérault, J. "Independent component analysis versus PCA" *Proc. EUSIPCO*, pp. 643 - 646, 1988.
16. Makeig, S. Jung, T-P. Ghahremani, D. Bell, A.J. Sejnowski, T.J. "Blind separation of event-related brain responses into independent components," Proc. Natl. Acad. Sci. USA, 94:10979-10984, 1997.
17. Nadal, J-P.and Parga, N. . "Non-linear neurons in the low noise limit: a factorial code maximises information transfer,". *Network*, 5, 565-581, 1994.
18. Nirenberg, S., Carcieri, S.M., Jacobs, A.L., and Latham, P.E. (2001) Retinal ganglion cells act largely as independent encoders. Nature 411:698-701.
19. Simpson, J.A. and Weiner, E.S.C. *The Oxford English Dictionary.* 2nd edn. Clarendon Press, Oxford, 1989.
20. Papoulis, A. . *Probability, random variables, and stochastic processes.* McGraw-Hill, 1991.

Asymptotic Distributions and Confidence Intervals of Component Loading in Principal Component Analysis

Shin-ichi TSUKADA[1] and Takakazu SUGIYAMA[2]

[1] Department of Information and Culture, Niigata University of Information and International Studies, 3-1-1, Mizukino Niigata-shi, Niigata, 950-2292. e-mail:tukada@nuis.ac.jp

[2] Department of Mathematics, Chuo University, 1-13-27 Kasuga, Bunkyo-ku, Tokyo, 112-0003. e-mail:sugiyama@math.chuo-u.ac.jp

Summary. In principal component analysis, it is quite useful to know the values of a correlation coefficient between a principal component and an original variable. We seek for knowing a meaning of each principal component from their values. However, we do not know how reliable the value of the component loading is. For this purpose we investigate the distribution of the component loading. But it is difficult to obtain its exact distribution. Therefore, we derive an asymptotic expansion for the distribution of the component loading, and also construct the confidence intervals from the result.

Key words: Component loading; Asymptotic expansion; Principal component analysis.

1 Introduction

Principal component analysis is a descriptive method that projects the data in high dimensional space onto two or three-dimensional spaces (principal components) preserving its original information as much as possible. The component loading is a correlation coefficient between the j-th principal component Z_j and an original variable X_i. So it is useful to know the meaning of the principal components and is also appeared in most of statistical software output. The component loading is often used in practice, but we don't know the reliability of the component loading. We need to obtain its distribution for this purpose, but it is difficult to obtain the exact distribution. Therefore, we derive the asymptotic expansion for the distribution, by perturbation method. Moreover, we may get an asymptotic confidence interval based on the result.

2 Asymptotic expansion for the distribution of the component loading

Let $X_1, \ldots, X_N$ be a random sample from p-variate normal distribution $N_p(\mu, \Sigma)$. Let $n = N - 1$, $S = (s_{ij})$ be the usual unbiased sample covariance matrix and $h'_\alpha = (h_{1\alpha}, \ldots, h_{p\alpha})$ be a latent vector corresponding to the α-th largest latent root l_α of S ($h'_\alpha h_\alpha = 1$). When we apply principal component analysis for the covariance matrix, the component loading between the α-th principal component and the β-th variable X_β is given by $\hat{F}_{C,\alpha\beta} = (l_\alpha/s_{\beta\beta})^{1/2} h_{\beta\alpha}$. This mathematical derivation is referred to Jolliffe(1986).

On the other hand, when we use the correlation matrix for principal component analysis, the component loading is given by $\hat{F}_{R,\alpha\beta} = \sqrt{e_\alpha} v_{\beta\alpha}$, where $v'_\alpha = (v_{1\alpha}, \ldots, v_{p\alpha})$ is a latent vector corresponding to the α-th largest latent root e_α of the sample correlation matrix $R = (r_{ij})$ ($v'_\alpha v_\alpha = 1$).

First of all, we derive the asymptotic expansion for the distribution of the component loading based on the covariance matrix. Let $\Sigma = (\sigma_{ij})$ be the population covariance matrix and $\Gamma = (\gamma_{ij})$ be an orthogonal matrix satisfying

$$\Gamma' \Sigma \Gamma = \Lambda = \text{diag}(\lambda_1, \ldots, \lambda_p), \qquad (\lambda_1 > \cdots > \lambda_p),$$

where we assume that all latent values of Σ are distinct each other. Then $S^* = (s^*_{ij}) = \Gamma' S \Gamma$ has the Wishart distribution $W_p(n, \Lambda)$. Let $h^*_\alpha = (h^*_{1\alpha}, \ldots, h^*_{p\alpha})'$ be a latent vector corresponding to the α-th largest latent root l^*_α of S^*. Then the relationships between the latent roots and vectors of S and those of S^* are as follows:

$$l_\alpha = l^*_\alpha, \qquad h_\alpha = \Gamma h^*_\alpha.$$

Sugiura(1976) obtained the asymptotic expansion of l^*_α and h^*_α in respect to $C = (c_{ij}) = (s^*_{ij} - \delta_{ij}\lambda_i)$, where δ_{ij} is Kronecker's delta.

Let $F_{C,\alpha\beta} = (\lambda_\alpha/\sigma_{\beta\beta})^{1/2} \gamma_{\beta\alpha}$ and $T = \sqrt{n}\left\{\hat{F}_{C,\alpha\beta} - F_{C,\alpha\beta}\right\}$. Using expansions in Sugiura(1976), we expand the component loading in respect to c_{ij} and obtain the characteristic function $M_T(t)$

$$M_T(t) = \exp\left(-\frac{t^2}{2}\tau_v^2\right)\left[1 + \frac{1}{\sqrt{n}}\left\{(it)D_1 + (it)^3 D_3\right\} + O(n^{-1})\right],$$

where the coefficients τ_v^2, D_1 and D_3 are defined in Appendix. Here we assume that τ_v^2 is not zero. Inverting the characteristic function, we have

Theorem 1. *Let the asymptotic variance τ_v^2 of the component loading be not zero and let all latent values of Σ be distinct each other. The asymptotic expansion for the distribution of the component loading based on the covariance matrix is as follows:*

$$Pr\left\{\frac{\sqrt{n}}{\tau_v}\left(\hat{F}_{C,\alpha\beta}-F_{C,\alpha\beta}\right)<x\right\}=\Phi(x)-\frac{1}{\sqrt{n}}\left\{\frac{D_1}{\tau_v}\Phi^{(1)}(x)+\frac{D_3}{\tau_v^3}\Phi^{(3)}(x)\right\}+O(n^{-1}),$$
$$(1)$$

where $\Phi^{(i)}(x)$ denotes the i-th derivative of the standard normal distribution function $\Phi(x)$.

Next, we consider the asymptotic expansion for the distribution of the component loading based on the correlation matrix. Let $\boldsymbol{\xi}'_\alpha=(\xi_{1\alpha},\ldots,\xi_{p\alpha})$ be a latent vector corresponding to the α-th distinct largest latent root ε_α of the population correlation matrix $P=(\rho_{ij})$. The population component loading between the α-th principal component and the β-th variable X_β is given by $F_{R,\alpha\beta}=\sqrt{\varepsilon_\alpha}\xi_{\beta\alpha}$ and the sample component loading is $\sqrt{e_\alpha}v_{\beta\alpha}$. As the same way of the covariance matrix, we have

Theorem 2. *Let the asymptotic variance of the component loading τ_r^2 be not zero and let all latent values of P be distinct each other. The asymptotic expansion for the distribution of the component loading based on the correlation matrix is*

$$Pr\left\{\frac{\sqrt{n}}{\tau_r}\left(\hat{F}_{R,\alpha\beta}-F_{R,\alpha\beta}\right)<x\right\}=\Phi(x)-\frac{1}{\sqrt{n}}\sum_{j=1}^{2}\frac{A_{2j-1}}{\tau_r^{2j-1}}\Phi^{(2j-1)}(x)+O(n^{-1}),\quad(2)$$

where the coefficients τ_r^2, A_1 and A_3 are given in Appendix.

Monte Carlo Experiment

We investigate an accuracy of the expansion (1) using Monte Carlo experiment. All simulation are carried out on Fujitsu S-4/20L. And we adopt the maximum length linearly recurring sequence as the random number generator. Let '

$$\Gamma=\begin{pmatrix}\cos\theta_1 & -\sin\theta_1 & 0\\ \sin\theta_1\cos\theta_2 & \cos\theta_1\cos\theta_2 & -\sin\theta_2\\ \sin\theta_1\sin\theta_1 & \cos\theta_1\sin\theta_2 & \cos\theta_2\end{pmatrix},\quad \Lambda=\begin{pmatrix}\lambda_1 & 0 & 0\\ 0 & \lambda_2 & 0\\ 0 & 0 & \lambda_3\end{pmatrix},$$

and the population covariance matrix be $\Sigma=\Gamma\Lambda\Gamma'$. We take the latent roots $(\lambda_1,\lambda_2,\lambda_3)$ of the population covariance matrix, (θ_1,θ_2), α and β as follows:

	$(\lambda_1,\lambda_2,\lambda_3)$	θ_1	θ_2	α	β	$F_{C,\alpha,\beta}$	τ_v
Case 1	(1.8, .90, .30)	45	20	1	3	.499	1.043
Case 2	(1.8, .90, .30)	58	10	1	2	.912	0.496
Case 3	(1.5, .90, .60)	60	30	1	3	.514	1.739
Case 4	(1.5, .90, .60)	65	10	1	2	.908	0.550

This table represents that in case 2 we treat the component loading between the first principal component and the second variable X_2 *i.e.* when

Table 1. Accuracy of the asymptotic expansion for the distribution of the component loading based on the covariance matrix.

	$n = 100$				$n = 200$		
	Term of	Term of			Term of	Term of	
x	$\Phi(x)$	$O(n^{-1/2})$	Total	x	$\Phi(x)$	$O(n^{-1/2})$	Total
Case 1 : $\alpha = 1$, $\beta = 3$; $F_{C,13} = 0.499$, $\tau_v = 1.043$							
.2848	.6121	-.0071	.6050	.2752	.6084	-.0052	.6033
.5388	.7050	-.0002	.7048	.5342	.7034	-.0002	.7031
.8207	.7940	.0093	.8033	.8257	.7955	.0067	.8021
1.185	.8819	.0189	.9008	1.211	.8869	.0137	.9006
Case 2 : $\alpha = 1$, $\beta = 2$; $F_{C,12} = 0.912$, $\tau_v = 0.496$							
.3165	.6246	.0030	.6276	.3022	.6194	.0016	.6209
.5363	.7045	.0179	.7224	.5360	.7046	.0126	.7172
.7641	.7779	.0360	.8139	.7869	.7848	.0267	.8115
1.032	.8493	.0546	.9039	1.098	.8642	.0410	.9052
Case 3 : $\alpha = 1$, $\beta = 3$; $F_{C,13} = 0.505$, $\tau_v = 1.739$							
.3024	.6188	-.0148	.6040	.2891	.6137	-.0108	.6030
.5499	.7088	-.0039	.7049	.5431	.7065	-.0030	.7034
.8172	.7931	.0103	.8034	.8246	.7952	.0075	.8027
1.154	.8759	.0251	.9010	1.189	.8827	.0185	.9012
Case 4 : $\alpha = 1$, $\beta = 2$; $F_{C,12} = 0.901$, $\tau_v = 0.550$							
.1358	.5540	.0253	.5794	.2177	.5862	.0199	.6060
.3643	.6422	.0356	.6778	.4488	.6732	.0291	.7023
.5915	.7229	.0518	.7747	.6915	.7554	.0422	.7975
.8508	.8026	.0714	.8739	.9853	.8378	.0563	.8941

$\alpha = 1$ and $\beta = 2$, we take $(\theta_1, \theta_2) = (58°, 10°)$ so that the population component loading is .912. Then the square of asymptotic variance denote .496.

Table 1 represents the approximate probability given by the main parts on the right hand side of (1) for the cases of $n = 100$ and 200. The points x in Table 1 denote the lower 60, 70, 80 and 90 % point which are obtained by ten million time simulation.

When the degree of separation of latent roots is large, the accuracy of the asymptotic expansion is good. For example, in the case of $n = 100$ the approximation of 90% of Case 2 is .9039 and that of Case 4 is .8739. Each difference between .9000 and the approximate value are .0039 and .0261. And the accuracy in the case of $n = 200$ is better than that of $n = 100$. In case 2 and case 4, the accuracy is not good. The reason may be that the asymptotic variance is small, though we assume that the asymptotic variance in theorem

1 is not zero. However we may use this expansion in the case that the sample size is about two hundred.

3 Confidence interval of the component loading

We consider the asymptotic confidence interval for the component loadings $F_{C,\alpha\beta}$ and $F_{R,\alpha\beta}$ by using the asymptotic variances which are included in the above results. We assume that substitution of consistent estimators for parameters gives $\hat{\tau}_*^2$. The component loading $\sqrt{n}(\hat{F}_{*,\alpha\beta} - F_{*,\alpha\beta})/\hat{\tau}_*$ is distributed as the standard normal distribution $N(0,1)$ for large sample size $n+1$. Let x_a be the upper $100(1-a)/2\%$ point of $N(0,1)$, then the asymptotic confidence interval for the component loading $F_{*,\alpha\beta}$ is as follows:

$$\hat{F}_{*,\alpha\beta} - \frac{\hat{\tau}_*}{\sqrt{n}}\, x_a < F_{*,\alpha\beta} < \hat{F}_{*,\alpha\beta} + \frac{\hat{\tau}_*}{\sqrt{n}}\, x_a. \tag{3}$$

We obtain the asymptotic confidence interval of the component loading using above equation.

Example.
Here we apply the above confidence interval for practical data, which is published in Sugiyama(1983). We have the results of 166 junior high school students examined in language, social studies, math, science, music, art, physical education, manual training and homemaking, and English. The mean vector and the covariance matrix are as follows:

$$\bar{x} = \begin{pmatrix} 52.4 \\ 39.4 \\ 45.4 \\ 50.1 \\ 42.6 \\ 62.5 \\ 57.8 \\ 47.1 \\ 39.0 \end{pmatrix}, \quad S = \begin{pmatrix} 470.6 \\ 363.8 & 459.4 \\ 384.9 & 407.8 & 583.6 \\ 333.5 & 383.8 & 426.9 & 462.1 \\ 356.2 & 369.9 & 421.6 & 391.1 & 531.9 \\ 259.0 & 229.7 & 245.9 & 224.5 & 263.3 & 300.1 \\ 248.2 & 113.2 & 106.3 & 66.2 & 186.7 & 201.8 & 708.3 \\ 321.4 & 326.6 & 320.3 & 344.7 & 301.7 & 209.4 & 95.3 & 500.7 \\ 493.6 & 501.6 & 576.5 & 485.3 & 479.9 & 304.7 & 232.3 & 404.6 & 874.7 \end{pmatrix}.$$

Applying principal component analysis based on the above covariance matrix, we have the following results, where U_i denotes the i-th principal component.

Latent vectors		U_1	U_2	U_3	U_4	U_5
Language	X_1	.338	.120	.093	.114	.492
Social studies	X_2	.339	−.121	.034	.000	.157
Math	X_3	.377	−.174	−.307	−.151	−.034
Science	X_4	.337	−.207	.100	−.177	−.211
Music	X_5	.349	−.003	−.005	−.668	−.332
Art	X_6	.227	.153	.171	−.251	.661
Physical education	X_7	.172	.926	.013	.028	−.248
Manual training and Homemaking	X_8	.298	−.126	.783	.347	−.260
English	X_9	.472	−.040	−.494	.550	−.105
Latent roots		3237.1	700.6	261.0	208.8	124.4
Contribution rate		.662	.143	.053	.043	.025

And the component loadings are as follows:

Variable		U_1	U_2	U_3	U_4	U_5
Language	(X_1)	.887	.147	.069	−.076	.253
Social studies	(X_2)	.900	−.150	.025	−.000	.082
Math	(X_3)	.889	−.191	−.206	.090	−.016
Science	(X_4)	.892	−.255	.075	.119	−.110
Music	(X_5)	.862	−.004	−.003	.418	−.161
Art	(X_6)	.746	.234	.159	.209	.426
Physical education	(X_7)	.367	.921	.008	−.015	−.104
Manual training and Homemaking	(X_8)	.759	−.149	.565	−.224	−.130
English	(X_9)	.908	−.036	−.270	−.269	−.040

Since latent roots are clearly distinct from these results, we consider the confidence interval of the component loading. Applying (3), we have the 95% confidence interval

Lower bound	component loading	Upper bound	$\hat{\tau}_v$
.799	$F_{C,11}$	.975	.580
.824	$F_{C,12}$	.975	.496
.813	$F_{C,13}$	.965	.499
.812	$F_{C,14}$	.972	.526
.761	$F_{C,15}$	.963	.666
.628	$F_{C,16}$	.863	.772
.326	$F_{C,17}$	.408	.269
.635	$F_{C,18}$	.822	.813
.822	$F_{C,19}$	.995	.568

4 Appendix: The coefficients of asymptotic expansion for the component loading

4.1 In the case of covariance matrix

$$\tau_v^2 = \sum_{\substack{i=1 \\ i\neq\alpha}}^{p} \frac{\lambda_\alpha^2}{(\lambda_\alpha - \lambda_i)^2} F_{C,i\beta}^2 + F_{C,\alpha\beta}^2 \left(1 - 2\sum_{\substack{i=1 \\ i\neq\alpha}}^{p} \frac{\lambda_\alpha}{\lambda_\alpha - \lambda_i} F_{C,i\beta}^2 \right) - F_{C,\alpha\beta}^4,$$

$$D_1 = F_{C,\alpha\beta}\left(\frac{3}{2}\sum_{\substack{i,j=1 \\ i<j}}^{p} F_{C,i\beta}^2 F_{C,j\beta}^2 - \sum_{\substack{i=1 \\ i\neq\alpha}}^{p} \frac{\lambda_\alpha}{\lambda_\alpha - \lambda_i} F_{C,i\beta}^2 - \frac{1}{4} \right) + \frac{1}{2}F_{C,\alpha\beta}^3 - \frac{3}{4}F_{C,\alpha\beta}^5,$$

$$D_3 = C_3 F_{C,\alpha\beta}^3 + C_5 F_{C,\alpha\beta}^5 + C_7 F_{C,\alpha\beta}^7 + \frac{5}{3}F_{C,\alpha\beta}^9 - \frac{9}{8}F_{C,\alpha\beta}^{11},$$

$$C_3 = -\frac{1}{8} + 2\sum_{\substack{i,j=1 \\ i,j\neq\alpha}}^{p} \left(\frac{\lambda_\alpha}{\lambda_\alpha - \lambda_i} + \frac{\lambda_\alpha}{\lambda_\alpha - \lambda_j} \right) F_{C,i\beta}^2 F_{C,j\beta}^2 + \frac{3}{8}\sum_{\substack{i=1 \\ i\neq\alpha}}^{p} F_{C,i\beta}^8,$$

$$-2\sum_{\substack{i=1 \\ i\neq\alpha}}^{p} \frac{\lambda_\alpha^4 - 3\lambda_\alpha^3\lambda_i + 3\lambda_\alpha^2\lambda_i^2 - \lambda_\alpha\lambda_i^3}{(\lambda_\alpha - \lambda_i)^4} F_{C,i\beta}^6 - 2\sum_{\substack{i=1 \\ i\neq\alpha}}^{p} \frac{3\lambda_\alpha^4 - 9\lambda_\alpha^3\lambda_i + 8\lambda_\alpha^2\lambda_i^2 - 2\lambda_\alpha\lambda_i^3}{(\lambda_\alpha - \lambda_i)^4} F_{C,i\beta}^2$$

$$+ \sum_{\substack{i=1 \\ i\neq\alpha}}^{p} \frac{15\lambda_\alpha^4 - 7\lambda_\alpha^3\lambda_i + 3\lambda_\alpha^2\lambda_i^2 + \lambda_i^4}{(\lambda_\alpha - \lambda_i)^4} F_{C,i\beta}^4 + \frac{3}{2} \sum_{\substack{i,j\neq\alpha \\ i<j}}^{p} F_{C,i\beta}^6 F_{C,j\beta}^2 + \frac{9}{4} \sum_{\substack{i,j\neq\alpha \\ i<j}}^{p} F_{C,i\beta}^2 F_{C,j\beta}^4$$

$$+ \frac{3}{2} \sum_{\substack{i,j\neq\alpha \\ i<j}}^{p} F_{C,i\beta}^2 F_{C,j\beta}^6 + 2 \sum_{\substack{i,j\neq\alpha \\ i<j}}^{p} \left(\frac{2\lambda_\alpha}{\lambda_i - \lambda_\alpha} + \frac{\lambda_\alpha}{\lambda_j - \lambda_\alpha} \right) F_{C,i\beta}^4 F_{C,j\beta}^2$$

$$+ 2 \sum_{\substack{i,j\neq\alpha \\ i<j}}^{p} \left(\frac{\lambda_\alpha}{\lambda_i - \lambda_\alpha} + \frac{2\lambda_\alpha}{\lambda_j - \lambda_\alpha} \right) F_{C,i\beta}^2 F_{C,j\beta}^4$$

$$+ \sum_{\substack{i,j\neq\alpha \\ i<j}}^{p} \left\{ \frac{1}{2} + \frac{\lambda_\alpha^2}{(\lambda_\alpha - \lambda_i)^2} + \frac{\lambda_\alpha^2}{(\lambda_\alpha - \lambda_j)^2} + \frac{5\lambda_\alpha^2 + \lambda_\alpha\lambda_i + \lambda_\alpha\lambda_j}{(\lambda_\alpha - \lambda_i)(\lambda_\alpha - \lambda_j)} \right\} F_{C,i\beta}^2 F_{C,j\beta}^2$$

$$+ 4 \sum_{\substack{i,j,k\neq\alpha \\ i<j<k}}^{p} \left(\frac{\lambda_\alpha}{\lambda_i - \lambda_\alpha} + \frac{\lambda_\alpha}{\lambda_j - \lambda_\alpha} + \frac{\lambda_\alpha}{\lambda_k - \lambda_\alpha} \right) F_{C,i\beta}^2 F_{C,j\beta}^2 F_{C,k\beta}^2$$

$$+ \frac{9}{2} \sum_{\substack{i,j,k\neq\alpha \\ i<j<k}}^{p} (F_{C,i\beta}^4 F_{C,j\beta}^2 F_{C,k\beta}^2 + F_{C,i\beta}^2 F_{C,j\beta}^4 F_{C,k\beta}^2 + F_{C,i\beta}^2 F_{C,j\beta}^2 F_{C,k\beta}^4)$$

$$+ 9 \sum_{\substack{i,j,k,l\neq\alpha \\ i<j<k<l}}^{p} F_{C,i\beta}^2 F_{C,j\beta}^2 F_{C,k\beta}^2 F_{C,l\beta}^2,$$

$$C_5 = -\frac{3}{4} + \sum_{\substack{i=1 \\ i\neq\alpha}}^{p} \frac{9\lambda_\alpha^4 - 30\lambda_\alpha^3\lambda_i + 35\lambda_\alpha^2\lambda_i^2 - 16\lambda_\alpha\lambda_i^3 + 2\lambda_i^4}{(\lambda_\alpha - \lambda_i)^4} F_{C,i\beta}^2$$

$$- \sum_{\substack{i=1 \\ i\neq\alpha}}^{p} \frac{5\lambda_\alpha^4 - 16\lambda_\alpha^3\lambda_i + 18\lambda_\alpha^2\lambda_i^2 - 8\lambda_\alpha\lambda_i^3 + \lambda_i^4}{(\lambda_\alpha - \lambda_i)^4} F_{C,i\beta}^4 + \frac{9}{2} \sum_{\substack{i,j\neq\alpha \\ i<j}}^{p} F_{C,i\beta}^4 F_{C,j\beta}^2$$

$$+ \frac{9}{2} \sum_{\substack{i,j\neq\alpha \\ i<j}}^{p} F_{C,i\beta}^2 F_{C,j\beta}^4 + 2 \sum_{\substack{i,j\neq\alpha \\ i<j}}^{p} \left(\frac{2\lambda_\alpha}{\lambda_i - \lambda_\alpha} + \frac{2\lambda_\alpha}{\lambda_j - \lambda_\alpha} - 1 \right) F_{C,i\beta}^2 F_{C,j\beta}^2$$

$$+ 9 \sum_{\substack{i,j,k\neq\alpha \\ i<j<k}}^{p} F_{C,i\beta}^2 F_{C,j\beta}^2 F_{C,k\beta}^2,$$

$$C_7 = \frac{21}{4} - \sum_{\substack{i=1 \\ i\neq\alpha}}^{p} \frac{6\lambda_\alpha^4 - 22\lambda_\alpha^3\lambda_i + 30\lambda_\alpha^2\lambda_i^2 - 18\lambda_\alpha\lambda_i^3 + 4\lambda_i^4}{(\lambda_\alpha - \lambda_i)^4} F_{C,i\beta}^2$$

$$+ \frac{9}{4} \sum_{\substack{i=1 \\ i\neq\alpha}}^{p} F_{C,i\beta}^4 + \frac{9}{2} \sum_{\substack{i,j\neq\alpha \\ i<j}}^{p} F_{C,i\beta}^2 F_{C,j\beta}^2,$$

4.2 In the case of correlation matrix

$$\tau_r^2 = \frac{1}{2} \sum_{\substack{i,j\neq\alpha \\ i\neq j}}^{p} \sum_{\substack{k,l\neq\alpha \\ k\neq l}}^{p} (\rho_{jk} - \rho_{ij}\rho_{ik})(\rho_{il} - \rho_{ik}\rho_{kl})f_{ij}f_{kl},$$

$$A_1 = -\frac{1}{2} \sum_{\substack{i,j\neq\alpha \\ i\neq j}}^{p} \rho_{ij}(1 - \rho_{ij}^2)f_{ij} + \frac{1}{2} \sum_{\substack{i,j\neq\alpha \\ i\neq j}}^{p} \sum_{\substack{k,l\neq\alpha \\ k\neq l}}^{p} \rho_{jk.i}\rho_{il.k}f_{ij.kl},$$

$$A_3 = \sum_{\substack{i,j\neq\alpha \\ i\neq j}}^{p} \{\rho_{ij}(3d_{ii} + d_{jj}) - 4d_{ij}\}d_{ii}f_{ij} + \sum_{\substack{i,j\neq\alpha \\ i\neq j}}^{p} \sum_{\substack{k,l\neq\alpha \\ k\neq l}}^{p} (d_{ij} - \rho_{ij}d_{ii})(d_{kl} - \rho_{kl}d_{kk})f_{ij.kl}$$

$$+ \frac{4}{3} \sum_{\substack{i,j\neq\alpha \\ i\neq j}}^{p} \sum_{\substack{k,l\neq\alpha \\ k\neq lP}}^{p} \sum_{\substack{q,r\neq\alpha \\ q\neq r}}^{p} \rho_{ir.q}\rho_{jk.i}\rho_{lq.k}f_{ij}f_{kl}f_{qr},$$

$$\rho_{ij.k} = \rho_{ij} - \rho_{ki}\rho_{kj}, \quad d_{ij} = \sum_{\substack{k,l\neq\alpha \\ k\neq l}}^{p} \rho_{ik}(\rho_{jl} - \rho_{jk}\rho_{kl})f_{kl},$$

$$f_{ij} = \left.\frac{\partial f}{\partial r_{ij}}\right|_{R=P} = -\frac{1}{2\varepsilon_\alpha^2}F_{R,\alpha\beta}F_{R,\alpha i}F_{R,\alpha j} - \sum_{\substack{k=1 \\ k\neq\alpha}}^{p} \frac{F_{R,\alpha j}F_{R,k\beta}F_{R,ki}}{\varepsilon_k(\varepsilon_k - \varepsilon_\alpha)},$$

$$f_{ij.kl} = \left.\frac{\partial^2 f}{\partial r_{ij}\partial r_{kl}}\right|_{R=P} = -\frac{1}{4\varepsilon_\alpha^4}F_{R,\alpha i}F_{R,\alpha j}F_{R,\alpha k}F_{R,\alpha l}F_{R,\alpha\beta}$$

$$+ \frac{1}{2\varepsilon_\alpha^2} \sum_{\substack{s=1 \\ s\neq\alpha}}^{p} \frac{F_{R,\alpha\beta}F_{R,si}F_{R,\alpha j}F_{R,sk}F_{R,\alpha l}}{\varepsilon_s(\varepsilon_\alpha - \varepsilon_s)} + \frac{1}{2\varepsilon_\alpha^2} \sum_{\substack{s=1 \\ s\neq\alpha}}^{p} \frac{F_{R,\alpha i}F_{R,\alpha j}F_{R,s\beta}F_{R,sk}F_{R,\alpha l}}{\varepsilon_s(\varepsilon_\alpha - \varepsilon_s)}$$

$$+ \frac{1}{2\varepsilon_\alpha^2} \sum_{\substack{s=1 \\ s\neq\alpha}}^{p} \frac{F_{R,\alpha k}F_{R,\alpha l}F_{R,s\beta}F_{R,si}F_{R,\alpha j}}{\varepsilon_s(\varepsilon_\alpha - \varepsilon_s)} + \sum_{\substack{s,t=1 \\ s,t\neq\alpha}}^{p} \frac{F_{R,\alpha l}F_{R,s\beta}F_{R,si}F_{R,tj}F_{R,tk}}{\varepsilon_s\varepsilon_t(\varepsilon_\alpha - \varepsilon_s)(\varepsilon_\alpha - \varepsilon_t)}$$

$$- \sum_{\substack{s=1 \\ s\neq\alpha}}^{p'} \frac{F_{R,s\beta}F_{R,\alpha i}F_{R,\alpha j}F_{R,sk}F_{R,\alpha l}}{\varepsilon_\alpha\varepsilon_s(\varepsilon_\alpha - \varepsilon_s)^2} - \frac{1}{2} \sum_{\substack{s=1 \\ s\neq\alpha}}^{p} \frac{F_{R,\alpha\beta}F_{R,si}F_{R,\alpha j}F_{R,sk}F_{R,\alpha l}}{\varepsilon_\alpha\varepsilon_s(\varepsilon_\alpha - \varepsilon_s)^2}.$$

References

1. Anderson, G.A. (1965). An asymptotic expansion for the distribution of the latent roots of the estimated covariance matrix. *Ann. Math. Statist.*, **36**, 1153–1173.
2. Anderson, T.W. (1963). Asymptotic theory for principal component analysis. *Ann. Math. Statist.*, **34**, 122–148.
3. Jolliffe, I.T. (1986). *Principal Component Analysis*, Springer-Verlag, New York.
4. Sugiura, N. (1976). Asymptotic expansions of the distributions of the latent roots and the latent vector of the Wishart and multivariate F matrices. *J. Multi. Anal.*, **6**, 500–525.
5. Sugiyama, T. (1983). An Introduction to Multivarate Data Analysis, Asakura Publishing, Tokyo. (in Japanese)

Text Segmentation by Latent Semantic Indexing

Tsunenori Ishioka[1]

[1]Research Division, National Center for University Entrance Examinations, 2-19-23 Komaba, Meguro, Tokyo 153-8501, Japan

Summary. We point out that the determination of the document boundary is possible by using Singular Value Decomposition (SVD) based on the idea of LSI (Latent Semantic Indexing), and show that the conditional entropy method is replaceable by the SVD method using illustrations from several well-known plays. If we use this entropy model, the homoscedasticity test can be available to detect the document boundary, because the entropy depends on the variance of k-variables of LSI.

Key words. entropy model, natural language processing, singular value decomposition

1 Introduction

In general, a certain range of sentences in a text, is widely assumed to form a coherent unit which is called a discourse segment. A global discourse structure of a text can be constructed by relating the discourse segments with each other. Identifying the segment boundaries in a text is considered first step to construct the discourse structures(Grosz and Sidner 1986).

Several proposed approaches to the text segmentation problem have been adopted. These can be summarized as follows:

1. Approach based on lexical cohesion, e.g., TextTiling algorithm (Hearst 1997),
2. Combing features with a decision tree (Passoneau and Litman 1997),
3. Topic detection and tracking (TDT) plot study (Allan *et al.* 1989).

Beeferman *et al.* (1999) examined the behavior of those 3 approaches, and introduced a new statistical approach using maximum entropy modeling.

We try to apply another statistical technique to text segmentation by using *Latent Semantic Indexing* (LSI) which has only been used for document or term retrieval. Our method may be called a statistical TextTiling algorithm. We also illustrate the text segmentation results applied to several famous dramas.

If we use LSI, potential discourse segment boundaries can be represent as k-dimensional vectors. Thus, we can easily obtain the Euclidean distance between two potential boundaries. The distance is an index that indicates the difference in meaning between the segments of text on either side of potential boundary.

We show the distance is similar to an entropy measure under the condition that the prior probability of the potential boundary is given. In addition, we refer the statistical criterion that we should identify the segment boundary.

In section 2, we describe singular value decomposition associated with LSI. In section 3, we present a new statistical text segmentation method and the relation with the conditional entropy. We show the text segmentation results applied to several famous dramas in section 4, and compare them to the actual chapter or section boundaries in these dramas.

2 Latent Semantic Indexing

2.1 Singular Value Decomposition Model

Latent semantic structure analysis starts with a matrix of terms by documents. This matrix is then analyzed by singular value decomposition (SVD) to derive our particular latent semantic structure.

Any rectangular matrix, for example a $t \times d$ matrix of terms and documents, X, can be decomposed into the product of three other matrices:

$$X = T_0 S_0 D_0' \tag{1}$$

so that T_0 and D_0 have orthonormal columns and S_0 are diagonal. This is called the singular value decomposition of X. T_0 and D_0 are the matrices of left and right singular vectors and S_0 is the diagonal matrix of singular values.

SVD is unique up to certain row, column and sign permutation and by convention the diagonal elements of S_0 are constructed to be all positive and ordered in decreasing magnitude.

2.2 Reduced Model

If the singular values in S_0 are ordered by size, the first k largest may be kept and the remaining smaller ones set to zero. The product of the resulting matrices is a matrix $\widehat{X}$ which is only approximately equal to X, and is of rank k. It can be shown that the new matrix $\widehat{X}$ is the matrix of rank k, which is closest in the least squares sense to X.

Since zeros were replaced into S_0, the representation can be simplified by deleting the zero rows and columns of S_0 to obtain a new diagonal matrix S, and then deleting the corresponding columns of T_0 and D_0 to obtain T and D respectively. The result is a reduced model:

$$X \approx \widehat{X} = TSD', \qquad (2)$$

which is the rank-k model with the best possible least-squares-fit to X.

2.3 Comparing Two Documents

The dot product between two column vectors of X reflects the extent to which two documents have a similar pattern of occurrence across the set of documents. The matrix of $\widehat{X}'\widehat{X}$ is the square symmetric matrix containing all these document-to-document dot products. Since S is diagonal and D is orthonormal, it is easy to verify that:

$$\widehat{X}'\widehat{X} = DS^2D'. \qquad (3)$$

Note that this means that the i, j cell of $\widehat{X}'\widehat{X}$ can be obtained by taking the dot product between the i and j columns of the matrix DS. Since S is diagonal, the DS space is just a stretched or shrunken version of the D space.

3 A New Statistical Approach

3.1 Text Segmentation based on LSI

If we use the reduced model, the coordinate position of a document is expressed by a vector whose number of components is not t (number of terms) but k, which is much smaller than t, because the vector corresponds to the i-th row of the matrix DS.

That means document i can be specified by one point in k-dimensional space. Thus, when we chain the coordinate positions of the documents, the magnitude of the linkage distance shows the dissimilarity between the two target documents, although LSI uses the cosine of the angle at which two target documents meet as the similarity measure. The cosine similarity corresponds to the correlation coefficient under the condition that the analyzed vector is composed of individual standardized variables.

We divided a larger document into several potential segments by using the delimiter of paragraph, page or section. These can be regarded as documents in LSI. Then, we can recognize where the text segmentation should occur by finding the two documents whose distance is more than certain threshold. This distance represents the degree of the change in the meanings associated with the two documents.

The contents of the text are changing progressively, even if it was written by same author. Therefore we can detect the text boundary by finding the part where semantic structure is changing a lot.

3.2 Entropy Model

The entropy for a continuous distribution is defined as follows:

$$H(X) = - \int f(x) \log f(x) dx, \qquad (4)$$

where X is a random variable, and $f(x)$ is the probability density function.

If we assume any k element in document i of the reduced model is under the normal distribution:

$$f(x) = \frac{1}{\sqrt{2\pi}\sigma} \exp\left[-\frac{(x-\mu)^2}{2\sigma^2}\right], \qquad (5)$$

the entropy becomes

$$
\begin{aligned}
H(X) &= - \int \frac{1}{\sqrt{2\pi}\sigma} \exp\left[-\frac{(x-\mu)^2}{2\sigma^2}\right]\left\{\log\frac{1}{\sqrt{2\pi}\sigma} - \frac{(x-\mu)^2}{2\sigma^2}\right\} dx \\
&= \log(\sqrt{2\pi}\sigma) \underbrace{\int \frac{1}{\sqrt{2\pi}\sigma} \exp\left[-\frac{(x-\mu)^2}{2\sigma^2}\right] dx}_{=1} \\
&\quad + \int \frac{1}{\sqrt{2\pi}\sigma} \cdot \frac{(x-\mu)^2}{2\sigma^2} \exp\left[-\frac{(x-\mu)^2}{2\sigma^2}\right] dx.
\end{aligned}
\qquad (6)
$$

We set

$$y = \frac{x-\mu}{\sqrt{2\pi}\sigma}, \qquad (7)$$

so that to be $dx = \sqrt{2\pi}\sigma dy$, the entropy is rewritten to the following using the transformed variable:

$$H(X) = \log(\sqrt{2\pi}\sigma) + \pi \underbrace{\int y^2 \exp[-\pi y^2] dy}_{1/(2\pi)} = \log(\sqrt{2\pi}\sigma) + \frac{1}{2}. \qquad (8)$$

If we assume that document $i(1 \le i \le d)$ is a potential segment, X_i obey a stochastic process. Under the assumption that the k-dimensional occurrence for document i is given as $X_i = r_i$, the conditional entropy for document j , where $j > i$, becomes

$$H(X_j|X_i = r_i) = \log(\sqrt{2\pi}\sigma_j) + \frac{1}{2}, \qquad (9)$$

where the occurrence for j is r_j, and the variance of the random variable $X_{j|i} = r_j - r_i$ is σ_j^2 .

Note that the conditional entropy is defined only by variance of the potential segment. Thus we can utilize a statistical homoscedasticity test to determine whether the conditional entropy changes significantly; the test should be performed by setting

$$\text{null hypothesis } H_0 : \sigma_{j-1}^2 = \sigma_j^2 \tag{10}$$

and

$$\text{alternative hypothesis } H_1 : \sigma_{j-1}^2 \neq \sigma_j^2. \tag{11}$$

Now we use the ratio of two samples as the test statistic, $F = S_{j-1}^2/S_j^2$. F obeys the F distribution whose degree of freedom is $(k-1, k-1)$. The critical region W of a significant level α is

$$W = \{S_{j-1}^2/S_j^2 > c_1\}, \tag{12}$$

where

$$c_1 = f(1 - \alpha/2, k-1, k-1). \tag{13}$$

By using the singular value decomposition model or the reduced model, we can reduce the t-dimensional term vector indicating whether each term is contained, to a k-dimensional vector showing a latent semantic meaning; k usually has a value from 50 to 100. An entropy model can further reduce to one statistic, which shows the randomness of the semantic meanings.

It is difficult to judge whether a k-dimensional coordinates position is changed significantly, even if we set the proper assumptions against the distribution of statistics. However by using the entropy model, the statistical testing becomes easier, because it allows a test of homoscedasticity of two samples.

The assumption of continuity and the further assumption of normality in this section may be difficult to be accepted without some proofs or justifications. However, when there is no prior information about the distribution, it is thought most appropriate to assume a normal distribution.

4 Illustrations

We consider the following classical famous dramas:

(a) Machiavelli's *"The Prince"* (English translation),
(b) Shakespeare's *"The Tragedy of Hamlet,"*
(c) Shakespeare's *"The Duke of Venice,"*
(d) Shakespeare's *"The Tragedies of Romeo and Juliet."*

These texts are available on the internet at http://www.gutenberg.net/. Table 1 summarizes the number of word types, word tokens, and pages in each text. A page is defined to consist of 50 lines including null lines; one page contains approximately 300 words. Potential segment(s) will be appear in the page.

As an example, Table 1 shows that Machiavelli's *The Prince* consists of 32,331 words, of which 3,666 are unique, and that we defined 64 "pages" of this text.

Table 1. dramas with which we dealt

drama's name	number of words	number of unique words	number of pages
(a) *The Prince*	32,331	3,666	64
(b) *The Tragedy of Hamlet*	31,974	4,631	98
(c) *The Duke of Venice*	22,253	3,178	64
(d) *The Tragedies of Romeo and Juliet*	25,917	4,035	81

We get a singular value decomposition of a matrix of terms by documents for each drama; the number of singular values we required is 50. The distance between neighboring pages, when we use this reduced model, is shown upper section in each part of Figure 1. The vertical axis shows k-dimensional distance, and the horizontal axis the sequential number of pages. We can recognize the page in which the text meaning is changed. The letters (a)-(d) associated with each title in Table 1 correspond with same labels in Figure 1.

On the other hand, the lower sections of Figure 1 show the conditional entropy under the condition that the k-variables from the previous page are given. When comparing two sections, we find the state of affairs are quite similar.

Euclidean linkage distance d_j, indeed, is shown as $d_j = \sqrt{(r_j - r_i)^2}$ and σ_j^2 in Eq. (9) as $\sigma_j^2 = (r_j - r_i)^2/k$. Thus, we can obtain the entropy for the document j by using d_j instead of σ_j^2; the formula is

$$H(X_j|X_i = r_i) = \log \sqrt{\frac{2\pi}{k}} + \log d_j + \frac{1}{2}. \tag{14}$$

This equation shows that the linkage (k-dimensional) distance is replaceable by the conditional entropy (that is only one statistics), under the assumption that the distribution of $(r_j - r_i)$ has the normality.

For further comprehension, we add vertical lines as the formal punctuation, e.g., ACT, SCENE, or CHAPTER (depending on the drama) at the specified pages. In addition, we append marks of '*' where the conditional entropy increases significantly (significant level $\alpha = 0.20$); the conditional entropy depends on the variance of different vector from the previous page, so the homoscedasticity test is adopted.

Machavelli's "(a) The prince", which include 26 chapters, deals with political theory. The beginning five chapters are mentioned about followings: Chapter 1, how many kinds of principalities there are, and by what means they are acquired. Chapter 2, concerning hereditary principalities. Chapter 3, concerning mixed principalities. Chapter 4, why the kingdom of darius, conquered by Alexander, did not rebel against the successors of Alexander at his death. Chapter 5, concerning the way to govern cities or principalities which lived under their own laws before they were annexed. Chapter 6, concerning new principalities which are acquired by one's own arms and ability.

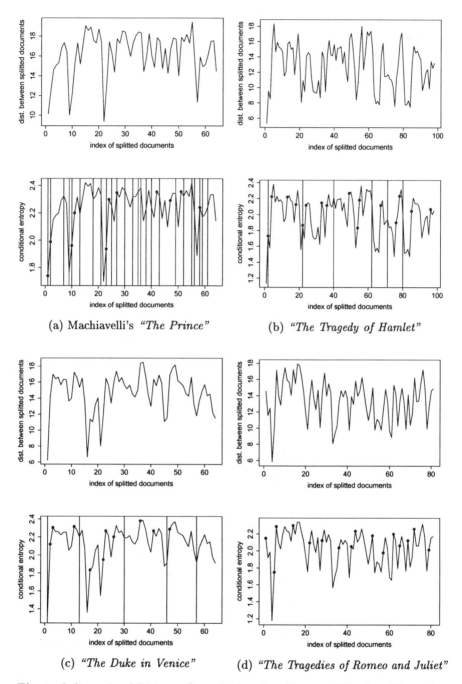

Fig. 1. k-dimensional Distance from the Previous Page, and the Conditional Entropy

Thus, we find that the context is changing in chapter 1, 2, and 6. And *
marks actually put there.

In "(b) The Tragedy of Hamlet", * marks are put on 16 places, that is
page 3, 4, 13, 18, 22, 24, 33, 36, 49, 54, 55, 67, 76, 78, 85, and 96; they coincide
with well the locations of "scene" in the drama on page 2, 3, 12, 15, 17, 24,
48, 54, 57, 63, 64, 66, 68, 74, 75 and 84; several vertical lines show "act" in
the drama.

In "(c) The Duke in Venice", * marks are put on 10 places in page 2, 3,
11, 17, 22, 23, 26, 36, 41, and 47; on the other hand, the "scene"s are located
in page 2, 3, 11, 17, 21, 23, 25, 27, 30, 36, 41, 42, 44, and 56; these are also
seemed to be coincident considerably.

The drama of (d) has no formal punctuation.

From these illustrations, we can obtain the following results:

- The sequential k-dimensional distances between two pages can be replaced
  by the conditional entropies; if we replace a k-dimensional vector with
  only one statistic, no lack of information is observed from the viewpoint of
  whether the semantic meaning of the document is changed or not.
- The pages in which the entropy is changed seem to correspond with those
  in the formal punctuation, e.g., ACT, SCENE and so on.

References

Allan, j., Carbonell, J., Doddington, G., Yamron, J. and Yang, Y.(1998) Topic
    Detection and Tracking Pilot Study: Final Report, *Proceedings of the DARPA
    Broadcast News Transcription and Understanding Workshop.*

Deerwester, S., Dumais, S. T., Landauer, T. K., Furnas, G. W. and Harshman, R.
    A.(1999) Indexing by Latent Semantic Analysis, *Journal of the American Soci-
    ety for Information Science* 41(6): 391-407.

Beeferman, D., Berger, A., and Lafferty, J.(1999) Statistical Models for Text Seg-
    mentation, *Machine Learning*, special issue on Natural Learning, C. Cardie and
    R. Mooney eds., 34(1-3): 177–210.

Berry, M. W., Dumais, S. T., and O'Brien, G. W.(1995) Using linear algebra for
    intelligent information retrieval *SIAM Review* 37(4): 573–595.

Gous, A.(1999) Spherical Subfamily Models, submitted, *special issue on
    Natural Learning*, C. Cardie and R. Mooney eds., 34(1-3): 177–210.
    http://www-stat.stanford.edu/~gous/papers/ssm.ps

Grosz, B. J. and Sidner, C. L.(1986) Attention, Intentions, and the Structure of
    Discourse. *Computational Linguistics* 12(3): 175–204.

Hearst, M.(1997) TextTiling: Segmenting Text into Multi-Paragraph Subtopic Pas-
    sages, Computational Linguistics, 23(1), 33–64.

Hofmann, T.(1999) Probabilistic Latent Semantic Indexing, *ACM 22nd Annual
    International SIGIR Conference on Research and Development in Information
    Retrieval:* 50–57.

Passoneau, R. J. and Litman, D. J.(1997) Discourse Segmentation by human and
    automated means, *Computational Linguistics* 23(1): 103–139.

Contributors

Keyword Index